The Growth of American Law
THE LAW MAKERS

The Growth of American Law

THE LAW MAKERS

by

JAMES WILLARD HURST

BOSTON

LITTLE, BROWN AND COMPANY

1950

PREFATORY NOTE

These essays outline the growth of the principal agencies of law in the United States. They cover the period 1790–1940, with occasional excursions beyond these points.

The emphasis is on the functions performed by legal agencies, rather than on their formal structure. Hence the same material is sometimes discussed in different contexts; I hope that such repetition as this involves is justified by a more full-dimensioned story of work done. The viewpoint is primarily that of a professional interest in law as an instrument of social values; I have tried to select for discussion lines of growth which have meaning for the middle of the twentieth century.

The order of the book follows the order in which the legal agencies discussed emerged into positions of leadership in successive periods of our history. In logic, the constitution makers should have first attention, since they make the fundamental law. Here they are discussed after the legislature and the courts, because in fact the growing point of our law — including our constitutional law — was first in legislative and then in judicial agencies. The bar rose to major status concurrently with the courts. Last to make its full weight felt was the executive branch, including administrative agencies.

This is not a study made chiefly from original sources. Primary sources have been tapped at various points. However, the general purpose is to interpret already available, but generally scattered, materials.

Grateful acknowledgment is made to the Social Science Research Council for a "Demobilization Award" which aided in the preparation of the book, and to Dean Oliver S. Rundell and the President and the Board of Regents of the University of Wisconsin for support in the enterprise.

Particular thanks are due to Frances Wilson Hurst for sustaining encouragement and patience; and to Harriet Foster Bunn for her care and skill in laboring to reduce the angularities of style in the second draft manuscript. My appreciation runs also to Professor Charles Bunn for reading parts of the manuscript; to the late Professor Eldon James and members of the staff of the Law Division of the Library of Congress for hospitality during several months of the work; to Mrs. Nellie Davidson, Misses Irene Kleinheinz, Virginia Dieball, Mary Strause, Emeline Ohnesorge, Mrs. Jean Nelson Squire, Miss Linda Pierce, and Mr. William Collins for the typing of various stages of the manuscript; and to Messrs. Robert Curtin, Paul Myerson, and Robert Dean for mimeographing the book in its interim form.

The bibliographical notes to chapters are generally limited to works specifically cited or referred to in the text. They express only a small part of my indebtedness to my teachers and to professional colleagues in the law and the related social sciences.

CONTENTS

I. Introduction

II. The Legislature

III. The Courts

IV. The Constitution Makers

VII. Conclusion: Prospectus for Legal History

I. Introduction

CHAPTER ONE

PERSPECTIVE

1. THE GROWTH OF INSTITUTIONAL AND SUBSTANTIVE LAW CONTRASTED

There is a great deal in the early history of the United States which has made it natural for people to think about public questions as legal issues. Men wanted national independence largely for economic reasons, but they said they wanted it because their legal rights were invaded. Since the pressures they fought against were first imposed by law, it was a natural way to express their resistance.

At the same time it is easy to exaggerate the part law has played in United States history. Now, as in the past, too many of us like to discuss politics and public morals largely in terms of legal issues. Too many have demanded their "rights" and at the same time concerned themselves in fixing the other man's "duties." In either case the solution has appeared to be another law on the books.

For one hundred years after independence people busied themselves occupying the continent, building towns and exploiting natural resources. Probably no one before them had mastered new territory less hampered by laws or customs of the previous occupants. As the settlers pushed farther west the older communities expanded behind them; men's lives touched at more and more points. People felt a recurring need to develop the elementary agencies on which peace depends.

Settlers from the Old World brought their old ways of life with them — the divisions of control among the family, church, neighborhood, school, and law. New social configurations stimulated social inventions. The mixture of cultural ideas diluted the strength of each. At the same time the pace of the industrial revolution in this country exceeded the capacity for change of institutions — like the family — which grow by time-consuming habit.

All this made people conscious of a need for legal regulation. The vastness of the United States as well as sectional differences made federalism a basic theme with Americans. The fact that men and women moved with such ease within the American class structure affected the place law took in their lives. It affected their attitude toward the lawyer. He always ranked high in our social hierarchy. As far back as 1830

Tocqueville considered the bar nearer to an aristocracy than any other group in American life.

The looseness of our class structure led not only lawyers but men and women in general to concern themselves with individual advancement. They enriched themselves on the new land and from the expanding markets, and were therefore content to leave public life to the lawyer. By training and means of livelihood he became one of the few who did the community's serious reading, spoke its thought, and struggled to bring together its diverse interests.

People did not regard either the state or the lawmakers with awe. To them government represented a tool to further ambition and energy. Because other institutions were weak, the law had much to offer in bounty and protection. Understanding this, we understand how it became natural for Americans to use law to win their partisan, business, or social ends.

We shall get a more realistic grasp of the part law has played in United States history if we keep in mind this readiness of Americans to use it as a means to bring about immediate practical results. In part, certainly, this was democracy's healthy insistence that the state exists for the people's benefit. Other sides of our highly instrumental attitude toward law were more difficult to read. This attitude reflected the depth and spread of change in our development, the pressure of events, the preoccupation with economic values and problems and with the nearest ends — those which people deemed the most practical. Paradoxically, the extent to which Americans put issues into legal terms and tried to use and control the legal agencies reflected a lesser role for the law. In the interaction of law and American life the law was passive, acted upon by other social forces, more often than acting upon them.

A timetable of the growth of law in the United States shows how far events and ideas from outside shaped it. If we think of those points at which the law bulks largest in the United States of the 1940's, a sharp division appears. As in other phases of our history, the 1870's mark the turn into a new society. From the pre-Civil War years we inherit a set of legal agencies and procedures: constitutions and the means of making or amending them; a federal nation; an elected executive; an elected, two-house legislature; a quite uniform pattern of courts, mostly elective; the grand jury and the petit jury; local law enforcement; a shapeless, still largely unorganized bar. But if we ask what jobs these agencies are doing, we find that their important work has to do with issues that scarcely existed before 1870.

A simple listing of the main fields of the law's work tells how the changing shape of American society moulded the jobs set for the law.

Law school catalogs tell the story. Their evidence is a conservative measure of the extent of change; the schools blend the intellectual's curiosity about what goes on under the surface of events with the practitioner's stress on current business. Take five notebooks representing the year's work of a student at the Litchfield Law School in 1813: one notebook was filled with real property matters; one the student gave to forms of action, pleading and practice; about three fourths of another to commercial law (especially bills and notes and insurance), about one third of another to contracts, with the remainder of the notebooks occupied by brief notes on a scattering of subjects (the headings of municipal law, master and servant, bailments, and chancery each taking less than 15 per cent of the contents of one notebook).

The Harvard Law School listed its texts for 1832–1833 as including real property, personal property, commercial and maritime law, equity, criminal law, civil law, the law of nations, and constitutional law. Its course list for 1870–1871 showed some widening of scope. The school required the study of real property, personal property, contracts, torts, criminal law and criminal procedure, civil procedure at common law, and evidence. The students might elect sales, bailments, agency, negotiable instruments, partnership, shipping, insurance, equitable jurisdiction and procedure, principal and surety, domestic relations, marriage and divorce, wills and administration, corporations, conflict of laws, constitutional law, and debtor-creditor relations, including bankruptcy. The list was a hodgepodge that had grown rather in response to the pressure of events than to an educational plan.

By 1940 the schools had widened their offerings in kind, as well as degree, but most legal education still lacked a broad plan. The schools still taught the staples: real property (but with more stress on the borrowing of the law of future interests in land for planned control of the passing of intangible wealth); contracts (but with greater bulk, and more stress on business deals); torts (with main attention now to accidental injuries from the use of machines); procedure, pleading and practice (but with stress on new remedies and efforts to simplify the field by legislation). New directions of emphasis in 1940 put the familiar titles in the shade. The corporations course had new prominence, and the teaching of corporation finance, taxation, antitrust law, and patents further reflected the importance of the corporation and problems of the concentration of economic power. Novel marketing patterns showed their effect in courses treating constitutional protections to interstate commerce, trade regulation, sales of goods, creditors' rights and sellers' security. Tensions of a tightly interlaced, mainly urban life prompted study of land use, zoning, municipal corporations, and due process of law in collision with regulatory legislation. Men in our society tended to group into more sharply defined interests; in the face of such divisions government within its limited capacity tried to bring the community together and to hold the balance of power. Law school catalogs gave indication of this pressure in the new fields of public utilities, civil liberty, labor relations, administrative law, and the new reach of constitutional law from high politics into the everyday affairs of the market.

Legal agencies and procedures of course changed a good deal before and after 1870. In the thirty years before the Civil War, the states turned from appointing to electing their judges; early bar organization and standards for admission to the bar fell apart; the President gained as a national and party leader; people voted into state constitutions restrictions which spoke a new distrust of the legislature. After 1870, in an effort to improve their courts, states showed some tendency to unify and specialize them. Lawyers formed voluntary, selective bar organizations, and a handful of the bar, together with law teachers, saved standards of education and admission to the bar from collapse. At the same time administrative agencies took over new fields of legal control, and statute making showed new life, thanks to the legislative committee and the organized interest group. Such changes in agencies and procedures continued within a setting which crystallized before the critical '70s. Legal history speaks mainly, in this aspect, of efforts to fit old agencies to new facts, to work under the handicap of old forms, or to fight inertia and vested interest in order to effect change.

The story of the substance of the law since 1790 is quite different. The questions that were live between 1790 and 1870 were not, by and large, the ones that were important after that time. What the law said in behalf of the public welfare before 1870 neither limits nor promotes what the public welfare called for after that period. This is taking the picture as a whole.

Particular subjects of interest in the later period are rooted in the first. This holds true, for example, in the law of land titles, sales of goods, or negotiable instruments. In general the timetable of our legal history teaches, however, that apart from the toughness of institutional structure, law has been more the creature than the creator of events.

2. THE PHYSICAL SETTING OF THE LAW
IN THE UNITED STATES

Geography set some problems for law in this country, made some matters here of no account, affected the direction and emphasis of others. It was not often a prime mover. The decisive facts were the vast land areas and the wealth and variety of natural resources.

For over one hundred years the land itself was a prize that stirred men to scheme and fight in making and manipulating laws and legal procedures; party ambition, economic interest, and hope of social advance all bore hard upon the law here. Men speculated or invested in land and used it as both a source and object of credit. Because of this activity, they were continually concerned with titles, they experimented with new business forms, they battled over banking and easy money, and the tug of war began between mortgagor and mortgagee. Because of the size of the public domain, the public land policy could not help but be an important kind of legal regulation of American economic life. Partly because there was free or cheap land on the frontier, we formed our own set of values and beliefs about how much respect was due to private and official power. These values and beliefs affected the ways in which law did its job in the United States.

Our law showed a belated concern over the fertility of the soil. But long before such a concern was manifested, men brought to law questions about minerals, timber, waterways, and water power. Sometimes the physical setting suggested the law. For example, the customs of gold miners formed the basis of mining law. Some Western states discovered that giving rights to the first taker made a more workable division of their scarce water than the English and Eastern states' rule of equal use of water for all owners of the banks of streams. More often, as in the case of oil and timber, the facts did not speak the answer so plainly. The natural wealth available excited proportionate greed and a grabbing for power. These forces fell upon legal agencies that, weak in tradition and rushed by events, were ill-equipped to meet them; this was particularly true of the legislatures. Thus the extravagance of our natural resources affected the growth of legal control as well as the people's attitudes toward it.

Communications were basic to national growth in a country of vast distances. Promoters early brought pressure on government to help transportation; later on, users of transportation pressed for its regulation. Some of the strongest political forces, some of the most warping influences, mixed with these issues. No one thing was more important in the rise of the administrative process, and nothing brought more discredit to the legislative branch, than the influence of "the railroad."

Measured by the few people who were on hand to claim and use them, we had a wealth of natural resources. At the same time, most men found life hard. But the country never came near the edge of subsistence, or even in sight of it. While individuals might have to be thrifty, public policy enjoyed opportunities for extravagance. We see this in the variety and strength of special interests that tended to divide rather than to unite our community life. We see it in our slowness to save natural wealth or to plan fairly and rationally for its use. It is reflected in the extraordinary scope our law gave to freedom of association and venture.

The physical setting worked to free us from legal traditions that might otherwise have bound us. The ocean limited the ideas freighted over from the common law and civil systems, great as was the effect of both. The country's size, rawness, and range of sectional differences in natural wealth and natural obstacles helped give our social relations a distinctive character.

Of course we cannot separate the physical and social settings in their effects upon our life and law. If the physical setting gave the frame for what went on, men's invention of machines and social institutions gave meaning now to one, now to another aspect of the country's geography. In 1825 the Supreme Court of the United States, speaking through Mr. Chief Justice Marshall in the case of the steamboat *Thomas Jefferson*, followed English precedent to decide that the admiralty jurisdiction of the federal courts went only to waters within the ebb and flow of the tide. In 1851, in the case of the *Genesee Chief*, speaking through Mr. Chief Justice Taney, the Supreme Court overruled the 1825 decision; the admiralty jurisdiction, it held, extended to all waters that were in fact navigable. Taney pointed out that "there were no navigable waters in the United States upon which commerce, in the usual acceptation of the word, was carried on, except tidewater, until the valley of the Mississippi was settled and cultivated, and steamboats invented." The 1825 case had been decided "when the commerce on the rivers of the west and on the lakes was in its infancy, and of little importance."

Behind Taney's opinion was the fact that the steamboat, which could push upriver against the current, had revolutionized inland transportation. Thereby it changed the theater in which there was practical demand for use of the federal admiralty power.

There was also interplay between the natural setting and social inventions. Large parts of this country produce almost nothing but raw materials. The people who settled these sections had very little capital. The pulling and hauling of debtor and creditor was an important factor in the story of our advancing frontier.

In these raw-material states, business, politics, and thinking swirled about the issues of the debtor-creditor relationship. Both in fact and in the eyes of their people, states like Wisconsin, Michigan, Oklahoma, or Montana stood, or still stand, in a colonial relation to the Eastern states. The Easterners had the capital, the manufactures, and the markets on which the younger states depended. Out of this background men made strong movements in the law. They wanted the state to dictate the law to railroads and other public utilities; they wanted the government to manage money and credit, to make them "easier"; they wanted government to take steps to save natural wealth and to plan the use of land for the greater benefit of average people; they wanted to tax wealth that was flowing out of their home states; they wanted the federal government to spend money where it would help to even out the level of national well-being.

3. THE TECHNOLOGICAL SETTING OF THE LAW

The man-made physical setting — technology —, was one of the great moving forces for change in American law. This was so before the Civil War, as the decision in the *Genesee Chief* shows. After 1833 the invention of the automatic reaper opened the way for a growth in farming that affected public-land policy and laid the basis for a tangle of speculation, credit, boom and bust, tariff and antitrust law; agriculture was thenceforth to be a major interest pressing upon the law. The rotary printing press and the telegraph made possible the modern newspaper. They facilitated vast circulation, broad markets, appeals to mass emotion and lewdness. Thus questions of trade-mark law, of libel, of free speech and press took on a new importance in our law.

The years after 1870 saw the truly massive impact of technological change. Men began to live always in the midst of machinery, the machines of factories, mines, railroads, street railways, and especially the automobile. Personal injury suits became of major importance. Who should bear the loss from personal injury was a legal issue with many facets; negligence became the greater part of the law of torts. The growth of cities was stimulated as well as limited by the improvement of transportation, building construction, and water supply. The expansion of the factory system and of commercial organization suitable to mass markets and to handling the immense paper work of national and international commerce, insurance, and finance spelled new demands upon law. Urban habits changed the kinds and amount of crime. They aroused urgent demands for legal controls to handle the dangers that crowded living created for health, safety, and fair dealing. Class lines sharpened, as the United States switched to mass-production industry, shifted emphasis from skilled to semi- and un-skilled labor, and found profit in concentrating ownership and control. The law had to consider labor relations, and monopolies and combinations to restrain trade. Patent law began by rewarding the ingenious individual and ended with concern for the uses that big business made of patent privileges. People found that, willy-nilly, they had lost power to fend for themselves and were dependent mainly upon others for things that had to be made or done if all were to have food, shelter, clothing, and the comforts of a rising standard of living. Society was more sensitive to the threat that vital services might be stopped, or ransom demanded for them; new means of mass communication made possible a new demagogy; unplanned, undesired, too-swift change could outdate machines and processes overnight and unsettle jobs and hopes. Through all these different channels came new demands that the law be used to guard social order and to direct the pace and direction of change.

What are the social and private interests that the law should recognize and protect? Here technological change set new problems and gave new urgency to old ones. The use of machines and the processes that go with them vastly increased the ways in which men depended on each other. What people did in this or that field of life had widespreading and at the same time intricate effects. The law had to alter many definitions of what was private and what was public interest.

Technology also affected the enforcement of law. The machine greatly added to the job of law enforcement, as in the new aid that the automobile gave to the criminal. In other ways the machine eased the enforcement job. The men who learned how to build hard-surfaced roads and how to draw a black line down the middle for mile after mile did more to enforce the rule of keep-to-the-right than all the police could do without these mechanical helps. The laboratory man set the pace for enforcing standards of health, safety, or fair dealing in foods, dangerous materials, and goods in general, as he found tests for inspection or objective measure. Those who invented the calculating, recording, and tabulating machines and the filing systems that go with scientific management made a lot of modern law possible. Without these mechanical aids, to collect taxes, to run state- or nation-wide systems of licensing activities (e.g., automobile driving), or businesses (e.g., insurance or securities), or to provide insurance against industrial accident, unemployment, or old age would be physically impossible on the scale needed to carry out modern legal policy.

The law has almost always been acted upon by, or has responded to, technological change, rather than controlled it. The patent lawyer may object that, in his field at least, the law helped shape technical history; but how far this is true remains to be proved. The relation between law and technical change was full of color and tension. But in almost every case, the scientist or inventor took the initiative, and the lawman came in only as complaints mounted that the new knowledge, or more likely its use, was too costly, might even, in fact, destroy life or security.

A key invention of the late nineteenth century was invention itself, as a systematized effort. People did not say seriously that perhaps government should plan, or at least control, the speed of technical change until the depression of the 1930's and the Second World War. At that time there was talk not only of control of the pace and directions of technical change, but also of government sponsorship for scientific research, through a National Science Foundation. In 1947 a Presidential veto killed the first bill that Congress passed to provide for such a Foundation. The veto went to the details of the project, however, and did not dispute the merit of doing something. It appeared likely, therefore, that in the mid-twentieth century the federal government would embark upon some new relation to scientific inquiry. What would be the vehicle of this governmental interest was uncertain; in default of a National Science Foundation, the armed services had obtained research appropriations of such scale as to give them at least temporary leadership in the field. In any case, it appeared that as invention itself had been a key invention of the nineteenth century, so a basic invention of the twentieth might be some effort by law to make technical change mesh in more smoothly with other aspects of life.

4. The Social Setting of the Law in the United States

The most creative, driving, and powerful pressures upon our law emerged from the social setting. Social environment has two aspects. First, it is what men think: how they size up the universe and their place in it; what things they value, and how much; what they believe to be the relations between cause and effect, and the way these ideas affect their notions of how to go about getting the things that they value. Second, it is what men do: their habits, their institutions. Ideas and institutions obviously are inseparable aspects of men's history. We do not have to try to decide which, if either, is the more powerful.

Section 1 of this chapter noted the contrast in the timetable of our legal growth, turning about the decade of the '70s. The effects of the social setting were the main cause of this contrast. Changing ideas and patterns of action in the outside society forced the reassignment of law jobs already mentioned and such changes led us to say that little substantive law before 1870 has meaning for our generation. On the other hand, it is the radical nature of this impact of ideas and institutions upon substantive law that makes clearer by contrast the area in which the law itself, as idea and institution, showed the toughest staying power, in the blueprints of the main legal agencies and their procedures.

The deeper we probe to explain shifts in legal doctrine, the less we are satisfied with what at first seem the practical answers. Neither changes in professional knowledge or tradition, nor even the march of objective facts, tell the whole story. As we search deeper, we have to give more weight to what men have in their heads concerning their wants and how they can satisfy their wants. And this seems true whether they have got these ideas more or less by consciously taking stock of their situation, or by simply rationalizing patterns of action that they have already formed without such conscious effort.

The different ways in which the law has defined interests at one time or another shows this importance of ideas. When the law says that this or that is a legally protected interest, it is putting into authoritative form the ideas that are acceptable in the society at one time or another about the comparative value of different kinds of activity and different kinds of security or advancement in personal standing or command over material goods. In the early nineteenth century, influential people believed that to treat men as independent, responsibility-taking individuals would best serve the general welfare. The lawmen drew the conclusion that if a man was to be held liable in law, it must be either because he had agreed to do something and did not do it, or because he had made a mistake in the choice or foresight by which he guided his conduct. In short, liability in a society of free-willing individuals must logically rest either on contract or on fault. But the prevailing temper of the twentieth century led to quite a different approach. We came to think that the general welfare was best served if we spread risk or loss broadly. This was the insurance principle, reflected in a broadening of common law categories of liability without fault, and in statutory workmen's compensation and social security systems. The law recognizes new interests and narrows old ones. Judges and legislators spell new results out of new principles. But the principles themselves are results and not causes of change. The change may show the effect of old legal doctrine upon new ways of acting, and vice versa. But men must pass experience through their minds, before they act on it in any but a reflex manner. First of all, the machinery of change turns over in men's heads.

Of course, men cannot think themselves beyond all limits of time, place, or habit, in forming their life in society. But we are concerned with what makes change rather than with the inert conditions that fix the frame within which its movements must take place. Consider what was behind the decision in the *Genesee Chief:* the interplay of (1) the physical setting (our network of navigable inland waters); (2) technological change (the invention and improvement of the steamboat); (3) shifts in the going ways of business (the growing business in inland water shipping); and (4) the legal precedent (the decision in the *Thomas Jefferson*). But a new rule as to federal admiralty jurisdiction could come from no automatic running-together of these facts. Change required that judges, charged with the duty of decision, should weigh the meaning of these factors. The Taney court elsewhere showed that it followed no dogmatic states-rights views. Specifically, as to interstate commerce, its decisions showed practical convictions about the desirability of keeping the flow of business among the states substantially free of the bonds of local interest or peculiarities of local policy.

It seems likely that the Court's main thought in extending the federal admiralty jurisdiction was the commercial value in a nationally uniform system of admiralty law. This is no less so, though Taney said that the commerce clause was not a source of Congress's power to pass the act that gave the federal courts their jurisdiction in admiralty. Taney was no dogmatist either of state or of federal power; he wanted to work out the lines of division cautiously and with regard to how rules operated in practice. His cautious pragmatism led him to deny a ground of decision that he thought might justify extending federal jurisdiction to contracts and torts on land in interstate commerce. Except for this caution, the opinion more than once stresses that government must give new weight to inland water shipping, and that division of jurisdiction according to the chances of the tide would be arbitrary. The case is only one of many in which the idea of a nation-wide free trade area showed itself strong in the background of constitutional and commercial law.

Law moves with the main currents of American thought. Of significance to legal history is the twentieth-century stress on security for the individual, in contrast to the nineteenth-century emphasis on getting ahead. Closely related is the fact that with the dawn of the new century men had a heightened sense of their dependence on one another, and were more keenly aware of the individual's helplessness against impersonal social currents; in contrast was the pride in self-sufficiency and localism that had marked America's earlier growth. At one time the people of the United States believed that they could speak their democratic faith through political action. They also believed in every man's use of his freedom to seek his own economic advancement. But with a changing society fewer men were able to use political power to advance their standing in the community or even to give them a satisfying sense of belonging and functioning in it. Hence they began to believe that there must be a wider popular share in making policy and in carrying it out, whether in industry, in the market, or in government. They began to grope for ways to express this new unease. On the other hand, men living in large, city-gathered masses according to standardized ways of life had lost much of an older sense of community. Urban living thinned people's feelings of group responsibility. Mingling with the new urge toward security, such facts fertilized the soil for enemies of democracy.

Changing ideas also affected the means as well as the choice of means for carrying out policy fixed in law. This last generation has less faith than its forebears in the possibility of making men moral by law. On the other hand it has more faith in the results of changing the material setting in which men live. Modern man finds less satisfaction in the theory that punishment is effective either as retribution or as deterrent. He is readier to believe that only preventive action strikes at the roots. He reassesses law enforcement in the light of new knowledge of the unconscious and irrational springs of action. Some tried to rethink the law of civil liberties in the light of new learning about the psychology and psychopathology of propaganda, prejudice, and mass emotion. We have already noted the shift from pride in self-sufficiency to a pervasive sense of individual inequality and helplessness before the accidents of life. If this shift in attitudes affected the weighing of interests, no less did it affect the ways in which law was put into action. Both laymen and lawmen showed less faith in the conventional private lawsuit as a means of protecting interests. They relied more on action by the state, through new regulatory uses of the criminal law, and through the amazing growth of the administrative process.

So far we have discussed the effects of ideas, general or specific, but in either case made explicit and more or less consciously directed. But ideas tie in closely with habits of action, and both change institutions. Institutional change was at least as important as alteration in the climate of ideas, in affecting the growth of law in the United States. So far as concerns the definition of interests, changes in economic institutions were probably most important. Thus the law cast the protection given to "property" about interests of more intangible kind, as businessmen found value in those intangibles. The growth of mass production industry, national markets, and nation-wide advertising moved the law to recognize broader rights in trade-marks and trade names, to which trade or customer acceptance had attached commercially valuable secondary meanings; and finally, the law began to give wider protection to the general reputation represented by an established mark or name. Industrial combination, and later financial manipulation of big industry and commerce, offered new prizes in profit, power, and social status. These presented altogether novel legal problems in marking the lines between public and private interest, and in trying to keep the balance of power that the vitality of a democratic society demands.

Institutional change posed problems no less striking in the field of law enforcement. The same prizes that encouraged the concentration of economic power spurred the invention of legal means that would bring about that concentration. So we got the "trusts," the holding company, the know-how in bringing about mergers or consolidations, the techniques by which managers could run the business with minimal stock control, the invention of restrictive licenses and patent agreements.

But economic change did not dominate the history of law enforcement as it did that of interests. Family and church lost ground as agencies of social control; this undoubtedly put greater demands on law for enforcing acceptable behavior. The public schools took in masses of students where they had once taught a comparatively small part of the people; they had to standardize methods in the process; and in consequence we had to size up with a new critical eye some of the law's assumptions as to the self-starting efficiency of free political processes and a free press. On the other hand, because both public and private education reached so many more children, we tended, whether wisely or not, to give the school more and more responsibility for keeping children out of trouble and policing what they did. And — to go back to the matter of interests — the wider spread of education also promoted those demands for security and status that gave the individual new rights and privileges in law.

It is clear that changes in machines and uses of machines are mixed in with shifts in ideas and in habits of action, as causes of much of what we have been discussing. And it is no less sure that the physical setting is often a more remote condition or cause of what goes on. But it is still true that the moving causes back of these kinds of events are men, and what they have in their minds, whether they are thinking things through more or less consciously, or are acting out of habit. Such causes may properly be said to fix the social environment, as distinct from the physical setting in which the law has grown. Because society, and law as a tool of society, are made by men, for men, they cannot help having the nature of men in them.

5. Key Characteristics of the Growth of Law in the United States

Certain basic features in the growth of law in this country are related to the social setting. First, change went on at a remarkable speed in American history. Because we forget how young this country is, we are often likely to be unfair in evaluating the job done by those who went before us here, and we are apt not to understand the causes that were at work. The earliest English settlement is less than three hundred and fifty years behind us. The law has been a significant factor in our life at the most for only about two hundred years. We took over the English common law about one hundred and fifty years ago, if we measure not by theory but by the length of time in which lawmen have made the common law a real working part of our legal doctrine. We became a nation within that same short time. Half of the present states of the Union were set up within one hundred years, the last two less than forty years ago.

If we look at other things than our basic political organization, we find that other important legal institutions, rules, and procedures don't date back many years. Look at the staple fields of law: We laid the bases of our rules in equity, conflicts of laws, torts, contracts, sales of goods, and real property as recently as 1810–1860. Corporation law began to take substantial shape only after 1830, and had its big growth after 1880. Basic procedural change dates only from the New York Code of Civil Procedure of 1848. We have seen that the main legal agencies, legislatures, courts, the executive branch — have changed very slowly in form. It is not until the turn of the century, and mainly after 1910, that we began to try new specialized courts to handle small claims, juvenile delinquency, and domestic relations problems; not till then that we heard serious talk of the one-house legislature, the initiative, referendum, or recall, or the executive budget and the centralizing of executive responsibility. The roots of the administrative process go down to the start of our national legal history. But the administrative arm did not begin to take on its present reach until Congress set up the Interstate Commerce Commission in 1887. Both in the nation and the states most modern administrative power dates from about 1910.

The relatively short time span back of most of our legal history shows the pace of change in the man-made setting of the law. We need only to recall the familiar story. Fulton's *Clermont* made its successful trip up the Hudson in 1807, and in 1831 a steamboat first traveled the upper Missouri. Steam trains began to run from Charleston to Hamburg, South Carolina, in 1833; in 1852 the first train ran from Philadelphia to Pittsburgh; in 1869 the first transcontinental line was finished; from 1860 to 1900 railway mileage grew from 30,000 to 166,000 miles, and to 240,000 miles by 1940. The first telegraph line opened between Washington and Baltimore in 1844; the first telephone message was sent in 1876; Edison's electric power plant began operation in New York City in 1882.

Population is an index that, like the growth of communications, marks the rush of change. Wisconsin had 305,000 people in 1850; 776,000 in 1860; 1,055,000 in 1870; 1,315,000 in 1880; and grew at the rate of about 300,000 each ten years, to 3,138,000 in 1940. From 1850–1860 Minnesota went from 6,000 people to 172,000. Population shifts were as great. In 1789 only about 3 per cent of the people lived in cities, and only 5 cities had over 8,000 people; by 1890 about one third of the people lived in towns of 4,000 or more; American life began to be overshadowed by the rise of great cities.

The use of natural resources typically followed the same headlong course of development. The law has no very proud story to tell of itself, for example, in connection with the destruction of the Wisconsin forests. There was no serious attempt to control waste of this natural wealth until the great damage had been done. But, in fairness, we must read this story in light of the fact that the lumber industry rose, flourished, and fell to minor rank in Wisconsin in about thirty years, and in a raw, youthful state, whose institutions had no seasoning to help them meet questions of the kind thrust upon them.

A second point to note is that we must use some caution in sizing up the part that particular individuals played in the growth of the law. We like to bring things down to life size by tracing what happened to the doings of specific people. This not only makes us feel more sure that we understand what went on; it also often adds drama to what seems, even if only superficially, to be otherwise a dull march of bloodless facts. We may be especially tempted to put too much weight on individual contributions in the law. For there the story deals usually with contest; and in a contest one naturally looks to see who are the champions on either side. The law deals always with decisions as to policy and as to carrying out policy; and to the logical mind it seems that we should be able to assign responsibility to someone in particular, where choices are being made.

But neither reason nor evidence supports any idea that the individual has played any greater or lesser role in the growth of law than he has in any other aspect of social life. If individual names seem to bulk large in English legal history, this is probably an illusion fostered by the relative smallness of the stage. The American story has more breadth and sweep, if a shorter time span. In it, we see that individuals have prominence according to how far they were able to express their time or foretell the generation to come, rather than according to their ability to change the direction of social currents.

There are a very few men in our legal history over whom one hesitates in making this general denial of individual influence: in the Federal

Constitutional Convention, Madison; on the bench, Marshall alone; in the presidency, Jefferson and Lincoln; in the Congress, or with respect to legislation, Jefferson, Hamilton, John Quincy Adams, Clay, Webster, Thaddeus Stevens (the list is not necessarily one of heroes), George W. Norris. If we keep a small list of men who have given creative direction to affairs, we do not deny due weight to moral courage or mental power; we simply sum up realistically the individual's relation to the forces that have shaped the United States. Generally what has made men "great" in our law has been that they saw better where the times led and took their less imaginative, less flexible, or less courageous brethren in that direction faster and with a minimum of waste and suffering. This is the merit of those names whose omission from the previous list will have stirred question or indignation: such men as James Wilson, Gouverneur Morris, Randolph, or Paterson, in the Constitutional Convention of 1787; such Justices as Johnson, Story, Taney, Curtis, Waite, Bradley, Holmes, Brandeis, Hughes, Stone, Cardozo; or, on the state bench, Kent and Cardozo (New York), Gibson (Pennsylvania), Martin (Louisiana), Blackford (Indiana), Shaw and Holmes (Massachusetts), Ruffin (North Carolina), Cooley (Michigan), or Doe (New Hampshire); such legislative leaders as Madison, Gallatin, Benton, Bingham, Sherman, Reed, LaFollette, Glass; such presidents as Jackson, Polk, Cleveland, Theodore Roosevelt, Wilson, or Franklin Roosevelt (reference is to domestic policy).

Particularly anonymous in the sight of history is the bar. Almost the only name that challenges this verdict is that of David Dudley Field, and his name more for the daring of effort than for achievement. Lawmen were leading figures in American history. But the leadership was that of the profession rather than of individuals. And for those who stood out, leadership was more in clarifying the direction and needs of change, than in controlling change. Whether things have ever been different anywhere else at any other time, this was the necessary result in the peculiar setting of American growth.

One more caution: unity and diversity have been a problem in United States legal history. The country is so big, and differs so in its sections, people, natural resources, local and regional traditions, that a diversity in legal institutions is entirely natural. Such differences developed. On the other hand, in face of the obstacles to uniformity, it is remarkable how much the country, or at least large parts of it, have had a similar growth. Our legal history has been so little studied that we must generalize about it with humility. If one looks for diversities, he will find them; if he looks for uniformities, he will find them, too. In either case, we must remember that we do not yet have the thorough studies of our general, regional, and local legal history that we must have if we are to see these conditions of likeness and unlikeness in their relation to each other. It seems fairly obvious that the likenesses have prevailed over the unlikenesses. But this is a proposition not without complexity. All differences are not necessarily opposed to union; indeed, differences that mesh together may make a division of functions that we have to have in order to be one. This has certainly been true in the United States to a large extent. Until we know our legal history better, we may fairly go on the hypothesis that there have been dominant trends toward uniformity in the growth of law in the United States, being ready at the same time to see that as we learn more we are likely to find more and more important local and regional variations.

This discussion has stressed the kinds of things outside the law that have materially affected its part in the growth of the country. This emphasis has been deliberate, to make up for the lack of balance that is likely to occur in favor of the central importance of any one phase of history when it is made the separate focus of study. Certainly the law has been a significant force. The idea here put forward, however, is that on the whole its role has been much more to organize, channel, legitimize, and in a substantial measure to redirect the course of changes that started outside the law. Realistically viewed, this does not take away from the importance of law in our society. Quite the contrary. Change is one of the few things men can be certain of. Any institution whose job is to deal directly, in as rational a way as possible, with this ceaseless flux, is to be counted one of the truly basic instruments of civilized living.

II. The Legislature

CHAPTER TWO

THE INHERITANCE OF THE LEGISLATURE

Logic might suggest that we begin our history with constitutional conventions: they made the "fundamental law." But as of our chosen base date, 1790, the legislature stands out as the first agency which exercised broad, creative influence in our law. So we shall begin with it.

Throughout the history of the United States, Congress has played a large, sometimes the leading role, in policy making and enforcement. State legislatures have had years of creative vigor. But as we measure this branch of our government against its historic endowment, it does not show the pre-eminent record we might expect.

The years from 1750 to 1820 offered legislators a chance to become the principal lawmakers for the nation as a whole and also for the states. In the War of 1812, during the years of the compromise over extension of slave territory and during Reconstruction, Congress led the country. Later on came the periods when the Senate dominated affairs, first between 1890 and 1910 as the "rich men's club" and between 1918 and 1926 as the seat of the party stalwarts. State legislatures also had their years of ascendency: when they tried to deal with banking and business cycles in the 1820's and '30s, when later they responded to the successive promotion of turnpikes, toll bridges, canals, and railroads, and finally in the 1870's, when they tried to curb railroad arrogance.

Yet we shall see, as we go on, that the story of the legislature becomes largely negative in the telling. Potential promise was not fulfilled. Where legislative leadership defaulted, judges too often acquiesced in the unregulated behavior of individuals or corporations. Later on much of the initiative passed to the executive and administrative branches.

1. ORIGINAL ADVANTAGES

The legislature began the postcolonial period with an impressive trinity of advantages:

1. its legitimacy in public opinion
2. its broad authority under the Constitution

3. its power as the grand inquest of the nation and states to inquire into matters of public concern.

The colonial years left a long memory in the first states of conflicts in which the legislature spoke for home interests against English trade and land policies that were designed to subordinate the American settlements to the British economy and ruling class. Moreover, in these contests, the legislature often spoke immediately in opposition to the colonial executive and courts, which were appointed agents of Crown policy. Because the other branches were creatures of the Crown, the legislative assemblies took direction of the gathering drive for independence, and of the war that followed. Through their committees they exercised a good deal of executive and judicial power. Success supplied a grateful tradition to cover the faltering, indecisive, often timid record which they made. The fight to enlist public opinion for independence planted deep in popular imagination the notions that the people were sovereign and that the locality was a natural unit for their representation. From these ideas the popularly elected, single-member-district assembly derived a firm acceptance as the most direct and authoritative voice of public policy.

The early constitutions gave the legislature broad power. There they bore witness to its high public standing. The first state constitutions simply vested "legislative" power in described bodies. The grant implied the historic sweep of authority that Parliament had won, except as this was limited by vague implications to be drawn from the formal separation of powers among legislature, executive, and courts.

Typically, the early constitution makers set no procedural requirements for the legislative process. They wrote a few declarations or limitations of substantive policy making. But these generally did no more than declare what contemporary opinion or community growth had already so deeply rooted as to require no constitutional sanction. For example, feudal tenure was abolished — beyond any need for the constitutional prohibitions — by the facts of unlimited free land and an absence of an inherited class structure. The same facts, more than the law's command, effected the separation of church and state. The first ten amendments to the Federal Constitution were adopted simply to put beyond question limits which by common opinion already bound the new government.

Theoretically, Congress was limited by the need to find in the Constitution a grant of any power that it desired to exercise. But the one hundred and fifty years of growth under the unamended terms of the Constitution testify to the sweep with which power was granted. The point was underlined when the framers included authority "To make all Laws which shall be necessary and proper for carrying into Execution" the powers vested in the federal government, without limiting this to laws in aid of powers expressly granted. The state governments inherited the Anglo-American political tradition without requirement of a grant, and were deemed to hold all power not denied them by their constitutions. This fact only emphasized the extent of power that was granted when a state constitution simply vested "legislative" power in one branch of government.

The Congress by express grant and the state legislatures by implication possessed the power of the purse. It was their proper inheritance from the English struggle for Parliamentary supremacy as well as from the American fight for independence. The battles fought over the power to tax and to spend measure the potentialities of this authority. Through the power of the purse the legislature could control all other agencies of government. But this emphasizes only the negative aspect of the power. More important, especially in face of the challenge of a new continent, control of the purse gave the legislature exclusive possession of the indispensable resources for making positive public policy.

The third advantage which the legislature held from the start of its career in the modern United States was the power of inquiry into matters of public concern. Law represents an effort — however short of the ideal — to order men's affairs according to rational weighing of values and the means of achieving them; how the lawmaker learns the facts of the living society in which he intervenes is, therefore, a point of fundamental importance regarding the manner of lawmaking. No agency in our government inherited a fact-gathering authority in any degree comparable to that of the legislature. As an essential instrument of its rise to control in the sixteenth and seventeenth centuries, the House of Commons established in practice a broad power to investigate matters that it felt relevant to the general welfare; likewise it developed the means to enforce its right of inquiry by contempt proceedings under its own hand against recalcitrant witnesses. Like the House of Commons, the colonial assemblies early assumed the right to look into the conduct of other parts of the government and into other matters of public concern; they, too, enforced their right of investigation by the contempt power. The authority continued to be recognized in the almost unchallenged practice of the Continental Congress, the Congress under the Federal Constitution, and the legislatures of the states.

Prior to the middle of the nineteenth century, there are no significant judicial decisions regarding the scope of the legislative power of investigation. The fact attests the strength of the unquestioned authority fixed by legislative practice of three hundred years. This authority plainly included the power to look for facts that the lawmakers believed relevant to their decisions as to what laws ought to be passed, as well as facts about the way in which the executive and judicial branches were working under laws that already existed. Holding the purse, the legislature had the means with which to start and support broad inquiries. This fact had another aspect: apart from traditional limits upon their fact-finding authority, other government agencies could in any case pursue only such inquiries as funds granted by the legislature might permit.

These were the factors that gave the legislature the opportunity to become the principal lawmaker in the United States. It began with preeminence in popular opinion, in sweep of constitutional authority, and in extent of the essential powers and means of investigation. Later, we shall consider the functions that the legislative branch performed in the growth of American law. But before this, we must consider the subsequent history of the trinity of advantages with which the legislature began, and the trends in personnel, machinery, and procedure which developed the institutions we call "Congress" or "the legislature."

2. THE INSTITUTIONAL FRAMEWORK

From 1787 to 1950 the structure of the legislature in both national and state governments changed little. This apparently unchanged structure produced different results at different times, according to the currents of events that played on it. Over this span the legislature kept the full measure of its inherited powers, both its authority to define the public policy of the community, and its important assisting power of investigation. But in its representative character, and hence indirectly in its public standing, the legislature suffered a real loss from its original inheritance.

a. The Lawmaking Power of Congress

The substantive powers of Congress were materially affected by formal amendment only in the changes made just after the Civil War, and in the income tax amendment of 1913.

The men who pushed through the postwar changes, notably the Fourteenth Amendment, clearly intended to revolutionize the balance of power in the federal system in two respects. They meant that the national government, rather than the states, should thenceforth hold the dominant authority to define and protect the rights of persons. And they meant that the Congress should be the principal agency of the national government to exercise this new authority.

The boldness with which the Supreme Court of the United States asserted power for itself under the due process and equal protection clauses of the Fourteenth Amendment in the generation following Reconstruction obscured the objectives of the Radicals who put through the postwar amendments. The latter, we shall see, were probably aware of the possibilities of an expanded judicial review under the terms of the Fourteenth Amendment, and probably accepted this as a desirable accompaniment of their work. But they spoke primarily for the enhancement of the power of Congress; they represented above all else a Congressional revolt against the President's Reconstruction plans and Congressional demand that the gains of the war be secured according to Congress's judgment of how this might best be done. To them the heart of the constitutional revolution that they were effecting in the federal system was the provision in each of the postwar amendments, that "The Congress shall have power to enforce this article by appropriate legislation."

Like the postwar amendments, the Sixteenth Amendment, regarding an income tax, was designed to increase rather than to narrow the scope of Congressional power. So far as the Congress suffered any loss from its original authority, this was due to judicial review, and not to the formal processes of constitutional change.

But the limiting effects of judicial decisions were not broad or lasting. Before the depression legislation of the 1930's, the Supreme Court had held acts of Congress unconstitutional in only about sixty cases. In less than a dozen was the matter sufficiently important to arouse serious public discussion.

In what respects did Court decisions put in question the powers of Congress? Apart from issues under the Civil War amendments, the principal questions concerned the power to tax and spend, and to regulate commerce among the several states, and the use of those powers for purposes of social regulation. The Court certainly did not curtail the very important spending power; on the contrary it insured that power the full scope that the broad terms of the Constitution allowed. This was achieved by ruling that neither a federal taxpayer nor a state had the legal interest requisite to challenge Congress's use of the authority. The taxing power had a more varied history at the hands of the Court. Obviously the Congress could not tax the governmental operations of the states; but the Court gave to this proposition a questionable extension when it was held to bar federal taxes on persons or institutions that were regarded as state instruments. At most, however, this was a minor limitation on federal revenues. Much more serious was the Court's ruling, in 1895, that Congress might not tax incomes. This was, indeed, a major limitation on the federal revenue power; it was twenty years before the limitation was effectively overcome, by constitutional amendment and new laws. The issue was then fought out primarily as one of social justice; it may be guessed that the Court's ruling would have been nullified much sooner, had the demands on the national government been such as to make the income tax the critical source of federal revenue that it thereafter became.

In 1870 the Court ruled that Congress lacked authority to make United States notes legal tender in the payment of private debts. The decision touched deeply both the government's financial policy and its control over interstate commerce. Within a year, however, the decision was overruled; the overruling followed the resignation of one Justice, and the appointment of two others known to hold views opposed to the 1870 decision.

Before the 1930's the decisions that seemed to raise the most serious barriers to federal legislation regulating the economy were those which, in 1918, denied Congress's power to ban interstate shipment of goods produced by child labor, and, in 1922, held that federal taxation of the net profits of persons employing children interfered with an exclusive power of the states to regulate their domestic affairs. Closely related in policy was a ruling of 1923: Congress, the Court said, could not, consistent with the due process of law required by the Fifth Amendment, provide for minimum wage standards for adult women employed in the District of Columbia. Those restrictive decisions had effect, however, for no more than fifteen years from the last of them. When economic disaster shook the nation in the mid-1930's, they fell before the demands of events.

Judicial review has its drama. That this may exaggerate its long-run influence was most strikingly shown between 1934 and 1937. In that period the Supreme Court first asserted, then renounced, the greatest degree of control over legislative policy that judges had ever claimed in the United States.

In the October term, 1934, the Court held invalid Congress's delegation to the President of power to forbid interstate transportation of oil produced in violation of state law. It held unconstitutional Congress's joint resolution requiring payment in paper of gold obligations of the United States and of private debtors, though it found no legal damage resulting therefrom, in view of Congress's lawful action in impounding gold and regulating the value of the currency. It held invalid the

National Industrial Recovery Act: the act was an unconstitutional delegation of power to the executive; the act exceeded the power of Congress when it regulated wages, hours, and other aspects of intrastate business; the act could not be upheld as an effort to cope with nationwide economic depression. The Court ruled invalid an act establishing a compulsory retirement and pensions system for employees of interstate railroads, on the grounds that the act bore no reasonable relation to the regulation of interstate commerce, and that it violated due process of law. It held unconstitutional an act that altered remedies under farm mortgages; the statute, said the Court, exceeded the bankruptcy power and ran counter to the due process clause of the Fifth Amendment.

The October term, 1935, saw the peak of the judicial veto. The Court ruled that Congress might not tax the processing of farm products where it appeared that the tax, the appropriation of the proceeds of the tax, and the conditions of their disbursement were parts of a plan to increase the prices of farm commodities by cutting production. The matter, declared the Court, was one within the reserved powers of the states. It held that Congress exceeded its power under the commerce clause when it used the tax power to control wages, hours, and working conditions in coal mining, as part of a plan to help that depressed industry; the majority Justices indicated grave doubt that Congress could take any comparable action to fix prices for the sale of coal. The Court ruled that the bankruptcy power did not extend to permitting local government units to become voluntary bankrupts, even with the consent of their states.

In two terms, thus, the Court stripped the national government of the legislative power to deal with threatened disintegration of the national economy. Its decisions of these two years reduced Congressional power more than had been ever intimated by dicta of one hundred years past.

But the judicial veto lasted only for these two years. The 1934 and 1935 terms and their immediate sequel offer our most significant testimony to the relative weight of judicial and legislative policy making in the face of crisis. The reality of power is in facts. The facts here were plain enough: the economic interdependence of the nation, the threatening social cleavages opened by economic distress, the ground swell of popular values and the demands based on those values as shown in Presidential and Congressional elections, the successful threat of an abortive "Court-packing" bill. By the end of October term, 1938, Congress was pronounced secure in its authority to deal with the national wage and price structure, labor relations affecting interstate commerce, railroad pensions, farm prices, and the enforcement of farm mortgages.

Also significant of the realities of the balance of legislative and judicial power is the one field in which the Court effected a major and lasting cut in Congressional power. The Radical Republicans plainly intended that the Reconstruction amendments should empower Congress to guard the political, economic, and social rights of all persons or citizens against invasion from any source, private or public. More particularly, they intended that Congress should be able to deal effectively with any legal or extralegal efforts of the defeated Southerners to regain power at the expense of the Negroes or their white supporters. But the Radicals pushed their revolution farther than even the Republican members of the Court would go. In the next fifteen years, with scarce dissent, the Court ruled that the Reconstruction amendments permitted federal protection only against wrongful action by a state or its officers; the broad field of rights between private persons remained for the decision of the states, at least so far as concerned the Thirteenth, Fourteenth, and Fifteenth Amendments. This clear departure from the intention of the proponents of the amendments stood. That it did so, seems due to the lack of a sufficiently urgent pressure, either in public opinion, or in the habits of the people, to upset the Court's counterstroke. This time it was the Congress and not the Court that had overstepped the practical limits of effective constitutional action.

b. The Lawmaking Powers of State Legislatures

State constitutional history tells an apparently more tangled story of limits upon the powers of state legislatures. But in fact the net of the situation is much as in the case of Congress. The formal record, it is true, shows a sharp contrast between legislative power originally granted in broad and unqualified terms, and later hedged by various procedural and substantive limits. However, these formal limitations had little practical effect on the total extent of state legislative power.

Without exception, the procedural limits proved unenforceable, and meant only as much as legislative convenience permitted. In a relatively few cases courts held legislation invalid for procedural defects appearing on the legislative journals; the greatest effects of these examples seem to have been the encouragement of litigation and the creation of needless doubts as to the validity of laws.

So far as constitutional limitations on special and local laws were effective, they increased rather than reduced the importance of the legislature. After 1870 the typical legislature was under constant pressure of detail and particular interests. Any device that offered some protection from these distractions could hardly do other than add to the legislature's potential capacity to take the lead in making important policy.

The most significant formal limits put on the state legislatures related to the power of the purse: i. e., the limitations, or the total prohibition, set upon state debt, on the lending of state credit or other subsidies to private enterprise; and the limits put on local government finance. These provisions touched the most sensitive area of traditional legislative power. That they had practical effect is evidenced in efforts to get around them, or to adjust public finance to them. Legislatures had to make formal declarations of emergency; they had to create self-sustaining projects for public service; they felt compelled to set up new taxing or borrowing units to support sanitary, park, or school services; they had to extend home rule to local government units. The reality of these financial limitations, and the dubious wisdom of thus freezing the financial powers of government, were brought sharply to attention in the depressed 1930's, when state and local governments struggled to find valid means for financing relief and recovery programs. Constitutional limitations on state financial policy undoubtedly contributed to the extension of federal influence since that time.

Judges had far more effect than constitution makers on state legislative power; the record of their influence was the judge-made constitutional law of the due process and equal protection clauses of the Fourteenth Amendment. Perhaps the courts would not have needed the vague principles of that amendment to rationalize their veto. In the 1850's state courts began to say that legislation was subject to general principles of right and justice, fixed by natural law or perhaps by that "law of the land" which some state constitutions invoked as a measure of lawful government action. Our English constitutional inheritance gave to the concepts under which judicial review operated the prestige of safeguards to the liberty of the subject. Time made clear the fact behind the new symbols offered by the Fourteenth Amendment: judges asserted their power to limit the efforts of late-nineteenth-century legislatures to regulate the conduct of business and to redress the balance of power between social or economic classes or interests. Few judicial rulings under the Fourteenth Amendment prior to the 1930's protected the civil liberties of the individual against legislative invasion. In part, of course, this was because legislatures were not yet interesting themselves in much that concerned civil liberties. But this fact only emphasizes that in their constitutional decisions the courts were setting their judgment against that of the legislature in the main field of late-nineteenth-century controversy — the relation of economic power to other values in the society.

In three particularly basic respects judges set marked limits to the legislature's right to fix public policy: (1) the prohibition of minimum wage legislation; (2) the strict definition of the category of business so "affected with a public interest" that its charges and practices might be regulated; (3) the frustration of statutory protection for labor's right to organize.

The courts never lost all sense of the caution needed to handle social issues that ran this deep. Even in their broadest assertions of power, the judges kept open the means to accommodate judicial review to necessary change. They regularly conceded that statutes must be presumed constitutional; constitutionality was to be judged only as a particular case required it, and then in the light of the existing social justification for what the legislature had done. Through the sounding adjectives of the opinions gradually emerged the simpler concept: that the basic issues of due process and equal protection were whether reasonable men could find that the facts showed a public interest in a given regulation, and that the regulation might be thought a reasonable means to effect the public interest.

This more pragmatic approach reflected the powerful pull of the facts and of public opinion toward more government intervention in the economy. The judges exerted their veto at its fullest between about 1875 and 1905. In that period they drastically limited the legislature's power over the economy. However, by 1910 the courts were on the defensive; by then — though now increasingly under executive leadership — the legislature was in the ascendant. The surest evidence of the undertow of events came in 1912 when that naïve opportunist, Theodore Roosevelt, made national issues of the proposals for the recall of judges and of judicial decisions. Power was in the balance in the 1920's. The depression '30s demanded affirmative government action in economic affairs. This cast the issue decisively in favor of legislative power as against the judicial veto, on the state as well as the national front. The Supreme Court of the United States set the tone for the handling of due process and equal protection questions the country over. It dramatized the turning point when, in the October term, 1935, it reaffirmed by a 5-to-4 vote that the due process clause forbade legislative fixing of minimum wages for women, and then in the October term, 1936, again by 5 to 4 overruled this and the previous rulings, to sustain such regulation. By 1950 it appeared that within the predictable future there was little likelihood that any legislation regulating economic affairs would be held unconstitutional.

In sum, then, for the first fifty years of modern, urban-industrial society in the United States, judicial review directly limited national and state legislative regulation of the economy to a material degree. But the judicial veto speedily collapsed under the impact of genuine crisis in the 1930's. At this point we are concerned only with the fact of the balance of power between legislature and court; we can better postpone analysis of the sources, strength, and weakness of judicial review.

c. Indirect Limitations on Legislative Lawmaking

Balanced analysis, however, requires note of ways in which judicial review since about 1875 had indirect influence on legislative power which may have been as great as its direct effect. Politicians deciding what issues should be pressed for action had constantly to weigh the threat of judicial veto. So also had draftsmen, concerned with their definitions of objectives and with the devising of the means to reach those objectives. Nor was the indirect effect of judicial review exhausted when a statute was drawn and passed. Judges made confident by the sense of ultimate power in their hands were the readier to express disagreement with the legislature's policy judgments by applying strict construction to the legislative product.

We need to know a good deal more than we know now about the history of legislative and judicial power in the United States, before we can appraise the true weight of these secondary results of judicial review. But their reality is sufficiently established. President Jackson faced up to it when he asserted that, under his oath of office, he was as much bound to use independent judgment of constitutional issues as was the Supreme Court; and that hence he would not sign national banking legislation which he believed invalid, though the logic of Court decisions might be argued to the contrary. President Taft came to the opposite result, when he vetoed the Webb–Kenyon Act, because he found that the logic of the Court's rulings raised doubt of the act's consistency with Court doctrine. President Franklin Roosevelt followed Jackson, rather than Taft: if, he declared, the Congress and the President found that a scheme of price regulation for the bituminous coal industry was wanted for the regular and continued flow of interstate commerce, they should act accordingly, though judicial precedent might seem opposed. Whatever the varying positions, obviously the shadow of judicial review falls heavily upon these legislative episodes. In the field of state legislation, the development of workmen's compensation laws offers a leading example. These laws were first cast in a form allowing the employer the option of entering the compensation system, or of preserving his common-law status, at the cost of losing important common-law defenses. This form of statute was wholly due to draftsmen's fears that a compulsory act would be held unconstitutional as contrary to due process of law.

The relative timing of the development of judicial review and of certain judicial doctrines of strict construction of statutes evidences the link between the two. In the late nineteenth century the courts gave prominence especially to the rules that (1) a statute in derogation of (i. e., changing) the common law must be strictly construed; (2) acts that would otherwise impose a drastic (i. e., a substantial economic) burden upon the one regulated must be interpreted to limit their scope; and (3) a statute must be so construed (even at the considerable expense of the policy it was obviously designed to promote) as to avoid any grave doubt of its constitutionality. These propositions all assumed importance in the Reports and kept their prominence in almost exact correspondence to the period when the courts most broadly asserted their power to review the constitutionality of legislation.

The indirect influence of judicial review was probably as great on the national as on the state scene. Probably, too, the indirect effect of the judicial veto was as great as the direct, in restricting legislatures' efforts to regulate the economy. It seems to have been subject to about the same history of fluctuating fortunes.

d. Growth of Legislative Power to Investigate

The constitutional history of legislative power also requires consideration of what happened to the legislature's investigating authority. This story can be told rather briefly. The fact-gathering power remained primarily the creation of legislative practice. No material changes or additions were made in this area by constitutional amendment. The courts were asked to declare the law of the subject in cases surprisingly few in number, compared with the extensive activities of legislative investigating committees and the often controversial nature of their inquiries. The reasons for this are probably various. The bar seems to have been less aggressive in this field than in its more familiar battleground of the courts. Lawyers in our system by training and tradition long regarded the legislative process as alien to the true body of the law; they seem, therefore, not to have been alert to the possibilities of practice before legislative committees, and not as vigilant there as in court to assert the claims of clients. Moreover, legislative inquiry often was armored against successful legal attack: the committee commanded publicity, the adverse effects of which might overweigh even a successful legal challenge to the committee's probing; events, too, might move too fast in a legislative inquiry to permit practicable relief by court action against unauthorized or unfair tactics.

That such factors had weight is suggested by the scant result of the one restrictive opinion of the Supreme Court of the United States:

Kilbourn v. *Thompson* (1880). The Court there indicated that Congress lacked authority to investigate matters not pertinent to a specific and impending proposal for legislation, and, further, that some inquiries were in their nature judicial and not properly to be pursued by a legislative body. The voice of the Supreme Court is respected; normally if it intimates broader defenses for the individual against demands of government, this is enough to alert private counsel to expand on the intimation. There were but a handful of federal cases after *Kilbourn* v. *Thompson*. In 1927 in *McGrain* v. *Daugherty* (a case growing out of the Teapot Dome scandal), a bench better informed of the historic basis of the investigatory power and of the legislature's practical need of it in effect overruled the 1880 case. Regardless of any specific, pending bill, Congress was entitled to examine into the conduct of government and the spending of public money; whether an inquiry bore any judicial aspect was irrelevant, if in fact it might reasonably be deemed in aid of a legislative function. The Court, in effect, gave full recognition to the authority of Congress as the grand inquest of the nation.

Nothing in the state decisions ever cast doubt on the scope of state legislative power in this regard comparable to that raised by the *Kilbourn* opinion. To the contrary, state courts from the first important rulings in the 1850's staunchly supported the full extent of the investigatory function.

Federal and state court decisions together, however, were too few to take on the significance that legislative practice had in marking the scope of this authority. After 1850 legislative practice broadened the scope of proper investigation. It firmly established the right to look into facts pertinent to possible lawmaking. Perhaps even more insistently it fixed the legislature's right, as holder of the public purse, to inquire into the conduct of all branches of government. And it went further, into a new function appropriate to an age of unprecedentedly large voting publics and unprecedented public problems: the function of public information and education. The power of the subpoena and of the publicity which the legislature could command brought to light facts otherwise hidden or inadequately understood or weighed. Such was the main practical meaning of an investigation like that of the Temporary National Economic Committee in the later 1930's, regarding the concentration of economic power.

Legislative practice thus put the existence and extent of the investigative function on a firm and broad basis. This development was oddly without parallel in the matter of the procedure of investigation. The only fundamental procedural limits that the courts enforced were those set by the Bill of Rights against self-incrimination and against unreasonable search and seizure. But, as has been suggested, the courts could probably accomplish little practical redress in most aspects of this subject; the immediate damage which might go with the publicity of a legislative investigation would of itself make most judicial relief of limited effect. Of necessity only the legislature could fix and enforce standards of decency in legislative inquiry.

In one respect legislative practice tended toward a marked standard of fair play. The courts declared that no one was entitled, as a matter of judicially enforced constitutional limitation, to notice or hearing before a statute was passed, however much it might affect his interest. Plainly such a ruling was dictated by necessity; statute making typically affected too many and too vaguely defined a group, and must proceed with too great flexibility, to be confined to the notice-and-hearing requirements for entry of a valid judgment on a cause of action in tort. But, beginning with the first years of this century, legislative practice made it the rule that any major piece of legislation be thoroughly considered by legislators in consultation with at least the main organized interests affected by the proposal; and this was to be done not only regarding general policy, but in hammering out the details. The decisive precedent was the co-operative method by which the first workmen's compensation and modern industrial safety statutes were shaped in the states between about 1908 and 1912. In the national government, the increasing importance of federal taxation, especially taxation of individual and corporate incomes, soon made this the familiar procedure in that important field. The rise of administrative legislation — delegated rule making by administrative bodies — reinforced the trend by analogy: conference was from the start a characteristic method of the modern administrative process.

Notice and hearing, so far as legislative practice thus established them, were desirable, minimum decencies of procedure. But beyond this minimum, legislative investigations, national and state, developed little or no tradition of fairness to limit their conduct. Committeemen were not disqualified, however obvious their personal, partisan, or interest bias. The order of calling witnesses, the control of irrelevant or prejudicial testimony, fair opportunity for rebuttal or justification to persons whose good name was attacked or cast into suspicion, the qualification of witnesses, the maintenance of dignity, plan, and decorum in proceedings — all were matters left to the practically unchecked discretion of a given legislative committee, or such minority of its members as might sit.

Clearly the needs of effective legislative inquiry could not tolerate subjection of legislative procedure to the detailed scrutiny of the courts;

this would not work on any basis, quite apart from the impossible effort to impose on a legislative hearing the many and technical limitations surrounding court proceedings. On the other hand, it would seem that legislatures, aided by the prominence of lawyers in their number, should have been able to develop standards of fair and orderly committee procedure; moreover, they might fairly have been expected to provide their own internal means of calling to account a legislative inquiry which broke the bounds of decency.

Legislative practice did not develop along these lines. The reason may be inherent in the method: the example of the common law suggests that the case-by-case, instance-by-instance way of building law makes for tough and enduring substantive principle but falters in the creation of rational procedure. But the inertia of lawyers may have contributed, too. The case-bred lawyer of our legal system long felt legislation to be an alien field. The bar devoted courage, persistence, and vigilance for individual rights to the building of a tradition of fair court trial; but such lawyers' activity was tardily matched in the field of legislative proceedings. This was not for lack of historic basis. Such could be found in many records of stubbornly contested procedural points in Parliamentary inquiries into charges of treason, for example; there had been a field where political abuse gave ample occasion for battling out the elements of a fair hearing. Why the American bar did not build on this tradition is a puzzle, especially because this was an area in which the American lawyer could have given natural play to his highly individualistic bent.

Whatever the causes, a firm procedural tradition was lacking here. In the absence of a broad history of the legislative process in the United States, we cannot estimate the extent of abuse, or its cost in individual rights and legislative standing. Such a contemporary example as the slandering of political liberalism by the Dies Committee and its successor bodies investigating "un-American" conduct suggested that the cost had always been high.

3. REPRESENTATIVE CHARACTER

a. Changing Popular Attitudes Toward the Legislature

The part of its inheritance in which the legislature suffered serious loss was its title of legitimacy, its claim upon the people's trust and obedience as the agency most representative of their common interests. That the state legislature suffered such a loss of standing, and that this dated from the generation of the 1840's was attested by the general movement to write into state constitutions various procedural and substantive limits on legislative power. This is no less true, though many of these limitations had little practical effect. Much structural detail, we have seen, was put into state constitutions simply as matter of course. But these constitutional limitations that began in the 1840's were not matter-of-course in origin: Typically they expressed real, if often inarticulate or directionless, controversy between the well off and the hard pressed — between those who had wealth or who were skilled in exploitation and those who had mortgage debts and an unsophisticated capacity for hard work.

This current of distrust touched the Congress both earlier and later than it did the state legislatures. The timing was related to the gifts which the state and national sovereigns had at their disposal at different periods. The organization of the national government brought chances to speculate in the public debt, to seek tariff favors for manufactures, and to spread the cost of government among different groups in the population (as, for example, the whiskey distillers of the Pennsylvania back country). The rise of the two-party system and the Jeffersonian revolution of 1800 showed that a good part of the voters did not accept Congress as a coolly dispassionate instrument of the public will. South Carolina threatened revolt against the tariff in 1832; and over a forty-year span North and South contested closely for control of Congress. These tensions introduced into popular attitudes another basic principle of skepticism toward the national legislature: Congress, it seemed, might be the instrument of sectional, as well as of class interest, rather than of the general welfare. The Civil War did not dispose of sectional politics; rather it insured that the increasingly vigorous claims of the West would be added to the previous clash.

The twentieth century brought new evidence of distrust of the representative character of legislative assemblies. This showed itself in a wave of what now appears a rather naïve faith in institutional reforms. In the states, we had the movement for the direct primary, and the initiative, referendum, and recall. In the nation, there was the fight for the direct election of Senators. Naïve or not, and regardless of their varying results, these changes, like the constitutional limitations of the nineteenth century, emerged from real conflict, and reflected profound questioning of the representative title of the legislature.

Back of the varying issues and reforms lay a momentous movement in popular attitudes toward the business of government. Politics was every man's business in the early-nineteenth-century United States, and the Massachusetts–Pennsylvania–Virginia dynasty of the first generation of national politics showed that public affairs were the proper outlet for ambition and ability. Soon men became increasingly engrossed in the exploitation of the continent and the command of economic power. Probably no less a proportion of able and honest men went into public life, but they did their work without the sustaining interest and confidence of an earlier day. Politics, and more particularly politicians as legislators, became stock figures of critical humor. Artemus Ward and Bill Nye, Mr. Dooley and Will Rogers immortalized many such. Significantly, business and businessmen never became similar "fair game," except in the clearly fringe character of the genial confidence man, Jeff Peters or Get-Rich-Quick Wallingford.

If the legislature lost in standing with the people, how far was this due to features of organization or operation peculiar to the legislative process, and how far to influences outside it? Institutional machinery is usually not a prime cause of events; society moves by currents deeper and more impersonal than any set going by men's contrivance. So here: popular distrust of the legislature rooted in two main facts: (1) that legislation almost always followed, rather than directed, the events of economic and social life; (2) that the legislature too often proved unable to set up against the divisive pressures of particular interests a positive, working idea of the general welfare.

The foregoing propositions are set out as an hypothesis. Obviously they involve complex factors, not to be summarized in a paragraph. They are set down in order to put in perspective an analysis of the characteristic organization and working features of the legislature as it figured in United States legal history.

The structural aspects of the legislature, which had special bearing on its representativeness were: (1) the single-member, geographical district, (2) the absence of an automatic, or easily worked machinery for periodic reapportionment of legislative districts, and (3) the existence of two chambers.

b. Localism in the Legislature

Localism was deeply engrained in our political structure: in part it was an inheritance from England; in part it was a natural accommodation to a frontier country of great distances and poor communications; partly, too, it was the natural frame within which to express the people's political power at a time when divisions of social class and economic interest were roughly alike in broad sections of the country. The legislature was not the only agency of government whose structure was affected by insistence on the locality as the governmental unit; we must later pay considerable attention to the same factor when we consider the organization of courts.

People, then, quite naturally took it for granted in the formative

years that the most numerous — and hence presumably the most representative — chamber of the legislature should be elected on the basis of
one member to one geographically defined constituency. By a combination of custom and express constitutional requirement, they made
standard the additional requirement, that each representative must be a
qualified elector of the district for which he stood. Localism was thus
doubly confirmed. Through our history, the situation remained unchanged, and on the whole little questioned. One practical exception
developed on the national scene. Because reapportionment of Congressional districts often did not keep pace with the growing population,
provision had to be made for election of congressmen at large, in order
that a state have its due representation in Congress. There was here the
seed of an important change in constitutional practice, by which representation at large might have supplanted or at least supplemented the
single-member district type. This possibility was never fulfilled, however.

If the single-member geographical district continued unchanged, the
facts that shaped the balance of power in United States society did not.
The contrast had profound effect upon the working significance of our
representative system. After the 1880's, the United States ceased to be a
chiefly rural and small-town country and became a nation mainly urban
and metropolitan. This meant factors that reduced the meaning of the
locality in urban areas as the unit of representation. Life in the metropolis was more impersonal and self-centered; it sharpened the contrasts
in class position; it involved the concentration of masses of recent im-
migrants, lacking resources and helplessly unfamiliar with the ways
of their new home.

Such factors gave power to the growth and effectiveness of the city
political machine, by helping an aggressive and knowing professional
minority to control political affairs. The conservatism of United States
politics was thus on the whole enhanced, for the professional politician
builds power normally out of shrewd use of the chances for compromise and balance of forces in the social situation as he finds it. The exception is in times of crisis, when genuinely deep currents of public
opinion may force him to rechart the course.

Another combination of factors that reduced the representative
meaning of the locality was: (1) the dominance of regional, sectional,
and national markets, (2) the concentration of financial and industrial
power, and (3) the increasing sensitiveness of all parts of the economy
to what went on in any one part of it. The interests for which men
especially seek political expression are their concern with how they
make their living, how they get some measure of economic security,

and how they win and hold self-respect by some conviction that their lives have meaning in the larger pattern of the society. These interests of men had less and less relation to the fact of where they lived, especially after 1870. The most tangible evidence of this was the rapid and broad development after 1890 of a new-style "lobby." The new pressure groups had permanent professional staffs, and they did not draw their greatest influence from the personal approach and direct money or political favors of the classic railroad lobbyist of the '70s and '80s. They carried weight, rather, because of, and in proportion to, the convincing quality of their claims to represent broad constituencies vitally united by common economic or social interest, regardless of the accident of residence. In fact, as our society became increasingly marked by specialization, the single-member legislative district kept its meaning largely to the extent to which the life of a given district was dominated by one means of livelihood. Such was the source of the "blocs" that wielded power now and again in Congress: the farm bloc, the silver bloc, the labor bloc.

c. Apportionment of Legislators

To set up a form of representative government, one must define the unit of representation and provide for the apportionment of representatives of these units. These are more than essentials of form. They determine also the political balance of power; this was shown early in our national history by the familiar use of the gerrymander, the manipulation of legislative districts in order to maximize one's voting strength by extending it to as many districts as possible, while minimizing the opponent's by concentrating it in as few as possible. Districting and apportionment were thus a conspicuous subject in the various constitutions. The single-member district was the general rule. Population was made the basis of apportionment for both chambers in most states, as in the case of the United States House of Representatives. Most state constitutions contained limitations aimed at the gerrymander; it was required, for example, that districts be formed of contiguous territory, or that they be equal, or compact, or the constitution might forbid division of certain basic units such as counties. But, inconsistently, most state constitutions also sanctioned some measure of inequality as to one or the other, or both, of the houses of the legislature; usually this was done by guaranteeing to every basic district some minimum of representation regardless of population.

There were many constitutional provisions and many lively battles in constitutional conventions; but withal, inequality of representation among legislative districts was the rule rather than the exception. More often than any constitutional provisions, the legislature's inertia was at the bottom of such inequalities. In 1938 Walter found inequalities in senate districts in 26 states, due primarily to legislative inaction, in contrast to only 15 states where constitutional provisions were primarily responsible. Similarly, constitutional limitations made for inequality of lower chamber districts in 14 states, but legislative inertia had produced noticeable inequality in 22. In 25 states then lacking an up-to-date reapportionment, 11 had not been reapportioned since the census of 1930, 8 not since 1920, and 6 not for a period of 35 to 45 years. Additional cases of inequality could be argued to exist where reapportionment had been carried out in form more than in substance.

What was the main effect of inequalities in districting and apportionment? Undoubtedly, it was the underrepresentation of interests that centered on urban life, and overrepresentation of rural and small-town interests and attitudes. Thus in 1938 the urban population was in the majority in 21 states, but in only 11 of these could it control the legislature. The political results of this tended to form a pattern: (1) overrepresentation of the small-town and rural districts in party machinery, the organization of which was often based on legislative districts; (2) the tendency for one party to control rural and small-town politics, while the other party controlled urban politics; (3) overrepresentation of rural and small-town districts in the processes of constitutional amendment, whether by convention or through the legislature; (4) greater chances for the rural and small-town areas to win senior posts in the legislative committees, especially since there seemed to be a tendency for legislators from these districts to come back a greater number of times to the legislature; (5) from all these elements, a more hospitable atmosphere for farm groups than for industrial or labor lobbies in many legislatures. Again, as in the case of the single-member-district system, structure contributed to build a fundamentally conservative spirit in United States politics.

Main responsibility for these inequalities in representation might in the first instance be assigned to the inertia of the legislature, or to politically motivated complacence. But the ultimate defect was the absence of some procedure to deal with these predictable factors. Ultimately 6 state constitutions authorized, and 30 plus the Federal Constitution required, apportionment of legislative districts after each federal census. Neither the Federal Constitution nor the state constitutions provided for enforcement of this obligation. Without exception the courts warily avoided the political battles and the impossible problems of execution that would have been involved if the judges had tried to make the legislators do their duty. Mandamus thus would not lie to command the passage of an apportionment act, nor quo warranto to challenge the title of legislators elected under an outdated apportionment, nor injunction to prevent payment of their salaries. Nor would the courts apply indirect pressure by refusing to recognize as valid the acts of a legislature elected under an out-of-date apportionment; failure to reapportion was held merely to pass the duty on to the next legislature, a body sitting under an outdated apportionment was the *de facto* legislature, and its acts under such color of authority were binding.

In decisions or opinions dated almost wholly in the '90s, courts in 22 states ruled, or indicated, that when the legislature had passed an apportionment act, its conformity to the constitutional requirements presented a justiciable question. But the traditional presumption of constitutionality applied to such a statute, as to any other. The courts ruled, therefore, that all they could decide was whether the apportionment provided might reasonably be deemed to meet the test of equality; whether the court itself would find the apportionment a fair one was not in issue. Even under this generous test, in 25 cases decided up to 1938, 17 laws had been held invalid, and only 8 approved.

The laying out of districts is too basic, and inherently too political a problem for any agency but the legislature to handle. It is another question to decide how many representatives should be apportioned to districts, when their populations vary over a period of time. This calls for the exercise of much narrower discretion. For this, the constitution makers might have provided a better solution. But improvement came late. Under the federal Reapportionment Act of 1929, the Bureau of the Census worked out an apportionment according to a statutory formula, and this apportionment became effective unless Congress overruled it by statute. This at least put the force of legislative inertia behind the cause of up-to-date apportionment, instead of against it. California and South Dakota — and once, Missouri — provided administrative action on apportionment, in default of legislative decision. Apart from working against inertia, the administrative device had the virtue of being enforceable. Mandamus could be had against laggard administrators without the practical enforcement difficulties that such a move would meet if directed against the legislature. A more ponderous machinery to get around the blocks to legislative reapportionment was the initiative; it was used for this purpose in Colorado and Washington.

d. Who Was Represented by the Second Chamber?

The third structural feature that particularly affected the representative character of the legislature was bicameralism. The two-chamber legislature grew at first out of theories of representation. One chamber

— the more numerous in membership — was to be directly elected by the most broadly defined electorate of the time and place. The other chamber was to have a smaller membership, elected either indirectly or by an electorate limited by a property qualification. Moreover, special qualifications were often set for the members of the second chamber: they must be of a minimum age higher than that set for the members of the more numerous chamber; or they must own a certain amount of land or other property. In the states the main object originally was that the upper house represent the propertied class, and check the taxing, spending, and leveling tendencies of assemblies subject to a broader suffrage. Like thinking was involved in the creation of the United States Senate, but there the primary factor was the political compromise between the large and small states.

Events worked great changes in the practical significance of the second chamber, both in the states and in the nation. The vote was steadily extended to more and more people; along with this went the demand that more and more offices be brought under direct election of the people; democratic symbols became the formal banners of all parties after Jackson. This meant the end of any practical effort to make the second chamber an avowed representative of property. The new temper was conclusively shown as early as the New York state constitutional convention of 1821. Kent and Spencer there took the floor in behalf of a proposal that a higher property qualification be set for election to the state senate. Bluntly they declared that this was necessary to preserve the power of the landed interest in the face of the rising tide of urban population. Debate was warm and lengthy, but only one other speaker rallied to the two stalwarts, and the final vote was 100 to 19 against their proposal. On the other hand, as we have seen, much constitutional structure was borrowed almost casually in the setting up of new states. This led to the adoption in some states of a second chamber designed, in superficial analogy to the federal situation, to represent localities of the state. This seems to have been done in Rhode Island in the creation of its second chamber in 1842. Over the years any differences between state chambers on grounds of sectional representation tended to disappear. In 1938 Walter found that "in fourteen states the senate represents population better than the lower house, in twenty-two states there is no difference, and in twelve states the lower house represents population more nearly than the senate."

Political growth also changed the role of the United States Senate. The original large-small state cleavage lost meaning almost as soon as the new government went into effect. Thereafter the equal representation of states in the Senate took on two meanings, both quite different

from the original plan. (1) Through all our national history the equal
representation of the states made the Senate the critical battleground
for the politics of sectional interest. Through it the less wealthy and
less populous South and West could bargain to some effect with the
Northeast and Central states. (2) With results generally almost the
same in expression as those that came from sectional division, the equal
representation of states enhanced the bargaining power of agriculture
and of raw-materials producers as against finance, manufacture, and
urban labor. Like interests recognized each other across regional and
sectional lines and often on a national scale in the kind of economy we
had after the 1870's. Overleaping state boundaries, they worked to give
a new functional meaning to the special representative character of the
United States Senate.

In the course of these developments the balance of power now and
again shifted. The Senate of the '70s and '80s was largely dominated by
sectional politicians. The Senate of the '90s and the early years of the
twentieth century was controlled by representatives of finance and big
business. In the 1920's the farm bloc and professional politicians made
the decisions, and in the depression '30s an uneasy alliance of labor and
farmers controlled.

In any case, experience developed a marked difference between the
role of the second chamber in the states and in the national government.
Though the lines varied, the Senate of the United States continued to
play a distinct representative role, because its members spoke for a
distinct constituency. In the states the second chamber lost any distinctive representative character that it ever had. By mid-twentieth century its chief meaning lay in the particular services it performed, and
the particular difficulties it presented, in the internal operation of the
legislature. Paradoxically, in the unfolding of state constitutional history, the part of the legislature's structure which was most directly
designed to affect its representative nature, in the long run least affected
it.

CHAPTER THREE

THE USES OF THE LEGISLATURE

1. MEMBERS

Who were the men who were Congressmen and United States Senators, assemblymen and state senators in the years after 1790? What was their representative character? What do we know of the factors that influenced them?

The only accurate answer is that we know little. Such studies as exist have dealt only with the few factors that are most easily measured — chiefly age, education, occupation, and previous government experience. Thus they give relatively superficial evidence about the representative character of the legislature, or the influences that played on the selection of its members.

People have sometimes tried to find trends in the quality of legislators over the years. Any answer may mislead. In the first place, we lack data. Furthermore the question invokes too general a concept to have much meaning. Legislation dealt at one time or another, in varying degrees of effectiveness, with most of the major problems in American history. Measured against such a range of challenges, legislative performance naturally differed considerably from one time to another and between different issues.

The legislature was the central and most accessible arena for the conflict or adjustments of interests. Hence it handled much humdrum but essential work as well as the dramatic issues of the time. Because of this and because its membership reached to all corners of its constituency, much of the legislature's meaning was in its corporate action. The years, however, cover up the mass of essential routine and the individually small, but totally meaningful, adjustments. There are left, in undue prominence, a few strong-willed or articulate individuals, acting on a few dramatic issues. On the other hand, we are well aware of the detail in the present which we easily forget in the past and are thus likely to magnify the number and importance of the individuals who loom up through the years, and to disparage unfairly the work of those closer to us, who are so clearly entangled in unimportant immediacies. Motives, too, are more obviously mixed among our contemporaries than they appear to be among the men of distant years; the latter we are more apt to judge on their own terms, whether we realize it or not, because we judge on the basis of a record that they made for themselves.

Such evidence as we have suggests that Congress and the state legislatures possessed about the same amounts of ability, integrity, and experience at all stages as they show today. There was some tendency toward a higher age level; but this was partly consistent with the general upward curve of long-livedness in the population. The proportion of college and professional school graduates or of men with some college or professional school education increased; this, again, followed a trend that could be seen in the general population. Lawyers and farmers consistently led all other occupations by wide margins in practically all legislative rosters analyzed; together they typically made up from 40 to 60 per cent of the membership. Lawyers apparently tended to number at least 20 per cent of the membership, and often more than a third. The percentage of lawyers in Congress was strikingly higher than in the state legislatures, and on occasion went as high as 75 per cent of the Senate and 65 per cent of the House. Lawyers' importance in both national and state legislatures was heightened by the importance of the committee assignments and the committee chairmanships which they usually held. Some tendency appeared for a higher percentage of lawyers in the chamber having the smaller membership and the longer tenure. No other occupational group apart from the farmers and the lawyers showed a sufficiently pronounced role to deserve special mention. The predominance of white-collar men was marked. Equally marked in all studies over all periods was the absence of any significant number of laboring men.

One half to two thirds of the legislators had prior experience in government on some level, either as party officials, or as elected or appointed officers in local, state, or national government. In sharp contrast, however, was the general lack of any substantial experience in the legislature itself. In the state legislatures about one half of the membership in the more numerous house was typically attending its first session. This percentage was lower for the upper house only because in it the term of office was ordinarily long enough to include two regular sessions; even there, however, at least one third of the men had typically served but one term. Studies showed few instances in which more than one third of the membership had served as many as four terms in either house. There was no convincing evidence that there was a significant difference in the rate of re-election as between rural and urban districts; legislators from the metropolitan areas did, however, show a slightly higher percentage of re-election.

The evidence was too scattering for safe generalization about any long-range trend in the legislative experience of state legislators. Some evidence suggested an increase in experience. In Illinois, for example, only 11.2 per cent of those elected to the lower house in the years 1850–1868 had served in the immediately preceding session, whereas in 1925–1933 that house averaged 27.6 per cent new members per session. Deming's figures for the Massachusetts lower house, on the other hand, show an unbroken drop in the percentage of members re-elected from the previous year, from 63.7 per cent in 1790 to 5.2 per cent in 1889, though the percentage climbed back to substantial figures from then on. Both houses of Congress tend to show a definite and increasing tendency toward higher percentages of re-election than in the states. Luce notes, for example, that whereas but 53 per cent of the members of Congress in 1871 had served before, in 1918 the percentage was 76.

The greater turnover in state legislative personnel naturally reflected itself in frequent changes in key committee chairmanships. Even though these were usually held by men of prior legislative experience, ordinarily there were not enough old hands to go around. Men could not be left to gain experience in the same committees but must be shifted from session to session to make the broadest use of the available knowledge of the job. On the other hand, the greater tendency of men to return to Congress was reflected in more stability in top committee jobs.

If we had all the facts about these measurable aspects of legislators' backgrounds, our criteria of legislative quality would still be limited. Greater age and more education raise some presumption of a broader base of information and general experience. They raise a less clear presumption of more trained judgment, and, unfortunately, little more than a purely theoretical assumption of greater objectivity, moral courage, or imagination. Studies which showed that the average age of members of Congress tended to exceed that of the electorate suggested an element that might contribute to make the legislature more conservative than its constituents.

A man's outlook is shaped by his experience, and his experience largely by his livelihood. Occupation thus may tell more about the representative quality of legislators. The evidence is somewhat suspect, since it is based wholly on legislators' own very general, and often probably colored or deceptive descriptions of their main occupations. Still, the data clearly shows their overwhelmingly middle-class background, and the accompanying lack of any nearly proportionate direct representation of the lower middle class, farm tenants, farm labor, or industrial labor. Contrary to common assertion, the evidence does not show that farmers enjoyed membership substantially out of proportion to their place in the total population. The high number of lawyers swelled the middle-class predominance. But the implications of this evidence require careful weighing, for the history of the bar shows the persistent tendency of all politically effective, organized interests to take the lawyer as their agent. No great difference appeared in this respect between rural and urban areas.

Occupational background thus suggested some material facts about the general class attitudes likely to be prominent in legislative operations. The evidence cannot safely be pressed further; on occasion a legislature might give quite direct expression to particular occupational interests of particular legislators, but in the large, there was little evidence for the specific influence of occupation on legislative performance.

Likewise conjectural was any estimation of the causes for the occupational selection of legislators. The single-member legislative district encouraged compromise; this perhaps made it more natural that lawyers — by profession accustomed to accommodation of interests — should go to the legislature in considerable number. On the other hand, no evidence showed that there were marked differences in the occupational line-up as between lower and upper house; bicameralism apparently did not affect the types of occupational background. The evidence did suggest that lawyers and farmers were so numerous among legislators, especially in the states, because their staple means of livelihood were more consistent with taking time out for a legislative career.

This last factor suggests what was clearly the main cause for the high turnover in legislative membership; at least, such was the indication of twentieth-century evidence, which was about all that was available. Hyneman found that in six sessions, 1925–1935, in eight widely representative states, only 16.1 per cent of 1965 house members and 14.7 per cent of 511 senators who quit service did so because they had lost at the polls; the figures were not much higher even in years of voting changes of landslide proportions, when two men were found to retire voluntarily for every one who lost at the polls. Most legislators gave financial reasons as the cause of voluntary retirement. No such poll exists for retiring Congressmen; the generally longer service there, however, suggested that finances were somewhat less of a problem, or had been more adequately taken care of.

There was little evidence of the effects of high turnover in membership on the nature of legislative performance. Presumably the comparative inexperience of a sizeable proportion of legislators worked to

the detriment of their job. Certain characteristics of legislative operation supported the inference, since they seemed likely to go with lack
of practiced firmness and tradition in the work: (1) Business typically
got under way slowly in each session, and was jammed at the end. (2)
Most committees worked without adequate investigation. (3) Much
proposed legislation was poorly drawn. (4) The legislature gave too
much time to detail in lawmaking — to petty bills, and to the minutiae
of bills of broader range — and likewise bogged itself in detail when it
examined the conduct of other branches of the government. (5)
Whether out of conviction or timidity, the legislature gave too much attention to the narrow concerns of particular localities or particular
persons or groups at the expense of attention devoted to general policy.
Such were marks of inexperience and reflected as much the lack of a
sound, sustaining tradition as they did the effects of partisanship and
special interest.

Apart from such circumstantial evidence of the effects of legislative
turnover some specific testimony appears. Such witness, for example, is
borne by Stewart's study of the work of the Kentucky lower house in
1932. Of 958 bills and resolutions introduced at that session of the
house, 270 were relatively unimportant measures, to name specified
local roads as "primary" roads. Rural members introduced the overwhelming bulk of these, and most conspicuous in this activity were the
members serving their first term. Among the remaining bills, the bulk
were introduced by a small number of experienced legislators. The men
who introduced most of the "primary" road bills introduced few bills
on other subjects; those who introduced most of the other legislation
sponsored few of the road bills.

These, then, were the more measurable qualities of legislative membership. Clearly these characteristics were important only as they
implied something about factors less easily measured — detachment,
disinterested concern for the general welfare, integrity, reach of imagination. On these deeper issues of appraisal, we have but one type of
evidence, and that of two divisions. It is opinion evidence. Contemporaries were never reluctant to have their say about legislators or their
work, and in a consistently critical tone. This suggests, for one thing,
that the great days of the elder statesmen were not so far above the
quality of our own time as we are sometimes moved to think. It suggests, further, that — barring such depths as those reached in the 1870's
— the legislative branch at any given time showed about the same adequacy to the challenge of its day as it did at any other period. This
inference finds support, on the whole, in the testimony of contemporar-

ies of greater experience, if not of greater objectivity, such as Maclay, John Quincy Adams, or Henry Adams. The best commentary on such elusive elements as the moral character and wisdom of the legislature is provided by the more impersonal record of the social functions that it performed in the successive phases of our national life. The last section of this chapter will attempt to analyze these functions.

2. Working Characteristics

Before we can appraise the social jobs that the legislature did, we must look at some features of its operation. These features derived partly from the legislature's constitutional structure, but more from its practice. They had weight not so much because they expressed the personal qualities of the legislators, as because they responded to conditions that set the framework of legislative action. These characteristics included the short session, the changing meaning of the two-chamber aspect of legislative structure, the concentration of leadership — especially in the parties and the committees — the legislature's working relation to the lobby, its lack of professional staff and of machinery for handling detail.

a. The Short, Intermittent Session

An assumption so ingrained as to call for no attention until well into the twentieth century was that a legislative body did not work continuously, but met only at regular intervals, or upon special call, and in either case for limited periods of time. This was implicit in the common constitutional provisions that defined the ordinary and extraordinary occasions for sessions. It was underlined from mid-nineteenth century on by amendments in many states that set rigid limits to the length of sessions. In origin, this concept of the legislature as an intermittent body reflected a time when people made only modest demands on government. There was not enough business, or enough urgent business, to call for a more continuous legislative agency. The same facts were reflected, also, in court organization; judges sat only when there were "terms of court," and these could be set for limited intervals and still handle all the business. Later this conception of the legislature's work was strengthened by the distrust with which both the people at large, and the conservatives of the community, came to regard the legislature; the constitutional provisions that limited the terms of legislative sittings expressed this distrust.

The idea that intermittent, relatively short sessions were the normal way for a legislature to work was never seriously challenged in principle. In practice there were departures from it. In the 1930's the growing volume of business, and the wider reach of the federal government, generated pressures that kept Congress in more continuous session than the accepted tradition would indicate. In the states, especially in the twentieth century, legislatures increasingly used joint interim committees to do the continuous labor necessary for major policy enactments. In some states the governors took away the practical effect of constitutional limits on the length of sessions by making liberal use of their power to call special sessions.

Such practices hinted at a new idea of the legislature — as a body that in effect, if not formally, sat continuously, in order to handle business faster and to explore issues more carefully. A full change in the tradition of legislative business seemed far off. But the tendency toward change was grounded in facts and not in theory.

The accepted idea of the intermittent, limited legislative session had great effect on the way in which the legislature did business, and the scope and quality of the work done: (1) It promoted the end-of-session jam of bills. This meant that there was much chance in the decision of what bills were enacted, much opportunity for undercover deals among politicians and special-interest groups, and too much control in the hands of the small, tight circle of inner leadership. (2) It handicapped the operation of the standing committees. In the absence of statute, their authority ran only for the life of the session, and their members lost the much needed experience that a continuing program might give. (3) It probably contributed to the lack of long-range policy planning and sustained execution that were main weaknesses of the legislature — though this last, and most important, point is hard to prove.

The lack of planning and follow-through is clearly established by the record. That the idea of limited sessions contributed to this result is suggested by the important role that the interim committee played in the most important state legislation of the twentieth century. The point is reinforced by contrast to the situation in Congress. There greater continuity of membership, plus the seniority rule in committee assignments, gave the standing committees of the House, and even more those of the Senate, somewhat the character of agencies of a continuously operating legislature. But the predominance of executive and administrative agencies in shaping twentieth-century legislative programs was the strongest evidence that the limited session had crippled the planning function of the legislature. Continuous responsibility was an essential part of the concept of executive power, and its expression was unhampered either by formal or traditional limitations.

b. The Working Significance of the Second Chamber

The two-chamber organization was by far the most conspicuous structural feature of the legislature in the United States, casually adopted by constitution makers and in late years much debated and studied. In the generation after independence, Georgia (1777–1789), Pennsylvania (1776–1790), and Vermont (1777–1836), had one-chamber legislatures. None of these seems to have abandoned the one-chamber form as a result of any deliberate or adequate examination of the merits of its performance as compared with that of the two-chamber legislature. Georgia seems to have dropped its one-chamber legislature because of a desire to put the new state constitution into apparent conformity with the Federal Constitution. In Pennsylvania there was vague talk that a one-chamber legislature did not offer enough opposition to the extremes of faction, and this is the most tangible residue of such talk as there seems to have been in connection with dropping the one-house legislature. The one-chamber form was set up in Vermont in 1777 under a constitution that followed the Pennsylvania constitution of 1776 so closely in form, as well as in time, as to suggest that Vermont had given little independent consideration to the kind of legislature it would provide. There is no evidence of any deep consideration behind the decision of the Vermont constitutional convention in 1836 to abandon the one-house form. That type of legislature seems to have stirred no popular or political reaction during the substantial period in which it functioned in the state; at the most, there are some indications that the switch to a two-chamber legislature, when it came, was favored by business and financial interests that were fighting contemporary agitation for regulation of banks. Revival of practical interest in the one-chamber legislature had to wait upon the long and energetic campaign that Senator George W. Norris waged to install it in his home state of Nebraska. He accomplished that change in 1937. Political scientists were interested in the change and its effects, but the concern which they felt seemed matched by complete apathy on the part of the public.

Apologists of the two-chamber legislature in the states claimed for it various features which they marked as virtues. The only one of these that can be shown to have been achieved was the production of delay. In practice this operated mainly to the interest of those who opposed extension of legislation regulating the economy. Even this accomplishment did not result according to theory. Delay, opportunity for obstruction, duplication of investigation and deliberation resulted from the simple fact that two relatively independent bodies must be moved to action, rather than one. But the classic case for the two-chamber legislature rested not on results to be had from mere multiplication of houses, but on the assumption that one chamber would differ in functional character from the other. Its supporters argued that the less numerous chamber, elected for a longer term (and, originally, elected indirectly or by a limited electorate, or from among persons of special property qualification), would show more moderation, more deliberate judgment, and greater experience and skill in the technical quality of performance.

Reliable studies of the second chamber in operation date only from this century. But for that time at least they unanimously confirm that the two chambers in the states evolved into substantial similarity, both in type of member and in function. Age and educational averages might run a bit higher in the "upper" house, but to no material extent. Lawyers might average a higher percentage in state senates than in assemblies, but no one proved any particular consequences of that factor; taken as a whole, the chambers showed no pattern of occupational or functional representation. Longer tenure naturally meant longer legislative experience, but in either legislative chamber there were few experienced men and they had to be spread thin through the key committee jobs in both houses. Other aspects of the representative character of the chambers showed equally inconclusive differences. In party complexion the two were usually alike, though the majority party might be stronger in the senate, because its members were usually elected from larger districts. The senate was apt to have a somewhat higher percentage of members from the larger cities, but in two thirds of the states the rural and small-town areas were generally overrepresented in both houses.

Evidence on performance was no more conclusive of any special virtues of the two-chamber organization. If a better product resulted, it came apparently from a double check on work done, rather than because the character of operations differed as between the two houses. The end-of-session rush marked all American legislatures after the early years. Primary responsibility for it probably could not be assigned to the delays of getting measures through two bodies. Though party or special-interest maneuvers might contribute, the main reasons for the jam seemed to be a combination of the volume of business that legislatures tried to handle, the inexperience of the bulk of their members, and their limited sessions. But if the two-chamber organization did not cause the jam, there was no evidence that it did anything to lighten it. In the face of the theory that a second chamber would bring less haste and more thorough consideration, both houses typically wound up a session by passing the bulk of measures, important and unimportant, in a hectic last two weeks.

A closely related theory was that the second chamber would critically review the work of the other house. We have only quantitative measures by which to test this theory — the number of bills rejected, the number of amendments made — and these suggest little as to the quality of such review as took place. We have seen that the two chambers tended to be alike in the age, experience, social and party background of their members; from this we might well infer that neither chamber was likely to show a more pronounced character as reviewing agency than the other. Other data support this inference. Most bills were killed in the house of origin. Of bills passed by one house, no high percentage — almost never more than 20 per cent — was rejected by the other. In some states the upper house typically rejected a higher percentage of bills originating in the lower than the latter rejected among bills originating in the upper chamber; but in at least as many of the sessions that were studied, the reverse was true. The executive generally vetoed a higher percentage of bills than either chamber rejected. This was especially telling evidence against the theory that the second chamber would insure more critical standards of legislative performance. Not only had these vetoed bills already passed through the double check of the two houses, but a marked percentage of the executive vetoes were normally for technical errors or crudities in the framing of the statutes; an effective second-chamber check should have caught such defects.

Unquestioning public acceptance put great weight behind continuance of the two-chamber structure. Party members built vested interests in a double set of committee jobs. The main demonstrated effect of a two-house legislature was delay. This meant, it is true, that the legislature presented an additional barrier to the pressure of lobbies. But this was by no means the self-evident virtue in the twentieth century that it may have been in the nineteenth. In the nineteenth century many important interests were mainly concerned with getting positive action out of the legislature — special corporate charters, for example. By the twentieth, the emphasis had changed for many of these interests, from getting to retaining their gains unimpaired. They were thus now more interested in minimizing than in promoting legislative activity. Senator Norris drove through the change in Nebraska to the one-house legislature mainly with the argument that the two-chamber form gave too much chance for obstruction of measures that were in the general interest. Ten years after the Nebraska change, satisfactory evidence was lacking to show its results.

The situation was different regarding the demonstrated justification for the two-chamber organization of the United States Congress. The Senate always represented different balances of forces than the House, and in different degrees of emphasis; this was no less true though the special representative character of the Senate shifted greatly from what the framers had contemplated. In operation, moreover, the Senate came much closer than did the upper house in any state to contributing through its longer tenure and smaller membership a more solid craftsmanship, in committee, on the floor, and both in policy and in technical detail. The relationship of the two chambers fostered rivalry that led the House to scrutinize more closely the Senate product. In this respect Congress showed the same tendency as appeared in the state legislatures; the two-chamber organization had its special effect, not so much from the distinctive character of the second chamber, as from the consequences of requiring double action on pending bills. Nonetheless, the United States Senate throughout its history kept an individuality that made it of peculiar influence on national policy. That this was not paralleled in the states was due to the fact that the separate existence of the Senate always represented political realities, whereas the second chamber in the states was, at least after the 1820's, an artificial creation.

c. Concentration of Control

The third main feature of legislative functioning concerned centralization of control within the legislature through more and more formal arrangements made for that purpose. This development paralleled at a tardy rate the mounting volume of legislative business.

For most of the nineteenth century, the parties furnished legislative direction. They did this mainly outside the regular legislative machinery, through the inner circle of party leaders, the boss, and the caucus. The inner circle and caucus were, for example, the directing forces in Congress in the Jacksonian period. After the Civil War the boss-ridden state legislature became common; Winston Churchill dramatized it in his novels of New Hampshire politics, *Coniston* and *Mr. Crewe's Career*. It is one of the most puzzling features of our constitutional history that, although colonial legislatures had known party control and party conflict, no constitutional provision was made to fit the party into the structure of government. To the contrary, the proponents of the Federal Constitution talked much of the dangers of "faction," and implied that a sound government would work through men who were sturdily independent in their judgment of the general welfare, but who were in such agreement on fundamentals that any deep division could come only from evil disposition. Such talk came oddly from men who showed great realism in framing and judging the new Constitution. The most likely explanation for ignoring the party in most of the new state constitutions, and in the Federal Constitution, is that the men who framed these were confident that they themselves would hold power under the new constitutions for an indefinite future. Hence specification was not only unnecessary but might hamper their plans.

The powers of the speaker or presiding officer afforded a traditional center about which some central control of legislative business might grow within the legislature itself. In the states there was the memory of the years before independence, when the speaker often represented the assembly in confronting the royal governor and council. The Federal Constitution singled out the speaker for mention as the presiding officer of the House, which was to choose him. The post was a natural vantage point in years when — as first under Madison — the balance of personal force and party fortunes inclined toward legislative rather than executive leadership. Practice gave to the office broad power over committee assignments, the choice of the committee to which a given bill would be referred, and recognition of those who might have the floor in debate. True, power was shared and diffused among the standing committees. But for the nineteenth century as a whole the speaker was the focus of party control within the House; the classic period of his power dated from Reed in the 1890's to Cannon at the turn of the century. Insurgent Republicans joined with Democrats in 1910 to curb the speaker's power. The revolt eventually produced a new instrument of majority party direction. This was the rules committee. To it was committed control over the priority, extent of time, and limits of amendment and debate under which business might come before the House. The rules committee became a familiar device for party control in the states as well, though with considerable variation in the extent to which it had to share direction with less formal circles of insiders. However, the United States Senate, exercising the traditional freedom of its more limited membership, resisted any such formal controls as a rules committee might impose.

Over the whole flow of legislative business — taking account not only of the major policy issues, but also of the detail of government housekeeping and the variety of matters of concern only to localities or particular persons or groups — the most striking centralization of control was in the standing committees. Nineteenth-century evolution made the main bodies of the Congress and the state legislatures chiefly agencies to review or ratify work done in their committees.

This was a revolution in constitutional custom. Until about the 1820's, both in the states and in the national government, determination of policy was strictly for the committee of the whole, that is, for the whole chamber, sitting under less formal rules of procedure for preliminary discussion. The subordinate role of the committee was reflected in the almost complete absence of standing committees. If facts must be checked, or detail considered, the chamber named a select committee for the particular job. This was the practice from colonial days; the Virginia House of Burgesses seems to have been the only colonial assembly that put the preparation of bills in the hands of standing committees.

We do not know much of the history of the change in the states, but in this, as in other matters of legislative practice, they probably followed the lead of the Congress. The Federalists began our national history with Hamilton's determined drive to put leadership in the executive, whereas Jeffersonian theory and early Jeffersonian practice maintained the importance of Congressional control of policy. The standing committees began their growth into principal agencies of Congress when, in the Fourth Congress under Gallatin, the Republicans moved to create means by which the legislature could wrest the initiative from the executive branch. Even so, the customary prerogatives of the committee of the whole showed that they had firm hold of men's minds. Apart from Federalist opposition, Republicans themselves objected to the new powers given to standing committees; they argued that the Constitution put on the whole house a responsibility that it could not delegate.

The demands of events led Jefferson to assume executive leadership as powerful as any in our history. But he did this by a tight system of control through the caucus and the work of loyal lieutenants in the legislative chambers. His method laid the basis both in practice and in machinery for the exercise of determined leadership within the Congress itself, should strong men appear to claim it. Strong Congressional leadership did come: under Clay, in Madison's second term. Clay's practical political imagination saw that more effective legislative procedure might be had from transfer of greater responsibility to the standing committees. The new emphasis showed in the comparative numbers of select committees (that is, those named to deal only with a particular bill or subject) and standing committees in Congress. At least 350 select committees were named in the Third Congress. The number had fallen to about 70 in 1813–1815. It stood at 35 in 1833–1835. From then on the number of select committees was negligible. In contrast, the standing committees rose from 2 in 1789–1791 to 6 in 1795–1803, to 10 in 1807–1813, to 20 in 1815–1817, to 30 in 1831–1833, to 45 in 1867–1873 and to between 50 and 60 in 1893–1921. Thereafter, until the Congressional Reorganization Act of 1946, the number stood consistently at 46 or 47.

With the expansion of the standing committees came reversal of the former role of the committee of the whole. This now considered measures only after the standing committees had shaped them both in policy and in detail. Moreover, after 1870 the trend was toward narrowing the matters discussed on the floor; by the end of the nineteenth century the overwhelming bulk of bills had their only real consideration in committee.

d. Committees at Work

If we could know the whole of its background, we would undoubtedly see, in the rise of the committee, a reflection of most of the great influences that played on the growth of the legislative process in the United States. The struggle for independence left a weak executive. On the other hand, it presented a legislative branch which, through its key committees, had assumed executive leadership of the politics of revolution. The beginnings of our national life saw broad powers given the legislature. These formed the basis and the stimulus for the legislature's ambition to control policy. Such control might have expressed itself naturally through standing committees, in a fashion closer to cabinet government than to the division of executive and legislative control that in fact evolved. Why didn't this happen? The outcome may have been due to the fortune that brought strong men to the Presidency at critical intervals. More deeply, it may be traced to the trends in affairs which gave steady pressure for broader intervention by government in the economy; this brought government into more continuous play on a widening front, and almost necessarily enhanced the executive power.

As the prize at stake in control of government policy became greater, party conflict sharpened. This made the committee structure more valuable, as a means of party control. Likewise the sheer volume of business, if nothing else, made it inevitable that the legislature as a whole transfer some of its burden to its agents. Once the committee system was well started, it took on momentum of its own. Committees earned power through experience, and gained power on less meritorious grounds as men sought the influence and perquisites, or at least the prestige, that attached to committee assignments. Both in Congress and in the states, experience proved it difficult to abolish or consolidate committees even though their practical function was gone or diminished. Experience also showed that here, as elsewhere, though concentrated authority might be more efficient, it made easier the capture of power. Hence interests that were actively concerned with getting benefits or diverting regulation were inclined to favor the committee system, since they could more readily influence a few committeemen than the whole legislature.

Certain characteristics marked the work of both national and state legislative committees in their contributions to statute making. The typical legislative chamber had many standing committees, but the bulk of business, both in volume and importance, was invariably concentrated in a few. In Pennsylvania in 1929, for example, 3 senate committees received over 57 per cent of all bills, and 8 committees considered over 85 per cent of the bills; at the other extreme 20 committees received less than 5 per cent of all measures referred. In the Pennsylvania house at the same session, 2 committees received nearly 40 per cent, and the 9 most active committees 80 per cent of all bills referred; more than half of the house committees together received less than 5 per cent of all referred measures. In New York in 1935 the majority of bills were referred to 6 committees in the senate, and to 5 in the assembly. The most active committees were typically those on finance (handling taxation, appropriations, and budget), and on the judiciary, to which were referred most proposals to change the existing body of law.

The committees came to perform most of the sifting of proposals laid before legislatures. Where the rules did not require reports, sifting took the form of letting bills die in committee files. Unfavorable reports and failures to report together usually accounted for at least a third of introduced bills. Another 10 to 20 per cent were reported with suggested amendments. Favorable or unfavorable, committee action was followed by the chamber nine out of ten times.

The foregoing were only quantitative measures of committee function and performance; though the few available studies afforded only limited samples, the results were nonetheless consistent and tangible. Consistent, but lacking the satisfaction of a measurable scale, were the judgments on quality of committee work. We noted the absence of established procedural traditions in connection with legislative investigations. This was as conspicuous in the drafting and consideration of bills in committee. There was lack of consistency in reference of bills; bills of the same nature did not necessarily flow through the same committee, and this hampered the development of specialized skill and knowledge. Generally there was no requirement that any meetings be open, nor was there any announced calendar of meetings. Committee members were apt to attend irregularly, from lack of sufficient advance notice of meetings, or because the numerous committees made for conflicting commitments, or because there was no discipline.

The legislative process showed itself far broader in the reach of its investigations, and far richer in resources for grappling with problems of social order, than did the process of lawmaking by judicial decision. However, there is no point in romanticizing the legislative process. In the states, on the whole, statute lawmaking was but a crude approximation of what it might have been. Testimony suggested that in the twentieth century Congress worked with more continuity, regularity, and experience. So far as this was true, it was chiefly because Congressional committee work reflected the longer tenure, the higher if still inadequate pay, the greater prestige, the more permanent party organization, which made for a smaller percentage in turnover in the membership of Congress, session by session.

Both in the state legislatures and in the Congress the committee, although the agent of the chamber, developed free from any continuously effective control. Most obvious evidence of this was the typical lack of any easy means for procuring the discharge of bills from committee. This was a sign of the extent to which the party had won control of legislative policy. An easy discharge procedure would in effect provide a way for the revolt of a bloc against party leadership, since it was the party leadership that fixed committee membership and, through the rules committee, directed legislative traffic.

Scarcely less effective in building committee autonomy was the absence of a tradition of regular modes of conducting committee business. Such states as Massachusetts and Wisconsin, which provided that committees keep calendars and journals, were notable as exceptions. Usually the legislature did not require committees to report on measures referred to them, or that they report out bills promptly instead of holding them until they contributed to the usual end-of-session jam.

Though this much can be said of the largely unchecked independence of committees, the record apparently must be reappraised on one count. Critics often pointed to the conference committee, a committee of members of both houses, appointed to compose their differences on a pending measure, as a sinister means for control by boss or special interest. However, the evidence gives scant support to the critics. Quantitatively, conference committees usually dealt with about 10 per cent only of the bills before Congress or a state legislature, and they seem consistently to have been used less in the states than in Congress. True, measures that went to conference were usually important ones, and in particular were apt to include appropriations acts. True, also, the conference committee through legislative practice gained a very favorable power position. English practice knew both "simple" and "free" conference committees, the first limited to exchange of views, the second empowered to strike deals. But in the United States the "free" committee was used from colonial days on, though conference committees were sometimes authorized to deal only with points of difference, while on other occasions they were allowed to alter any part of the bill before them. Conference committees also tended to take on the character of standing committees: Their members were often named from the senior members of the standing committees which considered the disputed bills, and since the bills sent to conference were apt to be the few important measures of a session, they generally came from the same standing committees from one year to another. Moreover, after mid-nineteenth century, the rules generally gave precedence to conference reports and much protection against any tampering with their recommendations on the floor. Possession of such power may raise suspicion of its abuse, but the evidence is elusive, and two careful studies failed to find that abuse was demonstrated.

e. The Legislature and the Lobbies

Power within the legislature thus tended to centralize in party leaders and a few committees. The power behind the community interests that played on the legislature likewise underwent a centralizing process. But in this case the total effect was an increasing dispersion of power. Each major economic or social interest drew more into itself as it organized itself for more effective action.

People in the United States most often displayed their political naïvete in recurrent surprise and indignation when they found that individuals or groups were seeking their own advantage from something which an agency of government — the legislature, where the stakes were highest — had it in its power to give. From colonial days on, of course, special interests sought to gain from the exercise or withholding of exercise of government power. There should be nothing surprising in this. The fact involves what, if not the most fundamental object of government, is at least an aspect of government's main purpose. Men are self-centered. A condition of their social living is that they be required to submit their conduct to the judgment of others than themselves. This is not only to set limits to the more predatory among them, but, perhaps more important, to provide for those prerequisites of civilized life that are so essential to everyone that no one attends to them. The purpose of government thus is that men should come to it, and all the more so because what they want may be against the general welfare.

Though pressure was constant, its forms changed much, becoming less direct both in focus and in method. As the term "lobbying" indicates, the typical nineteenth-century approach to the legislature was by direct contact with the legislator. One of the delayed effects of the extension of the vote to more and more people was to direct the attention of pressure groups to the people who elected the legislators. Movement in ideas also undoubtedly played its part here. The blows of economic depression and the contacts of closer living in an urbanized and interdependent society taught people intolerance of the grosser forms of plunder and arrogance. As the railroads and the power industry learned, this made it necessary to pay attention to public opinion, if only to deceive it.

The same causes helped redirect methods of influencing legislatures. There were occasions when direct corruption of legislators was wholesale, unashamed, and almost open. A notorious early example was the purchase of the Georgia legislature in connection with the Yazoo land frauds in 1795. The most widespread cases were in the generation after the Civil War, when the full tide of economic exploitation swept over institutions totally unprepared to deal with the resulting pressure. Proof of the point was inherently elusive, but standards of legislative morality seemed to have climbed up from the pit of the '70s and '80s to the point where, though any mid-twentieth century legislature almost certainly had its purchasable members, their number and influence were rarely material.

However, indirect approaches to legislators were many, though the evidence did not permit generalization as to their comparative weight in this and the previous century. Definite standards of ethical behavior for the bench crystallized in the nineteenth century, whatever the varying practical effect in different levels of courts. As late as mid-twentieth century, no comparably definite ideal had become set for the legislature. Substantial contributions to campaign funds came from interests that wanted specific gains from legislative action or inaction. Legislators took financial and other favors from sources that had business before their body. Lawyer-legislators were retained by clients for whom they apparently gave no service outside their influence as members of the legislature, and lucrative retainers likewise came to law firms of which legislators were partners. The line between influence and corruption was a hard one to draw in these forms of indirect influence. Even so they did not nearly approach the proportions of the improprieties of the last quarter of the nineteenth century.

These more dramatic aspects of pressure on the legislature were dwarfed in the twentieth century by types of activity almost wholly alien to the stereotype of "the lobbyist." The staple work of the representatives of major interests concerned with legislation began to center around detailed, technical craftsmanship in the drafting of bills, the gathering of statistics and descriptive material, collection and analysis of legislation and legislative documents from all over the country, the careful, bill-by-bill scrutiny of all that was fed into the legislative hopper session by session, the assembling of briefs on pending proposals and the formal appearance before legislative committees, the preparation and dissemination of large quantities of printed material presenting a point of view for the education of the members of an interest group itself or of the general public. The conduct of this sort of work required both more professional and more routine skills than the old-style lobbyist possessed. Hence there arose a bureaucracy of interest-group representatives. In its turn, this bureaucracy, by its own concentration of effort and its own ambitions, tended to strengthen the individuality and coherence of the various groups which it served. Sometimes the new lobbying bureaucracy took on a measure of independent power in policy making for its group, supported by the acquiescence or inertia of its principals.

In the face of such sizeable changes in the direction and methods of pressure groups, legislative efforts to reach a proper working relation with them were weak, fumbling, and of limited relevance to the real problems. Regulation began with the most obvious, and always the least effective device: criminal penalties. Proof was difficult, the normal inertia of the prosecuting machinery was often enhanced by politics, and it was hard to define prohibited kinds of pressure techniques in a way that would bar ready evasion.

The elder LaFollette led a more realistic effort to curb dubious pressure tactics through enforced publicity, chiefly by requiring lobbyists to register. This hit closer to the target, since it gave some promise of meeting pressure with pressure, instead of with formal instruments of control. But it proved hard to frame satisfactory definitions of the types of activity for which men must register, and enforcement was generally as lax as under the old-fashioned penal statutes. Publicity was a sanction whose possibilities were not fully explored. Under the usual regulation it was focused on the lobbyist rather than on the legislator. Requirements that the legislator make full disclosure of the sources and extent of his income and business connections during his term of office might yet prove more readily enforceable, particularly if fulfillment of such requirements were made a condition of eligibility for continuing legislative service, and if enforcement were put under steady administrative supervision. Again, publicity had been directed almost entirely at the lobbyist's relation to the legislator. Equally revealing might be administratively enforced disclosure of data which would show how justified were the lobbyist's claims to represent a fair cross section of the community interest for which he claimed to speak.

Much of the effort to regulate pressure groups was misdirected, because it expressed a naïvete unaware that pressures on government were normal and not an inherent evil, and that therefore the problem was to assure reasonably equal access to government by all who might want something from it. The most fundamental attack on the problem came after 1910, when the executive rose to leadership in social programing, and the administrative agency became the chief means for investigating the facts and enforcing the law in large areas of public concern. These developments abandoned an unrealistic, impossible neutrality of government in favor of positive use of government power to promote more equality among interests in the community. Similarly, from the 1920's on, many states set up legislative or judicial councils whose membership included legislators, judges, and executive appointees, to survey the fields in which law reform was needed.

The legislature joined this general trend toward affirmative action to equalize the pressure on government, by helping to generate opinion and effort where they otherwise did not exist or were hopelessly disorganized. Inadequate as most of these legislative developments were, they pointed in the right direction. Through most of our history the legislature lacked the permanent staff and facilities (libraries, librarians, research assistants, ample secretarial forces) that it needed to fulfill its responsibilities. New York founded a legislative library service in 1891. Dr. Charles McCarthy set up a much more active legislative reference library in Wisconsin at the beginning of the twentieth century, and Congress, after a flurry of opposition in 1912 to alleged encroachment of specialists on the legislative policy-making power, followed the Wisconsin example. By 1925 about 33 states, and by 1938 42 states had some type of legislative reference service. The quality differed widely, and no more than a dozen were substantial.

As initiated by McCarthy, the legislative reference library combined both fact gathering and advice and expert aid in bill drafting. With respect to the latter function the movement generally came to less than early hopes had prophesied. The political Progressivism which sponsored the movement had the weakness of believing too much in the power of facts and disinterested expertness. Apart from this, the legislative reference service typically lacked a strong and independent position in the states; usually it was attached to some administrative agency instead of enjoying status as a direct arm of the legislature. Its basic lack, however, was that in operation it grew to be concerned only with the technical level, and in most states did not courageously develop McCarthy's demonstrated idea of its function: McCarthy had believed and had shown in action that, consistent with full legislative responsibility for policy, a permanent staff might still take the initiative in presenting weighted appraisals of data and constructive recommendations for action, instead of confining itself to colorless assembly of raw materials on the chance requests of individual legislators.

In 1946 Congress strengthened its legislative reference and bill-drafting services. It indicated that it wanted these agencies to take a more positive role, and it created new permanent staff positions for research aides to its important standing committees, as well as providing a general administrative assistant for each Senator. The new facilities were modest. But the act was significant, for by it the Congress took its first major step in a generation toward improvement of the means for exercising its policy-making function. Too, the step had meaning as to the problems the legislature faced when it confronted unequally arrayed pressure groups, private or bureaucratic. Its own improved staff promised for it less dependence on such outside sources in gathering and ordering the data it needed and in drafting the measures that it considered.

f. *The Pressure of Detail*

One more feature of legislative operations must be mentioned: The legislature failed to develop procedures or agencies that would relieve it of detail and let it concentrate on the relatively few major issues of any session.

As a long-range trend, the volume of introduced bills steadily increased, though at least in some states the adoption of constitutional bans on special and local laws was for a time followed by a noticeable drop in the quantity of business proposed. After 1880 the typical, busy state legislature saw an increase of 200 to 400 per cent in the number of introduced bills, with the average annual total of bills introduced running above 1000. In Congress the total mounted from 813 bills introduced in the House in the period 1863–1865 to a peak of 19,209 in 1903–1905, and stood after the 1920's around 12,000 to 13,000 a year.

Samplings showed that most of the bills introduced, and most of those adopted, had relatively narrow meaning, and many were trivial. Despite formal constitutional limitations, much local legislation continued. The total of special laws was markedly less than in the mid-nineteenth century, but still swelled the total of business. A great proportion of bills concerned the internal housekeeping of government. Many represented minor tinkering with the crudities of earlier statutes. Probably the average state legislature confronted not more than twenty or thirty major bills in a session, and ordinarily the proportion was not much higher in Congress. But both in the states and in the national government, the important questions had to be dealt with under the handicap of the competing claims for time and energy made by the mass of lesser items. This meant a cost in lowered craftsmanship in the handling of business that did get before the legislature, and the delay or neglect of other pressing problems.

But the increase in volume of introduced bills was not the whole, or after 1890 even the most serious source of the detail that harried legislators. Government was intervening in a broadening area of affairs, and people felt its intervention mainly through contact with expanding executive and administrative offices. Individual citizens and organized groups had more and more adjustments to make with officialdom, and learned increasingly to seek specific advice or aid from government offices. Especially where there was conflict, the local representative in the legislature seemed a natural middleman for many of these dealings. As the activity of the national government grew, such demands became most marked on members of Congress, the more so because their constituents were apt to be many more miles away from Washington than from their state capitols, and because the relatively great size of the huge federal executive establishment confused the stranger who tried to find his way through it. So great had this middleman's role grown by the 1930's that a qualified observer of Congress expressed skepticism over the practical results for statesmanship that were apt to flow from reduction of the volume of detailed legislation: The most likely consequence, warned J. P. Chamberlain, was that Congress would spend still more time in the government departments, handling the affairs of individual constituents.

No problem better illustrates how little planning or deliberation went into development of the legislative process in the United States. Party and committee leadership arose in more or less instinctive response to the volume of business that flowed into the legislature. The policy-making role of the executive grew in large measure from the sheer default of a legislature that was swamped in details. Delegation of power to administrators came closest to a deliberate, major effort to free the legislators from the mass of particulars.

So far as concerned introduced bills, indeed, the administrative process suggested a really fundamental approach that was applied to a significant degree only in the federal government. By creation of the Court of Claims, the Court of Customs and Patent Appeals, and the Tariff Commission, Congress diverted a considerable amount of business that otherwise would have come to it as special or local bills or as amendments to general statutes. Invention was limited, though. We have yet to see in the states the creation of a local government board empowered to take final action on problems claimed to be peculiar to certain localities in the application of the general laws of the state. Moreover, such devices deal only with introduced bills. The provision of a well-paid assistant for each member of the Senate after 1946 was the first practical recognition that there was need to deal with the far more time-consuming job of acting as middleman between individual constituents and government departments.

3. Social Functions

What, in perspective, were the jobs that the legislature did in the law of the United States? It performed certain tasks which had so limited a history that we may dispose of them briefly.

a. Subsidiary Functions

The legislature was one, and sometimes the only, channel for initiating formal constitutional change, by individual amendment or revision of the whole document. Its contribution here was relatively small. So far as it tried to limit constitutional conventions in what they did, its efforts did not result in barring any important substantive changes that conventions strongly wanted. Whether in calling a convention or in exercising its own authority to propose constitutional change, as we shall see, the legislature was typically only an instrument of delay. Once we were past the generation of our origins, there was little real consideration of the structure of government. So far as substantive policy was written into constitutions, it generally represented hindsight wisdom, enacted after the movement of events had already robbed evils of their impetus.

Another function formally assigned to the House of Representatives was to elect the President where by reason of a tie or lack of a majority a candidate failed of election by the regular procedure. This power was latent with revolutionary possibilities, as the situation created by the tie between Aaron Burr and Thomas Jefferson in 1800 indicated. That it was rarely exercised was due to the development outside the Constitution of the two-party system. The only other time when the power was invoked was in 1824 when, despite the substantial plurality obtained by Jackson, no one received a majority of the vote in the Electoral College, and the House chose John Quincy Adams. Again the repercussions showed how much danger inhered in the extraordinary procedure.

A third formal function of the legislature comprised impeachment — analogous to the inquisitorial process of the grand jury — and the trial of impeachments — analogous to the judicial process. It is impossible to weigh the actual effects of the possession or exercise of this authority. It was not often used. In theory this is no evidence that it did not have practical effect, for the threat implicit in the very existence of the power might be expected to curb executive or judicial abuses. It was a very cumbersome machinery to put in motion; almost invariably official action against judges or subordinate executive officers who betrayed their trust was by criminal prosecution in the courts. Two instances in national political history were crucial in limiting the meaning of the impeachment process. The Senate failed to convict Samuel Chase, an associate justice of the Supreme Court of the United States in 1804–1805, and President Andrew Johnson in 1868, under impeachments brought in the heat of partisan conflict. The failure of these efforts established that impeachment might not be based on grounds of political difference, however deep or intemperate, in the absence of a showing of a specific crime or abuse of trust. Apart from this limitation, the practical ineffectiveness of impeachment when used for its proper purposes was attested by the slowly growing opinion that, except as to the highest officers, the trial of impeachment should be removed altogether from the legislature and entrusted to specially constituted courts. A constitutional amendment to this effect regarding impeachment of judges was adopted by the voters in New York state in 1947.

A fourth function was assigned to the upper chamber alone. It was to act as an executive council whose approval must be had, in the national government, for the adoption of treaties, and in both national and state governments for the confirmation of the more important executive and judicial appointments. We are concerned with law in the domestic history of the country; hence we shall not discuss the Senate's treaty-making role. By participating in the appointing process, the upper chamber gained importance both in party fortunes and in the development of public policy. The function was an executive one, but in at least one respect there were important results from placing it in a legislative body. The legislature in the United States had its roots in the locality; there the political fortunes of individual legislators were generally determined. There was reciprocity of interest among legislators, regardless of party lines, in building local political strength, and patronage was a staple of that strength.

Hence the review of executive appointments became less the function of the whole chamber than of those members in whose districts the appointee would operate, since without the approval of the members thus immediately affected, the chamber would not ordinarily consent to an appointment.

b. The Definition of Public Policy

Four functions emerged as the engrossing and peculiar contributions of the legislative branch in the United States: (1) the determination of general community policy, embodied in rules, principles, or standards to govern dealings among the people or between them and the government; (2) the creation of specific executive, administrative, and judicial machinery, and the scrutiny of its operation; (3) the performance of a middleman's role between particular constituents and the executive or administrative agencies; and (4) the investigation of facts of social interest.

Over the years the most important legislative function was the definition of general policy. This stood in the public eye as the characteristic job of the legislature: to "make laws." It might be argued that both in English and American colonial history an earlier function of the legislature was to look into the executive's conduct of affairs. But at least after 1790, weighed by the unique quality of the function and the importance of its consequences, "lawmaking" was the critical task.

What were the types of this lawmaking? In part it meant legislation that in the first instance affected private rights, as in the law of real property, sales of goods, or commercial transactions. These were important fields. But they formed the least fundamental area of legislative action, not only when compared to the fields covered by judge-made (common) law but also in comparison to two other types of statutes.

Until about 1910 legislation was the characteristic embodiment of the rights and duties of people in relation to the organized community. Pound, for example, rates the work done regarding criminal law and penal administration as the best work of the nineteenth-century legislature. Judged by importance rather than quality of result, policies fixed in legislation for the disposition of public lands and the exploitation of natural resources far overshadowed the significance of private-rights legislation. Legislation established the great service activities of government — education, roads, preventive health and safety measures, for instance — which supplied the foundations for all private activity. The legislature developed taxation into the most influential type of government regulation of the economy.

The third type of general legislation was closely related to the second. It included all the basic housekeeping of government: definition of the particular character of those agencies — especially the executive and judicial branches — whose general title only was set by the constitution; the establishment of important auxiliary offices, especially the multiplication of the modern administrative agencies; the definition and division of areas of responsibility among such institutions, and the appropriation of funds for their support; finally, the declaration of general policies and procedures which they should follow.

The lawmaking role of the legislature varied sharply in different phases. Through most of the nineteenth century the law dealing with the more private dealings or relations of people was common law. In the revolutionary years and the generation that followed, legislation in this field embodied some fundamental differences from the law of England. These were chiefly negative. Moreover, this legislation was not so much a moving cause, as a formal recognition of the consequences flowing from a radically new social environment. This was true of the abolition of feudal land tenure, or the establishment of the freehold as the basic kind of land title. It was true of the statutory abolition of imprisonment for debt. On the other hand, we must credit the legislature with innovations in the form of the homestead exemption and the mechanics lien. But much of nineteenth-century legislation regarding private rights and duties simply declared common law or equity doctrine, as in the "codes" that some states adopted. And a good deal of legislation simply incorporated into the general body of the law particular contributions of judge-made doctrine. Thus the married women's property acts were patterned after familiar equity principles.

Decisive for the nineteenth century in determining the relative weight of statutory and judge-made elements in the law of private affairs was the defeat of the codification movement in New York state. Three times between 1840 and 1887 the driving intellectual ambition and will to power of David Dudley Field brought New York within a step of adopting a comprehensive code of substantive law. With so powerful an example as New York behind it, the general Field Code might well have been copied throughout the country, instead of in only a handful of states (including California, the Dakotas and Montana). The nation-wide copying of Field's Code of Civil Procedure attested to the potential power of the New York example; though distorted by unsympathetic handling in the courts and by piecemeal amendment in the legislature, the Procedure Code became the model for the fundamentals of civil procedure in all but a few states of the Union. Indeed, this effort to simplify the system of remedies was the most sweeping legislative contribution in the nineteenth century to the law of private relations.

To its mid-point, the twentieth century was as conservative as the nineteenth in statutory innovation in the law of private transactions. Primarily on the initiative of the American Bar Association, in the years 1892–1912 a movement was begun for uniformity in the statute and common law of the states. This was to be achieved by adoption of uniform legislation. The Conference of Commissioners on Uniform State Laws won their outstanding successes in the Uniform Negotiable Instruments Law (recommended in 1896, adopted by 53 jurisdictions), the Uniform Warehouse Receipts Act (recommended in 1906, adopted by 52 jurisdictions), and the Uniform Sales Act (recommended in 1906, adopted in 37 jurisdictions). The Conference thus had its widest success in fields where the statutory and judge-made law was well settled and developed. Pioneering efforts, such as the Uniform Act on Contribution Among Tortfeasors, had relatively little success.

The significant legislation of the twentieth century in the field of private affairs affected not so much the substance of law as the provision of more economical, speedy, and active means for relief. This kind of development was exemplified by provision of new specialized courts and administrative agencies. In reality, it represented a broader recognition that there was in many of these "private" controversies a good deal more of public interest than the nineteenth century had realized. Viewed so, this line of development illustrated the second and third categories of legislative activity listed at the start of this discussion.

The constructive achievement that marked the law dealing with the individual's relation to the community was mainly written in legislation. This is not to say that the legislature was always the dominant factor; as we shall see later, the executive increasingly supplied the drive behind the most important changes. But certainly, as compared with the formal processes of constitutional amendment or of judge-made law, the legislature led in this area of the creation of law. In view of its command of the purse and the range of expedients that it could employ, this was a natural development. The constitution-making process and the courts did work in this field that was mainly negative — the definition of constitutional limitations, judges' case-by-case development of broad doctrines of judicial review and of restrictive rules of statutory construction.

Government intervention in affairs vastly increased after 1890. But there was no time when such legislation was not a material factor in United States law. In the first five years of the Congress, the Statutes at Large contain measures that levy taxes, impose a tariff, regulate the fisheries and the coastwise trade, establish a Bank of the United States, dispose of public lands, and set up such basic services as navigation aids, a patent system, and a post office. In a similar period in New York and Connecticut, for example, the session laws show a considerable variety of police measures that regulate practices thought to endanger public health, that license professions and trades, that provide rudimentary

standards of measurement, or that give bounties or special privileges
to encourage new enterprise. Compared with the range of twentieth-
century economic and social regulation, the statute books of the first
quarter of the nineteenth century make a meager showing of public
law. But the economy was limited, and problems of community living
were simple where there was plenty of elbowroom. Measured against
the time, the extent of regulation was always substantial, and was always
grounded chiefly in legislation.

The main developments in regulatory legislation amounted to
changes in emphasis within a pattern which still left the legislature the
chief policy maker. One trend was toward a great increase in the scope
and detail of statutory regulation. This was especially true of laws affecting the economy. A second, closely related change was marked by
the creation of the Interstate Commerce Commission in 1887. This was
the tendency for Congress to extend the area of economic regulation
faster and deeper than did the state legislatures. A third trend, about
equally pronounced in the states and in the national government, was an
increasing delegation of discretion to executive and administrative officers to make rules and regulations that had the practical range and effect
of legislation.

The last phase had the greatest possibility of a fundamental shift in
power among the branches of government. Especially after 1910 the
legislature granted to the executive the decision of many issues that
were not merely matters of detail but went to basic policy. After the
decision of the Supreme Court of the United States in the *Brig Aurora*
in 1813, and Marshall's opinion in *Wayman* v. *Southard* in 1825, the
firmly asserted doctrine was that a statute might be unconstitutional as
a violation of the constitutionally fixed separation of powers, if it conferred on the executive what the court deemed an unrestricted discretion to declare policy. But not until *Panama Refining Co.* v. *Ryan* and
Schechter Poultry Corporation v. *United States,* in 1935, did the Supreme Court hold an act of Congress unconstitutional as an undue delegation of legislative power. State decisions more often held state laws
unconstitutional on this ground. The judicial doctrine stood as an ultimate check to the legislature's abdication of responsibility. But measured by number of statutes overthrown, judicial review did not substantially impede the trend toward extensive delegation. And, judging
by the broad language of the statutes, draftsmen were not much
affected by the threat of a judicial veto.

The legislature's jealousy of the powers which it felt it must grant
was a more practically effective check on the scope of executive policy
making. This appeared occasionally in statutory amendments which

imposed specific policies on the executive officers. Thus in 1947 the Congress declared, contrary to rulings of the National Labor Relations Board, that unions of foremen should not be entitled to the protection of the National Labor Relations Act in their efforts to bargain collectively. The legislature exercised its check most often and most effectively, however, through special investigations of executive conduct, or through questioning executive performance when hearings were held on pending authorizations or appropriations of funds.

At this point, the housekeeping function of the legislature supported and enriched its lawmaking function. By practice, rather than according to any planned program, the legislature merged general policy making and administration. The merger of functions was most marked in the handling of the more complicated problems of public policy — in working out law concerning the concentration of economic power, the regulation of corporation finance or the national securities markets. A pattern of lawmaking grew in these complex fields of regulation: (1) With more or less of leadership from the executive, the legislative branch declared certain areas of conduct to be of public concern, and to require government intervention. (2) It delegated to executive officers or to specialized administrative bodies the job of working out the terms and machinery of regulation. (3) The executive or administrative officers in turn had to have funds from the legislature, and in obtaining them had to justify their programs, and answer questions, before legislative committees. (4) If there was special interest or pressure concerning particular aspects of the regulatory program, the legislature or the appropriate standing committee might investigate and consider changes in the law. (5) The grant of renewed or extended appropriations, or the expression of satisfaction with existing practice and the conclusion of a committee investigation might ratify executive or administrative implementation of the statute; or as a result of legislative displeasure expressed in the terms of appropriations or in committee reports, or sometimes by statutory amendment, a new direction might be given to the detailed development of the new field of policy. All this was not legislative policy making according to the old-fashioned textbook's description of a tripartite division of powers. But it was the practical way in which response was made to problems of baffling range and complexity.

c. Control of Government Housekeeping

Though it was the most important job of the legislature, the determination of general policy took but a small proportion of legislative time and energy. Both in Congress and in the states probably no more than 10 per cent of the statutory output added to, subtracted from, or amended the general body of law that defined people's relations to each other or to the government. Especially after 1890 the legislature gave the bulk of its time and effort to its housekeeping and its middleman functions.

Over 150 years of practice devolved upon the legislature two jobs concerning the internal affairs of the government. First, the legislature became the chief architect of all matters of structure and procedure not determined by the constitution. This meant a wide range of activity. Even at their wordiest, constitutions set out only a small part of the machinery that it took to run government in the United States.

This task of the legislature represented a considerable break with the past. The colonial legislatures of course concerned themselves with the establishment of local government. But it was inherent in the relation to the mother country that they could do little more than this; the King's government largely fixed the form and ways of the executive and judicial branches in the colonies, and the colonial legislature had to rely on its control of the purse, rather than on manipulation of the structure or procedure of other agencies of government, to try to enforce legislative notions of policy. The first state constitutions gave the legislature almost unlimited lawmaking authority. Naturally, therefore, the state legislatures began to determine the particular character of the institutions which were to interpret and execute the laws. Thus a marked feature of the executive, administrative and judicial branches, as well as of the pattern of local government, in the United States, came to be the detail in which the legislature created offices, allocated power, and set out procedure.

Consider, for example, the judiciary of the United States. The Constitution conferred on the Supreme Court a limited original jurisdiction. This apart, and within the types of cases or controversies defined in the Constitution, Congress has entire discretion to decide what parts of the allowable business the federal courts shall entertain. For example, Congress did not vest permanently in the federal courts until 1875 so important a jurisdiction as that over cases involving rights or claims under the Federal Constitution or statutes. Congress has full discretion as to the number, distribution, and relative judicial authority of all courts inferior to the Supreme Court. It has full control, as well, of the number and qualifications of judges both of the Supreme and inferior federal courts, and of the number, qualifications and terms of employment of all subordinate officers of the courts. History and precedent offer substantial support for the inherent power of Anglo–American courts to make rules for procedure in cases that come before them.

Nonetheless, statutory authorization was obtained before the Supreme Court of the United States promulgated rules for procedure in various types of proceedings in the federal courts.

Various incidents dramatized the extent of Congress's power over the federal court system. In 1802 a Jeffersonian Congress repealed the Judiciary Act of 1801, in large part to abolish courts which the Federalists had created to furnish secure posts for their partisans. In 1868 the Radical Republican Congress withdrew from the appellate jurisdiction of the Supreme Court review of certain judgments of the United States circuit courts, in order to avoid a Supreme Court decision on the validity of Reconstruction legislation involved in the pending appeal in *Ex parte McCardle*. McCardle's case had been argued and was under consideration by the Supreme Court when the 1868 act was adopted. Nevertheless, the Court held that that act deprived it of jurisdiction to decide the cause. In 1937 President Franklin Roosevelt sought to invoke the power of Congress over the number of the Justices of the Supreme Court, to increase the membership so that he might appoint men who would presumably vote to sustain new economic regulatory legislation.

The structure and procedures for exercise of official power are of course important. They affect the practical results of legislation, and they naturally concern the legislature. But United States history saw too much statutory regulation of detail in these matters, and difficulties followed. The legislature did not always have the expert knowledge needed to handle details wisely. Moreover, a legislature is ordinarily a ponderous machine to put into action, and detailed provisions were often long out of date before they were corrected by amendment of the statutes.

Again, the history of legislative control of judicial organization affords an illustration. The Field Code, adopted in New York in 1848, made a reasonably good start toward a simple and economical procedure in civil suits. But later the legislature burdened the Code with a mass of highly specific, unsystematic amendments, until it took some 50,000 sections of written law, in about 2000 printed pages, to set forth the whole. In most states in the latter nineteenth century statutes prescribed procedure in similar confusing detail. In reaction, the first decade of the twentieth century saw the beginnings of a movement to put in the courts responsibility for adoption of rules of procedure. At least the courts were given the power to make such rules in the first instance, subject to the approval or acquiescence of the legislature. Under the authority of federal statutes, the Supreme Court of the United States finally took the leadership in this reform. Its outstanding contribution was to promulgate in 1938 a body of rules governing procedure in civil actions in the federal courts. An advisory committee which represented the best talent of the bar and the schools assisted the Court.

After 1890 the expansion of the administrative process marked the greatest change from nineteenth-century emphasis on detailed statutory regulation of government machinery. The legislature generally granted the administrators broad substantive powers, aided by the general authorization to make rules "to effect the purpose of the act." This trend had both continuity and range; it marked the law in different sections of the country, and under both major political parties. These characteristics suggest that it signaled a permanent shift in practice. True, the 1940's saw Congress and several states adopt statutory "codes" which set out standards of rules regarding notice, hearing, and evidence in the conduct of administrative proceedings. Objections were raised to the enactment of such codes. But the primary objection was not that the legislature was trying to write too much detail into its procedural requirements; rather the fear was that difficulties would follow the effort to impose rigidly uniform rules or standards on agencies which faced diverse problems peculiar to different fields of regulation.

This is as much as we shall say about the first of the two legislative functions concerned with the internal affairs of government: the creation of organization and procedures. The second of these functions was the scrutiny of the work of other branches of government. This was done mainly in hearings on requests for the authorization or appropriation of funds, and also through specific investigations by standing or select committees.

This function had deep historic roots. But the legislature's watch over the operations of other parts of the government was episodic, and often superficial, or grossly distorted in the emphasis given to particular issues at the expense of broad surveys of the public business. Desire for publicity or partisan advantage was frequently a warping influence. We need a good deal more study of the legislative process before we can well estimate what effects legislative surveillance had on the work of the other branches of government. There can be no doubt but that there was a real measure of influence. But the twentieth-century movement toward the executive budget suggested that the legislative supervision fell far short of adequacy.

Before 1900 in neither national or state governments was there much systematic handling of appropriations. The House Ways and Means Committee exercised most of the control in Congress until the end of the Civil War. At that time the Committee on Appropriations took over control and held it until about 1882. Then began the practice of dispersing important appropriation bills among various committees concerned with the subject matter. Responsibility was not better focused until the Budget and Accounting Act of 1921, when appropriations were put back under the control of one committee in each house. In the states, reliance was generally on one appropriations committee in each chamber. But there was no regular system of control or appraisal of how the money was used. The first significant change in the states was the grant to the governor of the power to veto particular items in appropriation acts. Twenty-eight states adopted this device by 1900, and by 1930 thirty-nine states had taken it up. In 1911 California and Wisconsin led in a new change. They provided for a budget to be shaped by the executive, and by the 1930's about three fourths of the states had followed in this technique.

Though the practice was rooted in history, some argument was made over whether the scrutiny of executive or administrative performance was a proper job of the legislature. The argument lacked reality. Experience showed that, however haphazardly it might use the power, the legislature would not renounce the right of inquiring to what purpose and effect its appropriations were spent. The executive was too much an interested party, to be entrusted with the whole responsibility of investigating the administration of policy.

Apart from the lack of traditions of fair play in the conduct of legislative inquiries, the main weakness in the legislature's role as critic was its lack of adequate staff to permit it to probe intelligently. A line must be drawn beyond which legislative staff must not grow, lest administration be too much hampered by responsibility in details both to the executive and to legislative committees. But we had a long way to go in building up legislative staff, before this danger would be acute. The problem was practically untouched in the states. Congress took first, modest steps in that direction as late as the Legislative Reorganization Act of 1946, which provided permanent research aides and secretarial staff for key committees.

d. Legislator or Middleman

The housekeeping function of the legislature bore considerable relation to the middleman function of the individual legislator. Over the years the legislator tended increasingly to become an attorney to press particular claims of particular constituents before executive agencies. The Congressman made an especially effective advocate for the constituent because he was of the body which voted appropriations and whose committees might ask embarrassing questions. If the Congressman were a member of the standing committee which dealt with the work of the given agency, or was a member of the all-important appropriations committee, his word might carry great weight.

This middleman's or attorney's function was the single most amazing phase of the evolution of legislative practice in the United States. It became more marked in the Congress than in the states, though it was not unknown in the latter. The function did not have the historic roots of other legislative jobs. It probably first became important after the Revolution, with the extension of the suffrage, and with the new popular currents in political behavior that entered with Jacksonian Democracy.

Intercession for particular constituents developed along two main lines. In the mid-nineteenth century individual legislators gave much attention to promotion of special or local legislation. In the first quarter of the century, legislatures not infrequently exercised what amounted to judicial power, by special laws which fixed penalties, awarded new court trials, adjusted individual insolvencies, and granted divorces. No type of activity served more to lower the public standing of the legislature. The turn in public opinion was reflected in the commonly adopted constitutional bans on special and local laws. There was a substantial decrease in such legislation by the end of the century, and total elimination of that type which amounted to judicial business.

As special and local legislation declined, other kinds of middleman work for the legislators grew to enormous proportions. This involved interceding for the constituent before executive departments or administrative agencies — to expedite matters, to secure favorable treatment, or to obtain reversal or at least reconsideration of unfavorable action. In part this growth reflected the tardiness of the bar in developing the opportunities for legitimate practice before government agencies. But undoubtedly it was also inherent in the situation. Such at least was the thought behind the provision in 1946 of well-salaried executive assistants for Senators. The middleman's role probably more than any other factor diverted the time and energy of Congress from general policy. Experience suggested that it would continue to do so, and that still further provision should be made to handle it through the office of the individual member of Congress, to which the business flowed.

e. Legislative Investigations

In the twentieth century the investigating power of the legislature showed signs that it might develop a new, independent function for the legislative branch. For three hundred years in England and in the United States legislative practice firmly established the power of investigation, and defined it as an authority of breadth. True, in 1880 in *Kilbourn* v. *Thompson*, the Supreme Court of the United States indicated that the power might be narrowly restricted to investigation of matters relevant to immediately pending and specific proposals for legislation. But this did not prove to be the abiding pattern of the cases. In practice the courts put no barriers as to purpose or subject matter in the way of the full reach of legislative investigation.

Through the nineteenth century, however, the main use of the authority was to appraise executive or administrative performance. Of about 285 investigations made by select or standing committees of the House and Senate from 1789–1925, Galloway found that the greatest number concerned the War Department, 54 the Treasury, 41 the Department of the Interior (notably the Bureau of Indian Affairs and the Patent Office), and 23 the conduct of the President. Many other inquiries looked into the Navy, the Post Office, and the Government Printing Office.

A new emphasis in legislative investigations began with the Armstrong Committee of the New York legislature, which in 1905, under the direction of Charles Evans Hughes as committee counsel, investigated the financial operations of the great life insurance companies. In 1912 the House Committee on Banking and Currency named a subcommittee which became known, after the name of its chairman, as the Pujo Committee. Under the aggressive lead of its counsel, Samuel Untermeyer, the Pujo Committee inquired extensively into the concentration of control of money and credit in the United States. Both of these investigations sought in part to explore the need for new legislation. Both, however, were also obviously conducted with the purpose of informing public opinion of facts of significance to the balance of political and economic power in the country. New legislation followed both investigations. But their greatest long-range effect was their contribution to a new climate of opinion regarding government's proper role in the economy. The full results of this aspect of their work became apparent only with the legislation enacted in the first years of the administration of Franklin Roosevelt.

In 1937 an investigation of the concentration of economic power, made by the Temporary National Economic Committee, forecast a new type of inquiry — conducted by a group drawn from the legislative, executive, and administrative arms. The TNEC assembled a somewhat spotty record, and supplemented it with monographs produced by the Committee's experts. Such an inquiry brought general issues before the public; also, backed by the subpoena power, it brought to light for further scholarship source material that otherwise might never have become available.

In the past the many investigations of executive conduct were naturally directed in part to inform the public, especially when the investigators were of a different party than those under investigation. But there was a new stress in these more recent, deliberate inquiries into matters of broad public concern. In the face of the impersonality and self-centeredness of twentieth-century urban life, government faced the problem of creating a workable minimum of informed public interest in community affairs. The new function of the legislative investigation promised a substantial contribution to this problem. Especially might it be thus effective if it merged the resources of executive and legislative branches.

The functional role of the legislature can be fully considered only in comparison with the work of the other major branches. What we have seen so far amounts to a significant change in the legislature's status, compared with its position in the first generation of national independence. New functions arose — the middleman's role of the individual legislator, the use of the investigatory power to build informed public opinion. Historic functions continued — lawmaking and the review of the conduct of other branches of government. But the toughness of institutional forms concealed major shifts in practice. There was a definite transfer of initiative to the executive, and to a less degree to the administrative arm. Legislative approval was still prerequisite to most fundamental decisions in domestic policy. But the legislature turned over to the other branches much, if not the bulk, of the policy making of the second rank, without which basic decisions lack content. On the other hand, the legislature jealously held to its right to review, and ratify or veto, policy making on the second level. Thus, what went on was a sharing rather than a loss of power. The legislature in the United States showed a tough vitality that belied some of the gloomier bedside bulletins of the attending doctors of political science. Reports of its death were grossly exaggerated.

III. The Courts

CHAPTER FOUR

THE RELATIVE POSITION OF THE COURTS

When people thought of "law" they usually thought of the court as the symbol of law's authority, the lawsuit as the typical form of law in action, and the judge's opinion as the staple source of legal principles. At least, these were the popular stereotypes of "law" in the United States in most of the years after the 1830's. It may seem strange, therefore, that this chapter is not at the beginning of this history.

Contrary to popular notions the courts did not first take precedence in declaring or administering the law. From 1750 until about the 1820's the legislature led the growth of law in the United States. The courts did not fully capture popular imagination as the type and model of "the law" until after 1875. Then the popular stereotype took shape as aggressive judges played major roles in the drama in which courts measured legislation against the principles of the "constitution."

Actually, between 1820 and 1890 the judges were already taking the initiative in lawmaking. Far anticipating the leadership of the executive or administrative arms, the courts built up the common law in the United States — a body of judge-made doctrine to govern people's public and private affairs. At the same time the courts played a great role not only in declaring, but also in administering, policy. For this they used particularly the flexible doctrines and remedies of Equity. Especially through the injunction and the receivership, judges anticipated the later role of executive and administrative agencies. They assumed regulatory functions which involved so continuous a process of improvisation, bargain, and trial and error that they made the law in effect a partner rather than an outside regulator of large private interests.

There is no major agency of government whose role in United States history is harder to appraise than that of the courts. This is as much due to the wrong notions of the lawmen as to the mistakes of the laymen. If popular opinion tended to exaggerate the court trial and the court decision as the dramatic symbols of the law, this exaggerated emphasis was at least equally matched at the bar and among students of law.

The bar finally established itself in the United States in the years when judges were taking the lead in making law for the society. With a confidence bred of several generations of shaping a broad body of doctrine, nineteenth-century judges inclined to view a statute as a crude intrusion upon an ordered and symmetrical system of judge-made law. Out of its experience of the dominant rule of the judges, the bar was prepared to accept this evaluation.

In the last quarter of the nineteenth century a revived legislature and a newly vitalized executive began to challenge judicial leadership. Just then, however, the typical mid-century exaltation of the courts was powerfully reinforced by a revolution in legal education. In the '70s Dean Christopher Langdell installed the case method of instruction at the Harvard Law School. In the next generation it became the standard manner of instruction in the country's leading law schools. Explicit in Langdell's thinking and implicit in his selection of teaching materials was the thesis that the essence of "law" lay in the decisions and opinions of appellate courts.

To the case-trained lawyer, statutes, executive or administrative rules or orders, the facts of community life, all had meaning only as they were filtered through the work of the appellate courts — all had importance only as they furnished the humble materials from which judicial craftsmanship fashioned "the law." As late as the 1930's in the best American law schools it was the exception to find courses that dealt explicitly with legislation, administrative law, the merged study of law and economics, or of law and politics, or of law and psychology.

Against this background, there is more danger that we shall exaggerate than that we shall underestimate, the place of the courts in United States legal history. To redress the balance, we must weigh several factors.

Popular consent and trust gave to the legislature the initiative in lawmaking until the 1820's. Indeed, during the Revolution the legislature often took on even the ordinary tasks of the executive branch, so far as these were performed at all.

This popular attitude was compounded as much of distrust for the courts as it was of faith in the legislature. In the later colonial years, the courts were apt to share with the executive the disfavor that people put on agencies which the Crown created and supported. An incident in the growing tension in Massachusetts, for example, was the legislature's demand that the judges take their salary from it and not from royal taxes. The Revolutionary War was followed by disturbed economic and political conditions. Debtor farmers found the obvious symbols of their hard burdens in the lawyers and the courts through which their creditors moved upon them. It was an effort to close the courts by force that brought discontent into sharp focus in the autumn of 1786; taking Daniel Shays for their leader, mobs of western Massachusetts farmers sought to halt the debt proceedings and mortgage foreclosures against which they had fruitlessly asked legislative relief. Eastern Massachusetts easily put down Shays's Rebellion. But the farmers' revolt marked the practical importance of the courts, and the divided attitudes toward them in the formative period of the nation.

The federal judiciary was a prime object of Jeffersonian suspicion and attack. The single fact that so resourceful a Federalist as John Marshall was Chief Justice might have made Jefferson's party feel that it must reduce the power of the federal courts. But the Federalists insured that the courts would become a political target. In a last-minute effort to hold a bastion in the government, they passed the Judiciary Act of 1800, creating new courts which would offer jobs for the faithful of their party. Repeal of this law was one of the first successful objects of Jefferson's program.

As the frontier moved west, new states took it as a matter of course that they must set up courts along with other institutions of a settled community. But their ready acceptance of courts did not mean that they regarded judges as above the political battle. Thus in Kentucky in the 1820's, there were fierce contests over the election of a supreme court which could be relied on to sustain debtors' stay laws; plainly a substantial part of the frontier community held very pragmatic views of the role of the judge. Following Mississippi in 1832 and New York in 1846, the states generally provided that all judges be elected by popular vote. It is one of the paradoxes of our legal growth that this most basic assertion of the people's control of the courts came at the threshold of the greatest period of judicial power in our history.

If we are accurately to weigh the role of the courts, there are other factors to consider. None of our major institutions developed with less deliberation as to structure or its relations to the jobs to be done. Men judged the courts' influence in affairs with a confidence that the available evidence did not justify; reliable data about the courts' business before the twentieth century is fragmentary. We must ask not only what the judges did, but what they failed to do, and look not only at the issues which they met but also at those they avoided or failed to see. This is with no intent to deny that the idea of the court was very important in our political and social attitudes. That idea dominated popular, and to a surprising extent scholarly, notions of "the law." The latter fact is relevant to the history of thought in the United States. But we still must ask whether courts actually played the role in the growth of our law that common opinion attributed to them.

CHAPTER FIVE

STRUCTURE OF STATE COURT SYSTEMS

In 1950 state courts had about the same structure and powers that they had one hundred years before. They presented a notable example of the toughness of our legal institutions as contrasted with the movement that went on in substantive policy; the judicial systems of the United States were one of the most important parts of our pre-1870 inheritance. The persistence of certain features of state court organization was the more striking because so little deliberate thought was ever given to them.

Before 1870 the only matter that had general, considered attention was the attempt to simplify procedure. This movement took impetus from New York's adoption in 1848 of the Code of Civil Procedure which David Dudley Field drew and drove through to acceptance. In a few instances of local significance, court organization was for a time an issue: Georgia early refused to set up an appellate court; Pennsylvania distrusted the extent of equity power and would not give it to the judges; New Jersey set up separate courts of equity. Such instances apart, the state constitutions and statutes adopted a uniform plan of courts with the same casual, unquestioning acceptance by which the two-chamber legislature became standard government apparatus.

After 1870, as the city and the concentration of economic power dominated the society, new problems pressed fast upon the courts. But the need for change was recognized slowly and piecemeal. In 1906 Roscoe Pound, in a classic speech before the American Bar Association, placed the defects of the court systems high among causes of popular dissatisfaction with the administration of justice. But not until 1913 was the American Judicature Society formed, to promote better judicial organization. The main response in court organization to the pressure of new demands was the specialization of courts; this developed only after the beginning of the twentieth century, and showed vigor only between 1920 and 1930. The tardy pace of change in judicial structure ill matched the drastic changes in social life and the sharp criticism of the courts' work. Probably the tough vitality of pre-1870 judicial patterns was another reflection of our tendency to adopt familiar government forms with scant deliberation, in order to concentrate on "getting ahead" in personal wealth, power, and social standing.

1. CONSTITUTIONAL PROVISIONS

State constitutions and statutes included vast and various detail about the scheme and powers of courts. But certain common characteristics stood out boldly. First, the constitutions typically set forth judicial organization so specifically as to hinder desirable change or experiment. The Federal Constitution was in sharp contrast. It specified the allowable types of federal jurisdiction, but this was essential in a document which marked out the zones of authority in a dual system of government. On the other hand, it directly created only one court, the Supreme Court of the United States, and directly established for it only a very limited original jurisdiction. It left to Congress unqualified discretion in the creation of inferior courts and in the determination of how much of the allowable jurisdiction should be vested in the federal courts.

The states found judicial reform hampered not only by constitutions which specified the classes of courts, their number, and their jurisdiction, but also by constitutional limits on local legislation. The latter made it particularly hard to adjust to the peculiar problems of the great cities. Constitutional amendment was difficult. This meant that needed change was delayed. It meant, also, that when change came, it was apt to be distorted by the compromises that were politically necessary to push it through.

Court reform for the Chicago metropolitan area was a notable instance of these troubles. The court structure in the Chicago area grew by unplanned addition of one item after another. The outworn justice-of-the-peace courts became a source of scandal and waste. It took a generation of agitation to produce a simplified scheme of courts for Chicago. Always in the background was the struggle of "downstate" Illinois to hold a preponderance, or at least a balance, of power with the metropolis; this struggle was reflected, for example, in the fact that, with well over half the state's population, modern Chicago was allocated but one of the seven members of the state supreme court. Within Chicago, forces were divided. There were substantial political interests vested in the *status quo*, and this promoted trading with downstaters in the legislature. In addition "downstate" was usually apathetic toward, or did not understand, the problems of the metropolis. These factors defeated a strong attempt in 1890 to set up a municipal court and abolish the justice of the peace in the metropolitan area. The Illinois constitution barred local legislation, and this added to the difficulty of framing a law which could muster enough votes to pass; an act could not deal with the Chicago courts alone, and the downstate districts, while they might be willing to see certain changes in Chicago, often did not want them at home. For example, the old law provided that probate court decisions could be reviewed *de novo* in the circuit court. Downstate distrusted the professional quality of its probate courts and wanted to keep this full scope of review; to those familiar with the higher standards of the metropolitan probate court, the full review was wasteful and unnecessary. Finally, in 1904, Illinois amended its constitution to permit special reorganization of the Chicago area courts. A popular referendum gave overwhelming approval thereafter to abolition of the Chicago justice-of-the-peace courts and the creation of a Chicago Municipal Court.

2. LEGISLATION AFFECTING COURT STRUCTURE

State constitutions had much to say of court structure. Scarcely less significant was the extremely detailed legislation which in the typical state allocated jurisdiction, designated venue, fixed the number and length of terms of court, created, modified, or abolished remedies, and above all else, regulated procedure.

With vague breadth state constitutions vested the three great departments with "legislative," "executive," and "judicial" power, and made little more definition of these grants. Given the legislature's ascendency in public confidence until the 1820's, it was not surprising that legislators seized the initiative in fixing the details of both the executive and judicial branches. In 1825 Marshall put the weight of his name and court behind this trend. In *Wayman* v. *Southard* he indicated that the legislature could fix rules of court procedure itself, or delegate this function to the judges; in any case, he indicated, the determination of such rules was not exclusively in the courts by any virtue inherent in the grant of "judicial" power. His opinion did not clearly concede to the courts a nonexclusive, inherent authority to make rules even in the absence of legislation.

Practical sense generally marked the growth of unwritten constitutional doctrine in this matter. The courts later asserted their inherent, if nonexclusive, rule-making power, as a necessary and proper incident to the grant of judicial authority. Judges developed greater self-confidence throughout the nineteenth century, and between a fourth and a third of the state courts eventually claimed inherent rule-making power superior to legislative interference. But, in practice, the enactment of the Field Code in New York in 1848 set a fashion which in the next generation overrode any theoretical allocation of power, and led most states to adopt statutory codes.

Few changes begun with such high ideals of reform yielded such ambiguous results. Critics had assailed the judge-made procedure before the statutory codes for its complicated and confused rules, and for its tendency to treat errors of procedure, however trivial, as fatal to the proceedings. Unfortunately, both criticisms became equally applicable to administration under the codes. Both courts and legislatures seem to have been at fault. The legislators were not content to adopt a relatively simple code and leave to the courts the inevitable adjustments in detail. As a result, in New York the Field Code expanded from 393 to 3441 sections in two generations. Moreover, a legislature is a ponderous machine to set in motion; to put procedure into statute form invited the handicaps of rigidity and outdated provisions. This was an additional reason for drastic simplicity in a statutory code. Instead, the codes often froze into permanent form some of the most dubious features of common-law procedure — for example, the cumbersome writ of error as the form of appeal.

For their part, the judges were reluctant to accept the code in the full measure of its ideal of a simplified and flexible procedure. We noted that before the codes procedural errors were often treated as necessarily vitiating the proceedings; the courts took this attitude the more strongly when procedural law came from the superior authority of the legislature. Judges in effect gave litigants substantive rights in procedure questions. The mounting pages of procedural points noted in nineteenth-century Digests show that the courts gave increasing time to issues that were wholly apart from the merits of the controversies before them.

Judicial failure to apply the basic policy of the codes was most marked in the first generation after the Field Code. If the codes could have been used only by lawyers and judges who had known no other system of procedure, perhaps they might have been handled with more sympathetic attention to their purposes. But by the time that a generation of lawyers and judges had grown up under the codes, their chance to bring a more sympathetic interpretation to code provisions had been limited by the legislative developments. By then the pattern of detailed and unplanned statutory additions to the codes had become settled.

Opinion now turned to a fundamentally new approach. English judicial reform in 1873 suggested the grant of full rule-making power to the courts. Beginning with the 1908 report of a committee to suggest remedies against unnecessary delay and cost in litigation, and continuing for twenty years, the American Bar Association fought to secure full rule-making powers for the courts. Particularly the Association sought to persuade Congress to grant this power to the Supreme Court of the United States with reference to procedure in the federal courts. Congress gave the authority to the Court in 1912, as regarded equity procedure. But not until 1934 did it give the Court complete rule-making power in civil and criminal cases.

In the meantime, however, the states had progressed. By its Practice Act of 1912, New Jersey gave rule-making power to its courts, and a number of states followed this example. By 1940 a full rule-making power over procedure had been exercised by or conferred on the courts in fifteen states (Arizona, Colorado, Delaware, Indiana, Maryland, Michigan, Nebraska, New Mexico, North Carolina, Rhode Island, South Dakota, Texas, Washington, West Virginia, and Wisconsin). Incomplete but broad power had been conferred on the courts in California, New Jersey, Ohio, and Pennsylvania. In some of these states the authority lay dormant or was not used with full and imaginative vigor. But an obvious trend had been established; the legislature had begun to relax its century-old dominance over the details of judicial administration. In the first quarter of the present century there was more evidence of this trend. "Judicial councils" developed as instruments for continuing appraisal of judicial administration by a body drawn from the legislature, the judiciary, the executive, the bar, the schools, and the public.

3. Localism in State Court Organization

Within this frame of constitutional and statutory detail, certain characteristics marked the pattern of state court organization. These were: (1) localism, (2) hierarchy, and (3) emphasis on the right to appeal. They were closely related elements, and they meant costly, wasteful, unsupervised administration of justice.

Anglo–American lawmen traditionally defined jurisdiction in terms of territory. In the formative generations after 1776, the peculiar circumstances of the United States gave a special slant to this territorial-mindedness, as it applied to the creation of courts. In a sparsely settled country, with poor communications and people of small means, men naturally sought to bring the administration of justice close to home. The early and widespread adoption of the justice of the peace meant that one kind of court was set up almost on a neighborhood basis. County and circuit or district courts were the first instance courts, respectively, for minor criminal and civil or probate matters, and for the more important criminal and civil business. The states set up these courts by districts. They measured the districts by about the distance that a man could travel in a day on horseback. Likewise they fixed on a local basis the offices whose assistance the courts required — the clerks of court, record offices, and the enforcement officers.

Certain corollary features went with the adoption of the locality as the unit of judicial organization. Each locality came to regard as its particular possession the state courts which sat there. Did business increase? The obvious answer was either to divide the locality and make two local courts where there had been but one, or to increase the membership of the local bench. Was business slack? So much the easier for the local judge; whether or not he should lend a hand in an overcrowded, neighboring circuit was wholly up to him.

The state supreme court invariably had traditional supervisory powers over the inferior courts. These it exercised by the writ of error, appeal, mandamus, prohibition, or the like. This supervision was designed to see that particular cases were properly handled. Neither in law nor in practice was it an authority to survey the flow of business and the efficiency of its disposition in the state judicial system as a whole. The states increased the number of courts and the number of judges, but they did so in no accurate adjustment to the types and location of court business. State law fixed venue, the reach of process, the details of practice according to the restricted limits of the circuits or districts that had become century-old traditional units of the court system.

Chicago court organization provided an example. Even after the creation of the unified Municipal Court, there were in the 1930's 556 autonomous courts in the Chicago metropolitan area. Cook County alone had 205. These courts generally overlapped in jurisdiction, were ill-arranged relative to the distribution of business, operated with varied rules of procedure, and fixed their calendars on no unified plan. At the widest reckoning, the judges required to man this hodgepodge of courts numbered but a fifth of the persons who directly served in the courts; of 3416 persons so employed in the Chicago area, 146 were judges and 505 were justices of the peace or police magistrates.

In 1931 England and Wales, with a little under 40,000,000 people, had about 92 judges in the county courts and the principal trial courts. New York state, with less than 13,000,000 people by the 1930 census, had about 127 judges in the principal trial courts alone, excluding judges of inferior and city and county courts. In New York City, with about 7,000,000 people, (including the suburbs, nearly 8,000,000), there were 58 judges of the first instance court of general jurisdiction, 211 of the city court, 8 in the county courts of the Bronx, Kings, and Richmond; in addition there were 9 judges of the Court of General Sessions, 16 of the Court of Special Sessions, 6 of the Court of Domestic Relations, and 63 judges of the Municipal Court.

The states met increase in the volume and complexity of judicial business by sheer multiplication of judges and courts, rather than by planned reorganization. Nor did this locality-by-locality and quantitative approach characterize only the early periods. It was the typical attitude taken toward judicial organization well into the twentieth century. When, for example, Ohio looked favorably on the unified municipal court, the state did not incorporate the change into its judicial scheme by any single comprehensive statute. Cleveland set up the first municipal court system in Ohio in 1910. It was regarded as a success. For twenty years thereafter nearly every session of the Ohio legislature saw the creation of a similar court in one or more of the other cities of the state. By 1932 thirty-three cities had a municipal court with civil and criminal jurisdiction, and seven other cities had municipal police courts. Each of these courts had been set up by a separate statute; each presented variations in jurisdiction and procedure. In 1930 a careful survey of the expenditure of public money for the administration of justice in Ohio reflected how firmly the local principle continued to rule the court system. Of the total public expenditure for the courts in Ohio, the state paid 12.1 per cent, the counties 69.4 per cent, the cities 17.6 per cent, and the villages and towns 19 per cent.

Thus a characteristic cluster of features grew about the central factor of the locality as the unit of judicial organization: (1) a tendency to increase the number of courts and judges in rather mechanical response to the pressure of business; (2) complications of venue, process, and varied local procedure; (3) almost complete autonomy in each judge as to the efficiency, energy, and volume of work done in his court; (4) the absence of any central authority empowered to shift judicial manpower from underworked to overworked circuits.

This development had not been for lack of a different model. Before 1873 the English courts had also shown the tangled piling of one specialized tribunal on another, with much independence among the various courts. Still, the English system offered the example of the King's Bench, with its one body of judges, now riding circuit, now gathering as the full bench at Westminster. In 1873 English judicial reform presented a new and more impressive model; England abolished its old independent courts, merging them into one High Court of Justice, empowered to act throughout the country with members assigned to divisions according to the needs of business and the call for special skill or experience.   ✓

Economic reasons, we noted, gave a firm hold to the rule of autonomous, local courts in the United States. Once the practice was set, inertia and our characteristic lack of interest in government forms accounted for the continuation and expansion of the local emphasis. Economy prompted successive Territories in their early days to adopt a system like that of the English migratory judges, who heard facts on circuit and met centrally to decide the issues of law. Thus in the Northwest Territory the judges rode circuit to hold trials on the facts, and met as one bench to resolve difficult issues of law. The lineage of this system has been traced back through the state of Pennsylvania to Pennsylvania colonial organization, derived in turn from the English model. Such defects as appeared in its operation seem to have been due to nothing inherent in the system, but to the judges' distaste for rigorous and dangerous travel, and their consequent refusal to hold court in the more distant counties. The experience suggests the practical considerations which reinforced the system of local courts. In any case, there is no evidence that the existence of such unified courts in the territories reflected any substantial opinion favoring such a system. And the territorial experience made no permanent mark on judicial organization.

Some men tried to substitute a rationally ordered and administered state court system for the old pattern. Their efforts roused little public or professional interest, and led to relatively little change.

After 1900 some leaders called for the unification of state courts: They would locate courts and apportion judges in planned response to the distribution and varied demands of the different kinds of judicial business; they would have the whole administered by a chief justice with authority to direct judicial man power where it was needed; they would supervise the methods and efficiency of such assisting officers as the clerks of court. Roscoe Pound was the leading spokesman of this effort. In 1913 the American Judicature Society was established, with the benediction of the American Bar Association; its primary purpose was to promote the unified court idea.

Actual changes in state court structure were limited. Early in the nineteenth century most states merged in one trial court jurisdiction in law, in equity, and in major criminal cases. This was not, however, on the theory of the value of a unified court system as such. The move reflected the burdensome expense on a meager public purse, of providing separate courts for these different types of jurisdiction. Where jurisdiction was not thus merged in form, it was in substance, by vesting the separate powers in the same local judge. In the case of the probate courts, however, history overrode economy. These were generally kept as separate courts; nevertheless, there was a degree of unification here, by putting in the one probate court the authority which in England had been divided between the law, equity, and ecclesiastical courts. Often, for economy, probate jurisdiction was joined with petty civil and criminal jurisdiction, though this meant an unfortunate loss in dignity and tended to encourage appeals from the probate court to a higher tribunal.

Some tangible results came from the twentieth-century agitation for unified, centrally administered court systems. A number of larger cities adopted unified municipal courts. An increasing number of states created judicial conferences or judicial councils, to consult and plan concerning the administration of justice. We shall not discuss the details of these developments at this point, but we should note their place in time. The municipal court movement began with the adoption of the pioneer system in Chicago in 1906. In the next twenty years municipal court systems — unified and centrally administered with varying degrees of effectiveness — were set up in a substantial number of the great cities, notably in Detroit, New York, Cleveland, Kansas City (Missouri), Milwaukee, Buffalo, Pittsburgh, Philadelphia, and Atlanta. But the movement never became universal, and by 1930 it appeared to have lost impetus.

The judicial conference began in Wisconsin in 1913, when a statute provided that the state's circuit judges should meet annually to adopt rules for the better administration of justice in their courts. A later statute provided that this body elect a chairman, who should have the duty to try to expedite and equalize business, and to request judges with light calendars to aid those who were overburdened. A closely related development, which began with Massachusetts in 1924, was the creation of judicial councils. These were composed of representative judges of the state, members of the bar, and sometimes members of the legislature or persons chosen to represent the public. Judicial councils were set up mainly to collect statistics of judicial administration and to survey needed law reforms connected with the operation of the courts. Rarely was there any explicit provision — as in the legislation that created the Wisconsin judicial conference — for recommendations regarding the shifting of judges to meet overcrowded dockets. We shall see later that the most concrete action of this last type was taken in the federal court system. Altogether, the accomplishments in the movement for unified, centrally administered judicial organization in the states had very limited effect.

4. INDEPENDENCE OF AGENCIES AUXILIARY TO COURTS

Related in effect to the extreme decentralization of courts, was the courts' relative lack of control over important assisting agencies. Jacksonian Democracy inaugurated in the 1830's a resistless demand for the popular election of public officials, great and small. It thus became typical that the clerk of court — though an indispensable agent to efficient operation of the court — owed his office to the electorate, and was not accountable even to the local judge, let alone to any state-wide supervisor of judicial record keeping. Not until the development of judicial councils in the first quarter of the twentieth century was there any move to subject the clerks of court to a degree of central supervision. As late as the 1930's the states had made almost no provision for the kind of records or statistics needed for continuous, scientific study of judicial administration; this fact alone condemned the decentralized and largely irresponsible clerical staffing of the courts.

More dramatic was the independence that the nineteenth century gave to the trial jury — and thus indirectly to the contending lawyers, whose tactical freedom before the jury was much expanded. Our tradition included distrustful memories of masterful English trial judges. To this we added pioneer faith in the average man's capacities, and pioneer skepticism for the claims of specialized skill or knowledge. Out of this background we wrote into state constitutions and statutes a very limited role for the trial judge. He must not comment on the evidence, nor could he strive in his instructions to the jury for simple directness which might disclose his own view of the merits. He was to be little more than an umpire. The attorneys had the real management of the case.

On the whole this continued to be the situation of jury trial in the states. Such change as occurred was mostly indirect; the jury became less important, because it was less used. But the jury's independence had far-reaching effects. It stimulated efforts to control the jury, and these in turn encouraged the growth of a complex body of rules of evidence. The jury's independence was attested by judges' reluctance to review the facts of the case. This encouraged very technical rules to limit review on appeal to what was contained in the formal record of the case; later, when the temper of the courts favored greater control over the jury, the technical intricacy of appellate procedure was used to upset judgments based on jury verdicts.

5. HIERARCHY IN THE COURTS

A third characteristic of state judicial systems was the creation of sharp differences of rank among judges, according to their authority. The hierarchy of judges had formal evidence in different methods of selection, different salaries, titles, and tenure. These formal distinctions had more important meaning in their effect on public opinion. Public opinion put different valuations on the different ranks of judges, and this in turn increased the effects which the formal distinctions had on the character of the judiciary. Lawmen and laymen learned to make commonplace reference to "inferior" courts and judges, and to speak of "the court below." These terms held unfortunate significance. In one sense they simply described the limited jurisdiction assigned to certain courts; but in another sense they implied that such courts were less important and could get along with something less than first-rate judges or standards of operation.

Where an organization must handle a great volume of diverse business, there was sense in division of labor, decentralization of policy administration, specialization in function, opportunity for review of decisions. Less by deliberation than in response to the pressure of facts and imitation, the states worked these organizational ideas into a standard pattern: They provided justices of the peace for minor civil and criminal matters, with police magistrates in the larger cities; they set up county courts, or — their urban counterpart in latter years — municipal courts for probate matters, for the smaller civil suits, the trial of misdemeanors, and the *de novo* review of justice-of-the-peace cases; they provided circuit courts with general original jurisdiction in law and equity and in the trial of felonies, and with power to hear *de novo* appeals from the county courts; finally, they created a top appellate court, which might have original jurisdiction in a limited range of matters of high public concern, but which existed primarily to exercise a broad appellate jurisdiction, aided in a few states by intermediate courts of appeal which sifted out the more routine appeals.

Many charges of waste and injustice could be sustained, against this pattern of state court organization. On the other hand, there was sound management instinct in distinguishing jurisdiction according to the gravity of issues or their special character; and there was sense in providing some degree of review and supervision over action of single judges. But there was another aspect of the situation which was not sound, nor at all a necessary consequence of these distinctions of function among courts. This was the idea and the practice — which developed their own parallel, almost unexplored, but stubborn life — that it was satisfactory and proper that judges of "inferior" jurisdiction should be chosen by less exacting standards of character and ability than judges of superior jurisdiction. Lay and professional opinion particularly came to draw a broad distinction in importance and dignity between the supreme court of a state and all courts "under" it.

English example probably contributed to these ideas. But two related factors peculiar to the United States undoubtedly contributed more. During our cross-continent growth, as one new state after another set up its basic legal institutions, the courts were at the high point of their creative, lawmaking function. The authoritative declaration of a body of judge-made law for the state was a task which naturally focused attention on the appellate bench. On the other hand, at a time when men knew their neighbors and issues were relatively simple, the decision of the run of disputes in the local courts did not seem to call for special talent. Rural and small-town experience dominated nineteenth-century American ideas about government. Out of the necessities of that experience, the average man in the United States acquired a large confidence in himself as a Jack-of-all-trades. What, then, was so special about judging a case: any good man could do it.

Complaints of the ignorance, prejudice, or venality of justices of the peace date from as far back as the early nineteenth century. But after 1870 deeper currents of change challenged the adequacy of the conventional standards for "lower" court judges. An increasing proportion of people were living in cities; as legal control was applied to a widening area of complicated social and economic issues, increasing demands were made on the integrity, skill, and learning of officials.

Again, the English judicial reform of 1873 gave impetus to re-examination of our system. England had put all members of the High Court of Justice on a substantially equal level of dignity and perquisites, whether they sat in courts of first instance or on appeal. The English reform also gave high status to the county courts, both in the care given the selection of their judges, and in the pay and tenure of the judges.

The contrast between English and United States courts of "inferior" jurisdiction was brought to the front by shocking revelations of corruption, inefficiency and injustice to the poor and foreign-born in the great cities which more and more set the tone of the society. Revolt against Tweed's grasp on the New York City courts in the 1870's spurred the creation of the powerful Association of the Bar of the City of New York. "Muckraking" journalists of the turn of the century — such men as Lincoln Steffens and Brand Whitlock — spread wide the consciousness of unsavory local government. When in 1906 Pound called for a unified judicial system, and when the formation of the American Judicature Society in 1913 gave formal expression to this demand, the motive was in part to lift the status and quality of the "inferior" courts. In 1922 the Cleveland Crime Survey hammered the thesis that there was great need for high standards of character and competence in the courts of petty jurisdiction. Here, it was emphasized, most people had their only contact with the judiciary; from that contact, for better or, more likely, for worse, they would form their idea of the administration of justice. In later years this point was underlined by every major survey of judicial administration in the states.

Informed laymen and lawmen thus recognized the problem. But improvement was not impressive. In the greatest cities — where, indeed, the failure of justice had been most flagrant — promising changes took place between 1910 and 1940. Where a more or less unified municipal court was set up, the justice of the peace departed and at least potentially higher status was given the inferior courts. Specialization of small claims, juvenile delinquency, and domestic relations courts helped raise the status of those critically important phases of judicial work. Judges of first instance courts of general jurisdiction received more adequate salaries; sometimes, as in New York state, increases were sufficient to leave a narrow margin only between their salary level and that of appellate judges.

Up to the mid-twentieth century the great cities had not yet found how to reconcile an elected bench with freedom from grandstanding tactics and shady political affiliations. Nor had the typical municipal court system yet given to the chief judge or any other administrative authority assignment and disciplinary power sufficient to provide the possible means for raising standards within the judiciary itself. In any case, such marked changes as had occurred in internal organization, specialized status, or salary had on the whole touched only a few of the cities of first rank. It would be unwarranted to assume that rural justice was generally administered under old forms with competence, efficiency, and honesty. And — the big cities and the country areas apart — well over a quarter of the people of the United States by the 1930's lived in urban communities of the intermediate range from 5000 to 250,000 population; here, throughout the land, there had been almost no substantial reordering of the judicial system during the national lifetime.

6. The Emphasis on Appeals

Closely related to the relative indifference toward "lower" courts was a persistent emphasis on the appellate side of judicial administration. This emphasis was not inevitable. We had from the start an English example which reduced the stress on a formally separate hierarchy of appeals courts: This was in the King's Bench system, whereby, on a reserved question or on motion for a new trial, the judges *en banc* might hear disputed questions of law that arose out of the facts of a case which one of their number had tried on circuit. Some states, such as Massachusetts, and some of the territories, like the Northwest Territory, followed this example. Indeed, for many years some states did not sharply separate original and appellate jurisdiction. From 1814–1852 in Virginia the highest appellate court was composed of judges who presided over trial courts; members of the Illinois Supreme Court tried cases until 1848; members of the Massachusetts Supreme Judicial Court tried capital cases with a jury from 1804–1872, and in modified form this practice continued until 1891; members of the New Jersey Supreme Court, who were also members of the Court of Errors and Appeals, had general trial duties well into the twentieth century.

On the other hand, it was the exception when no provision was made for some sort of review of proceedings at trial. Georgia had no appellate court until 1846; there was no right of appeal in criminal cases in Delaware until 1897, nor any in Louisiana during the period 1812–1843; in New York the Senate, the Chancellor, and the judges of the Supreme Court formed the court of last resort until 1847. The New York system was the last token of the fact that just before and after the Revolution the legislature was commonly the appellate tribunal. After the Revolution, however, the trend was toward the creation of a separate appellate bench; the membership of these appellate courts became more and more separated from that of the trial courts, as the latter were decentralized.

No part of the history of United States courts presents such a tangle of detail as does the handling of appeals. Nor does the tangled story unwind toward a happy solution. A distinguished student of the problem, as it stood in the 1930's, rated the United States as the possessor, even at that late date, of probably the least efficient system of review in the world. To attempt an adequate survey of the varied aspects of appeals would lend the subject an emphasis disproportionate to its proper place in this book. Certain features will be mentioned because they throw some light on more important currents in our legal development.

The opportunity for successive appeals was a conspicuous source ot waste, cost, and delay in our judicial system. There was, first, appeal — with the opportunity for a trial *de novo* — from justices of the peace to county courts, and from county courts or probate courts to circuit or district courts. There was in some states review by intermediate courts of appeal. In all states there was the possibility, and often the right, of review by the top court.

This elaboration of appeals in part showed how much laymen and lawmen had accepted less exacting standards of quality in the "lower" courts, and how far in consequence they distrusted the unchecked discretion of those courts. The twentieth century saw some improvement in this respect, though it was along lines that strongly suggested how far we were from creating a strong bench in the inferior courts.

Improvement lay chiefly in simplifying appeals and eliminating duplication, rather than in narrowing resort to review. Some states created appellate divisions, or appellate terms, of courts of first instance in probate and small causes, and provided therefor a simple appellate procedure and limited review authority so that it no longer involved a *de novo* re-examination of the lower court's work.

The other change came in the dozen states which had intermediate appellate courts. These jurisdictions consistently tended to cut down the right of double appeal, and gave finality to the judgments of the intermediate review courts in an increasing range of cases. Sometimes the intermediate court's rulings regarding fact findings were made final. Sometimes all of its judgments were made final, subject to power to certify important issues to the highest court. But the main tendency was to reduce double appeals as a matter of right, by giving the supreme court discretionary power — usually through the statutory writ of certiorari — to order up cases for review according to the highest court's judgment of the importance of the questions involved. The less significant cases were thus disposed of by denial of certiorari, and the top court could limit opinion writing to the more important issues.

Appellate organization and operations in the nineteenth century were much influenced by the lawmaking done by the judges between about 1810 and 1880. Those were the years when the creation of one new settled community after another demanded also the creation of a body of law to govern everyday affairs in the new states; this was the formative period of our common law. People came to regard appellate courts primarily as lawgivers, rather than as agencies to secure the best adjustment in the particular case. This function, and the attitude which was both created by it and supported it, were reflected in the readiness with which the states allowed even successive appeals. They were reflected in the unprecedented flood of reported opinions in all cases, whether the cases were trivial, peculiar in setting, or of broad policy importance.

It was accepted without question that the prime responsibility of the appellate court was to declare the law, rather than merely to decide the case. Thus it was one hundred years before the states began to relieve their highest courts of this indiscriminate burden, by adopting some form of discretionary review, as by grant of certiorari.

This concentration on the lawmaking job of the top courts was especially shown in the intricate and restrictive forms of appellate procedure, and in the approach taken to procedural issues on appeal. For example, appellate courts were very reluctant to pass at all on questions of fact; they saw their proper task as centered on questions of "law," however much this involved disregarding the merits of the concrete dispute before them. Likewise, they were unwilling to dispose of the whole case, and ready to see a given lawsuit wind its laborious way upward on successive appeals, as successive issues were brought to the front by the logic of nice procedure and the meticulous observance of the limitations of the record.

Always in the background was the most stubbornly formal of the limitations that hedged the appellate process: as its early model for appeals procedure, the United States selected from the store of English examples the writ of error. This strictly limited review to matters that appeared on the formal record of the case; it was a costly and delaying procedure, all the more so because it invited a highly technical approach. No one has yet fully explained why we took this unwieldy device as the general foundation of our appellate procedure. Pound saw the answer in the contemporary suspicion of Equity, and the consequent reliance on the familiar learning of Coke's *Institutes;* Coke taught distrust of all tribunals except the superior courts of common law, and exalted the procedures of the latter as the safeguards of English liberty. Perhaps so. But surely also the economic factor had weight. The difficulty and cost of travel, we have noted, led to extreme decentralization of court organization. Therefore, it was perhaps more natural in providing for appeals to follow the model of the King's Bench in reviewing on writ of error the judgment of the Common Pleas, than to choose the procedure of the King's Bench in reviewing, on simple motion or reserved question, a trial that had been held on circuit before one of their own members.

In any case, the adoption of the writ of error proceeding brought many troubles. It became easy to treat an appeal as an independent proceeding, almost as a new lawsuit — with its own summons, pleadings (assignments of error), printed records suited to the dignity of a high-ranking and distinct reviewing court, and a transcript of evidence instead of the simple transfer upstairs of the original papers in the suit. And it brought what Pound called "record worship":

> . . . as late as the first decade of the present century, there were still jurisdictions where the record alone would be tried on a proceeding in error and so a judgment would be reversed which would have been affirmed had it been possible to get the real case before the court.

Eventually such technicality bred countertechnicality, as courts resorted to fine points of procedural doctrine to escape those confines of the record to which the appellant or appellee might try to hold them. The *Century Digest* of 1896 shows about 4 per cent of all the cases noted turning on points of appellate procedure.

Not all these difficulties could be attributed to lack of flexibility or imagination on the part of appellate judges. Legislatures contributed, by insisting on fixing the details of procedure. In the law's formative years in the newly made states, to insist on procedural nicety was to take one means of curbing trial courts' discretion at a time when a reasonably broad body of substantive law was not yet developed to do that job. Some of the use of fine procedural points to dispose of appealed cases was probably an indirect effort to check the broad powers of the early-nineteenth-century jury. In criminal appeals, strict insistence on procedural correctness may have been used to counteract what many saw as an excessive development of protections to the accused on trial. At best, however, such elements only support pleas in mitigation.

In the twentieth century the states improved appellate procedure along two lines of change. The grant of full, or generous, rule-making powers to the courts made reform simpler and more flexible. Toward the end of the nineteenth century a few states pioneered in making one type of review proceeding applicable to all cases; in the twentieth century the codes tended to make this the rule.

More significant than these changes, or than any of the simplified procedures adopted under them, was a shift in attitude. People began to take an increasingly pragmatic view of government in general, as an instrument of service. In particular, men treated procedure more and more as a means to the better handling of a case, and less as a source of substantive rights. Legislatures prescribed that reversal should be only for prejudicial error, and courts over the years applied these prescriptions with greater sympathy than they first showed toward them.

New rules of court had their greatest meaning in the extent to which they reflected this new practicality. By rule, courts abolished formal process to bring in the appellee; they adopted a simple procedure in the trial court, to supplant the assignment of errors in fact; they generally relaxed the requirements of new trials for errors in the record; they permitted use of the lawyers' briefs to state abstracts and specifications of errors, in place of the old assignments of errors as a separate pleading; they allowed documents or articles put before the trial court to go before the reviewing court by stipulation, or by some easy mode of authentication, without a formal proceeding or order below making them a part of the record.

Their nineteenth-century lawmaking role and their cumbersome, controversy-breeding procedure brought the appellate courts a great volume of work. The burden of appellate business grew especially as population increased and changed technology and economic organization after the Civil War created whole new areas of conflict and adjustment.

More in response to the pressure of facts than out of any considered plans, various expedients were tried to match appellate organization to the flood of work. The most mechanical response — taken at one time or another in two thirds of the states — was simple increase in the membership of the highest court. However, all this really did was lighten the individual judge's load of opinion writing.

First New York, in 1870, and subsequently eighteen other states tried the appointment of temporary "commissioners" as aides to the regular judges. The "commissioners" either sat separately or with one or more of the regular court. The system found no lasting approval in professional circles though the grounds of opposition were never clearly established.

A third device was given substantial trial only in New York and Virginia, though it would seem one of the most obvious and sensible ways to relieve overcrowded appellate dockets. This was the temporary designation of lower court judges to sit with members of the supreme court. Where this was tried, especially in New York, its results were found to be good; in New York the procedure served in some notable instances to train and test men for future selection to the highest court.

During most of the years of our national lifetime, some states employed intermediate appellate courts. But the experience of the twelve states which used them created no apparent trend to their further adoption. Intermediate appellate courts added to jurisdictional uncertainty, and it took a long time to limit the double appeals which they made possible.

As another expedient to meet the burden of appeals, twenty of the highest, and six of the intermediate appellate courts in the states at one time or another sat in divisions. There was general satisfaction with the operation of the divisional scheme, and it proved easy to handle antici-pated difficulties. Some semi-automatic docketing procedure was neces-sary to keep litigants from choosing their division. Conflicts of doctrine were avoided by provision that the chief justice sit with each division, or that judges be rotated, or that hearing by the full bench be had on request of one or more of the judges or on dissent in the division that first heard the appeal, or by provision for frequent conferences of the whole court. There was no substantial increase in motions for rehearing following adoption of the divisional system.

Finally, one method of adjustment to increased appellate business was the occasional provision of trained research assistants for the judges. Despite the simplicity and potential worth of thus staffing the courts, the measure was not generally used.

Few states granted their courts of review any discretionary control of the volume of their business — a fact indicative of the stress that both the public and the bar put on appeals. The states, of course, did set various absolute limits on the time within which review might be had. A third of the states set minimum requirements as to the amount in controversy in some kinds of suits. But they fixed such financial limits only in a restricted area of litigation; they made many important excep-tions to the limits — as of questions involving the title to, or possession of, a freehold or franchise, and of questions involving constitutional issues; and they usually set the required amount in controversy too low to have much meaning as a limit on the volume of appealable cases. Most states barred appeal by the prosecution in criminal cases — though about half of them came to allow appeal by the prosecutor on questions of law — but this barrier did not relieve the courts of a relatively large amount of work. Most states provided that the loser must pay the costs of appeal as well as court fees; but cost schedules were obviously far below actual costs, and no state taxed full actual expenses on appeal. Many states provided that if the appellate court was satisfied that the appeal had been solely for delay, it might tax added costs or lay a pen-alty. But there is no substantial evidence that the courts ever enforced these provisions to any material extent.

Except for New Jersey, each of the states which had an intermediate court of appeal, and eight other states had by 1940 adopted some form of discretionary authority in the top court to control such cases as might be brought to it. We have noted that this meant a saving of time, chiefly, in the lessened labor of writing opinions; the appeals court in effect still had to review all the cases in order to sift out those to be given extended hearing. Beginning with the Circuit Courts of Appeals Act of 1891, Congress granted the Supreme Court of the United States increasingly broad discretion in the control of its business. This might have been expected to give a weighty precedent for the spread of this method through the states. That so few states gave discretionary control of business to their appellate courts marked the tenacity of the idea that a man was entitled to at least one appeal as a matter of right.

CHAPTER SIX

STRUCTURE OF THE FEDERAL COURT SYSTEM

Federalism put its mark on almost every aspect of our law, including the development of our court systems. From 1789 on, we had distinct systems of state and federal courts; their coexistence posed problems of relative jurisdiction and comity; and these facts contributed to the unique role of the courts in our history.

The novelty of the federal experiment insured that the federal courts would follow their own course of growth. There was here no tradition, to substitute for conscious creation. Here, as in the history of the state courts, one can find inertia, heedless sentiment for the past, shortsighted response to the immediate pressure of facts. But these did not figure in the federal court story to the same great extent that they did in the growth of the state judiciary. To a degree unique in the development of our major government institutions, the history of the federal courts was marked by explicit, deliberate decisions of policy.

1. Constitutional Provisions

The Federal Convention made decisions critical to the development of the national judiciary. That there should be one Supreme Court of the United States was accepted without debate. The unquestioned acceptance of this testified how far our political thinking assumed that government must operate under formal processes of law. That this Supreme Court might be granted powers to review state court rulings in matters of national right was recognized in Convention debate; there was some suggestion that the way should be left open for even broader review powers, to be used to promote uniformity in the general law.

The Convention took a more controversial decision when it voted into the Constitution the provision for creation of inferior federal courts. The dispute which this provoked led to the third critical determination — to leave to Congress full discretion as to setting up these inferior courts. The latter decision was taken for the immediate purpose of compromising the difference between those in the Convention who feared undue encroachment on state authority, and those who believed that the national government must have its own courts, for the sure enforcement of its laws. This was the immediate purpose, but the decision had deep implications for the future of the federal courts. It meant that in their development there would be possibilities for flexible experiment and adjustment which the typical state constitution denied by its rigid specification of the details of state court structure. The decision meant also, however, that in any ultimate test of strength between the federal courts and Congress, Congress (and the President, insofar as at any given time he held effective leadership) could prevail. Finally, consistent with its decision on the creation of inferior courts, the Convention left full discretion to Congress to decide how much of the permissible federal jurisdiction it would confer on the federal courts; the range of this discretion put into relative insignificance the specified, limited original jurisdiction of the Supreme Court.

2. THE FIRST JUDICIARY ACT

A Senate committee headed by Oliver Ellsworth of Connecticut drew the First Judiciary Act, that of September 24, 1789. The act set up a federal court organization which lasted almost unchanged for nearly one hundred years.

The First Judiciary Act embodied two decisions of policy which proved basic in federal court history. First, Congress exercised its power to create inferior federal courts. It divided the country into thirteen districts (two each for Massachusetts and Virginia; Rhode Island and North Carolina were still not members of the Union) with a district court for each district. The restriction of district courts to state boundaries was followed ever thereafter. The act also divided the country into three circuits in each of which a circuit court, consisting of two Justices of the Supreme Court and one of the district judges of the circuit, was to sit twice a year in the respective districts of the circuit. The system of circuit courts, with various changes, lasted until January 1, 1912.

More important than the most enduring of these organizational details was the founding of the tradition that the federal government should have its own first instance courts throughout the nation. Likewise established was Congress's full authority to decide how much jurisdiction should be given the inferior federal courts. The First Judiciary Act set this jurisdiction in quite limited terms — emphasizing thereby the measure of Congressional control of the matter. The substance of this first grant consisted of cases in admiralty, allotted to the district courts, and cases resting on diversity of citizenship, allotted to the circuit courts, with a limited appellate jurisdiction in the circuit courts

over district court decisions. Thus, from the start practice gave no support for the theory later sponsored by Mr. Justice Story, that Congress
was under some obligation derived from the spirit of the judiciary
article of the Constitution, to give the federal courts the full possible
jurisdiction allowed by the Constitution. Nor did later practice give
countenance to this high Federalist doctrine.

Section 25 of the First Judiciary Act embodied the second basic
decision written into that statute. This was the proposition that under
the supremacy clause of the Constitution the state courts were bound to
faithful enforcement of the Constitution and laws of the United States,
and to that extent were in effect subordinate agencies of the federal
government. For Section 25 provided that a final judgment in the
highest court of a state:

> where is drawn in question the validity of a treaty or statute of, or
> an authority exercised under the United States, and the decision is
> against their validity; or where is drawn in question the validity of
> a statute of, or an authority exercised under any state, on the
> ground of their being repugnant to the Constitution, treaties or
> laws of the United States, and the decision is in favour of such their
> validity, . . . may be re-examined and reversed or affirmed in the
> Supreme Court of the United States upon a writ of error, . . .

Unlike the basic decision to establish inferior federal courts, this second
decisive step under the Judiciary Act of 1789 did not go uncontested.
Jeffersonian attacks on the judiciary as the last Federalist stronghold
climaxed in a full effort in 1825 to repeal Section 25. The attempt
failed. In 1831 another such effort met severe defeat. Thereafter in practice Section 25 was established in the constitutional tradition of the
United States.

3. THE HIERARCHY OF FEDERAL COURTS

We can best sketch the development of the federal courts by looking
at their structure, then at their jurisdiction — at the anatomy and
the physiology of the system. One characteristic remained through all
changes: There was always an hierarchy of courts of first instance,
of intermediate appellate jurisdiction, and of final review. But the relation of the first two courts changed materially over the course of years.

We noted that the district court began with quite limited first instance jurisdiction, and that the circuit court had both first instance and
appellate jurisdiction. The circuit court was first composed of two
Justices of the Supreme Court, and one district judge. The act of

February 13, 1801 made this circuit court consist of one Justice and
one district judge; and it allowed either of these to hold court alone.
In practice, under increasing pressure of Supreme Court business, the
circuit court came to be held most often by a district judge. This in
effect often abolished its appellate jurisdiction, since the district and
circuit courts were held by the same officer.

Though the 1801 provision, that one judge might hold circuit court,
introduced desirable flexibility, the formal tie of the circuit courts to
the membership of the Supreme Court was an artificial limit on the
ready addition of circuits to meet the needs of a growing country. Repeatedly the membership of the Supreme Court was increased to meet
the need for more circuits. This meant that the composition of the highest court was being determined by considerations irrelevant to the
appellate work which early became its main concern.

Men complained of the structural inadequacy of this system; they
did not like the unchecked power which district judges wielded on
circuit; they noted the mounting arrears of Supreme Court appellate
business. But not until 1869 did the complaints prevail against Congressional inertia and the competition of more clamorous demands on
legislative attention. Even then Congress made no fundamental reform.
It created a new panel of nine (later ten) circuit judges, to join the
district judges in holding circuit court; and it kept, in attenuated form,
the theoretical obligation of the Supreme Court Justices to sit on
circuit.

For over twenty years, in the face of increasing demonstration of the
inadequacy of this outworn structure, Congress allowed it to continue.
The ten new circuit judges were not enough to handle the business of
sixty-five districts. The statutory duty of the Justices to attend circuit
could not stand against the demands of the swollen appellate docket at
Washington. By the late '80s single judges, mostly district judges, were
disposing of almost 90 per cent of litigation in the circuit courts. The
volume of appeals that came direct from the circuit courts to the
Supreme Court, swamped the high court's docket beyond hope of relief
under the existing system; from 1884 to 1890 the cases docketed at the
opening of each term moved steadily up, from 1315 cases to 1800.

The Senate urged improvement of the federal court structure. But
this movement became entangled in counterefforts to cure the situation by cutting down federal jurisdiction. It was not by accident that
the countermovement was pushed most vigorously by Southern and
Western members of the House; for their various reasons, these sections
distrusted federal power.

Not until the Circuit Courts of Appeals Act of March 3, 1891 did

Congress work any substantial relief out of this stalemate. The district and circuit courts were kept, as a tribute to sentiment; but the act abolished the appellate jurisdiction of the circuit courts. In further deference to sentiment, the Justices were in form still to be assigned to the circuit courts. Congress created nine intermediate courts of appeals, and divided the stream of appellate business. Restricted types of issues that were deemed intrinsically more important might go straight to the Supreme Court from the district and circuit courts. But the bulk of cases would henceforth go to the circuit courts of appeals for final disposition, subject to certification to the Supreme Court, or subject to the Supreme Court's allowance of a hearing by grant of the writ of certiorari. The 1891 act set a basic structure which has lasted to date. The anachronism of two courts of first instance (the district and circuit courts), now of substantially equal weight, was ended by the Act of March 3, 1911. This abolished the circuit courts as of January 1, 1912, and left the district courts as the first instance tribunals of the federal system.

Aside from the matter of circuit duty, the formal organization of the Supreme Court of the United States changed after 1789 only in the number of its members. The Court began with a Chief Justice and five associates. The Act of February 24, 1807 increased its number by one; it erected a seventh circuit to handle the growing federal judicial business in Kentucky, Tennessee, and Ohio, and this automatically called for a sixth Associate Justice for the new circuit. Western pressure for additional circuits brought the Act of March 3, 1837, which divided the country into nine circuits and added two members to the Supreme Court. In 1863, partly as a war measure to acknowledge the loyalty of California and Oregon, Congress added a tenth circuit, and thus a tenth Justice.

In 1866, out of its bitterness toward President Andrew Johnson, Congress reduced the Court again to seven members, and the circuits to nine; declining to face the possibility of Johnson appointees, Congress provided that no vacancy should be filled "until the number of associate justices shall be reduced to six." After the death of Wayne, from July, 1867 to February, 1870 the Court stood at eight members. However, the Act of April 10, 1869, in addition to creating the new circuit judges, again increased the membership of the Supreme Court to nine. The Court continued at that figure. Experience upheld the number nine as the probable maximum consistent with effective action as a body.

Early in 1937 President Franklin D. Roosevelt proposed to Congress that it authorize the appointment of as many as six additional Associate Justices. At first the administration ineptly rationalized the proposal as a needed supplement to the flagging energy of older members of the existing Bench. A crisp letter addressed to the chairman of the Senate Judiciary Committee by Chief Justice Hughes and Justices Van Devanter and Brandeis easily disposed of this point, on the facts. This was all byplay. The administration proposal was actually its countermove to the abuse of the judicial veto by a majority of the Court in the previous two terms; those years had seen a majority of the Justices apparently ready to block attempts to combat national economic collapse by novel uses of national financial and regulatory power. After a spirited fight that ran through the summer of 1937, the proposed measure was defeated. Its defeat was due largely to the fact that in the spring of 1937 the changed votes of Mr. Justice Roberts turned into a majority the former Court minority, which in 1935 and 1936 had vainly opposed substitution of judicial for executive and Congressional policy making.

The growth of the federal court system offered one particularly constructive example for the improvement of judicial organization in the United States. This was in the development, after 1920, of means for central, planned control of the administration of federal court business.

In the assignment of Supreme Court Justices to circuit duty, the First Judiciary Act took a much earlier step toward a unified, centrally supervised system. The unfortunate experience under that scheme, however, showed that unification was not a good in itself. That plan put too much work, over too large and diverse a geographical area, on too few men; it provided no defined means to check regularly the quality of local court performance; and it gave no one authority to dispose judicial man power throughout the system in the most efficient manner. Moreover, at most the circuit Justice represented a very small move toward a unified judiciary. The assigned circuit was the limit of the powers and activity of the Justice. As a whole the federal courts stood for the same emphasis on local autonomy as did the state systems. Congress kept federal judicial districts congruent with state lines; district judges were at first entirely confined in authority to the districts in which they resided; and before 1920 the statutes permitted senior judges to assign district judges to duty outside their circuits only in narrowly defined emergencies.

The states felt the first impetus toward a more rational administration of judicial business; this showed itself early in the twentieth century in the drive for unified municipal courts. That the movement was soon carried into the federal system and there was given its most notable achievement, was due first to the interest and conviction of William Howard Taft, and later to his prestige as Chief Justice, when he cast that into the balance.

The Act of September 14, 1922 introduced into the federal court system two important new instruments of administration. Together these marked the first effort to treat the system as an entity. The act gave the Chief Justice authority to assign district judges to service anywhere in the country. Even so, Congress made concessions to the vital tradition of localism: The Chief Justice's authority was conditioned on a certificate of need by the senior circuit judge or circuit Justice of the district that requested aid; and also there must be a certificate from the circuit judge of the supplying circuit that the services of the assigned judge could temporarily be dispensed with.

Secondly, the 1922 act provided that the Chief Justice should call to an annual conference in Washington the senior circuit judge, or his representative, from each circuit, to discuss the functioning of the federal courts. Though this Judicial Conference of Senior Circuit Judges had only a modest endowment of formal authority or means of action, over fifteen years' practice developed for it an expanding role. Assignment of judges was more flexibly handled, and on the basis of more assured information; improvements in rules of procedure and practice were effected; the practice was adopted, and widely extended, of tendering the co-operation of the Conference in movements for the improvement of federal justice, through participation in joint committees of the bar, the bench, and the schools.

So far as there was such progress, it became increasingly clear that the lack of a comprehensive, reliable system of statistics of federal judicial administration limited the future. On the recommendation of the Conference and of the Attorney General, Congress passed the Administrative Office Act of August 7, 1939. A distinguished federal judge characterized it as "probably the greatest piece of legislation affecting the judiciary since the Judiciary Act of 1789."

The 1939 act did four things. First, it ended an awkward budget situation. The federal courts were an independent, co-ordinate branch of the government. But before 1939 the Department of Justice had prepared and presented to Congress the budget for the judiciary. This was a particularly anomalous situation, since the Department was the legal representative of the chief litigant before the federal courts. The new statute put on the Conference of Senior Circuit Judges the duty of passing on the judiciary budget; it committed the preparation of the budget to one branch of a new Administrative Office of the Federal Courts, responsible only to the Conference. Secondly, the 1939 act placed in the Administrative Office the responsibility of gathering statistics as to the work of the federal courts; when the new Office was set up, this job was entrusted to a second principal division of the Office, co-ordinate with that which handled the federal court finances. Third, the act created in each circuit a Judicial Council, composed of the circuit judges of that circuit, charged to supervise the efficiency of all *3.* business; and the act charged the district judges to carry out the directions of the Council as to the administration of their courts. Fourth, the act required that in each circuit there be an annual conference of all the *4.* district and circuit judges together with representatives of the bar, to consider the state of business therein and the improvement of its administration.

Of the various phases of the 1939 act, that which provided for the regular, planned, and reliable collection of judicial statistics carried the broadest practical implications. The importance of the task was reflected in the energy with which the new Administrative Office pressed the development of this work. The implications of change were not confined to federal judicial administration. Meetings of the National Conference of Judicial Councils discussed the application of the federal scheme to the simpler problems of state judicial administration. New drive was given to the pioneering statistical work of such states as California, Iowa, New York, and Pennsylvania.

What the Conference of Senior Circuit Judges did, and what the Administrative Office of the Federal Courts did, had meaning for the general problems of judicial organization and operation in the United States, rather than for the special problems of federalism. From the latter standpoint — granted the basic importance of the early establishment of the tradition that we should have a system of inferior federal courts — what most determined the role of the federal courts in the community of nation and states was the extent of jurisdiction that Congress from time to time conferred. At this point we are concerned with jurisdiction as the essential complement to court structure, in setting the character of the system.

4. THE JURISDICTION OF LOWER FEDERAL COURTS

There were two long-range trends in the story of federal jurisdiction. One was the expansion of the jurisdiction of the federal courts of first instance. The other was the restriction of review as of right in the Supreme Court of the United States. These were seemingly polar points about which clustered the intricate details of the history of authority from time to time granted the federal courts by Congress. The apparent divergence in emphasis was reconciled in a ground common to both developments; the increased importance of the federal courts in the life of the country, an importance expressed both in the wider reach of national law, and in the convergence on the major national agencies of issues of the deepest impact.

The Judiciary Act of 1789 gave to the district and circuit courts jurisdiction in admiralty and in suits between citizens of different states. It conferred little of the potentially broad jurisdiction allowed by the Constitution over all cases arising under the Constitution or the laws or treaties made thereunder. Thus it gave the lower federal courts jurisdiction over penalties and forfeitures under the laws of the United States, and over a small number of federal crimes.

The next chapter was as drastic, although brief, as the first was cautious and lasting. The Federalists wanted to expand the courts in order to find posts in which to entrench their party, which was now about to pass control of the executive and legislature to the Jeffersonians. In addition, the Federalists wished to give the full possible jurisdiction to the federal courts so that local feeling would not bar enforcement of federal laws. Accordingly, the Act of February 13, 1801 not only created new circuit judgeships, but also expanded the jurisdiction of the federal courts to the limit of the Constitution. By the Act of April 29, 1802, the Jeffersonian Congress repealed this broad grant of power; such changes as it made in the system were limited to court structure.

Mr. Justice Story — by this time as good a Federalist as if he had been appointed by John Adams instead of by James Madison — authored a bill (1816) for which he obtained the approval of his colleagues, which again sought to give the circuit courts the whole jurisdiction possible under the Constitution. The effort failed, apparently more because Congress was not interested than because it was actively opposed. In contrast was the cautious expansion of the jurisdiction under temporary provisions at the end of the War of 1812, by which federal tax collectors might remove from state to federal courts suits in which their duties involved them. In 1833 a provision of the "Force Bill," passed in reply to South Carolina's threat to nullify the tariff of 1828, renewed this grant in general form, regarding all suits against United States officers on account of any acts by them under the revenue laws.

Court structure and jurisdiction are not likely to engage continuous legislative interest; action was typically delayed until fairly compelled by the pressure of events. Thus the next step in expansion of federal jurisdiction did not come till after the Civil War. But, with complete political logic, it then finally came in full measure.

The vast commercial and industrial growth after the war greatly expanded the volume of business that came to the federal courts under their existing jurisdiction. In addition Congress largely extended the authority granted the federal courts. Several acts of the war and Reconstruction years brought a flood of cases that were removed from state courts because they involved action of federal officers. For ten years the Bankruptcy Act of 1867 added to the volume of business.

Overshadowing all else, however, was the Act of March 3, 1875. By it Congress gave the federal courts the full range of constitutional jurisdiction. Not only might any suit be brought in a federal court, if the action asserted a right under the Constitution or the laws or treaties of the United States. In addition, any such action brought in a state court might be removed to the federal courts for disposition. So natural a concomitant of the trend of the times was this vast expansion of jurisdiction, that it passed with little contemporary notice.

Expansion had now gone about as far as possible; further history must necessarily be retreat. From the late '70s, the return of Southern power in Congress, and growing Western feeling against the federal courts as the resort of wealthy interests led to efforts to curtail original federal jurisdiction. In 1887 there was an attempt to remit to the state courts the large business that came from suits by foreign and federally chartered corporations. This effort failed, but Congress did eliminate national bank litigation from the lower federal court dockets by its declaration that these banks should be "deemed citizens of the States in which they are respectively located."

Otherwise, the only material restriction of jurisdiction was by successive increases in the minimum value of the matter in controversy, which had always been a requirement of jurisdiction in first instance federal courts. The Judiciary Act of 1789 set the amount at $500, exclusive of costs; in 1887 Congress increased it to $2,000, exclusive of interest and costs; and in 1911 to $3,000, exclusive of interest and costs.

There were those who repeatedly urged that Congress cut out all jurisdiction based on diversity of citizenship; this was urged most strongly after the '90s. A more limited proposal, usually sponsored by the West, was to withdraw the litigation brought to federal courts by the fiction of the common citizenship of corporation stockholders. Neither of these proposals ever came near passing.

5. APPELLATE JURISDICTION OF THE SUPREME COURT

By the mid-twentieth century legislation governing the appellate jurisdiction of the Supreme Court of the United States clearly reflected the idea, and the fact, that that Court was no ordinary appellate tribunal. Implicit in the statutes which finally set the lines of its appellate burden was recognition of the Court's unique responsibilities: that it was one of the prime agencies to hold the federal balance in adjustment; that it was imperative, therefore, that the Court be free of cumbering detail so it might treat the issues of high policy that came before it with appropriate care and yet with reasonable speed.

However, this concept did not begin to emerge with clarity until well after the Civil War. The First Judiciary Act gave the Court appellate jurisdiction of all classes of cases that might lawfully be reviewed, both from the lower federal courts and from the state courts. From the start of operations under the act of 1789 to the Circuit Courts of Appeals Act of 1891, the story was monotonously the same; the details need not be related. There were the burdensome circuit duties of the Justices; the economic growth of the country brought a swelling tide of litigation to the lower federal courts, even under their early, restricted jurisdiction; the act of 1875 brought enormous business, under claims of federal right; Section 25 was the basis for a continuing stream of important issues on appeal from the state courts. There resulted a consistent history of overloaded dockets, long-delayed decisions, and lack of the freedom from pressure which was needed for wise treatment of major issues.

For one hundred years the only response was in terms of structural tinkering. Terms of court were successively lengthened; the circuit duties were grudgingly whittled away; the number of Justices was increased from one time to another; and the Court was left to such limited control as it could effect by its own rules of practice, such as by limiting time for argument. The only notable occasions when an attempt was made to reduce the scope of the Court's appellate jurisdiction were those, as in 1825 and 1831, when an effort was made to repeal Section 25 of the Judiciary Act. Here, however, the motive was entirely the drive of states'-rights extremists to cut down the powers of the national government; there was no concern in these efforts for the proper adjustment of the Court's appellate docket to its responsibilities under the Constitution and the First Judiciary Act.

There was no consistent policy behind this insistence on tinkering with court structure and avoiding the more fundamental approach, through jurisdiction. Inertia was mainly responsible. No interest group was concerned to put steady or substantial pressure back of a drive to rationalize the federal judicial scheme. Congress found it easier to change structure than jurisdiction, because it could follow apparently simpler patterns in devising structure.

When Congress finally moved to consider a basic change in the

Supreme Court's appellate jurisdiction, live interest at last awoke; but it was an interest almost wholly negative. The proposed change linked structural and jurisdictional reform — by creation of intermediate appellate courts and the grant to the Supreme Court of wide discretion over the matters it would take on review from these new courts. This proposal awakened strong feeling among lawmen, against depriving litigants of their "right" to review by the highest court; this sentiment was urged even as to ordinary cases, where issues were in the federal courts not because they involved any peculiarly important policy issue, but only because the suitors were citizens of different states, or because of a right claimed under a federal statute. This reaction was sufficient to require a compromise in the Circuit Courts of Appeals Act of 1891: The act provided that a considerable number of what were deemed the more important federal claims might be reviewed directly from the district courts by the Supreme Court. We noted, in discussing the state courts, that this country had early fixed a tradition which stressed the distinct character and importance of top appellate courts. Probably the compromise in the 1891 act reflected this tradition. In any case, the stubborn persistence of the idea that every man should be able to take his case to the highest court as a matter of right cannot be attributed to any deliberate discussion of policy through the years.

The 1891 statute was important because it cut at the jurisdictional roots of relieving the Supreme Court's burden. The statute fixed two principles: that there should be powerful intermediate appellate courts, and that the Supreme Court should have broad discretion, through grant or denial of the writ of certiorari, to decide which decisions of these intermediate appeals courts presented matters of an importance deserving the highest court's attention. The statute thus expressed a radically new principle concerning the Supreme Court's function: that the business of the Supreme Court was, not to see justice done in every case, but to decide the more important policy issues presented within the frame of a "case" or "controversy," concerning the federal balance, the relations of the branches of the federal government, or the fundamental rights of the individual in relation to government. This was an idea which ran counter to our traditionally easy resort to appeals, and even the bar was slow to be convinced that the Supreme Court of the United States was an appellate court of unique function. As late as the mid-twentieth century the high percentage of petitions for certiorari denied reflected the undisciplined efforts of litigants to press on the Court a great quantity of trivial or narrow matters.

Those who understood the Court's problems sought still further to curtail its appellate load even after the 1891 act. This was no reflection on the soundness of the approach taken in that statute. Mainly this continued trend toward limitation of the Court's appellate business reflected the vast expansion of state and national government economic regulation, and the consequent increase in the number and difficulty of issues pressed on the Court.

As always in this field, Congress did not distinguish itself by foresight or by action of a breadth equal to the scope of the problems that developed. The simplest solution to the Supreme Court's overcrowded docket was to reduce the cases in which appeal lay as a matter of right — that is, where a disappointed suitor could automatically obtain review of an adverse decision merely by filing formal appeal papers. But Congress went at the problem piecemeal. In 1915 Congress barred review as of right in the Supreme Court in bankruptcy cases, cases under the trade-mark laws, and appeals from the District Court of Puerto Rico. The act of September 6, 1916 effected more important, but still piecemeal, restriction of review as of right. The Court now gained discretionary control, through the writ of certiorari, over review of the voluminous litigation under the Federal Employer's Liability Act, and related statutes, as well as over cases from the Supreme Court of the Philippine Islands. The 1916 act also drastically limited the scope of the review that might be had under Section 25 of state court decisions that denied claims of federal right; review might now be had as of right only where a state held that a treaty or statute of the United States, or an authority exercised under the United States, was invalid as in violation of the Federal Constitution. Thus the 1916 act left to the writ of certiorari all cases that involved simply the application of federal legislation or authority, as distinguished from their constitutionality.

Drastic change was left to the act of February 13, 1925. The Court itself took the initiative in obtaining this legislation. It was pressed to this action. The increase of business following World War I was consistently putting its docket over a year in arrears. The new Chief Justice, William Howard Taft, had long vigorously advocated further limits on the Court's business. He now lent the weight of his office and prestige to advancing a bill drawn by a committee of three of the Associate Justices, primarily by Mr. Justice Van Devanter. The prestige of the bill's origins and sponsors, plus the competition of matters politically more engrossing, eased the passage of the 1925 act, and it went through with an amount of discussion that was surprisingly meager in view of the great changes effected.

The 1925 act finally settled the dominant principle that should shape the Supreme Court's appellate jurisdiction: that the Court should have almost complete discretionary control of the extent of its appellate business, through grant or denial of the writ of certiorari. The act eliminated a substantial number of cases in which appeal had laid as of right from the circuit courts of appeals, and made all cases disposed of in those intermediate courts reviewable in the Supreme Court only on grant of certiorari. It preserved direct appeal from the district courts only in four types of cases deemed of exceptional importance: suits under the antitrust and interstate commerce laws, appeals by the United States in criminal cases (thus preserving the Criminal Appeals Act of 1907, which had so provided for cases where a district court quashed an indictment on a ruling of constitutionality or interpretation of a statute), suits to enjoin the enforcement of state legislation or state administrative action, and suits to enjoin orders of the Interstate Commerce Commission. The 1925 statute cut off burdensome sources of less important business by putting the Court of Appeals for the District of Columbia on a level with the circuit courts of appeals, and by putting Court-of-Claims decisions under the certiorari power. It effected a uniform distribution of appeals from United States dependencies among the appropriate circuit courts of appeals, replacing previous patchwork legislation and completely relieving the Supreme Court of obligatory review in this field. It clarified somewhat review of state court decisions, by restricting review as of right to cases that involved the validity of legislation; it committed to the certiorari process cases that involved the validity of other types of state action.

So far as the burden of Supreme Court business could be relieved by extension of the Court's discretionary control of appeals, the 1925 act went as far as it seemed desirable or practicable to go. After 1925 the Court continued to have a heavy docket. Lawmen considered limiting the original jurisdiction of the lower federal courts, for this of course largely fixed the sources of appellate business. Particularly, it was suggested that Congress should cut out jurisdiction based on diversity of citizenship. Argument on both sides of this question suffered for lack of facts to show the practical significance of the diversity jurisdiction in recent years. In any case, there was little evidence that Congress would make the change. Barring the possibility of a strong "Judges' Bill," like that of 1925, by mid-twentieth century federal jurisdiction had apparently reached another of its typically long periods of stability. In the past such lack of change had rested mainly on inertia. Now more than at any time since 1789, with the background of the 1925 act and the potentially more efficient judicial administration under the Administrative Office Act, this stability rested on a reasoned adaptation of the system to its tasks.

CHAPTER SEVEN

SELECTION AND TENURE OF JUDGES

The methods and ideas concerning the selection and tenure of judges in the United States present a story that can be told briefly. But, for lack of satisfactory evidence by which to weigh the results, the story is disappointingly abstract and barren.

Two pair of opposites were woven together to make up the formal story: appointment versus popular election, as the manner of selection; tenure during good behavior versus tenure for a term of years, as the manner of holding. Appointment and life tenure tended to go together, as did election and limited tenure. The second grouping dominated the long-run trend, up to mid-twentieth century.

1. Constitutional Provisions

Despite much variation in details, the first state constitutions provided a selection either by the legislature (which still enjoyed its popular favor as champion against the Crown's representatives), or by the governor (who was himself named by the legislature in some states). Most constitutions stipulated tenure during good behavior. Vermont first provided for popular election of some judges, in 1777. Ohio, in 1802, provided for selection by the legislature, but for a term of seven years. In 1812, Georgia and, in 1816, Indiana declared for the popular election of some of their judges, as later did Michigan. Only Mississippi (1832) had adopted popular election for its entire judiciary. In 1846 New York followed suit and opened a trend. Within ten years fifteen of the twenty-nine states which then made up the Union had followed New York. Every state which entered the Union after 1846 stipulated the popular election of all or most of its judges.

Indiana, in 1816, followed Ohio in setting a limited term of years to the tenure of elected judges. This became the usual accompaniment of the switch to popular election; by the Civil War twenty-one states had thus adopted limited tenure. Thereafter the trend continued, though with a more conservative attitude toward the length of term; the average range increased from four-to-seven years to eight-to-fifteen.

Georgia was for long the only state which voluntarily abandoned popular election, once having adopted it. Then in 1934 California changed from the elective method, to provide that judges of the highest and intermediate appellate courts be appointed by the governor, subject to approval by an ex officio commission composed of the chief justice, the attorney general, and the presiding justice of one of the intermediate courts of appeal. In 1940 Missouri adopted a somewhat similar system.

As of 1944, in twenty-one states all judges were elected by the people; in another fourteen, all except some inferior court judges were popularly elected; and in thirteen states there were appointment systems of diverse extent and procedure. In contrast to the change and variety in the state scene, the formal plan set up by the Constitution for the federal judiciary was never altered: appointment by the President with the advice and consent of the Senate, and tenure during good behavior. The Constitution fixed the guaranty of tenure. But Congress apparently held a residual discretion over appointments, though it had never exercised it. The Constitution said that "the Congress may by Law vest the Appointment of such inferior Officers, as they think proper, in the President alone, in the Courts of Law, or in the Heads of Departments"; and this would appear to include the judges of inferior federal courts.

2. CIVIL IMMUNITY AND PAY OF JUDGES

From English common law and constitutional history we inherited three matters which bore so closely, along with selection and tenure, on the quality and independence of the Bench, that we should note them here. From the common law we adopted the principle that no civil liability attaches to the judge because of his acts as judge, even though he be guilty of fraud or corruption. From the Act of 12 and 13 William III, of 1700, American constitutions generally drew the principles that a judge's pay might not be withheld or reduced during his term of office, and that a judge might be removed only for cause, established in a formal proceeding. The first state constitutions the more readily adopted the doctrines of the Act of William III because the colonial judiciary had been the subject of bitter complaint, grounded largely on the facts that colonial judges held office at the King's will, and were not removable by colonial assemblies.

Within this formal framework judges were selected and held their offices in the United States. What were the results, in judicial quality?

For any help on this question, we must look not only to the formal structure, but also to the patterns of behavior that developed about the forms.

With respect to the last three items discussed, the historic institution closely fitted the form. Judges were, in fact, exempt from civic liability for their acts as judges, and on the most sweeping terms. As to security of pay: In the Massachusetts constitutional convention of 1820, Mr. Justice Story of the United States Supreme Court found it necessary to cast his influence as a leading citizen of the state into successful leadership of a fight against giving the legislature power to reduce judges' salaries. But, in general, the constitutional ban on tampering with judges' pay was so clear-cut that even expediency dictated that no serious effort be made to evade it. Indeed, over the dissent of Holmes and Brandeis, the United States Supreme Court went so far as to forbid imposing on a federal judge a federal income tax which, though laid equally on his fellow citizens, had been first enacted after his appointment.

3. REMOVAL OF JUDGES

Practice made no substantial inroad on the requirement that judges be removed only by the constitutionally defined procedures of impeachment or removal on joint address of the houses of the legislature. There were some threats to regular procedure, however; these came, under color of authority, through efforts to abolish judges' jobs, instead of direct removal action against the sitting judges. The threats came to little and in their outcome thus provided practical precedent to sustain the constitutional principle.

The issue of abiding by regular removal procedures was fought on three notable occasions. By the act of March 8, 1802, the Jeffersonian Congress repealed the Second Judiciary Act of February 13, 1801. Thereby it abolished the 16 new circuit judgeships which President John Adams had already filled with trustworthy Federalists. The Federalists, of course, bitterly attacked the constitutional propriety of thus abolishing the new jobs. But if there was a breach of principle, there were at least strong, mitigating circumstances. However sincerely some Federalists may have identified the fate of their party with that of the nation, their creation of the new judgeships had been an act of sheer party jobbery. Repeal followed as swiftly as was practicable. And the judgeships were abolished for what they stood for in origin, and not to reverse or penalize decisions of the sitting judges.

The next case emphasized these points by its difference. In 1822 the

Kentucky Supreme Court held unconstitutional certain debtor relief legislation passed under imperious local demand in the depression following 1819. The Kentucky judges held life appointments and were removable only by two-thirds vote of the legislature. Unable to muster the necessary vote, the legislature passed a statute that purported to abolish the old court and to create a new one. The "old court" refused to recognize its abolition, however. For several years two courts claimed to function as the lawful supreme court of Kentucky, while the issue became the focus of state politics. The "old court" party finally won control of the legislature. In 1826, over the governor's veto, the legislature repealed the act that had abolished the "old court." The "old court" party, now in the legislative majority, cited the election defeat of their "new court" opponents as a popular decision that the act of abolition had been unconstitutional.

The third major incident of irregular removal of judges was, like the first, one involving the federal government. In the first generation of federal railroad regulation, one of the thorniest problems was that of judicial review of Interstate Commerce Commission orders. By the act of June 18, 1910 Congress set up the United States Commerce Court, made up of five judges, who were given exclusive original jurisdiction to review Commission action. Proponents of the new Commerce Court argued that it would mean a speedier and more expert review; opponents argued that to concentrate review thus in one inferior court would merely help the railroads to dominate the regulatory effort.

The Commerce Court found itself confronted from the start with a docket loaded with many highly controversial issues, which would have tried the mettle of a long-established institution. The Supreme Court frequently reversed the Commerce Court during the latter's brief career; and while this was perhaps largely inevitable in the face of natural doubts and ambiguities involved in fitting so novel a court into the federal system, it did not help the Commerce Court's standing. Thus the new body was from the beginning a political storm center and had little chance to prove itself by experience. In 1913 one of its judges was impeached, convicted, and removed, because he was found to have used his influence to get favors from carriers litigating before him. This incident added powerful, if really irrelevant, weight to the drive against the Commerce Court. In 1912 President Taft, who had recommended its creation, vetoed an attempt to abolish it. But when the Democrats took power, abolition followed in short order, October 22, 1913.

In the debate that accompanied this step, a central issue was what to do with the Commerce Court judges; Congress, it was argued, could

not constitutionally deprive a judge of his office except by impeachment. This contention was mingled with other arguments. Some urged
that the Commerce Court judges could be kept to the useful purpose
of relieving congested circuits, and that it was unjust to abolish what
all had assumed to be lifetime jobs.

The final decision was to keep the Commerce Court judges, as roving
circuit judges; but it is impossible clearly to disentangle the effect of
the constitutional argument in producing this result. The 1912 act
which Taft vetoed had made this provision for the judges. It was
accomplished in the 1913 act only by a narrow margin; at first the
House voted to abolish the judgeships as well as the court; the Senate
voted to keep the judges as circuit judges, though it did so by a vote
of only 25 to 23; in conference the House conferees refused to agree
to retention of the judges, and the point finally prevailed only by appeal
to the floor of the House.

4. Changes in the Number of Judges

Article III of the Federal Constitution directly creates the Supreme
Court of the United States. That article also gives Congress authority
to fix the number of the members of the Supreme Court. Under color
of this authority Congress could in substance abolish the Court. We
noted a qualified instance of this in the Reconstruction period — when
Congress, wishing to bar appointments by President Johnson, provided
that no vacancy on the Court should be filled until the Court should be
reduced to seven members from its then total of ten. In this case, however, Congress was putting pressure on the executive rather than on the
Court.

An incident which soon followed is also distinguishable from Congressional purpose to coerce the Court. In 1870 President Grant nominated, and the Senate confirmed, William Strong and Joseph P. Bradley
as Associate Justices. The two men were believed to hold constitutional
views that would permit Congress to make paper money legal tender;
by a 4-to-3 vote in the First Legal Tender Cases, the Court had earlier
denied that Congress had the power. On reargument of the full issues
in 1871, the Court reversed its prior decision and upheld the Legal
Tender Acts, the two new Justices joining with the former minority
to make up a majority of five.

The instance certainly shows that a man's views on policy may affect
his practical chances of appointment to the Court. But the case is not
one in which the Court was "packed" by increase of its number. One
of the vacancies which the Bradley–Strong appointments filled had been

created by the retirement of Mr. Justice Grier. Both the posts involved represented an exercise of Congress's power over the Court's number. Under the act of 1866 Grier's retirement would simply have reduced the Court to the stipulated seven members. But Grant had now become President, and Congress had passed the act of April 10, 1869, which increased the number of the Court to nine. A majority of the Court did not reach a decision in the First Legal Tender Cases until November 27, 1869, and the Court held the decision in the secrecy of conference until it announced the decision and opinions on February 7, 1870. This was the day on which Grant sent to the Senate the names of Bradley and Strong. There is substantial evidence that Grant knew the nature of the pending decision in the First Legal Tender Cases a month or more before it was handed down. But the decision had not been reached in conference until months after passage of the act of 1869 which created the new judicial positions, and there is no evidence of any connection between the 1869 act and the legal tender issue.

In contrast to any previous incident was the proposal of President Roosevelt early in 1937, to increase the membership of the Court to a potential fifteen justices. The purpose was to overrule the abuse of power by a majority of the Court in 1934 and 1935. The proposal was in form constitutional. In substance it violated constitutional policy; by assuring tenure and undiminished pay, the Constitution clearly meant that the members of the Supreme Court should enjoy the independence to be wrong. The proposal put no personal penalty on any Justice. But its immediate practical effect would be to take away the effective vote of certain Justices; at least this would be true in respect to those policies regarding which the President and Senate could fairly predict the views of the new appointees.

Congress's control over the Court's numbers was, as Bryce commented, "a joint in the court's armour through which a weapon might some day penetrate." To argue over the intent of the Federal Convention brings us to no conclusive result. Plainly the framers intended the independence of the Bench; but equally plainly they gave Congress control of the number of the Justices, and neither their words nor their debates are helpful to outline limits or qualifications on this Congressional authority.

A complex of causes brought the defeat of the 1937 proposal. The primary influence was the decisions of the spring of 1937 in which a new majority, created by the vote of Mr. Justice Roberts, sustained the economic regulatory power of the federal government. But there was more to the story than this. Fervor for principle rang hollowly from some of the spokesmen in this debate. But Congress reacted to a substantial opinion through the country, which was genuinely concerned that the 1937 measure would destroy a valued principle of judicial independence.

The outcome of the 1937 battle furnished no practical precedent to justify the method there proposed to correct judicial arrogance. The strongest justification for the President's proposal was not in the logic of argument; the long debate showed a relatively even balance on that score. Justification lay rather in the support which the proposal had from men wise in affairs, of learning, and of good will. That fact must temper all criticism of the method taken to discipline the Court. It underlined the political truth which Mr. Justice Stone had soberly restated, prefacing his dissent in *United States* v. *Butler*, in 1936:

> The power of courts to declare a statute unconstitutional is subject to two guiding principles of decision which ought never to be absent from judicial consciousness. One is that courts are concerned only with the power to enact statutes, not with their wisdom. The other is that while unconstitutional exercise of power by the executive and legislative branches of the government is subject to judicial restraint the only check upon our own exercise of power is our own sense of self-restraint. For the removal of unwise laws from the statute books appeal lies not to the courts but to the ballot and to the processes of democratic government.

We have now looked at three safeguards of the courts' position: civil immunity, assured pay, and freedom from arbitrary removal. These protections were firm elements of all save the lowest judicial positions in the United States from 1790 on. Though they received little attention, they probably had more effect on the quality of our courts than the more prominent questions of selection and tenure. Certainly form and substance were much farther apart, in the matters of selection and tenure.

5. THEORY AND PRACTICE IN SELECTION OF JUDGES

Where constitutions provided that judges be appointed they were in fact appointed; there was no *de facto* conversion of appointment into some disguised practice of popular selection. But in practice the appointing power was often exercised by someone other than those formally invested with it. The prime example was the development in the federal government of that Senatorial "courtesy," under which, if any Senator of the President's party found a nominee personally objectionable, his fellow Senators would join in refusing confirmation.

This in effect placed the nomination of federal judges for service within a given state or region in the hands of the administration-party Senators from that area. After the wry experience of a presidential term, Mr. Taft observed that: "The appointing power is in effect in the Senators' hands, subject only to a veto by the President." Political tradition even broadened this practice, by analogy. Where a judge, especially a district judge, was to be named in a state whose Senators were not of the administration party, the President began to refer the appointment to the local Congressmen of the administration party, or to the state's party leaders, with first voice probably to the national committeeman.

We have no detailed study of practices under the appointing power in the few states in which it prevailed. Impeachment proceedings against a first instance judge in New Jersey in 1934 made a matter of record the accepted operation of "Senatorial courtesy" regarding New Jersey judicial appointments. In Massachusetts, Maine and New Hampshire the governor's judicial appointments must be confirmed by an executive council; the latter was a body distinct from the upper house of the legislature, was popularly elected in Massachusetts and New Hampshire, and elected in joint legislative session in Maine. Haynes found evidence that in these states there developed some tendency to permit individual councillors to name nominees for local judicial offices, and for the governor to choose nominees for offices of state-wide importance. Political trading entered, where governor and council were of different parties.

With all such qualifications, appointment in form proved to be appointment in practice. Where constitutions provided for popular election of judges, the formal method underwent much more profound changes in operation, and became largely selection by covert appointment. This judgment is framed conservatively. Reliable evidence is spotty, drawn almost wholly from the last thirty years, and consists mostly of opinion. If we treat the available evidence as probably reflecting what went on throughout the United States after 1870, the conclusion must be that popular election of judges became almost wholly a matter of form; and that the form covered two main types of *de facto* systems of appointment of judges. Both of these *de facto* appointment systems were products of the rise of the political parties.

Generally, and especially in metropolitan areas after 1870, election of judges meant the formal ratification by popular vote of appointments made by party leaders. A prudent leadership would always reckon with the possibility of popular rebellion at the polls, and this possibility was some check — on prudent leadership — even in the most tightly controlled machines. But experience repeatedly showed that as a rule people were not much interested in judicial elections; this was the more true in proportion as they lived in thickly settled communities where the courts, as well as other more technical aspects of government, seemed remote from daily living.

The most definite influence which the average voter's attitudes had on the *de facto* system of appointment by party leaders was in the strong presumption which generally favored the renomination and re-election of sitting judges. This was a matter of general feeling and tradition. Only one more or less organized check on the operation of party appointment developed after 1870. This was through the activity of bar associations in the larger cities, chiefly after 1900; some associations undertook to appraise candidates' qualifications, to offer association support to approved candidates, and opposition to those deemed not qualified. This bar association activity was evidence of the extent to which the most critical problems in judicial elections came out of the shift to an urban society. We shall see later that the modern organized bar itself originated as a response to the shocking levels of politics and legal administration in the great cities in the later nineteenth century. Bar activity in judicial elections was definitely an urban phenomenon. In 1932 a count showed such bar activity in all but 2 cities of 450,000 or more population, and in 27 of the 42 cities of over 200,000 population.

However, the bar associations had only limited effect on the operation of the party appointment system. Their clearest influence was probably in the improvement of the general standards which the law set for qualification to judicial office. Early-nineteenth-century America did not put its faith in courts or lawyers, and distrusted most claims for specialized knowledge or abilities. Thus many states laid down no professional qualifications as requirements even for judges of their highest courts. In the latter part of the century, bar associations began to urge higher standards of legal education and admission to the bar; and as a collateral product of this movement to raise professional standards, the states generally adopted the requirement that all judges except those of some courts of petty jurisdiction must be members of the bar. This was a modest requirement; its minimal nature is emphasized in the fact that up to mid-twentieth century less than a third of the states had adopted any requirement that a man have some experience at the bar before taking judicial office. In their efforts to influence judicial elections, bar associations, it is true, emphasized the quality of candidates' legal education and experience in practice. But at most, the bar's influence was indirect. The bar associations generally did not try directly to influence the party leaders' choice of candidates; frequently, therefore, the bar found itself in the not-too-happy position of publicly recommending that the people accept the lesser evil.

For all of these limitations, judicial elections were not without some quality. As one student of metropolitan judicial elections observed, "The Judiciary is the only group of major elective offices for which progress has been made in requiring specific qualifications other than age or citizenship."

The foregoing summary has of necessity been rather abstract; some comment on a particular situation may add another dimension to the analysis. The best studies of twentieth-century courts under the test of adverse conditions were made of the judicial system in the Chicago metropolitan area. Granted that Chicago conditions were not typical for the country as a whole, they served by the sharpness of their outline to clarify the relations between some of the assumptions on which judicial elections proceeded and the working conditions under which they occurred.

The basic facts in the Chicago situation were the speed and extent of the city's growth, and the sprawling reach of the court "system" which was created in response to that growth. Chicago grew tenfold in population before 1870; to match that increase, the legislature provided a special court system for Chicago and Cook County, with ten judges.

In 1870 Illinois adopted a new constitution. The judiciary article of this constitution was a political compromise, whereby vested interests in existing courts were preserved, to the confusion of later judicial growth. From 1870 to mid-twentieth century, the population of the Chicago metropolitan area expanded over 11 times, and Cook County went from 13.8 to over 52 per cent of the state's population. Parallel to this went increased demands on the courts, which were met by unplanned, more-or-less-mechanical addition of new courts and of more judges for the old courts.

The largest single increase in the Chicago court system, and the closest approach to a rationalization of the system, was the creation of the Municipal Court, in 1905. This court replaced the appointive justices of the peace, and at one stroke raised the number of elective judges from 29 to 57.

By the 1930's the average voter in the Chicago area was asked to cast ballots for 88 judicial officers, 85 of whom had 6-year terms, and to nominate for 39 of these offices in primaries. In a sample 6-year cycle, Chicago voters were asked to choose among 997 Republican and 787

Democratic candidates, as well as to vote on 124 bond issues, and 34 propositions of public policy. In this period 423 individuals sought 146 judicial offices in 15 contests.

From 1870 to 1887, Chicago's judicial elections seem to have worked rather satisfactorily. For this there were a number of reasons: regular newspaper publicity regarding the conduct of judges on and off the bench, a considerable tradition of nonpartisan coalition where a single office was in question, and the regular renomination and almost complete re-election of sitting judges. Prominent individual lawyers — and to a less extent the fledgling local bar association — provided the drive for nonpartisan elections in 1873, 1885, and 1897. This type of influence had its high point in 1887, when a bipartisan fusion slate of very dubious character lost to an independent ticket which had been put in the field entirely on the initiative of a lawyers' group. After 1900 only one such striking success was scored for bar influence. In 1921 the bar association, allied with the Democrats, successfully waged an aggressive campaign against an effort of the "City Hall" Republicans to oust satisfactory sitting judges, in a blatant assertion of machine power. Probably only the sheer effrontery of the defeated politicos, which presented an unusually clear-cut issue, accounted for the result.

After 1900 the Chicago political machines effectively turned judicial election into judicial appointment by party leaders. This was helped by the long ballot. The important offices of circuit and superior court judges sometimes drew no more than 40 per cent of the voters; in 3 "normal" elections, separate elections for the superior court attracted to the polls slightly over 23 per cent of the voters. Even in general elections as many as 21 per cent of the voters failed to make a choice for the prominent post of chief justice of the Municipal Court. The background and diversity of the Chicago electorate also helped the parties to control judicial elections; well into the twentieth century over 82 per cent of the voters were no more than one generation removed from foreign origin. At least 17 distinct national voting blocs plus marked racial and religious cleavages, could be counted. This gave the politicians an acquiescent or readily manipulated body of voters. Party appointment was strengthened by coalition tickets. These reflected deals that were based on the current balance of power between machines. In "taking the bench out of politics" such bipartisan slates ended even the formal pretense of election.

One measure of the independence of the party leaders in appointing Chicago judges was the gap between their appointments and what the bar association recommended; the gap was the more significant, because the bar association followed quite modest standards in deciding

whom it would back for judicial office. A related fact was the absence
of any clear-cut evidence that the bar association's recommendations
had substantial influence on the voters. About 70 per cent of the Chicago judges elected in 103 contests from 1887–1934 had bar-association endorsement. But the percentage was less in the latter part of this
period; in 43 primaries, involving nominations for 175 judicial offices
between 1910 and 1934, only 57 per cent of the successful Republicans
and 63 per cent of the successful Democrats had the bar association's
endorsement. Over a 20-year span 16 candidates whom the bar association openly opposed ran 67 times with only 14 defeats; some of these
defeats, moreover, were in party primaries, some were incidents of
political landslides.

The parties' weight showed itself in variations in the record between
different courts in Chicago. Over the course of forty years, the bar
association endorsed only two persons who held county-court judgeships, and six of ten successful candidates were opposed by the association. Illinois law gave the county court jurisdiction over questions
arising in the administration of elections; this factor clearly made party
loyalty the critical measure in selecting candidates for these judicial
jobs. The branches of the Municipal Court were the tribunals which
came closest to the most people. In these courts the opportunity was
broadest for the kind of service that builds party strength. On the
average, during the years of bar-association activity in Chicago judicial
elections, 63 per cent of the party nominees for Municipal Court
judgeships failed to win the association's endorsement.

We noted earlier that throughout the United States popular tradition
favored the re-election of sitting judges. This popular feeling was
strong enough in Chicago, no doubt refreshed by the emphasis which
the bar association put on it, to make it to the party's interest to return
men of satisfactory record. About eight of every nine candidates who
sought re-election to one of the highest courts in the Chicago area won
it; but only about five of every nine judges who sought re-election to
the courts of lesser jurisdiction were successful. The most substantial
evidence that the bar association had some effect on judicial elections
was the fact that endorsed candidates consistently led, among the winners, in the total of votes; in the Municipal Court during twenty-five
years no unendorsed candidate led the winning slate. But the number of
voters influenced by the recommendations of the organized bar was
usually too small to overcome party or bipartisan support.

There was a second, less broadly operative, way in which judicial
election worked out as a de facto system of appointment. State constitutions commonly gave the governor power to fill vacancies, pending

election, both in the supreme court and in the lower courts. Especially where the term of office on the supreme court was a long one, vacancies by death or retirement from illness were frequent, for men were usually already of mature years when they came to the highest court. Thus in some states a high proportion of men who attained the highest court did so originally by the governor's interim appointment following a vacancy. Benefiting by the tradition in favor of returning a sitting judge, they were then likely to win if they ran in the succeeding election, especially if their interim term had been of substantial length. Bar association activity, as in Minnesota and Wisconsin, contributed to this outcome. In Minnesota in 1940, for example, all members of the Supreme Court and thirty-one of the fifty district court judges had come to the bench in the first instance by interim appointment. There seems to be no study which measures for the whole country the practical extent or effect of this combination of interim appointment and ratification by election.

The scheme thus evolved by the accident of events coincided with, and stimulated, what promised to become the model plan advanced by those concerned with improvement of the selection of judges. In 1914 Albert M. Kales, distinguished Illinois practitioner and professor of law, proposed to combine the appointive and elective methods for judicial selection. Kales suggested that some proper appointing authority name the judge for an initial term of years, and that at intervals after the expiration of this first period, the judge submit to popular election on the question of his continuance in office. If the vote were against him, his term would end forthwith. The appointing power would then name a new judge who, after the designated initial period of service, would come before the popular vote. In the election phase of the process, thus, a judge would run only against his own record. The Kales proposal was in substance adopted by constitutional amendment in California in 1934. California applied the new plan directly to judges of the supreme and intermediate appellate courts. It allowed the counties local option as to whether they would adopt the plan for selection of the principal trial judges. In 1940 Missouri likewise adopted the Kales principle, in a somewhat more complicated form than that taken in California.

6. Theory and Practice Regarding Tenure of Judges

Where office was held during good behavior — most notably, of course, in the federal courts — political practice over the years did not modify the stipulated tenure. In the hot party battles of the first generation of our national life, however, it was by no means certain that this would be so.

The Jeffersonians, convinced that the Federalists would wreck the Republic for their ambition, distrusted a federal bench which in the normal course of years of Federalist control of the government had been well staffed with men of that persuasion. A number of the Federalist judges behaved themselves so intemperately as to spur the reforming zeal of the Jeffersonian Congress which came in in 1800. Under the guise of charging grand juries, Federalist judges had delivered political harrangues against their partisan opponents; and in several trials brought under the Alien and Sedition Acts, Federalist judges had given the defendants some rough handling.

In the debates over repeal of the Second Judiciary Act, of 1801, Jefferson's supporters had committed themselves to the proposition that impeachment was the sole constitutional means of removing a federal judge. The Constitution defined the causes for removal as "treason, bribery, or other high crimes and misdemeanors." Though the words were very narrow in scope, the debates in the Federal Convention indicated an intention that the grounds for impeachment should be broader than the scope of the technical law of crimes. On the other hand, in the Convention, "maladministration" was withdrawn as a suggested addition to the defined grounds of impeachment; Madison objected that this vague term would in effect put the tenure of all federal offices at the pleasure of the Senate. Out of the Federalist–Jeffersonian clash came two questions: Did the Constitution permit impeachment of a judge because he held, or expressed, or intemperately expressed certain political views on or off the Bench? More serious, might he properly be impeached because he applied these views in strong-handed or arbitrary rulings from the Bench?

The denial of a fair trial through partisan rulings would have presented the most solid argument for impeachment and conviction. But the prosecutors failed to make out such a case. Two attempts were made. In 1804 upon impeachment, the Senate removed from office John Pickering, judge of the federal district court for New Hampshire. The trial of the impeachment was managed in the full intemperance of party spirit. Nonetheless, the prosecution proved that the judge had been guilty of serious irregularities in the conduct of his court. The removal was undoubtedly proper, though not for the reasons which the prosecution had hoped to establish, since it became clear that Pickering was insane.

The critical test of the scope of impeachment was reserved for the trial, in the same year, of charges brought by the House against Justice

Samuel Chase, of the Supreme Court. Dogmatic in opinion, choleric in temper, Chase had repeatedly voiced his Federalist contempt for all Republicans and their notions; in the exercise of his circuit-riding duties he had been foremost in delivering political diatribes to grand juries; and he had given rough treatment to his political opponents and their counsel, when he found them before him in court. But upon trial of the impeachment, the evidence reduced itself essentially to the matters of the Justice's expression of political views and his overbearing manner. The state of the case produced division among the Jeffersonian Senators. William Branch Giles, of Virginia, spokesman for the extreme Jeffersonian position, put the issue frankly in a conversation noted by John Quincy Adams. Giles argued that claims of judicial independence under the Constitution were sheer aristocratic pretension, and that the power to impeach and to try impeachments stood without limitation. According to Adams's account, Giles then revealed the full implications of what was afoot:

> . . . and if the Judges of the Supreme Court should dare, AS THEY HAD DONE, to declare an act of Congress unconstitutional, or to send a mandamus to the Secretary of State, AS THEY HAD DONE, it was the undoubted right of the House of Representatives to impeach them, and of the Senate to remove them, for giving such opinions, however honest or sincere they may have been in entertaining them. . . . A trial and removal of a judge upon impeachment need not imply any criminality or corruption in him. Congress had no power over the person, but only over the office. And a removal by impeachment was nothing more than a declaration by Congress to this effect: You hold dangerous opinions, and if you are suffered to carry them into effect you will work the destruction of the nation. *We want your offices*, for the purpose of giving them to men who will fill them better.

This proved too strong doctrine for six of the Jeffersonian Senators who joined the Federalists in voting acquittal on all counts. With twenty-three votes required for conviction, the prosecution could muster no more than nineteen against Chase on any count.

The outcome of the Chase impeachment settled the issue as a matter of the practical political construction of the Constitution. No serious attempt was ever made thereafter to impeach a federal judge on grounds of his political opinions, his conceptions of public policy, or his interpretation of the laws. We noted that in 1913 the Senate convicted Judge Archbald, of the United States Commerce Court, under impeachment for use of his influence as a federal judge to obtain favors from litigants in his court. This conviction in nowise impaired the limitation implicit in the result of the Chase impeachment; on the other hand it served perhaps to remove any implication that impeachment must be limited to grounds adequate to support an indictment for crime.

State political practice through the first half of the nineteenth century made a much less clear-cut record regarding judicial tenure. On an impeachment brought in 1802, the Republican legislature of Pennsylvania removed Alexander Addison, President Judge of the Fifth Pennsylvania Circuit, primarily because of the unpopularity of the Federalist speeches which Addison insisted on delivering from his bench. In 1803 the Pennsylvania Republicans failed in a like attempt to remove all but one Republican member of the state supreme court, for alleged arbitrary error in a contempt case. In Ohio, in 1808, two circuit judges were impeached for presuming to hold a statute of the state unconstitutional; both were acquitted, though the legislature by less than a two-thirds vote declared their offices vacant.

Other state incidents are distinguishable, because they turned on exercise of the power which some constitutions granted the legislature, to remove judges by joint address of both houses. This authorization was even less defined in historic scope than the power of impeachment. At the end of the eighteenth and the start of the nineteenth century, Kentucky was the scene of a number of attempts to use this power broadly; none of these came to a clear-cut result. In Maine, in 1856, a member of the state supreme court was removed upon address of both houses, because the governor and legislature objected to his opinion on a constitutional question. A few years later in Massachusetts, after a long controversy, the legislature by joint address removed Probate Judge Loring; this action was founded in the hostility in which abolitionists held Loring, because in earlier years, as a United States Commissioner, he had enforced the Fugitive Slave Law. Removal by joint address generally fell into disuse, however. This was in part because it came to be hedged about with procedural requirements which made it not much simpler than procedure by impeachment.

After the 1850's there was no serious effort in the states to use impeachment to remove judges for unpopular opinions or decisions. On the other hand, opinions and decisions formed the campaign material in a fair number of judicial elections where there was an effort to oust sitting judges. This suggests that it was the spread of the limited-term, elective system, rather than any precedent to be implied from the ambiguous record before 1850, which in practice eliminated a state judge's policy views or rulings as permissible bases for impeachment.

On the whole, tenure during good behavior, where it existed, was not substantially altered in political practice. In contrast, the limited-term tenure which accompanied the adoption of popular election of judges did undergo substantial modification in practice. In many states tenure which in form was for a limited term of years became in practice tenure during good behavior, due to the strength of the popular feeling that satisfactory sitting judges should be returned to office. There was at least one objective measure of how real and deep this tradition became — at least with regard to judges of the courts of general jurisdiction — in the practical respect paid to it by the metropolitan political machines, as in Chicago. No one, apparently, has studied the effect of this popular attitude the country over. But the available evidence all testified that it was a significant influence affecting the personnel of the more important courts, especially of the top appellate courts.

The continued vitality of the tradition of re-election promised in mid-twentieth century to affect the future structure of the courts. For it prepared the public mind to accept a combined system of official appointment followed after a term by an election in which the appointee would run only against his own record. The popular tradition apparently helped to obtain the adoption of this plan in California in 1934, and in Missouri in 1940.

7. COMPARISON OF TYPES OF SELECTION AND TENURE

Given these formal plans of judicial selection and tenure, and the patterns of behavior and tradition which more or less modified them, how appraise the results that form and practice had on the quality of the courts? There is little reliable information from which to draw even inferences. And even to such conclusions as may be ventured, two important qualifications must be made. First, judges numbered probably no more than 20 per cent of the people who over the years were directly concerned with the administration of justice through the courts. There is almost no information on which we can weigh the contributions to policy and administration over the years, made by the retinue of clerks, commissioners, masters, referees, secretaries, marshals, constables, bailiffs, probation officers, and others. Secondly, studies made of the quality of judges focused on selection and tenure almost exclusively; they ignored the likelihood that the three protecting elements which entered into all our judicial systems — civil immunity, protected pay, assurance against arbitrary forms of removal — gave all our main judicial posts more in common than they had in difference due to variations in manner of selection or tenure. At least, this unexplored question should caution further against our treating selection and tenure as if they comprise all that is relevant to a judgment of the quality of judges.

If the limited evidence bids us hesitate over objective judgment on the quality of our courts, there is, on the other hand, no doubt what was the history of opinion on the matter in the two periods of our history in which any substantial number of people were enough interested to hold opinions. Between 1800 and 1850, at different times and places, thanks to the vigorous emotions aroused between those who favored and those who opposed, first, Jeffersonian, and then Jacksonian Democracy, there was a lively concern with the quality of the Bench. This quality the adversaries estimated in terms of the judges' known or surmised political philosophies. The verdict was heavily in favor of an elected judiciary.

Prefaced by a generation of pioneer bar association activity in reaction against corrupt city politics, the twentieth century saw a revived interest in the quality of judges. The interest was partly political, partly professional. Popular control of the Bench took on new life as a political issue, when early-twentieth-century political insurgents promoted the idea of the recall of judges and of judicial decisions. Their campaign was in reaction against the judicial zeal of the late nineteenth century, for transmuting *laissez faire* into constitutional dogma, to bar social welfare legislation. In 1912, Theodore Roosevelt's advocacy brought the recall to its peak of challenge. Abhorrence of the proposals inspired the American Bar Association to its first major effort to influence public opinion; from 1911 through 1916 (by which later year it was evident that the proposal had lost all major drive), a special Association committee waged an energetic campaign against the recall. Some echo of this fight was heard in 1924 when, seeking the Presidency, the elder LaFollette proposed that Congress be empowered to override the judicial veto on legislation. But LaFollette's issue, like that which Franklin Roosevelt posed in 1937, so centered on the peculiar functions of the Supreme Court of the United States that it did not count in the currents of general judicial reform in this country.

After the recall movement lost its impetus, the only sustained interest in problems of the quality of judges was that of a handful of scholars and professional men. Politics touched the subject mainly in the form of a sentimental presumption in favor of the elective system.

The overwhelming verdict of scholarly and professional opinion — evidenced, for example, in Kales's writings and in the publications of the American Judicature Society — was that appointment produced a much higher quality on the bench than did election. But this was a verdict of opinion; it rested on no substantial evidence of historical inquiry, and the best of the opinion was necessarily qualified by circumstances of time, place, and the point of view of the observer. The opinion, that is, expressed the judgment of men who had an intelligent, conservative-minded concern for the condition of the administration of justice as they saw it in courts operating in great cities in the twentieth century. Thus to emphasize the setting of their judgment is not to prove it in error. But it does suggest that their opinion cannot be taken as the equivalent of an adequate historical comparison of the elective and ap-pointive courts throughout the country in the past one hundred years.

In weighing the merits of the two systems of judicial selection we get little help from examining the history of their adoption in most juris-dictions. Like our two-chamber legislatures, our state judicial organiza-tions were adopted mainly by default.

The men who drew the early state constitutions and the Federal Con-stitution were conservatives who distrusted popular control of affairs in general; to them the provision for appointed judges was not a matter that called for much debate. The bulk of such discussion as there was in the Federal Convention concerned the question, whether the framers should put the appointing power wholly in the Senate, or in the Presi-dent, subject to the Senate's approval.

In its origin, the shift to the election of judges that took place in the states after the 1830's marked a highly self-conscious choice of policy. This shift was one phase of the general swing toward broadened suf-frage and broader popular control of public office which Jacksonian Democracy built on the foundations laid by Jefferson. As such, the movement was based on emotion rather than on a deliberate evaluation of experience under the appointive system. There were colorful epi-sodes of controversy centering on appointed judges — such as the Chase impeachment in 1804, or the Kentucky "old" and "new" court battle in the middle '20s — and these help explain the emotion back of the Jacksonian shift. This does not prove that a broad popular opinion in favor of elected judges had grown out of any widespread, consistent experience of dissatisfaction with the way in which appointed judges handled the day-to-day grist of business. Nonetheless, the original swing to the elected judiciary did come out of self-conscious, if scantly deliberated, choice.

So much cannot be said for the continued march of the elective sys-tem. There is no evidence that the spread of the elected bench after 1850 was the result of anything but imitation and sentiment. Take, for example, the Minnesota constitutional convention of 1857. This body was close in time to the vital origins of the movement for elected judges. Yet it made a choice between the two systems of selection in a fashion which stands as a good example of the almost casual way in which the later states generally adopted their basic institutions. The drafting committee of the Minnesota convention recommended that judges be appointed. The elective system was substituted by amendment on the floor of the convention, without reference back for further committee consideration. The floor discussion produced praise of election as a "great principle," citation of precedent for the elected judiciary from other states, and expressions of tender regard that no slight be put on the wisdom of the people. With no more than this, the convention forthwith approved election as the method by which Minnesota's judges should be selected.

One difficulty in appraising the quality of the bench in the United States was the lack of agreement, or even of any considerable thought, on the qualities which make a good judge. A few names came down the years as familiar — at least to the more well-read members of the bar — Marshall, of course, and Story, Kent, Shaw, Gibson, Blackford, Ruffin, Doe, Cooley, to cite only from the fore part of the nineteenth century. Asked to specify wherein lay the greatness, or the common thread of distinction of such a group, opinion faltered and took refuge in vague generalities from the moralists. One of the few comments that said anything was, characteristically, from Holmes, speaking of Shaw:

> The strength of that great judge lay in accurate appreciation of the requirements of the community whose officer he was. Some, indeed many, English judges could be named who have surpassed him in accurate technical knowledge; but few have lived who were his equals in their understanding of the grounds of public policy to which all laws must ultimately be referred.

Those who listed "great" judges almost always mentioned only judges of appellate courts. They did not thus honor the trial judge — at least not for his work as such. Judges of appeal, of course, could point to the Reports as witness of their achievement. The declaration of policy gave them the more authoritative and more prominent role. But policy got meaning from application and the qualities that made the measure of the appellate judge were not necessarily those most important in courts of trial jurisdiction.

Obviously we wanted our judges, of whatever court, to be men who did not sell justice. If this was a negative rather than a positive characteristic, it was not less important. Appointment proved no automatic guaranty of this elementary honesty, as was shown at least by the proven case against Senior Circuit Judge Manton of the United States Second Circuit Court of Appeals in 1938. But over the years the instances in which even a substantial charge of corruption was raised against federal judges were trifling.

There is no need to recite the classic instances of corruption in the elective state courts. By repetition the books exaggerated the significance of such examples as Tweed's corruption of judges in New York which provoked the formation of the Association of the Bar of the City of New York to fight for the decency of the courts. When all the state *causes célèbres* were added together their total, like that in the federal courts, was trifling. If a critic hints at unrevealed cases, he may fairly be asked to produce evidence. In fact, there is no evidence, nor has there been a study from which to make any historical generalization about the extent of corruption in the state elective bench.

Metropolitan conditions put judges to as hard a test as ever in our history. Critical investigators for the pioneer survey of Criminal Justice in Cleveland reported of the municipal court (1922) that "the judges are generally above the suspicion of taking direct bribes, but find it difficult to forget the coming election." A careful student of the operation of the Chicago area courts in the 1930's came to about the same conclusion. No major investigation of twentieth-century great-city justice differed from these findings.

But, as the Cleveland survey indicated, there were subtler means of suborning the administration of justice than through the offer of money. However, here again the state of the evidence calls for caution in judgment. Surveys of metropolitan justice in the first half of the twentieth century agreed that by a combination of influences the elective process had had bad effects upon trial courts; especially, the practical requirements of re-election encouraged types of behavior on the bench that impaired the integrity and dignity of the administration of justice. This was true particularly of metropolitan courts of limited jurisdiction — magistrates courts, for example — but the fact was noted also of the first instance courts of general jurisdiction.

In proportion as men owed office to the party leadership, often very specifically to a particular party leader, they disposed of cases according to the nod of their sponsor where his will was made known. Elected judges must keep in the public eye, must in particular situations defer to national, racial or religious groups, must find time and energy for recurrent campaigning. Such demands diverted attention from judicial duty, took away security, encouraged conduct in and out of court not marked by detachment and sobriety nor easily consistent with self-respect.

The appraisal of debits against metropolitan judicial elections called for some qualifications. Most evidence of lowered standards related to the administration of criminal justice. The available studies were limited. But they indicated that most of the tremendous volume of civil business was not directly affected in disposition by factors peculiar to the elective judicial system. The sheer size of the civil business to be done in great-city courts created pressure for impersonal, matter-of-fact handling; the pressure of steadily mounting dockets was in itself a force to discipline judicial performance.

Political influence did show itself in the civil dockets, where litigants had close ties to the party, or where — as in large-scale receiverships — the business before the courts provided political patronage. For example, in Chicago during the depressed 1930's the appointment of receivers became a high political stake. There were tens of thousands of attorneys, janitors, and domestic help to be employed, and countless contracts to be awarded by receivers, in the operation of insolvent apartment houses. On the other hand, this patronage problem was not peculiar to elected courts. During the same period sharp questions were also asked about the patronage use which some federal district judges made out of similar opportunities.

We have no broad studies concerning judges outside the great cities; nor have we such studies of judicial performance anywhere, prior to about 1900; nor have we studies which single out the elective appellate courts. As to the last, it is not hard to find colorful examples of hot campaigns to defeat sitting judges because of decisions over controversial policy. An instance is the unsuccessful campaign of 1861, to unseat Judge Orsamus Cole of the Wisconsin Supreme Court, because he had voted to upset legislation which sought to relieve farmers of mortgage debts they had incurred in aid of railroad expansion. But it is hard to prove instances where such election pressure affected decision. And in any case, the matters involved, however important, were an insubstantial fraction of the general business of the courts.

Moreover, the history of the appointed Supreme Court of the United States did not lack examples of the impact of politics on the role of the Court: On occasion, men failed of nomination to the Court, or if nominated failed of confirmation, because they ran afoul of party opposition, or objections which went not to their professional qualifications but to their actual or supposed notions of public policy. The enemies of Andrew Jackson in 1835 defeated Taney's nomination as Associate Justice; a Democratic Senate in 1852 for purely partisan reasons rejected three nominations sent to it by the Whig President Fillmore; in 1861 the Republicans as a party matter rejected Buchanan's nomination of Jeremiah Black; in 1866 the Senate would not even consider the nomination of Henry Stanbery, and Congress passed legislation which in effect barred further nominations by President Andrew Johnson. Such were but a few of many incidents and these merely from one thirty-year period.

There is, of course, a more subtle kind of honesty which we would like of our judges: the honesty of self-examination, which makes a man conscious of his own limitations of imagination and sympathy, and which keeps him from playing the Pharisee. This is an element too intangible for measurement over the whole scope and span of our judicial history. But at least it is clear that neither elected nor appointed courts monopolized self-righteousness. The moral complacency which exalted *laissez faire* dogma over human claims in the late nineteenth century was nowhere more marked than in some elected state supreme courts, which in theory might have been supposed to be closer to the needs of the people. And on the other hand, the great judicial spokesman against cant and smug dogma was Oliver Wendell Holmes, Jr., whose whole career on the Bench was on two great appointed courts.

Granted standards of honesty, self-respect, detachment, dignity — what other values go into the estimation of the good judge? Learning. But this is less important surely, than the quality of original and penetrating thought. And intellect can be dry, or, alternatively, dangerous, if it is not joined to those qualities of personal viewpoint which lead us to call a man wise. How measure such imponderables, during years of judicial work in the United States, in federal courts, in state courts, from the justice of the peace and the probate judge to the judge of highest appeal?

There was little attempt at objective measurement of the quality of judging; and the results, when one had them, were plainly of limited value. Surveying the record of Illinois trial judges, Neitzert found that "the popular supposition that the character of the bench is on the decline is without foundation." He examined the percentage of successful appeals in Illinois, from decisions of trial courts of general jurisdiction, over the years 1819–1934. After 1872, he found that never more than 50 per cent of cases appealed were reversed; this percentage of reversals compared favorably with the prevailing twentieth-century ratio of one-third reversals on appeal in the appointive federal and English court systems. In volume of work disposed of, Chicago trial courts showed increased efficiency on the civil side in the first third of the twentieth century, and they held their own at least on the criminal side of the docket. In length of service (ability to get re-elected), the judges of Illinois trial courts of general jurisdiction showed a steady rise in average length of service from 1831 to 1934; in the Chicago area this was true for the lesser, but still substantial, span from 1871 to 1934.

We have almost no reliable judicial statistics in the United States for any period before 1900. But scattering studies confirm these Illinois findings. Thus, Vernier and Selig, examining the reversals in criminal cases in the California courts (an elected bench during all the time studied), found a general downward trend in the percentage of reversals, 1850–1926, with an average of 27 per cent for the whole period, and a high of 52 per cent in the 1860's. Through the first half of the twentieth century the jury played a diminishing role both in civil and criminal cases. The fact suggested that, measured by comparison with that traditional seat of common sense wisdom, the average performance of the trial bench in jury-type cases at least had shown superiority.

If honesty involves self-examination, so too does wisdom. We do not call a man wise if he lacks the humor or humility to see his own bias and discount it. This is an important element in humane administration of a trial court. But it is a value which our history put at a special premium on the appellate bench, because of the power of our judges to review the constitutionality of legislation under such vague formulae as due process and equal protection of the laws. The point must not be exaggerated: Constitutional issues were central probably to a good deal less than a quarter of 1 per cent of the cases that came to our appellate courts from 1790 to 1940. But when such questions arose, they were apt to involve matters of broad consequence, and at any rate they presented an unusually clear test of the judicial temper.

What was the record? In the fifty years after 1880, legislation responded to the new problems of a crowded and interdependent society, and was met by sweeping and dogmatic use of the judicial veto. The ultimate barriers were raised by the Supreme Court of the United States. *Lochner* v. *New York* (1905) and *Adkins* v. *Children's Hospital* (1923) stood at about the central span of the period as symbols of the substitution of judicial for legislative determination of social policy.

But some caution is in order before we conclude from such cases that social conservatism was inherent in an appointive court. *Lochner* v. *New York* in effect repudiated the liberal doctrine of the "presumption of constitutionality" which the same Court had fashioned and brought to full strength in 1887 in *Powell* v. *Pennsylvania*. The Court made the presumption again operative doctrine when in 1932 it upheld a Minnesota mortgage moratorium, and when in 1934 it sustained a New York milk-marketing control system. The decisive turn in the Court's decisions in the spring of 1937, following the brief but almost catastrophic abuse of the judicial veto in 1935 and 1936, made the Court again the forthright exponent of judicial self-restraint which it had been in *Powell* v. *Pennsylvania*.

Moreover, in the years in which the Supreme Court most broadly asserted its veto on legislative policy decisions, it did not stand alone. In the fifty years after 1880 the most conspicuous and drastic judicial condemnations of social legislation came from states which had elected judges. Notable instances were the 1895 Illinois decision in *Ritchie* v. *People*, and the 1907 New York ruling in *People* v. *Williams*, which invalidated laws which regulated the hours of labor of women. On the other hand, no state courts exceeded in liberality toward the legislature the appointed supreme courts in Massachusetts and New Jersey.

The record at least showed that appointment did not guarantee a more conservative bench than election. The whole evidence indicated no direct relation between the liberality of the courts toward legislative judgment and the circumstance that the judges were elected or appointed. The ideas and feelings prevailing in any given generation in those levels of the community from which judges came offered far more convincing explanation of judicial policy.

CHAPTER EIGHT

COURTS FOR THE PEOPLE

Court organization in the United States reflected the remarkable lack of concern of lay and professional opinion in this country regarding the shape and functioning of the basic agencies of government. Inertia and the momentum of going institutions were the main influences. Though familiar, the fact is especially striking as it applies to the courts. Of the major agencies of government, for over one hundred years, at least, the courts came closest to the life of many people; their primacy in this respect was materially challenged only with the twentieth century, by the rise of the administrative process. Because they were so close to the people's living, the courts might have been expected to be under some consistent and lively attention. To the contrary, nowhere were the force of inertia and toughness of accepted institutions, the tardiness of practical planning and direction, more shown than in the handling of problems which most brought the average person to court.

This chapter reviews the story of the justice of the peace, and of the urban courts of minor criminal and civil jurisdiction. Their history reminds that court structure and court personnel are inseparable parts in a common problem. The jurisdiction of these courts was "minor" in the sense that they were authorized to impose only limited penalties or to dispose only of cases that involved relatively small sums. But only in this sense were they minor courts. In terms of human welfare and the practical experience that masses of people had of "justice" in our society, these courts dealt in issues of first importance.

1. THE JUSTICE OF THE PEACE

During most of our national history, the justice-of-the-peace court was the court which the states set up to handle the small disputes of the average man. The title invoked a long English history. It was a misleading reference, however, for there was never much more than a resemblance in name between the English justice and his American namesake. The English justice of the peace was, typically, a knight, or at least a man of property, though he was likely not learned in the law. He had no civil jurisdiction; his primary function was to keep the peace, trying petty offenders and binding over those against whom more serious charges were laid. The office had been an important instrument by which the Crown extended its power at the expense of the barons; the justice's commission thus of course ran from the Crown, and his tenure, though indeterminate, was usually equivalent to holding during good behavior.

In all essentials, the justice of the peace in the United States was the opposite of the English officer. In the United States the office was the arch symbol of our emphasis on local autonomy in the organization of courts. Its widespread adoption responded to the practical need, in a time of poor and costly communications, to bring justice close to each man's door. Consistent with this demand, the states granted the justice of the peace jurisdiction in small civil cases, as well as in criminal matters. One could expect to find neither many established landholders nor many law-trained men in the new states; from the first the law set no qualifications for the office — a condition which prevailed in substance in 1940 in forty-five of the forty-seven states in which the justice of the peace existed — and the spread of the elective system barred development of anything like the traditional standards set by the practice of executive appointment in England. As a natural accompaniment of elective status, the justice was given a short term of office. Moreover, the justice court represented an effort to bring law administration close to a scattered population with minimum expense to a slender public purse, and in a way adjusted to a volume of business that was likely to be small and irregular in the individual court. Thus it was natural to put the office on a fee rather than salary basis, and so it continued in every state.

The justice's commission ran from the state, but this was pure form. In the twentieth century, England put new meaning behind the fact that the central government commissioned the justices, by providing a practical measure of central supervision of justice court administration. Given the familiar decentralization of our court systems, it was not surprising that no such development took place here.

In 1790, it is true, the judges of the Northwest Territory provided that the justices of the peace should meet collectively in a general quarter sessions of the peace, to hear the more serious criminal charges. But this move toward a co-ordinated body of minor courts was short-lived, and did not survive the creation of new states out of the Territory.

In the 1930's, Warren's survey of the handling of traffic cases in justice courts in thirty-seven states showed that in thirty-two states there was no agency which had any supervisory duties over the justices' work, though five states entrusted some supervision to a county officer. The states invariably made no provision, or at least no adequate provision, for justice court records, so that in any case control was practically impossible. There is no evidence that in practice any state developed any regular, planned supervision of the judicial work of the justices of the peace. With so little in justice court organization to assure fair or efficient operation, it is not surprising that the states invariably provided *de novo* review of the justices' decisions in the county or circuit courts.

Structurally, the happiest feature of the justice of the peace system was that the states rarely froze it into constitutional status. Though forty-four state constitutions finally gave some mention to the office, thirty-two of these expressly permitted the legislature to fix justice court jurisdiction, and three allowed the legislature to abolish the office; in but nine states did the constitution give the office standing beyond the legislature's control.

2. Administering Justice in an Urban Society

In all essentials, the justice of the peace was and remained a judicial officer who was appropriate to a relatively simple society of rural character. After the turning point of the 1870's, great cities grew, and all people of whatever neighborhood began to find themselves in an increasing and unaccustomed dependency upon their fellows. New demands of desperate urgency were made on administration of justice in fields that most closely touched the lives of the mass of the people.

One major area involved wage claims, landlord-tenant problems, and the wage assignments, rights of repossession, garnishments, and other creditor's security devices bearing on people of small means. Economic strain and the distractions of an urban way of life challenged the traditional sanctions of church, neighborhood, and school, weakening the internal union of marriage and family life. Out of this background came another cluster of problems in the administration of justice, new in their volume and in the disquieting threat which they held to the integrity of community life: There were separation proceedings, divorce, proceedings for nonsupport ("The poor man's divorce"), the prosecution of youths and even children for "petty" offenses that were anything but petty in the implications they held for the future life of the delinquents. A third new field of challenge in urban justice was close to the new technology. New machinery in transportation, mining, lumbering, and manufacture spelled a vast and beneficent rise in the standard of living; it also added the fear of death or disability of the wage earner to the shadows about workingmen's homes, and in a generation transformed the social importance of the law of torts, which had been a rag bag of problems on the periphery of the law.

The foregoing were issues primarily in the lives of city people of small means. Other matters — small in the individual case but of weight in their total impact on the society — affected the lives of people of more varying fortunes, whether they lived in rural or urban neighborhoods. Most conspicuous were problems that arose out of modern technology and the related growth of mass markets. It was now possible to distribute dangerous foods and drugs on an unprecedented scale; the traveling medicine show was the insignificant forerunner of fraudulent use of new mass means of communication, and of more callous appeals to fear, vanity, and insecurity, to sell worthless or grossly overpriced goods to thousands. Within twenty years, the automobile created great and novel problems of mutual accommodation in crowded living, and grave, unforeseen threats to safety of body and peace of mind. Were all such issues to be handled in the old courts, in conventional lawsuits, under familiar actions for breach of warranty, fraud and deceit, negligent injury — or in criminal prosecutions under classic charges of public nuisance, larceny, assault and battery, or disorderly conduct?

As problems flooded in on the tide of a new society, adjustment was bound to be complex, and to call for much shifting of policy and redefinition of values and of the rights and duties which would express those values. Here we are concerned with the issues of court organization that grew out of the new social problems. Response was slow, spotty, powered by a feeble sense of public responsibility at the bar; and what was done was generally not radical enough to get to the bottom of the troubles.

The new problems in the administration of justice came mainly out of the great cities. They were felt at least from the 1850's on. But for almost thirty years the only reflection of new demands on the judicial system was the easiest and most mechanical of reactions — the multiplication of new courts, largely on the model of the old. In the cities the justice of the peace — unsupervised, looking to fees rather than to a fixed salary for his pay — allied himself to politicians and to collection agencies, and under the protection of the impersonality of city life, turned his court into a business.

Even if corruption or money getting had not tarnished urban justice, the condition of a large working class would still have changed the situation fundamentally from the simpler, more easygoing administration of rural justice. The states adopted the idea (of long ancestry in English statute law) that each litigant must pay fees to get justice, and that the loser must pay his opponent's costs. Fees and costs developed haphazardly. They varied from state to state and among the courts of the same state. The legislature typically failed to adjust them according to any rational theory of revenue or of making the courts pay their way; nor were they changed to take account of labor- or time-saving developments in communications or in reproduction of documents or in the handling of office work.

Most fundamental point of all, no substantial consideration was ever given to the wisdom of thus setting a price on obtaining justice. English statutes had permitted paupers to sue without paying costs; and at least two courts in the United States found these laws old enough to have been adopted as part of the common law in this country. But in practice, so far as relief from court costs was given the poor in the United States, it was by statute. So far as it was given, it was much hedged about, limited to particular kinds of cases (such as wage claims), or to proceedings in certain courts, and was often not applicable to cases on appeal. As late as 1923 over one third of the states provided no relief at all to the poor litigant. And in any case, provision for costs never covered adequate allowance for employment of a lawyer, though as the procedure and the substance of the law grew more complex, a lawyer's aid was more and more often the practical prerequisite of effectual assertion of a right or a defense.

From mid-nineteenth century on there was some promise of improvement in urban justice through the creation of new, full-time, salaried magistrates courts, city courts, or other local courts of various titles. Sometimes states attempted halfhearted reform of the justice court. Thus in 1891 an Ohio statute made justices of the peace in first-grade cities salaried officers. But the act left justices of the peace generally with county-wide jurisdiction in attachment cases, and rural justices kept city quarters and sought trade to such effect that the salaried justice jobs proved to be sinecures.

Throughout the country, statutory tinkering with the lower courts' structure was invariably limited to given localities: Such legislation left each court to the practically unsupervised conduct of the business that came to it, and multiplied issues of jurisdiction, venue, practice and procedure, under the arbitrarily varying terms of the individual statutes. The outcome was a crazy quilt of inferior courts, wherever city growth had pressed hard on old institutions.

Allegheny County, Pennsylvania, furnished an example of the patchwork of courts that resulted. By the late 1920's there were in that county 14 Common Pleas judges, 3 judges of the Orphans Court, 6 county court judges, 242 justices of the peace in the rural parts of the county, 46 aldermen as their urban counterparts, and various municipal executives who exercised judicial or quasi-judicial functions directly or through their representatives, including 4 mayors, 68 burgesses (executives of boroughs), and 8 police magistrates (delegates of the mayor of Pittsburgh). All this made a total of 391 offices involving judicial power. There was no office which was responsible for, or had any powers over, the way in which these officials did their judicial work; the secretary of the commonwealth could not even furnish an authoritative list of all the men who held the various offices at a given time.

This situation was not peculiar to the older Eastern states. The late 1920's found Hamilton County, Ohio, with a total of 55 judges of 49 courts of limited jurisdiction, elected in 36 independent governmental units. Included in the confusing picture were 7 judges of the Cincinnati Municipal Court, 22 city and village mayors who had judicial powers, and 26 justices of the peace in 13 townships.

The patchwork creation of new inferior courts might offer some chance that judicial business would be handled with more skill or honesty than in the justice courts, which were ill-fitted to a city environment. Otherwise the new courts were in procedure, practice and tradition no different from any other familiar judicial bodies. In them there were still fees, costs, and expense of counsel to be met; in them, too, were procedural delays before trial, in trial, and on appeal; and in criminal cases there was all this plus the stigma of the criminal law and the crudity of the remedies or sanctions that it provided. These factors spelled denial of justice to more and more people, and failures in social engineering whose consequences broadened and ran deep into community life.

3. LEGAL AID

In the 1870's and 1880's the only substantial move toward improvement was the limited beginnings of legal aid work. The common law, and in some states a few early statutes, held out to the poor the help of counsel assigned by the court. But by the later nineteenth century this practice had long fallen into disuse in civil cases. In criminal cases, the glaring unfairness of lack of counsel had kept the practice alive. However, it was limited, in practice if not in law, to the offenses that carried the most serious penalties; and in the great cities it was often the means by which police-court hangers-on victimized the families or relatives of the accused.

The roots of modern legal aid work were in the service first tendered by a German immigrant aid society in New York in 1876, and during the slow growth of the movement over the next thirty years this limited origin was characteristic. The founding of the Detroit legal aid unit in 1909, by the city bar association, marked the first recognition by the organized bar that it had some responsibility to do something to make justice more available to the poor. As late as 1910 there were still but fourteen legal aid societies in operation. But here, as in so many other respects, 1910 was a threshold year. In the next three years the number of legal aid organizations doubled. The lead now passed from the single-mission or proprietary groups which had done most of the work theretofore, to the unorganized charities, which now saw legal aid as one phase of their broad programs. By 1918 there were forty-one societies and four public defender offices.

The public defender offices, and the several publicly supported legal aid bureaus, indicated still a further, and more fundamental shift in the thinking behind the legal aid movement; to support legal aid with public money was to put it on the basis of right, and not simply of friendly help or charity. Thirty years later this last change in policy, however desirable, was still in advance of lay or professional opinion and interest. In the light of some intervening experience, it was apparent that the wisdom of publicly supported legal aid depended for each community on the level of local politics, and the willingness of the local bar to keep an alert surveillance of the work.

In 1934 Smith and Bradway found that "legal aid was definitely established in all of the 21 cities having a population over 350,000 in 1930, in 15 of the 20 cities having a population of 200,000 to 350,000, in 5 of the 10 cities with 150,000 to 200,000 population, and was fairly well established in 47 of the cities having populations of 25,000 to 150,000." There was no completely satisfactory measure of the adequacy of legal aid coverage in these areas. The "rough standard" which the National Association of Legal Aid Organizations adopted out of years of experience in the various societies, was that there should be annually one case per one hundred inhabitants. By this test the great bulk of the societies were serving less than the theoretical need in their areas, by substantial to very large margins; municipal bureaus and societies sponsored by bar associations showed the highest service ratios.

For all the limitations of the legal aid movement, its record was impressive. As of 1933 legal aid societies had handled 3,912,146 cases; had collected $13,604,855; had spent $7,860,746. The then-existing organizations served territories in which 39,000,000 people lived; in these areas they annually aided over 300,000 persons, and collected for them nearly three quarters of a million dollars, or an average of a little over

$15 per case, at an average cost of $1.45 per case. The societies did all this work with incredibly small staffs; in 1933 full-time legal aid employees numbered about 81 lawyers, 70 clerks, and 25 investigators, throughout the country.

However much the legal aid societies did with limited means, their assistance was limited to those who could afford to pay nothing, or only a nominal fee, for legal service; this was from the start a basic policy in the legal aid movement. Not until the 1930's was there any substantial recognition that there was a problem of people of small means and small cases, who could not qualify for legal aid, but who yet could not pay what, under conventional conditions of law practice, a lawyer must fairly charge for his work. The problem thus so tardily considered was one aspect of the general concern for the economics of the bar which the 1930's depression stimulated. Since the matter may be more adequately considered in the context of the economics of the legal profession, discussion of it is postponed to the chapter which deals with the bar.

4. THE MUNICIPAL COURT

Legal aid was a social invention of the middle 1870's. It was almost a generation after that, before we saw any equally promising new step in the administration of justice as this touched the lives of the city masses. What came next was compounded partly of a drive for local government reform — bred of the "muckraking" journalism of the early twentieth century — and partly of the effect of the rise of professional social welfare work. Thus in 1905, in Chicago, after a long fight against political vested interest, the office of the justice of the peace was abolished, and the legislature created the Chicago Municipal Court, as the first unified metropolitan court exercising limited civil and criminal jurisdiction under the administrative supervision of a chief justice. In the next generation many of the larger cities copied the Chicago example, in varying degrees of thoroughness; in particular they copied Chicago's creation of a specialized division of the Municipal Court, to handle small claims under simplified procedure. The professionalization of social work was paralleled by growing emphasis on the rehabilitation of social relations that had gotten out of joint, in place of the older simple resort to decree and penalty. These currents found expression in the judicial structure through the creation of special courts — or, more desirably, special divisions of existing courts — for cases involving juvenile delinquency and domestic relations.

5. THE JUVENILE COURT

Volunteer probation work and the establishment of reformatories had their beginnings about the middle of the nineteenth century. These steps foreshadowed concern for separate treatment of the juvenile offender. But no jurisdiction tried to modify conventional criminal court proceedings involving young people, until in the 1870's Massachusetts provided that they be tried separately. In the next twenty-five years only New York, Illinois, and Indiana joined in this change. Moreover, the change still left the youthful offender in the status of a criminal. In 1869, however, the Illinois legislature adopted a radically new concept of the young offender as a ward of the court, rather than as one charged with crime; it gave special jurisdiction of such cases to named courts; and in particular, it singled out one of the circuit judgeships in Cook County for special assignment to such work in the metropolitan area.

After this there was a rapid spread of the movement for separate juvenile courts with flexible and informal procedures aimed at education, guidance, and rehabilitation, in place of the stigma of criminal proceedings. By 1904 ten states, by 1914 twenty states and the District of Columbia, by 1920 all but three states, and by 1927 all states except Wyoming had authorized probation systems; all but Maine and Wyoming had authorized juvenile courts, and the last two states had made special provision for children's cases.

But formal progress far outstripped practical accomplishment. At mid-twentieth century there was still great need to expand and generously implement the use of juvenile courts and their techniques, especially in rural areas. Nor, experience confirmed, would the most generous changes in judicial organization repair most of the social damage that had been done before the child came to court. The most constructive aspect of the juvenile court was in its powers to act preventively; its greatest strength was in its authority to use other means than confinement, to correct the situation.

6. DOMESTIC RELATIONS COURTS

There were two main aspects to the developments that went on in the handling of domestic relations problems. One side of the story concerned readier access to the courts by people of small means. Several factors converged on this problem. After the opening of the twentieth century, the criminal law broadened to cover more adequately the matters of nonsupport and desertion. This meant that the aggrieved wife who lacked means could have a possible remedy through the help of the district attorney and the follow-up of the probation officer; and this assistance she could have without cost to herself, with comparatively little delay, and generally without need of private counsel. Similarly, the provision of domestic relations courts, staffed with their own investigators, foretold a lessened need for lawyers' services in handling the more complex questions of divorce, separate maintenance, and custody of children. Such developments in the interest of the domestic relations litigant of small means were the more important since from the start legal aid societies usually adopted the policy of defending, but not initiating divorce proceedings.

The other aspect of changes in treatment of domestic relations issues more directly concerned court organization. The problem here was the general question, apart from the problems of the poor litigant, of the social efficiency with which domestic relations matters were handled in court. In 1910 a domestic relations division was set up in the city court of Buffalo with jurisdiction in all criminal cases involving the family, including bastardy proceedings. Similar action was taken in the Chicago Municipal Court in 1911. In 1914 the Domestic Relations Court was set up in Cincinnati, with sweeping civil and criminal jurisdiction. A court of the same title was established in New York City in 1933, with a broad jurisdiction which did not, however, include separation or divorce. In 1934 a separate branch of the circuit court in Milwaukee was designated for domestic relations cases, and was given the aid of trained investigators.

In these instances, and in several other cases where such courts, of varying breadth of authority, were created, the practical drive apparently came from faith in specialization in procedure, experience, and expert staff work, rather than from some felt need for unification of functions. It was true that in those courts which were given the broader grants of jurisdiction, it was possible to handle in one court the various phases of a family breakdown; in such jurisdictions, for example, it would not be necessary to try the husband in criminal court for disorderly conduct, while divorce must be sought in circuit court, and a dependency or delinquency hearing held in a juvenile court. Some of those who urged the creation of domestic relations courts put much stress on the desirability and need for unified treatment of all the angles of a family breakdown. On the other hand, there is no evidence that such many-sided problems occurred in sufficient volume and importance to account for the movement for the domestic relations court.

The communities which set up the more adequately staffed juvenile and domestic relations courts equipped them with trained social workers, investigators, psychiatrists, and ample office forces. Such aides could provide the court with background information, advise on its decrees and check obedience to its orders, as well as give counsel and affirmative help to an aggrieved wife or husband or a dependent child against a noncomplying defendant. The growth of such staff work became so important in the work of the best of these courts that it appeared as if the traditional judicial process might disappear in these fields to a great extent, and merge into administrative handling of these problems.

The quality of a few of the new special types of courts must not obscure the fact that they were relatively rare. Up to mid-twentieth century, most of the juvenile and domestic relations courts lacked adequate staff or suitable co-ordination with related facilities for the administration of their business. And, over the country as a whole, such specialized courts were still the exception.

It helps for a realistic picture of the total situation, to look at the court organization that existed in the middle 1930's in a state, and in a metropolitan community of that state, which had experimented in the creation of better instruments for the administration of justice. Consider, for example, Michigan, and the Detroit area. Only in its juvenile courts had Michigan made substantial provision for special investigation of the social context of family cases. Even there the typical case reports in a sampling of nonmetropolitan counties were superficial and of slight value; on the other hand, pre-trial social investigations in the Wayne County (Detroit area) Juvenile Court met high standards of social case work. Michigan circuit courts handled important domestic relations problems. The only important pre-trial investigation available to these courts in their dealings with such matters as divorce, separation, and annulment was through an office known as the "Friend of the Court." In some districts, particularly in Wayne County, this office did valuable inquiry work; but its investigations were limited mainly to obtaining background for the fixing of decrees for alimony or the custody of children.

Except in Wayne County, Michigan provided no important agency to help the courts in criminal cases involving the family; there was no auxiliary office on which the judge could rely to attempt informal adjustment of family difficulties, or to provide the judge with information on the social, economic, or emotional background of cases.

In Wayne County, several agencies did contribute to the criminal courts useful information and help — but less than might have been given under a co-ordinated plan. By collecting information from all social agencies and doing some independent investigation, the small staff of the Detroit women's police division screened complaints and cases that came to the attention of the authorities, to decide which should be prosecuted. But the division lacked the resources to follow or supervise cases in any continuing way. The adjustment division of the Recorder's Court — a branch of the probation staff — sought informal adjustments in nonsupport cases, and as a by-product made some efforts at reconciliations. The adjustment division did not have the staff to investigate cases thoroughly; this was especially unfortunate, because the regular work of the division put it in a strategic spot to act as a domestic relations clinic. The domestic relations division of the Recorder's Court — another branch of county probation work — made no pre-trial investigations, but did make a social study of cases before sentence; a statute required such investigation in all felony cases. The Recorder's Court also had a psychopathic clinic which, though it made no pre-trial investigations, did make findings and recommendations on the medical and social aspects of cases at the stage of sentence.

In all these respects, Wayne County sought to bring modern science and administration to bear for the more effective disposition of certain difficult business of the courts. What it did, it did without a general plan; and the logic of its experiments called for doing a great deal more than was attempted.

7. Administrative Agencies

The rise of the administrative process was the latest major development which responded to the problems of justice in the everyday affairs of average people in an urban-industrial society. The administrative agency had roots in Anglo–American law that reached back at least to the Tudors. It assumed its modern meaning as late as 1910. In some specialized forms it was aimed directly at winning justice for people who had too little means to pay to fight their own battles. Of such nature, for example, was the authority which Massachusetts gave its commissioner of labor to bring summary criminal proceedings where an employer wrongfully withheld wages. Of such a character, too, was the help given the injured workman, when an industrial compensation commission represented him on appeal to the courts from an administrative award in his favor. So, too, commissioners of agriculture used statutory licensing powers to enforce payments which licensed commission merchants owed farmers; agencies empowered to license loan companies acted to protect small borrowers; local boards of health could proceed in cases where otherwise private persons must have brought actions to abate a nuisance.

But the administrative power was used also in situations of wider range: It gave special, continuous supervision and enforcement in fields where the total community impact of undesirable practices might be serious but where the effect on individuals was too slight or haphazard in incidence to make it economical for them to protect the general welfare by enforcing their own complaints. This was so, for example, of false advertising or the marketing of dangerous foods and drugs. The difficulty was broader than that of the individual too weak to battle for his rights; the problem was of grievances individually too small or occasional to provoke private suits, though in the whole sum presenting substantial damage to the society.

In both these aspects, the administrative process differed from other developments discussed in this chapter in that it did not so much represent a movement to improve court organization as it did a challenge to the inherent capacity of the courts to meet the mass problems in the administration of justice presented by a new society. A later chapter will further consider the implications of this challenge for the place of the courts in our legal structure.

8. SMALL CLAIMS COURTS

We have now looked in general terms at the history of the uneven response made in terms of court organization to problems that arose in the handling of great volumes of "small" matters in a society dominated by the city and by industry. The story may take on more tangible meaning if we look at the developments that took place in the judicial administration of two particular kinds of everyday law business — small claims, and traffic violations. The small claims problem was one of justice for the man of little means; the traffic violations problem was one of socially efficient treatment of a mass of cases that involved all classes directly. In both instances, the seeming pettiness of the individual case tended to conceal problems of grave social concern.

Most civil business in the first tier of city courts in the twentieth century consisted of wage claims and creditors' claims against wage earners. Samplings of justice court suits in Allegheny County, Pennsylvania, in 1913 and 1926, for example, showed that over 99 per cent of the actions were in contract, and the large majority of these were for wages or for goods sold and delivered. Over three fourths of the civil suits in justice courts in Hamilton County, Ohio, 1925–1929, were of the same character. The amounts in suit were typically small; about three fourths of the actions involved in the two studies just mentioned were for less than $100.

Representative studies showed that at least during the second generation of the twentieth century the justice of the peace functioned in civil cases in certain uniformly characteristic ways. By the least count, judgment went for the plaintiff in two thirds of the cases; the more usual count showed the plaintiff almost automatically the winner — in 90 per cent or more of cases — where the suit was pressed; many more cases typically went for the plaintiff by default than by trial.

Justice courts disposed of cases speedily, and in this sense were cheap; and since they almost all remained fee-supported, they were economical, from the standpoint of the state treasury. But litigants had to pay relatively heavy costs of suit, considering how small were the sums usually involved. A study in Hamilton County, Ohio, showed a range of costs from $6.09 to $11.93, with a median of $7.44; three of the four busiest Hamilton County justice courts showed average costs of $9 in ordinary civil suits — a fact which suggested that the underlying motive in the conduct of these courts was to make them a good-paying business proposition. Justice court litigation was costly even to successful plaintiffs, when regard was had to the low record of satisfied judgments. At the best, satisfied judgments amounted to 60 per cent of those entered, and the figure was usually closer to one third.

Suits tended to concentrate in a very few of the many justice courts which had formal existence in a given area. The fact emphasized the anomaly of permitting courts which did a regular business to operate on a fee basis. It also reflected the temptations to commercialize the justice court, and to invite collection agency business by giving reliable service. Two of twenty-six justice courts in Hamilton County handled 69 per cent of the garnishment and attachment proceedings, 1925–1929. A 1934 study of small-town and rural justice courts in Illinois showed that there also business was as much concentrated in a few courts as it was in the big cities.

Justice court proceedings were simple, if not by law, then because the typical justice of the peace lacked the learning to make them otherwise. Indeed, where the defendant appeared, there was a tendency for the proceedings to be less of a trial than an effort by the justice to negotiate a settlement. This tendency was in line with recent policy affecting trial courts of general jurisdiction. But the practice was open to strong suspicion when it was conducted by a judge who was likely to be little restrained by professional tradition or knowledge, and who was paid by fees, and particularly by fees of collection agencies which would naturally take their lawsuits where they got results. Often there were no proceedings in justice court; instead the justice would write what amounted to dunning letters on behalf of the creditor, and would rely on the intimidating effect of a formidable letterhead (sometimes printed so as to appear to be a form of legal process) to bring the debtor quickly to terms.

State statutes carefully preserved a full measure of appeal from justice court decisions. Invariably the appeal was *de novo;* the reviewing court had authority to try the case all over again, with no binding effect attached to what had been done in justice court. This gave strong inducement to a well-off or callous defendant to permit the plaintiff to wear out his money and energy in a futile proceeding in justice court. In fairness, it must be added that appeals were generally taken in but a small percentage of justice court cases. On the whole, therefore, the justice court could be credited with a final, as well as a speedy, disposition of the business that came to it, however much other qualities might be lacking in the handling of that business.

The small claims court was perhaps the outstanding success among judicial innovations of the first half of the twentieth century. This was true whether it was set up as a separate court, or, more desirably, as a division of a unified municipal court. At the mid-century mark, the small claims court was but a generation old. But in this time it had a nation-wide growth. By 1940 over a third of the states, including many of the more populous ones, had statutes which authorized such courts; and small claims courts had been established and had made good records in such cities as Cleveland, Portland (Oregon), Chicago, Philadelphia, Boston, Milwaukee, and Minneapolis.

We must look with some caution at the enthusiastic verdicts passed on these new courts, since there are no detailed studies of their operation. But in structure, procedure, and personnel, they made a strong presumptive case for themselves.

The statutes usually gave the small claims courts general jurisdiction in contract and tort (libel and slander excepted), within a value range of $20 to $200; some acts limited these courts, however, to contract or wage actions. Ordinarily the law made it optional with the plaintiff, whether he sued in the small claims court. The advantages of a simple and summary procedure made the court a strong competitor for judicial business; this was evidenced by the readiness of many plaintiffs to scale down their claims in order to come within the jurisdictional limit of the small claims court.

The new court offered informal proceedings administered by a full-time professional judge. Generally the plaintiff did not have to file a

complaint or serve the defendant, since the clerk of court would attend
to both matters, on the basis of the facts of the case given him by the
plaintiff. Service was frequently by registered or ordinary mail, or even
by telephone. Usually the defendant was not required to file an answer.
A counterclaim or setoff could be presented as informally as an original
claim. Action was fast. Ten days would ordinarily be enough to bring
a claim through the whole process of trial. Some laws required no payment of court costs. Where costs were assessed, they were very low as
compared with those familiar in justice courts; Boston showed small
claims court costs as low as $1.20, Cleveland $1.40, Milwaukee $1.70,
and the state of Vermont $2. The extreme simplicity of procedure and
the help which the court and its staff gave the parties further cut
expense, by almost completely eliminating the need of lawyers; in half
a dozen states the statutes, with unwise rigidity, went so far as to forbid
the appearance of counsel in the small claims court.

Small claims court laws made judgments more collectible by providing that they might be paid in installments, and sometimes by providing
as part of the court's staff a "trustee" to collect the debtor's earnings
for pro rata distribution among his creditors. The delays which indirectly added much to the cost of ordinary lawsuits were mitigated in
the small claims court by provisions encouraging the waiver of jury
trial, and by the elimination of appeals or the limitation of appeals
strictly to questions of law.

Informal procedure and the absence of counsel required that a court
be under responsible and professional administration. This was a critical
point of distinction between the small claims court and the justice court.
Small claims courts were usually set up only where there was a well-
organized municipal court or system of inferior courts qualified for the
responsibility. The importance of proper administration in a court of
such informal procedure was noted by the secretary of the American
Judicature Society. As of the 1930's he estimated that for every place
where a small claims court could be set up with promise of success,
there were perhaps ten places where it could not be, for lack of a responsible, qualified judicial organization into which it might fit and
from whose tradition it might draw support and discipline.

The creation of the small claims court bore on only a small part of
the money problems which people of little means brought to law. The
worker with a small wage claim was still the person most heavily imposed on by the inevitable delays and expenses of collection. Experience
suggested that his best remedy, despite the small claims court, lay in an
administrative office authorized to enforce wage collections. Wage
claims apart, there were other situations where the question of the

remedy available was at least as important as the question of what
agency was available to apply the remedy. The farmer-debtor was a
persistently potent figure in United States politics, and his pressure
showed in exemption and homestead laws. Legislatures gave much less
heed to adapting the law to the troubles of the debtor who lived in the
city. The poor debtor in the city had much reason to be interested in
the regulation of the small loans business, in the possible provision of a
bankruptcy or personal receivership procedure for the wage earner,
in regulation of consumer credit. But the city debtor lacked ties to an
effective pressure group, and such matters had scant effective attention
from the legislature, at least before the 1920's.

In praise of the small claims court, then, we must not forget that at
best it was only a very limited answer to the money troubles which
average people brought to law. Granted this, it may fairly be said that
the small claims court appeared to accomplish the limited purpose of its
creation, to an extent rare in reforms of the administration of justice.

9. The Traffic Court

The traffic court was another agency significant for the handling of a
great volume of everyday law business.

The treatment of automobile traffic cases showed how great was the
force of inertia, and how little there was of plan or direction, in the
growth of the courts in the United States. The example was the more
clear-cut because the administrative issues were not blurred by controversy over policy: Everyone wanted safety and mutual accommodation
in auto traffic; the difficulty was indifference and lack of imagination
or foresight regarding the organization required to implement these
policies.

Trouble came partly from the huge volume of traffic cases, and
partly from the fact that at a deceptive first appearance most individual
traffic cases seemed to involve rather petty matters. In 1942 it was
estimated that 1 in 8 persons in United States cities went to traffic court
every year. By that time traffic cases in cities of any size throughout
the country totaled over 6,500,000 annually. Accidents involving the
operation of automobiles were bringing death to about 30,000 persons a
year, and serious injury to about 1,250,000; annual property damage
from such accidents was running around $1,500,000.

Traffic violations were involved in at least half of all traffic accidents.
From the 1920's, the engineers made great strides in building safer
roads and cars. With the 1930's belated efforts began to educate people
in automobile safety. But as late as the fourth decade of the automobile

century there had been the tardiest and least widespread or effective efforts in the creation of well-considered traffic laws or enforcement programs. This lack was the more striking because all the evidence was that effective enforcement of sound traffic standards was prerequisite to keeping whatever gains were made by engineering or educational advances. There was progress in police methods of dealing with automobile traffic problems. But little progress could be credited to judicial administration in this field.

The corrupt or money-grabbing rural or suburban justice of the peace, who operated a "speed trap" with the aid of his constable, was a colorful villain of early motoring days, and he did not wholly disappear. But the public probably always exaggerated his importance. At any rate, by the time the auto came of age, in the 1920's, the justice court was of steadily diminishing importance in traffic cases. As late as 1940, justices of the peace still handled more traffic cases than any other judicial officers in thirty of the less populous states. But in the heavily populated areas, full-time local courts dealt with the great bulk of traffic offenses.

Where the justice court predominated, familiar defects were sharpened by the nature of traffic cases. The fee system promoted commercialization of justice, where opportunity invited to a new, larger scale of returns. Typically no more than 10 per cent of the justice courts in a state got most of the traffic business. Such concentration might mean sensible economy in handling the work. Given the history of justice courts, however, the fact invited the suspicion that the concentration of business rested on an unjudicial collaboration with the police, who naturally would bring cases where they could get convictions. Justices were characteristically men unlearned in the simplest aspects of the law which they administered; to over two thirds of them their judicial duties were a minor source of income. Justice court administration showed the results of such background factors: The disposition of cases often ignored the statute book; sentences lacked uniformity and were often not proportionate to the offense; there was almost no pretense at constructive correction; convictions averaged about 98 per cent. Any conviction ratio over 80 per cent was regarded as excellent, and sometimes unobtainable by most cities in the same states where such justice court records were made.

In the face of its dubious performance, the justice court lost much of its traditional excuse for being, as both the automobile and the hard-surface road system developed in efficiency. The states could now centralize the administration of justice without undue cost or delay in transportation; too, these factors made it exceptional that a community might be both too small to afford a regular court and too isolated to share a regular court with others. The anomalous character of the justice court was heightened by the fact that the best justices were in the more populated areas where a steady flow of business promoted higher standards of personnel and administration. In other words, where the justice court functioned with reasonable satisfaction, it was because it had lost its traditional character and amounted to a regular city court.

In almost a fourth of the states — where most of the auto traffic cases went neither to justice courts nor to special traffic sessions — the county or state court dealt with traffic violators as part of the regular flow of criminal cases. Procedure here was geared to more serious offenses. The courts were not located with reference to the volume of traffic cases, nor were court terms adjusted to speedy disposition of the steady flow of traffic charges. Where the regular courts thus handled traffic cases, they made no formal distinctions in the treatment given traffic violators as compared with other lawbreakers, though in community opinion the traffic violator had not committed a "crime" nor was he a "criminal."

To handle traffic cases through the regular courts generally meant that no attention was given to devising special penalties or corrective measures adapted to enforcement of highway safety. No special training was given county or circuit court judges in handling traffic matters, nor was any special system of court records set up to check repeaters or to aid study of local traffic problems. Quite plainly, where traffic business was thus casually turned over to the regular criminal courts, the prevailing attitude was that traffic prosecutions were a petty annoyance: They hampered the more important business before the courts, and they should be disposed of with summary routine, or be postponed, or the defendant be discharged if any plausible excuse appeared.

The sheer volume of traffic cases, more than anything else, forced more sensible arrangements for the administration of traffic justice. From the middle 1920's the larger cities — where the bulk of traffic cases arose — began to provide specialized treatment in varying degrees for traffic violators. Of municipal courts in 76 cities which Warren surveyed in 1942, 11 devoted 1 or more branches of the municipal court exclusively to traffic matters; 18 set separate days or hours for the hearing of such cases; 14 undertook to group traffic cases for trial in the same session; 2 (Danbury, Connecticut, and Baltimore) had set up special traffic courts; 30 made no effort to differentiate traffic matters.

Segregation of traffic cases was only a first step toward revised administration. But Warren found that few cities had done anything more than this to adapt court organization to the automobile problem. Few judges had special knowledge of traffic matters; most judges held office for short elected terms, and in unified municipal courts duties were often rotated, so that in either case judges had little chance to accumulate experience. Salaries of judges in courts that dealt with traffic cases were typically low; about 70 per cent of the minor court judges with traffic jurisdiction supplemented their judicial salaries with earnings in law practice, and this brought inevitable embarrassments in the conduct of their courts.

In 42 of the 76 cities that Warren studied, prosecutors were assigned to traffic courts, but the attention given traffic prosecutions varied considerably. Few efforts had been made to adapt criminal court procedure to the trial of traffic offenses. Except that no indictment was had, typically as many other steps were involved in the trial of these minor cases as in prosecutions of major crimes. To start the prosecution, there was the unnecessary formality of a summons, or alternatively the accused was brought in by arrest, to the loss of police time and the promotion of bail bond abuses; only a few cities adopted such sensible procedures as to make the policeman's "ticket" the summons, or to hold the driver's license as security for his appearance. Generally a return day was set, which involved the waste of another appearance, for trial, by one who pled not guilty. Formal complaints were often used, though the offense was rarely grave enough to warrant this, and despite the fact that the accused would generally know what the alleged offense was, from the policeman's on-the-spot charge. Usually the courts kept no dockets, which might be used to segregate cases according to their complexity, or to keep records for the ready checking of repeaters and the continuing study of enforcement.

Traffic courts typically did their business in crowded, dirty, and ill-ventilated quarters, with lack of dignity or order. They were apt to dispose of cases in a slipshod or purely routine fashion: Nonappearances averaged one in eight cases and were not consistently followed up. At least a third of the courts were excessively liberal in granting continuances. In over half the jurisdictions he studied, Warren found that "the fix" was a serious problem, and though the police had a large share of responsibility for this, the wide discretion that the judge inevitably had in traffic cases allowed much room for abuse. Conviction typically ran high, averaging around 80 per cent, but in many cases no penalty was actually inflicted, or the penalty was a fine set so low that it could have little possible effect. Warren found that less than 15 per cent of the courts he studied made regular use of drivers' records to help fix punishments. In only a few instances was imagination applied to the development of new enforcement techniques, as in the creation of "violators' schools" where some planned effort might be made to correct the lack of driving skill, or to instill proper attitudes toward traffic regulation and the driver's responsibility.

Many cities did develop "violations bureaus" or "cafeteria courts." This growth was striking evidence that substantial changes in legal organization might be hammered out in unplanned response to the pressure of facts. But it also illustrated the dangers to sound procedure that lay in such a course of events. The violations bureaus or cafeteria courts represented an entirely new practice in criminal law administration: the payment to a police clerk, sometimes even by mail, of a penalty for the violation of a law, without the necessity of a court appearance. In most instances this practice grew out of the practice of the offender's posting a bail bond with the understanding that upon forfeiture it would be accepted as a fine. The amount of the bail bond was, accordingly, set with this purpose rather than that of insuring the defendant's appearance. In 1942 Warren reported that seventy-three of the seventy-six large cities which he had studied followed this practice; the violations bureaus handled probably over 60 per cent of all traffic cases in the medium and large cities.

So long as there was no planned adaptation of the court machinery to the disposition of the great volume of urban traffic cases, a case could be made for the violations bureaus. At least they represented something of a workable response to the serious defects in conventional court handling of traffic cases. They saved time for the public and the police; they did not help to lower public esteem for the law by subjecting citizens to odorous, milling, disorderly courtrooms; they did not make enemies to traffic law enforcement by imposing the incidents of a criminal proceeding on ordinary people who, in general rightfully, did not regard themselves as criminals; and they despatched a large amount of business without jamming court dockets or indulging in the meaningless and undignified fiction of ninety-second "trials."

But administrative disposition of law business had no intrinsic value which made it in itself superior to judicial disposition. Whatever it was, procedure must be appraised according to the policy which the agency enforced, and the standards it observed to protect both public and private interest.

In the administration of traffic law, plainly the important objective was to correct faults and prevent trouble, rather than merely to punish. But most violations bureaus operated mechanically, with emphasis on their clerical functions, and with no regular effort to get at the root of the difficulty which a case might present. Typical violations bureau procedure did not even require that the violator sign a waiver of trial or file a guilty plea; the transaction, in other words, had simply the atmosphere of bargain and sale, a violation-for-a-price. Again, traffic law administration in its nature required the exercise of discretion to a degree which called for surrounding it with some of the safeguards of a judicial process. But over 60 per cent of the cities that had violations bureaus left them entirely under the control of the police. This was probably in part because the violations bureaus began in an adaptation of bail bond procedure, and the police department had traditionally handled the taking of bail; probably it was in part because the ordinary city courts lacked space or staff for the job.

In any case, police administration of violations bureaus, without judicial supervision, typically meant that no one undertook to separate for court trial those traffic cases that involved the public safety, as distinguished from offenses (like overtime parking), that concerned merely the public convenience. At least half of the time it meant that no one regularly checked offenders' records, so that repeaters might be sent before the judge. It meant that no one supervised the desk sergeant's discretion in varying the amounts of fines, so that there was increased chance for "the fix" to operate. All this spelled a situation where the judge had lost ground to the administrator, not because anyone had rationally planned it that way in the public interest, but as a result of sheer drift toward the achievement of certain obvious and not unimportant advantages, at the expense of the really basic purposes which legal control was supposed to serve.

10. DRIFT

Drift was the common note both in the adaptation of urban justice to the small claimant or the poor debtor, and in the kind of mass social regulation that the traffic law exemplified. Indifference rather than opposition, mainly accounted for the slow response to very practical problems. We should neither be surprised, nor glib with moral judgments, over this fact: Inertia is one of the given facts, or even one of the conditions, of social life.

But to overcome such inertia is one of the essential jobs of men who have special knowledge or skill, and it is one of the justifications for men's association into groups organized to do particular jobs. It was in return for this action-against-inertia that, in increasing measure after the twelfth century, western society allowed scope for the increase and use of individual knowledge and skill and the powers gained by association for common ends.

In this light, we should take note of how slowly and to what limited effect lawyers, as individuals or as an organized bar, acknowledged any responsibility for the correction of obvious defects in the machinery of justice. We need not be surprised at their tardy response to such social problems; we shall see in a later chapter that there were assignable reasons for this lack of professional spirit, in the social environment of nineteenth-century United States. But the fact inevitably provokes some moral judgment.

As seems always true, we owe a heavy debt to a more sensitive and energetic minority for progress; there were lawyers' names which stood out in the lists for constructive change. But the general verdict held. Except during the brilliant first years of the nation, in the field of legal structure and administration which was peculiarly his own, it was only in the twentieth century that the lawyer in the United States began to earn his keep. Nowhere was this more so than with respect to the organization and operation of the courts.

CHAPTER NINE

SOCIAL FUNCTIONS OF THE COURTS

We can with assurance appraise the relative importance of the different functions which judges performed in the growth of the United States only when we know a great deal more about our legal history than we do now. Those functions extended widely through the life of the country. Though this text tries to avoid exaggerating the role of the judge, his story cannot be told in any summary fashion. This is the more so because even a sketch of the judiciary requires that we consider in relation to the courts the role of other agencies and institutions; one of the marked characteristics of United States legal history was the extent to which the judicial function was interwoven with the functions of other agencies of the law.

If we must be cautious about the relative weight we give to various judicial jobs, we need not hesitate over listing those jobs. For, despite the theoretical separation of powers, the kinds of work that courts did included every major function of government. We are here concerned with the kinds of jobs the judges undertook, both those formally assigned to them, and those they, in fact, performed regardless of formal assignment. We are only incidentally concerned with the quality of the performance of these jobs; that inquiry can be made only in the context of particular fields of policy administered by the courts and other legal agencies.

Available information for study of the main court functions is very limited. There are almost no statistics of judicial administration for the country as a whole, prior to 1920. Judicial statistics in the United States practically began with the restricted data on federal litigation published in the annual reports of the Attorney General of the United States from 1870. The Conference of Senior Circuit Judges, after it was set up in 1922, took steps which provided more useful data. But a truly broad and scientifically arranged plan of federal judicial statistics had to wait on the creation of the Administrative Office of the Federal Courts, in 1939.

The situation regarding state judicial statistics is no better. In 1885 David Dudley Field reported to the American Bar Association on the desirability of provision for civil judicial statistics in the states. In 1912

New York took some first steps to that end. But throughout the country, except for statistics on divorce actions, the states collected no material amount of data on civil cases until the spread of the judicial council movement in the 1920's. Some statistics on judicial administration in criminal cases are available back to the mid-nineteenth century. But as late as the 1930's only a few more than half of the states had made broad provision for collection of such data. Before the 1920's, moreover, there were no substantial statistics concerning the administrative, as distinguished from the more traditionally judicial, work of the courts — as in receiverships or bankruptcy, for example.

With regard to substantive policy — the development of the common law, the determination of constitutional issues, the interpretation of statutes — judicial performance was inherently less open to quantitative study. Dogged commercial and scholarly effort, occasionally marked by brilliantly comprehensive skill in analysis, produced a mountain of texts from the early nineteenth century on, in the effort to reduce these policy areas of judicial activity to a plausible symmetry. But with such rare exceptions as Holmes's *The Common Law* (1881) or Pound's early writings, until the 1920's legal scholarship threw little light on the actual functioning as distinguished from the formal surface of the law in the courts.

1. Deciding Civil Disputes

Traditional practice as well as lay and professional opinion clearly marked out the central job of the judge: It was to dispose of particular disputes by applying the law to the facts of the parties' situation. This job was commonly thought of as the "trial" of cases; it centered on the drama of the courtroom. Actually, at least within the years for which we have reliable data, this judicial function made itself felt more outside the courtroom than in it.

Of course, judges did an astronomical volume of business in hearings and trials in court during the years of our national history. Even a brief cross section of time presented a staggering total of business done in court. Professor Leon Marshall pointed this out, looking at the situation in 1933:

Annually, these trial courts have not far from 300,000 cases in divorce litigation. They have perhaps an equal number of criminal actions in the courts of general criminal jurisdiction of our states (and a hundred thousand in the federal courts), and millions upon millions in the minor courts — how many, no one knows. In civil actions other than divorce, one can only guess the number; say it is a million in the courts of general jurisdiction and many millions in the minor courts. If we go back only a generation, the grand total for all types of action begins to sound fanciful.

Nonetheless, this vast amount of business disposed of in court was a minor part of the total civil and criminal proceedings begun. Clark and Shulman made a pioneer study of civil suits in New Haven County, Connecticut for the years 1919–1932. Their analysis showed a pattern which was confirmed by later studies elsewhere. Of the cases filed in New Haven County, 1919–1932, 27 per cent were withdrawn and 20 per cent were discontinued, before any court considered them. Excluding mortgage foreclosures (generally disposed of by default), only 40 per cent of the total cases filed were terminated by court consideration; even this figure included as "considered" cases, the border-line categories of cases disposed of by judgment on the pleadings or summary judgment, as well as uncontested divorce decrees. Eighty per cent of divorces and 90 per cent of foreclosures were uncontested, so reducing their call on the court's time. Only 17 per cent of contract cases, and but 16 per cent of automobile negligence cases were disposed of on court consideration; 21 per cent of negligence cases other than auto, and 36 per cent of other miscellaneous suits, were ended with court consideration. In New Haven County, 1919–1932, the pattern of case disposition stayed about the same, except in the particularly novel category of automobile suits. There the percentage of cases considered by the court showed a marked decline over the years, as the total number of such cases and of all other cases mounted.

The New Haven figures as a whole suggested that judges had their widest influence on the disposition of people's disputes by exerting background pressure for the parties to settle cases by negotiation. Over 80 per cent of automobile cases were disposed of without court consideration: The fact suggested that the lawsuit was used as a device to bring the parties together to work out situations in which blame was at least not all on one side or equally distributed. Over 80 per cent of suits about debts or breach of contract were disposed of without court consideration: The fact suggested that the lawsuit was primarily a dunning device, to force the payment of admitted obligations.

If one asked who won the cases that did go to court, the facts supported the same general inference about the nature of the courts' function. In cases considered by the court (omitting mortgage foreclosures, changes of name, actions for construction of wills, or for declaratory judgments), 83 per cent resulted in judgments for plaintiff. In divorce suits, 92 per cent went for plaintiff; but nearly all of these were un-contested cases. In the fields where contest was more the rule, plaintiffs were still mainly the winners — to 82 per cent in the contract cases and 75 per cent in the automobile negligence cases (though only to 54 per cent in other negligence actions). In few types of cases did plain-tiffs win less than defendants; one example was actions for specific per-formance of contracts, where plaintiffs won in 49 per cent of the cases. The general record of plaintiffs' victories further supported the in-ference that the main practical importance of judicial disposition of disputes was in creation of a background pressure for settlement of matters among the parties themselves. But the tendency toward plain-tiffs' victories also suggested that there were practical reasons why more attention should be given to summary procedures to handle much of the business that came to court.

From the 1920's on, the twentieth century began to provide some evidence that there might be a declining trend in the volume of private civil litigation in the states. There were practically no data prior to 1900, however, and the twentieth-century figures were too limited to allow more than a suggestion of the possible trend. In Wisconsin, taking cases filed in 1880 as a base (100), an index of civil suits filed in all courts of record went down steadily from a peak of 364 in 1934 to 216 in 1939–1940; the last figure was at the level of the early 1920's. The drop in cases before the Wisconsin Supreme Court was sharper, from a peak of 174 in 1932 to 109 in 1939–1940, the lowest point since 1890. Califor-nia and Kansas showed similar figures. One might expect decline from the peak volume of the depressed 1930's, as distress litigation gradually passed away. But by 1940 the California, Kansas, and Wisconsin indices had gone to the level of years well before the depression. Business in several state supreme courts showed a like trend. The Supreme Court of Kansas showed a continuing decline in the docket which brought it down 41 per cent from 1922–1937; in Indiana the decline was 46 per cent, 1925–1939; in Massachusetts, 36 per cent, 1926–1938; in Mis-souri, 45 per cent, 1927–1936.

Civil litigation between private parties in the federal courts showed steadier volume. From 1873 to 1920 private civil cases there begun ranged from about 12,000 to 14,000, and thereafter gradually rose to-ward a new, higher level. In 1929 slightly under 21,000 such civil cases were begun in all United States district courts. The total rose slowly to 26,000 in 1933, and declined to 22,000 in 1940, a little above the 1929 level.

In one respect the civil business of the courts seemed to be in a long-range expansion. This was at the expense of the participation of the jury. According to the limited data, the jury was waived in a steadily increasing percentage of cases over the years. To some extent this trend was promoted by the law itself. Statutes set special fees as the price of jury trial; other laws provided that jury trial was automatically waived if suit was filed in certain courts (notably small claims courts), or if no affirmative demand for a jury was made. But allowing for such official encouragement, the trend was marked enough to show that it grew largely out of the independent choice of suitors. The Clark–Shulman figures on New Haven County litigation, 1919–1932, showed that the jury was playing a minor role there. Of the total cases examined, less than 4 per cent ended in a jury trial; of the total cases where jury trial was available, less than 8 per cent were tried by jury. Negligence actions accounted for 73 per cent (automobile negligence actions for 48 per cent) of the jury trials, and contract suits for another 13 per cent. In 97 per cent of the negligence suits it was the plaintiff who claimed jury trial; in about a third of the contract or debt actions the claim was by the defendant. The contrast perhaps implied that people believed that juries sympathized with the underdog. In the contract cases the special advantages of delay might be another factor in defendants' requests for the jury.

2. DECIDING CRIMINAL CASES

In the criminal docket, the courts' case-deciding job developed along a pattern like that in civil litigation. Here, too, the court finally considered only a small fraction of the cases that started through the official mill. Here also it appeared that the courts exerted their widest influence by indirection: By their presence in the background, they contributed pressure toward disposition of most alleged violations of law through out-of-court action among the police, the prosecutor, and the accused.

The overshadowing fact here was the dominant and largely unsupervised discretion of the district attorney, or public prosecutor. This officer was an American creation. The English common law generally left the prosecution of criminal offenses to the initiative of private persons immediately offended by the alleged violation of law, subject to the Attorney General's right to file a nolle prosequi where he deemed this private initiative not in the interest of the Crown. Connecticut created the public prosecutor in 1704, and by the end of the eighteenth century the office was established in American practice, with a function which has been described as a combination of the powers and duties of the English Attorney General and the French *procureur du roi*. From the start the federal government had its prosecutors. The United

States Attorney General first attained some centralized power over the federal district attorneys at the time of the Civil War. But in practice not until about 1909 did the Department of Justice establish ultimate control of federal prosecutions.

None of the states effected a responsible, central supervision over local public prosecutors, comparable to that which the Department of Justice came to exercise in the federal system. The fact that in the states the public prosecutor gained his office by local, popular election reinforced his independence. The judge, according to his force of character, could be master of his courtroom, in control of the conduct of the prosecutor therein. But the prosecutor enjoyed a broad power before matters reached the trial stage. He decided what matters he would present to the grand jury, or in what cases he would file an information; he determined which matters he would press for trial, which he would let slumber in the files, in which he would file a nolle prosequi, and in which on the basis of bargaining with the accused or his counsel he would accept a plea of guilty to a lesser offense than that originally charged. At none of these points did the law typically give the judge any surveillance of the prosecutor's conduct of his office. This omission was particularly remarkable in connection with the filing of the nolle prosequi or the acceptance of a lesser plea; in both instances the prosecutor must formally declare to the court his decision on the handling of the matter, and this might well have led to a requirement that the prosecutor at least file his announced reasons for the action taken.

Where the prosecutor was indifferent, the discretion of the committing magistrate was to that degree enhanced, also at the expense of the practical scope of the trial judge's function. As a result of these various factors, reliable surveys of criminal justice after 1920 showed that only between 15 and 50 per cent of initiated criminal cases reached a final determination of guilt. Moreover, where the accused was found guilty, in the overwhelming number of cases this was on his own plea, and not by a finding of a jury or judge after contest. Though the percentage varied among localities, about 80 per cent of those found guilty in felony cases had pleaded guilty. This pattern was as marked in rural as in urban districts.

Implicit in the scope of power wielded by prosecutor and committing magistrate was the much restricted importance of the jury. Of 13,000 felony prosecutions begun by arrests in Chicago in 1926, for example, less than 500 resulted in jury trials. Moreover, after 1900 a growing number of states in effect increased the trial judge's field of operations, compared with the jury's, by giving the judge broader powers in the selection of jurors, and by permitting the accused to waive jury trial in favor of trial before the judge alone. Defendants used the waiver privilege in such varying degree within the adopting states that one can make no firm generalization about the results. But the tendency seemed to be toward more waivers of jury trial both in felony and misdemeanor cases. In some states — as in Connecticut, Maryland, and Wisconsin — trial by the court became practically the general rule. In 1930 the Supreme Court of the United States indicated that a defendant might waive jury trial in a federal court even in the absence of statutory provision therefor. Up to mid-twentieth century, however, though waiver of the jury had by then been recognized by statute and rule of court, the practice had not become of material consequence in federal courts.

3. TRENDS IN VOLUME OF COURT BUSINESS

That we have reliable statistics for the history of the judicial function only from 1920 is important enough to bear repeating. From that point on, the data, though obviously limited, showed enough consistency to bring out certain framework facts, revealing a comparatively stable pattern in the business of courts in the second quarter of the twentieth century. For the whole time before 1920, one may properly view with skepticism directly proportioned to the confidence of the assertion any generalization about the extent, distribution, and trends of judicial business. Some tentative statements may be made for the years before 1920 on the basis of scattering figures and the contemporary reflection of court work that one finds in letters, reminiscences (usually sentimental and anecdotal), and bar association reports and speeches (usually long on assertion and short on fact).

It is a reasonable hypothesis that courts disposed of steadily, even vastly increasing, volumes of civil litigation through 1900. Thereafter the competition of administrative decision and commercial arbitration began to cut the proportion of dispute business that went to court. Probably operating to the same result after 1900 were important shifts in the prevailing public temper: The country community had emphasized and insisted on the drama of the county courthouse; city people, rich or poor or middling, looked at their legal problems from a viewpoint that was more impersonal, more cost-conscious, more hurrying and business-results-minded. It is true that the growth of cities increased the civil business of the law tremendously, but in the twentieth century it did not bring proportionate increases in business for the courts.

The timing of growth in the criminal docket was probably somewhat different. Criminal court business seems to have been rather stable through the mid-nineteenth century. The sharp upward curve here coincided with the curve of the city's predominance. Of 100,000 persons arrested on criminal charges in Chicago in 1912, for example, over one half were charged with offenses that had not been on the books 25 years earlier. In the criminal cases appealed to the Supreme Court of California in the 1850's, 20 different crimes were involved; the figures for succeeding decades reflected the expanded scope of the criminal law — the criminal appeals of the '60s involved 28 different offenses, those of the '70s 30, those of the '90s 50, and the appeals that came to the court in the years 1900–1926 involved 75 different offenses.

Regular statistics of criminal business in the federal courts began with the Attorney General's report for 1871, on the threshold of the urban-industrial United States. The volume of business increased almost three times by 1895, though for unknown causes it then declined sharply for three years, and leveled off until about 1910. Draft cases in World War I brought a sharp increase in 1917–1918. From then until 1933 the federal courts were flooded with the backwash of Prohibition, both on the criminal and civil dockets. In 13 representative federal districts whose business was studied for varying intervals over the fiscal years 1925–1930, 80.1 per cent of the total criminal cases involved liquor; in the same districts, quasi-criminal cases were 44.1 per cent of the government civil cases decided, and 88.6 per cent of these were based on the liquor laws.

It seems likely that for the country as a whole the great quantitative growth in the criminal docket came later and more abruptly than did the growth in civil business. But after 1910 the story of the criminal docket is like that on the civil side. More and more enforcement activity centered in the work of executive or administrative agencies — before trial, the police and the prosecutor; at and after sentence, the social worker, the probation or parole officer, and the psychiatrist.

4. Deciding Appeals

If common opinion tended to make the trial court the center of drama in the decision of controversies, it assigned central importance to the appeal. Fact and common opinion were not in accord. The available studies showed that in the second quarter of the twentieth century only a minor fraction of the total decided cases went to appeal. As of 1935 it was estimated that in one year more than ten times as many cases were being recorded in the United States as had been reported since the first Reports of decisions were published in this country 150 years before;

since reported decisions were almost all those of the appellate courts, this gave some measure of the small percentage of cases on review. Clark and Shulman found that appeals were taken in only 1.7 per cent of the civil cases that reached decision in the trial courts in New Haven County whose business they studied for the years 1919–1932. If divorce and foreclosure proceedings were omitted in the New Haven County tabulation (these being generally uncontested proceedings), appeals were taken in 13 per cent of the remaining total. A sample of federal district court civil cases, terminated in the year ending June 30, 1930, showed that the losers took to the circuit courts of appeals between 2.5 and 4.5 per cent of the suits under various jurisdictional heads; a little over .1 per cent were taken to the Supreme Court. The average of criminal appeals in a sampling of federal districts for different years between 1925–1930 was 6.9 per cent of the liquor cases and 19.8 per cent of the nonliquor cases. In California from 1929–1935 the number of criminal appeals decided on the merits averaged 157, compared with average felony convictions in between 7000 and 8000 cases.

To put the number and proportion of civil and criminal appeals in still better perspective, we should recall that only a minority of cases filed ever reached decision even by a trial court. The studies, moreover, indicated a strong presumption that the result of a civil or criminal appeal would be the affirmance of the judgment below. The New Haven County study showed 33.8 per cent reversals or modifications of judgment over the 14-year period examined; in 66.2 per cent of the cases the trial court decision was affirmed. In the study of civil cases in the federal courts, it was found that 50 per cent of the decisions appealed were affirmed (a few with judgments modified), 21 per cent were reversed in whole or in part, and in 27.5 per cent appeals were dismissed or withdrawn; disposition figures for the federal criminal appeals were not tabulated. The California figures, 1929–1935, showed 10.6 per cent reversals in the appeals decided on the merits.

5. Judges as Administrators

Certain developments after 1870 gave color for asserting that the courts had added to their basic job of deciding cases a related but distinctive field of administration. The English justice of the peace had administrative duties that were as important as his judicial ones. But from an early date in the United States, even this traditional link between judicial and executive authority was broken — perhaps as a reflection of the distrust of executive power that grew out of contests with Crown officers — and the justice of the peace was generally restricted to judicial power. But from the last quarter of the nineteenth century, a number of changes blurred the lines of the separation of powers as these outlined the scope of the judge's job.

On the civil side, the outstanding development was of the equity receivership. This was primarily in the federal courts and came as a device whereby the management of a railroad in financial difficulties might, with the help of friendly creditors, continue operations for years without being unseated by rivals. On the criminal side, the outstanding event — not of material effect, however, until well into the twentieth century — was the tendency to shift the emphasis from what went on before sentence to what went on in connection with and after sentence. The old stress was almost entirely on the trial of the accused's guilt. The new emphasis was on the effort — helped by special investigators, doctors, and probation and parole officers — to fix sentence in the light of what might increase the chances of rehabilitating the offender; and in addition there was the attempt to treat "sentence" less as a single disposing act, and more as a process of continuing adjustment, which might go on for an unspecified time according to the need.

In between these leading developments of the civil and criminal dockets — and also a twentieth-century product — were efforts to apply more effective methods to the handling of domestic relations problems. Traditional litigation did little except ratify a breakdown in the family. Now the attempt was more at reconciliation, or at getting at the roots of tension through homely adjustments of the family budget, or through more subtle analyses by social worker or psychiatrist. Some jurisdictions provided for special investigations where the custody of children was in question, or set up special staff facilities to check compliance with support money or alimony decrees.

Since these developments made a new core of activity centering originally on the courts, they require notice in this chapter. But this much notice will do. The underlying reality of these various activities was that the court served mainly as the formal source of authority for administrative officers who did the substance of the job. Whether in the operation of a railroad in receivership, or in the treatment of one convicted of crime, or in the repair of a broken home, it was increasingly not the judge but officers who were his subordinates who in the name of the law did the things that most affected the social or human situation involved. So appraised, the work of such new administrative aides of the courts may be viewed in better perspective in the later discussion of the executive branch.

6. The Scope of "Judicial Power"

Our survey has referred almost entirely to certain quantitative indications of what was involved in the courts' job of deciding particular disputes. There was a sense — both formal and substantial — in which this adjudicative job was the sole function of the federal courts, and practically the sole function of the state courts. Article III of the Federal Constitution vested "the judicial power of the United States" in one Supreme Court and in such inferior courts as Congress might from time to time establish. Article III further provided that "The Judicial Power shall extend" to "all Cases" or "Controversies" of defined types. Twice in the first years under the Constitution the Justices of the Supreme Court of the United States were called on to assert that their judicial authority was limited to the decision of bona fide lawsuits.

The first occasion was in response to Congressional legislation which granted to the circuit courts jurisdiction to hear claims for soldiers' pensions, directed the judges to send their findings to the Secretary of War, and provided "That in any case, where the said Secretary shall have cause to suspect imposition or mistake, he shall have power to withhold the name of such applicant from the pension list, and make report of the same to Congress, at their next session." With varying expressions of their common opinion, the Justices in their respective circuits declined to entertain applications under the act, as matters brought before them of right in their judicial capacity.

The circuit court for the Pennsylvania district (Wilson and Blair, Circuit Justices, and Peters, District Judge) rendered the most forthright "opinion." In a joint letter to the President, the members of the court explained that the court could not proceed because the business directed by the act was "not of a judicial nature," and in addition because under the statute the court's findings were subject to the revision of an executive officer and of the Congress. This last feature the judges deemed "radically inconsistent with the independence of that judicial power which is vested in the courts." The issue was presented finally to the Supreme Court in *Hayburn's Case* (1792), on motion for a mandamus to be directed to the circuit court for the district of Pennsylvania, commanding that court to proceed on petitioner's application to be placed on the pension list of the United States. The Supreme Court gave no decision in the matter, since while it had the case under advisement following argument, Congress provided another procedure for handling pensions.

The second, early occasion for the Court to consider the scope of its constitutional authority was provided by action of the President. The use of United States ports by French privateers as bases for operations against English shipping set an embarrassing problem for President Washington. He was anxious to find authoritative support for his interpretation of the country's obligations as a neutral under its treaties and under international law. Deferring to the wishes of his Secretary of State, Thomas Jefferson, the President addressed to the members of the Supreme Court twenty-nine questions relating to the definition of our neutral position. He sought "to know, in the first place, their opinion, whether the public may, with propriety, be availed of their advice on these questions. And if they may, to present, for their advice, the abstract questions which have already occurred, or may soon occur, from which they will themselves strike out such as any circumstances might, in their opinion, forbid them to pronounce on."

After an interval of consideration, the Justices respectfully but firmly refused to give opinions on the questions submitted. They emphasized "the lines of separation, drawn by the Constitution between the three departments of the government."

> These being in certain respects checks upon each other, and our being Judges of a Court in the last resort, are considerations which afford strong arguments against the propriety of our extra-judicially deciding the questions alluded to, especially as the power given by the Constitution to the President, of calling on the heads of departments for opinions, seems to have been *purposely* as well as expressly united to the *Executive* departments.

The full rationalization of the position so early taken awaited elaboration in later opinions. But the Supreme Court had thus established that the terms of Article III were words of limitation as well as a grant of power.

The state constitutions varied in the formulae under which they created systems of courts, and in the extent of power reserved to the legislatures to alter the constitutional arrangements. But, in the absence of constitutional exception, the state courts invariably interpreted their authority as limited to the decision of bona fide lawsuits. The notable constitutional exception to this doctrine was the provision under the laws of a fourth of the states for the rendering of advisory opinions by the judges of the supreme court on important questions of law, at the request of the governor or legislature.

In the United States we early put the doctrine of the separation of powers upon a constitutional basis. This gave special meaning here to the issue of the scope of "judicial" power. Though some of its elements had analogy in English precedent, the concept of what made a valid lawsuit within the constitutional authority of a court to decide, had its own growth in the United States. It is impossible to draw a clear line between those elements of the concept derived mainly from the felt requirements of the constitution and those derived mainly from a sense of judicial proprieties and the desirability of preventing outsiders from imposing on the dignity of the court. Particularly where the constitutionality of legislation was in issue, it was apparent that judges sensitive to the problem were as much concerned for the proprieties as they were for the theoretical limits of power.

The Kansas court made a representative, if not altogether complete statement of the concept of the judicial function when it explained that "Judicial power is the power to hear, consider, and determine controversies between rival litigants as to their personal or property rights, and must be regularly invoked at the instigation of one of the litigants." A court, as such, would decide an issue of law only in a suit between parties who had a legal interest in the determination (in the sense that their past or proposed conduct might be within the scope of the pertinent legal doctrine), who also had an interest-in-fact in the determination, and whose interests were in fact opposed. The issue must be a living one in the parties' interests; it must not have become moot by change of circumstances which robbed the point of any practical concern to the parties, and the issue must not rest too far in the speculative future to make it a matter of tangible, present importance. A court, thus, was not a self-starting agency, nor was it, even when put in motion by the forms of a lawsuit, an agency to declare general doctrines of law. It was an agency to decide bona fide lawsuits, and to declare and apply the law insofar as this was essential to that task.

Legislatures or executive officers did not often put to the test the doctrine which thus limited "judicial" power. The issue was most widely raised after 1920 when statutes provided for the declaratory judgment. The Supreme Court of the United States and the state courts found little difficulty in ruling that such relief was within the bounds of the "judicial" power vested by the constitutions.

Lawyers and their private clients, far more than the agencies of government, felt the practical impact of the doctrine that courts could decide only matters presented within the frame of a "case" or "controversy." What the doctrine meant to them was reflected partly in the Reports and in the Digests, with their thousands of points noted on the pitfalls and obstacles that confronted one who would assemble an adequate record on which to get a court decision.

So much in general the evidence shows. We do not yet have studies which would allow a more discriminating appraisal of the realities of the judicial function — studies which might inquire how frequent were collusive suits or test cases skirting the edge of propriety or judicial power; studies which might explore how often and how effectively courts narrowed their business by refusing to pass on issues that were either moot or too far in the future; studies which might inquire how far suitors and judges stretched the definition of the legal and factual interest that a litigant must show to have standing to raise a given issue.

The Federal Judiciary Act of 1937 provided that the United States might intervene and become a party to present evidence and argument and to appeal, where the constitutionality of an act of Congress affecting the public interest was drawn in question in any court of the United States, in a suit to which the United States was not originally a party. The 1937 statute was in itself evidence that the traditional concept of the "judicial" function had not worked without fault, at least in the area of judicial review. There had, in fact, been efforts to obtain court rulings against the constitutionality of important federal legislation in suits to which the government was not a party, and in which the ostensible adversaries were united in common desire to overturn the statute. Such incidents made the immediate background for the 1937 statute. But it did not prove much, to show that the system did not work without fault: What system did? A good deal of study must be done, before we could venture any really discriminating appraisal of the concept of the judicial function as it affected action. Litigation was certainly important enough in the development of law in the United States to warrant more detailed examination of its premises.

7. FACT AND OPINION REGARDING JUDICIAL FUNCTIONS

What social functions did the courts perform, within this basic framework of the litigious process? In large measure we can answer only with a summary of what men thought about the courts' work, rather than with a recitation of what that work was. We noted that for considerable parts of our history we lacked adequate statistics of judicial administration. This was only part of the difficulty. At best, statistics could not measure the full extent of the courts' social functions. Statistics, if we had them in fullest measure, could only help frame questions, by suggesting trends and distribution of emphasis, leaving still the matter of their explanation. This is true, indeed, of an inquiry into the functions of any social institution that involves the varied and ramifying activity characteristic of a major legal agency. Such an institution in its nature is open at countless points to the impact of other social forces, and in turn at countless points contributes its weight to a social momentum gathered from many sources.

Our best evidence of the courts' social functions over the years of United States history is, then, opinion evidence. Its guaranty must be the quality of the witnesses. Here, unfortunately, we find as sharp a break in the evidence as we did regarding judicial statistics. Every generation has to decide for itself what it believes to be a realistic jurisprudence. To a mind schooled in mid-twentieth-century ideas about the law-in-action in the United States, there was no observer before Holmes (*The Common Law*, 1881), whose word on the judicial process carried much conviction of depth or mature understanding.

The first generation after independence saw a brilliant series of lawyers' disputes and debates about law and the ends of government. But it offered little to our immediate concern regarding the peculiar functions of the judges. The acute distrust which Jeffersonians had toward a Bench filled with Federalists gave them a lively appreciation of the fact that judges had much room for making policy under the forms of declaring law. But this led chiefly to constitutional polemics and provoked no helpful analysis of the general, going business of the courts. The same may be said of later, recurrent crises centering on the judicial power to pass on the constitutionality of legislation — such controversies as rose over the Dred Scott decision, for example, or the Legal Tender Cases. Lawmen in the United States showed early concern with the principles which should guide the "reception" of English common and statute law into our body of law; and early discussions on this matter sometimes touched the power of the courts to lay down community policy. But this talk was general, and often reflected the same political heat as marked the constitutional issues.

In mid-nineteenth century the ambition and energy of David Dudley Field stirred debate over the movement for codification. This discussion necessarily involved certain assumptions as to the nature of the judicial function, and in particular it directed men's attention to the fact that judges inescapably exercised a considerable discretion in the interpretation and application of statutes, however inclusive and detailed the legislation. But this debate proceeded, too, in generalities. And the dispute over the code movement obviously enlisted as much emotion as reason; hence we cannot give full weight to what men then said about the work of courts as evidence of how the courts of their day were operating.

Altogether the nineteenth century produced little fruitful thinking about the social functions of the judges. Men were preoccupied with getting on, and with opening up the country. So far as there was a prevailing legal philosophy it was of a superficially practical and conscience-resting kind that fitted the temper of the time. It divorced the law and its agents from the grubby conflict of interests: The law was a self-sufficient system, its premises lawyer-made, its growth requiring only the logical development of what could be found in the Reports and the treatises. This estimate of the law found classic expression in Langdell's first casebook, on Contracts, in 1871, and Langdell later put in terse summary the principles on which he founded his conquering method of teaching law: "First, that law is a science; secondly, that all the available materials of that science are contained in printed books. . . ."

Though we have no great amount of evidence, and though most of it is, at best, opinion, as to the social functions of the courts through most of the years of United States history, still the evidence supports some propositions with rare unanimity.

8. Courts as Lawmakers

Both trial and appellate courts were major lawmakers in United States history. In the first half of the nineteenth century, within the confines of a "judicial" power limited to disposition of particular disputes, the courts did the vast job of fashioning a body of common law for the main affairs of everyday life. They defined the bases of rights in real property; they laid the foundations for the law of business contracts and commercial instruments; they shaped rudimentary doctrine for such fields of new importance as the law of negligence or of the conflict of laws. From the logic and decisions of John Marshall, in the third quarter of the century the judges made good their title to pass on the constitutionality of legislation; and they used the power to such effect as to make it a material factor in the social balance of power. To 1937 judicial review continued to be a tangible influence on what the legislature did and how it did it, especially in regard to economic regulation. This was nonetheless true, though the effects of judicial review were often misconstrued; its long-range influence was overrated, and what was in practice only delay was sometimes treated as an effectively definitive veto. But, through the drama of judicial review, the courts made the idea of constitutional limitations one of the most powerful elements in our political thinking.

The task of statutory interpretation took on increasing importance in the role of the courts. This development paralleled the growing importance of judicial review in the late nineteenth century; it was a response to the same heightened activity in social legislation which had stimulated the obstructive talents of the "constitutional lawyers."

The interpretation of statutes offered a truly creative job for the judges. But the chances of events long obscured the creative opportunity. The legislature and its works fell far in popular standing in the second quarter of the nineteenth century. But at the same time the newly forming states felt the urgent pressure of practical needs for law to meet their everyday needs and the everyday problems of the people. The response to this pressure afforded the first great manifestation of judicial lawmaking in the United States. Out of this period of policy leadership, the courts learned confidence in their own capacity to decide what was best for the community. For example, in the late nineteenth century, judges were not inclined to look favorably on legislation which, like the married women's property acts, changed doctrine which judges had made the law of the land. There was more involved than a conflict of policy ambitions. Social conservatism brought the full flowering of due process doctrine at the end of the century; the same impetus also inclined the courts, where they were not ready boldly to declare social legislation unconstitutional, to interpret it so restrictively as to narrow its effect.

These factors found expression in the abstract canons of statutory interpretation which liberally ornamented judicial opinions after the '70s: strict construction of statutes in derogation of the common law; strict construction of penal statutes, or of legislation that imposed "drastic" burdens, or of legislation that imposed special damages, or of legislation that could be fitted to one or another of various tags.

The effect was to put a primarily obstructive, if not destructive connotation on the process of statutory interpretation. And insofar as this was not the temper of approach, nineteenth-century lawmen tended to rate legislation or its proper handling as of secondary importance in the law. This depreciation of the statute book was promoted by the preeminence of case-made, judge-made law in the formative first half of the nineteenth century; and this was reinforced, first, by the office-apprentice system of legal education, and then by the spread of the case method in the law schools. Legislation was an intrusion on a symmetrical system of learning properly found only in the Reports. One could to general satisfaction summarily distinguish a cited case if he could brush it aside as merely "turning on the particular statute involved."

The slowness with which courts drew on the full resources of legislative history in the interpretation of statutes was a measure of their lack of interest or sympathy toward the legislative process; or, equally, it measured their failure to understand what was implied in a true effort to carry out their often-announced duty to find "the intention of the legislature." As late as 1897 a leading opinion of the Supreme Court of the United States noted "general acquiescence in the doctrine that debates in Congress are not appropriate sources of information from which to discover the meaning of the language of a statute passed by that body."

But it was in the trend of events that statutory interpretation should form one of the positive contributions of the courts to the making of law. Only the legislature — with its control of the purse, its powers of investigation, and its varied array of benefits and sanctions — could begin to cope with the demands made on government after the 1870's. But experience taught that the best-drawn statute was only the starting point of effective regulation; this was inevitable, out of the limits set by language and men's foresight, as well as by the infinite variety of events and causes. The measure of understanding, sympathy, and vigor with which the executive or the judges implemented a statute decided how far it became a living fact of the community life.

Between about 1880 and 1920 legislation again became, as it once had been, the main growing point of the law in the United States. By 1920 administrative legislation shared this distinction. In either case, after 1880 the leadership in making general policy had passed from the courts; their creative opportunity had become the subordinate, but essential, task of imaginative, firm implementation of legislative policy.

The decisions after 1900 began to reflect a more affirmative and practical, a less negative and literal, approach, in response to the pressure of this shift in the political situation. Tangible witness of the change was in the shifting techniques of interpretation. The canons of construction whose elaboration filled the pages of nineteenth-century treatises began to disappear from judges' opinions. After 1920 it became hard to assemble from the Digest any substantial citations to so familiar a late-nineteenth-century shibboleth as the rule that statutes in derogation of common law must be strictly construed. Before it had explicitly validated the change, in practice the Supreme Court of the United States began to drop the barriers to full use of the history of a statute as light upon its meaning. Where there had been absolutely phrased rules of competency that barred use of hearings, debates, committee reports, there appeared by the 1930's more or less explicit recognition that almost any official source contemporary with the passage of a statute might be used in its interpretation. The effect of such background evidence was to be gauged by its credibility, and not by its compliance with formal rules of competence.

Significant of the realism of the new approach was the particular weight given to materials that directly reflected how a modern legislalature worked. This meant according particular attention, on the legislative side, to committee reports and to the remarks made in debate by leading committeemen; it meant, on the executive side, particular weight to executive messages and letters, in reflection of the executive's growing leadership in the legislative program; it meant, on the administrative side, attention to evidence of a long-continued, uniform, practical construction of the statute by men who, charged with immediate responsibility for effecting its objects, might be deemed aware of what was needed to make it work, men who oftentimes had sponsored the statute before the legislature as a response to their administrative experience.

In the law at least, mere technique guarantees no one result; there remains inescapably "the sovereign prerogative of choice." In 1940 as well as in 1890 the interpretation of statutes inevitably demanded that the courts share in making policy. One could still find examples — one was the restrictive interpretation of state statutes which curbed the use of the injunction in labor disputes — where judges hostile or distrustful toward the legislative judgment clearly shaped construction to minimize the effect of a statute. Only the naïve could not see that in adroit hands the "history" behind an act might be read in different ways: The new technique of using legislative history in interpretation might widen, rather than narrow, the judge's discretion.

Nonetheless, the new approach lent itself less than the old to manipulation in the interests of the judge's personal values. It was most insistent on a demonstrated basis in fact, for the interpretation given the legislation. And in any case its basic importance was that it showed a shift in the prevailing attitude toward statute law. Late-nineteenth-century judges rationalized their interpretations under abstract canons of construction which had no necessary relation, and required no showing of any specific relation, to the legislation in question. Clearly there was a drastic change in approach, when courts sought to view an act in terms of its own particular genealogy, and in effect to fashion their principle of construction from the materials of the statute's own environment and origins.

The change perhaps reflected the pragmatism which characterized thought in the United States after the turn into the new century. Certainly it evidenced a shift in the climate of opinion affecting the balance of power. Perhaps the judges merely shared the self-doubt of their generation. Perhaps they yielded more or less consciously to the weight of events which had thrust the initiative in policy on the legislative and executive branches. In any case, in the second quarter of the twentieth century judges plainly lacked the serene self-confidence and assurance of wisdom and rightness with which their predecessors had made a native common law and, firmly and sometimes arrogantly, had explicitly or under guise of interpretation wielded a veto over legislative judgment.

The foregoing catalog of judicial lawmaking — in common law, constitutional limitations, or statutory interpretation — does not distinguish the functions of appellate and trial courts. Since few trial court decisions or opinions were reported, the appellate courts naturally had the more prominent role in the declaration of policy. But, if there were no other evidence, the contrast between the huge volume of trial court business and the small percentage of cases appealed would have suggested that a large share of the working policy shaped by judges was made in the unappealed cases. The largest body of reported trial court decisions — those of the federal district courts — offered evidence to support this inference. The scant studies of lower court law in the states confirmed the point.

9. THE SPECIAL FUNCTIONS OF THE FEDERAL COURTS

A special question was presented by the policy-making role that the federal courts played in holding the federal balance. The First Judiciary Act gave to the district and circuit courts jurisdiction, respectively, in admiralty and over suits between citizens of different states and over criminal or quasi-criminal prosecutions brought by the federal government. Thus the act implied the three main special tasks which the lower federal courts were to share with the Supreme Court in making a workable system out of a dual sovereignty.

Congress granted the admiralty jurisdiction because it wanted uniform doctrine in what was then the principal field of commerce. But it was the Supreme Court, rather than Congress, which most strikingly asserted that federal judges had a responsibility to create uniform legal doctrine affecting commerce. In 1842 in *Swift* v. *Tyson*, Mr. Justice Story, speaking for the Court, ruled that in suits between citizens of different states the federal courts were free to follow their conception of the law rather than any particular doctrines announced by the courts of a state, at least so far as concerned the general principles of commercial law. The years brought much debate as to how much uniformity the Supreme Court achieved through the assertion of this independence. There was no clear proof that it promoted any substantial harmony of doctrine that would not otherwise have developed. In 1938 in *Erie*

Railroad Co. v. *Tompkins,* the Court reversed *Swift* v. *Tyson.* It declared broadly that, save as the Federal Constitution or statutes governed a situation, the federal courts must apply the law of the appropriate state.

Congress apparently granted the federal courts jurisdiction in cases between citizens of different states because it feared that nonresident suitors would find prejudiced treatment in state courts. Particularly from the 1870's on, it was recurrently argued that this jurisdiction should be withdrawn. It was said that, whatever its onetime validity, the original reason no longer had substance, and that the diversity jurisdiction put a substantial burden of no federal concern on courts that were heavily enough laden with business peculiarly their own.

The argument never brought serious threat that the Congress might abolish the diversity jurisdiction; nor did the discussion produce satisfactory evidence on which one might weigh the merits. Some claimed that diversity jurisdiction had been essential to the growth of nationwide commerce and investment; this was a more up-to-date version of the original rationalization for its creation. Its supporters also argued that diversity jurisdiction had promoted uniformity in legal doctrine, especially as to commercial questions. However, there was no way to separate the possible influence of the federal courts on the country's economic growth through their diversity jurisdiction, as compared with their decisions under the commerce clause, for example, or under federal legislation affecting the economy.

The most common thesis was that in practice diversity jurisdiction chiefly served the interest of corporation litigants. After the 1840's the Supreme Court, by legal fiction, was willing to treat a corporation as the equivalent of a citizen of the state of its incorporation, for purposes of diversity jurisdiction. Thus, said critics of the jurisdiction, the Court had given corporations the chance to harass local suitors by removing proceedings from a state to a federal court, or by bringing suit in a more remote federal court. Thus, too, said the critics, corporations could bring their cases before judges thought to be more sympathetic to business interests. There are no complete surveys of diversity-jurisdiction cases for different periods. But in the 1930's one half to three quarters of these cases involved foreign corporations; nearly 90 per cent of the cases removed from state to federal courts under this jurisdictional claim were removed on motion of a foreign corporation. Such facts, however, did not of themselves reveal the role that diversity jurisdiction might be playing — whether as a legitimate protection or convenience of interstate business, or whether as a means by which the more wealthy and knowing suitor might oppress the weaker. Despite much confident assertion both ways, no one knew.

In giving the federal courts original jurisdiction of federal criminal and quasi-criminal proceedings, the First Judiciary Act implied that they had a special responsibility to see that national policy was loyally enforced. Not until 1875 did Congress put on the federal courts the full possible extent of this responsibility, in civil as well as in criminal matters.

We must distinguish two aspects of this responsibility as federal agents. Congress occasionally put special reliance on the federal courts where it foresaw serious danger that state courts might be unsympathetic, or actively hostile, to enforcement of a locally unpopular national policy. Such was the background of jurisdiction conferred by the Force Act of 1833 and under some Reconstruction legislation. The proof is lacking that in this respect the federal courts materially affected any crises in the relation between nation and states. Of course, they may, by their mere existence as close-at-hand symbols and national instruments, have contributed to temper local attitudes. However, this is speculation.

On the other hand, the national government grew to need its own judicial agents for more constant, if less dramatic reasons. As it extended its regulatory activity, the volume of litigation involving its policies expanded enormously. Federal courts undoubtedly handled federal business more thoroughly and speedily than could state courts which were already burdened with local concerns. This seems a reasonable hypothesis; we could test it, however, only in the wholly improbable event that Congress should abolish the lower federal courts and throw all federal-rights litigation into the state courts.

From the time of John Marshall the Supreme Court of the United States held a position of unusual authority. The First Judiciary Act empowered it to review decisions of the highest state courts in matters of federal right. Against this background, the Court over the years performed a function which, of all the aspects of federal judicial business, most plainly related to the peculiar problems of a dual sovereignty. With characteristically dispassionate appraisal of his own institution, Mr. Justice Holmes once observed:

> I do not think the United States would come to an end if we lost our power to declare an Act of Congress void. I do think the Union would be imperiled if we could not make that declaration as to the laws of the several States. For one in my place sees how

often a local policy prevails with those who are not trained to national views and how often action is taken that embodies what the Commerce Clause was meant to end.

Holmes, that is, did not believe that the peculiar function of the Court in the federal system was to protect property or business within the states, through the Fourteenth Amendment; rather, it was to safeguard the national free-trade area and the channels of communication among the states, under the limitations which Marshall had fashioned from the commerce clause.

The commerce clause, in terms, simply granted power to Congress. In theory, Congress might legislate against Balkanizing laws or practices of the states. In a measure Congress did do that, as in the Interstate Commerce Act. But Congress proved a slow and ponderous machinery with which to meet the frequent, complicated, and varied challenges which parochial interests presented to nation-wide commerce. The normal inertia of legislation was the more important in this field, because local interest was likely to be tangible, immediately felt, and ardently pursued; the general interest was diffuse, hard to organize into equally effective counterpressures. For the guarding of national social and economic unity, there was, therefore, special merit in a body like the Court. It was almost always in session, was compact in numbers for speedy decision and action, was insulated from local pressures, and was by tradition a national institution.

In exercising this peculiarly federal function, the Court acted mainly under the commerce clause. However, particularly after 1890, it made creative use of other constitutional sanctions. It broadened the resources of the full faith and credit clause, and it invoked due process doctrine to limit the states in their efforts to regulate transactions which the Court felt lay too far outside the proper concern of the regulating state to warrant its impositions.

The Reports offer some measure of the impact of the Court's federal function. In 1932 Gavit listed well over three hundred cases in which the Court had upheld state regulation, and well over two hundred in which it had declared state laws invalid, under the tests of commerce clause doctrine. But, as in other connections, existing studies do not provide a fully satisfactory basis for appraising the job done. We do not know how much of the total of state legislation hostile to commerce clause principle was brought to court, or what was the practical compliance with the Court's rulings and doctrine throughout the country.

On a related question, however, the answer seemed more clear. In theory, the Court might be as alert to check encroachment by the central government on the constitutionally reserved powers of the states as it was to bar state interference with nation-wide concerns. By 1932 in only a few more than a score of cases had the Court held that Congressional laws exceeded the Congress's authority under that broadest of peacetime grants of power, the commerce clause. No more than three or four of these cases involved matters of fundamental importance. And up to 1932 the Court had found in the commerce clause authorization for over three hundred and fifty challenged acts of Congress. The Child Labor Cases (1918, 1922) intimated a sterner exercise of the judicial veto, and in 1934 and 1935 the Court made spectacular assertion of its authority over Congress. But as the sum stood in 1937, the Court had effectively renounced any function of close supervision over Congressional acts challenged as encroachments on state power. Its renunciation could be read in its broad interpretation of the substantive powers granted to the federal government, and in its restrictive definition of the standing of federal taxpayers to challenge the spending of federal funds. Barring very basic shifts in doctrine, the Court seemed ready to limit its future function as federal balance wheel to the job of curbing local interest.

10. DECIDING CASES WAS PART OF LAWMAKING

What, in all of this, happened to the elementary job of the courts, of disposing of the everyday run of disputes at law? By authoritative definition, this was the sole proper business of men who held "judicial" power: Even the grandest display of judicial policy making must proceed within the framework of a lawsuit.

The more dogmatic late-nineteenth-century philosophy — if it can be so dignified — asserted that the courts made no policy: They found the facts (or allowed the jury to do so); to the facts they applied rules of law which, if not plainly at hand, were inexorable deductions from a self-contained body of legal principle. In the shaping of that self-contained body of principle, no given court had scope for creative effort. In the most strict sense, this analysis insisted that courts did nothing except dispose of particular disputes.

This became a wholly inacceptable theory, to twentieth-century observers. It is impossible to accept it as a realistic account of what went on in courts at any stage of our history. To the contrary, we may reasonably take the hypothesis that each of the millions on millions of cases which courts disposed of over past years inevitably represented some creative contribution to the forming of public policy. However clear the "law," the applicable law must always be selected by the determination of the "facts" of the case, since it is only in terms of the facts found that a given rule becomes the relevant guide to decision. The infinite variety of circumstance and the hazards of proof, if nothing else, would insure that value judgments must be made even in what appear the most straightforward cases, in the finding of the "facts."

If we agree that policy making or lawmaking inhered in the whole range of the judicial process, we need not therefore deny that the simple disposition of disputes also involved the performance of social functions. The courts allowed the peaceable end of wasteful conflict, and contributed to men's ability to rely on certain expectations arising out of other people's conduct. These seem reasonable inferences, for example, from the fact that the overwhelming proportion of filed suits was typically ended without the need of court consideration — or from the fact that the overwhelming percentage of cases that did go to court never went beyond the trial court. There was certainly evidence of serious defects in the system — for example, in the high percentages of unsatisfied civil judgments, and the high proportion of criminal cases in which after sentence no penalty was in fact imposed. But the defects did not disprove the positive contribution.

Perhaps the most profound social function which the courts served, through the simple fact that they were available to hear and decide disputes, was the strength that this imparted to popular confidence in law in the United States — that is, to the legitimacy of government. The shrewdest observers of society in the United States repeatedly commented on the central place that law held in people's thinking about public affairs in all periods of our history. People in the United States were anxious to reduce public issues to legal issues, and to justify their notions of policy by appeal to legality. Behind such thinking was a widespread popular conviction that in a meaningful sense men had "rights" which they could go to court to enforce. We noted the tough vitality of localism as the organizing principle of the court systems in this country. This fact evidenced the inarticulate insistence of popular tradition and opinion upon the courts as guarantors of the individual's security, and the consequent feeling that, as his courts, they should be close to him. Despite occasional scandal, and despite characteristic American skepticism of the virtue of all public officers, no men holding official power stood so consistently high in public trust as did the judges. Given the colorful controversy that swirled about judicial review, this popular status of the judges seems to have grown in spite of, rather than because of, the judges' overt policy making. It rested on the respect which people accorded to officers whom they viewed as primarily responsible for giving honest decisions of controversies under the law. Not the least disquieting aspect of our judicial history was the extent to which this sturdy regard for the courts may have been shaken since 1890 — not by corruption or evil-doing, but by the demonstrated inadequacies of the system in making justice available to the poor and to people of small means, and by the weakness of its procedures, its investigating processes, and its available sanctions for coping with issues presented by the concentration of economic power.

IV. The Constitution Makers

CHAPTER TEN

THE CONSTITUTION-MAKING PROCESSES

1. The Idea of Constitutionalism and the Agencies for Making Constitutions

This history began with the legislature and the courts, because it was these agencies which dominated the growth of the law for 100 years after the start of the period with which we are concerned. In the generation before 1790, and for nearly a generation after 1790, the legislature commanded the scene; by the 1820's the courts had begun two generations of leadership.

During their respective periods of command, legislatures and courts controlled the making of constitutional law. Early constitutions were often made by legislative bodies; in any case they were made in a legislative atmosphere, of practical compromise and adjustment. Both legislative and judicial practice and philosophy shaped the working content of constitutional law.

On the other hand, the constitution-making process had a character of its own, which calls for separate examination. The first state constitutions and the Federal Constitution embodied elementary, and therefore powerful, ideas about the frame of government, the relations which government agencies should bear to each other, and the general limitations on official power.

At the outset we must distinguish between three methods of constitution making: (1) by convention, (2) by legislative proposal, and (3) by the initiative, in the three or four states that adopted this form and put it to use.

We must also distinguish between these institutions for making constitutional law and the idea of constitutional government. This chapter tells of the institutions rather than the idea, except as the latter helped form the institutions. As we continue, we shall see why people went to the trouble of using the formal processes of constitution making in order to pass what amounted often simply to specific legislation.

The fact that people in the United States insisted that their government rest on written constitutions stems from certain political ideas that were strong at the start of our national life. The founders organized the colonies under trading-company charters, proprietary grants, or royal charters. People thus became used to the idea that a government owed its moral power to formal grant from a higher authority. In the great debate leading to independence, our spokesmen rationalized this acceptance of past practice. Borrowing from political philosophy, notably from that of Harrington and Locke, they added the idea of "the people" as the natural source of the grant of authority.

So, when the colonies became states, eleven of them adopted constitutions as one of the first items of business, even though they were in the rush of a revolution. The other two, Connecticut and Rhode Island, did not neglect the matter of a fundamental law. They contented themselves with some changes in their old royal charters, under which they already held considerable powers.

On the other hand, a constitution for the nation grew less out of accepted ideas than from the practical need to put into tangible form an agreement on the terms on which we should carry out what was a very new sort of venture. The framers of the Articles of Confederation and the Constitution responded to very practical needs. But they also added finality to the idea of constitutionalism in the United States. Both documents, and especially the Constitution because of its success, put it beyond question that henceforth legitimate governments in the United States must rest on written constitutions. Thus was provided the occasion for development of distinctive machinery for making constitutions.

The people fixed the requirement of a written constitution in tradition rather than in law. There is no formal requirement that a state have a constitution. Article IV, Section 4, of the Federal Constitution does say that "The United States shall guarantee to every State in this Union a Republican Form of Government . . ." But the Supreme Court refused to decide whether the frame of government in a state met the test of Article IV, Section 4. This is a political and not a justiciable question, said Mr. Chief Justice Taney, in *Luther* v. *Borden* in 1849. In 1912 the Court reaffirmed this ruling, and refused to decide whether by making the initiative and referendum part of its constitutional machinery a state departed from a "Republican Form of Government."

Congress in effect decides whether a state has the republican form of government that the Constitution guarantees; it does this when it decides to admit new states, and when from time to time it admits the Senators and Representatives elected from the states. The President might have to decide the question, by using or withholding federal troops; President Tyler was ready to do so in 1841 when Rhode Islanders of different factions disputed the title to their government in the contest that gave rise to the case of *Luther* v. *Borden*.

But neither President nor Congress could find support in the history of Article IV, Section 4, for requiring that a state adopt a written constitution. The framers debated and reworked the phrasing of the guaranty clause in the Constitutional Convention; they were anxious to make clear that, in effect, the only authority thereby given the federal government was to resist violent efforts to overturn state governments. By their careful choice of words they quite plainly meant to exclude interference with peaceful political processes. Of course Article IV, Section 3, says that "New States may be admitted by the Congress into this Union," and the Supreme Court said this allowed Congress to set the terms of admission. Congressional practice early conditioned the entrance of a new state on the adoption of a constitution satisfactory to Congress. This requirement, of course, gained peculiar urgency from the long effort to hold the balance between North and South.

The idea of government-under-a-constitution marked the processes of constitution making in another way. Constitutions have on the whole proved to be difficult to change, partly because their framers made the machinery of change hard to work. Both the nature of the machinery and the slowness of change were due partly to the fact that a lot of people believed such was the proper characteristic of constitutions. *The Federalist* expressed such an idea of constitutional government; the same idea figured in many a state battle over the calling of a constitutional convention; and men had much to say about it when they debated whether they should provide for constitutional amendment by popular initiative.

But except in these ways, the general idea of constitutional government did not decisively shape the form of the constitution-making machinery, or the way in which it worked. For example, there is the important question, what makes people regard a government as legitimate, and entitled to obedience. Legitimacy deals with a very practical fact of politics: a stable and enduring government rests only on the acceptance, if not the active consent, of most of the people who live under it. People accept or consent to a government that they believe shows some title that they feel carries some moral conviction.

Plainly the idea of legitimacy, in some form, is inherent in the general notion of a government that exists subject to constitutional limitations. You might expect, therefore, that one of the first things that would concern those setting up constitution-making machinery would be this: that they would fix a procedure that would insure against sub-

stantial cloud on their title to make a constitution or on the validity of
what they made. But this did not happen; we built our constitution-
making procedures out of a generation of practice, rather than out of
the logical development of any clear-cut idea of constitutionalism.
Men did not for some time realize that independence was going to
come out of their fight with England; too, they had no precedent for
the jobs they faced, of making new states and a new confederacy; and
what they had to do, they had to do in a hurry and amid confusion.
So there was much legally dubious procedure and a good deal of difference in practice when the first states called constitutional conventions between 1775 and 1789. Most of the bodies that framed constitutions adopted in this formative period had not originally been elected
to do any such job, nor had they been given any specific mandate for
it. Most of them did not submit to popular ratification the constitutions
that they drew.

The Continental Congress, by its resolutions of May 10 and 15, 1776,
perhaps meant to recommend that the legislatures in the states adopt
permanent instruments of government. From 1776 through 1778 eleven
constitutions were so framed and adopted in ten states, by bodies that
were, in view of their lack of a mandate for this work, revolutionary
in a legal and not merely a rhetorical sense. Only five of the state constitutions adopted by 1789 were put into effect through machinery
specially made for the purpose, and one of these was submitted to no
form of popular ratification. After 1789, at least thirteen conventions in
twelve states newly formed from United States territories were irregularly called, because they were not authorized by Congress; of
course in effect Congress later ratified these constitutions when it admitted the states. There were striking departures from regular procedure in the revision of existing constitutions in Pennsylvania in 1789,
Delaware in 1792, Rhode Island in 1841, and Maryland in 1850. Six
of the constitutions adopted in the formative period before 1790 contained no provision for their amendment. Clearly, the procedures for
constitution making in the states did not spring full grown from some
ideal conception of constitutional government. Rather, they grew in
fifty years of practice formed by experience.

If we look at what people put into their constitutions, we find a second case where an idea logically inherent in the concept of a constitution did not take hold in practice. Ideally, a constitution embodies only
the fundamentals of government. Opponents of proposed amendments
often raised this argument in the states. But, at least after the 1840's, the
states amended their constitutions to include large amounts of procedural detail and specific legislation. That they did so was remarkable on

two counts: Not only did the practice depart from the general notion of the dignity of constitutions; it also violated the proved practical wisdom of not freezing detailed policy into a form hard to change.

When we compare the idea of constitutionalism with the ways in which the constitution-making machinery worked, by far the most important contrast concerns the origins of the popular reverence for "the constitution." Our constitutional law begins in a very practical setting. Men framed, fought over, and adopted the first state constitutions and the Federal Constitution in an atmosphere of the utmost political realism. They saw they were dealing with the balance of power between interests, and they were frankly skeptical of the permanency of what they had done. The sanctity that came to surround the idea of constitutional principles was the growth of years and of many influences. It was fostered by the logic and prose of *The Federalist*, Marshall, and Webster; by the reverential histories of Fiske, Hildreth, and Bancroft; by the gathering of emotion and tradition about symbols by which generations fought their political battles; by the crystallization of doctrine by Cooley, and its practical development at the hands of big-business lawyers of the late nineteenth century.

Popular reverence for the "constitution" had important results in our law. For one thing, it secured broad and deep acceptance of the courts' role in enforcing constitutional limitations. In turn, the activity of the courts in appealing to the higher law undoubtedly strengthened people's belief in the value of constitutional limitations. Thus the idea of constitutionalism shaped, and was shaped by, the institutions of constitution making. But, however much it owed to the court, the reverence attached to "the constitution" gained little force from the operation of the more formal process for making constitutional law, by convention or amendment. Nor did the idea of constitutionalism substantially affect the way those processes worked.

This is not quite the paradox that it first appears. Except for the late invention of the initiative, the methods of formal constitution making became well established before 1850. But it is not at least until then, and mainly after the 1880's, that the constitutional idea fully enters the catalog of basic American beliefs. Only after 1880 does it become a powerful weapon in political and economic battles. Moreover, as has been suggested, we went about writing our early constitutions in a very practical atmosphere. Madison's notes of the Federal Convention, Elliot's records of the state ratifying conventions, and the history of such important early state conventions as those that produced the Massachusetts constitution of 1780 and the revision of 1820–1821, the Connecticut constitution of 1818, or the Pennsylvania constitutions of 1776, 1790, and 1838 show a uniformly realistic approach to the job. Like their successors, the first makers of constitutions saw their work in terms of contests for power and advantage, or the security of power and advantage already won. Sanctity, legend, symbolism did not spring from the immediate operations of formal constitution making, nor did they substantially direct those operations.

2. THE CONSTITUTIONAL CONVENTION

There has of course been but one Federal Constitutional Convention in our history, and never any serious effort to hold another. But since 1776 over 200 state conventions have met to adopt or revise constitutions. It is hard to make a reliable count of those conventions that produced working constitutions, because so many different kinds of circumstances were involved. But by any tally at least one third of these conventions produced no addition to the law. Such a count includes those conventions that adjourned without recommendations, those whose recommendations were rejected at the polls, those that were called only to ratify constitutions proposed by others, and those that were revolutionary bodies whose ventures failed.

The total of creative conventions was still impressive; the convention was not an insignificant member in our hierarchy of legal agencies, though its importance was sometimes exaggerated. Moreover, we used conventions enough to develop quite a body of practice as to procedures. This body of practice was the main stuff of any analysis of the working structure of the institution. There were few court decisions to help: Lawsuits did not often arise over the mechanics of making constitutions. The courts cautiously refused to decide the more far-reaching issues in this field; they labeled rather than explained their caution by calling the questions political and not justiciable. The area was notable as one of the few in which judges consistently practiced self-restraint in the exercise of judicial review.

a. The Proposal of Constitutions

A constitution might be amended by proposals passed by the legislature and submitted to the people; such was the standard practice. Theoretically, legislators could thus propose an entirely new or completely revised constitution. The Nebraska territorial legislature drew and submitted to the people the Nebraska constitution of 1866. But, with this exception, we firmly fixed the practice of using conventions to prepare an original or to make a general revision of an existing constitution.

The agencies that drew most of the constitutions adopted during the War for Independence had not been specially called for this purpose. This was largely due to the pressure of the times. Massachusetts set the enduring pattern by its procedure in adopting its constitution of 1780: It submitted to the voters the question of calling a constitutional convention; it used that distinct agency for the framing of a constitution, and submitted the convention's product to the voters. This constitution was the political testament of John Adams; as might be expected there was an unusual measure of intellectual leadership behind the whole venture. But the careful double submission to the voters and the use of the separate agency of the convention seem to have come from a wide belief that this was the proper way to do the job.

The central idea of the convention took hold readily. But there was much variation in the procedures for calling such bodies and approving their work. Men showed little sense of the high danger of allowing any question to exist about the legitimacy of agencies charged with so basic a task. Potentially, the most serious question was, who might lawfully take the initiative in calling a convention. From the late nineteenth century on, constitutions commonly said that this authority was in the legislature. Before that time the matter was often uncertain. The courts seem never to have claimed the power. Presidents Lincoln and Johnson called conventions in certain seceded states. They claimed authority as commander in chief; Congressional partisans contested the claim, and students have doubted its merit. With these exceptions, the executive branch did not take the initiative in calling constitutional conventions. Pennsylvania, for a brief time, and Vermont until 1867, experimented with a Council of Censors especially charged with the proposal of constitutional changes; in neither case was the device found satisfactory.

The legislature might thus have appeared to hold the initiative in constitutional changes, if only by default of other agencies. But two difficulties remained. One was readily answered. Many constitutions, and almost all of those adopted after the 1820's, provided that the voters should pass on amendments proposed by the legislature; from this it was argued that such was by implication the only proper way to amend. The courts held this to be a justiciable question, and found little trouble in answering it. They ruled that a general revision of a constitution, done in convention, was so different from specific amendment that the provision for proposal of specific amendments could not fairly be interpreted to bar general revision by convention. This recognized what had become well-settled practice, backed by popular acceptance; in 1887 Jameson noted twenty-seven conventions that had been called for constitutional revision under the general authority of the legislature. Rhode Island had a long history of trouble over its constitution, and there alone had judges denied the legislature's power to call a convention. But in 1935, in a decision not without political overtones, the Rhode Island Supreme Court overruled local precedent and held that the legislature might summon a convention even though the constitution did not expressly authorize it.

The second challenge to the legislature's power was more rare, but far more serious. If the people were sovereign, why might not they initiate constitutional reform by direct action? Rhode Island provided the test case. By 1840 constitutional change was long overdue in that state. Upon gaining independence, the state kept the form of government set up under royal charter. Under this, the right to vote was sharply limited, and those who held power under this limited franchise blocked demands for constitutional revision which might extend the right to vote. Thomas Wilson Dorr, a courageous lawyer of principle, led a popular party in the drive for change. The blind opposition of the party in power seemed to bar all hope of reform through a convention called by the legislature. Therefore after due notice the Dorr party ran a state-wide election of their own contriving, for selection of a "People's Convention."

In 1841 this convention framed a constitution and submitted it to popular vote. The "People's Convention" constitution was adopted in December, 1841 by a claimed vote of 13,944. This was a clear majority of the 23,000 adult male citizens of the state; and the Dorr party claimed that 4960 of the 13,944 favorable votes were cast by persons who had the vote under the existing charter, and who amounted to a majority of the approximately 9000 voters qualified thereunder.

Dorr was elected governor, and a legislature was elected with him, both asserting authority under the new constitution. The two parties armed and prepared to make good their titles by force. The old charter government had the larger and more resolute army. Dorr's band was broken up in a skirmish, and Dorr was later convicted of treason against the state and imprisoned for life. It was an action for trespass, arising out of the activity of the charter government militia, that occasioned the opinion of the Supreme Court of the United States in *Luther* v. *Borden*. There the Court declared that the legitimacy of a state government presented a political and not a justiciable issue.

The Dorr party's efforts were not in fact vain. The old charter party called a constitutional convention in June, 1842. The convention met in September and submitted a liberalized constitution, which was adopted in November. A wave of political change brought Dorr unconditional release after a year's imprisonment. He was physically broken by his experience, and lived in retirement until he died nine years later.

No other American state came so close to falling apart because of irregular constitutional change. But Rhode Island's example showed plainly that uncertainty and violence might attend departure from regular procedure in amending the fundamental law. Of course it showed also a more fundamental political truth: the peril of unreasonably damming up change. Granting this, it was still true that if the regular constitution-making procedure were not followed, there was danger of losing the great stabilizing value of public acceptance of the legitimacy of the government.

Other instances skirted this result. Almost invariably this came, as it did in Rhode Island, because a great many people became impatient with slow advance toward changes that they deeply wanted. Twelve states adopted their first constitutions by conventions that were called irregularly, because they lacked the sanction of enabling acts of Congress. In each case, however, Congress ratified the action by admitting the state. In Pennsylvania in 1789, in Delaware in 1792, and in Maryland in 1850 conventions were called in disregard of unduly rigid procedures under existing constitutions. In the Maryland instance, violence threatened several years before the popular party won its changes. But in all of these cases the conservatives gave ground faster than in Rhode Island, and hence there was no actual disorder. And in all of these cases, though change was irregularly initiated, at least it was brought about through the legislature.

b. Submission of Proposed Constitutions

Less serious were questions concerning submission of constitutional change to the voters. Many state constitutions required that the calling of a convention be put up to the electorate. Historically, this was the trend, but there were many cases where such a preliminary submission was not made. An often cited incident involved the New York Council of Revision, of which Chancellor Kent was a member. In 1820 the Council vetoed legislation that made direct provision for a convention. It put its veto on the ground that the convention would be inexpedient at that time, and not upon the claim that legality required a prior referendum. Three constitutions (New York, 1894; Michigan, 1908; Missouri, 1920) provided for a popular referendum on the calling of a constitutional convention every twenty years, without resort to the legislature.

The overwhelming weight of practice involved the submission of the product of the convention to the voters. There was obvious excuse in circumstances for not doing this with the constitutions adopted by revolutionary legislatures in 1776–1778. The submission of the Massachusetts constitution of 1780 seems to have been in response to genuine popular feeling. This set the later pattern, and the Jacksonian trend to put more power directly in the voters reinforced the practice. The most marked departures from this procedure were not of a type that put in question the worth of the general practice. Constitutions were not submitted in Mississippi in 1890, in South Carolina in 1895, and in Louisiana in 1898; the new constitutions were intended to deprive the Negro of his vote and some of the framers feared they might be thwarted if they put their work to popular referendum. The same motive figured in the decision not to submit the Virginia constitution of 1902, though fear of opposition from other adversely affected interests seems also to have been involved.

New constitutions were almost always submitted to the decision of those who were entitled to vote under the existing constitution. The practice helped assure the legitimacy of the constitution-making process. In the Revolutionary and Reconstruction periods, those in power barred from the polls persons who could not satisfy the requirements of a loyalty oath. This was consistent with maintaining the legitimacy of government in those cases, though very partisan motives were also involved. Absent soldiers were, on the other hand, included among those qualified to vote upon submission of several proposed constitutions during and just after the Civil War; political considerations apparently controlled in these instances. On at least five occasions, new constitutions enlarging the electorate were submitted to the vote not only of those already enfranchised, but also of those for whom the new voting right was proposed. The procedure offended logic, but it probably was the higher wisdom where the suffrage question had evoked deep feeling. These varying aspects of the problem of submission are worth noting primarily because they underline a truth too often blurred by uncritical reverence for constitutionalism — that constitution making was deeply enmeshed in the conflicts of interest in the community.

c. Powers of Conventions

Debaters on convention floors now and again sharply disputed the powers of conventions. But in practice the definition of these powers made little trouble. A constitutional convention was a distinct agency of the existing government, charged with the responsibility of proposing revision of the basic legal document of government. Logic and practice agreed that it had no title to executive, legislative, or judicial power. It is true that several bodies that adopted state constitutions in 1776–1778 also exercised these other powers of government. They did so, not because they were constitutional conventions, but because they were in the most literal sense revolutionary assemblies. Emotion stirred by Secession and Civil War led one distinguished student to warn that the constitutional convention was "an institution, that, however hedged about by legal restraints, obviously exhibits more features that are menacing to republican liberty than any other in our whole political structure." In the light of all our experience this horrendous picture seems the product of a too lively conceptualism. Constitutional conventions were charged with framing the fundamental law. But this did not mean that they were free or likely to revolutionize society. Mr. Justice Holmes observed that he had "no belief in panaceas and almost none in sudden ruin. I believe with Montesquieu that if the chance of a battle — I may add, the passage of a law — has ruined a state, there was a general cause at work that made the state ready to perish by a single battle or a law." Our constitutional conventions worked within limits of constitutional tradition, party resistance to changes in government structure, and the jealous watchfulness of interest groups.

Most questions of convention powers arose over relatively prosaic matters. For example, the issue was raised when a legislature tried to set a time limit for the convention, or to require that the convention product be submitted to the voters, or to specify how it should be submitted, whether as a whole or by parts. Legislatures did not do this often. And conventions generally followed the terms set by the statutes that called them. In a few cases courts said that conventions must keep within such limits as the legislature set. In fact, the conventions probably followed the statutes largely because the latter did not require anything that the convention would not have done anyway. Practically there was no direct way in which the legislature could control a convention once the convention met; the Federal Convention most strikingly showed this. The exception was the admission of new states, where Congress could condition admission upon the adoption of satisfactory constitutional provisions. Of course, if a convention disobeyed limits set for it by the initiating statute, conceivably the courts might thereafter refuse to recognize the convention's handiwork. At best this would be an indirect, remote means of enforcing the statutory limits. In practice, it was also a theoretical one; precedent was lacking for such judicial action, and the courts were unwilling to decide "political" questions involving the validity of whole governments. That conventions generally followed the terms of the initiating statutes had little weight as a practical precedent, for only rarely did anyone explicitly consider whether such obedience was required. Where the point was expressly considered, as in New York in 1894 and Michigan in 1908, convention leadership asserted independence of legislative control. If the convention were to have a function of its own, this was the sound position regarding its authority to decide the content, if not all aspects of the procedure, of constitutional change.

3. LEGISLATIVE PROPOSAL AND POPULAR INITIATIVE

The legislature might propose amendments for the voters to adopt or reject. When it did this, the legislature in effect exercised a distinct function, as a constitutional organ; it was well established, hence, that executive approval was not necessary for the legislature to propose an amendment.

This became by far the largest source and the most frequent occasion of constitutional change. One count lists 595 amendments proposed by this method in the states from 1895 to 1908. The voters accepted about 60 per cent of these proposals. Another count shows 1500 amendments thus proposed in the states from 1900 to 1920. Of these the voters also accepted about 60 per cent.

Between 1902 and 1918 thirteen states adopted the initiative as an additional method of constitutional amendment. This was when the Progressives were revolting against the tightly organized party machines of the late nineteenth century and asserting faith in the political capacity of the average voter. People had had the idea of using the initiative for constitutional amendment before the Progressives took it up, but it was its association with the Progressive movement that put the initiative onto the books.

Amendment by initiative was used on a comparatively large scale during this period of adoption, 1902–1918; it was used almost not at all from 1926–1932; and again became a substantial factor from 1932–1938. Some states that adopted the procedure made little or no use of it; Massachusetts and Nevada were examples, of which Massachusetts was the more striking case, since the adoption of the initiative was one of the hottest issues surrounding the constitutional convention of 1917. Men became deeply engrossed and passionate over issues of government structure, with little concrete intention or imagination as to what they would do with their new instruments when they got them.

CHAPTER ELEVEN

THE USES OF THE CONSTITUTION-MAKING PROCESSES

1. How the Constitution-Making Machinery Worked

So far we have considered mainly the product of the constitution-making processes, particularly their results upon the fixing of power among the more everyday agencies of government. But the constitution-making processes themselves amounted to distinct organs of government, and their manner of operation as such deserves attention.

a. The Independence of Constitution Makers

Both in theory and in fact the formal institutions for making constitutional law had in marked degree a separate life of their own; they showed a distinct capacity for influencing decisions of public policy. As a matter of law, constitutional change originated outside the regular channels of the day-to-day agencies of government. A constitutional convention would generally be called only if the legislature called it; the exceptions were in those few states that provided for a popular vote on the calling of a constitutional convention at set intervals, and in the never-used power of two thirds of the states to apply to Congress for a national convention. Experience showed that this was a powerful discretion that rested in the legislature. Many states had a history of years of abortive effort to get the legislature to call a convention or to hold a popular vote on the issue. Years of fruitless effort to move the legislature to summon a convention in New York finally made the matter a leading political question in 1846. As a result, the constitution was amended to provide for a public referendum on the calling of a convention every twenty years. In more recent years Pennsylvania gave other examples of the legislature's power over the calling of a convention. Early Pennsylvania practice was simple. The legislature asked the voters whether a convention should be called; if the vote was "Yes," the legislature then provided for the apportionment and selection of delegates and other details of the convention's operation. But in later years the Pennsylvania legislature learned to submit the question of calling a convention only after it had fully prescribed how the convention should be made up. The legislators could thus set conditions that they knew would raise substantial opposition to the calling of a body so constituted. Thus in 1921 the vote went against a convention, in part because voters who desired substantial constitutional changes distrusted a convention in which, as the legislature had provided, the governor would appoint twenty-five delegates. The voters again rejected a convention in 1935, apparently in large part because they disliked the proposed make-up of the convention.

But if the legislature held the key to the convention door, once a convention was called, it took on a life of its own. The legislature probably lacked authority in law to control the procedure or content of a convention's work. Certainly in practice conventions did as they saw fit, wherever a real issue of control arose. This independence in law and in fact was most marked in conventions summoned by use of the initiative; indeed, this was one reason why that device was adopted in a number of states. Where the initiative was used, people who wanted a convention might frame and submit their proposal wholly outside the control of the regular branches of government.

After about 1890 most constitutional amendments were initiated by the legislature. This process was also formally outside the regular channels of government operation. In this capacity, the legislature acted alone, as an agency of the constitutional process, free of the requirement of executive approval or the threat of executive veto. Of course the party leadership of the time was likely to have the say as to what amendments the legislature submitted to the people; action by this channel was therefore not likely to stray far from the paths laid out by those who controlled the ordinary machinery of government. But in a time of crisis there might be the highest practical meaning in the formal independence that the legislature had in framing and proposing constitutional amendments. The most dramatic demonstration of this, of course, was the imposition of the post Civil War amendments upon the Southern states by a Radical Republican Congress that would stand no opposition from the President.

In any case, by its final appeal to the voters the constitution-making process, in whatever form, introduced a distinct, and often unpredictable, factor. However wide the right to vote, the voters were not the whole people. They were a part of the population, charged with specific legal functions that affected all of the people. They acted for others, not simply for themselves. Both in form and in practical effect, therefore, the electorate invited consideration as a separate organ of government.

Only a minority of the voters generally bothered to vote on proposed constitutional amendments; this was the teaching of all our constitutional history. Any sampling told the same story. In Indiana, in 1846, issues of real public interest were involved in the proposal to call a convention, but less than half of those who voted for governor voted one way or the other on the convention question. A call was rejected in Virginia in 1922 with 25,000 less people voting on the issue than had voted to call the Virginia convention of 1900. The small 1922 vote was the more remarkable because the adoption of woman suffrage had doubled the Virginia electorate and a population increase had added still more to the number of potential voters. Of 8 convention referenda in Tennessee, 2 called forth over 40 per cent of the total vote cast at the general elections then being held; on the other hand, on the 7 occasions for which data are available, the average vote in favor of a convention was not over 28 per cent of the total cast in the current general election, and at no time did the total vote on the convention question reach over 80 per cent of that for governor. Once it was as low as 25 per cent. On 10 legislatively proposed amendments to the Tennessee constitution, a large vote was recorded only on a prohibition amendment in 1887; the other proposals never attracted a total vote exceeding 25 per cent of that cast for governor. In the 50 years after the Texas constitutional convention of 1875, the average vote cast on proposed amendments was about 20 per cent of the total qualified vote in the state, though somewhat larger percentages were recorded after 1926. In 1902 a proposal requiring a poll tax receipt as a condition of voting, and in 1919 an amendment increasing the legal tax levy for small towns brought out total votes of over 300,000, at a time when the vote for governor was seldom over 500,000. But the most representative votes were cast on two proposals concerning state-wide prohibition, and after long and exciting campaigns. In Nebraska, proposals submitted by the constitutional convention of 1919–1920 were voted on by about one sixth of the electorate. Proposals of the Missouri convention of 1922–1923 attracted a total vote only one third as large as that cast two years before for the election of the state superintendent of schools.

Even where a sizeable vote was cast, there might always be the question, how far it represented an informed decision. Data were usually lacking to weigh this aspect of most constitutional votes. But it seems likely that the percentage of informed voting varied in direct proportion to the amount of organized, intelligent leadership the voters had from political forces or interest groups concerned with a given issue. In the 1870's California farmers and laboring men had hot grievances against railroads and big landowners. They sought redress of their grievances through the constitutional convention of 1878–1879. About

145,000 out of an electorate of 161,000 voted on the convention's proposals. These were adopted by a rather narrow margin. But despite the general interest in the campaign, there is no evidence that many voters had much notion of what they were voting for or against. On the other hand, New York voters showed a very discriminating choice among amendments submitted to them in 1938. Thus they adopted amendments which reflected an increased demand for state services (health insurance, grade-crossing elimination, low-cost housing, for example); but they also approved provisions for the better regulation of the state's finances, and in approving several additions to the bill of rights they showed that they were alert to the dangers of abuse of executive power. On the other hand, they voted down a very technical proposition, which might easily have passed under the guise of another guaranty of individual rights. By this proposal, courts might have been permitted unlimited, *de novo* review of the findings of fact made by administrative bodies in determining rights under such modern social legislation as the workmen's compensation act. A well-directed campaign against this proposition had made tens of thousands of voters aware that the amendment threatened to upset the administration of laws touching their rights and welfare; if an extended range of protections and services were demanded of government, broad discretion must be allowed to the specialized administrative agencies that were needed to carry out these policies. The defeat of this amendment showed how well a vigorous educational campaign could teach a large electorate to see the policy implications behind a highly technical proposition.

The initiative gave results that apparently confirmed this lesson. In California, Oklahoma, and Oregon considerably more people tended to vote on amendments submitted by initiative than on those submitted by the legislature. Probably this was because, due perhaps to the practical difficulties of setting it in motion, the initiative was used only in matters like taxation, liquor control, and home rule, where the issues drew general interest and the leadership of political parties and interest groups. Initiative proposals were not adopted without discrimination; rather, the voters tended to favor amendments submitted by the legislature. In general the initiative worked well only on matters of state-wide importance and common agreement. Measures bearing the label of a narrow group or sectional interest, or advancing broad and untried economic or social reforms, failed. Whether it be informed or uninformed, the electorate was a quite conservative organ of government in the United States.

The New York example of 1938 showed that a large and informed public vote could be had under proper conditions; but as we have seen, ordinarily only a minority, and sometimes a very small minority, of the voters bothered to vote on constitutional amendments. In two contrasting ways this fact increased the significance of the electorate as a separate organ of government. Conservatives sometimes made this fact the sturdiest bulwark of things-as-they-were. They did this by providing that a constitutional convention might be called, or constitutional changes adopted, only by a majority or even two thirds of the total vote cast at a general election. This long blocked change in California, for example. There was increasing discontent there over many years because of the political control exercised by railroad and large landed interests; nevertheless, the inertia of the voters was such that, combined with the active opposition of the "interests," it proved impossible in 1857, 1859, and 1873 to get the required two thirds of the votes at a general election in order to call a constitutional convention. The voting of a convention in 1877 was charged to have been brought about finally by a measure of trickery, since one party had printed "For Convention" on all its ballots. Amendment also proved difficult in Minnesota after the state in 1898 adopted the requirement that a majority of those voting in a general election approve any proposed change in the constitution. The 1898 requirement has been attributed to the pressure of liquor interests, concerned to avoid constitutional prohibition of their business.

Where a majority of those voting on a proposed amendment was enough for its adoption, the electorate provided the professional politicians and defenders of the *status quo* with a new and unwelcome source of uncertainty in their calculations. The initiative was of course designed in large part to get around vested interest, political or otherwise. But the constitutional convention introduced incalculable items into the political equation. Once a convention sat, it showed a tendency to develop items of business not on the original agenda, or to fashion its own solutions of previously discussed questions, and to propose matters that, without the momentum of the convention behind them, would never alone stir the legislature to act. We shall consider the reasons for this independence of the convention at a later point, when we examine the ways in which conventions operated. Here it suffices to point out that: (1) when a majority of those voting on a submitted amendment was legally sufficient to adopt the amendment, and (2) when typically only a small minority of the electorate bothered to vote on such proposals, it followed that an aggressive group in convention and on the hustings might push through changes that would stand little chance if they required the co-operation of the political regulars.

Fear of the unknown possibilities in a convention once it got under way marked much opposition to calling such bodies. This was especially true at times when there were waves of popular protest against the "interests" or the bosses. Such a real, if vaguely defined, movement brought the California convention of 1878, and that body produced measures on taxation and control of railroads which had not been specifically framed as issues in the fight over calling the convention. The nature of the proposed amendments was so little understood by many of their supporters as eventually to cause them grievous disappointment in what they had accomplished; but the 1878 convention remained an example of the unheralded propositions that a convention might grind out once its mill started to turn. The hard-fought Massachusetts convention of 1917 was another example. It was called rather in response to the emotional flood tide of Progressivism than to any concrete program of action. The two central issues which emerged from it — adoption of the initiative and referendum, and a ban on state aid to sectarian (that is, Roman Catholic) institutions — became prominent only after the drive for a convention had already become strong. Again, there was the case of Tennessee: Much of the detail that the 1870 convention put into the Tennessee constitution has been attributed to the convention's felt need to justify its existence, in face of the fact that it had actually been called as a political stroke to recapture control of the state from the Radical Republicans. And the fact that there was no convention in Tennessee from 1870 till 1907 has been traced primarily to opposition of corporate interests and officeholders, fearful what unpredictable changes in the balance of power a new convention might bring about. Virginia told the same story in 1888, 1897, and 1922. In Nebraska, the railroad and the liquor trade headed the opposition that blocked a legislative call for a convention from 1897 to 1917. The defeat of movements for constitutional conventions in Pennsylvania in 1921 and 1935 has been linked in part to conservative fears that the unsettlement of the times would lead to radical changes.

b. Working Patterns of Constitution Makers

Since these constitution-making institutions showed independence in operation, there is reason to look into the ways in which they worked. This examination will focus mainly on the constitutional convention. Legislatures, it is true, proposed most of the constitutional changes after about 1890. No one has made a broad study of how legislatures behaved when they acted in this special capacity; but samplings indicated no marked difference between their handling of legislation and of proposed constitutional amendments. There were the same battles of interest groups, and about the same measure of control by the party leaders. We noted that the executive had no formal part in the amending process, and that this might be important if relations between the executive and legislative branches were in crisis. But ordinarily the executive was likely to wield his new-found power as a party leader to guide policy in constitution making as well as in legislation. Nor did the use of the initiative involve any radical changes. In fact, because of the difficulty and expense of getting a proposition on the ballot and of campaigning for it, change by initiative if anything tended to be more sensible than by the other two methods of constitutional amendment. It was not the initiative that cumbered state constitutions with undesirable detail and unenforceable limitations.

Over the years the constitutional convention was endowed by popular faith with legendary qualities contributing to the constitution worship that figured so much in our legal history. Such legends called for realistic examination. Republican government could counter its challengers only with real and not with mythical strengths. If people began to question fundamental ideas, popular myth might prove a great danger to political stability.

The legend of the constitutional convention was detailed and lofty, and almost completely divorced from reality. According to legend, the people — or at least the wisest of them — called constitutional conventions; they called them out of a belief that they needed to effect a revision of the fundamental structure of government; they selected delegates who typically represented a superior average of intelligence, experience, and disinterested zeal for the general welfare; the convention, being called, with a minimum of partisanship or self-seeking deliberated only upon general principles; it did this dispassionately and thoroughly; and finally it submitted its results impartially to the judgment of the whole electorate. Because of the truly remarkable extent to which it met this description, the Federal Convention of 1787 contributed mightily to this legend. That there was only one model Federal Convention, and that apart from it federal constitutional law was dominated by the reverential symbol of the Supreme Court, were facts that reinforced the stately tradition.

Not popular demand, but the concern and vision of a few able men, notably Madison and Hamilton, brought about the Federal Convention. In education, thoughtfulness, and political experience, the fifty-five delegates were at the least a cross section of the country's best talent. No official body that met thereafter in the United States equaled the quality of its deliberations. These deliberations did concern the basic principles of the proposed government — necessarily so in view of the novelty of what the Convention was about. But even here a constitution became the vehicle for particular legislation: witness the treat-

ment of the slave trade, and the provision for counting the slave population for apportionment and taxation. And though the Constitution
recorded important decisions on the structure of government, these
decisions came out of the pressure of social, economic, and sectional
interests, seeking a favorable adjustment of the balance of power. The
Federal Convention set a standard of concern for the general welfare
that was as high as one could ask human nature to produce. But it was a
standard which in concrete respects (e.g., the contracts clause, the national control of interstate and foreign commerce, the national control
of coinage, and of defense) honestly identified the general interest with
the welfare of certain political, social, mercantile, and speculative interests. Madison's "Notes" show that despite sharp clashes the delegates
debated on a high plane of reason and persuasion. But we must remember that most of our evidence is of what went on in convention; we
know little of the inevitably important sessions of twos and threes or
small groups, in lodging houses, taverns, or across the dining tables of
Philadelphia homes.

When men came to debate the proposed Constitution in state ratifying conventions, discussion was bitter rather than sharp, passionate
rather than cool. The atmosphere of reasonable deliberation pervading
the Convention records was due to the fact that though the delegates
had their differences, these were in sum far less than their agreements.
For one reason or another, the Convention overwhelmingly represented that opinion which urgently desired a new national government.
The state ratifying conventions represented a much greater diversity
of opinion. There were hot charges and countercharges over the manner in which some of these conventions were called. And if debates
in the ratifying conventions were often on a high level, they were also
marked by as much rancor, class feeling, emotional appeal, and soph-
istry as ever colored an American political campaign.

If these qualifications are necessary to an honest estimate of the bodies
that framed and adopted the Federal Constitution, what of the more
than two hundred state constitutional conventions that sat in the
course of the years after 1775? Only a fourth of these have had more
than cursory study. But samplings of the available data gave the same
answer. Though the legal effect of their product might be different,
the state constitutional conventions did not differ markedly from the
state legislatures, in types of business, or in quality of deliberation. The
state constitutional convention was an additional legislative body, with
certain political characteristics of its own.

Few conventions were called primarily to consider the basic structure of government. This was in large part necessarily an object of the first conventions in the states, and may have occasionally been true of later ones. The outstanding examples where there seems to have been real popular demand to settle upon the basic governmental institutions were when very rapid growth brought a lively sense of the need for institutions more settled than those of the frontier. Tennessee in 1796 and California in 1849 showed this. But almost always the particular interests of particular groups prompted the call of conventions. Sometimes the impetus was partisan, to supply more offices for the dominant party (Iowa in 1844 and 1846, Oregon in 1859); or to ratify an upset in political power (the overthrow of the Radicals in Tennessee in 1870, and in Texas in 1875); or to define voters' qualifications or apportion legislative districts in a way that would favor a given party, class, or section (as in the conservative efforts to limit the foreign-born vote in Indiana, from the 1850 convention into the twentieth century; or the deadlocked Illinois convention efforts of 1920–1922 to find an acceptable balance of power between Chicago and "downstate"). Sometimes the driving force was the resentment of a class or section that felt itself underprivileged, and demanded specific panaceas, or some vaguely defined shuffling of the balance of power; examples were the California convention of 1878–1879, the Arizona convention of 1911, the Massachusetts convention of 1917.

Whatever the particular pressure, the calling of a convention almost always became a party issue, whether or not it was so at the outset. Once a convention was called, the selection of its delegates, and the control of its machinery, likewise became a party matter. This was so even where, as in New York in 1938, the convention was called without any party backing, in obedience to a constitutional requirement. Whether they were at the start indifferent or hostile, the parties could not ignore a convention once it was summoned. For it might affect the political balance of power through reapportionment; it might develop issues good for later campaigns; and in any event it carried with it some valuable patronage.

The extent of party activity upon submission of the convention product to the voters varied greatly, depending on the stakes. Where so critical a political matter as apportionment was involved campaigning took little account of the special dignity of the constitutional process. In Rhode Island in 1936 the Democrats wanted to turn out a large vote to call a convention whose main business would be reapportionment. To the convention referendum, therefore, they added referenda to declare as legal holidays New Year's Day (for the French Canadian vote) and Columbus Day (for the Italian vote). Their ingenuity, however, went unrewarded.

The books often say that constitutional conventions have had memberships superior to the roll of the average legislature. However, there seems to be no general proof that this has been so. Occupation is about the only matter on which full data have been gathered. A sampling of convention personnel shows the usual proportion of one-fifth to one-third lawyers; farmers were usually the next most numerous, and sometimes the preponderant group. The average legislature showed the same occupational backgrounds. Most constitutional conventions included a number of elder statesmen — perhaps some judges many years removed from active politics, perhaps a handful of leading citizens who had held no other office. But this did not prove that the conventions enjoyed an average superiority in quality of members. Wherever careful study was made, the verdict was that convention membership resembled the cross section of a typical legislature.

Even a substantial number of superior men would not guarantee superior performance. Character and intelligence are no substitute for organization, and it was in this aspect that constitutional conventions showed their most distinctive operating feature. George Wharton Pepper tells the experience of a distinguished commission which in 1919 studied the revision of the Pennsylvania constitution. Any convention might have been content with the commission's roster of scholarship, public spirit, and experience:

> We sat in the Senate Chamber of the Capitol and week after week were watched with curiosity by spectators who came and went. Years afterward I heard from "Charley" Snyder, a politician of an eminently practical turn of mind, what seems to me an excellent summary of our activities. "One day," said Charley, "I took one of my workers into the Chamber to listen while you people chewed the rag. You were debating some reform proposal which, if adopted, would have cramped our style in Schuylkill County. 'This is terrible,' said my friend, 'can't we stop it?' 'Let 'em alone,' says I, 'they ain't doin' no harm.' " Neither were we. We produced after much labor a draft of a new constitution which was submitted to the legislature for consideration. That body, after having received all sorts of protests from all sorts of critics, determined to submit to the people at the primary election in the fall of 1921, the question, "Shall There Be a Constitutional Convention?" A huge majority at the polls said "No." And so the big printed volumes which recorded our labors were consigned to upper shelves in libraries and the commission itself passed into history.

We do not know enough to generalize confidently about the leadership and control of constitutional conventions. Probably most operated under the lead of the prevailing political organizations. But the convention had features that were likely to weaken party control of its proceedings to a degree rarely seen in a legislative chamber; in the legislature, at least if one party lost leadership, this usually meant that its opponent seized it, but in a convention there was apt to be no strong leadership by any party.

O'Rourke and Campbell show this situation in their fine study of the New York constitutional convention of 1938. Except in regard to convention patronage, party control was markedly lacking. This was not because the membership was nonpartisan. Not more than 30 of 168 delegates were without some ascertainable party service or connections; two thirds had sometime held elective office, and one third then held elective or appointive office aside from their convention seats (including 26 judges and a considerable number of other public employees). The membership showed the sectional, ideological, and economic divisions commonly found within political parties, as well as the normal amount of personal animosities and personality conflicts. These normal divisive factors were, however, aggravated by elements peculiar to the convention. Many delegates were county leaders of the party, accustomed to independence. Many were judges, also used to much independence in tenure and management of their official business. A small but influential number of elder statesmen were delegates, enjoying personal freedom of action. Many delegates held no elective state office, and they had no interest in the party support, patronage, help on personal and local bills, and committee appointments which were the prizes with which the party leaders kept the average legislator in line. The convention was a body of but one term, and few delegates faced impending re-election to any other offices. The convention, finally, attracted public notice which made it an important platform, and hence a natural trial ground for aspirants for the governorship; this gave some prominent members the motive for going their own ways.

Other conventions — Virginia in 1900, Massachusetts in 1917, Illinois in 1922 — showed a similar lack of the kind and degree of party control normal in the average legislative session. This, plus the typical lack of interest of any but a minority of voters when the convention's results were submitted to the polls, helped account for the distrust with which conservatives and party leaders viewed the calling of constitutional conventions. The fact that parties had less certain control over conventions also meant that conventions sometimes by-passed legislative log jams and enacted policies long successfully blocked in the legislatures. This point leads us to examine the special functions which the formal processes of constitution making performed.

2. Social Functions: Fixing the Structure of Government

What social functions were performed by these institutions whose formal job was the making of constitutions? The question relates to the formal institutions: constitutional convention, legislatively proposed amendment, the initiative. It is not the same as asking what was the influence of the general idea of constitutional government; nor is it the same as inquiring into the vastly important, informal processes of constitution making through the practices of the judicial, executive, and legislative branches.

For perspective some preliminary points need to be made. When we consider the processes of making constitutions, we are not dealing with institutions which were always on the job. Many states had but one constitutional convention in their history, few had more than three. Legislatures proposed an impressive total of amendments, measured by decades the country over. But none was proposed in many states during considerable stretches of time, and the greater amending activity in other states at most brought the typical annual average to about one amendment per state. The initiative came on the scene amidst spectacular political fireworks, but only four states used it very much.

We have to take account, also, of the timetable. If we take the original document and the first ten amendments as one, the Federal Constitution saw only two major periods of amendment. There was the great shift in the federal balance sought by the Radical Republicans through the amendments that came after the Civil War, and in the early twentieth century there was the costly side show of national Prohibition. When we consider state constitution making, we are even more clearly in the nineteenth century. Most of the existing state constitutions were drawn and adopted before 1900, almost one half before 1880. Over 80 per cent of the constitutional conventions that met in the United States after 1775 convened before 1890. Legislatures proposed amendments in a rather steady flow from mid-nineteenth century on, but on the whole their work dealt with limited topics. The initiative was too recent and local a product of this century to have made a broad mark by 1950, if it was ever to do so.

Finally, to put our inquiry on constitution making into right focus, we must note that we do not know as much as we should about how this machinery worked. At most no more than a fourth of the constitutional conventions that sat in this country have been given more than cursory study, and there are no more than half a dozen thorough analyses of particular state conventions. There have been at least two good studies of the use of the initiative for constitutional amendment. But there is no good study of what has been accomplished by legislatively proposed amendments to our constitutions. Given this state of the materials, conclusions may be wrong because they rest too much on study of the conventions. However, the studies that have been made agree so completely on certain matters as to justify at least a core of generalization.

Theory and practice agreed in defining the most important jobs of the constitution makers. These were: (1) to set up agencies to exercise the power of the politically organized community, (2) to allot authority among those agencies, and (3) to mark limits to the use of that authority. But theory and practice diverged sharply, when one examined the matters on which constitution makers spent most of their effort, and the ways in which they went about their business. There was an early period of inventiveness in the making of our constitutions. But little creative use was made of these processes after the 1830's. And constitutions most affected the relative power of the legislative, executive, and judicial branches not so much by direct allocation of authority among them, as by furnishing conveniently vague formulae under which these agencies had the chance to show their own creativeness. By their own operations, the constitution-making agencies affected the balance of power within government more by enacting quite specific public policy than by announcing general principles. And in the course of enacting specific policy, they showed little aloofness, but rather most of the characteristics of the rough and tumble of contemporary politics and practical legislation.

a. Creating Institutions of Government

The years in which constitution makers in the United States gave much thought to shaping the main branches of government were early and few. Article XXX of the Massachusetts constitution of 1780 was the classic, explicit statement of such concern:

In the government of this Commonwealth, the legislative department shall never exercise the executive and judicial powers, or either of them: The executive shall never exercise the legislative and judicial powers, or either of them: The judicial shall never exercise the legislative and executive powers, or either of them; to the end it may be a government of laws and not of men.

To the degree that this famous statement was not a tautology, it was inaccurate as a description of the actual allocation of authority in American governments at any time, including that made by the Massachusetts constitution of 1780. But this was the most carefully considered state constitution of the formative period, and its Article XXX was a mark of the attention that men were then giving to the theory and the practical judgments involved in setting up their frame of government.

This classic period in our political thought reached its climax in the preparation for, and the framing of, the Federal Constitution, and in the ratification debates in the state conventions. This was natural in view of the pressures that led to the Federal Convention. Men wanted a new national government; they wanted this government to secure property, to safeguard interstate and foreign commerce. In their nature these demands directed attention to the structure of government. And the tangible means for securing these benefits were new agencies and new allocations of power. The status of the executive, the creation of a two-chamber national legislature, and the authorization of a separate federal judiciary reflected no mere borrowing from colonial experience, or the history of the Achaean League. However much the framers drew upon the past, their work was creative, under the spur of the high novelty of the problems they confronted.

But on the whole there is little evidence that most state constitution makers deliberated their choices of governmental structure. From 1776 the typical story was of the taken-for-granted borrowing of a three-branched structure of government, with elements drawn from colonial experience, legitimized by the prestige of a handful of early constitutions (notably that of 1780 in Massachusetts), and bulwarked by the example of the Federal Constitution and the sonorous debate that swirled about it. New Jersey wrote a constitution in 1776 under wartime haste, mainly adapting colonial-charter provisions to the new form of an independent state. Tennessee in 1796 took its constitution largely from that adopted in 1776 by North Carolina. The Louisiana constitution of 1812 came substantially from that of Kentucky of 1799. New York and New England influences were great in the Michigan constitutional conventions of 1836–1838. Illinois based its first constitution largely on those of New York, Kentucky, and Ohio; in 1875 Nebraska drew most of the content for its first constitution from that of Illinois. Excluding the parts defining the state boundaries, of 136 sections of the first California constitution, about 70 could be traced to the Iowa constitution, and about 20 to that of New York. There was a sort of *stare decisis* about this making of constitutions; it was altogether natural in a country in which men moved about readily, taking with them the learning and institutions of their former homes.

This is not to say that state governments were set up in a casual fashion. Conflicts of political and economic interest surrounded constitution making in every state. As the frontier advanced, one area after another went through a familiar cycle; there was increasing settlement, increasing distaste for frontier violence, increasing desire for the roads, schools, courts, and other institutions of established government. There was, for example, popular pressure for organization of a state government in California in 1848 and 1849, given special impetus by the conditions of the gold rush. This was only a more dramatic instance of the elementary desire for protection of life and property that, for example, put drive behind the movement for the Tennessee constitution of 1796.

These practical-minded men knew that they wanted certain immediate, tangible benefits of government; that they wanted their governments to be popular governments; and that beyond this there were no serious problems of theory. The details of structure could be taken, were taken, with little discussion, from the older states. Or they might copy the federal structure, with little apparent regard to its real applicability to the local situation. Thus in 1842 Rhode Island created a senate, in superficial analogy to the United States Senate; set up to give equal representation to the towns of the state, it created in Rhode Island a rotten borough problem that plagued state politics for generations.

This odd coupling of forces runs through state constitutional history to the present: a real demand for strong, popular government, at least as conceived in elementary terms; but with this an almost complete lack of interest in any thorough exploration of the policies which should shape the institutions of this government. One of the most politically conscious, hard-fought constitutional conventions ever held was that of 1878–1879 in California. From his careful study of its proceedings, Swisher concludes that the California constitution makers took for granted most of the important structural points they wrote into their document — the framing of a Bill of Rights, the division of the branches of government, the continued use of the two-chamber legislature, and the familiar hierarchy of courts, for example. "Some of the customary arrangements were questioned by weak minorities, but the major portion of the delegates looked upon them as matters which were settled, and which could not and should not be otherwise."

The creation of court systems furnished many points that show this lack of deliberation over the basic structure of government in typical state conventions. The choice between elective and appointive judges, for example, was a structural matter of importance, and one on which different decisions were made, and much professional discussion spent. But the student will search constitutional records in vain in most states for evidence of any substantial consideration of the issue. It is clear, for example, that the Iowa constitutional convention of 1846 wanted to follow public opinion in the matter. It compromised by providing that district judges be elected by the people, and supreme court judges by the assembly. There is no evidence that it based the compromise on any tangible public demand; on the other hand, there is no evidence that Iowans favored appointment of judges by the governor. In 1857, Iowa provided that its supreme court also should be elected, by general popular vote. Again, there is no evidence that this step resulted from any particular deliberation or any deep public feeling.

b. The Comparative Influence of Constitution Makers and Judges

In view of this characteristic lack of deliberation over even basic structure, and considering the speed of social change in our short history, it is not surprising that the practical operations of the legislative, executive and judicial branches did more than the formal processes of constitution making to fix the distribution of power and functions within our governments. Beyond doubt the most important effect of the constitution makers was to enhance the power of the judges. They enhanced it more or less unconsciously, to be sure, when they put into constitutions both broad and detailed procedural and substantive limits on the legislature, as well as specific decisions upon public policy. For, under our tradition of broad judicial competence, it fell to the courts to interpret and enforce these limitations and provisions, and thus ultimately to shape their practical meaning. This was a phenomenon not marked until after the 1830's. Not until past 1850 did it become certain that public opinion would fully support the judges' claim of right and duty to review the constitutionality of actions of other government branches.

Leading members of the Federal Convention apparently believed that the Supreme Court of the United States would have the authority to disregard an act of Congress which it found to violate the Constitution. The framers thus contributed to a climate of opinion that eventually supported the judges' power. To this extent the framers may be said to have directly promoted the establishment of judicial review. Beyond this, all that can be said is that they provided a court, and broad definitions and limitations of power, to which bold and ingenious judges could apply their talent.

It is harder to weigh relative responsibility for the growth of the judges' power in later Federal Constitutional history. Clearly the Radical Republicans intended the post Civil War amendments to revolutionize the federal system at one stroke, by giving the national government unchallengeable control of affairs. The plans and words of statesmen ultimately had less to do with the outcome than did the improvement of communications, the growth of national markets, the concentration of economic power, and the increasingly sensitive interdependence of all parts of the economy. Nonetheless, for their own reasons, the Radical Republicans did their best to legislate these events into being. The puzzle has been how broad a role they planned for the Supreme Court of the United States. Ostensibly the postwar amendments were primarily to protect the right of freedmen and loyal whites in the South. But responsible historians have suggested that a more subtle "conspiracy" was behind the vague phraseology of the due process and equal protection clauses of the Fourteenth Amendment: that able Republican lawyers who directed the Joint Congressional Committee in 1866 sought by this language to provide a new basis on which federal judges might protect business, and particularly corporations, as "persons" whose "liberty" or "property" must not be infringed under state legislation.

The evidence is tangled, and the issues subtle, but on the whole it may be said that the "conspiracy" is not proved. Representative John A. Bingham of Ohio was almost alone responsible for the phrasing of the critical first section of the Fourteenth Amendment. He expressly emphasized above all else not any role of the courts under the Fourteenth Amendment, but the power given by that amendment to Congress to legislate to protect the rights that it declared. As to the scope of the amendment, it appears that the framers probably could foresee that it might be used to protect both the substantive and procedural interests of "persons," and more particularly of corporations. But there is no evidence that this was a primary motive. Arguments in terms of due process were used in a substantive sense in Negro rights controversies in the later '50s and in 1866. Earlier in the century, but especially in the '50s, corporation lawyers (notably counsel for insurance companies), had argued earnestly, if with indifferent success, that due process clauses of state constitutions gave their clients substantive protection. Resort to substantive due process in the Negro rights cases may have been suggested partly by the earlier usage in corporation cases; thus in 1866 the framers probably saw the possibility that their language was broad enough to include corporations as well as natural persons, and substantive as well as procedural guaranties. In 1866, while the amendment was being shaped, more than two hundred insurance companies petitioned Congress separately. Some of these petitions were received by members of the Joint Committee, and all were referred to a House committee whose chairman was a member of the Joint Committee. The companies prayed the protection of federal legislation against the state legislation which they had challenged on due process grounds in the state courts; they appear to have urged upon Congress their arguments from due process. At the same time the Ohio and Pennsylvania delegations in Congress received other petitions. A federal court had decided that a Pennsylvania statute repealing the franchise of the Cleveland and Mahoning Railroad violated the contract clause of the Federal Constitution and the "due course of law" provision in the state constitution; the petitioners wanted Congressional help to enforce this ruling. The railroad lawyer who had successfully urged the protection of the state due process clause was Reverdy Johnson, leading minority member of the Joint Committee. Thaddeus Stevens later shepherded the railroad's bill through the House, where Stevens, Bingham, and Conkling (all leaders in the drive for the Fourteenth Amendment) voted for it; indeed Bingham's home district was interested in the completion of the petitioning railroad. These coincidences of events are the most tangible, contemporary evidence we have of the background against which the Fourteenth Amendment was framed, so far as concerns the protection of business. The evidence does not prove that the framers had a primary purpose to draft the amendment in terms that would allow the courts to extend new protection to business interests. It is sufficient to suggest that the framers may have foreseen that this was within the possibilities of their language.

The "conspiracy theory" of the Fourteenth Amendment is worth this much detail because it deals with the single most important contribution that the formal processes of constitutional amendment made to the allocation of governmental authority after 1787. Obviously it is hard to decide how far the Amendment's sponsors planned the great development of the power of the federal courts under the authority of the due process and equal protection clauses, and how far the result was the work of strong-willed judges, seizing their opportunities. The difficulty typifies the embarrassment one has in assigning definite importance anywhere to the formal processes of constitution making.

This is true with respect to the growth of judicial review under the state constitutions. Most constitutional changes worked to increase the power of the judges, by giving them broader scope for their interpretation and application of the fundamental law. But there is little to suggest that most proponents of constitutional change in the states had this as their main purpose, if indeed they foresaw the result at all. Rather, the record more often suggests that in the typical case they naïvely believed that the words they put into their constitutions would execute themselves, that merely by writing those words they were settling all the questions that their propositions involved.

This naïveté marked the wide movement, from about 1835–1895, to impose many specific procedural and substantive limits upon state legislatures. Thus state courts used wide discretion in passing on the validity of hundreds of statutes challenged as violating constitutional bans upon "special" or "local" legislation. From 1835 on, men distrustful of legislatures wrote into the constitutions such procedural requirements as that a quorum must be present to do business, that the yeas and nays must be taken on certain occasions, that every bill must go through three readings, that every bill must be referred to committee, and the like. The practical result of these limitations was to extend the power of judges over legislation in those states whose courts held that they might look back of the statute book to the legislative journals to see whether these procedural requirements had been obeyed. In 1892 in *Field* v. *Clark* the Supreme Court of the United States cast its influence against this expansion of judicial review. It ruled that the enrolled bill was the final evidence of the existence of a valid act of Congress, and that evidence from the journals or other sources could not be used to impeach a statute even by showing that the text of the bill signed by the President varied from that voted by Congress. About half of the state supreme courts followed this leadership in judicial self-restraint. But in the rest, the reports were studded with procedural challenges to the validity of legislation.

The story of the tax reforms attempted by the California convention of 1878–1879 shows how constitutional revision often, if unwittingly, expanded the powers of judges. The farm debtor party in the convention secured the provision that the amount of any mortgage debt should be deducted from the valuation for taxes assessed against the mortgagor. However, the convention exempted railroads from this provision. It argued that their bonds were mainly held out of the state, and hence the mortgagees of railroad property could not be reached for taxation. After the constitution was adopted, the railroads held up their taxes for years and won great bargaining power in getting adjustments, because they claimed that the constitutional provisions violated the equal protection of the laws guaranteed by the Fourteenth Amendment. Railroad lawyers, seeing that some unfavorable tax provision was bound to pass, may in fact have helped get into the constitution language that would ensure lengthy lawsuits. In any case, nothing is clearer than that the farmers had no intent to delegate to the courts the decisive voice on railroad taxes. But that was in large part the result of their efforts. The evidence from this and many other instances shows that the more state constitutions went into detail, the more they limited the power of the legislatures and increased that of the judges. That this was more often than not a result not foreseen or desired by the constitution makers did not alter the fact.

Without substantial exception, the emphasis all ran toward increased judicial power. True, beginning in the 1830's, with the flood tide of Jacksonian Democracy, the states turned to electing rather than appointing their judges. But there is no satisfactory evidence that this greatly changed the directions, or narrowed the scope, of judicial policy making. Again, there were times when specific constitutional amendments were adopted to overrule court decisions on particular issues of constitutional power. But these cases amounted only to occasional, limited intervention in a judicial process that, in contrast, was strong largely because it had continuity and covered potentially almost the whole field of public policy.

c. The Comparative Influence of Constitution Makers and Legislators

Compared with these indirect, and largely unplanned, effects upon legislative power through increasing the scope for judicial review, any direct influence of the constitution makers upon the legislature was inconsiderable. Again, in fact, their main influence was indirect; they furnished a setting for legislative growth, the content of which was chiefly the result of legislative practice. Their most obvious contribution to the legislative branch was the adoption of the two-chamber legislature as the standard type. The Congress under the Articles of Confederation had but one chamber. By creating a House and Senate the Federal Convention of 1787 took one of the critical decisions without which a new national government would have been impossible. In the states, since the Revolution only Georgia (1777–1789), Pennsylvania (1776–1790), Vermont (1777–1836), and Nebraska (1937), have set up single chamber legislatures.

There was deliberate policy behind the adoption of the second chamber in the Federal Constitution and in some of the early state constitutions. The second chamber was used to balance large and small states in the federal government, and in both the federal and state governments was regarded as a check on the executive and the lower house. In these capacities, it was to protect property and the higher social standing of certain groups in the community. But there is no evidence that the two-chamber legislature was adopted in the bulk of the states as the result of any such deliberation. It was taken up in one state after another, so far as the record shows, in relatively thoughtless imitation and acceptance of the familiar.

Social change, new political patterns, new channels for exerting pressure on government largely destroyed the basis and possibility of the second chamber's role as special guardian of the *status quo*. At least by the 1930's there was no great practical difference in the way in which the two houses worked, and one was as likely to be a restraining influence as the other. Over the years there were meaningful shifts in power within the legislature and between it and the other branches of government. But these came in no material degree from the laying out of two legislative chambers in constitutional blueprints. They came from the years of co-operation and jousting within and between the agencies of government in practical operation; they came from the force that political parties and nonpartisan interest groups directed upon the government; they came from deep-running popular attitudes toward law and politics, such as the people's acceptance of the courts' power to review the constitutionality of action of other officers.

When they set up the United States Senate, the constitution makers performed a creative act that influenced the growth of the Congress. This was because what they did here was more matched to social and economic realities than what the states did in establishing second chambers. For example, the longer term of office in the Senate added to the influence of that body, because it helped give continuity of policy and experience and promoted independent judgment. On the other hand, a different estimate must be made of the change from indirect to popular election of United States Senators. On its face this was an important product of the formal constitution-making process. Judged realistically, however, it did not so much make the change as record a shift that had already occurred in the balance of political power and in the climate of public opinion. In the Senate as elsewhere in the government, some of the most important changes came about without benefit of the formal processes of constitutional amendment. Thus grew the practice of "Senatorial courtesy," by which in effect one or both of the Senators from a state, when they were of the President's party, made, or held a veto over, the important federal appointments within the state.

The Federal Convention affected the future when it gave the states equal representation in the Senate. It thus ensured that the Senate would stay relatively small. The framers apparently thought that the Senate would be more of a council to the President than an active legislator. Senatorial practice defeated this expectation almost from the start. But it was nonetheless true that because of its small size the Senate showed superiority in deliberation and debate, as well as in workmanship. On the other hand, the framers' intent to affect the interstate balance of power by setting up the Senate worked out in ways much farther from their foresight. Not their creation, but the rush of events in the growth of the country decided what should occur. The framers had posed "small" against "large" states in relatively simple juxtaposition. Instead, we had the more complicated and more difficult relations of sections, as the heart of the balance of power issue in the Senate. The framers believed that competition for political power as such was the problem they must meet. Instead, we saw the Senate become the battleground of much more sharply and narrowly defined interests cutting across state lines, as in the farm and mining blocs.

With the unhappy exception of the Prohibition experiment, the Federal Constitution kept its original simplicity and generality. The state constitutions started with like simplicity. But they sprouted detail in their growth. Nowhere was this more so than in the provision of procedural and substantive limitations on the legislature. These limitations broadened the opportunities for the judges to exercise power. What practical effect had they on the way in which the legislatures worked?

This story has two well-defined parts. In the main, despite such action as the courts took, the procedural limits proved to be worth only what the legislature chose to make them, and they were easily and widely evaded. This was true of such requirements as that bills be read in full three times, that they be referred to committee, or that they stand over for specified periods. Limitations calling for journal entries to show compliance — such as the requirement for entry of the yeas and nays in certain situations — were better observed.

Substantive limits on legislative power (notably the fixing of debt limits, bans on the lending of state credit or on local or special legislation) had a more varied career. All considerably affected the technical problems of the draftsman. Sometimes, as in the case of the prohibitions on local and special acts, this was the practical extent of the influence of the constitutional limitations. Legislatures learned how to give "general" form to statutes that in practical operation affected but one city in the state (where the city was, for example, the only community that fell under a statutory reference to "all cities of over five hundred thousand population").

The debt and credit provisions, on the other hand, stated limits that apparently stuck. This was partly because the courts generally enforced them rigorously. It was also, however, because some of the offending practices against which the provisions were directed had ceased to have practical political importance; this was true, for example, after the '90s so far as concerned the lending of state credit to aid in railroad building. Similarly, legislation granting some special privilege or exemption to a particular person or corporation almost disappeared from twentieth-century session laws, whereas in the early nineteenth century such laws were a large part of the legislative output. But this could not be traced in any definite measure to the effect of the constitutional bans on special legislation that were put into most constitutions after 1850. Other factors certainly had at least equal effect: a livelier public opinion checked legislative performance, and people were beginning to doubt the social desirability of an every-man-for-himself philosophy; there was less chance for certain special privileges, as natural resources, including the public land, were more and more taken up, and as the railroads became established; the promoter lost in political power with the new challenge of farmer and labor organizations. From 1880 on our society was increasingly marked by the gathering together of large interest groups — chiefly economic, but also racial, national, and religious. The serious problem ceased to be the classic "special" legislation, in favor of one or a few persons or corporations. The competition now was for laws that would give to one broad-interest group, as against others, the benefit of the state's money, tolerance, or police power. Because of the breadth of the interests involved, the "special" legislation bans had no historic application in such situations. To some extent, and rather blindly, the courts grappled with these new centrifugal drives in the society, invoking against special-interest legislation the checks of the due process and equal protection clauses. The framers of these vague constitutional standards had done their work before the root problems of our urban, industrial society disclosed themselves. So far as concepts of due process and equal protection supplied any basis for checking the new kinds of "special" legislation, the creative work was clearly that of judges and not of those who drew and adopted the constitutions.

Another aspect of "special" legislation and the constitutional prohibitions thereon may help us to weigh the comparative influence of the constitution makers and of events outside formal constitutional processes. "Special" legislation, in the historic sense of the term, ceased to be a major problem. On the other hand, legislatures continued to enact many "local" laws — laws that expressly or in practical effect were confined to a limited area of the state. And as to these, the courts made the constitutional ban largely a matter of form: If the act was phrased in general terms, it would almost certainly be sustained in most states, though it could be shown clearly that the act would affect, and was undoubtedly intended to affect, but one locality. Why this contrast to the lost importance of the "special" act? Whatever else may have been involved, it seems clear that the same social pressures did not operate in the two fields. In most matters what the locality wanted was not opposed by effective, state-wide pressure groups, nor by any broad public opinion. As a rule no one but the locality was much interested in what the locality wanted. On the other hand, local areas continued to have their special needs or ambitions, springing out of the inevitable peculiarities of local geography, politics, and community growth. Significantly, when large cities found that outside sectional or political interests were getting on the books laws that were to the disadvantage of the cities, or at least interfered with their running their own affairs, the cities successfully pressed for constitutional guarantees of "home rule." And the courts gave more substantial enforcement to these guarantees than they had to the general prohibitions on local laws. Since there was substantial pressure behind the "home rule" amendments, they brought about some substantial results.

From the formal record, it would seem that the evolution of the state constitutions markedly affected the power of the legislature. Such early constitutions as those of New Jersey and Virginia of 1776 granted unqualified power to the legislature, and in contrast set up a weak executive and left the position of the courts uncertain. In sharp distinction were state constitutions written after 1840. On their face, the latter, setting detailed procedural and substantive limits around legislative action, showed prevailing distrust of the legislature.

But in operation, these constitutional limitations were of doubtful effect. Legislators generally evaded or followed the procedural limits according to convenience. They reduced some of the substantive limits to matters of draftsman's form. Where they observed others, more often than not, they seem to have done so because strong-minded judges called them to account or because community pressures so changed as to make it politically unnecessary or unwise to do what the constitution forbade. There remain the cases where the constitution makers limited the legislature by legislating specific matters into constitutional form. In doing so, however, the constitution makers did not modify legislative structure, but simply acted as a separate organ to review particular cases of legislative action or omission. The framework of the legislative branch was not touched. We shall consider this function of *ad hoc* review of legislative conduct hereafter when we look at the ways in which the constitution-making machinery operated as a distinct organ of government.

d. The Comparative Influence of Constitution Makers and Executives

The executive branch changed more fundamentally than either of the other arms of government both in its structure and function. This is not to deny the great growth in judicial power; but the development of judicial review simply fulfilled a role for which the judges were cast from the start. Nor does this judgment of executive history ignore the course of the legislature. But despite its ups and downs the legislative branch never changed so drastically as the executive in power and function; the legislature began as the most powerful agency, suffered in public esteem and in formal freedom, but it remained throughout our history the main arena of debate and group conflict over policy.

It is true that in the national government the Presidency had the promise of power from the start, through the Constitution: for example, in the veto, the authority as commander in chief, the power of appointment. In the states, on the other hand, constitutional history begins ten years closer to memories of conflict with royal governors. Accordingly, the early state constitutions set a pattern of a weak executive, often lacking the veto (as under the Pennsylvania constitution of 1776), being denied control of appointments (which were put in a "council of appointment" by the New York constitution of 1777), and lacking any control over important executive officers of the state, or over the extremely decentralized machinery for local law enforcement.

The constitution makers played an essential part in the growth of executive power by providing the structural bases for power. The Federal Convention did the job for the national government. It gave the Presidency the potentiality of power deliberately and as a matter of responsible choice among alternatives; that it did so is the more clear in the light of attacks made in the state ratifying conventions against the dangerous promise for power in the Presidential office. By 1950 the job had not yet been done with equal thoroughness in the states. But the evolution of state constitutional law brought marked changes that were essential to any growth in the power of the governor. He was given the veto. In the twentieth century, several states strengthened the governor's veto power by adding the authority to veto particular items of appropriations. In many states such important executive officers as the attorney general or secretary of state were independently elected. This made for undesirable blurring of executive responsibility. But the governor's appointing power was broadened; it was no longer put in such hybrid agencies as the original New York "council of appointment." The governor also strengthened his direction of state policy. In New York, for example, he received power to shape an executive budget which the legislature might cut, but not increase.

Nevertheless, the overshadowing facts behind the rise of the executive were the political forces that produced these constitutional changes and put them to use. The President owed much of his direction of national policy to the fact that he alone was in effect the directly elected representative of a nation-wide constituency. He attained this position through the growth of national political parties; the party system grew outside the forms of the Constitution, and the new status that it gave the President completely nullified the elaborate system of indirect election set up by the framers. To a less, but still marked degree, the governor came to enjoy a similar prestige and political power in the states through direct election by the state at large.

The President's relation to Congress varied. It depended on the urgency of the times, the strength of the particular executive, and the amount of patronage at his disposal. In any case it is safe to say that all the main factors that molded the tradition of our strong Presidents came from outside the formal constitutional machinery. The strong chief executive did not often appear on the state scene until much later than was the case with the national government. And the reason was undoubtedly in large part that the governor lacked the potential of power that the Constitution gave to the Presidency. But after the turn into the twentieth century, the governor has emerged as a legislative leader. The immediate impetus to this was the Progressive reaction against the old-style boss. Coupled with this were demands for legislation and administrative reorganization needed to make overdue adjustments to the problems of an urban, industrial society.

It is also true that the modern governor benefited from favoring aspects of his constitutional position. He had the prestige of state-wide election. He had broader powers of appointment, which put in his hands the instrument of some patronage. He developed the veto — as did the Presidents — from a device merely to resist legislative encroachments on his powers, into a weapon to enforce a positive program and to resist special-interest legislation. From his authority to call special legislative sessions and define their business he added to his control of the state program. And the governor enjoyed the advantages of a full-time, more professional public servant over legislators who typically had only brief and intermittent experience of public life. Obviously constitutional and extraconstitutional powers and practices were inseparably interwoven in this executive growth. It is no less true that the formal constitutional processes made a more positive contribution to the development of the executive than they did to the growth of the legislature or the courts.

3. Social Functions: Constitutional Legislation

We have seen that the Federal Constitution as a rule kept its original character as a document which fixed the basic frame of government, allocated power among the major agencies, and stated some general limitations on official power. But after 1830 state constitutions were filled with increasing amounts of specific legislation. Often these were the products of intense party or interest-group conflicts. State constitutional change occasionally, of course, involved revision of governmental structure, but when this was so, it was with little deliberation or debate.

A great variety of specific matters were written into state constitutions. But the matters of real controversy which gave the formal constitution-making process its distinctive role in legislation, fell into two categories: suffrage and apportionment, and economic regulation. State constitutions were used in effect to decide where and how the weight of votes should be felt in party and class conflict. Sometimes this was done by the way in which the right to vote was defined. Sometimes it was done through the apportionment of the districts in which the people's representatives were to be elected. State constitutions were also used, more or less haphazardly, to decide particular questions about the role that the government should play in the economy; some interests sought to write into constitutions stronger guarantees of property and limitations upon the extent of public regulation; other interests sought to broaden the authority of the state to regulate or perform services, or wanted the constitutions to limit more strictly state favors for special groups.

a. Suffrage and Apportionment Battles

In one of the persistent trends in our constitutional law, all adult citizens gained the right to vote. In theory this concerns the structure of government: Why, then, does it belong in this analysis of the use of constitutions as vehicles of legislation? The answer is in the practice rather than the theory of politics. The vote was not extended to broader classes of citizens as a result of any dispassionate pursuit of a political ideal. Party battles and class feeling went into the trend, with as much of opportunism as of principle. Those who fought for extended suffrage often wanted to write it into the constitution simply to put a political victory of the time and place into the form most difficult for their opponents to upset.

Hot class conflict swirled about the adoption of white male suffrage in the first state constitutions after 1776. The social and political conditions of the succession of frontier states then, however, made it a taken-for-granted point. Next, prejudice against the foreigner was fanned for political advantage; definition of the voting rights of the foreign-born became an issue in constitution making in Michigan in 1837, for example, and in Indiana in the 1850's and for a generation thereafter; on the West Coast from the 1870's into the twentieth century men saw no incongruity in writing race prejudice into their constitutions by denying the vote to Asiatics. Some of the militant idealism of the Abolitionists went into the Fifteenth Amendment, but the more immediate and practical pressure for it came from passionate, partisan determination to keep the Republican party in control of the Union for an indefinite future. Women's suffrage ran its eventually successful course into the first quarter of the century. Back of this battle for the vote, of course, were strong ideas about women's social status. But these were no more important to the outcome than the very specific, if naïve, conceptions that many politicians and interest groups, as well as reformers, held about the effect that the women's vote would have on such "moral" issues as control of liquor.

An expanded suffrage was closely related to the tendency to put an increasing amount of legislation into state constitutions. The constitution-making process showed more sensitivity to popular political currents, and hence a greater readiness to write into constitutions more detailed limits on government authority, and more specific authorizations for government services and protections.

As pervasive, and oftener a matter of contest than the right to vote, was the issue of apportionment of legislative seats. Sometimes, in a completely opportunistic way, the constitution was brought into an out-and-out contest for party control. Thus, in the Massachusetts 1853 convention all previous lines between radical and conservative were confounded in a debate over apportionment of the House. The Democrats and Free Soil Whigs formed a coalition, representing the liberal side, but since the coalition's strength was in the small, interior towns, it defended the reactionary scheme of town representation. On the other hand, the old-line Whigs, representing conservatism, supported the modern-type system, by which each district of the state would be represented according to population; the Whigs wanted this because they controlled the large manufacturing towns.

Apportionment issues typically involved a tangle of sectional and partisan advantage. It is hard to define realistically the sectional interests concerned. The division is usually labeled town on one side, and country on the other. But there seems almost no time in our history in which this simple division adequately describes the contending forces. There was long dissatisfaction with the Connecticut constitution of 1818 for its handling of apportionment. But the small towns rather than the country led the stubborn resistance to calling a constitutional convention. In an apparently nonpartisan way, the towns defeated convention bills in 1855, 1867, and 1873. In 1891 the Democrats made the call of a convention a party issue, and since town control meant Republican control, the Republicans denied even grudging concessions in the old apportionment scheme. More recently, the towns figured in Rhode Island struggles over apportionment. Vested interests in town power overrode even party loyalty: In 1936, though the Democrats had made a convention a prime party objective, Democratic Senators from several country towns contributed strong opposition to a convention bill.

Other instances could be cited which, like that of Massachusetts in 1853, show that the division was more likely to be small-town-and-country versus city than the simple division of town and country. Moreover, after 1870, in states like New York and Illinois, great metropolitan areas developed, and the deepest cleavage came to be between big city and "downstate" or "upstate"; the latter category invariably included many cities of large population, now allied with small town and country.

Many states saw sharp battles over apportionment where different sections fought for offices and public money for internal improvements. Especially was this so in states that had at the same time a frontier, or newly settled region, and an older, more populous section controlled by an established industrial, or mercantile, and professional class. In the early years after independence the Pennsylvania back country constantly complained that it lacked fair representation that would get from the legislature the troops and money needed for defense against the Indians. Apportionment between the eastern and western parts of Virginia was a leading issue of the state constitutional conventions of 1829 and 1850; the tax-paying east feared the internal improvements that western leadership would demand. Like divisions were behind apportionment battles in Georgia in 1833 and 1839, in North Carolina in 1835, and in Maryland in 1836. In California a north-south cleavage figured in apportionment contests from 1849 on, when the state's first constitutional convention revealed division between the large landholding areas of the south and the mining population of the north.

Apportionment troubles explained the tensions back of many state constitutional conventions. But there was likely to be a very tangled web of pressures and motives behind the apportionment problem. The

struggle in Illinois, for example, cannot be summed up simply as between Chicago and "downstate." Party considerations were involved.
Democratic strength was in Chicago, Republican strength in the nonmetropolitan urban and rural areas. Each party thus opposed change
which it could not control. Moreover, both Chicago and "downstate"
politicians had a number of rotten boroughs to protect. Another factor
was the division between those who wanted public services, and those
who thought primarily of paying for them; "downstate" was generally
concerned to keep services at a minimum cost to itself. Regional allegiances cut through the nominal unity of Illinois, too, with the southern
portion linked to Kentucky, the central and western sections to the
Iowa–Missouri farm area, the east to Indiana. Interest groups were not
concerned to press for reapportionment; as the legislature stood, powerful groups could promote or block legislative action more easily than if
Chicago were more strongly represented. In the background was the
curious mixture of ideas and emotions with which rural America reacted to the rise of the great city. "Downstate" did not understand, and
therefore the more distrusted the varied interests, the mixed population,
the new types of political and professional reformer, the press, and the
morals of the metropolis; therefore it feared all the more its control by
big city political machines.

b. Contests Over Economic Regulation

Property — the getting, distributing, and holding of it — was the object of most of the substantive policy and limits on power that were
written into state constitutions. The preponderance of such issues in
constitutional legislation testified how far the law in the United States
was concerned with the economic balance of power.

At first analysis, surprisingly few of these constitutional enactments
of economic policy could be labeled of conservative origin. Most of
them were products of the liberal politics of their times, expressing
either the liberal's hopes or his disillusioned reading of experience. The
explanation of this "liberal" background of constitutional legislation lay
in the judge-made law of the constitution. Conservatives had their constitutional protection from judges rather than from the specific terms
of constitutions. Operating under a few broadly phrased constitutional
declarations, judicial review provided the more ready, and flexible protections for property. Among the specific constitutional limitations, the
notably conservative ones were the limits put on taxation and public
expenditure. Even here the picture was confused; in their origin most
of the limits on spending, in particular, marked revolt against the earlier
excesses of the promoter; in the 1930's, however, they provided points

for conservative attacks upon spending policies with which states tried to meet the downswing of the business cycle.

Whether regard be had to those constitutional provisions resulting from liberal or from conservative drives, the main note was negative. The fact was not without meaning for appraisal of the strengths and weaknesses of political liberalism in the United States. In their definitions of policy for the general welfare, our constitutions were overwhelmingly negative. They stated limits on power rather than objectives of power. They showed more distrust than confidence in the uses of authority.

This was partly a consequence of the form of our governments. The federal government was wholly one of delegated powers; of necessity thus the Federal Constitution stated positive objects of national policy and spoke of grants of power. The state governments inherited the historic authority of general government. The state constitutions naturally, therefore, dealt largely with the limitation of powers that resided in state governments without the need of affirmative grant.

But government and politics do not move just to vindicate a legal theory. The negative emphasis in state constitutions continued because it fitted strong, if more or less inarticulate, beliefs among the people as well as the social setting which shaped those beliefs. At first, not much positive government seemed to be needed in this wealthy new country. This was no less true, though the people's practical attitude toward government led them to make some affirmative demands on it even at the outset. Too, in this setting, it was right for the individual to stand on his own feet. In every community there were some bad men whose badness must be punished or controlled. But this kind of thing was abnormal, and should be handled by specific prohibitions and regulations as the need appeared.

Until the 1930's the prevailing political notion was in terms of the bad men and restriction. New ideas stirred before this; but they did not control during the years when our formative constitutions were written. The New York constitutional convention of 1938 was concerned to declare that government had positive responsibilities, and powers accordingly, to provide health insurance, highway safety, urban transport, slum clearance, and low-cost housing. But this expressed a new current of thought concerning government's role in society, a current that did not begin to gather force until close to the end of the nineteenth century.

The persistent theme of the limitations written into state constitutions after the 1840's was the desire to curb special privilege. The trend began with general or detailed prohibitions on the enactment of "special" and "local" legislation. The related fear, that special favors would be sought under cover, was expressed in requirements that every bill bear a title clearly stating its subject matter, and that every bill deal with but one subject. The same fear was behind insistence upon many requirements, hopefully designed to insure full publicity and open deliberation of the merits of legislation, through three readings, reference to committee, recording of the yeas and nays, and the like.

Real, if naïve, public protest spoke through such provisions; its stimulus was in revealed fraud and corruption in public-land dealings and in the getting and granting of franchises, subsidies, and rate privileges for turnpikes, canals, river improvements, toll bridges, and, of course, especially railroads and street railways. So also between 1840 and 1880 banking was singled out, either as a wholly prohibited subject of legislation, or at least as one on which there must be no "special" laws. People's attitudes toward banks wavered in the nineteenth century, more or less according to the swings of the business cycle. Banks were vastly unpopular when the "colonial" frontier saw in them the grasping representatives of the settled and wealthier parts of the country; they were popular when, as local institutions, they seemed to offer easy money; but when the collapse came, they were blamed for speculative excesses. On the whole, during this period, the net judgment was unfavorable, as the constitutions testified.

The rapid, vast, and ruthless expansion of the railroads in the thirty years after the Civil War brought the second wave of constitutional limitations. States and local governments responded to early popular enthusiasm and to the pressures of railroad promoters, and liberally and often heedlessly granted land and money subsidies, subscribed to stock, and lent the public credit to build railroads. Railroad building proved very expensive, the more so because in conspicuous instances it was conducted for the greatest profit of the promoters. Lines were laid out in areas that could not for many years, if ever, support them. State and local governments found themselves out-of-pocket and burdened with long-term debts. The people found that the railroads for whose building these sacrifices had been made were often not completed; or, if they were built, were in such precarious financial condition that they could not bring the expected cheap and efficient transportation. The public reaction was the more intense because the railroads used their power arbitrarily, allowing rebates and fixing discriminatory rates, to the favor of some shippers and localities and the injury of others.

State constitutions first reflected these facts in amendments strictly prohibiting the grant of public money or credit by the state or local governments to private enterprises. These provisions first appeared in the '70s, but were enacted mainly in the late '80s, and thence to the end of the century. Other amendments set almost absolute bans upon the borrowing of money by the state or, less often, by local governments; government henceforth was to pay as it went, out of current revenue. There appeared new recognition that taxes were in their effects an important form of economic regulation, affecting the distribution of wealth and power. Constitutional amendments limited or forbade tax exemptions. They defined taxable subjects more broadly, and occasionally expressed an effort to lift the tax load somewhat from the farmer mortgagor and put it on the mortgagee.

In a score or more of states another kind of constitutional change grew out of the railroad expansion. This was the creation of regulatory commissions, protected by constitutional status against legislative tampering. This, it is clear, came from no abstract idea that the symmetry of government structure required constitutional provision for the new administrative bodies. The men who put these enactments into constitutions did so to settle contests between popular parties and the railroads for control of the government machinery, and to settle these in a way that they hoped would stick.

4. SOCIAL FUNCTIONS: THE MOTIVES FOR CONSTITUTIONAL LEGISLATION

Why did people go to the trouble of using the formal processes of constitution making in order to pass what often amounted simply to specific legislation? Mainly, they used this alternative channel for lawmaking because it offered new opportunities for change and promised permanence. Where constitutional amendments dealt with the structure of government power — which, theoretically, was the only thing that constitutions should deal with — there was also the desire to put basic decisions into permanent form; there was sometimes also a recognition that such changes should be in a form that firmly established the legitimacy of the government. Generally, however, as we have seen, when the people used the constitutional forms to set up state government structure, they did so out of a rather matter-of-fact acceptance of the practical need for adopting certain familiar institutions. The specific legislation written into state constitutions was often prompted by much more particular motives.

The two factors, of permanence and a new avenue to change, were closely related in the use of state constitutions for the enactment of particular policies. Men felt that legislation in constitutional form would be harder to upset, because the procedure for amending a constitution was more involved than passing a statute. Curiously, this stress on permanence often only illustrated a more general motive for putting legislation into the constitutions: that because of its independence from the everyday institutions of government, the constitution-making process might offer opportunities for changes that could not be had through other channels. This independence might not only facilitate certain changes, but also insure that, once made, they would stay.

When certain interests sought permanence for their policies by putting them into constitutional form, they expressed their distrust of what they could accomplish through the ordinary agencies of government; they expressed also their fears of what their opponents might be able to accomplish through the ordinary agencies. Plainly this was behind the constitutional amendments that forbade government to loan public credit, incur long-range debt, or spend public money to subsidize private promotions. A similar concern led many states to grant constitutional status to railroad regulatory commissions. In California, for example, such a commission was first set up by statute, but the railroads caused its repeal. In the California constitutional convention of 1878–1879, farmer and labor groups united to re-establish a railroad commission on a basis secure from legislative restriction; the delegates saw themselves as truer representatives of the people, enacting the people's legislation in a form that would last. A contrasting example appeared in the provision of the New York constitution of 1821 that fixed the taxes to pay debts incurred for building canals. Here the impetus to constitutional enactment was conservative. The more settled part of the state feared that after the canals were built, the relatively new and poor western regions of the state would try to cut taxes needed to pay off the canal debts.

The constitution-making process was used not only to conserve a victory won, but to skirt obstacles in the ordinary agencies to the enactment of new policy. Sometimes the effort was to break a log jam in the legislature. The Massachusetts convention of 1917 furnished an example. A leading issue there was whether the constitution should be amended to prohibit the grant of money to aid sectarian institutions. Those who sought this action from the convention apparently did so because they had tried for more than fifteen years without success to induce the legislature to propose such an amendment. Virginia offered another instance. The railroads for years fought efforts to abolish the fellow-servant rule by statute. Proponents of the change, however, finally made it plain that if they could not win via the legislature they were probably going to win through the constitutional convention that met in 1901–1902. At that point the legislature abolished the rule.

It was not always the legislature which was by-passed through constitutional enactment. The process was used also to overrule judicial decisions adverse to some substantial interest or demand in the state. Compared with the influence that judicial review had upon United States law and politics, the number of such instances was not impressive. But their existence reminded that change could not be dammed up indefinitely.

Federal constitutional history supplied two notable examples: The Eleventh Amendment overruled *Chisholm* v. *Georgia*, to make plain that a state could not be sued without its consent by a private party in the federal courts. The Sixteenth Amendment overruled *Pollock* v. *Farmers' Loan & Trust Company*, to establish that Congress might tax incomes. Examples of this constitutional "reversal" of decisions could also be seen in the work of the California constitutional convention of 1878–1879. In suits brought by banking interests, the California court had ruled that the old constitution did not permit "property" taxes to be laid on intangibles, including the value of a mortgagee's interest in mortgaged land. The farm debtors in the 1878 convention insisted that provision be made for taxing intangible wealth, especially mortgage interests. Another enactment of the 1878 convention set up a state board of tax equalization. This replaced a board created under legislation which the California court had declared unconstitutional; the court held that the statute attempted an invalid delegation of power, and that it also violated a provision of the old constitution which put the assessment and collection of taxes in locally elected officials. Under the old system certain localities, notably those dominated by large landholders, had shifted state taxes to other sections by reducing assessments; local needs were met by raising local tax rates on these assessed values. The 1878 convention seemed for the moment to have corrected the situation. But it did not clearly state the powers of the new state board of equalization. The court thus had to interpret the provision, and in doing so considerably restricted the new board's power to interfere with local assessors' favors to special interests. At best the slow-moving process of constitutional legislation was not equipped to match the more flexible power of the courts.

Constitutional amendment was sometimes used to forestall possible judicial challenge to legislative action. This was probably one reason why the New York constitutional convention in 1938 adopted various provisions declaring the legislature's authority to provided added public services in the state. Because the California constitution could be amended rather easily, this approach seems to have been taken often in that state; the California legislature proposed as constitutional amendments some measures that amounted to statutes, where the legislature feared that the courts might question their validity if they were passed as legislation.

Legislation enacted into state constitutions often involved the deepest political and social feeling of the time. Men often felt that it was critically important to give constitutional status to some declaration of policy which to them embodied a matter of principle or symbolized a great victory. Such efforts helped to exalt the idea of the constitution among our political beliefs. Nevertheless, a realistic appraisal of the bulk of the constitutional legislation did not add up to a very impressive estimate of its importance. In most cases such specific enactments of policy did not direct, but merely recorded, the currents of social change. Most of this constitutional wisdom was the wisdom of hindsight. So far as much of this constitutional law was obeyed, this was because it was enacted when particular conflicts had reached a peak, and comparatively soon thereafter men's interests had so shifted as to relieve the pressure. Or the constitutional provisions merely registered an already formed public opinion whose weight, rather than the force of the law, changed the operations of government.

Even where constitutional legislation had force, the verdict was still a mixed one. It was undoubtedly worth while that it be demonstrated now and then that change too long dammed up through ordinary government channels could be effected by constitutional amendment. It is extremely dangerous to social stability for a substantial opinion to find the regular channels of political action blocked. But experience suggested that the constitution-making process should be used only occasionally, if it were not itself to produce dangerous rigidity in government. Constitutional change was likely to be relatively difficult and slow to achieve. Specific policy, enacted in this resistant form according to the judgment and passion of the time, might prove a dangerous barrier to flexible treatment of later situations. The rigidity of some early prohibitions on banking, and of some later limitations on public financial operations, demonstrated the point. The processes for the enactment of policy into constitutional form served best by the reminder of their existence rather than by frequent use.

V. The Bar

CHAPTER TWELVE

THE CHARACTER OF THE LAWYER
IN UNITED STATES SOCIETY

When we talk of the constitution-making processes, the legislature, or the courts, it takes no great effort to define the framework of discussion. These are institutions of precise form; indeed, their tough vitality of form as against changing demands or pressures was their common feature.

Paralleling the successive rise to influence of these agencies, however, was the continuous but extremely varied effect of another institution — the bar — whose lines are harder to fix. "The bar" means, of course, lawyers. But, who is a lawyer? What distinguishes him from other people who do jobs in the community? When we speak of lawyers in the United States, do we mean men set apart by social class, political favor or monopolistic grant? Do we distinguish lawyers by education, by guild organization, or state-imposed corporate character? Are they set apart by economic power or affiliation to economic power, by common ideas or habits of thought and action, by particular functions in market place, forum, or meetinghouse?

At one time or another in the country's history each of these features, and various combinations of them, marked the position which distinguished the lawyer. At other times, the strong trend was to wipe out even the minimal distinctions which might be thought proper or necessary to set lawyers apart. One main theme in the history of the bar in the United States must be to trace those elements which gave it such identity as it had at different periods.

1. POPULAR ATTITUDES TOWARD THE BAR

Popular opinion has consistently accorded the lawyer a separate character — more often than not an unflattering one. The full history of American thought and folklore must have its chapter on the lawyer's place in the community. That chapter has not been written, but we can see some of its incidents.

People in the United States of all social levels and at all times mingled respect for law and for doing things in a legal way with an unashamedly practical attitude toward the law as an instrument. They would use it when it effected a purpose and otherwise dispense with it more or less openly. This paradox appeared with reference to the status of the bar. As we shall see in more detail, the tide of early-nineteenth-century democracy carried before it almost all previously existing standards of admission to the profession: Every man was as good as every other, and everyone should find open the gate to self-advancement in any field. Indiana made the most extreme statement of this policy. From 1851 to 1933 the Indiana constitution declared that "Every person of good moral character, being a voter, shall be entitled to admission to practice law in all courts of justice." But even this extreme statement did not declare the practice of the law to be any man's right; he must be "admitted" to it. There was deference here to what must have been a tenacious popular acceptance of the idea that practice of the law was not just another means of livelihood; that it was a calling over which the community, even in its most liberal mood, must assert a residual right of control. It is consistent with this underlying attitude that lawyers were accorded, as much as they took, a prominent place in public affairs from the early years when they led in speaking the purposes and contriving the means of national independence.

Since colonial days another thread woven into the pattern of the lawyer's position was the social status of the profession as an object of ambition. In the late eighteenth century the bar was an acceptable career for the sons of well-off planters and merchants. In the nineteenth century, as many biographies testify, it was second only to the role of captain of industry as the road to success for the poor boy of the Horatio Alger legend. What matter — this being popular myth and not hard fact — that the poor boy almost always began his upward climb from at least respectable, lower-middle-class station? In the twentieth century the most authoritative evidence of popular standards attested the continued social prestige of the lawyer's career: Moving-picture romance had its closely limited catalog of suitable occupations for its heroes; in this select list, the career of lawyer shared eligibility with that of doctor, architect, or advertising executive.

The combination of the lawyer's popularly recognized political and social standing impressed Tocqueville. His views were perhaps colored by the fact that he had most contact with the middle- and upper-middle-class United States. Still, his estimate is corroborated by other evidence. In 1835 he wrote that: "The special information which lawyers derive from their studies ensures them a separate station in society; and they constitute a sort of privileged body in the scale of intelligence. . . . In America there are no nobles or literary men, and the people are apt to mistrust the wealthy; lawyers consequently form the highest political class and the most cultivated circle of society . . ." Given their social status, and the conservatism fostered by their training and position, Tocqueville had no difficulty in placing the lawyers on the social ladder: "If I were asked where I place the American Aristocracy, I should reply without hesitation, that it is not composed of the rich, who are united by no common tie, but that it occupies the judicial bench and the bar." Bryce confirmed this appraisal as largely true for the end-of-century social structure in the United States. And it was significant that critics of the bar's status in the mid-twentieth century described it as having lost moral and political leadership, but did not deny its continuing, distinctive social prestige.

From colonial days popular attitudes conceded to the bar a marked measure of honorable distinction. Yet this was always matched in popular lore by a character for sharpness, pettifogging, and greedy manipulation of technicality to oppress the weak and ignorant.

Early colonial legislation showed the beginnings of this distrust of lawyers in provisions that restricted or discriminated against the practice of law. This distrust was reflected at its peak after the Revolution in Shays's Rebellion. It could be found in the overwhelming insistence of Jacksonian Democracy on the "democratization" of the bar — expressed, for example, in the provision already quoted from the Indiana constitution. The existence of an unfavorable popular stereotype of the lawman was evidenced by the stock figure of the lawyer as the villainous forecloser of mortgages and pursuer of maidens in nineteenth-century melodrama. Most lately the lawyer's ambiguous position in public standing was revealed at more serious levels. There was evidence that widespread popular distrust had cut down the effect of the bar's efforts to influence the election of qualified men to judicial office. There was evidence, too, that popular suspicion was a leading cause in dissuading people of small or moderate means from bringing to lawyers much preventive and adjustment work on which in their own interests they should have had counsel.

The popular stereotype probably at all periods and in large measure had little support in fact. Unfairly, and with much hypocrisy, it assigned moral responsibility to the bar for conditions outside lawyers' control, or for which the community must share responsibility. Records showed few disciplinary proceedings for lawyers' misuse of funds. Even if there was a substantial margin of undetected or unprosecuted cases of breach of trust, it was yet clear that the bar over the years handled huge amounts of other people's money with faithfulness at least equal to, and probably not matched by, any other fiduciary group. As so

often, popular opinion ignored the more real points for moral indictment. For example, common criticism did not often strike at the
intellectual dishonesty with which influential parts of the bar now and
again supported private against public interest. Common criticism generally had little to say of the inertia of lawyers in the face of patent
defects in the administration of justice, though such defects robbed ten
thousand of their due for every one whose money was misappropriated
by a faithless counselor. So far as criticism singled out the lawyer because of his zeal for his pocketbook, the criticism came with poor grace
from generations that subscribed to the ambitions they saw in others.
Lawyers and judges developed a law of fiduciary relationships which,
even if outpaced by the rush of nineteenth-century economic developments, still imposed on the market place standards which business could
not or would not develop within itself.

The business cycle had a good deal to do with criticism of lawyers.
They were natural, because they were obvious, whipping boys for the
successive breakdowns of the economy before 1900. The bar was one
of the great institutions which carried the administrative burden of our
society. As such, it was always to the front when social arrangements
were badly out of joint. Lawyers invariably had a good deal of business
out of economic depression — in collections, foreclosures, insolvencies,
reorganizations, and other clean-up work. This business came at least
to some lawyers when other men were conspicuously not busy or
profiting. From the bar's unpopularity in the severe depression after
the Revolution, to the distrust of farmer politics after the 1870's toward
"railroad" and "corporation" lawyers, the bar in general reaped a har-
vest of disfavor from the downswing of the business cycle. It was an
unjust, but an understandable, result of work which, given the nature
of the economy, was a proper part of lawyers' useful functions.

Whether mistaken, unjust, or hypocritical, the unfavorable popular
image of the lawyer was a reality throughout our social history. It contrasted oddly with the people's readiness to make a place at the bar an
object of public honor and private ambition. Both faces of the image
combined to make the bar a distinctive functional group in the community. Though this may not tell us much of the basis for this distinctive
identity, the stubborn vitality of the image indicates that the lawyer
played a part of practical importance.

2. THE PLACE OF THE BAR IN THE SOCIAL STRUCTURE

The bar in the United States never was a group determined by family
lineage or government-granted monopoly. This was, of course, natural

in a new country which was free of a feudal inheritance and characterized by a highly mobile class structure. The closest approach to a status
based on inheritance or monopoly grant came in colonial Virginia, New
Jersey, and Massachusetts. Particularly in the generation before the
Revolution, there were some slight beginnings of a native adaptation
of the English distinction between the barrister or advocate and the
solicitor or client-caretaker. In Virginia the roots of a possible social
distinction of this type lay in the practice of well-to-do planters to send
their sons to the Inns of Court in London. In the Northern colonies
there were the roots of a self-perpetuating, more-or-less closed class of
lawmen. This was grounded in the system of admitting lawyers to
practice in the higher courts only after a preliminary period of admission to practice in inferior courts, the whole under the strict scrutiny
of strong local bar associations. But the Revolution and the revulsion of
popular feeling against things English effectively cut off the American
supply of young men qualified at the Inns of Court. In the North the
departure of many leading lawyers of Royalist sympathies and the general disfavor of the bar in the hard days after the Revolution broke up
the influence of the local bar associations. The eighteenth century gave
us a strong bar; its influence was felt in the quality of the legal education
that young men had in the better offices under the apprentice system,
and in the public leadership that we had in the Revolution and in the
first years of the Republic from many of the older lawyers and from
young men who had read law in their offices. But by 1790 there were
left only a few formal marks of the budding barrister-solicitor distinction, and in the generation that followed, these lost all practical
meaning.

We can surmise the probable position that lawyers held in the
country's class structure at various periods. However reasonable, the estimates rest on thin and scattering evidence. It was not until the mid-
eighteenth century that the growth of commerce and of land speculation gave the basis for a full-time, professional bar. Before then, law
business was apparently done mainly by "attorneys" who were in
fact laymen under no professional discipline, who depended chiefly on
shrewdness with tongue or pen to qualify to speak for others in court
and attend to their affairs outside it. Plainly such men were not high
on the social ladder. In contrast were the successful lawyers of some
pretensions to formal training, who devoted themselves exclusively to
the profession, and who began to appear mainly after 1750 — such figures as Andrew Hamilton of Pennsylvania, Theophilus Parsons of Massachusetts, or Zephaniah Swift of Connecticut; these men were clearly
at least of the middle and upper-middle class. And in such figures as

George Wythe of Virginia, or John Jay or Robert R. Livingston of New York, the bar could claim men who belonged to the top level of American society.

Over the years, the bar ranged upward through the social hierarchy, beginning with the lower-middle class; the workingman or small-farmer lawyer was never a material factor, and so far as ambitious young men attained to the bar from lower-class status, they took on the color of middle-class values. The perennial complaints of overcrowding at the bar suggest the constant pressure of a lower-middle-class group trying to raise itself. Nonetheless, the preponderant weight of the lawyer in American life — as reflected, for example, in his notable role as spokesman and guardian of traditional values — was felt as part of the well-off, striving, complacent and yet restless middle and upper-middle class.

Significant of this character of the bar was its continuing role as one of the main roads of self-advancement for ambitious young men. The typical leader of the bar — Judah Benjamin, John G. Johnson, Daniel Webster, William Evarts, Benjamin Curtis, William Seward, David Dudley Field, Stephen J. Field, Joseph Choate, Elihu Root, John W. Davis — rose to community influence from a background that was economically modest, if often above average in culture. The older cities regularly had a number of men born to the law or bred in it as a position suitable to a gentleman — a Moorfield Storey of Boston, or a George Wharton Pepper of Philadelphia. Some of these men made valuable contributions to tightening professional standards and meeting the lawyer's public responsibilities. But, as a group, they never had a determining influence on the working values and behavior of the bar as a whole. For better or for worse, the bar in the United States was middle class — in its outlook, predominantly upper-middle class. That implied an unresolved mingling of the urge to get on, with an only partly articulate and partly practiced sense of social obligation such as men could afford to have who came from a point above the margin of subsistence.

Income is by no means the only thing that fixes class position, especially in the upper strata. But it is certainly of great weight. We have only very recent and quite incomplete information on lawyers' incomes. Toward mid-twentieth century, however, it was plain that except for beginners the bar was economically better off than any other professional group except the doctors. As a whole, lawyers stood in the upper economic level of the population. United States Department of Commerce data in 1936 showed 18 per cent of lawyers with net professional incomes under $1000, 42 per cent under $2000, 81 per cent under $5000. In itself this did not appear to show a particularly high status. But two thirds of the families in the United States then had incomes under $1500.

Class position and attitudes are shaped largely by contacts. Here again income figures were suggestive. A National Resources Committee survey in 1938 showed that 14 per cent of families in the United States received less than $500 yearly. Clearly this group's only dealings with lawyers would be through legal aid. Over 73 per cent of families, or over 100,000,000 of people, had annual incomes between $500–$2500. These figures took on special meaning when they were correlated with a study made about the same time by the United States Department of Labor, of the things for which wage earners and small-salaried people in thirty cities spent their money. With an average income of $1500, one third of these families owned homes, over one half owned automobiles; the families averaged $30 annually for personal care (spent, for example, at barbershop or beauty parlor), and $60 for health, but less than $1 for legal service. In a given year only 1.5 per cent consulted a lawyer. Plainly, lawyers were getting their paying clients largely from the highest-income groups, including only about 13 per cent of the families in the United States. The mass of the people had practically no contact with the lawyer in a client relationship.

Over the years the bar shared the prevailing religious, racial and national prejudices of middle-class Americans. Charles O'Conor had to win his way to prominence at the New York bar in the early nineteenth century against the bitter prejudice that surrounded the son of an Irish immigrant. A century later arguments favoring avowed quota systems for admission to law schools and to the bar were under sharp suspicion as covert devices of anti-Semitism. Law and fact combined to limit law practice to white men, before 1863; in this the bar as such had no special part. On the other hand, the bar played no leading role in opening up the opportunities of the profession to the Negro after the Civil War. By administrative practice, the American Bar Association effected their exclusion from the chief body of the organized bar. Women presented another minority problem. One of the stubborn battles which they fought for their emancipation in the late nineteenth century was that to secure admission to the legal profession. Opposition to their entry — as reflected, for example in the outraged opinion which Mr. Chief Justice Ryan wrote for the Wisconsin court on the matter in 1875 — rested squarely in bench and bar as self-appointed guardians of a man's world.

3. The Distinction of a Professional Education

Besides popular opinion and class position, three other factors more sharply marked the lawyer in our society — his education, his admission to his calling, and the organization of the profession. (1) The lawyer possessed a special body of learning, and special skills or techniques in the application of his learning. (2) He did not practice his profession as a matter of inherent, personal right, but only after he had satisfied some standard set by the state. (3) He was linked to his fellows by some measure of internal organization of the profession.

These elements showed strength over the course of our history in the order in which they have been named. There was always some central core of professional knowledge and skill, even when standards of admission sank close to insignificance. Even at lowest ebb, as we noted of the provision of the Indiana constitution, the concept of an admissions requirement remained. But, as to the third factor, there was a long period in which an organized bar could scarcely be said to exist, and organization at its strongest up to mid-twentieth century embraced only a minority of the profession, and these in tenuous bonds. However, the three elements were closely interrelated in development, and tended to be strong or weak together. Of necessity, therefore, we must weave some of the whole story into telling any part of it.

Well past 1850, the chief method of legal education was the apprenticeship: The student read law in an older lawyer's office; he did much of the hand copying of legal instruments that had to be done before the day of the typewriter; and he did many small services in and about the office, including service of process. Sometimes the older man might take these incidental services as his pay for his preceptorship. But stiff fees were paid for the privilege of reading in the office of many a leader of the bar. Legal biography amply witnesses that such training was of widely varying thoroughness and quality; that it was typically not of great length of time; and that much of it, as in the interminable copying of documents, was of a rote character.

Many men, Abraham Lincoln among them, prepared for the profession almost entirely by self-directed reading. The example of the leading New York conveyancer, Charles F. Southmayd, showed that this was by no means only a recourse of the rude frontier. In the early nineteenth century the appearance of influential treatises gave great impetus to apprenticeship and self-imposed reading, at the expense of any expansion of training in formal law schools. Most important was the edition of Blackstone, annotated with the American authorities by St. George Tucker, successor to Wythe as professor of law at William and Mary College. Tucker's *Blackstone* was published in 1803. Blackstone was already a classic tradition of the bar in the United States. Tucker's Americanization of a work which purported to put all legal knowledge in a single treatise seemed to offer the ready instrument for the apprentice or self-trained lawyer.

Such were by overwhelming preponderance the methods of elementary legal education almost to the end of the nineteenth century. Over these years, however, there were beginnings of more formal law training. These had an importance of quality that was disproportionate to the few students whom they reached.

The earliest step was the inclusion in the faculties of a few colleges of a professor of law, who lectured and wrote in the tradition of Blackstone's Vinerian professorship of English law at Oxford. Two of these chairs led to work of special influence. Thomas Jefferson caused the creation of a law professorship at William and Mary College in 1779. It was first held by Jefferson's old teacher in law, Chancellor George Wythe. Wythe's influence was felt particularly through his students, who included John Marshall, Spencer Roane, John J. Crittenden, John Breckenridge, Henry St. George Tucker, and George Nicholas. The second holder of the chair was St. George Tucker, whose edition of Blackstone we have already noted.

In 1793 James Kent was elected to a professorship of law established at Columbia College in New York City. In 1795 Kent published a volume based on some of these lectures. However, he had few students and he resigned his chair in 1798. But in 1823 Chancellor Kent again began lectures at Columbia, and in 1826 he published the first, and in 1830 the fourth and final volume of his *Commentaries,* based on the lectures. This immediately became the standard general treatise on law in the United States, and reinforced Tucker's influence in apparently denying the need of formal schooling in the law. The *Commentaries* dealt mainly with constitutional law and the law of real property. As a constitutional law treatise, they were widely used for college instruction, apart from their usefulness to lawyers; their use in this respect evidenced the place that lawyers had made for themselves and their point of view in American affairs. As a real property treatise, the *Commentaries* reflected the business that was the mainstay of law practice throughout the country throughout much of the nineteenth century; their influence waned as real property law ceased to be the center of the lawyer's livelihood. Kent's volumes went through repeated editions to the end of the century; the most noteworthy of these was the twelfth (1873), edited by a young Boston lawyer, Oliver Wendell Holmes, Jr.

A third college professorship in law should be mentioned, though more for its promise than its fulfillment. In 1790 the College of Philadelphia appointed as Professor of Law James Wilson, then an associate justice of the United States Supreme Court. Wilson's lectures were discontinued after a second series in 1791, probably for lack of student interest. The lectures were published in 1804, but because they dealt mainly with general jurisprudence and constitutional law, they never became familiar tools of students.

The work of Wythe, Tucker, and Kent was marked by a breadth of treatment which did not again appear in formal legal education until the 1920's. These men saw legal education as a proper part of a liberal education. Accordingly, they introduced their students and readers to a framework of general ideas in jurisprudence; and they gave them some picture of the law of nations and of constitutional law, not as a superficial adornment of more bread-and-butter matters, but as necessary to a lawyer's proper grasp of his subject.

Quite different in approach was another type of formal education in law, which ran its brief career in the late eighteenth century and the first third of the nineteenth. In these years, in various towns up and down the East Coast, individual lawyers set up private law schools, and held themselves out to furnish an essentially "practical" education for law students. These schools were little more than an extension of the office-apprenticeship type of training, more systematized, and made available to more men by use of lectures. First and most influential was the school which, after ten years of less formal office instruction, Judge Tapping Reeve set up in 1784 in the little town of Litchfield, Connecticut. Judge Reeve ran the school after 1798 with the aid of a former pupil, James Gould; and from 1823 until the abandonment of the school in 1833, Gould was in sole charge.

From 1784 to 1798 the Litchfield school is estimated to have had a total of about 210 students; from 1798 through 1833 its students numbered in all 805; its largest entering class, that of 1813, counted 55 men, the next largest, in 1823, numbered 44. A student usually completed the whole course at the school in fourteen months, including two vacations of a month each. The field of instruction purported to cover the whole of the law, under 48 titles; most of these necessarily had quite cursory treatment. Instruction was mainly by lectures, which the student attended for about an hour and a half in the morning; the several volumes of notes which a diligent student would take from these lectures would supply him with a set of elementary handbooks to carry with him into the practice. Instruction was supplemented by moot courts over which the schoolmaster or his assistant presided. The school gave informal examinations at the end of each week, but it does not seem to have issued diplomas. Its students usually took their bar examinations in their respective communities shortly after they completed the course.

Circumstantial evidence suggests that the Litchfield school had an influence disproportionately large in comparison with its small attendance and its modest course of instruction. Its students came from a broad range of states: Of the total, Connecticut naturally supplied the most, 275; but New York claimed 128; Massachusetts about 100, Georgia 70, South Carolina 45, Maryland 37, and Louisiana 7; and a scattering few came even from such new communities as Alabama, Ohio, Indiana, Kentucky, Missouri, and Tennessee. We lack information by which to judge the professional leadership of the school's graduates. But there can be no doubt of the outstanding record of public service totaled up by this comparatively small number of men. Two of them became vice-president of the United States; 3 sat on the United States Supreme Court; 34 became members of the highest courts of their states (including 16 Chief Justices or Chancellors); 6 served in the cabinet; 2 were ministers to foreign countries; 101 were elected to the House of Representatives, and 28 to the Senate; 14 became governors, and 10 became lieutenant governors of their states. Many Litchfield graduates who did not practice law engaged in activities related to public affairs. Several founded or were identified with various law schools; at least 24 entered the ministry; several were editors, writers, or teachers, presidents of banks, insurance companies and railroads; at least 3 became college presidents.

The private law schools of the Litchfield model were at their peak in the first quarter of the nineteenth century, and declined rapidly thereafter. In part this was due to the greater availability of good texts — notably Kent's *Commentaries*, and the amazing series of treatises produced by Story, on *Bailments* (1832), *The Constitution of the United States, Conflict of Laws* (1834), *Equity Jurisprudence* (1836), *Equity Pleadings* (1838), *Agency* (1839), *Partnership* (1841), and *Bills of Exchange* (1843). Such books robbed the schoolmasters' private lecture notes of most of their salable value.

In part the Litchfield-type schools lost to the competition of the more regular instruction provided in the colleges. Apart from the beginnings at William and Mary and Columbia, Harvard in 1817 and Yale in 1824 established law professorships. However, law instruction at both Cambridge and New Haven was dominated by the desire to meet the most immediate demands of the would-be lawyer. Thus, though the instruction was on a college campus, it was, like that at Litchfield, little more than an expanded form of office apprenticeship training. But it did eliminate the more rote, time-wasting clerical features of office learning.

In the new college law courses, instruction was almost entirely by lecture, based on an assigned text. The course was not long, and the student could begin and end it with little formality. For example, Benjamin Curtis broke off his law training at Harvard in 1831 to take a desirable opportunity in practice, and returned for a brief time, to sit through the lectures in Equity. For William Evarts, in 1838, the Harvard Law School was an appendage to a previous office apprenticeship. Joseph Choate, recalling law training at Harvard in the 1850's, was impressed with the lax standards for passing work. The law degree counted for little; the training offered was in competition with office apprenticeship, and largely met the terms of the latter.

In terms of what was accomplished, until the 1870's legal education in the colleges and universities was part of the era of apprentice training and proprietary schools. And, taking the bar as a whole, all types of schools contributed but a trickle of men. It has been estimated that in 1833 the whole number of law students under any kind of school instruction in the country numbered about 150. The record of the Litchfield alumni suggests that school-trained men in general probably played a role in public affairs that was disproportionate to their numbers. And probably the schools contributed much to keep alive some minimum tradition of the bar as a learned profession, even at the lowest ebb of admission standards. Granted this, still the day-to-day working load of the bar was plainly carried by men educated in the law by their own reading or by office apprenticeship.

Fundamental change in legal education went naturally with the drift of law business and of main currents of thought in the United States after 1870. Leadership fell to the Harvard Law School through the accidents of personality; if it had not come there, some other school must shortly have taken the lead under the driving force of the times. Events now demanded of the bar knowledge and skills not within the sonorous phrases of the "constitutional lawyer" of mid-century or the black-letter learning of the conveyancer. After the Civil War industry and finance grew fast; the states and then the nation, faced by unprecedented problems presented by the rise of the cities and the concentration of wealth, embarked on new kinds of economic regulation; the structure of corporate business and of credit and investment took on new complexity. The new problems brought a pressure for more thorough and rigorous intellectual training in the law. This happened at a time when people were acquiring a great faith in "science"; to raise the standards of legal education fitted this temper. Dispassionately collecting, analyzing, classifying their materials, inducing therefrom certain laws to explain the order inherent in the world and to guide men in accommodating themselves to it — the natural sciences were viewed even by learned men with undiscriminating enthusiasm, as the model for the study of all phenomena. Why not, then, for the study of law?

At New York University Law School between 1865–1867 young Elihu Root studied law under John Norton Pomeroy. The course consisted in reading assigned cases and participating in discussion of them in a small class under the lead of Pomeroy's questions. Pomeroy's approach was radically different from the prevailing text-and-lecture method. But it did not fall to him to shape the whole program of a leading school to a new technique, and thence both to redirect and to warp the course of law training in the United States. That distinction and responsibility came to Harvard, through the conjunction of two striking personalities.

In 1869 Charles W. Eliot, late professor of analytical chemistry at the Massachusetts Institute of Technology, was elected president of Harvard University. In 1870, under Eliot's nomination, Christopher Columbus Langdell was elected Dane Professor of Law at the Harvard Law School. In the same year he was named Dean of the school. Langdell was then forty-three years of age. He had studied at the school from 1851 to 1854, and at the completion of his course had promptly been admitted to the New York bar. He did little court work, was a constant student in the library of the New York Law Institute, and was often employed by leaders of the bar in the preparation of opinions, briefs, and pleadings. When, from 1858 to 1870, he became a member of a partnership, he continued to devote himself almost exclusively to the office and the library; he even set up his bedroom in connection with his law office. Sixteen years after Langdell's appointment, Eliot recalled his selection in terms deeply significant of the temper of the new leadership thus given the law school world:

> I remembered that when I was a Junior in College in the year 1851–1852, and used to go often in the early evening to the room of a friend who was in the Divinity School, I there heard a young man who was making notes to *Parsons on Contracts* talk about law. He was generally eating his supper at the time, standing up in front of the fire and eating with good appetite a bowl of brown bread and

milk. I was a mere boy, only eighteen years old; but it was given
to me to understand that I was listening to a man of genius.

In the year 1870, I recalled the remarkable character of that young
man's expositions, sought him in New York and induced him to become Dane Professor. So he became Professor Langdell. He then
told me, in 1870, a great many of the things he has told you this
afternoon; I have heard most of his speech before. He told me that
the way to study a science was to go to the original sources. I
knew that was true, for I had been brought up in the science of
chemistry myself; and one of the first rules of a conscientious student of science is never to take a fact or a principle out of second
hand treatises, but to go to the original memoir of the discoverer of
that fact or principle.

In the speech to which Eliot referred, Langdell stated the central
propositions of his educational philosophy: "First, that law is a science;
secondly, that all the available materials of that science are contained in
printed books." In the preface to his classic *Selection of Cases on the
Law of Contracts* (1871), Langdell defined the conditions which he believed made possible the teaching of the law from class discussion of
selected cases:

> Law, considered as a science, consists of certain principles or doc-
> trines. To have such a mastery of these as to be able to apply them
> with constant facility and certainty to the evertangled skein of
> human affairs, is what constitutes a true lawyer; and hence to ac-
> quire that mastery should be the business of every earnest student
> of law. Each of these doctrines has arrived at its present state by
> slow degrees; in other words, it is a growth, extending in many
> cases through centuries. This growth is to be traced in the main
> through a series of cases; and much the shortest and best, if not the
> only way of mastering the doctrine effectually is by studying the
> cases in which it is embodied. But the cases which are useful and
> necessary for this purpose at the present day bear an exceedingly
> small proportion to all that have been reported. The vast majority
> are useless and worse than useless for any purpose of systematic
> study. Moreover, the number of fundamental legal doctrines is
> much less than is commonly supposed; the many different guises
> in which the same doctrine is constantly making its appearance, and
> the great extent to which legal treatises are a repetition of each
> other, being the cause of much misapprehension.

That is to say, the law was a slow accretion from the history of a people of the material of a few basic principles, reflected at critical stages of

development in a comparatively small number of reported opinions of appellate courts.

With equal firmness Langdell asserted a principle for the qualification of the law teacher that was radically different from the Litchfield tradition of part-time instruction by practitioners or judges:

> I wish to emphasize the fact that a teacher of law should be a person who accompanies his pupils on a road which is new to them, but with which he is well acquainted from having often travelled it before. What qualifies a person, therefore, to teach law is not experience in the work of a lawyer's office, not experience in dealing with men, not experience in the trial or argument of causes — not experience, in short, in using law, but experience in learning law; not the experience of the Roman advocate or of the Roman praetor, still less of the Roman procurator, but the experience of the jurisconsult.

Langdell contributed greatly to legal education. Consistent with his dictum that law had the dignity of a science, he revolutionized the low standards of the schools by installing annual, written examinations, making these cover separately the work of each year, and using them to determine the student's eligibility to further study. Before this time, the best schools had nothing more than one, final-degree, oral examination. The written, graduated examination system became a standard feature of the modern American law school. Under the influence of this example, the written examination also became the central device of modern machinery for determining admission to the bar.

If the study of law fitted the dignity of a university curriculum, it must be done in depth. Between 1870 and 1890 the number of year hours of instruction offered at the Harvard Law School just about doubled. But the number of courses fell off. Langdell pursued the logic of his conviction that the essentials of law could be found in a relatively small number of principles; rather than increasing the courses as he increased the hours, he ruthlessly sheared off such faint beginnings as his predecessors had made in political and economic studies allied to law. At least, however, the doubled instruction time thus went into more thorough exploration of a few fields, in place of the smattering of many which had marked mid-nineteenth-century law schools. Later, the law schools began to offer students some election of courses. This was in more or less planless response to the pressure of increasing specialization of problems in the law. This development presented a difficult issue of integrating the student's legal education. But introduction of elective courses did not impair the basic principle that Langdell had fixed, preferring a firm grasp of a relatively few fields to a superficial scanning of many.

In 1873 Langdell set another precedent for the development of the modern American law school. With the support of President Eliot, he secured the appointment as assistant professor of James Barr Ames; Ames was then twenty-seven years of age, a graduate of the law school of only a year past, with no experience in the practice. Previously law teachers had always been men of long experience at the bar or on the bench, who taught on a part-time basis or as full-time instructors after their retirement from the practitioner's or judge's career to which they had given the fullest vigor of their maturity. Ames, later dean of the Harvard Law School, brilliantly justified the faith of his sponsors. More important was the assertion implicit in his appointment: Modern legal education called for the full-time devotion of able men who would give to scholarship and teaching not simply the fortunate residue of an active life lived elsewhere, but their full, sustained strength, and the continuity and specialized study which the challenge of the field required. Langdell's precedent inaugurated, as a new branch of the legal profession in the United States, the career of the scholar-teacher of law.

Langdell's name is chiefly associated with the introduction of the case method of the study of law. He did not invent the idea that the student should learn law from critical analysis of selected reported opinions of courts; some before him had stressed study from this kind of raw material, instead of from the predigested summaries of treatises. Langdell's contribution was to translate the idea into the prevailing method of a whole law curriculum.

Langdell's administrative accomplishment involved three principles of operation; and it rested on a rationalization which changed drastically under pressure of experience. By the late nineteenth century the printing press had already created a wilderness of reported judicial opinions. The case method demanded of its sponsors the daring responsibility of selecting from this mass a comparative handful of opinions, as those which embodied the essentials of the law; these selected opinions must then be made available for the simultaneous examination of a class, through their publication in "casebooks." The pioneer volume was Langdell's, on *Contracts*, in 1871. Inherent in this approach was a bold challenge to the extreme emphasis on peculiarities of local law, which had accompanied the apprentice training and the decentralized court systems of the mid-nineteenth century. The core of sound principles was the common inheritance of all the United States; the best English and American court opinions should be drawn on to illustrate the development of these principles, regardless of jurisdictional lines. A university law school should be a school in the Anglo-American legal tradition, and not the voice of a parochial sovereign. Herein, at least, Langdell's approach set an ideal of generous sweep.

The case method relied not on the lecture, but on class discussion of successive court opinions, arranged to unfold the basic doctrine in the field; the instructor was simply discussion leader. The method demanded of the learner a maximum of self-reliant study. The earlier casebooks were as bare of assisting or amplifying footnotes as a Dissenter's chapel of sacred ornament; the student must make his own synthesis of the subject matter out of the casebook and his class notes.

Measured by subjects treated, this was inherently a time-taking procedure; it took fully twice the time required by the text-and-lecture method of instruction. The original theory of the case method was that because only a few basic principles underlay the whole law, students could thus be taught the whole body of important doctrine. As the schools had more experience of the time cost of the case method, and became more aware of the protean reach of modern law, the rationalization of the case method changed. The shift was toward terms that spelled a more realistic, if not yet altogether satisfactory, conception of what was the law school's job. The claim now was that the case method best served to train men in a sound and efficient technique for bringing to bear on a problem of counseling or advocacy the principles and rules to be found in reported decisions. The case method provided not so much a map to point the road over rough ground, as a compass by which to take bearings, and an axe with which to hack through the underbrush.

Such a change in teaching technique was bound to meet inertia, distrust, and hostility. As against such obstacles, the case method spread with a speed that was the best testimony to the fact that it had a solid core of virtue. Langdell converted the whole of his own school to the method within a decade. By 1909 Ames was able to note that a majority of the country's law schools had adopted it in whole or in part; these schools included nearly all those of first rank.

Compared with the spoon-fed dogma of the earlier text-and-lecture instruction, the case method won its spectacular success fairly. It gave qualified students a tough-minded and self-reliant craftsmanship in handling the materials they could find in the Reports.

But in implicit philosophy as well as in technique, the case method was far too limited to become — as it did without serious challenge for a generation after its nation-wide acceptance — the organizing principle of the whole law curriculum. All criticism traced to one radical defect. The case method isolated the study of law from the living context of the society. The student of law needed to be aware of the pressure of politics, the strands of class, religious, racial and national attitudes woven into the values and patterns of behavior with which law dealt; he needed some appreciation of the balance of power within the community, the clash of interests, and the contriving of economic institutions, as all these influenced and were influenced by the effort to order the society under law. But of all this, so far as the law school was concerned, the student was made aware only incidentally — as he glimpsed the social context through recitals of fact and appraisal, of widely varying accuracy and imagination, in the reported opinions of appellate courts.

The typical apprentice-trained or self-read lawyer of the earlier nineteenth century had a narrowly technical training out of a few ill-assorted books. But there had been a time when the best legal instruction — whether under a Wythe or a Tucker or some learned leader of the bar — recognized that breadth of study was no matter of ornament, but an essential for a professional grasp of the law. The course assigned John Quincy Adams for his study in the office of Theophilus Parsons in 1788 embraced Robertson's *History of Charles V*, Vattel's *Law of Nature and Nations*, Gibbon's *Rome*, and Hume's *England;* then, closer to the immediacies of the practice, Sullivan's *Lectures*, Wright's *Tenures, Coke on Littleton*, Wood's *Institutes*, Gilbert's *Evidence*, Foster's and Hawkins's *Pleas of the Crown*, Bacon's *Pleas and Pleadings*, Buller's *Nisi Prius*, and Barrington's *Observations on the Statutes;* finally, returning to the broad canvas, the *Institutes of Justinian*. The titles ring with some quaintness in our ears, but the underlying principle was one with revived efforts of one hundred and fifty years later, to inform the study of law with closer understanding of main currents in the environing society.

Why was the best leadership in legal education in the United States content to give the field so narrow a definition in the fifty years after 1871? The answer must take account of our long inheritance from the English bar; it must look, also, to the demanding pressure of our own social development, and to the climate of ideas in which the university law schools won their way to control of standards at the end of the nineteenth century.

English legal education was led by practitioners. Geography, and the politics of royal and national ambition, spelled the refusal of England to receive the body of its law from Rome through the universities, which on the continent were the medieval custodians of the civil law system. With university leadership foreclosed, the student naturally sought instruction among the lawyers who lived in the "inns" that clustered about the courts at Westminster. Teaching in the Inns of

Court was tied, both in materials and in firsthand observation, to what was the primary concern of the practitioners who gave the instruction. Their concern was with prediction of what judges would do with the instrument which the solicitor prepared, or the cause which the barrister argued. Despite the narrow emphasis of the training they offered, the Inns of Court might have contributed to the bar of the United States their medieval tradition of a firm organization for the education and discipline of the profession. Unfortunately the years during which young men went to London from the colonies to study law were mainly years of decadence in the Inns. By the time the Inns returned to strength students from the United States were no longer minded to come to them. So much of the Inns' tradition as crossed the sea was the tradition that legal education and practice were independent of university influence, and that the practitioner was the sole and sufficient leader of the profession.

The chair of law which Wythe occupied at William and Mary was founded under no guiding tradition from the Inns; on the contrary, it was set up in response to the innovating imagination of Thomas Jefferson, who was no admirer of the English legal system. The breadth of approach among the first great teachers of law and among such preceptors as Theophilus Parsons did not come from the Inns, but expressed the passing acknowledgment of America to the Age of Reason.

The most imperious circumstances of the first half of the nineteenth century combined to enforce a limited, and wholly technical, conception of training for the bar. A few men, such as Jefferson, found the challenge of a great vision in the opening up of a new country. But the business at hand made the run of men disdainful of matters that did not bear immediate fruit; people were engrossed in the detail of the job, and the chances for wealth and economic power were peculiarly attractive in a fluid society where wealth and economic power were fast becoming the most accepted marks of status. Popular feeling had driven irresistibly for extension of the right to vote. The same feeling demanded that all men have free access to all means of earning a living; and this attitude, together with the frontier's faith in individual versatility, led to the minimum of requirements of special learning for admission to the bar. The wholly "practical" curriculum of the Litchfield school was the highest response to this climate of opinion; the programs of university and college law schools in mid-century, after the proprietary schools had declined, were in essence no different.

The Civil War and the economic expansion it brought, despite the mismanagement and corruption, began to make men more conscious of problems of management and efficiency. This was no less true, for all that events had not yet spurred people to broader concern with the values to which this efficiency should be devoted. There is a suggestive correlation in time and idea between the movements for civil service reform and for tighter standards of legal education and admission to the bar in the later nineteenth century. Both reflected a dawning sense of the technical difficulty of operating the new society that was emerging; both in some measure expressed a naïve faith in technique as such.

This measure of naïveté, as applied to the law curriculum, was undoubtedly reinforced by the current uncritical enthusiasm of learned men for the (generally undefined) method of the natural sciences. This "method" set hard conditions for its use; it worked only on material that could be isolated for study. The will to study law "scientifically" thus created a strong, if unspoken, bias to look only at that part of law materials which seemed most capable of defined and orderly examination. At first this meant almost exclusively the reported opinions of appellate courts. This new provincialism of the law curriculum went unchallenged because it fitted — indeed it was an outstanding early step in — the tremendous growth of universities in the United States about the turn of the century. This university growth consisted in the addition of successive specialized schools which had little in common except that they were located in the same place and were administered by the same president. Furthermore, most major branches of social science were raw novelties in the 1890's. Clearly the tides were all against any early, effective integration of the study of law with study of related aspects of society. Even so, it is a fair criticism of the trend which Langdell gave to legal education, that it closed the approaches to related knowledge, and encouraged treatment of law as a self-sufficient body of learning.

Nor was the answer to cast on the college the full responsibility to provide the future lawyer with the framework for his technical knowledge. For a generation after 1871 the law schools faced a hard enough job in tightening their own standards while keeping their students, without a premature attempt to set entrance requirements that would involve college training. As late as 1890, of 61 reporting law schools only 18 set any entrance requirements; only 4 of these 18 required substantially as much as was then asked for admission to the liberal arts colleges of their respective universities. Only after 1890, led by Harvard, a considerable number of law schools began to require candidates to present some preliminary college training. It was as late as 1921 that the American Bar Association declared that at least 2 years of college work should be a condition of admission to law school. By 1936, 55 of the 94 schools approved by the American Bar Association demanded the minimum of 2 years of college work for admission, and 39 exceeded the Association's minimum standard by requiring 3 or more years of college preparation. But if the schools now felt strong enough to set such requirements, thinking was uncertain and confused as to how far these should go. A division between liberal and technical studies had become a traditional inheritance. As late as 1937, over one half of the member schools of the Association of American Law Schools expressed opposition to any formulation by the Association of required prelegal social science study.

On the other hand, by the 1930's thoughtful men at the bar and in the schools were questioning the fundamentals of existing patterns of legal education. It seemed clear that the current was toward a far deeper re-alignment of the relation between college and law school than could be met by any mere definition of prelegal study requirements. There was much talk, and some inconclusive experiment, with a four-year law course; in theory at least, the added time was to be given to integration of law and social science learning. "Casebooks" appeared which hereti-cally departed from the stripped model of Langdell's *Contracts,* and in-cluded sizable text material, much of which sought to place the legal problems in their social and economic setting. A few catalogs showed seminars conducted jointly by lawyers and economists, lawyers and political scientists, lawyers and psychologists. There was only slow progress toward agreement on objectives or the broad planning which might be expected to accompany such agreement. But the general di-rection of change seemed toward a working partnership, rather than a formal treaty, between college and law school. The twentieth century was inching its way back up to the conception of professional learning held by the best preceptors of late-eighteenth-century America.

The radical defect of the case method, when it was treated as a self-sufficient principle on which to form a law curriculum, was that it isolated law study from other threads in the pattern of United States society. Corollary to this root defect, Langdell's model involved grave limits when it was considered simply as technical training for the prac-tice of law. Among the principal agencies of the law, it focused the student's attention almost exclusively on one highly specialized type — the appellate court. Behind this was a tacit, untested assumption, that the problems and techniques reflected on the appellate level adequately represented what went on in the trial courts or in judges' chambers, and that nothing more need be explored. What the executive or legislative branches did was not treated as significant for the law student, except as statutes or executive orders provided grist for the judicial mill. The student saw statutes only as occasional references in opinions; as late as the 1940's it was the exceptional school that offered any course in legislation. The law curriculum did not bring administrative law into distinct focus until past 1900. And except for Ernst Freund's pioneering, for twenty years administrative law was restricted almost entirely to the problems of judicial review of administrative action.

In no respect was the case-method curriculum more narrow than in ignoring the bulk of the lawyer's special skills. A lawyer must draft documents; he must untangle complicated tangles of raw fact (and not merely handle the predigested "facts" stated in reported opinions of courts); he must weigh facts for the formulation of policy in counseling clients, and know how to choose and employ legal tools as positive instruments of policy. But of all these things, the student learned under the case method only as neglected by-products of reading the assigned opinions, or from passing classroom references drawn from his instructor's experience. The new law curriculum put a firm intellectual discipline in place of the lax apprenticeship; but it offered no substitute for other aspects of training that had been a valuable part of the better office education.

Because it isolated legal from general social studies, and because it singled out the study of appellate courts from that of the whole interlocking system of major legal agencies, the classic law curriculum after 1871 had a third marked limitation. Artificially delimited in subject matter, it taught largely in artificial terms. Its prime tool was logic, and the limited usefulness of the tool set the limits of study. The law course was organized by concepts which were primarily the intellectual creation of lawmen — "Contracts," "Real Property," "Personal Property," "Torts," "Equity," "Future Interests," or "Crimes." There was little to suggest that these concepts did not exist for themselves. There was little to reflect that troubled people did not come to lawyers for acute essays on legal doctrine, but for help in organizing a business, getting credit, realizing on security, effecting a working arrangement with creditors, planning for the devolution of property to dependents, winding up a broken home, dealing with the district attorney, settling the bills for a wrecked automobile, or fitting the tax assessor's probable figures into a decision to buy or sell, to form a partnership or corporation, to declare a dividend in cash or in stock.

Langdell believed that "the number of fundamental legal doctrines is much less than is commonly supposed." This principle implied a restricted field of instruction. But it was not necessarily inconsistent with studying legal doctrine in terms of the social functions to which it was put; it was not, for example, inconsistent with welding the study of wills, future interests, and trusts into a co-ordinated examination of problems of estate planning. But Langdell also believed that "all the available materials" for inquiry into the "science" of law "are contained in printed books" — by which he meant the Reports. In this exclusive emphasis, the approach he took was necessarily inconsistent with studying law in functional relation to social situations that embraced more than the lawman's play with his own peculiar body of learning, technique, and tradition.

The first years of the twentieth century saw the case-method curriculum established in practically unquestioned command of the field. But events outside the law schools moved too fast into difficult new problems of social adjustment to permit any long disregard of discrepancies between legal education and the contemporary realities of law practice. The second quarter of the century found a ferment of questioning, skepticism, and generally unco-ordinated planning and experiment in the law school world. By mid-century, one could trace emerging trends for reorganization of law study itself, apart from its better integration with other social studies.

The law student must learn a certain body of information, but the case method was clearly an uneconomical way to learn it. Hence law teachers openly, though cautiously, reintroduced some text and lecture material. The case method offered valuable intellectual discipline. But once the average student had sufficient opportunity to acquire this discipline, continued use of the case method not only wasted time, but induced boredom and lowered morale. Thus schools began to introduce into the third year of the law course more seminars or other individualized instruction. The lawyer's most used, and most needed, skill was in administration and adjustment, in situations complicated by the crosscutting of interests that so marked the interdependent economy into which the country had grown. To give the student grounding in such skills, schools and casebook makers organized instruction increasingly around the problems on which the lawyer must bring to bear his various tools and techniques. Such headings as "Credit Transactions," "Land Use," or "Labor Relations" appeared in law school catalogs.

Exacting critics thought that even such measures only tinkered at the edges of the problems. At mid-century no one could be assured how far revolution might go in the law curriculum. In any case, even such change as had occurred was in but a minority of schools, and in none of these in full degree. Fifty years after the victory of the case-method curriculum it stood as the avowed guide and standard for the average school that claimed professional respectability.

Within this frame, and despite the common deference to it, twentieth-century legal education in the United States was by no means a unity. True, school education had decisively displaced apprentice training. Of the approximately 22,000 persons who took the New York state bar examination between 1922 and 1931, for example, only 769 had graduated neither from college nor from law school, and but 193 qualified to take the examination entirely on the basis of law office clerkship. But an experienced law school dean could say in 1939 that among the almost 200 law schools then operating in the United States ("most of them being able to secure the licensing of a fair proportion of their students"), the variation in quality was "almost unbelievable."

The battle for improved law school standards began with the organization of the American Bar Association in 1878; indeed, this was a principal objective of the serious-minded initiator of the Association, Simeon E. Baldwin, of the Connecticut bar and the Yale Law School. Against the weight of inertia, progress was painfully slow, even in the first step of securing authoritative agreement on standards. The impetus came consistently from teacher-members of the Association, supported by a handful of bar leaders. These men grew impatient with the lack of progress through the parent Association. Hence in 1893 they caused the organization of the Association's special Section of Legal Education. In turn, in 1900 the Section caused the organization of the Association of American Law Schools, and thus provided a still more continuously effective exponent of higher standards.

Even with these developments, it was not until 1921, and then only under the strongest advocacy of such powerful figures as Elihu Root and William Howard Taft, that the American Bar Association was brought to adopt the minimum standards under which the recognized law schools of mid-century operated. And twenty years later neither public opinion nor bar admission requirements had enforced nation-wide educational standards in law comparable to those that prevailed in medicine after 1920. There were 102 degree-conferring law schools in the United States in 1900, 124 in 1910, 146 in 1920, 190 in 1940 — close to a 100 per cent increase in the span of 40 years. Over the same period, under the pressure of reform of standards, the number of medical schools fell about 100 per cent, from 160 in 1900 to about 80 in 1940. By 1940 only 6 institutions in the country offered a medical curriculum not recognized by the American Medical Association or the medical examining boards of most of the states. But in 1936, of the 190 law schools operating in the United States, only 94 were approved by the American Bar Association, and but 91 were members of the Association of American Law Schools; only about half a dozen states had definitely refused to recognize law office study as sufficient preparation to take the bar examination; only about half a dozen states required study in a school meeting the minimum standards of the American Bar Association. In 1936 only 55 per cent of the law students in the country were in approved schools; at that, this figure represented progress since 1928, when the figure had stood at one third.

The most striking cleavage in the law school world was between full-time and part-time schools. Full-time law schools were those which offered instruction in the morning and early afternoon, and where of necessity therefore the average student gave most of his working time to law study; part-time schools generally held classes in the late afternoon or evening, for the convenience of students most of whom were self-supporting and who gave to law study only a minor fraction of their time. Some schools of mixed type also developed, offering morning sessions for full-time students and afternoon or evening sessions for others. Part-time schools increased at a rate that was spectacular, and particularly ominous, relative to the growth of full-time schools. In 1890 there were 51 "day" schools and only 10 night, or mixed-type, schools together. In 1900 the respective figures were 77 and 25; in 1910, 79 and 45; in 1920, 80 and 62. Counts vary according to definitions; another tally lists 40 full-time and 20 part-time schools in 1890, and 83 full-time and 107 part-time or mixed schools in 1936.

The rise of the part-time schools showed how social institutions may change their substance, though not necessarily their form, in unplanned response to events. The "night law school" developed in the larger cities partly to suit the purse of students, but also to carry out a "practical" concept of legal education; part-time students were at first usually men who were clerking in law offices. There were no uniform or supervised standards for the office side of such mixed law training, and toward the end of the nineteenth century a revolution in office techniques wholly changed its social character. Law offices substituted the stenographer for the longhand copyist. This brought a gradual, but in the long run a very substantial decrease in the law offices' demand for student clerks. But meanwhile the part-time schools had become established, and now the students who came to them were more and more young men who were earning their living outside the daily atmosphere of law offices. No longer was the average student's part-time law school study enriched and supplemented by his daytime earning activity.

Thus deprived of the strengthening element of concurrent law office experience for the bulk of its students, the part-time law school presented a serious problem in lowered educational standards. A low-cost education was now practically the whole of its drawing attraction. It operated typically on a small budget, with inadequate library facilities. Its faculty was ordinarily made up largely, or entirely, of men in active practice who gave but a part of their time to teaching, and who both for limitations of time and philosophy taught in the dogmatic tradition of the Litchfield school, even though the school might follow the forms of case-method instruction. Many such schools operated for private profit. In any case competition for students pressed them to offer a degree in no more time than was required in the full-time school. This was, however, partly offset by the tightening of bar admission rules through a general lengthening of the prescribed period of study; this notable improvement was probably brought about the sooner because of the existence of the part-time schools.

That there was a serious problem of standards in legal education was reflected in data on schools and their attendance. In 1936 of the 94 law schools in the United States which were approved by the American Bar Association, only 18 were of the "mixed" type, and only 1 was a part-time school. Of the 96 unapproved law schools then existing, 8 were full-time, 17 were of the mixed type, and 71 were part-time. Plainly the 45 per cent of law students who in 1936 attended unapproved law schools were concentrated mainly in the part-time institutions.

It was no simple matter, however, to define standards of "progress" in legal education. Many people urged that one clear advance would be to abolish part-time law schools. Proponents of this view pointed to the comparative quality of full-time and part-time school students, as reflected in bar examination experience. In New York state, 59 per cent of all those who took the whole bar examination for the first time in the years 1922–1931 were successful. Among the 7,048 college and law school graduates in this total group, 70 per cent succeeded on the first try; among the 14,563 who were law school graduates but who lacked a college degree, 55 per cent were successful the first time; among the 769 who had graduated neither from law school nor from college 48 per cent passed their first examination; among the 193 candidates who qualified to take the examination wholly on the basis of clerkship in a law office, 33 per cent succeeded the first time. But despite these varying initial percentages of success at the first try, of the 22,827 applicants for admission to the New York bar in the decade 1922–1931, 87 per cent had passed by the end of the decade, thanks to the privilege of repeated efforts at the examination. It might be granted that bar examinations had limited value as tests of professional qualification. Nonetheless, such results gave evidence that different levels of education for the bar made marked differences in qualification for admission. They indicated, too, that most of the marginally prepared men who eventually passed the examination by repeated efforts were men who had the less satisfactory training backgrounds in general schooling and in professional education.

On the other hand, the policy was firmly rooted from the early nineteenth century, that access to the bar must not become the exclusive privilege of the well-to-do. Standards of education and admission fell to excess, under the uncritical application of this attitude after 1800. But the bar was important in public life and in the protection of individual rights and the administration of affairs, and its position thus reinforced the fundamental soundness of the democratic institution.

Moreover, as a more critical eye was cast on the case-method curriculum, it was pointed out that the full-time schools might learn something from the greater emphasis which the practitioner-led, part-time school put on the going uses of the law. And the question was raised whether legal education should be all of one pattern. If well-defined and enforced standards could prevail, perhaps there should be more than one kind of law school; there was much routine law business whose practitioners need not be trained in the same broad and rigorous discipline desirable for the preparation of future judges, barristers and policy counselors. In short, it might not be inherently wrong that law schools were of different type and function; the difficulty came when adequate standards were not set or enforced.

Mid-twentieth century found a tendency to look critically at legal education since 1871. This viewpoint perhaps failed to do justice to the truly remarkable contribution which the university schools had made to law in the United States. Viewed simply as an educational enterprise, the leading American law schools of that time offered professional training of an intensity and discipline that was unique in the Anglo-American legal world. Indeed, competent observers of the schools of medicine and law in the United States treated the development of such professional training as the one distinct contribution which this country had made to the general field of education.

However, our primary concern is to consider how far legal education fixed the character and social functions of the bar in the United States. Clearly legal education contributed distinctly to the bar only in those periods in which it achieved a character measurably distinct from the bar. There was a long mid-nineteenth century span in which the schools were little more than an extension of office apprenticeship, and teaching was merely the avocation of practicing or retired judges and lawyers; in this time legal education simply reinforced a parochial tendency to follow the idiosyncracies of local law and practice, and the schools showed no leadership in even limited reforms in the administration of justice. At its best, practitioner-led education — as at Litchfield, or at Harvard under Story — kept alive the idea of law as a field of truly professional learning.

In contrast were such experiments as those under Wythe or Tucker, in establishing instruction in law as a part of a liberal arts curriculum. Such efforts contributed to the most brilliant generation of public leadership which the bar had to its credit in the United States. It was not chance, nor was it without future significance, that the Langdell period began in 1871 and the American Bar Association was founded close by, in 1878, under the spur of a teacher-practitioner, Simeon E. Baldwin. The improvement of legal education was the earliest and most sustained policy objective of the new Association. Conversely, the growth of the Association and the emergence of some reborn sense of corporate being in the bar of the United States owed much to the common experience which the law schools gave to a widening circle of lawyers, and to the public policy initiative that stemmed from the new branch of the profession, the full-time teachers of law.

In the 1930's some lawyers spoke alarm at what they saw as a growing gulf between practitioner and teacher. The record did not warrant their disquiet; theirs was probably only an immediate reaction against the liberal politics of outspoken law teachers. In the first half of the twentieth century there were three main areas of public policy activity which gave to the bar some sense of a nation-wide, corporate purpose. These were the improvement of standards of legal education, the drafting of proposed uniform or model state laws, and the preparation through the American Law Institute of "restatements" of the principal fields of common law. In each of these, teachers and practitioners worked in close partnership. Economic regulation and civil liberties presented more controversial fields. In these the teaching branch of the profession tended to fill a role of disinterested public service like that traditionally associated with the English barrister or higher civil servant; it was a role which the peculiar emphasis on client-caretaking had made difficult for the practitioner in the United States. Even so, there was some evidence that a more socially conscious legal education, conspiring with the currents of affairs, was preparing an opinion at the bar that was receptive to such public service from the schools, and that a closer integration of all branches of the profession was a fair prospect.

4. Standards of Admission to the Bar

What was the effect of the requirement that men pass through some distinct procedure for admission to the profession? This factor was of less substantial influence than the possession of a special body of professional learning in giving a separate character to the bar. Nonetheless, it was a continuing thread in the distinctive life of lawyers in the country.

Even in the mid-nineteenth-century period of most nominal standards of admission, the states did not treat the practice of law as an activity that was an inherent, private right of any person who chose to follow it. There were early efforts in some colonies to forbid all law practice. But as the development of commerce and land speculation brought the first demand for full-time professional legal service, the colonial legislatures provided that the courts should control admission to the bar. Local procedures varied, but by the eve of the Revolution a relatively strong beginning had been made in creating some meaningful standards for admission to the practice. However, this beginning broke down during the Revolutionary years when a number of factors combined to turn public opinion against measures which might build up a strong legal profession. Many leading lawyers adhered to the Crown; English-based institutions, including the common law, were politically unpopular; debtors associated lawyers with the hardships of the depressed years after independence. The imperious demands of the democratic opinion which gathered force in the Jeffersonian years and came to full expression in the Jacksonian 1830's, brought extreme relaxation of professional standards.

As in so many other instances, so here the generation that began with the '70s was a turning point. It brought a new emphasis on the rationalization of private and then of public affairs, which showed itself in the matter of bar standards. Improvement in standards for admission to the bar was part of a general movement in which old callings regained professional status and new ones sought it.

Before the Civil War the only professions in this country that were not freely open to all comers were law and medicine (the latter category sometimes included dentistry), and in a few cities pharmacy. In all of these callings restrictions that earlier had some meaning wore very thin during the mid-nineteenth century. But between 1868 and 1878 the first State Board of Bar Examiners was set up (in New Hampshire), and medical licensing laws were for the first time paralleled by general laws of like type which affected dentists (New York, Kentucky, and Ohio) and embalmers (Massachusetts). New York led in licensing accountants, in 1896. Licensing acts for architects dated from about 1900, for engineers from 1908. By the 1930's, "professional" licensing had so far extended as to suggest that there was more zeal to use this as a means to limit competition than to define areas that could be accurately described in required learning or standards as professions. A count in 1932 showed that 1 or more of 18 representative states had by then licensed a total of 210 occupations or businesses. But if the observer might be skeptical of the motives behind the marginal extensions of this movement, clearly the drive to professionalize callings of special public importance was firmly rooted in the circumstances and attitudes of the twentieth-century United States.

At no stage in this country was formal control of bar admissions given to the profession itself. This was the more notable because it departed from the strong contrary English tradition of guildlike organization of lawyers under their own discipline. On the other hand, we showed the English inheritance in the fact that control of the profession did not come to rest in the schools, as it did in large degree on the Continent. After 1750 in some Northern states, especially in Massachusetts and New York, the courts delegated their responsibility for admissions to county or other local bar organizations to such a degree as to make the bar the controlling authority. Such precedent might have broadened into general bar control. But this *de facto* authority was exercised in so drastic a fashion as to spread the conviction that it was the instrument of a selfish monopoly. On the eve of the democratic revolution in standards, Massachusetts required, before complete privileges of law practice were granted, a course of training and practice that totaled eleven years for a man who had gone to college, or nine years for one who had not. New York required ten years in either case. Such terms of preparation fitted 1940 standards; plainly they were not justified by the available education of 1800. They quickly fell before the prevailing temper of relaxed standards. Not until the American Bar Association, in 1921, made its first firm assertion of recommended minimum admissions standards was there any substantial return to control of the situation by the organized bar. The organized bar in the twentieth century again exercised *de facto* authority in the matter — in the sense that its pressure on public opinion and on legislatures and courts won such improvement in standards as was achieved. But the bar's influence was limited, and it was in all respects exercised through the public authority and not by the sole discipline of the profession itself.

It is hard to define, either in law or in fact, the comparative relation which legislatures and courts bore to the control of admissions. From colonial days on, statutes set down at least the general form of requirements for admission to the bar. Until the 1870's the administration of admissions, and sometimes a measure of specification of standards, was committed to the courts. When states tightened requirements by installing written examinations, a new agency, the board of bar examiners, appeared. It was generally set up by statute. It was usually the legislature which also added committees to review the character qualifications of candidates for admission. In operation, these various bodies were ordinarily closer to the courts than to the legislature.

There was a separation-of-powers issue involved in control of bar admissions and discipline, but judicial opinions did not set clear-cut doctrine in the matter. Most of the cases arose after 1920. The courts did not seem sensitive to the issue until agitation for procedural reform through rules of court gave practical importance to the definition of the authority which courts might acquire under constitutional provisions vesting "judicial" power. The opinions generally refused to concede that the legislature had plenary authority, or any defined degree of authority, over the bar. On the other hand, the courts in effect approved reasonable statutory regulations, though they sometimes blurred the force of their acceptance by treating the statutes as advisory or as gratuitous aids, to be graciously acknowledged as such. This last approach was the one which the judges usually took when they accepted provisions which set up boards of bar examiners or character committees. They ordinarily denied that the legislature could compel them to admit men to practice merely because the candidates met legislatively defined qualifications. But the judges acceded to negative provisions set by the statutes, treating them as merely setting minimal tests for admission. Consistent with this last position, the courts generally did not object to statutes which fixed causes for disbarment, but they refused to recognize that bodies created by the legislature might wield final authority to enforce such discipline on lawyers. No court squarely challenged the legislature's power to require that lawyers be members of one incorporated bar association; and such statutory organizations were affirmatively upheld by the courts in about half a dozen of the score of states which had adopted them by 1940.

The matter of centralized versus decentralized administration of bar admission standards had more practical importance than any separation-of-powers dogma. Primarily because communications were difficult, for the sixty years after the Revolution the states tended to decentralize control of admissions, putting authority in the local courts. In some states admission by one local court conferred no general right to practice before others; more usually, admission by any one court of general jurisdiction opened the door to any court of the state. As travel became easier, there was more centralization of admissions, but for many years this went on only in a minority of the states. Technically, admissions were centralized in 8 of 30 jurisdictions in 1840; in 10 of 39 jurisdictions in 1860; in 16 of 49 jurisdictions in 1890; but in actual operation

admission was decentralized in many of these. After 1890 a strong movement toward centralization set in. By 1914 only Indiana and Kentucky
kept the system of admission by independent action of local courts;
thirty years later these states, too, had centralized control. Centralization was by no means necessarily the same as higher admission standards. Indeed, some states adopted it in order to bring particularly high
local-court requirements down to an easier general level. But, especially
where the certificate of one court admitted a man to practice before all
courts, decentralization promoted laxity because it diffused responsibility. A centralized administration was more readily applied to the raising of standards, once there was the will to do so. After 1890 the central authority was almost invariably, in the first instance, a state board
of bar examiners.

Most attention was given to those admissions requirements which
dealt with study in preparation for the practice of law. Despite their
weaknesses, the schools consistently ran ahead of the prevailing official
standards. Indeed, over most of our history there were no official
standards of preparation for the bar, and such standards as existed in
fact were largely the product of the schools' traditions. Of 19 states and
organized territories in 1800, 14 required a definite preparatory period
of professional study. But such a requirement was made by only 11 of
the 30 states and territories that existed in 1830; and in 1860 only 9 of
39 states and territories had even nominal requirements of professional
preparation. By 1890 nearly one half, by 1920 about three fourths, and
by 1940 all states required some professional study preparatory to admission. The spread of this requirement was gradually attended by a
lengthening of the period of professional preparation, up to the three-
year requirement which by 1940 was fixed in forty states.

Naturally, through the years in which most states did not even set
minimum requirements of professional training, they set no requirements for prelegal study. In 1921 the American Bar Association first
committed itself to a substantial declaration in favor of higher standards.
As late as this, only fourteen states had any requirements of preliminary
general education, and only ten required the equivalent of graduation
from high school as a condition of eligibility for admission to the bar.
But advance was fast after the Association's action. By 1940 over two
thirds of the states had adopted the requirement of at least two years of
college preparation or its equivalent, as a prerequisite for admission.

Once a firm initiative was taken in 1921, progress toward higher
preparatory requirements for the practice of law came with amazing
speed. Twenty years saw change little short of a revolution. Of course
this advance had more meaning for the future than for any immediate

large-scale change in the background of the bar as a whole. Legal biography showed that, before he entered practice, the average lawyer of 1800 had a basic education a year or so short of finishing what the twentieth century would call grammer school, plus 6 to 14 months' training in law. A random sampling from over the country in 1931 showed an average basic education that reached through about one year of college and two and a quarter years in a law school or in office training. Clearly, during the whole period of 131 years the well-trained men from good law schools had been "a tiny stream — emptied into an ocean of inadequate preparation." Clearly, too, when one allowed for the comparative educational facilities of the times, and for the increased complexity of the society, the 1931 average of education was no startling degree beyond that of 1800.

The examination was throughout the main official instrument for enforcing standards of preparation for the bar. Before 1870 it was typically oral. In any case, oral or written, it was administered with casual leniency; the approach was characteristic of times and communities that were close enough to the frontier so that they had no awe of formality or specialized knowledge, and small enough so that personal acquaintance and relationships were a substantial check on conduct. Salmon Portland Chase — distinguished at the Ohio bar and as Cabinet officer and Chief Justice of the United States Supreme Court — recalled the circumstances of his examination in 1829 for admission to the bar in the District of Columbia. His recollection catches the prevailing atmosphere. He was examined before the federal court sitting for the District:

Very seldom, I imagine, has any candidate for admission to the bar presented himself for examination with a slenderer stock of learning. I was examined in open court. The venerable and excellent Justice Cranch put the questions. I answered as well as I was able — how well or how ill I cannot say — but certainly, I think, not very well. Finally, the Judge asked me how long I had studied. I replied that, including the time employed in reading in college and the scraps devoted to legal reading before I regularly commenced the study, and the time since, I thought three years might be made up. The Judge smiled and said, "We think, Mr. Chase, that you must study another year and present yourself again for examination." "Please, your honors," said I, deprecatingly, "I have made all my arrangements to go to the western country and practice law." The kind Judge yielded to this appeal, and turning to the Clerk said, "Swear in Mr. Chase." Perhaps he would have been less facile if he had not known me personally and very well.

Jonathan Birch of Bloomington, Illinois, recalled the circumstances of his examination for the Illinois bar by Abraham Lincoln, a member of the board of examiners by appointment of the state supreme court. The candidate found the examiner in his hotel room, partly undressed, and so far as the facilities permitted, taking a bath, which proceeded during the examination.

> Motioning me to be seated, he began his interrogatories at once, without looking at me a second time to be sure of the identity of his caller. "How long have you been studying?" he asked. "Almost two years," was my response. "By this time, it seems to me," he said laughingly, "you ought to be able to determine whether you have in you the kind of stuff out of which a good lawyer can be made. What books have you read?" I told him, and he said it was more than he read before he was admitted to the bar.

This prompted a typical Lincoln story, after which the examination was resumed.

> He asked me in a desultory way the definition of a contract, and two or three fundamental questions, all of which I answered readily, and I thought, correctly. Beyond these meager inquiries, as I now recall the incident, he asked nothing more. As he continued his toilet, he entertained me with recollections — many of them characteristically vivid and racy — of his early practice and the various incidents and adventures that attended his start in the profession. The whole proceeding was so unusual and queer, if not grotesque, that I was at a loss to determine whether I was really being examined at all or not. After he had dressed we went downstairs and over to the clerk's office in the courthouse, where he wrote a few lines on a sheet of paper, and, inclosing it in an envelope, directed me to report with it to Judge Logan, another member of the examining committee, at Springfield.

> The next day I went to Springfield, where I delivered the letter as directed. On reading it, Judge Logan smiled, and, much to my surprise, gave me the required certificate without asking a question beyond my age and residence, and the correct way of spelling my name. The note from Lincoln read: "My dear Judge: — The bearer of this is a young man who thinks he can be a lawyer. Examine him, if you want to. I have done so, and am satisfied. He's a good deal smarter than he looks to be."

The movement to lengthen the required period of professional study went on for a generation after the Civil War before it was accompanied by a substantial effort to improve the examining machinery. Before 1890 only four states had boards of bar examiners, and in no more than half a dozen had written examinations been used. However, when the leading law schools began to use the written examination, this encouraged adoption of the practice in the states, where it became the invariable method of examination after 1900.

Tighter examination standards involved important secondary issues. In the pattern typical of our legal growth, these questions were not squarely faced or planned for, but were allowed to work themselves out under the pressure of events. First was the problem of bringing the law curriculum and the bar examination requirements into reasonable relation. Second, and closely related, was the need to devise machinery which would make the examinations produce the selective result hoped of them. For forty years the schools and the state authorities had no regular channel of communication through which to seek agreement on the standards of legal education and of examinations. There was considerable friction. Until the 1930's, bar examinations tended to stress rote learning and details peculiar to the jurisdiction; both emphases were wholly foreign to what the leading schools and the American Bar Association standards envisaged as proper lines of professional training. This problem could not be separated from that of the organization of the bar examining machinery. Bar examiners were part-time workers at their task; they received no pay or inadequate pay; they were selected by no standard criteria; they served terms so limited as to prevent their building experience in the job. Although from 1900 on, the schools had their association, a National Conference of Bar Examiners was not created until 1931, to work to improve standards and to co-operate on a national basis with the bar and the schools.

We thus had a long history of easy access to the bar; applicants pressed eagerly forward; there was little organization or tradition to stiffen the administration of admissions requirements. It was not surprising, then, that the bar examinations worked directly to exclude only a small part of those who were willing and able to make repeated efforts to pass them. The examinations lacked the practical support to effect a quota system, if that was desired — as it was by a substantial opinion at the bar. In 1937, 81 per cent of the country's practitioners were in the 35 states which had adopted the American Bar Association standards for minimum qualifications for the bar.

As tests of professional preparation, examinations excluded impressive percentages of applicants on the first attempt — from 46 to 52 per cent the country over in the 1930's, for example. But the states invariably allowed persons who failed, to repeat the examination; only a few began to limit the number of attempts that might be made. When allowance was made for repeaters, survey in five states showed that about 90 per cent of all who applied from 1922 to 1925 eventually passed. Under the relatively well administered system of New York state, 87 per cent of those who attempted the examination in the decade 1922–1931 had passed by 1931. A careful student of the system cautioned in 1930 that, realistically appraised, what the bar examinations "actually do is to act as an informal equalizer of law school standards, assuring admission to the best qualified men promptly, and forcing the more poorly equipped to prepare themselves for a year or two longer. The failures try, on the average, four times, and though before they pass, they must meet the standard set by the best men in the class, they eventually pass."

Even when admissions standards sank to their lowest point, eligibility was conditioned on the "good moral character" of the applicant. Though the states continuously insisted on this factor, up to mid-twentieth century they had not found adequate means to test "character." In their nature the bar examinations were not adapted to this end. In simpler communities where life went largely on everybody's knowledge of everybody else, common sense could take care of most of the problems. But to require letters of recommendation, or to post publicly the names of applicants were requirements that became largely meaningless in the impersonality of modern city life. So far as social science could contribute, it only warned that no satisfactorily objective tests of "character" had been invented. Only the naïve or the hypocritical could disregard this warning. The inherently arbitrary nature of the criteria meant that "character" tests might easily serve as numbers quotas, or quotas based on racial, religious, or other social prejudice. So few states had done much to carry out the character requirement that this danger of abuse was generally potential rather than operative; a 1934 survey concluded that only eleven states provided substantial "character" examinations. But in the face of perennial cries about an "overcrowded" bar, and because the bar mirrored the prejudices of its society, the integrity of the examination system required careful watch.

The depression of the 1930's promoted widespread, if generally superficial, talk in favor of open quotas on admission to the practice. The merits of an avowed quota plan are inseparable from analysis of the economics of the bar in relation to its social functions; discussion of quotas may better be postponed, therefore, to a later consideration of these other matters. But it is here pertinent to note that, as in the case of the character examination, there were serious, unsolved administrative questions.

A quota system that was drastic enough to win the desired economic effects might have deep effect on the social character and function of the bar. Lawyers continued to play an important role in the politics of the country. This factor alone would require very careful definition of the bases of any quota, in order to keep the profession open broadly to talent regardless of class or social sympathies. Scholarship funds must be greatly liberalized, probably from public money; care must be taken that the quota would not destroy worthy smaller law schools whose graduates were needed to supply local leadership in the face of the tendency for the great cities to drain off the talent that passed through the larger schools.

Coupled with the political tradition of democratic access to the bar, the administrative problems posed by an avowed quota system were such as to raise doubt that a quota would ever be adopted. Experience suggested that the more likely trend would be in effect to limit the number at the bar by tightening prelegal and professional educational requirements. But this only pushed back one or two levels further the knotty administrative issues raised by an avowed quota. If nothing else, in the absence of much more liberal scholarships, higher educational requirements amounted to a means test for admission to the practice of law; the financial abilities of candidates would fundamentally determine their access to the bar. This was a result which plainly could not be tolerated as an avowed policy in a democracy. The practical issue was how far the drift might go in such a direction without fair and explicit consideration of what it implied.

5. Bar Associations

During most of the years after the American Revolution, in the local communities, in the states, and in the nation, there was no bar in any but a courtesy use of the title. A "bar" implies internal organization and cohesion, and on the whole lawyers in the United States were among the most unthinkingly and stubbornly individualistic members of the loosely organized American society. In the late eighteenth century the more populous places had local bar associations, which the lawyers formed for social, library, or disciplinary purposes, or for a combination of these ends. In the Northern states some local bar associations — for example, the Suffolk County bar in Massachusetts — attained a high degree of guild organization, and for a generation firmly controlled admissions and professional conduct. In the first two generations after independence the popular temper demanded relaxation of bar standards, and most of these local associations disappeared, or became wholly social.

In the rural districts, between about 1800 and 1870, geography and technology provided the setting for a measure of local bar organization. Settlement was sparse; court thus must be held at various county seats within a judicial circuit. Travel was hard, dangerous, and lonely; it was natural that the judge and the lawyers should ride the roads together, put up at the same tavern, share the same table. Each little county seat did not yet offer enough business to support a local bar or any sizable number of lawyers; hence the same group of men, making the common round, was likely to do most of the law business through the circuit.

The circuit-riding days were the most colorful in the history of the bar of the United States, and they naturally yielded a great stock of reminiscence. These accounts undoubtedly somewhat romanticize the life on circuit. Still, they make clear that under these conditions there grew a substantial corporate sense in the local bar of rural circuits. There was not only professional fellowship, but also a close sense of what was done and what was not done. If there was little formal discipline, there was nonetheless pressure to conform to group standards — pressure that made itself felt in the long discussions and exchanges of professional talk as horses stumbled or wagons bumped their way over the indifferent roads between courthouses; pressure that was expressed through the mock courts that were held of an evening at the tavern, to call one of the brethren to account for conduct that day in court. But in the last quarter of the nineteenth century law business grew enough to support a stay-at-home bar in the local communities, and improved communications fast began to put an end to the common circuit round. Because the former corporateness of the local rural bar had arisen only in unplanned response to circumstances, there was no tradition to give a basis for organization when the circumstances changed.

Planned bar organization revived first in the great cities. It marked a reaction against the corruption in local government. In 1870 a number of leading lawyers organized the Association of the Bar of the City of New York, primarily to fight the Tweed ring. The activities of a notorious fringe of unlicensed practitioners gave impetus to the formation of the Chicago Bar Association, in 1874. Between 1870 and 1878 eight city and eight state bar associations, in twelve states, were formed largely under the motive of reform of municipal government and of conditions within the bar.

But the first-generation history of the first national bar association showed how formless the urban bar in the United States had become; the point was the natural result of nearly a century in which admissions had been almost uncontrolled, standards undefined, discipline nonexistent, and the lawyer simply another runner in the nineteenth-century race to get ahead. At Saratoga, New York, in August, 1878, seventy-five lawyers from twenty-one jurisdictions organized the American Bar Association. They responded to a proposal made earlier that year by a small group which owned no authority beyond its conviction that such a national organization was desirable.

Behind the event was a curious mixture of motives. The prime initiator was Simeon E. Baldwin, of Connecticut — conventionally conservative in politics, a conscientious legal servant of the new concentration of financial power, a teacher of law and legal historian, a judge, sincerely concerned to improve legal education to rebuild professional spirit in the bar, within the framework of unquestioning acceptance of the society as he found it. Francis Rawle, of Philadelphia, joined Baldwin in long shouldering the administrative burden of the new organization. Rawle belonged to a family prominent at the Pennsylvania and federal bar since the formation of the republic; he was bred in the real, if limited, sense of public duty which was traditional in the socially elect inner circle of Philadelphia practitioners; he was treasurer of the American Bar Association from 1878 to 1902, and its president, 1902–1903. The influence of a handful of such men as Baldwin and Rawle was reflected in the Association's initial and continuing concern with improvement of legal education and standards for admission to the bar. Thus from the start the new body attended to a public service function; the emphasis was significant even if for the first generation nothing happened beyond a few committee reports.

A different thread of motive was implicit in the founding of the American Bar Association. The Association was organized in the vacation month of August at the best known, if not the most fashionable, summer resort of the country, and the annual meeting was held only at Saratoga Springs until 1889. A convivial group of Southern lawyers, accustomed to vacation every year at the Springs, formed the largest single element in the original membership. For many years election was a highly selective, personalized matter; for at least twenty years the atmosphere of the Association was mainly social. The objective evidence of this was the fact that there was almost no effective formulation or execution of policy in the name of the Association until in the years 1911–1919 the Association campaigned to rouse public opinion against the Progressive movement for adoption of the recall of judges and of judicial decisions.

By 1890 there were 20 state or territorial bar associations in the United States. By 1900 there were 40; by 1916 there were 48; by 1925 all the states and territories could claim some sort of association. It was hard to get reliable counts of city or county bar organizations, either of those which claimed formal existence or of those which in fact functioned. Estimates put the total at 159 in 36 jurisdictions in 1890, at 623 in 41 jurisdictions in 1916, and at above 1100 by 1930. The great growth in numbers in both cases came after the turn of the century. However, like the American Bar Association, most state and local associations originated primarily for social reasons; and, like the national organization, most of them held to this character until the 1920's. With such rare local exceptions as the Association of the Bar of the City of New York, on the record of functional achievement it is fair to take the American Bar Association as the strongest representative of the organized bar as it grew after the 1870's.

As the symbol of the bar's own sense of corporate being, and as the institution most likely to stand for the bar in the public view, the American Bar Association suffered grave limitations of structure and function. In 1934 Mr. Justice Stone observed that the comparatively disappointing record of the organized bar in this country was the more striking because public policy had conceded the bar so free a hand to form its ranks and fix its policy: "While it has not inherited the completely independent status of the English bar, to no other group in this country has the state granted comparable privileges or permitted so much autonomy."

Structurally, the organized bar was weak because of the ill-considered adoption of the practice of a select instead of an all-inclusive membership; it was weak, also, because it failed to solve the characteristically American problem of federalism. The stronger local bar groups of the late eighteenth century won so complete a control of admissions and professional discipline that they grew to include almost all lawyers in their areas. The 1870's brought revived efforts at formal organization of lawyers in local, state, and national associations. But by then the bar had been too long without standards, and in this condition it was too formless and varied in character, to make practicable or desirable any effort at organization embracing all licensed lawyers. Quite naturally, therefore, those who started the new bar organizations invited only selected lawyers to join. For fifty years thereafter the firm tradition was that the individual lawyer had neither the right nor the duty to join a bar association; membership was a privilege, conferred by election of the existing membership.

The defect was not in the original adoption of the practice of selective membership, but in the failure to turn the practice into a principle. The new associations did not fix reasonably objective, uniform, and defensible criteria for the selection of their members. Hence they weakened their authority to speak either to laymen or to lawyers, as representatives of the profession. In 1880 the American Bar Association had 552 members, or 0.9 per cent of the lawyers in the United States; in 1890 it had 943 members, or 1.1 per cent of the country's lawyers; in 1900 it had 1540 members, or 1.3 per cent of the country's lawyers; in 1910 it had 3690, or 3.0 per cent of the lawyers in the United States. As late as 1915 the total membership of all state bar associations in the country was reckoned as but 20 per cent of the lawyers; and even when membership in local associations was estimated in addition, only about 30 per cent of the country's lawyers in 1915 belonged to some bar organization.

In 1912 the American Bar Association began a new phase of membership policy. It held to the selective idea, but sought nonetheless to add substantially to its rolls. By 1920 it had 15,000 members (about 12 per cent of all lawyers), by 1930 about 27,000 (about 18 per cent of all lawyers), by 1940 about 31,000 (approximately 17 per cent of all lawyers). In the earlier years of smaller rosters, attendance at annual meetings averaged a little over 10 per cent of the membership; after the total membership expanded, a little over 5 per cent typically attended the annual sessions.

After 1910 state and local associations also sought broader membership. Some of them went from the extreme of restriction to an extreme in which they emphasized merely quantitative growth. By 1935 it was estimated that 60 per cent of lawyers in the United States belonged to some professional association.

There were large claims in behalf of the representative character of associations. But the claims were unsupported by proof regarding the distribution of members according to area, income, class, or types of law business. There was some evidence that not all lawyers would concede the representative character of the established associations. Between 1887 and 1891, the American Bar Association met a short-lived rival in the National Bar Association, which justified itself on the claim that it had a more representative structure. In 1936 the National Lawyers Guild was organized under the claim of speaking for liberal political thought at the bar. Some effort was made to avoid the appearance of a clash with the older national organization. But the formation of the Guild was plainly grounded in dissatisfaction with attitudes which the American Bar Association was thought to represent in public affairs. This reaction exaggerated the extent to which the Association had adopted any clear policy line. Even so, it evidenced the failure of the older organization, after fifty years, to establish for itself a clearly outlined and generally accepted sphere of authority as spokesman for the bar.

Although of course any organization tends to be run by a minority, the control of affairs by a self-perpetuating inner circle accentuated the restricted character of the American Bar Association. During its early years the Association was run by the same executive committee, with the same committee chairmen continuing in office, and though the constitution provided that the president be changed annually, until 1888 there was not even a provision that the new president sit on the executive committee. The Executive Committee had power to act between annual meetings. Thus it became the policy-making body of the organization, and its membership was of high importance.

After the first decade the apparent clique leadership of the Association was reinforced for years by an unplanned development which grew out of the Association's main field of public policy work. Though the Association early began discussion of reforms in legal education, its outstanding field of action during its first generation was in the preparation and recommendation of uniform laws for adoption by the states. The Association took the initiative in forming, and chiefly financed the operations of, the Conference of Commissioners on Uniform State Laws. The "commissioners" were in form appointed by their respective state governments. In practice they were self-selected from among those members of the Association who were willing and able to give time and effort to considerable uncompensated work. For over twenty years the Conference was the one branch of the Association in which work was always going forward. It regularly met during the week before the annual meetings of the Association, and out of the cohesion of its membership came the political direction of the succeeding meeting. About one third of the Association's presidents over a twenty-year span came from the Conference group, and the election of scores of Executive Committeemen and other officers was there determined.

This evolution of affairs was without sinister cast. But it did not tend to build up the representative title of the organization as a whole. As part of a general reorganization of structure in 1936, the policy-making authority for the Association was taken from the Executive Committee and vested in a representative House of Delegates. The step reflected the reality of the problem of wider participation in the shaping of the Association's programs; whether it would bring marked change could only be tested by experience.

In a broadly based organization clique control might have been effectively checked by the normal contests of ambition and power. Thus the more fundamental structural defect of the American Bar Association may be seen in its failure to effect an integration with local and state bar associations which might have given it a broader base. At least until 1936 the Association was in effect simply another group competing with local and state groups for status and membership; it was not the nation-wide co-ordinator of the organized bar of the country.

When the American Bar Association was formed, it is true, there were not enough state or local organizations in existence to make possible the creation of an effective general federation. But from 1878 to 1919 the bylaws permitted state or local associations to send delegates to the annual meeting with full privileges of members for the occasion. Nevertheless, no special effort was made to promote closer relationships through this provision, and few state or local organizations were ever thus represented. In 1916 the American Bar Association created a Conference of Bar Association Delegates, to which all organized bar groups were invited to send representatives. However, the Conference had no power to bind the organizations represented in it; its only practical function was to serve as a forum and an educational device. The annual meeting of the national Association itself continued to fall far short of the representative, authoritatively federal character needed if it was to make policy effectively. In the 1930's a sympathetic observer of the Association and its (then) 25,000 members observed that:

> When two thousand of them arrive at a meeting, it scarcely knows what to do with them. As a deliberative body, they can do little. On a close issue their vote would not be convincing, since the state in which the meeting is held usually furnishes about a third of the attendance. In practice, those who are delegates from other associations depart from their homes without instructions and arrive to find themselves possessed of personal influence only. The whole notion of leadership of the American bar by precept and example and voicing its opinion, much less binding its conscience, by the device of annual assemblies, belongs to a bygone century.

Plainly there was need for a more broadly based, more continuously operative procedure to make policy. In 1933 the national Association set up a "National Bar Program" to promote co-operation among bar associations on all levels, by bringing them together to consider and advance specific projects; the American Bar Association supplied an administrative office for the program. The "National Bar Program" evidenced a new sympathy toward federation. This was further shown by the new constitution which the American Bar Association adopted in 1936. This document placed control and administration of the Association in a House of Delegates in which the state bar associations and a few large county and city organizations were given substantial representation. That the government of the Association was not entirely vested in representatives of state and local groups reflected a continuing distrust of federalization on both sides. But at least — about one hundred years after the medical profession had begun its successful federative organization — the organized bar seemed finally committed to a steady, if slow, approach toward nation-wide federation.

Within the states there was as little federal joinder of state and county or city bar associations as there was on a national scale. Nonetheless, in the states events came full circle, back to the idea of an enforced, all-inclusive membership of lawyers in one organization. Perhaps this was because in that more neighborly context, the existing voluntary organizations were more immediately aware that they lacked authority with laymen or lawyers, to speak for the profession.

In the early 1920's several selective state bar associations campaigned successfully for laws establishing the "integrated bar." The movement began in a number of Western states. By 1940 such a plan was in force in 20 states and in Puerto Rico, covering about 40,000 of the 177,000 members of the bar in the United States and its territories. Five states had such limited population and compact boundaries as to remove the practical impetus to compulsory bar organization. Among the rest, by 1940 over half had seen active promotion of the idea.

In origin, the "integrated bar" plan was advanced primarily as a means for better discipline of lawyers in their relations with clients. The inflexible remedy of disbarment was typically the only remedy theretofore provided to deal with professional misconduct. For it the integrated bar laws substituted a range of measures, from disbarment to suspension or reprimand. Old-style disbarment called for cumbersome proceedings in court; in place of these, the new type of law authorized proceedings by agencies of the bar itself, to apply the various remedies provided. Court proceedings inevitably meant publicity which might greatly damage the accused even if he were finally found innocent. In place of this the new laws provided unpublicized proceedings carried on within the organized bar.

Discipline was the primary consideration in the integrated bar plan. But the secondary argument was made, that thus the bar would for the first time have a unified means to express opinion and define standards and policies on professional matters. For the first time — because of the inclusive character of the group taking the action — a professional organization could command public attention and respect as speaking for "the bar."

In return for these advantages, it was argued, the only new, positive obligation put on the individual lawyer was to pay modest annual dues, according to an equal scale. No limits would be put on his individual freedom of speech or action in opposing decisions of the organization of which he was required to be a member.

Such defensive arguments touched the most debatable area of the plan. If the integrated bar engaged simply in routine discipline — checked ultimately by the courts, according to ordinary standards of a fair hearing — it might offer a hopeful substitute for the previous inadequate methods of policing the profession. But the bar would not fulfill its traditional functions in politics and in shaping public policy, if its activities did not range beyond routine discipline. Yet it was in the realm of politics and policy that one hundred years' indifference of the individual lawyer toward the collective responsibilities of the profession might readily permit an inner clique to control, and abuse, power. Perhaps, however, this no more than stated the danger common to all efforts at self-government. And the presumption favored a fair effort to regain leadership forfeited over many years for lack of the moral authority that only responsible, cohesive professional organization could confer.

Education, admissions policy, and organization wove together to form main strands in the character of the bar in the United States. The history of admissions policy and bar organization created a challenge to legal education. The decline in admissions standards, and the disappearance of dominant local bar associations, gave the law schools the opportunity to assert a leadership in regard to bar standards and law reform that was without parallel in the Anglo-American legal world. The history of admissions policy affected the course of bar organization. The relaxation of admissions requirements in the mid-nineteenth century contributed to the formlessness of the bar, its loss of the sense of cohesion and the corporate morale needed for effective organization. Education did not always benefit by what happened regarding admissions and bar organization. The decline in professional standing — both in terms of admissions requirements and bar organization — reacted on the schools; they were impelled to make concessions to immediately "practical" demands in law training, at the expense of a broad grounding of the student in the social, political, and economic context of his subject. Yet, for all its limitations, legal education continued to furnish the most consistent thread of unity among lawyers, and it was the initiative of educators, supported by a handful of men influential in the organized bar, which slowly regained lost ground in admissions standards.

However, after all allowance is made for the factors so far discussed, the law jobs done by lawyers remain as essential to definition of the part the bar played in the growth of the United States. But before we can inquire into the social meaning of these law jobs, we must see what law business amounted to in its own terms. What kinds of matters made up the practice of the law over the years? What was the economic organization of legal service, and how was it related to standards of professional obligation?

CHAPTER THIRTEEN

THE USES OF THE BAR

1. The Types of Law Practice

Almost up to mid-twentieth century the work done by lawyers had never been comprehensively studied. Reliable research in the business flowing through law offices dated mainly from the acute concern with the economics of the profession which was stimulated by the depression of the 1930's. For the years before then, what we know of lawyers' work comes chiefly from legal biography, and secondarily from political and economic history. Legal biography offered only limited evidence. It drew almost wholly on the careers of those lawyers who were most successful, financially or in influence or political power. It was disproportionately concerned with lawyers of the Northeastern United States. Most biography was written of men whose force was felt before 1900. And since the biographer naturally stressed the drama of an individual career, he told more of events in the spotlight than of the day-to-day accretion of instances which in the long run set the stage for the spotlighted moment.

a. The Subject Matter of Law Practice

So far as the evidence goes, the practice of the law throughout our history closely reflected the main concerns of the society as of any given time. The fact marked the degree to which law was woven deep into the growth of the United States. It was not surprising, therefore, that the bulk of law practice consistently dealt with economic affairs — with property, business institutions, and economic conflict.

As was natural in the opening of a new country, land and commerce provided the grist of law office activity well past the Civil War. Thereafter both continued to supply much of the sustaining business for law offices of all sizes and consequence, but in much more run-of-the-mill fashion, with less challenge to the profession; and after the 1880's much of the routine of realty transactions shifted to abstract and title insurance companies, to real estate dealers, and to trust companies.

The vast resources of the public domain made public-land policy one of the first main fields for the lawyer-politician and the lawyer-lobbyist. Neither land speculator, frontiersman, nor homesteader was noted for understanding or ready acceptance of formality in dealing with titles, nor were the land laws adequate to orderly development. Vermont offers an example. For many years that state lacked a recording office; hence there was much fraud in local titles, and this, together with a dispute with New York over Vermont's sovereignty, made the question of possible federal court action on Vermont land titles an important factor in Vermonters' doubts about joining the Union. Kentucky affords another case of lawyers' business that grew out of land-title confusions. In the eagerness to promote settlement, Kentucky permitted settlers to survey their own tracts, of any size or shape, and allowed them on filing their surveys to obtain a land-office warrant for the ground. No account was kept of the land for which warrants were issued, and the Kentucky Court of Appeals referred to "the notorious fact that a great portion of the land in the state had been patented more than once."

Apart from countless individual snarls, time and again lawyers fought out the title — and hence the politics and the livelihood — of whole cities, counties, and regions. In the early nineteenth century Alexander Dallas successfully contended for the title of the Holland Land Company (purchasers from James Wilson), as against Pennsylvania squatter interests whose claims were supported by the radical wing of the Democratic party. The Pennsylvania legislature gave the state supreme court special jurisdiction to pass on the western land patents; Dallas refused to enter his Dutch clients' appearance before what he deemed a prejudiced tribunal, and the land company lost before the state judges, only to win an ultimate victory in federal court. Judah P. Benjamin, Edwin M. Stanton, and Jeremiah S. Black led in an array of lawyers who between 1840 and 1870 fought through to the United States Supreme Court the exposure of fraudulent Mexican land claims that involved huge areas of southern California. The Osage Land Case — with a history that ran from 1825 to 1875 — involved the titles of thousands of small settlers in Kansas; Black successfully defended their interests in the final stage before the Supreme Court of the United States. Matthew Carpenter first won public attention in litigation which involved the title to much of the town of Beloit, Wisconsin. Seargent Smith Prentiss made one of his leading appearances in litigation which drew in question the underlying titles to a great part of Vicksburg, Mississippi. In the years when Matthew P. Deady distinguished the federal court for Oregon, an important body of land litigation before him concerned titles to much of the city of Portland, which were in confusion because of dealings that squatters had in the land in years when title was still in the United States. Such matters were familiar, and of great economic and human importance, the country over. Lawyers further entangled themselves in the land question because they were prominent among land speculators and investors; while William H. Seward practiced in upstate New York in the early nineteenth century, he lost successive law partners to the greater lure of land operations.

Marked specialization in fields of practice did not develop until the end of the nineteenth century. But from an early date the inherent diversity of commerce was reflected in the growth of particular types of law business in particular localities. Commercial instruments, security documents, and collections were familiar items in the work of city lawyers by 1825; in his early days in Portsmouth Daniel Webster made collections no small part of a growing practice. Philadelphia became a center for the insurance of goods and capital invested in commerce, and war years spawned insurance controversies; Horace Binney began his progress to the leadership of the Philadelphia bar with the successful handling of a major insurance lawsuit. That law practice was sensitive to the going needs of business was reflected in the prominence of marine insurance cases in states as far from the seaboard as Kentucky. Owners of cargo vessels on the Mississippi and Ohio furnished a market which was met as early as 1802 by the formation of inland marine insurance companies. Under the same impetus admiralty law figured to a marked degree in law business far from tidewater. Commerce and industry grew and became more complex, and with this growth went recurrent depressions. Lawyers found more and more work in untangling financial affairs and in handling the problems of insolvent debtors; Morrison R. Waite found much of such business in the Miami Valley of Ohio in the depressed 1830's, as did William Evarts in New York of the 1850's. The increasing importance of credit meant more law business for and with banks; Salmon Portland Chase and another lawyer launched a partnership in Cincinnati in 1833, based largely, it seems, on the assurance that they would have the business of the local branch of the Bank of the United States.

Industry and finance gave decided direction to the growth of new types of law business after 1870; and, as we shall later note, this development was paralleled by marked specialization in law practice. The "railroad lawyer" was the first symbol of change. For a generation after the Civil War to be general counsel of a railroad was to hold the most widely esteemed sign of professional success. When William Joseph Robertson left the Virginia supreme court at the end of the war, it was taken as a measure of his further professional advancement that he became general counsel of two railroads; in the early '80s Judge G. W. McCrary left the federal bench to become general counsel of the

Santa Fe; and when Albert Howell Horton resigned as Chief Justice of Kansas in 1895, with the announced intention of better providing for his family, he became one of the chief attorneys for the Missouri Pacific.

But ambitious men soon found that the centers of power were closer to finance. Able lawyers began to sit on boards of directors. As early as the 1850's Richard Blatchford brought business to the Seward firm in connection with railroad consolidations, through his service as trustee for various bond issues. In the '70s and '80s Charles M. DaCosta played the newly important role of counsel in helping pilot railroad expansion and the attendant financial arrangements. Another bench mark of change was the span of years from 1885–1893 in the career of Francis Lynde Stetson; it was indicative of a broad shift in law practice that over those years a leading advocate should withdraw from trial work to specialize in counseling on the plans and conduct of large corporate affairs, notably in matters of corporate reorganization. In marked contrast to such names as Robertson of Virginia, McCrary of Missouri and Kansas, or Horton of Kansas, those of Blatchford, DaCosta, or Stetson were all from the roster of the New York metropolitan bar. The distribution of the most influential new law business responded to a shift in the center of gravity in the economy. Railroad mergers and railroad finance were the avenue to a whole new field of corporate counseling, and the centers of this work were in a handful of great cities east of the Mississippi.

Important developments in law practice of the late nineteenth and early twentieth centuries clustered about the growth of unprecedented concentration of industrial and financial power. Seaboard cities had early seen the founding of great family fortunes; and from early years lawyers had counseled regarding the descent of large properties through wills and trusts. But in the last quarter of the nineteenth century this business first became a main specialty. It was most clearly exemplified in the dry precision and exaggerated caution of that archetype of the English family solicitor, Charles F. Southmayd, of the New York bar. In the 1840's and '50s William H. Seward and William M. Evarts, as general advocates, took in their stride such important patent questions as presented themselves; after the war George Harding and Edmund Wetmore represented the beginning of a specialized patent bar, reflecting a revolution in technology. Before the '70s lawyers had relatively little personal injury business, though in the 1840's the first railroad fellow servant cases warned of new problems. The spread of mechanized transportation, mining, and industry made the personal injury field a major challenge to legal adjustment. The reality of the problems was attested by the spread of safety laws, employers' liability legislation, and finally workmen's compensation systems. After 1920 the automobile still more drastically revolutionized the personal injury business that passed through law offices.

Population continued to move toward several score of great cities, and this drift provided another focus of change in law jobs. Thus small claims, landlord-tenant disputes, issues arising out of broken homes presented vast totals of potential work for the bar; the work was no less real or important because most of it could not be handled economically as the profession was organized to deal with it. The growth of cities changed the nature of law practice in criminal cases. Through most of the nineteenth century the average practitioner took his quota of cases in defense of persons accused of crime; even lawyers most occupied with large affairs appeared for the defense in criminal cases. But in the twentieth century the defense of accused persons became more and more the specialty of a small part of the bar, even as the reach of the criminal law greatly expanded. Only in cases that involved the new types of economic crime, turning on the conduct of business, did the average or leading practitioner continue to play a role.

From 1790 on, law practice included a material amount of dealings with or affecting the government. Such business varied much in type and extent. In the first quarter of the nineteenth century, Alexander Dallas of Pennsylvania made lobbying a substantial part of his practice. The self-consciously upright Horace Binney of Philadelphia acted for the first Bank of the United States in its efforts to secure from Congress renewal of its charter; one could ask no stronger testimony that from an early date such activity was regarded as professionally proper. At first government was primarily the potential source of gifts. This shaped the kind of business that lawyers had before legislatures and executive officers. The high point, as well as the most abused type, of such effort concerned the obtaining of special corporate charters, franchises, and privileges, especially between about 1820–1890. In his political novels, particularly in *Mr. Crewe's Career*, Winston Churchill graphically pictured the efficient partnership of political boss and "railroad lawyer" at the end of the century.

After 1850, as emphasis turned from government bounty to government regulation, new issues began to bring lawyers before government. The Seward firm offers a significant example. One of its clients was the Adams Express Company and on behalf of this client the law firm had many dealings with Congress; after the 1860's the express company lawyers gave as much time before Congress to matters affecting the taxation of their client as to any other single subject matter. To take another example: We may see the prophecy of a new type of client representation in the statement which William D. Guthrie drew for the Pinkerton detective agency to make before the House committee which investigated the Homestead riot. This incident suggests that the bar had a way to go, to learn prudence in its new fields of counseling; the historian of "the Cravath firm" comments that Guthrie's statement "brought down on 'Pinkertonism' more ill will than Homestead." These were early examples of a kind of client representation which steadily grew in importance. Government at all levels in the United States extended the scope of its regulation of business in the twentieth century. In turn this vastly extended the work of lawyers before administrative bodies, as well as before legislatures and courts. Lawyers appeared before new official agencies not only in formal contests, but even more importantly for the purpose of steering clients' affairs through proper procedures of compliance with detailed regulations, and in negotiating and adjusting disputed points outside the traditional framework of litigation.

It was not only the big city law offices which saw the changed emphasis on law business which touched government. Let us look at the office dockets of leading law firms in a moderate-sized Illinois city at three intervals from the late nineteenth century on. In 1874 one firm's docket showed that it handled 143 items of business, which included 3 partition proceedings, 1 divorce, 1 petition for a writ of mandamus, 3 specific performance cases, 3 attachments, 1 arbitration award, and a petition to sell real estate to pay debts. All the rest of its cases involved collections, whether by negotiation or by suit, in justice, county, or circuit court; these included 23 mortgage foreclosures. Thus throughout 1874 this firm appeared in but three courts; knowledge of these courts' procedure served to do the year's business.

At the turn into the twentieth century, the office docket of a law firm in the same locality reflected the development of tort law. In 1904 this firm had suits which involved personal injuries arising out of coal mine accidents and from defective sidewalks, and it defended a libel action, and another for malpractice. It saw to the incorporation of two companies. It conducted one proceeding for an injunction. But, aside from the incorporation proceedings, the firm needed only to know court procedure, to handle its clients' contacts with government.

In sharp contrast was the record of a similarly situated Illinois law firm in 1934. During that year this office was in the federal court to handle a suit regarding the liability of a stockholder in a national bank; it negotiated adjustments with the federal income tax officers; it collected a claim for excess railroad rates, through the Interstate Commerce Commission; it qualified certain securities under the state "blue sky law"; it defended a workmen's compensation case; it litigated an inheritance tax case; it conducted a suit in the state court of claims; it sought a reduction in a corporation franchise tax, through court proceedings; it represented the defendant in a noncompliance proceeding under the National Industrial Recovery Act. The 1874 firm had dealt solely with the local courts. The 1904 firm had its only dealings with government outside the courts in procedures to obtain two corporation charters. But the 1934 firm made only 30 per cent of its appearances before government agencies in the courts; 70 per cent of its appearances were before agencies that had not existed a generation earlier, and whose operations reflected a vast increase in economic regulation.

Parallel to the extended reach of government regulation was of course a great expansion in the volume of the government's own law business. In the early years of the republic, the Attorney General was the federal government's sole lawyer. From this beginning expansion was gradual, until it began a rapid upward climb in the last quarter of the nineteenth century. In 1940 the Department of Justice had over 1200 lawyers on its staff. By then the federal government had well over 5000 legal positions formally recognized in organization charts; and this total did not allow for the many administrative and policy-making posts which lawyers occupied. In 1940 the New York State Law Department and the office of the Corporation Counsel of New York City together employed about 1000 lawyers.

New types of government regulation and services involved individual actions and adjustments, taken under the laws, which ran into figures which would have seemed astronomical to lawyers or administrators of a century earlier. Consider only a limited part of the field of federal taxation: In 1939 the United States Treasury received 7,600,000 income, estate, and gift tax returns; government officers made hundreds of thousands of tax adjustments; 4854 appeals were filed before the (then-styled) Board of Tax Appeals, and 900 appeals were filed in the courts. The percentage of tax matters that went to formal controversy was small. But behind the tremendous flow of such kinds of business — intimately touching the lives and fortunes of hundreds of thousands of people, as well as major sources of government revenue — was a great amount of lawyers' work on both sides of the relationship.

b. Lawyers' Skills

We have thus sketched some of the subject matter of law business at different stages since 1790. But this does not suffice even for an outline of lawyers' work. We must at least also look at the things people wanted

lawyers to do for them in connection with the matters they brought
into lawyers' offices. This raises some questions which we can better
deal with in later discussion of the economics and social functions of
the bar. At this point we shall look only at the immediately professional
learning and techniques which lawyers were called on to apply.

Within this purely professional frame of reference, the most basic
change in the nature of lawyers' professional work was the shift in emphasis from advocacy to counseling. Of course lawyers always did office
work as well as court work. They drew documents, planned the descent
of property, negotiated bargains and settlements, and attended to their
clients' compliance with procedures and requirements which the law
set for the accomplishment of desired results. But before 1870, both in
their own eyes and in the common opinion of laymen, lawyers' distinctive business was contest in court; the criterion in handling most matters
out of court was how the arrangement would stand up under a later
challenge in court; by common consent in the typical community the
prizes in reputation, public influence, and wealth were the due of the
able advocate.

To call the roll of leaders of the bar in the first part of the nineteenth
century is to list men who without exception won pre-eminence not in
office conference or around a board-of-directors table, but in court or
in politics: Luther Martin, (1748–1826), William Pinkney, (1764–
1822), William Wirt, (1772–1834), Jeremiah Mason, (1768–1848),
Daniel Webster, (1782–1852), Rufus Choate, (1799–1859), James
Louis Pettigru, (1789–1853), Horace Binney, (1780–1875), Reverdy
Johnson, (1796–1876). It may be objected that the list is drawn too
exclusively from the Eastern seaboard. Consider, then, Abraham Lincoln, who progressed from an extemporizing circuit-riding pleader to
a place in the late 1850's as a leading courtroom attorney for the Illinois
Central. Or take as an example the first president of the American Bar
Association, James Overton Broadhead of Missouri, (1819–1898):
"There is great talk in eulogies of his being an outstanding Constitutional lawyer. Everybody in that day was a Constitutional lawyer."

Men brought business to a lawyer's office when they were ready to
fight in court. They expected their lawyers to fight in court. Clients
and lawyers carried through to the highest appeal matters which in the
mid-twentieth century were thought too small to warrant appearance
in an inferior court. The years after 1870 showed a more matter-of-fact
attitude, a prevailing distaste for litigation as a costly luxury, and increasing effort to use law and lawyers preventively. Why this should
have been so is a problem in the social functions of the law. Here it is
enough to note the fact.

Whatever was the full explanation for the shift in emphasis from advocate to counselor, it came mainly from the more complicated demands that the business world made on the law. It is in this realm that we see the first signs of a new type of lawyer. Looking back from a time when the balance had definitely shifted to the counselor, Joseph H. Choate recalled how rare it was to find special experience or talent in business among mid-nineteenth-century bar leaders. Choate singled out Sidney Bartlett and Charles G. Loring of the Boston bar, and William Curtis Noyes of New York, as among the first of the modern business lawyers. By the 1850's leading law firms began to take on a characteristic make-up. One partner was the advocate; another was the "office man." This was something of an approach to the English distinction of barrister and solicitor, though we shall later see that law firms in the United States never reached the clear-cut English distinction. It was likely to be the "office man" who gave the continuity to a firm; a case in point is that of George W. Strong, who for forty-nine years directed the affairs of a great New York City law office.

There was another sign of the times in the extent to which in the late 1850's and '60s business clients sought "opinions" from leading advocates on issues pertinent to business policy. This became a material part of the practice of William M. Evarts in New York and of Benjamin R. Curtis in Boston. Through 1900 the writing of opinion letters was a transition toward the lawyer's participation in business policy making. But it was not to be the last stage of that movement. In a formal "opinion" the lawyer took no responsibility for determining or evaluating the facts of the situation or the practical wisdom of any course to be followed; he merely gave his opinion on the law of a situation as it was presented to him by a client's question. In the long run this was not what was wanted by clients who were trying to steer their way through a maze of legal and economic complications. So the lawyer was more and more asked to share the responsibility for appraisal of facts and choice of policy in the shaping of his client's business.

There was no more striking symbol of the new style of bar leader than Paul D. Cravath. From 1899–1940 he was a partner in the Seward firm, which in its twentieth-century career became identified with his name. "Six feet four inches in height, he weighed well over 200 pounds. He had a massive head, with wavy brown hair which turned iron-gray as he reached his fifties, a ruddy complexion, and piercing blue-gray eyes behind gold-rimmed, later shell-rimmed pince-nez." Cravath disciplined a large law office, to produce a professional product of high technical quality, through businesslike organization His personal strength and interest lay in what went on around the business conference table. His partner De Gersdorff noted Cravath's "passion for organization," his immediate grasp of the implications of the lawyer's new responsibilities toward his corporation clients.

De Gersdorff summarized Cravath's working philosophy:

> He sensed that a big law firm which attempted to cover the whole field of general practice could not attain the best results for its clients or for itself unless, in addition to men with broad experience in various fields, it contained specialists in those narrower fields which, with the passing years, became both more and more important and more and more complicated. Prior to the time when Cravath took control as the active head of the firm there had been little attempt at scientific organization in the office. There had been many good men and not a few distinguished members of the firm, but for the most part each of them worked independently by and for himself, with his own assistants, seeking to cover all the varied problems of the particular clients with which he dealt. Cravath's organizing genius gradually transformed the firm into a cohesive team containing men both with training and experience designed to give them a comprehensive view of the problems of the office clients as well as specialists highly trained through concentration in particular fields such as corporate organization and security issues, corporate reorganization, the preparation of wills and trust agreements, the trial of cases and argument of appeals, and, of increasing importance in later years, Federal and State taxation.

Such was the base of operations. With so highly perfected a technical instrument at his hand, Cravath fixed a new role for the lawyer, as he entered the field of business conference and negotiation. Let no one think that he resigned the advocate's role out of distaste for conflict. "Cravath was essentially an extrovert, with unbounded determination and self-confidence, intolerance of incompetence or inefficiency, and contempt for mediocrity." Robert T. Swaine, his partner and historian of the firm, graphically sketches the field which Cravath took for the new, rightful domain of the lawyer as counselor and policy maker:

> Unlike the scintillating and contentious Guthrie, Cravath had no instinct for litigation. On its merits he thought it was something to be avoided at any reasonable price; and he had neither liking nor capacity for courtroom forensics. Cravath's forum was the conference room. Seldom was he a party to a conference that he did not dominate by his driving personality, with its ruthlessness tempered by persuasiveness and patient regard for the opinions of others. He would first try to convince and argue away opposition, but he

could ride roughshod over those he could not convince. Usually
he succeeded, one way or the other, though feelings often were
hurt. In abstract reasoning of a pure question of law, Cravath was
not the equal of either Guthrie or his later partner Henderson;
but in diagnosing a practical corporate law problem he had no
superior among his contemporaries.

Of course this is to look at the top bracket of the bar, as measured by
financial success, material influence, and professional esteem. We noted
at the start of this discussion that there were only limited data available
for any broad survey of lawyers' business through the years. However,
the evidence that we have confirms that the great city business law
offices of the early twentieth century set a pattern which simply put in
clearest form certain trends which marked the more lucrative and influential practice of the law throughout the country. The first reliable
investigations of the economics of the profession were made in the
1930's. These studies tended to confirm the new picture of the lawyer
as primarily advisor, counselor, administrator of affairs — in contrast to
the image of the frock-coated Daniel Webster, which was the mid-
nineteenth-century stereotype of the bar. We shall consider at a later
point how far law practice took on the characteristics of the "administrative process"; and this will further confirm the new outlines of the
lawyer's role. That the picture is more matter-of-fact, less dramatic,
than the nineteenth century would have drawn it, adds to the conviction that it is true to its time.

2. The Economics of the Legal Profession

The economics of a profession is a subject which is perilously tempt-
ing to hypocrisy, cynicism, or naïveté, in the thinking both of the practitioner and of the layman. The historic concept of a profession includes
the ideas of organization, learning, and public service, to which making
a living is incidental. This concept translates the abstractions of morals
into far more tangible terms than frail human nature is usually asked to
meet. And the professional idea sets these moral obligations as the
framework for handling not merely the great moral crises but also
the more difficult daily grist of relentlessly material and often ambiguous incident. As if the inherent difficulties were not enough, in the
United States the professional idea had to make its way in a society
dominated by middle-class attitudes — a society, that is, which was
characteristically distrustful of speculative thought and the grand manner in action; a society which was interested in what could be accumulated, counted, and used; a society that had concern for righteousness,

but under a scale of values formed in a period highly individualistic and competitive in its measure of a man. We should not be surprised, therefore, to discover that — failing to rationalize even the plain economics of its operations — the bar achieved a somewhat less than satisfactory working relation between its characters as profession and as business.

a. The Size of Law Firms

The economic organization of the practice of the law was relatively simple through the country's history. In the conditions that prevailed after 1870, it was a simplicity which, without any plan or malice, deprived many people of legal services which they might advantageously have enjoyed.

Through the years, most lawyers practiced as individuals. From the first quarter of the nineteenth century on, there were partnerships. But no firms of large membership appeared, even in the great cities, until the end of the century. The typical partnership was a two-man affair; it usually had its "office" member and its "court" member; and it ordinarily operated without a formal agreement of partnership, or under an agreement of the simplest kind.

Joseph H. Choate tells of the modest circumstances of the leading New York City firm in which he became a junior lawyer about mid-nineteenth century:

> The conduct of law business in those primitive days was very different in every particular from the strikingly commercial methods into which the profession has fallen, or risen, in recent years. [Choate was speaking as of 1914.] For instance, the office of Butler, Evarts & Southmayd consisted of four very moderate-sized rooms on the second floor of 2 Hanover Street . . . cashier's and accountant's rooms would have been thought absolutely unprofessional, as the lawyers of the establishment did their own work.

Another distinguished New York lawyer recalled that even toward the end of the nineteenth century a successful big city office was relatively small — staffed with "but few law clerks, one or two stenographers, and perhaps an engrosser. Often the arguments and briefs were written out in longhand."

In a dramatic contrast to such simplicity was the growth in size of later metropolitan law firms. The firm of Strong and Cadwalader was formed in New York City in 1878; it then included 2 partners, 4 members of the legal staff, and 4 of the nonlegal staff. In 1913 its successor firm numbered 52 persons. These included 8 partners, 15 members of the legal staff, and 20 of the nonlegal staff. In 1938 this firm's roster totaled 142 persons. These included 13 partners, 44 members of the legal staff, and 85 of the nonlegal staff. The "Cravath firm" rose from 3 partners and 16 associated lawyers in 1906, to 22 partners and 72 associated lawyers in 1940, and in 1940 it had a clerical staff of close to 150. As early as 1910 it was estimated that the overhead cost of a large city law office was 60 per cent of its fees.

The historian of a great New York City firm counted the growth of large-scale law offices at their mid-twentieth century peak. Mr. Robert T. Swaine noted that the Martindale–Hubbell Directory for 1948 listed 284 law firms in the United States with 8 or more partners, located in 57 different cities. New York had 73 and Chicago 25 of such large firms; 7 cities had 10 or more. On the largest scale, firms with 12 or more partners totaled 99, in 21 cities; New York had 33 of such large offices, and Chicago 15. A quite different type of large-scale law office was that staffed by full-time salaried lawyers in the employment of corporations. Mr. Swaine counted nearly 70 lawyers in the parent legal department and the legal department of one subsidiary of a New York utility holding company; one insurance company maintained a New York legal department of 70 members, and another had a legal staff of 52; an oil company had 28 lawyers in its legal department, a railroad 25.

Such great law offices in the first part of the twentieth century symbolized a new role of the bar. They reflected the demands of big business clients. They expressed a businesslike temper which had grown to mark the financially successful lawyers in cities throughout the country. On the other hand, only a handful of lawyers were members of highly organized offices. Several studies were made of the organization of law offices in different parts of the United States in the early 1930's. These studies showed only between 18 to 25 per cent of lawyers in partnerships. And they showed only between 24 to 40 per cent of lawyers employed by other lawyers, even in the first to the fourth year of practice — although these beginning years were those in which, under conditions of nineteenth-century apprentice training, most young lawyers would have been found in the offices of older members of the bar.

Data published by the Office of Business Economics, United States Department of Commerce, in August, 1949, showed continuation of the earlier pattern of law firm organization. In 1947 three fourths of non-salaried lawyers practiced without partners, according to the sampling taken by the Department of Commerce. Of the rest of the bar, 15 per cent were in firms of two partners, 5 per cent in firms of three partners, and 2 per cent in firms of four members. The larger the firm, the larger the average income of its members — a fact which, of course, did not prove that it was the size of the firm which produced the larger incomes. In 1947 the mean net income of lone practitioners was $5759; that of members of two-partner offices, $8030; of members of three-partner offices, $12,821; of members of firms having nine or more partners, $27,246.

b. The Overhead Cost of Legal Service

The overhead cost of conducting a successful law practice greatly increased in the course of a century. Books were the lawyers' tools, and work with books occupied much of his time. Ours was a common-law (case-law) system, and our lawyers traditionally emphasized case precedent even in handling legislation. Whatever its virtues, this was a legal system which was inherently costly to work with. It required time-taking search for authorities. It called for expensive law libraries. And libraries grew to include not only the reported decisions of courts, but also digests, treatises, legal newspapers, advance pamphlet editions of judicial opinions, and expensive loose-leaf publications embracing the output of administrative agencies. In the United States we had our many separate jurisdictions, state and federal. This meant that, at high cost, there must be published many separate sets of reported decisions, statutes, and executive or administrative materials.

Clients brought more and more problems to lawyers which called for specialized knowledge or skill. This was a natural reflection of the greater reach, detail, and complexity of legal regulation and of business. It was another factor in the mounting cost of legal business. If a lawyer was careful both of his client's interests and of his own reputation, he must educate himself in new fields for which the staples of an old-style law training no longer sufficed. The many lawmaking jurisdictions in the United States contributed to the specialization of knowledge that was involved in the practice.

We may date the revolution in the cost of legal service after the 1870's. Before then a lawyer did not have to have very many books. Before then lawyers could educate one another to a large extent, in the regular interchange of the circuit-riding or small local bar. Before then the intricate web of administrative regulation had not been woven. After the '70s the printed sources of the law became a flood; the bar shared the growing impersonality of a society that was plunged headlong into urban ways; and the reach of government vastly expanded.

c. *The Division of Labor at the Bar*

Despite these changes in conditions of law practice, in 1940 the bar was organized just about as it was in 1840. It was still a profession of highly individualistic practitioners. The average lawyer practiced alone. In a minority of cases, he practiced with one or two partners. In the typical instance, he relied on building up his individual resources — in books, knowledge, skill, and experience — in order that he might operate as far as possible as a completely self-sufficient unit.

Division of labor within the profession came slowly. Up to the 1940's it had developed to a marked degree only in a small inner circle of law firms that were close to the seats of financial power in the great cities. The comparative lack of specialization was the most striking evidence of the gap between the economic organization of the bar and the range and difficulty of potential law business in the first part of the twentieth century. In 1938 a special committee of the American Bar Association surveyed the economic condition of the bar. Summarizing the few reliable studies available, the committee observed that "A general absence of specialization, a fairly miscellaneous clientele, and a large amount of work in the fields of property, collections, and torts, appear to be characteristic of the run of the bar." Very few lawyers were ready to call themselves specialists. This was so even when to assert the claim might bring in business; for example, relatively few lawyers enrolled as specialists under a lawyers' reference plan which was set up under bar association auspices in Illinois in the 1930's.

The roots of the nonspecialized character of the bar in the United States ran deep. The colonial bar had before it the example of the English distinction of barrister and solicitor. The English barrister was the courtroom advocate; he rendered "opinions" on questions of law involved in facts presented for his opinion by a solicitor; he belonged to the group which traditionally supplied nominees to the Bench. The English solicitor was the client-caretaker; he alone had direct relations with clients; he did all the grubbing for facts and the briefing needed to "instruct" the barrister who would present the case in court; he drew and cared for the documents under which lands and estates passed and commerce was carried on. The barrister-solicitor distinction originated in accidents of circumstance. It began probably because the courts were concentrated at Westminster. This brought the ablest practitioners together, to form the Inns of Court. Legal education was controlled by the members of the Inns, and these lawyers early began to specialize in advocacy, which was then the most desirable part of law practice. Despite its chance beginnings, the barrister-solicitor distinction grew into a maze of social, legal, and economic elements. The barrister was the social superior of even the distinguished solicitor; a rigid line of etiquette separated the types of law work which each might do; the barrister practiced in proud independence, never forming a partnership even with a fellow at the bar, let alone with a solicitor. Specialization also developed within each of the two classes of English lawyers, according to the different courts before which men appeared and according to the distinct types of business they handled. This further specialization in the English legal profession arose mainly after 1776.

In the second half of the eighteenth century the colonies saw the slender beginnings of the English barrister-solicitor distinction. The Southern bar included men trained at the Inns of Court. In some Northern states distinctions were taken between different levels of practitioners; there were "attorneys" who might practice only before the inferior courts, and there were "counselors" who, having passed a substantial probation in the lower courts, might appear before the higher tribunals.

The Revolution broke the Southern tie to the Inns of Courts, and it swept away the close organization and strict discipline of the bar in Northern states. The political and social temper of the times opposed any guildlike exclusive organization of the profession. In 1790 the country was poor, scattered and sparsely settled, and engrossed in exploiting its natural wealth; conditions would not allow law practice to develop according to the costly etiquette of the peculiar English type of lawyers' specialization. These circumstances put a lasting stamp on the character of the profession in this country. One hundred years later Bryce was impressed that an ambitious beginner at the law in the United States had earlier and broader opportunities to advance than his counterpart in England. The young lawyer in the United States was free to deal directly with clients, and no dignities of professional class forbade him to pick up such small, experience-building and practice-building business as came his way.

In the nineteenth century the advocate emerged as the model of the leader of the bar in the United States, and successful firms typically included a "court" lawyer and an "office" lawyer. Such a partnership was itself a development that differed basically from the English pattern. Neither in fact nor in form was the advocate in this country confined, as was the English barrister, to appearing in court and giving "opinions."

After 1870 leadership at the bar in the United States went to men who more resembled the solicitor. But, as in the early case of the advocate, these "solicitors" were not confined to the role that English etiquette would have assigned them. In such men as Elihu Root or Louis

D. Brandeis the bar of the United States developed a type of leader peculiarly its own. Such men mingled the roles of barrister, solicitor, business adviser, and statesman.

So far as the first half of the twentieth century developed any further division of labor at the bar, it was not along the lines of a distinction of barrister and solicitor. The demand for specialization was in terms of subject matter rather than in terms of litigation. There were of course some lawyers who still were courtroom specialists. But in no respect did they dominate the profession or form an exclusive branch of it. Moreover, this modern courtroom specialist was likely to be a man who possessed not so much a general forensic skill as a special ability to handle particular subject matter (torts, patents, or corporation law, for example).

d. Lawyers' Incomes

There was little reliable information on lawyers' incomes, until the depression of the 1930's stimulated studies in the economics of the bar. In the nineteenth century leaders at the bar earned substantial, and occasionally very high, professional incomes. In Connecticut in 1789 the top income was reputed to be only $2000. By contrast, in Philadelphia Dallas was making $10,000 by 1801, and double that by 1814. From New Orleans in 1811 François Xavier Martin wrote a friend that "A lawyer of common talent makes from $4 to $5000; several make $8 or $10,000. What is understood as a fee in ordinary parlance is $500. They call a good fee $1000 or $1500." Also in New Orleans, by the 1850's, Judah P. Benjamin was making between $40,000 to $50,00 a year from a practice based largely on commercial affairs. In New York in 1869 Elihu Root and his partner, in the first year of their firm, each drew $5000 from the practice. At about the same time, the records of the well-established Seward office indicate that it had a net income for 1870 that was "considerably less than $150,000 a year." At the peak of his practice, just past 1850, William M. Evarts was making about $75,000 a year. In Boston Benjamin R. Curtis's professional receipts for the period 1857–1874 were estimated at $650,000.

The position of the top bracket of the nineteenth century bar is thus fairly clear. As to the generality of lawyers we have only scattering information. Of Philadelphia's 1500 lawyers in the 1880's less than one third were said to be self-supporting, and not more than 100 were thought to have an income over $5000 a year. In Boston of the 1890's it was estimated that half a dozen men made $20,000 a year, a dozen more $10,000, and perhaps another quarter of the bar had incomes of $5000. For about the same period Bryce estimated that not more than

30 men in the country made over $100,000 from the profession. In 1936 the United States Department of Commerce sampled net professional incomes. It found 18 per cent of lawyers with net professional incomes under $1000, 42 per cent under $2000, 81 per cent under $5000. In the same period ⅔ of United States families had incomes under $1500.

There were many respects in which data on lawyers' earnings were incomplete. For no period was it reliably known how many men were in practice, how many wholly in practice and how many only partly, how many practiced part time for lack of business or because of profitable side lines or from ill-health, how many were retired or in semi-retirement, how many men admitted to the bar had never practiced, or what men who practiced earned in various localities or according to age groups or types of practice.

From local studies some additional detail could be added to fill out a picture of lawyers' economic status in the 1930's. Such studies indicated that, apart from the highest and the lowest brackets, lawyers in cities earned about the same amounts throughout the country over a stretch of years; the chances of earning big incomes in the large cities were not so promising as to deserve much weight in the choice of a place in which to practice. Except in the smallest towns, lawyers on the whole enjoyed a more comfortable and stable financial situation outside the great cities than in them. Young lawyers had very low incomes during the first five years of practice; the best income years ranged quite evenly through the eighth to the thirty-seventh year of practice. Torts and corporation law work yielded better fees than the average items of practice in relation to time spent on them; in other types of work income seemed about proportionate to time invested.

In August, 1949, the Office of Business Economics of the United States Department of Commerce published a summary of sample studies of lawyers' incomes which tended to corroborate but also to go beyond the general findings of earlier inquiries. In 1948 the mean net income of all nonsalaried lawyers, according to the sample studied, was $8121; the median income (probably a more representative figure) was $5719. Summaries of data, 1929–1948, showed that the average net income of such lawyers corresponded very closely with the fluctuations of general business conditions. Lawyers' incomes were more unevenly distributed within the profession than were incomes of other professional groups, but the greatest inequality showed itself in depression years; in prosperous times lawyers of small or moderate income enjoyed greater relative increases of income than lawyers of larger income. The 1936–1947 figures showed a tendency toward greater equality of incomes within the bar. Average income tended to increase with the size of the community; however, the 1949 study noted that surveys in depression years had shown some tendency for lawyers' incomes to fall more in the larger cities than in those of intermediate size. Salaried lawyers showed less inequality within their ranks than existed among independent practitioners. Salaried lawyers also showed markedly higher incomes; the median income for salaried lawyers was 16 per cent higher than that for independent lawyers.

The most striking implications of the mid-century income data for the social functions of the bar concerned the relation between income and type of clientele. Nonsalaried and part-salaried lawyers received about half of their professional fees for services to business, about half for services to individuals; in 1941 about 48.5 per cent of their total gross income from fees was from service to individuals, in 1947 about 52.1 per cent. But seven of every ten nonsalaried lawyers depended on individual clients for the major part of their gross receipts. Hence lawyers who concentrated on personal service types of business earned considerably less than those whose major income came from service to business. This appeared graphically from a table of:

Percentage of Total Gross Income Received for Services to Individuals: Relation to Income

% of Gross	% of Lawyers	Mean Net Income	Median Net Income
Less than 50%	29.4	$11,737	$9014
50% and over	70.6	5,650	4226
90% and over	32.5	4,456	3390

e. The "Overcrowded" Bar

To lawyers the overshadowing economic aspect of their profession was the competition to earn a living and win standing. In one form or another this concern showed itself in all periods of our history. In earlier years lawyers worried about competition within their own ranks. Toward the end of the nineteenth century they first began to talk about new competitors outside the legal profession. By the 1920's this new concern had been given a label, and the bar took first steps to oppose the "unauthorized practice of the law."

Lawyers invariably attributed competition from within the profession to its "overcrowded" state. The perennial character of this complaint cast some doubt on its validity. Young John Adams looked darkly on his prospects in mid-eighteenth century; every county of the Province of Massachusetts swarmed with students and young lawyers. About 1800 an acid observer claimed that only the excessively litigious nature of the people in Connecticut supported the sizable bar there. In 1839 George W. Strong thought that the law was made uncertain in New York because an overcrowded bar encouraged too many lawsuits. As bar associations revived, there were further expressions of concern over the numbers admitted to the profession. Such views are of record in Wisconsin in 1881 and 1914, for example; and in 1940 polls showed that there was a general conviction among the organized lawyers in Michigan and New Jersey that too many newcomers were being licensed.

The respectable age of the belief did not prove it true. The matter was among those considered in 1938 by the American Bar Association's "Special Committee on the Economic Condition of the Bar." The committee pointed out that there was nothing more than opinion to support the belief that the bar was "overcrowded"; such standards of measure as had been used to demonstrate overcrowding were found to be untrustworthy.

In the first place, there was no reliable information on the number of lawyers in practice; and without this data, there was no base line from which to gauge the "crowding" at the bar. After 1850 the census gave some figures. But there was reason to doubt their adequacy; a detailed check of data from other sources on the number of lawyers actively practicing in Wisconsin from 1848–1932 showed that the census much understated the totals for that state.

If the census data were accepted, as the only general figures available, they showed that on the whole from 1850–1900 lawyers increased in number faster than did the population. After 1900 the story was different. The 1910 and 1920 census figures showed a ratio of lawyers to total population that was below the ratio of 1880. The 1930 census showed a sharp increase in the relative number of lawyers, but their ratio to the population was still well below the peak of 1900. From 1880–1920 there averaged throughout the country 786 persons to 1 lawyer; in 1900 the relation was 704–1; in 1920, 863–1; in 1930, 764–1; in 1940, 745–1.

The census of later years also showed that lawyers were unevenly distributed. Of 66 cities with populations of 120,000 or more in 1930, 17 had less than 400 persons per lawyer. The 93 cities of over 100,000 population in 1930 accounted for 29 per cent of the population, but had 48 per cent of the lawyers. Communities under 25,000 population, including all rural areas, made up to 60 per cent of the population, but only 38 per cent of the bar. A contemporary sample indicated that in the rural districts lawyers concentrated in the county seats, and that many small communities had no lawyer. The data on area distribution of lawyers suggested that "overcrowding" was primarily a phenomenon of certain large cities.

Lawyer-to-population ratios were actually not very useful measures of the state of the bar. Law business depended on many other factors in addition to population. Chiefly it depended on the economic activity in a given place at a given time. Little study had been made of the relation between such facts and the number of lawyers. For like reasons, it was unsatisfactory to measure the relation between the numbers of lawyers and the per capita wealth in an area. Law business depended on the use rather than the mere amount of wealth credited to a given place at a given time. Wealth in the United States was often distantly controlled; the law business connected with it might thus be done in cities far away from the site of the mines, factories, or shops that immediately produced the wealth. Where population was dense, per capita wealth might be less, but law jobs might be the more numerous.

Such evidence as existed of the quantity of law business done at different times in the United States cast doubt on the claim that the bar was overcrowded. There were some indices of the probable extent of law work through the years — the number of documents filed with registers of deeds, the number of divorces, of workmen's compensation suits, of suits in local federal courts, and of suits before state appellate courts. Such indices were studied in Wisconsin for the years 1880–1933, and in California for the years 1910–1933. They showed that over those periods the volume of work for lawyers tended to outstrip the number of lawyers. The total quantity of probable law business seemed to have grown at least as fast as the profession. Even such data did not carry full conviction. There was no accurate measure of the undoubted increase in the overhead cost of law practice; nor was there an accurate measure of the undoubted increase in lay competition. Some observers noted a tendency for the greater bulk of law business and the better fees to go to fewer law offices of larger size. But if this trend existed, there was no accurate measure of it. Finally, the effort to gauge opportunities in the practice of law was complicated by evidence which suggested a declining trend in litigation, and an increasing relative emphasis on office work.

Though complaints of overcrowding went back to the eighteenth century, there was one essential element in the matter which was not recognized until after 1930. Lawyers had discussed their "overcrowded" profession on the tacit assumption that the only possible variable in the situation over the long run was the size of the bar. Discussion assumed that the pie was baked; the only question was, into how many pieces to cut it.

In 1934 members of the Yale Law School faculty made a pioneer study in New Haven, Connecticut, to determine whether there might not be a great deal of untapped business for lawyers. The results of this and some other like studies over the next ten years suggested that there was.

Studies of incomes and spending in the United States in the middle 1930's indicated that lawyers' paying clients came largely from higher income groups that included only about 13 per cent of the country's families. The 14 per cent of families with annual incomes less than $500 were apt to get legal service only so far as it was available without fee from legal aid bureaus or individual lawyers. There remained 73 per cent of the families in the United States, receiving 56 per cent of the income; if these people needed legal service, they could afford to pay moderate fees for it. The United States Department of Labor sampled the spending of wage earner and small-salaried families of average income of $1500 in 30 cities in the middle 1930's. The sample showed that one third of the families owned homes, over one half owned automobiles, and others bought furniture and other goods on secured credit. These items spelled potential need for legal advice, to prevent or adjust difficulties. These families averaged $60 a year for health expenditures, and $30 for such personal services as barbershop or beautyshop care. They spent less than $1.00 per year per family for legal services. Only 1.5 per cent of the group consulted a lawyer in the course of a year.

Such facts implied the need for a fresh analysis of law business. The New Haven study of 1934 first undertook such a new approach. The Yale researchers interviewed 50 lawyers, 412 householders, and 61 neighborhood businessmen in New Haven. Their sample was designed to represent lower- and middle-class incomes. The object was to find out from these people (1) in how many transactions they had been involved in the past year where a lawyer's advice might have been of service to protect their interests and prevent trouble; and (2) how many actual trouble situations they had experienced in the past year, in the adjustment of which a lawyer might help.

The householders and businessmen interviewed reported 557 matters that fell within the scope of the survey; 299 of these were situations where preventive advice might have been in order, and 258 were situations where some kind of trouble had already occurred and there was need to adjust it. In only 11 per cent of the prevention situations and in 47 per cent of the trouble situations had the people sought outside advice: and these instances included those in which advice was taken from someone other than a lawyer. In the 557 matters noted by the survey, 28 per cent were handled with, and 72 per cent without, the advice of some third person. The businessmen's annual affairs showed a higher proportion of matters in which preventive advice might have been appropriate, than did the year's record of the householders. Yet the businessmen had taken outside advice in only 6 per cent of these prevention situations; the householders had sought outside advice in 19 per cent. Where actual trouble had occurred, the householders took outside advice in 45 per cent of the situations, the businessmen in 52 per cent. There was some indication that members of the sample group who were in the higher income bracket (especially the businessmen) were most likely to seek outside advice.

Where the householders sought outside advice, they went to a lawyer in 78 per cent of the prevention, and in 83 per cent of the trouble situations; the businessmen chose a lawyer as their adviser in 64 per cent of their prevention, and in 85 per cent of their trouble situations. When people sought outside advice, they expressed much more satisfaction than dissatisfaction with the outcome. When the adviser had been a lawyer, they tended to be more critical of the results, but they still expressed much more satisfaction than dissatisfaction with the help received. Both householders and businessmen showed that they were at a loss as to how to select a lawyer. Generally they did so on the chance advice of friends.

The New Haven survey inquired only as to civil matters that might involve legal questions. The householder seemed most likely to seek outside advice, preventively, when he bought or sold real estate, or made a will or some other property arrangement. Occasionally he would consult a lawyer in connection with a mortgage, usually where the mortgagee was a bank or other financial institution. When the householder found himself in actual trouble, he most often took outside advice when the trouble involved an accident, a question of inherited property, or an issue between landlord and tenant. The businessman was likely to be involved in a considerable range of situations where advice might protect his interest or ward off future trouble. His problems might involve income and other taxes, rentals, government permits, insurance, loans received, endorsements, automobile sales or purchases, installment buying, business purchases, investments, mortgages, property arrangements, or incorporation. In contrast to this array of situations, however, the survey showed that the businessmen sought outside advice only in a number of cases of income taxes and leases, one case of a property arrangement, and one case of an incorporation. When the businessmen used outside help in trouble cases, the matter was usually about uncollected bills, with a few disputes over delivery of merchandise.

The New Haven findings deserve summary at this length because, though the sample was limited, the results offered a refreshing breath of fact in an atmosphere fogged with generalities. Scattering evidence after 1934 tended to confirm that there was a considerable area of untapped law business among people of moderate means. A study made in Columbus, Ohio, in 1940 showed that only 14 per cent of a sampling of householders, and only 39 per cent of a sampling of downtown businessmen (excluding department and chain store operators) had consulted a lawyer in the preceding year. In 18 months following the opening of experimental, low-cost, "neighborhood law offices" in Philadelphia, 82 per cent of the clients stated that they had never before entered a law office, either of a private attorney or of the legal aid society. A large percentage of these Philadelphians came for preventive advice; less than 5 per cent brought matters involving litigation; and less than 2 per cent actually litigated. They were a broad cross section of lower-income people, including school teachers, clergymen, day laborers, skilled laborers, and civil service employees.

In 1940 the Chicago Bar Association set up a referral office to help the layman to find a competent lawyer to handle his problem. In its first year the office handled 400 inquiries. By its sixth year it was handling some 16,000 telephone, mail, and personal inquiries. Since the secretary of the office was a competent lawyer, he was able to answer 80 per cent of the inquiries without referral. In 1945 the Committee on Legal Aid of the Association of the Bar of the City of New York reported that two thirds of the time of one lawyer in the legal aid office was required to tell people who were not seeking legal aid, but who could and wanted to pay a reasonable fee for service, where they could find competent counsel.

In the first six months of 1946 the legal assistance system of the United States Army handled matters in the following categories:

Adoption	8,145	Personalty	21,896
Affidavit	53,690	Power of Attorney	46,712
Citizenship	10,007	Real Property	17,749
Contracts	15,556	Taxes	423,682
Divorce	74,392	Torts	12,540
Estates	6,616	Wills	34,065
Insurance	42,633	Miscellaneous	48,492
Marriage	31,362		

This random sampling of the difficulties of a large body of citizens who happened to be soldiers, of course omitted such familiar civilian problems as questions over wages, rents, possession of real estate, partnership relations, and business questions in general. Nonetheless, the totals were suggestive of the scale of legal questions arising in everyday affairs. As matters stood about mid-twentieth century, a qualified observer concluded that by a conservative estimate there was unsatisfied need for legal services among "at least one third of all our citizens."

f. Lay Competition for Law Business

Our story so far has concerned questions centering about competition within the ranks of lawyers. Competition from outside the profession began to figure as a material element in the economic situation of the bar in the 1880's. Real estate transactions, and particularly the examination of titles, provided an important and profitable branch of law business. The expense of the transfer of property became burdensome; in New York City, for example, fees for title examination ran at 1 per cent of the purchase price or mortgage loan amount. Furthermore, business clients wanted title insurance, which individual lawyers or law firms were financially unable to supply. In the last quarter of the nineteenth century, title guaranty companies were established, and grew in number, size, and efficiency. In the larger cities the examination of titles according to the old method and the old fees practically disappeared. Lawyers still figured in the closing of substantial real estate transactions, but on a much reduced scale of services.

The collection of debts was another branch of law business that changed drastically. Change paralleled the vast growth of dealings between great commercial cities and their tributary trade areas after the Civil War. No longer were collections a simple dunning for small claims due the local merchant. The credit structure of the wholesale trade of the country was involved. The volume of collection work that originated in such forwarding centers as New York, Chicago, Philadelphia, Detroit, or St. Louis, where large interstate concerns had their main offices, ran to impressive totals. In response, there developed lay specialists in collections. They claimed specialized knowledge of the economic situation and practices of different lines of business; they gathered information on the credit standing of debtors; they negotiated with, and pursued the reluctant or evasive debtor. In the last resort, the services of a lawyer might still be needed. However, in practical effect the lawyer was now retained by the collection agency onto whose shoulders the creditor had cast his concern for the claim. A new business relation grew up between collection agencies and a part of the bar. Firms appeared which published "law lists"; in their columns, for a charge finally fixed by the business obtained through the listing, a lawyer might in effect advertise that he was available to do collection work. The law lists sought close relations with collection agencies which could furnish business in quantity; the listed lawyers, who could find profit in collection work only on a volume basis, were anxious to please the agencies, whom they regarded as their actual clients. Law-list business grew to sizeable proportions. In 1926 one list handled $100,000,000 of forwarded claims, another $40,000,000, another $10,-000,000; in 1938 about 200 lists were being published in the United States, and they received about $15,000,000 from lawyers who inserted notices in their columns.

Other fields in which lawyers claimed special competence were invaded by lay competitors in the early twentieth century. Trust companies took on broader responsibilities for estates and trusts, and for a time showed readiness to draft wills. Certified public accountants won increasing business as they advised on tax questions in which law and facts often were mingled beyond separation. Automobile associations offered members legal services in the defense of traffic violation charges, and in adjustment or litigation of property damage claims. Lay specialists appeared to represent clients before administrative agencies which dealt with new fields of regulation or government bounty, such as the control of public utility rates or the grant of veterans' benefits. On the fringes of the main areas of lay competition were a varied and growing number of lay counselors in problems that touched the law — interpreters, notaries, consuls, social workers, political fixers. Most of these various developments responded to problems that accompanied the interdependent economy and the urban pattern of living that marked modern society in the United States.

Over the span of 1880–1940 lawyers thus became increasingly conscious of the growth of lay competition. But they did not have the basic information to make an accurate appraisal of what such competition meant. In the first place, if they appealed to history for an authoritative definition of "the practice of the law," they found history mostly ambiguous or silent. One of two things was likely to be true in a given case: (1) a particular job, by practice and tradition, had come to be done both by lawyers and laymen — collections, for example; or (2) the work in question was new with no pre-emptions fixed by usage or custom, as was the case with income tax counseling or representation of veterans' benefits claimants.

Between 1919 and 1940 the state statute books grew to include an impressive list of bans on the unlicensed activity of real estate brokers, tax adjusters, collection agents, claim adjusters, notaries, conveyancers, probate attorneys, law students, law clerks, and legal aid associations, as well as of banks, trust companies, title companies, collection agencies, mercantile associations, insurance companies, and incorporated legal aid societies. This legislation was conveniently vague as to the boundaries of the conduct prohibited to these persons. The typical statute merely forbade them to engage in "the practice of the law." The laws, it was said, were so written partly to prevent evasion; surely, also, they were vague because the draftsmen did not know how to make them any more definite.

Thus it was difficult to measure the field of law business on which lay practitioners were claimed to be making illegitimate inroads. Furthermore, there was almost no reliable information from which to estimate how much of this undefined law business they had taken away. Some of the contested matter — as in the field of trusts and estates — almost certainly represented new business, developed by the enterprise of such outsiders as the life insurance and trust companies. Some of the contested business — like much of the modern tax work — represented wholly new matters; for example, whatever work the lay counselors did regarding income tax problems could not be counted a subtraction from traditional areas of "law practice." However "unauthorized" might be its form, some lay competition was the competition of one group of lawyers masked behind trust or insurance or real estate companies or collection agencies, against other lawyers conducting their professional work in more traditional style.

The few reliable surveys of the economics of the bar failed to show any large amount of lay competition. The 1934 New Haven study found that the householders sampled had gone to a layman in only 22 per cent of the prevention situations and in only 17 per cent of the adjustment situations in which they had sought outside advice; businessmen had gone to a layman in 36 per cent of the prevention and in 15 per cent of the trouble situations in which they had sought outside advice. In Wisconsin a state-wide survey of the bar in 1934 "found a good deal" of unauthorized practice, "mainly of the small order"; the survey found no convincing evidence that total elimination of this competition would materially increase lawyers' clientele or incomes. The 1940 Columbus, Ohio, study found no evidence of any general, unauthorized practice of law. The Columbus householders in the sample group had gone to lawyers in 15 per cent of the prevention and in 30 per cent of the trouble situations they had encountered in the year studied; they had gone to lay advisers in less than 2 per cent of cases of either type.

The Columbus businessmen had sought a lawyer's advice in 15 per cent of their prevention and in 36 per cent of their trouble situations. They had gone to a nonlawyer for counsel in 13 per cent of their prevention and in 21 per cent of their trouble situations; of 113 identified lay advisers whom the businessmen had consulted, 54 were collection agents and 44 were accountants, leaving a miscellany of 15 persons, mainly relatives and friends. By any estimation, much of the collectors' and accountants' services were not of a type to which lawyers could fairly assert any exclusive claim.

g. Ethics and Economics

So far we have sketched some main features of the economic organization of the practice of the law. The economics of the profession had implications for the public as well as for lawyers. The economic organization of the bar could not but affect the bar's social functions, and the bar's own concept of those functions. This was true in both aspects of the lawyer's social job — his services to his client, and the public implications of this client-caretaking. In neither aspect did the bar make an impressive response to the problems posed by the economic facts of the profession.

The bar made one notable accomplishment in putting its own house in order. This was the tardy, but eventually substantial effort to raise standards of legal education and of admission to the bar. There was real professional idealism in the origins and leadership of this movement. But in the depressed 1930's there was the suspicion of more selfish motives in talk of quotas on entry to the profession.

The absence in the United States of the English barrister-solicitor distinction had diverse implications for the quality of legal service. Making a critical comparison with the Chicago bar of about 1900, Albert M. Kales felt that in England litigation was handled with more dispatch and competence by a class exclusively devoted to such law work. On the other hand, Bryce reached a different sum of the account. He conceded that barrister and judge made a good combination for the speedy and expert disposal of courtroom business. But he felt that in the United States the client's affairs were handled more skillfully, speedily, and economically in the office stage under a system in which one law firm took care of all phases of a matter, through men who had perforce learned skill in a varied range of lawyers' tasks.

Whatever the net assessment of debits and credits, the absence of the barrister-solicitor division within the profession in the United States was the result wholly of circumstance. Apart from standards of legal education and admission to the profession, until the 1930's the bar developed no conscious program regarding its economic problems.

Its narrowly negative approach to competition within and without its ranks could not be dignified by the title of program. Many lawyers supported the schoolmen and bar leaders in the movement for better educational and admission standards out of a belief that thus competition might be limited. Vocational guidance in the stage before law school might have been a constructive measure against true overcrowding of the profession. Such a step would have required the continuous, reliable collection of data on numbers of lawyers in active practice, and the provision of some meaningful indices of law business by localities. As late as 1940 only a handful of such experiments had been attempted — in Illinois and in Wisconsin, for example.

Sensitivity to the "unauthorized practice of law" (i. e., outside competition) was not sharpened to the point of action until in 1914 the New York County Lawyers Association appointed the first standing committee on unlawful practice. In the 1920's there was scattered interest in the matter, especially with regard to the "practice of law" by corporations. Widespread concern did not appear until after 1929. The American Bar Association gave no vigorous attention to the problem until it appointed a committee on the subject in 1930. In 1933 the Association made the topic an item of its "National Bar Program" which it had designed to draw to a focus the interests of all bar organizations in the country. By 1940 over 400 bar association committees had been appointed to consider the unauthorized practice of the law.

Reflecting how recent was the activity in this field, a 1937 compilation of virtually all court decisions dealing with the subject devoted 98 pages to cases before 1930, and 838 pages to cases after that date. The depression of the 1930's stimulated the first really widespread and organized concern of the bar with its lay competition. This coincidence of events ill fitted claims that this activity was moved simply by regard for protecting the public against the incompetent or unscrupulous. The speedy development of the drive against "unauthorized practice," set against the circumstances of the time, suggested that the movement was born more of an emotional desire to do something in the face of social catastrophe, than out of any deeply reasoned analysis. Evidence of this was to be found in the almost complete lack of any scientific fact gathering out of all the sudden bustling of committees and associations.

The drive against unauthorized practice found expression in both formal and informal sanctions — all of a purely negative character. State laws forbade "the practice of the law" to a wide range of specified individuals and corporations. The statutes invariably fixed criminal penalties for their violation. There were few prosecutions, probably because it was feared that the public reaction would be unfavorable. The commonest, and generally most successful, approaches were (1) proceedings for contempt of court, on the theory — where unlicensed practice before a court was not directly involved — that the offender had infringed the court's general control of the bar by holding himself out without authorization as one ready to offer legal service; (2) suit for injunction, to protect the franchise of the licensed profession, or — the more usual theory — to safeguard the administration of justice. Quo warranto, though an applicable and flexible remedy, was not as often used. The prosecuting party was usually a public prosecutor or a bar association; proceedings for contempt also carried the psychological advantage — and hazard — that they made the court in effect the party plaintiff.

Another avenue of official control of unauthorized practice of law was through regulations of administrative bodies that controlled fields on the fringes of the law. Thus a state banking commission which had regulatory power over collection agencies might by its rules limit unauthorized law practice by such agencies. A state board of registration might warn architects or engineers against trespassing on lawyers' ground. In all such instances, enforcement was likely to be the more effective because the enforcing agency held the drastic power to revoke or suspend the licenses of those whom it regulated.

There were also informal methods of enforcement. Bar association committees disposed of minor complaints by warning letter. This approach might be particularly effective in the hands of a committee of a state bar association; such a committee could act in situations in which, as a matter of local public relations, a city or county bar organization might feel it must hold its hand. Especially in the 1930's, national, state, and local bar associations negotiated agreements with various lay organizations, to demarcate the fields of lawyer and lay adviser. For example, the Trust Division of the American Bankers Association put into its code an article which forbade the practice of the law by its members. Bar associations secured agreements for co-operation from organizations of abstract and title companies, clearing houses, and corporate fiduciaries. Most of the agreements created committees of conference or arbitration, to hear complaints and pass on alleged violations.

No one could say with assurance what was the total effect of the formal and informal sanctions thus brought to bear against the bar's lay competition. No organization made provision for continuous collection of reliable information in the matter, either as to the extent of lay competition or the practical importance of steps taken against it. No more was known of the economic situation of the bar, in consequence of fifteen years' bustle about "unauthorized practice," than had been known before.

All this dealt with negative aspects of law business. Up to 1950 only few tentative steps had been taken toward a positive program to strengthen the economic basis of the profession. Apparently it had occurred only to a few men that lawyers might find more income and security and a wider opportunity for service, through efforts to make legal service better understood among laymen, as well as more competent and less costly.

There was no organized attack on the mounting overhead cost of the books and current pamphlet and periodical matter essential to a modern, working law library. There was little attention to the possibilities of developing more retainer business, such as might be had under group- or insurance-type plans for the rendering of legal service. An example of rare experiment was the plan set up in 1940 by the Illinois State Bar Association under which lawyers might list themselves with the Association as specialists in stated fields, available at set fees for consultation with brother lawyers who found themselves confronted by unfamiliar problems. The theory of the Illinois experiment was that if specialized experience could more readily be tapped, this would expand the capacity of the bar as a whole to render service, with reduced costs of finding the law and learning how to use it. One other notable exception to the bar's general unconcern toward the costs of legal service was the support which the American Bar Association gave to legislation effectively implementing commercial arbitration. However, even in this case the bar seemed not so much to have taken the initiative, as to have recognized a demand of businessmen that could not be withstood.

All such thinking or experiment at most dealt with the profession within its existing framework. Probably nothing short of the development of new business would basically change the economic position of the bar.

The few reliable surveys indicated the existence of much untapped law business among people of small or moderate means. The surveys showed also that city people knew little of when it might be to their interest to seek legal advice, that they had no idea how to choose a lawyer, and that they were afraid to go to a lawyer because they had unfounded and exaggerated notions of what it would cost and what consequences would be involved. Professional ethics banned individual advertising by lawyers, and there was no reason to doubt that this was sound doctrine. However, to say this gave no answer to the problems of the average city dweller in need of legal advice. In the small town or country community the individual lawyer's reputation could get around; people could know, from firsthand acquaintance with their whole community, where to go for help; everybody could know something of everybody else's business, and this knowledge could curb the layman's natural suspicion of professional mysteries. None of this was easily or naturally true of modern city living. Nonetheless, institutional advertising by the bar was unimaginative, limited, and too sporadic to have lasting effect.

In the 1930's imaginative young Philadelphia lawyers experimented with the creation of supervised, low-cost "neighborhood" law offices, designed to bring legal service closer to the average person in the large city. The neighborhood law office was aimed to serve the client who could pay a moderate fee, but who through fear or ignorance was unlikely to go "downtown" for the help he needed. In 1940 the Chicago Bar Association established a referral service, with panels of lawyers passed upon by the Association, and a referral officer, to bring together people looking for competent legal advice at reasonable fees and lawyers prepared to offer it.

The Philadelphia and Chicago experiments together suggested that bar associations might guide the development of low-cost legal service offices in large cities. Such offices would not do the work of legal aid societies, whose clients were people too poor to pay anything but nominal fees. The new type of office would seek to provide, on a self-supporting basis, for handling the work of clients who could pay moderate charges. It seemed likely that competent, lower-cost legal service could come only (1) through such standardization as the stubborn variety of human problems would allow, coupled (2) with the development of special skill in the main types of work that a large volume of business might permit. There was some evidence to support this hypothesis. Accumulation and standardization of experience, and specialization of skill and knowledge were largely at the base of the economic success of the large business law firms; the same factors were involved in the advance of principal lay competitors of the bar, such as collection agencies, tax bureaus, and trust companies. The lawyer-secretary of the Chicago Bar Association's referral office was able to dispose of about 80 per cent of the inquiries that came to his office every year, without need to refer the matters to further counsel. The fact indicated how much simple consultation business there was to be done, in a volume which should make possible the self-sustaining operation of a new type of city law office, adapted to handling it for relatively small fees.

In its 1938 report, the American Bar Association's "Special Committee on the Economic Condition of the Bar" recommended that experiments be made in the creation of new types of low-cost legal service offices. The organized bar was not yet ready for constructive action of such scope. However, several city bar associations did set up referral offices. This was done in Los Angeles in 1937, and in Chicago in 1940. Eight more associations set up less developed reference plans, 1941–1945. In 1946 the House of Delegates of the American Bar Association revived the suggestion made by the special committee in 1938. It put the sanction of the Association behind a degree of experiment so far little known to the bar, when it:

> Resolved that the Association approves and sponsors the setting up by state and local bar associations of lawyers' referral plans and low cost legal service methods for the purpose of dealing with cases of persons who might not otherwise have the benefit of legal advice.

The resolution expressed a revolutionary change in approach to the profession's economic problems and the related questions of its service to the public. It remained to be seen by how many years the national Association was in advance of thinking on the state and local levels where action must occur. By 1948 about 20 referral plans operated.

As the profession proudly asserted on all formal occasions, the bar did not exist merely as a livelihood for its members, but to do jobs of social importance. Inevitably its economic organization affected both its conception and its execution of its social responsibilities. It was natural that men who had constantly to take the responsibility of decision should be highly self-conscious individualists in their professional attitudes. Moreover, this individualism, and the almost complete lack of professional organization and internal discipline at the bar through most of the nineteenth century, were rooted deep in the political thinking of the United States from 1800–1850. Due allowance must be made for such factors. It is also plain that individualism and a lack of professional cohesion were natural to the temper of a society whose members were bent on personal gain in the feverish exploitation of a rich new continent. The economic organization of the bar — which, translated, meant the lack of professional organization at the bar — offered no great barrier and to the contrary encouraged men to treat the law as only another road to personal gain. What this implied regarding the social functions of the legal profession may best be considered after we look at the main law jobs which lawyers did in the course of the country's growth. The next section of this chapter will consider that matter. Here it is enough to note certain immediate relations between the economics and the professional standards of the lawyer in the United States.

The bar held itself out to serve people who were in legal difficulties or in need of legal advice. Up to 1850 probably most white residents of the United States who needed a lawyer's services got them. After 1850 the same was probably true in the small-town and rural United States — if one overlooked the situation of the tenant farmer and the migratory farm laborer. But after 1850 a steadily increasing proportion of the people lived in cities. We have little direct, reliable evidence, but there is reason to believe that among city dwellers there was great, unsatisfied need for legal help, and much injustice, waste, and suffering for lack of it. Such is the inference — with a plausible reach back into the years before — from the first studies made in the 1930's of the legal needs of people of small means above the legal aid level. Throughout our history ran the denial of justice to the Negro.

Against the challenge of unsatisfied needs for legal help, the record of the bar was one of long inertia. The organized bar did not originate the legal aid movement, and was slow to give it even limited support. The bar became concerned with lay competition, largely under the spur of lawyers' economic distress; it then busied itself with attempts to suppress its lay competitors, and did little self-searching, to find out wherein lawyers were so inadequately serving people that they should turn to other advisers. The bar did not initiate the first well-done studies of untapped fields of law business, in the 1930's; only fifteen years later did it begin to support work to develop the promising leads which these pioneer studies had opened up.

Concerned for "the extent to which devotion to private interests has obscured our vision of the public welfare," Mr. Justice Stone in 1934 cited as a prime failure of the bar in the United States that it had "done relatively so little . . . to make law more readily available as an instrument of justice to the common man." A distinguished lawyer, weighing the profession's public service record as of 1938, commented with restrained exasperation that:

> while very few practitioners fail to recognize that in the practice of advocacy, the interest of the client is always to be preferred to that of the advocate, quite a number forget that the general public is the collective client of the Bar, and that where there is a prospect of the improvement of judicial procedure the Bar should be the first to welcome the change though it be at the expense of its members.

In the 1920's and 1930's, for example, there was discussion of the possibility of substituting for the lawsuit some system approximating workmen's compensation, to handle automobile accident claims. These discussions often brought expressions of fear that the bar would lose business from the change. This, observed Mr. Arthur E. Sutherland, Jr., was a frame of reference which showed little vital professional feeling at the bar:

> The fact is that the general public quite properly feels that if its interests are best served by some change in governmental arrangements, the incidental embarrassment or elimination of some or all the lawyers as a result of that change is quite unimportant. . . . one can scarcely imagine a speaker at a meeting of a county medical society discussing the possible elimination of some disease by public health measures, and then qualifying his observations by the statement that many practitioners make a living out of treating the disease in question; and that unless the physicians are vigilant to prevent the adoption of such measures, this source of business will be taken from them. Yet speakers at bar association meetings are frequently heard to make similar observations about the effect of proposed reforms.

A profession may be defined by reference to functions historically performed, or by reference to some theoretical justification for its status and privileges. In any case the concept of a profession has included the recognition of obligations owed to the society, above and beyond the personal advancement of its practitioners. At the lowest ebb in standards of education and admission, lawyers in the United States never wholly lost the tradition — expressed in 1854 by Sharswood's *Essay on Professional Ethics* — that the practice of the law involved at least formal concession to standards of conduct which specially bound the bar. Yet the stated ethical principles of the profession lacked breadth and penetration; particularly were they inadequate before the challenge of the urban, industrial United States that grew after 1870. We shall consider later the going facts of law practice. Here it may be said that this deficiency in the formal standards of the profession was not unrelated to the economic organization of the bar, and to the economy-dominated values of the society.

Sharswood's little book, *The Canons of Professional Ethics* adopted by the American Bar Association in 1908, and the principal additions to the *Canons* in 1928, authoritatively spoke the articulate conscience of the profession in the nineteenth and early twentieth centuries. In emphasis, in relative detail, in the proportionate attention given to various topics, they expressed a conscience which at its best was directed to the honorable relations between individuals, and which took little concern for the lawyer's role in his community. They paid relatively brief, and very general, respects to the lawyer's obligation to maintain "the law." They reserved their most full and specific directions for the guidance of the lawyer in his relation to his client, and to his fellow lawyers.

The accepted canons emphasized the lawyer's prime obligation to put his best advice and advocacy fearlessly and vigorously at the service of his client's interests. In this respect, they restated a fundamental civil liberty. The canons required of the lawyer an undivided loyalty to his client; he must fully disclose any possibly conflicting interest, and he must scrupulously handle and account for his client's funds separate from his own. Such matters might not touch any policy so significant as the client's basic right to representation; still, they were important elements of professional obligation, and in these respects the lawyer's canons spelled out fiduciary standards that were sharply distinct from the customs of the market place. Yet the individualistic attitude of lawyers toward the opportunities and obligations of the profession was a subtly pervasive influence. It made itself felt even in this most-emphasized field of relations to the client. The nineteenth-century cases regarding lawyers' liability for bad advice or mishandling of affairs sought a rationalizing principle. They found it more often in what they interpreted to be the terms of the contract of service between lawyer and client, than they did in the incidents of a professional relationship. This approach reflected some loss of sensitivity to the idea of an overriding professional obligation. The stress on the lawyer-client contract, rather than on the lawyer-client relationship, was consistent with the disappearance during most of the nineteenth century of any strong or disciplined sense of corporate existence and responsibility in "the bar"; it fitted into the pattern of a diminished sense of the social responsibility of the profession.

Beyond this point, in bulk the canons of ethics focused on matters that had practical and human meaning, but which all revolved within a small orbit. The canons spoke of bargains with the client (fixing the fee, the permissibility of a contingent fee), competition with other lawyers (advertising, stirring up litigation, serving lay competitors, holding out as a specialist), and the etiquette of professional relations (personalities between lawyers, punctuality and speed, taking technical advantage of opposing counsel). Some of the most prominent ethical problems existed only within the unquestioned and unexamined framework of the traditional economic organization of the bar. Collaboration with lay competitors or solicitation of business (e.g., "ambulance chasing") in considerable degree presented problems not of morals but of economics. A more rational economic organization of the bar might make certain ethical problems no longer of practical importance. For example, "ambulance chasing" could not be intelligently handled as a simple problem in morality; it reflected also the inability of laymen of small means or knowledge to get competent legal help at reasonable cost within the conventional pattern of legal service.

The canons of ethics put dominant emphasis on the lawyer-client and lawyer-lawyer relationships. Their next most striking emphasis was the overwhelming extent to which they focused on situations arising out of litigation. Most of the problems they envisaged directly related to the conduct of a lawsuit, or to steps likely to lead to suit. Litigation held a decreasing relative, if not absolute, position in lawyers' business, compared with matters of office counseling and compared with lawyers' relations to legislative, executive, and administrative bodies. Despite this shift in the direction of law practice, the formal thinking of the profession about its ethical problems clung to the early nineteenth-century stereotype of the lawyer as advocate. It had little to say — and that in most uninformative generalities — about the main currents of law practice as these took direction after 1870.

In detailed application the ethical thinking of the organized bar moved in the same narrow channels. Of about 150 opinions rendered by the Committee on Professional Ethics and Grievances of the American Bar Association between 1924–1936, 42 dealt with advertising or solicitation of business, 16 with relations between lawyers and lay competitors, and 11 with fees. Almost half of these opinions, that is, dealt simply with the business aspect of the profession. Of the rest, 31 opinions dealt with questions of etiquette or good faith in the conduct of litigation, and 29 with matters of conflicting interest, most of which involved or looked toward impending litigation. About a third more of the opinions treated specific points connected with the lawyer's role in court. When the ethical pronouncements of the spokesman for the national association fell within so limited an area, it was not surprising that the "Questions and Answers" on ethical problems published by a leading local bar committee (that of the New York County Lawyers Association) concentrated overwhelmingly on professional advertising, fees and fee splitting, and collections. If one took as representative of the ethical problems of law practice the listed causes for discipline of lawyers in New York, 1914–1924, he would conclude that the moral issues of the profession had to do with only a few well-worn, familiar, and relatively simple problems, common to lawyer and layman alike.

The overwhelming bulk of these disciplinary cases centered in one way
or another on the mishandling of funds, or on the perpetration of lies
or other outright frauds on laymen or officials. In fact, of course,
neither the society nor the lawyer's role in it had remained on so elementary a level of moral challenge.

The lawyer's growing participation in business policy and business
risks complicated the problem of serving two masters, and of disclosing
remote and indirect interests possibly adverse to those of a given client.
As lawsuits were used as tactical maneuvers or as parts of a strategy of
campaign in broad and involved questions of public policy, lawyers
faced problems as to what they should disclose to the court regarding
the full relations of the parties and of facts that bore on the reality or
representativeness of the contest that was being staged. As lawyers
dealt with bodies of mixed judicial and executive character, they faced
questions as to the proper limits and types of approach that they might
take in representing a client's interests before such officials. There was
need to evaluate the lawyer's effort to pre-empt fields of work in which
such lay specialists as accountants made plausible claim to a share. There
were difficulties in defining the line between advising or helping a client
to arrange his affairs in such a way as to avoid a conflict with law, and
assisting him to contrive his affairs so as to evade the law. As a new
economy grew headlong after 1870, problems thus multiplied which
could not be dealt with adequately within the context simply of the
lawyer-client relationship or of professional etiquette. But the accepted
cannons made no answer in most cases. How was it, Mr. Justice Stone
asked in 1934:

> that a Bar which has done so much to develop and refine the tech-
> nique of business organization, to provide skillfully devised methods
> for financing industry, which has guided a world-wide commer-
> cial expansion, has done relatively so little to remedy the evils of
> the investment market; so little to adapt the fiduciary principle of
> nineteenth century equity to twentieth century business practices;
> so little to improve the functioning of the administrative mech-
> anisms which modern government sets up to prevent abuses; so
> little to make law more readily available as an instrument of justice
> to the common man . . .

A clue lay in the seeming paradox of the highly individualistic organization of most of the bar and the highly organized, businesslike atmosphere of the small circle which practiced within the realm of concentrated economic power. Both reflected the subordination of the
professional attitude to an absorbed concentration on the workaday

world of client-caretaking, as this appeared to men in the circumstances of their particular distance from or nearness to the seats of power.

In any case, whatever the answers to the question posed by Mr. Justice Stone, the facts bore out his further warning, that the bar had responsibilities far broader than those which the traditional codes of ethics encompassed:

> . . . the very conditions which have caused specialization, which have drawn so heavily upon the technical proficiency of the Bar, have likewise placed it in a position where the possibilities of its influence are almost beyond calculation. The intricacies of business organization are built upon a legal framework which the current growth of administrative law is still further elaborating. Without the constant advice and guidance of lawyers business would come to an abrupt halt. And whatever standards of conduct in the performance of its function the Bar consciously adopts must at once be reflected in the character of the world of business and finance. Given a measure of self-conscious and cohesive professional unity, the Bar may exert a power more beneficent and far reaching than it or any other non-governmental group has wielded in the past.

No less severe because it came from a deep and friendly concern with the future of the profession, was Stone's verdict on the failure of the traditional ethical formulae to meet the challenge of the times:

> . . . we cannot expect the Bar to function as it did in other days and under other conditions. Before it can function at all as the guardian of public interests committed to its care, there must be appraisal and comprehension of the new conditions and the changed relationships of the lawyer to his clients, to his professional brethren and to the public. That appraisal must pass beyond the petty details of form and manners which have been so largely the subject of our codes of ethics, to more fundamental consideration of the way in which our professional activities affect the welfare of society as a whole. Our canons of ethics for the most part are generalizations designed for an earlier era. However undesirable the practices condemned, they do not profoundly affect the social order outside our own group . . .

3. SOCIAL FUNCTIONS OF THE BAR

Lawyers did certain jobs, and used certain skills that were important in the building of American society, and that were especially, even though not exclusively, identified with the legal profession. Thus we can define the profession in large part in terms of its social functions.

a. Individual and Corporate Contributions

In this effort we immediately encounter difficulties sketched earlier in this chapter. Lawyers' work was woven so closely into the fabric of the community life that it is hard to distinguish the threads the lawmen contributed. As if this were not trouble enough, there is confusion latent in talk of "the lawyer's" contribution. Do we refer to the work of creative individuals, to the contribution of a class united by the loose ties of common education and interest, or to the functions of a guild organized to effect conscious policy?

The bar had its creative individuals. There were men who devised new legal tools, as John G. Johnson was credited with the invention of the modern equipment trust certificate. There were men who explored new fields of counseling, as Francis Lynde Stetson led in broadening the lawyer's role in corporate reorganization. There were men who adapted the advocate's technique to a new challenge — for example, Louis D. Brandeis by his brief in *Muller* v. *Oregon*, with its two pages of conventional legal argument and its one hundred or more pages of social and economic facts and analysis.

There was individual creativeness at the bar, but it is hard to trace. The evidence of the activities of a busy lawyer is largely ephemeral; much of his work disappears in the unrecorded words spoken around countless conference tables or in unnumbered, unrecorded hearings; much of it disappears into the scattered files of numerous clients. From the mid-eighteenth century on, the successful lawyer was a man of affairs living in a rush of days that left little time or inclination to preserve documents or reflect on experience. The historian partner of a great New York firm of one hundred and fifty years' lineage wrote of the difficulties of re-creating the activities of a law office that had taken more pains than most to keep records; even there the historian found incomplete office registers, suit registers that yielded only skeleton facts, great gaps in the files of papers and briefs concerning office and court business, the practical impossibility (and dubious benefit) of searching court records to trace the firm's appearances, the necessary reliance on the personal letter file of a founding partner, on the diary of a firm member, on a broken file of drafts of office business letters, on "memorials" of deceased members preserved in bar association or court proceedings. Legal biographers uniformly lamented the scant evidence of the grist of daily practice.

These difficulties were so consistent and stubborn as to suggest that more than mere lack of evidence was involved. The individual creativeness of the lawyer was so hard to trace in large part because what the bar gave to the growth of American society was inherently a corporate contribution. This is not simply to say that among lawyers, as among all men, creative individuals were rare. It is to suggest that the lawyer's special function was characteristically that of a mediator of forces. In its nature his success was merged in results the essence of which was that they were not peculiarly his creation. His activity ran into so many aspects of the society, especially on its economic side, as to blur the drama that might have accompanied a more isolated role.

To say that the bar's contribution was corporate rather than individual requires further definition. "The bar" implies an organized, cohesive, self-disciplined entity. Such an entity existed — whether on a local, state, or national basis — only to a limited extent and only for a few of the years in the span from 1790 to 1950. The United States had many lawyers, but little of a cohesive legal profession.

The social contributions of the organized bar were limited even more than the relatively short span of its influence in time or territory might suggest. The main force of lawyers was not felt through the work of a few men of creative genius. It did not come through an organized professional guild. It came from the cumulative influence of many able men who were effective because they had a common body of learning, tradition, and techniques, and because together they concentrated on and developed special skills and feel for the process of adjustment in social relations.

The positive record of the profession, defined in this last sense, was formed by usage and the pressure of events, rather than by conscious planning. This process of development was accompanied by grave limits of vision and usefulness. Yet the manner in which it proceeded was evidence of the unforced, vital relation that lawyers' work bore to the society. That relation was far broader than the customary public view recognized; common opinion put too exclusive an emphasis on what lawyers did in the courtroom and in public office. A fuller appraisal must take stock of lawyers as makers of institutions, of social tools, and of patterns of action; it must see them as skilled in the analysis of situations, and in adjustment of social tangles or contests (sometimes by litigation, but oftener by more effective, if less colorful, methods); it must credit them as carriers of social tradition, and as a main source of the administrators needed to carry on the complicated affairs not only of modern government but also of modern business.

b. Social Inventors

The institutions of society in the United States — the ideas, emotions, and patterns of behavior in which its vitality consisted — were of course formed by circumstances far beyond the reach of any group of men. Like any other members of their society, lawyers could claim no more than that to a degree they had channeled or harnessed forces which they had not created. "Sonny," Holmes in legend replied to his inquiring law clerk, "I just remember, I'm not Lord God Almighty."

Even so, in our years of national life, lawyers could show a record of social invention that was matched only by that of the more restless and vastly larger class of businessmen. Two distinctions must be drawn. First, as to time: As in other respects, the 1870's made a watershed decade that divided periods distinguished by great acceleration in the range, depth, and speed of social change. Through most of the nineteenth century, for example, entrepreneurs could legitimately complain of the clumsy and limited forms available to organize, control, and finance business. But for fifty years after the 1880's the tide of lawyers' inventions overflowed the levees that the law had so far erected to protect investors, consumers, labor, and everybody in the community who had reason to be concerned about the swings of the business cycle.

Secondly, in appraising lawyers' invention, we must distinguish at any given time the relative extent and success of their innovations in different fields. Here is a significant gauge of variations in the bar's social allegiances and professional morale. After the creative generation that followed the Revolution and until about 1910 lawyers contributed little effective invention in the devising of government institutions and regulatory techniques. The Jacksonian "revolution" expressed itself in conspicuous changes in public institutions, notably in the extension of the right to vote and the extension of the number of elective public offices. Even so, the Jackson era was marked by the lack of lawyers' craftsmanship to shape the new forces for effective use. Indeed, an important aspect of the popular and lay character of the Jackson "revolution" was the destruction of formal professional standards at the bar; this undoubtedly helped to dull the sense of professional obligation toward the legal order among its sworn guardians. Most nineteenth-century state constitutions were the product of unconsidered borrowing of taken-for-granted patterns of legal institutions. The Reconstruction amendments to the Federal Constitution were lawyer-drawn institutional invention on the grand scale. However, after the first fervor of Radical Republicanism had passed, legal virtuosity was not devoted to implementing the public purposes of the amendments but to making the Fourteenth Amendment a defense for private purposes against social regulation. In the generation after the Granger laws of the 1870's the lack of lawyerlike realism was apparent in every aspect of the first efforts at social and economic regulation. One could see this deficiency in the naïve reliance that men put upon general declarations of right and duty, without providing machinery or funds adequate to implement their principles. One could see it in their undue reliance on the crude simplicities of the criminal law, and in their simple confidence that the initiative and resources of aggrieved individuals or of the local public prosecutor would suffice to put the control machinery into action. First-rate institutional invention by lawyers did not appear in the field of public affairs until the full-scale development of the administrative process after 1910.

There was no such drought of creation in what lawyers did for private clients. Invention was most fertile in relation to business, especially in commerce and finance, as distinguished from industry. Lawyers contrived or adapted institutions (the corporation), tools (the railroad equipment trust certificate), and patterns of action (the reorganization of corporate financial structure or the fashioning of a price structure for a national market). The lawyer's contributions to business were many, though we lack the detailed studies that would permit assessment of the relative creativeness of lawyer and entrepreneur in the teeming fields of business invention.

Much, if not most, of lawyers' inventions consisted in making old institutions serve new needs. Obviously that did not derogate from the practical importance of their work; to the contrary, it placed it in the normal pattern of social change. Under the stress of the depression of the 1890's the cumulated ingenuity of counsel in a number of great railroad reorganizations substantially settled the form in which the real estate mortgage was transformed into the basic security document of corporation finance. In commodity dealings, the businessman contrived the bill of exchange and the bill of lading. On the other hand the lawyer devised the means by which a lender might have security in goods, while the borrower had their beneficial use in transactions from whose profits he might meet his debt. To this purpose he adapted the law of trusts to the creation of the trust receipt — first as an instrument of domestic commerce, then of foreign commodity deals, finally as a device for the novel problems of automobile sales finance. Such growth was typically a product of the continuous application of many skilled and ingenious minds to the details of a multitude of transactions. Hence it went on mainly in law offices rather than in courtrooms. Llewellyn sketches the pattern of invention in the case of the trust receipt:

You can see its growth, follow its invention, its steady stepwise spread. First in financing grain from upper New York to the sea. The early litigation that went unnoticed. The crucial case that caught the eye of metropolitan counsel. The introduction of the device, now modified, elaborated, into the importing business. The major firms that participated in its development, and the development itself, case by case, in litigation, clause by clause, in the increasing adequacy of the drafting. And in the course of the past ten years [1920–1930] we can trace out its spread and readaptation to the financing of automobiles. Again we know the men, the means, the problems. In this one history we can see something of the energy, thought and originality that must go into creation of even such a single, simple tool as this.

With no less technical skill lawyers provided the rationalization for the judicial policy making that went on from 1870–1930 in the name of review of the constitutionality of legislation. The treatise writers (notably Cooley, Tiedeman, and Dillon) and the "constitutional lawyers" showed a remarkable range of doctrinal inventiveness. In their books and briefs were first outlined such classic formulae as freedom of contract and its haven under "property" in the Fourteenth Amendment, the distinction between the "direct" and "indirect" relations that various regulated subject matter bore to interstate commerce (with consequences for the allocation of power between the nation and the states), the concept that government was inherently limited to action within a closed catalog of permissible purposes, and the "public purpose" requirement that hedged the taxing power.

It is hazardous to apportion creative credit among scholars, counsel, and judges, for the erection of these doctrinal bridges to decision. Judicial opinions typically do not acknowledge such indebtedness. Thus the main evidence of the lineage of a formula is apt to be the fact that it is found outside the Reports before it is sanctioned in them. It would be presumptuous to claim that John Marshall could not, or would not, have developed the argument of his basic rulings without Webster's promptings. On the other hand there are plausible reasons for crediting the lawyer with a substantial role in fashioning the doctrinal tools of law. Briefs display an abounding fertility of invention; few judges are of the stamp of Marshall; at best the judge is much removed by even a few years on the bench from the currents of the times, and hence must necessarily rely on the lawyer for the concepts which will make intelligible the on-going world of affairs which suitors bring into the courtroom. If we are to credit the lawyer with notable invention in constitutional doctrine, no less must we do so regarding the shaping of the general body of common law to govern the everyday and the out-of-ordinary transactions of life.

c. Master of Fact

"Know thoroughly each fact," Louis D. Brandeis cautioned himself in a memorandum on "What the practice of the law includes," set down in his years at the Boston bar. He expanded upon and returned to the initial theme: "Don't believe client witness. Examine documents. Reason; use imagination. Know bookkeeping — the univeral language of business; know persons. . . . Know not only specific cases, but whole subject. Can't otherwise know the facts. Know not only those facts which bear on direct controversy, but know all the facts and law that surround."

The emphasis was characteristic of Brandeis. This was not only because in his own counseling and advocacy he made himself the exemplar of his text, but also because more than any but a few men he appreciated the deep-running currents of his time. "For the rational study of the law the black-letter man may be the man of the present," Holmes observed in 1897, "but the man of the future is the man of statistics and the master of economics." In practice Holmes found his diagnosis too much at odds with temperament to apply it. He had nonetheless surely perceived the same truth which his younger colleague had fastened on as the mark of the age in the law.

Before 1850, in his then most prominent role as special pleader and advocate, the lawyer — and the courts also — dealt with situations that were rather simple. A sampling of briefs and judicial opinions will show that their main focus was not on the facts but on "the law." Facts were simpler because men's interests did not yet interweave to the extent that they did later when urban living and a highly specialized economy complicated patterns of living. In the early nineteenth century men still saw their relationships largely on a one-to-one basis (buyer-seller, lender-borrower, grantor-grantee); they had little familiarity with multicornered dealings; they had little sense of individual helplessness in the face of great impersonal social currents; they felt little awareness that the public might have concern with matters wholly "private" in origin.

Interest centered on the rules of law in part because facts were relatively grubby, and hard to come by in comparison with the superficially greater ease and intellectual challenge in devising general principles. However, it was also true that the times presented an overriding need to elaborate doctrine, and to do it rapidly, to deal with the going affairs in raw new states which tumbled into being one on the heels of another. The appeal of intellectual ease might underlie Horace

Binney's elegant disdain of time spent in investigating facts which he found of no meaning to anyone but the parties. It might also explain why bar memorials honored as a "constitutional lawyer" any deceased colleague who had been gifted with a tongue for sonorous truths. On the other hand, one senses a very different attitude behind lawyer Lincoln's characteristic concern for the underlying principle in relatively simple troubles; there was a felt need to make "law" in new communities. As early as 1849 we may detect a greater sophistication, in the more studied work which Lincoln did after he returned from Congress. Yet, in the Illinois of 1820–1850, it made sense in terms of community need, to subordinate the full individuality of individual trouble cases to their usefulness as vehicles for declaring the law.

After 1850 the handling of facts took on a new importance both in advocacy and in counseling. By the 1890's the complex facts of the economy in particular offered both the setting and the pressure for the lawyer to take on a new role — as a specialist in incisive, accurate, fast appraisal of snarled or complicated situations. Law was too close to affairs for the lawyer ever to have been wholly a man of books. Nonetheless, there now came a change in emphasis that amounted to a change in function. As advocate, the lawyer was typically called in after trouble was full-blown and a last-ditch fight seemed the only recourse; his job then was to cull from past events those aspects which would support his client's position and color the problem to his client's view. As counselor, he might weave the facts of family into the pattern of will or trust; or he might draft the instruments that dealt with the crisis of a business — the papers of its creation, its reorganization, its composition with creditors, or its dissolution. Even these limited activities were usually done according to the single dominant criterion of meeting a possible challenge in court. What the job demanded typically was not evaluation of a total situation; it was enough that the lawyer had sufficient grasp of certain aspects so that by proper procedure or draftsmanship he might set the situation in a mold that the law would acknowledge — in a deed, a contract, a mortgage.

The upper bracket of the profession, close to the seats of the new financial and industrial power, first felt demands that took the lawyer beyond the conventional limits of law practice. Later years then brought similar pressures on all lawyers who advised business clients, guided substantial properties, or counseled organized groups. What caused the new demands on the legal profession? There was the crowding of an urban society, the sensitive interdependence of its parts, the reach of its markets and the maze of its channels of finance and supply. There was the relative increase for everyone in what was staked on the risks taken and the objectives sought — what was at stake in terms of people's security, self-respect, faith, and ambitions, as well as the material capital that was put in play. Matching such factors was an enormously extended government intervention in affairs. This came particularly through executive and administrative action marked by pervasive detail and pragmatic flexibility.

This new society required more long-range planning, even of individual affairs. It called for heightened awareness of causes and interests that might operate — at third- or fourth-hand, or more remotely still — to affect a business firm, a proposed course of action, a position of present power. It put more emphasis on preventive action. And when conflict was submitted to the decisions of some state agency, the pressure of the society worked toward the presentation of issues in terms which, if partisan, were nonetheless relevant to the community realities of which the legal solution must become a part.

To deal with the crosscurrents of the new century called for an imaginative, accurate grasp of facts. This did not only mean the ability to find the facts, and to see their relationships. The counselor must also be skillful in using what he knew to measure the probable extent and importance of what he did not know about the situation he confronted. Only thus could he plan to deal with the alternatives that his evolving problem might present. A variety of developments bore evidence that the effort to master the bewildering facts of the new society was recognized as a prerequisite to effective action in it. This was the meaning of the growth of the social sciences in the universities. It was behind the appearance in the business world of new ranks of specialists — market analysts, public relations counselors, house economists, personnel experts, management advisers, public accountants, trade-association and lobbying bureaucracies.

The lawyer was by professional tradition a specialist in handling evidence and diagnosing trouble. He naturally assumed a leading part in responding to the challenge to master the intricate facts of the twentieth-century United States. The law was inextricably mingled in the headlong growth of the economy; if the law needed insight into the life with which it dealt, what the law did and the direction in which it moved were important facts in almost any social equation.

Chief Justice Holmes, of the Massachusetts Supreme Judicial Court, put the matter in broad context in a speech which he made in the first year of this century of complexity:

Until lately the best thing that I was able to think of in favor of civilization, apart from blind acceptance of the order of the universe, was that it made possible the artist, the poet, the philosopher, and the man of science. But I think that is not the greatest thing. Now I believe that the greatest thing is a matter that comes directly home to us all. When it is said that we are too much occupied with the means of living to live, I answer that the chief worth of civilization is just that it makes the means of living more complex; that it calls for great and combined intellectual efforts, instead of simple, unco-ordinated ones, in order that the crowd may be fed and clothed and housed and moved from place to place. Because more complex and intense intellectual efforts mean a fuller and richer life. They mean more life. Life is an end in itself, and the only question as to whether it is worth living is whether you have enough of it.

Holmes did not fear to look upon change; and as a lawman he found zest in the challenge to order so turbulent a society. But a generation later, a distinguished lawyer found it necessary to rebuke futile complaints about complex legal regulation:

The network of laws and ordinances and regulations that surrounds a civilized people can no more be eliminated than the tangle of pipes, tubes, cables, and beams that underlies a street in lower New York City. They are both the result of an effort to make life simpler for the individual by means of infinitely complex devices.

d. Administrators of Social Relations

The lawyer's new service as a man of facts emerged during a great expansion of his role as an adjuster of social relations. This adjustment function was not limited to the settlement of disputes; a fortiori, it concerned more than the lawyer's skill in litigation. After 1870 a revolution occurred in the nature of law practice, shaped by the same pressures which in government produced the rise of the administrative process.

In function as well as in homily, the lawyer had been mainly "an officer of the court." Even the office lawyer worked principally with an eye to what a judge might rule upon the document or plan he was contriving. But the requirements of his clients now forced and invited the lawyer — as the pressure of events compelled the administrative officer — to become legislator, judge, and executive, in the handling of affairs. After the 1880's the lawyer became a familiar figure on boards of directors; first the railroad general counsel, and then the lawyer for the investment banker led the way into this new role as corporation director. Dos Passos observed in 1907 that: "The lawyer now boldly enters into the business end of his client's transactions — he sells him prudence and experience, sometimes even usurping the client's discretion and judgment." The reach and detail of new social regulation, the higher stakes, and the wider range of interests which must be reckoned with in guiding affairs — all these emphasized the lawyer's planning function. Also they put a premium on the hardheaded objectivity of the policy advisor; more and more this was what the client's interests demanded rather than the zealous partisanship of an advocate. Clients were no longer satisfied to put to their lawyers a statement of facts on which to obtain an "opinion." They wanted the lawyer to share the responsibility of deciding what were the determining facts in their situation, to bear part of the weight of fixing policy in the light of the facts so assessed. The "opinions" for which such leaders as Curtis or Evarts received good fees in the 1850's and 1860's represented merely a transition toward the function of the modern counselor.

Of course lawyers in the United States were always active in business; the formal dignities and etiquette of the English barrister-solicitor distinction never hampered them in their contacts with the market. James Wilson speculated in land in the late eighteenth and early nineteenth centuries. One after another of William H. Seward's law partners in upstate New York of the early nineteenth century drifted into business and out of the practice. In the 1840's Richard Blatchford pioneered in exploiting the profits to be had in promoting companies based on patents. But this sort of thing had been personal venturing. The new emphasis was in the lawyer's widening participation in making business policy as a counselor rather than as a coadventurer.

There is an early touch of the new emphasis in the letter which Clarence Seward wrote (January 28, 1870) to Samuel Simpson, who was opposing counsel in "the Ice Pitcher Case":

I had a visit day before yesterday from Mr. Harding in which he asked me to ask you if you did not think it was better to keep the Ice Pitcher trade in the hands of a few persons of ability to supply the market and by bringing suits against the smaller dealers, close them out, than to litigate our suit and if we succeed therein, to open the market to every one who might choose to make and sell Ice Pitchers. He intimated something with regard to the arrangement between himself and the Meriden Britannia Co. having proceeded upon this view of the case; and that if this view struck you as favorable, he would be prepared to receive a proposition from us of a confidential nature, to pay so much for stamps, and take a license.

A cross-licensing arrangement was made in this instance. Much more forthright in intervening in business policy was the driving William

Dameron Guthrie. Guthrie took a leading part on occasion in the financial arrangements leading to corporate mergers; he plunged ardently into the policy issues presented by the "fairness" of reshufflings of corporate financial structures; savoring "the many internal intrigues" in the management of the Chicago stockyards company, he interested himself actively in the company's policies on expenses, executive salaries, and advertising.

In the public causes in which Louis D. Brandeis interested himself while he was at the bar, his inventive concern for policy was even more notable than his skill in thrust and parry in committee hearing or courtroom proceeding. For example, in his hands the Boston traction franchise contest of 1897–1911 put at issue a long-range program for public versus private control of the transport system. In the gas rates fight, Brandeis's emphasis was on developing a rate-making formula that would take the gas company out of politics and obviate the need for public ownership. Concerned with the cost and inadequacy of life insurance for people of small means, he devised and successfully pressed for legislative authorization of the issue of low-cost life insurance through savings banks. These were cases in which Brandeis took the responsibility of appearing for the public interest. He carried the same approach into private counseling. He would represent a liquor lobby in its battle against prohibition only on condition that there was rigorous control of the use of lobby funds. He took prime responsibility for the drafting of a railroad reorganization plan concerning his client, the Wisconsin Central. His advice to his shoemaker client, W. H. McElwain, when McElwain confronted labor troubles, dealt not with the tactics of battle, but looked toward reorganization of the firm's production schedule to regularize employment and provide a fair annual wage.

Representation of interests before legislative bodies became a field of increasing significance in twentieth-century law practice. In this phase, the lawyer moved directly into broad areas of policy making. How wide-ranging was this phenomenon may be seen in the activity of legal aid societies before legislatures; their work in this respect was the more striking because they spoke for a clientele which might not have been expected to share the bar's services in its policy-making role. Out of their experience with the legal troubles of the poor, the legal aid societies effectively urged changes in the statutes to facilitate wage claims, to curb body execution by installment sellers, and to regulate small loans.

The lawyer's office served in all periods as what amounted to a magistrate's court; what was done in lawyers' offices in effect finally disposed of countless trouble cases, whether preventively, or by discouraging wasteful lawsuits, or by settling claims over the bargaining table. After the 1870's, as the lawyer assumed a broader responsibility in his client's business decisions, a corollary result was to extend the occasions and degree to which the lawyer was called on to judge the rights and duties of his client, with a decisive effect on future action. "Of course a lawyer's chief business is to keep his clients out of litigation," Elihu Root remarked; on another occasion this exemplar of the new leadership at the bar put more bluntly the positive aspect of this job: "About half the practice of a decent lawyer consists in telling would-be clients that they are damned fools and should stop."

Lawyers' independence of judgment on their clients' decisions was of course affected by the nature of their practice. John G. Johnson, lion of the Philadelphia bar in the first generation of this new kind of counseling, was an "officer of the court" in more than a technical sense. His biographer notes that:

> The volume of his business brought about a subtle change in his attitude toward the public, in his conduct in the office and courtroom. It made orderly habits of work and thought indispensable. It made each day a complete, compact design. The businesslike lawyer became more businesslike. He no longer was waiting for the main chance — eager for a case that would bring recognition and money. His initial reaction to new business was a detached appraisal of the merits, disinterested, impartial.

The pressure of business and responsibility might enforce the lawyer's insistence that he control the situation in which he represented his client; the fiery Guthrie took a sharp tone in rebuking the executive of his greatest banker client, for independently discussing settlement with the defendants in a pending contest.

Yet there was another side to the picture in the last quarter of the nineteenth century. It was epitomized in Commodore Vanderbilt's "What do I care about the law. Hain't I got the power?" It was summed up in the no less blunt statement — variously attributed to the elder Morgan, to Thomas Fortune Ryan, and to William C. Whitney — that a good lawyer was one who would tell his client not what he could not do, but how to do what he wanted to do. Waiving judgment on what professional obligation might enjoin, there can be no doubt that the empire builders of the exploitative era after the Civil War conceded no great independence to their counsel.

Nonetheless, as in Elihu Root, there appeared evidence that lawyers were assuming broader responsibility of judgment, parallel to their broader participation in public and private policy making. By the 1930's the intervention of government in the economy spelled consequences of material, sometimes of life-and-death, significance to business. This was true especially regarding taxes, regulation of rates and prices, and control of trade agreements, financial structure, and the marketing of securities. As government regulation raised such grave issues, its effect was to enhance the independence and force of counsel in appraising the client's affairs. A parallel development appeared in the role that the lawyer played inside official agencies. In the interest of uniform craftsmanship and policy, government tended to unify control of its litigation, as federal litigation was largely centralized in the Department of Justice. On the other hand, there was a no less pronounced trend to develop separate counsel for each major office of government; and it was indicative of the kinds of legal service that the agencies wanted, that typically they made counsel a staff officer directly responsible to, and in continuous contact with, their policy-making heads.

The modern lawyer was called on to be legislator and judge in handling his client's affairs; he was also required to be an administrator. Samuel Williston described the able Boston lawyer of the 1890's in whose office he served his apprenticeship as "not in any sense a learned lawyer," but one who "when law was needed for his purpose . . . could secure it from others. In his own phrase about another he was 'a man who brought things to pass.'" In the complex society that took form in the United States after the Civil War, what the client needed more and more was a man skilled in bringing together the tangled threads of a situation — whether the problem was negotiation, compromise, arrangement, or plan, or whether the call was to steer some affair through the gathering intricacy of public regulation. Increasingly the lawyer made himself useful as an administrator, both in the myriad small affairs that went with the elbow-to-elbow living of cities, and in the patient attention to detail and the continuing adjustment and improvisation required to effect great schemes.

Legal aid societies exemplified one aspect of the administrative burden carried by the bar. Despite their relatively brief history and limited coverage, by 1933 legal aid societies had handled an estimated minimum of nearly 4,000,000 cases, with an annual average then running over 330,000; their work concerned mainly wage claims, difficulties over installment credit and small loans, and landlord-tenant relations, and about 95 per cent of these matters were concluded without litigation. The late-aroused concern of the bar over its lay competition afforded other evidence of the range of administrative detail in everyday life with which lawyers had become involved — tax advice, debt collections, real estate deals, adjustment of automobile accident claims, the drafting of wills. The bar figured prominently in the necessary clean-up in the wake of every depression; such work found lawyers acting largely as adjustors and executors of distressed business, with litigation of decreasing importance.

All this was administrative detail in the mass. Lawyers also contributed a variety of executive talent to events and plans which had weight of themselves. G. P. Lowry, general counsel to the Western Union Telegraph Company for many years, met Thomas A. Edison through contract dealings and lawsuits, admired his ability and rallied financial aid to Edison at critical times, led in suits to enforce Edison patents, and by his knowledge of affairs supplied much of the managing ability needed to make business application of the inventor's work. The public utility consolidations, which from the 1880's were a significant part of the business lawyer's work, were largely a matter of executive direction and administrative detail. The erection of such new business structures and the development of new patterns of commerce drew on the lawyer's administrative skill: for example, in the invention of such tools as the corporate trust indenture, the equipment trust certificate, the trust receipt.

Well-conducted litigation might of course be a necessary instrument of the execution of vast schemes. In connection with the building of the New York Elevated over 2000 damage claims of abutting property owners were tried and nearly 1000 appeals argued under the direction of Julien T. Davies. The historian partner of Davies's firm comments that "but for his brilliant efforts in restricting the amounts recovered against the Company, its control would have passed permanently from its owners into the hands of judgment creditors."

Litigation might be used tactically, as a means to bring contending interests together in a bargain. In the 1880's the railroads threatened to carry on their own express business; thus they sought a stronger position in negotiating the payments that the independent express companies must make to continue their exclusive arrangements with the roads. Under the direction of Clarence Seward, the express companies countered with a wide array of lawsuits. They sought mandatory injunctions (usually with success) to compel the railroads to perform existing exclusive contracts; however, Seward could not induce the railroads to stipulate for one test suit, to reduce costs. The railroads countered by opening express company safes and chests, and attempting to charge regular freight rates on the contents as well as full fares for the express company employees. Express company lawyers then obtained a ruling that such conduct was in contempt of the court's mandate that the railroads fulfill their contracts with the expressmen. Seward caused the president of Adams Express to buy stock in one railroad, in order to qualify to bring a stockholder's action to enjoin the road from wasting its assets by handling its express business otherwise than through Adams. At the same time Seward waged a successful proxy fight against the railroad management which had started the war. Seward also acted for the president of Southern Express in a flank attack on the Gould railroads of the Southwest, which had been among the leaders in the contest. He intervened in a Wabash receivership, to attack Gould control; he brought stockholders' suits on charges of mismanagement of the Iron Mountain road, which had leased Wabash and guaranteed its mortgage; he won the co-operation of the attorney general of Missouri, in bringing quo warranto proceedings to assail the interrelationships of the Gould lines and their interlocking directorates; he began another diversionary stockholder's action, to prevent the purchase of another railroad and its consolidation with the Iron Mountain. Then the Supreme Court of the United States decided in the main lawsuit, about which all these maneuvers had swirled, that the railroads were not obliged to carry the traffic of independent express companies. Thereupon the various diversionary lawsuits were dismissed, and the warring parties promptly agreed on new contracts.

Policy making and administration might merge in counsel's work, particularly in transactions of great consequence. This merger was most likely to appear in the office aspect of law practice. Explaining the bill which counsel had rendered for service regarding the organization of the Western Pacific Railway Company, Paul D. Cravath wrote to a banker client (July 14, 1905):

As you know, the Western Pacific business proved to be unusually complicated, and more novel and difficult questions were presented than in any corporate transaction with which I have had to do for several years. The fact that the mortgage was made by a corporation which as yet has no railroad, and that the real responsibility behind the bonds was being furnished by three other railroad companies, none of whom were willing to be formal guarantors of the loan, placed a very serious responsibility upon counsel. We had to deal with four railroad corporations each organized under the laws of a different State, and to fully consider the laws of four States. The mortgage — the preparation of which was assigned to my office — was, on the whole, the most difficult and complicated railroad mortgage I have ever drawn. The nature of the transaction was such that a great deal of the negotiating which is usually done by principals fell upon the lawyers, and many days were spent in consultations and negotiations. While the fact that three law firms were employed involved some duplication of work, still the transaction was strengthened by that fact and by the fact that the bonds will be reenforced [sic] by the opinions of three law firms instead of one.

However, litigation as well as office work might be both an instrument of fixing policy and a tactical device in its execution. It might be so used quite apart from the simple theory of its older function, to enforce rights and duties according to an existing body of "law." This invasion of the advocate's role by the role of planner and negotiator was implied in the rising percentage of cases that involved three or more interests, in contrast to the older style of one-to-one litigation. In the Supreme Court of the United States in 1900 6 per cent of all cases involved three or more parties. In 1920 the figure was 17 per cent; in 1939, 23 per cent; in 1944, 36 per cent.

Skilled lawyers had always made the most of cases that might serve to define important principles. Usually on such occasions the spotlight was on political issues; this was true of the many partisan-tinged cases which Alexander James Dallas defended in a Pennsylvania that was warm with Federalist-Republican battles of the early nineteenth century; it was true also, for example, of Jeremiah Black's masterly handling of *Ex parte Milligan* in 1866. Moreover in earlier years the typical "great" case was not the product of a planned use of litigation as a tactical maneuver in a campaign of policy. Ordinarily the case represented the exploitation of an opportunity cast up by events; this was no less so despite the occasional strong atmosphere of a test case, as in *Brown* v. *Maryland*.

In the later nineteenth century there was more marked use of lawsuits as planned, and even contrived, instruments to shape and execute economic policy. The record of Philadelphia's John G. Johnson was full of suits over "tremendous trifles." There was the action to compel acceptance of perpetual ground rents in the originally specified (now thoroughly depreciated) Spanish dollars — in a lawsuit over $14.25. There was a $12 claim of a guardian, which involved the constitutionality of the estates statute. There was an appearance for a hunter convicted in justice court for using an automatic gun contrary to a statute whose regulation of sporting weapons was not well regarded by great powder companies. There was Johnson's appearance for the state in a prosecution for the sale of a ten-pound tub of oleomargarine in violation of a challenged statute. There was his representation of a small shopkeeper whose conviction under a Tennessee act banning cigarette sales interested tobacco manufacturers.

Before the advent of modern administrative regulation, litigation was used in a wide range of corporation regulation. Men resorted to court in attempts to control railroad consolidations and reorganizations, through injunction or quo warranto. There were efforts to enforce corporate morality by litigation; notable instances were the stockholders' suits which Evarts brought in the post Civil War decade against the looters of the Erie, or the suits incident to the Hazen–Alexander fight for control which broke open to public investigation the affairs of the Equitable Life Assurance Society of New York in 1905.

Control of a lawsuit was recognized as a valuable prize where high policy was at stake. On the suggestion of William D. Guthrie, a stockholder's suit was brought in federal court to enjoin a Chicago gas company from complying with a city rate-fixing ordinance claimed to be invalid. The company was formally a codefendant, alongside the city. In a letter to brother counsel, Guthrie expressed annoyance when the city raised, in defense, the contention that the suit was a collusive one, arranged between the plaintiff stockholder and the company:

> I should be very much distressed to have one of my cases dismissed on the ground that it was collusive, as I have been particularly careful not to undertake litigation which I felt was an attempt to impose upon a federal court jurisdiction of a case which did not properly belong to it. At the same time, I was very glad to have the company decline to sue, for it gave me the opportunity of controlling the new litigation. If the company had brought a suit in compliance with Mr. Mills' request [the plaintiff stockholder], I would have been a mere outsider whose views would be followed or turned down as other counsel in their own wisdom might see fit. You will appreciate how I felt, for you must have frequently been in the position where you wanted to be alone and to control litigation. I always prefer to be in control, even though this involves responsibility and invites much criticism in many cases when one does not succeed.

The dynamic Guthrie had at this time already been principal architect of one of the critical policy-making lawsuits of the modern United States. The federal income tax, created anew by the Wilson–Gorman tariff act of 1894, adversely affected many clients of the Seward firm. In correspondence Guthrie urged most of the firm's clients, and many of its correspondent law firms in other cities, to contribute funds for a test suit to challenge the constitutionality of the measure. A federal statute forbade injunctions against the assessment or collection of any tax, and this act had already been held to bar a pending action in the federal courts in the District of Columbia. Guthrie wanted to bring to the Supreme Court the clear-cut issue of the validity of the income tax, unencumbered by any question arising under the statute involved in the District of Columbia litigation. He arranged that the directors of the Farmers' Loan & Trust Company, and the directors of the Continental Trust Company (both New York corporations) should vote to provide for payment of the tax despite acknowledged doubt of its validity. After some difficulty Guthrie then found a stockholder of the Farmers' Loan & Trust — Charles Pollock of Boston — and a stockholder of the Continental — Louis H. Hyde of New Jersey — who were willing to sue in federal court as plaintiff stockholders, to enjoin alleged wasting of the assets of their respective companies. Guthrie's further worry was that the pending District of Columbia litigation might reach the Supreme Court before his case. However, he was able to make an arrangement with the Solicitor General of the United States which took care of this possibility. The Collector was a codefendant in the Pollock and Hyde cases; on his behalf the Solicitor General demurred; as had been anticipated, the trial court sustained the demurrers, and thereupon a direct appeal to the Supreme Court was expedited. Solicitor General Maxwell failed to consult the Attorney General of the United States about this arrangement; and this fact may have figured in the Solicitor General's resignation soon after. However this may have been, *Pollock* v. *Farmers' Loan & Trust Co.* sped on its way to the Supreme Court where it furnished the occasion on which a sharply divided Bench held the income tax law unconstitutional.

The lawyer's most traditional function in the execution of laws is to assist courts to proper decisions of litigated matter. Though this is the lawyer's oldest task, it is the one about which the available materials permit the least reliable generalization. Until we have perceptive histories of the law in action in representative localities, states, and regions, we can judge little of how the bar fulfilled its responsibilities toward the courts.

There are some scattered points to be noted. One of the expressions of the Jacksonian demand for popular control of government was pressure to extend the discretion of the jury and to curb the control of the trial judge. In practice this meant that the lawyer gained at the expense of the judge in the conduct of the trial. Toward the end of the nineteenth century the bar saw the development of "the railroad" and the "insurance company" lawyer; and this specialization in defense of particular interests encouraged the development of specialized "plaintiffs'" lawyers. These shifts in law practice created tactical pressures to reinforce the earlier trend toward curbing the trial judge. Now the plaintiff's lawyer wanted the broadest opportunity to get his case before a jury, where he felt he could best use his eloquence and his skill in the adroit shading of fact. Now the defendant's lawyer bent his skill to diverting the case from the merits — on which it would go to the jury to procedural points. In either case the result was to limit the scope of the trial judge.

In both trial and appellate courts, most markedly in the appellate courts, much of the nineteenth century witnessed an excessive insistence on local peculiarities of doctrine and procedure. Undoubtedly this was due in large part to the loss of professional standards at the bar, and the victory of a rule-of-thumb attitude toward the administration of justice. Any sampling of appellate briefs from the late nineteenth century on showed a discouragingly small percentage of craftsmanship. The main item to the credit of the courtroom lawyer was his fertility in the invention of the tools, procedures, and doctrinal bridges by which law was put to new uses.

e. The Bar as a Source of Leadership

Another function of the bar throughout our history proved to be the supply of a considerable percentage of the directing personnel needed in large public and private affairs. This was not an unnatural aspect of a profession which was so directly and regularly called on to exercise wide-ranging skill in adjustment of human relations.

The legal profession seems regularly to have supplied leadership in government in a measure that far exceeded its proportion in the population. This seems a fair generalization, even though as usual we lack adequate data for all periods and places. For example, lawyers' prominence in public office, though often exaggerated, was nonetheless impressive.

From 1790 to 1930, about 66 per cent of United States Senators were lawyers, and about 50 per cent of the members of the House; the percentages appear to have been about the same over the whole time span. Lawyers numbered between one half and two thirds of state governors. Southern state legislatures had notably high percentages of lawyer members and metropolitan areas in general sent a high proportion of lawyers to represent them in legislatures; lawyer legislators were least numerous in agricultural areas, outside the South.

Especially after 1850 lawyers' influence in legislatures tended to be specialized. Lawyers generally controlled or were especially prominent in rules or steering committees, directing the general procedure and order of business, and in judiciary committees, handling matters which related particularly to institutional structure and the general body of law affecting private rights and duties. This pattern meant that lawyer members had great power in the management of legislative programs. On the other hand, it probably meant a lessened influence on policy in important areas dominated by modern interest groups and voting blocs (such as those concerning agriculture or trade practices), and in important fields of the service activity of modern government (as in education).

Law-trained men enjoyed a practical monopoly of all save the lowest rank of judicial offices, at least after 1870. In contrast, the administrative branch of government was recruited mainly from nonlawyers. This reflected the extent to which in the twentieth century the administrative process responded to the need for specialized knowledge or experience in a wide range of economic and social fields. Nonetheless, lawyers were prominent in high, policy-making administrative posts. They constituted at least a plurality in almost every case, and often a majority, of those who became undersecretaries or assistant secretaries of departments of the federal government.

In civil life, there were some marked trends for law-trained men to take leadership outside of the profession. A sampling of business leaders in the United States in the second quarter of the twentieth century showed that about 13 per cent were men classed occupationally as professional men; the bulk of these were probably lawyers. In the academic world the practical needs of the legal profession and the vision of a handful of its leaders created a new professional group, the full-time law teachers, who became a significant element in the energy of law reform and in the appraisal of many lay social institutions.

Lawyers played an important part in public affairs outside of public office and off the platform. From the first days of the republic lobbying was an important item in the practice of the more influential and financially successful lawyers. Law-trained men figured in the inner circles of party politics, from the days of Jefferson and Hamilton to those of Taney and Webster, Jeremiah S. Black and Thaddeus Stevens, John P. Altgeld and Elihu Root, John W. Davis and Charles Evans Hughes, Benjamin Cohen and John Foster Dulles.

Probably as important as these more obvious public activities was the cumulative weight of lawyers' unofficial unpaid, nonpartisan service. Intellectual pride and regard for the public welfare entered, in imponderable mixture, into the amazing, single-handed battle which David Dudley Field waged for codification of the laws from the 1840's to 1887. In the post Civil War generation an aristocrat at the bar, William Allen Butler, concerned himself with housing, hospital, and charity problems that came with the growth of great cities. The paradoxes of the New England conscience appeared in Moorfield Storey, who was active for civil service reform, anti-imperialism, and the National Association for the Advancement of Colored People, who sharply criticized lawyers' inertia toward procedural ills and their abusive practices in lobbying and in handling corporate reorganizations, and who yet also was prominent in opposing the confirmation of Louis D. Brandeis as Associate Justice of the United States Supreme Court, in 1916. Other lawyers whose success at the bar gave them leisure for public service devoted themselves to technical reforms in the law, through the work of the Commissioners on Uniform State Laws, and, later, through the activities of the American Law Institute.

Despite such public and private display of civic consciousness among some of the profession, certain twentieth-century observers saw a material decline in the bar's general participation in public affairs. As he looked back from 1907, Dos Passos felt that the Civil War marked "the commencement of an era of professional change — perhaps I am justified in saying, an intellectual decadence — in the Bar. There certainly was a transformation, from a profession to a business." Addressing the American Bar Association in 1910, Woodrow Wilson warned that specialization, particularly on the model of the corporation lawyer's practice, was withdrawing the lawyer from his traditional contact with public issues. A few years later, Julius Henry Cohen, no unfriendly critic, wrote of the question: "The Law: Business or Profession?" and commended to his fellow lawyers the annual rereading of Wilson's warning. From the vantage point of 1932, James Grafton Rogers regarded the career of James Hagerman of Missouri (1848–1913), twenty-sixth president of the American Bar Association. In Hagerman the biographer saw a lawyer of a bent of ideas and action that was no longer familiar:

> His command of speech, his faith in the usefulness of party allegiance, his abstention from office, his vigorous opinions, his railroad employment, his strong loyalties to public causes are all part and parcel of the successful lawyer of the cities that crystallized behind the frontier. This sort of man has now been superseded even in the West by a business lawyer who is suspicious of political affairs, almost non-partisan in politics, less vocative, less individual and even timid in public causes. The new lawyer had traded for security some of the opportunities of the barrister's position which Hagerman enjoyed to the full.

Sharpest of the critics was A. A. Berle, Jr. In his view, after the period that began with the Virginia dynasty and ran perhaps to Webster, social

leadership in the United States passed from the lawyer to the entrepreneur. "Traditions of public service, such as are found in the medical
profession, insensibly disappeared. . . ." As Berle saw the situation in
1933: "Intellectually the profession commanded and still commands
respect, but it is the respect for an intellectual jobber and contractor
rather than for a moral force." In 1934 Mr. Justice Stone expressed his
sober appraisal that:

> . . . candor would compel even those of us who have the most
> abiding faith in our profession, and the firmest belief in its capacity
> for future usefulness, to admit that in our own time the Bar has not
> maintained its traditional position of public influence and leadership.

The unanimity of such testimony from responsible observers was
impressive. On the other hand, though there was a plausible case for the
proposition that the bar had lost much in public influence, the case
rested largely on opinion. So far as anyone sought to produce tangible
evidence, it tended to be directed mainly at an attempt to show that
there were fewer lawyers in public office. However, it was hard to
establish even this last point by quantitative evidence; available data
were incomplete.

The fundamental question was, what net effect did lawyers have in
public affairs. The mere number of offices held did not answer this.
There was more telling evidence in the record of major legislation after
1870; the bulk of important modern regulatory laws dealt with the
reform or control of practices or institutions of which lawyers had
been, if not the initiators, at least the architects and master builders.

Toward mid-twentieth century, however, it appeared that events
might be maneuvering lawyers back toward a greater position of constructive public influence. It was an irony of our legal history that this
should have been so because of the expansion of federal regulation after
1933, which aroused at least as much emotion as it did reasoned opposition from the upper brackets of the profession. The first reaction, it is
true, was almost purely negative; this phase was expressed in the cru-
sade of the American Liberty League to write the commerce, taxing,
and spending powers of Congress out of the Constitution by judicial
construction. In 1937 the Supreme Court finally affirmed Congress's
control of the national economy. In a large measure this only shifted
the battleground, but at least it shifted the fight toward more constructive efforts to reach working accommodations between private and
public direction of affairs. The lawyer had won his public leadership
in the past largely because his profession helped make him a more ob-

jective and resourceful mediator of forces. Perhaps he was returning to this basis of leadership. Writing in 1949, the leader and historian of a famous New York law firm seemed in effect to say this. Mr. Robert T. Swaine saw a critical challenge presented to the bar:

> Today the American lawyer deals with the problems of his business clients on a much broader basis, considers substance as more important than form and attempts to relate legal problems to their political, economic and social implications. . . . The clients of today also generally recognize the interrelation of legal questions with political, economic and social questions. . . .

> Big Business, Big Labor and Big Government are all here to stay. But in the gigantic concentrated power of their aggregate collectivism there is real danger that they may be leading us along the road to state collectivism. If we believe that such an end would be a tragedy, and that individual freedom of opportunity in a system of private enterprise should be maintained, it behooves all of us who render 'specialized service to business and finance' to seek such solutions of the legal problems of our clients as are compatible with the changing social concepts and as will avoid the abuses of economic power to which our profession too often contributed in past decades.

It was too early to express assured judgments on the social role of the bar. However, the available evidence did not give basis for complacence in appraising the part that lawyers as a group had played in the United States after the full impact of industrial-financial-urban change burst upon the society in the '70s. For that matter, there was little evidence by which to check the accuracy of the prominent role conventionally assigned the profession even in the classic generation of its leadership, after 1790. The further back one looks, the more the boldest figures stand out, and the harder it becomes to place them in proper perspective to the profession as a whole. We must have adequate local and regional legal histories, before we can pass confident judgment on the social leadership of the bar in any period of our history.

f. Symbol Makers

Finally, in this sketch of the social functions of lawyers in United States society, we must look at lawyers in relation to the symbols by which the society lived. Like all communities, the American community had a common core of values which held it together. It needed ready means by which to express those values, to apply them, and to invoke them for reassurance. Lawyers were leaders in the formulation of the symbols which expressed what the American community believed in; they were leaders in shaping and maintaining rituals which helped preserve those symbols.

Yet the way in which lawyers fulfilled this particular function probably had much to do with that diminished public influence of the profession which struck so many critics of the bar. Events early accustomed people in the United States to analyze and debate public questions in terms of "law." However, they regularly mingled reverence for "the Constitution," "the law," and "the courts" with a working attitude toward law as something to be used for individual and group purposes; and when they reached for law as a tool of everyday business, they were apt not to be meticulous about the public implications or the procedural proprieties of the uses to which they put it. The speed and extent of change, and the social mobility in American society contributed to this combination of attitudes toward law. And there need not have been anything unhealthy in the combination; it was the American expression of the everlasting problem of striking a balance between stability and change.

Lawyers did not create these prevailing attitudes toward law, but they had a unique opportunity to harness the power generated by the popular views, and put it to work in the directing of public policy. If it was to do this, the bar could not afford to forget that it was dealing with a somewhat paradoxical combination of popular attitudes. People in the United States were looking for beliefs to which they could hold fast, in a country of change; they also wanted change which would fulfill the promise of a new continent and advance their personal fortunes.

Unfortunately lawyers as a whole demonstrated little realization of the practical implications of these diverse popular attitudes. After 1870 the bar seemed to take as its exclusive role the exaltation of things as they were. It was not surprising if lawyers tended either to lose contact with the mass of their community, or to lose the community's confidence.

Such a bias was not apparent in the lawyers' golden age of public leadership — in the generation that founded the republic. The Constitution represented change which would stabilize the institutions under which commerce, land speculation, and industry might move ahead. For all the suspicions of those who opposed the new government, this was change which went with the current of the dominant temper of the whole people; their main concern was the exploitation of the continent. But Jeffersonian and then Jacksonian Democracy roused strong emotion, in attack: Witness Mr. Justice Story's lament for himself as the last of the old judges; witness the virulent partisan attacks on Taney for his role as Jackson's lieutenant. This emotion marked a time when successful men at the bar became identified in their own minds and in the popular view as the natural adherents of the comfortable and powerful, who would not see things changed except on their own terms.

The bar showed its conservatism in scenes quite removed from the drama of class conflict. Leading lawyers sternly opposed, and prophesied dire consequences from the adoption of married women's property acts, the grant to mothers of rights with respect to the custody of their children, the enactment of homestead laws, the effort to simplify procedure and merge legal and equitable remedies, the establishment of women's suffrage, the creation of juvenile courts, the adoption of the initiative and referendum.

The activities of the foremost advocates of the late nineteenth and early twentieth centuries dramatized lawyers as a group that opposed almost all legislation for the public health and safety and against gross abuse of superior economic power, in the face of grave challenges to the integrity of the society that arose out of the growth of the cities and the concentration of wealth. Lawmen's resistance to rational change neared high tide in New York state in 1911–1912. The New York Court of Appeals then held that that state's first workmen's compensation act was so unreasonable a departure from fundamental principles as to amount to a violation of due process of law. A group of eminent lawyers solemnly warned the public that it would imperil social stability to attempt to overrule that decision even by constitutional amendment.

It might have seemed that legal standpattism could go no further. But the next generation saw a contest in which leaders at the bar still more stubbornly identified the profession in the public mind with opposition to use of public power for the general welfare. In the 1930's counsel for the concentrated industrial and financial power of the country associated themselves with their clients in an American Liberty League. The lawyer members of the League thus undertook to lead a campaign of slogans and emotion, to combat efforts to use the fiscal and regulatory power of the national government to fight a national depression. The year 1937 brought the climax of this contest, in the battle over President Franklin Roosevelt's proposal to increase the membership of the Supreme Court by enough members to sustain the administration's economic recovery and reform measures. The astonishing aspect of this 1937 contest was not that the Roosevelt proposal lost, but that it so nearly won. Against it were the tremendous symbols of "Constitution" and "Court." That at one stage the contest could nevertheless be so close was evidence of how far lawyers — most of whom fought the

Roosevelt Court bill — had lost public leadership even in a field that was by tradition peculiarly their own.

This development was not inevitable. Law is an attempt systematically to order social relations. By their profession lawyers are immersed in this effort. It is a working environment inherently conservative, in that it seeks regularity and predictability in affairs. No less inherently, it involves the constant experience of adaptation to change; it is the restless pressure for change in human relations that largely creates the felt need for law. Where lawmen made creative contributions it was, as in the Federal Constitution, by combining unafraid and even daring readiness to innovate with tough-minded insistence that the need and direction of innovation rest firmly on fact. Such an approach is at the pole opposite to standpattism. Sheer resistance to change, by only damming a gathering current, does not conserve, but insures destructive flood when the dam finally breaks.

g. Lawyers as a Pressure Group

Where lawyers had living influence on society in the United States it was because they channeled and directed change, rather than trying simply to damn it. A constructive working philosophy was never wholly lacking in the profession, and showed itself among men of such diverse outlook as Roger Brooke Taney, Samuel F. Miller, Morrison R. Waite, John P. Altgeld, or Elihu Root. It was, in the true sense, a "conservative" philosophy, and, appropriately, it was best expressed by one of the greatest reformers in the law in the United States. Writing to Robert W. Bruere (February 25, 1922), Mr. Justice Brandeis spoke his philosophy with a freedom which he rarely allowed himself after he went on the Bench:

Refuse to accept as inevitable any evil in business (e.g., irregularity of employment). Refuse to tolerate any immoral practice (e.g., espionage). But do not believe that you can find a universal remedy for evil conditions or immoral practices in effecting a fundamental change in society (as by State Socialism). And do not pin too much faith in legislation. Remedial institutions are apt to fall under the control of the enemy and to become instruments of oppression.

Seek for betterment within the broad lines of existing institutions. Do so by attacking evil *in situ;* and proceed from the individual to the general. Remember that progress is necessarily slow; that remedies are necessarily tentative; that because of varying conditions there must be much and constant inquiry into facts . . . and much experimentation; and that always and everywhere the intellectual, moral and spiritual development of those concerned will remain an essential — and the main factor — in real betterment.

Its sharper critics were likely to label the organized bar reactionary. The label was not accurate. In the relatively brief span of its effective existence, after 1870, the organized bar was by no means as blindly conservative as the general body of lawyers. This was nonetheless true because it was probably due mainly to inertia and lack of corporate feeling in the profession. Since the bar had little organization through most of its history, it could achieve coherence and drive only with great difficulty. In any case, whatever the cause, by mid-twentieth century the organized bar had developed little of the role of symbol maker, apologist, and guardian of the *status quo*.

The most tangible, continuing activity of the organized bar concerning public policy was its efforts to affect the election of judges. This was chiefly the work of local bar associations. They sought to hold up to the voter the ideal of an honest and competent bench. And they publicly endorsed selected candidates, even if their endorsements often seemed a wry recommendation of the lesser evil rather than the better choice. Such activity in judicial elections grew naturally out of the origins of the revival of bar organization in the '70s; it was indignation against corrupt local government that spurred the creation of the Association of the Bar of the City of New York, and the formation of other local organizations, in the later nineteenth century. As was noted earlier, the bar scored only occasional success in efforts to affect the course of judicial elections; its indifferent success was evidence of its tenuous claim to public influence.

Activity in judicial elections was the most specific item in a very general interest of the bar in good government. This interest was good in intention, and honest in motive; but it produced little long-range accomplishment. This was not surprising, since the bar dealt with good government in terms of symptoms rather than causes. State bar associations did little or nothing to foster desired ideas or attitudes toward public institutions or public affairs. From 1911–1916 a special committee of the American Bar Association worked vigorously against the movement for the recall of judges. This campaign in the name of the Association was credited with a considerable share in the defeat of the recall proposal in various states. The 1920's, with their nostalgia for older ways of politics and business, brought another campaign of faith and ideas. The Association then conducted a widely publicized educational program, to inform the public of the nature and values of our government as embodied in the Constitution. There was little tangible result, except that most of the states adopted statutory requirements that the Constitution be taught in the schools.

Thus the organized bar made very limited contributions to public thinking about public affairs. It contributed hardly more to the profession's own working philosophy — its aims, standards, and evaluation of its own performance. The American Bar Association was founded in 1878; there was no movement to adopt a code of professional ethics until 1905. A code was adopted in 1908. Except for brief platitudes neither this code nor subsequent amendments to it dealt with the bar's social responsibilities. The first widely awakened interest in "ethics" coincided with a new sensitiveness to lay competition during the depression of the 1930's.

If it was not to be a promoter of ideologies, the organized bar might have been expected to become a new center of energy for law revision or reform. Particularly was there a job to be done in technical fields — in matters of court procedure and administrative organization, for example — where inertia rather than opposition blocked changes that might benefit the community.

The record of the American Bar Association might fairly be taken to measure the most sustained work of the organized bar in law reform and revision. One could not accurately or fairly label this record reactionary or radical, conservative or liberal, in the ordinary meaning of any of these terms. It was not a record of a comprehensive, long-range program, though on particular fronts the Association put forth organized, coherent activity. Certainly it was not the record of a pressure group that could show energy, internal discipline, or staff work comparable to the activity of the contemporary spokesmen organizations for industry, commerce, labor or agriculture. As a pressure group, the lawyers were crude amateurs. With few exceptions they busied themselves with matters which they took up in isolation from the social context, and matters which were generally of secondary social importance, concerning issues merely instrumental to the basic institutions and powers of the time.

The American Bar Association's most important contributions to law reform developed slowly. They concerned the regulation of the legal profession itself, the procedure of the courts, and the enactment of uniform laws among the states. Simeon E. Baldwin's convictions that legal education and bar admission standards must be improved was a prime factor in the founding of the Association. Nonetheless, for years the Association had little to show in these matters except a few committee reports. In 1893 a handful of members especially interested in the educational issue and impatient with the inertia of the main body, caused the formation of a separate Section of Legal Education. Still, little happened beyond discussion and the filing of recommendations which were left unimplemented. The few teachers and lawyers in the Association who were interested in an energetic program looked for another instrument for action. Finally in 1900 they hit upon an effective device; they caused the Association to sponsor the creation of an Association of American Law Schools. Thereafter the law school organization supplied initiative and persistence in the effort to raise educational standards. The role of the American Bar Association as a whole was simply to lend prestige to the activity of a small group of interested people, rather than itself to supply the direction and motive power for change. Even after the schoolmen took the lead, it was not until 1921 that the parent Association endorsed any really substantial advance in defined standards of legal education.

Higher educational standards were a powerful influence toward higher admissions standards. The initiative of the bar associations and of the schools eventually supplanted the nineteenth-century local control of bar admissions by the twentieth-century system of centralized bar examinations. In 1931 the American Bar Association gave further impetus to the new movement by sponsoring the organization of a National Conference of Bar Examiners.

Reform of procedure ultimately became a proud boast of the American Bar Association but it was not always so. When Roscoe Pound made his path-breaking analysis of "The Causes of Popular Dissatisfaction with the Administration of Justice," at the Association's 1906 meeting, he outraged the Old Guard. Pound was charged with an effort "to destroy that which the wisdom of the centuries has evolved." The stalwarts tried, unsuccessfully, to defeat a motion that the address be printed and circulated. In 1907, despite this flurry of opposition, the Association created a committee to investigate delay and expense in the administration of justice. In 1909 that committee reported a series of recommendations for reform of court organization and procedure which for the next quarter century furnished the guide lines to change in those fields.

One of the main proposals was to give the courts broad powers to make rules of procedure. The Association persisted for a generation in pressing Congress to put such power in the federal courts; such a step would furnish a pattern and a weighty precedent for like action in the states. In despair the Association finally abandoned its long effort to persuade Congress to this action. At that juncture, in 1934, a sympathetic federal executive prodded Congress into conferring on the

Supreme Court of the United States broad rule-making authority for the federal court system. The Federal Rules of 1938 were the result.

The drive for uniform state laws produced the American Bar Association's outstanding contributions in substantive law revision. The work of an Association committee appointed in 1889 led to the creation of the Conference of Commissioners on Uniform State Laws. Thereafter the Association partly financed the work of the Conference. There was tangible accomplishment in this field; an impressive number of states adopted the uniform acts proposed in such important areas as negotiable instruments, sales, and warehouse receipts. Plainly, however, the work was not legislative reform of prime importance. Significantly the notable successes were scored in commercial law, and concerned the working legal tools of institutions whose basic framework was not in question.

Outside of the matters of procedure and uniform laws, the American Bar Association made only an episodic, spotty record of efforts to affect public affairs. Consider, for example, the positions that the Association took on various public matters over the years 1896–1937 that might be classified, roughly, as "conservative." It opposed the capital gains feature of the income tax act of 1913. It campaigned against adoption of the recall of judges. In 1913 it refused to sponsor a model workmen's compensation act reported to it by one of its committees, on the ground that this presented a "political" question not proper for Association action; in 1914, however, it advocated adoption of a Uniform Workmen's Compensation Act. It resolved that injunctions should be available in labor disputes as in any others, and opposed special treatment of labor in the law. In 1918 it approved the Uniform Flag Act. In 1922 it unanimously adopted as its own a committee report on Americanism, launched a campaign of popular education regarding the Constitution, and pressed state legislatures to pass laws requiring that the schools teach the Constitution. In 1923 it opposed any limitation of the powers of the Supreme Court to review the constitutionality of legislation. It opposed the federal Child Labor Amendment, though it coupled this attitude with support of state control of child labor. It opposed legislation to regulate fees received by lawyers for the prosecution of claims against the United States. Throughout the depression of the 1930's it urged softening modifications of the antitrust laws. In 1932 it criticized the national government for putting main reliance on the income tax as a source of federal revenue. In 1933 it recommended that federal tax law should make more liberal allowance for charitable gifts. In 1934 it made alarmed report of the growth of "bureaucracy," alleged the existence of undesirable administrative procedures, and supported legislation to hedge about administrators' discretion. It opposed limitations on the jurisdiction of federal courts, especially in constitutional cases. It declared itself against expenditure of federal funds in aid of research by the American Law Institute.

Over the period 1896–1937 an observer could also note that the Association took positions that might, in conventional terms, be classed as "liberal." Examples were the Association's interest in legal education and procedural reform. In 1903 it adopted a committee report condemning monopoly. In 1912 it resolved in favor of state legislation patterned on the federal food and drug law of 1906. In 1922 it expressed hope that the United States would support the Permanent Court of International Justice. In 1921 it gave approval to provision for declaratory judgments. In 1924 it supported legislation to implement arbitration contracts and commercial arbitration treaties between the United States and South American nations. In 1920 it advocated regulation of air navigation and in 1925 it supported the establishment of the first administrative regulation of air traffic, in the Department of Commerce. As early as 1921 it urged that the Constitution be amended to abolish the "lame duck" session of Congress. In 1928 it showed interest in legislation to facilitate the peaceful adjustment of labor disputes. In the 1920's it expressed readiness to see further regulation of modern business on such varied fronts as radio, interstate motor transport, uniform state aeronautical codes, and improved food and drug legislation.

Such, then, was the tally of "liberal" and "conservative" positions to which the American Bar Association committed itself in the course of some forty years. Regardless of the analytical pigeonholes into which one might thrust the various commitments, they expressed little pattern or philosophy. This was the mark made by the weightiest of the country's organized bar groups. Aside from the Association of the Bar of the City of New York, no local or state bar association could show a record of public interest comparable to that of the national organization. After seventy-five years from the rebirth of professional associations, the organized bar as a whole had made for itself no clear-cut or influential function as a source of public policy.

Internal discipline of the profession was the narrowest of the likely functions of an organized bar. It was also the function that the organized bar might most naturally be expected to perform. Here, too, the record was at best inconclusive.

Some of the early local bar associations (for example, in Chicago) were founded to correct undesirable conditions within the profession.

However, before 1910 the local, state, and national associations were little more than social clubs. We have noted the tardy adoption and the limited and even superficial character of the canons of ethics which the organized bar finally sponsored.

There was no clearer example of belated, narrow, and shallow treatment of the bar's "ethical" problems than in the matter of making legal service available to people of small means. Toward an issue which challenged the professed ideals of the profession and of American society the organized bar was inert, insensitive, unimaginative.

The most obvious problem was that of the poor. After 1870 the rise of great cities fast multiplied the number of people whose ignorance and defenseless economic position made them easy objects of oppression or neglect. The bar as a whole did nothing of consequence for the legal aid movement for the first fifty years of its existence. Finally, in 1917, the first Conference of Bar Association Delegates sponsored by the American Bar Association resolved that all bar associations should foster legal aid societies. In 1920 the American Bar Association created a special committee, following this with a standing committee on legal aid in 1921, and strongly endorsing the legal aid movement. In 1922 the national Association urged all state and local organizations to name standing committees on legal aid. These were all desirable expressions of interest. What they represented in tangible contribution was not so clear. From the late 1920's on, the organized bar as a whole gave some regular attention to legal aid. But as late as 1934 competent observers found that existing legal aid societies still fell far short of meeting the need of poor people for legal help. By then there was ample administrative experience in legal aid work. Finances were the main obstacle to a complete and businesslike provision for the problem; there was little evidence that the bar felt this financial problem as its responsibility. Apparently the professional conscience was not yet sufficiently aroused to finish the job begun by the belated acceptance of formal responsibility in the 1920's. Even slower to develop was any consideration within the organized bar as to whether more could be done to make legal service available at lowered cost to people of small means, above the legal aid level.

Up to 1950 the only thoroughgoing activity of the organized profession with reference to its own housekeeping was the drive for the "integrated bar." This was a movement to substitute for the voluntary bar association an organization to which all lawyers must belong. Experience was still too slight and too little studied to detect what that change might mean for the fulfillment of professional obligations. It was characteristic that, at least in these beginning years of the integrated bar movement, its main emphasis was negative rather than affirmative. Concern seemed to be chiefly with improved internal discipline of the profession. Voluntary bar associations had "grievance committees." Their action was typically sporadic and haphazard. The tighter organization and the financial resources of an "integrated" bar association might promote more inclusive and efficient policing. This might improve the service that the community had from the bar. Still, traditional discipline dealt almost wholly with simple problems of the lawyer's fidelity to his client and good faith toward other lawyers and the courts. The essential narrowness of this approach was emphasized by its inherently negative quality. The integrated bar movement would add little substance to the social functions of the organized bar, if it did not promote more positive examination of the economics of the profession, or of the profession's obligations to the general welfare in addition to the obligations of client-caretakers.

h. The Working Philosophy of Lawyers

Thus far we have talked of lawyers' social functions primarily in terms of lawyers' behavior. Realistic appraisal of those functions requires also some examination of the professional values and beliefs involved in that behavior. This is especially so because the most characteristic functions of lawyers in the United States related to the mediation and adjustment of social forces. The temper in which such work was done would necessarily affect the kind of results that followed.

History had no record of the minds and hearts of the hundreds of thousands of men who practiced law in the United States; we must not forget this in generalizing about attitudes of "the bar." However, in their working philosophy some men made so consistent a pattern with other factors of their age that we may justifiably draw from their careers hypotheses about the main trends of thought and action among their contemporaries.

In the profession's golden age of public leadership — the years from 1765 to 1830 — we find qualities of independence of judgment, and pride in the responsibility and dignity of legal counseling and the shaping of social institutions, such as were not manifested with equal vigor later on. Men like James Wilson, Alexander Hamilton, and John Marshall spoke with the conscious authority of those who found institutions. They had neither the overbelligerent nor the anxiety-tinged dogmatism of men who feel themselves only the agents of a situation to whose fortunes their own are committed.

A more ambiguous tone became evident in Webster. We need not lose ourselves in speculation on ultimate motives. His biographer found him a "healthy" extrovert, his "personality neither subtle nor inexplicable," with "attention . . . fixed, not in his own reactions but on externalities . . ."; however, the biographer saw also that "Throughout his life, Webster attached perhaps an undue importance to material possessions." In any case, one is almost never quite sure, unless in the speech of March 7, 1850, that he is hearing the true conviction of the master of the law or the hired pleading of the advocate. It was Senator Webster who, when renewal of the charter of the Second Bank of the United States was at stake, wrote as a lawyer to his client Nicholas Biddle: "I believe that my retainer has not been renewed or *refreshed* as usual. If it be wished that my relation to the Bank should be continued, it may be well to send me the usual retainer."

On the other hand, through the middle nineteenth century there also continued the note of independent, consciously responsible judgment. We find it in such men as George W. Strong or William H. Seward, of New York, or David Davis and Abraham Lincoln of Illinois, or Samuel Miller and George Grover Wright of Iowa. The careers of some of the leading "railroad lawyers" of the post Civil War generation caution most remarkably against putting glib labels on "the bar" of a given period. Though he was many times counsel for railroads, Jeremiah S. Black early fought for more effective public regulation of railroads. He led the battle on the issue in the Pennsylvania constitutional convention of 1872. And before he appeared in the legislature in 1883 to oppose certain measures sought by the roads, he refused to accept the railroad's retainer at a fee which they left for him to name; he was, said Black, pledged to the people on the issues at stake. James Hagerman of Missouri was successively a general attorney for the Santa Fe, general solicitor for the "Katy," and finally general counsel for the latter. He also believed in and spoke out boldly for Free Silver and Bryan, at a time when conservative lawyers saw in both the disintegration of society. Edgar H. Farrar of Louisiana, railroad lawyer and practitioner chiefly in matters of corporate finance, interested himself in a broad range of municipal and state political reform. In an open letter to President Theodore Roosevelt, toward the end of Roosevelt's last administration, Farrar urged federal legislation to curb the great railroad and financial corporations. Stephen Strong Gregory, a leader of the Chicago bar, spoke out vigorously against the hysteria generated against the Haymarket Riot defendants. Against a storm of newspaper criticism Gregory sought habeas corpus to bar the execution of the assassin of Mayor Carter H. Harrison, claiming that the defendant was insane. Gregory also was one of the three defense counsel for Eugene Debs, in the contempt proceedings that grew out of the Pullman strike.

There was no time when the bar altogether lacked men of independent and inquiring spirit, concerned with public issues. By and large, however, the ambiguities in personal philosophy and allegiances which marked Webster characterized those who set the tone, and stood as models of professional success in the late nineteenth century. We cannot know their ultimate motives. In action these men showed either the technician's sheer absorption in his craft, or the partisan's single-minded devotion to his principle or his party.

John G. Johnson, of Philadelphia, and Elihu Root, of New York, represented the master technician in law. George Wharton Pepper estimated Johnson as the complete Machiavellian, seasoned with "an impish delight in successfully making the worse appear the better reason." More likely Johnson was by temperament a man too practical to be concerned with the meaning of what he was doing. In any case, he was his own master, taking clients large and small, refusing to become a director or officer of any business firm, fighting with detached ruthlessness men who had been or might thereafter be his clients in other matters. He had the simple independence of the strong man who takes his strength for granted and stands ready against any comer.

Root was no less his own master, but in a different temper. His family background produced a New England bred concern alike for morals and mind; the environment of his youth was the simplicity and intellectual devotion of the Hamilton College faculty community, to which his father belonged. Naturally, Root held to his personal independence as a matter of moral responsibility, rather than of simple pride of strength. The more striking, therefore, was his ability to put into separate compartments his views and his work regarding the public welfare, and his undivided devotion of a superb lawyer's craftsmanship to the service of a client. As a young man he assisted the defense of Tweed; probably he enjoyed the professional compliment and the responsibility that went with association in a major case with leaders of the bar. As an established leader himself, he scorned to become salaried counsel of any economic empire. However, he stood ready to handle legal problems as they came, and on their own terms, with little regard to the identity of the client. Thus he handled the legal affairs of the Hannibal & St. Jo throughout that railroad's vicissitudes at the hands of various financial war lords; Root served the railroad at first when its president was his friend, later when Gould had seized control, and again when Gould was forced to sell to the CB&Q. And the decision as to the interest he would represent in the winding up of the Northern Securities case characteristically turned on the chance that one party offered him a retainer earlier than did the opposing interest.

To Root the technician, a case was just a job to be done in work-manlike fashion, and one case generally speaking was as good as another. His technician's approach to the practice was thrown into sharp relief by its contrast with his genuine concern with issues of public policy which he encountered outside his law office. In the New York constitutional convention of 1894 he strongly supported broad regulation of election expenditures; he spoke bluntly of the need to regulate corporations' political contributions; and he supported the ban on the grant of railroad passes or other free services by public utilities to legislators. He argued for street railway clients against the constitutionality of a franchise tax whose passage under Governor Theodore Roosevelt he had approved; later he expressed his belief that the court correctly upheld the tax. He represented great financial interests; on the other hand, as early as 1879 in a public address he frankly discussed deepening class cleavages in the United States growing out of the concentration of economic power, and deplored the trend as a threat to the republic. He was skeptical of regulation; in 1898 he wrote to a correspondent:

> You are quite right in supposing that no amount of professional employment by corporations has blinded me to the political and social dangers which exist in their relations to government and public affairs. It has seemed to me, however, that most of the attempts to cure the evil have been like jerking at a tangled fishline, which only makes the hard knots harder.

Nonetheless, in his Union League Club speech in New York City in 1904, he praised Theodore Roosevelt's policies as true conservatism, because they sought to prevent the development of social schism.

To Mr. Justice Brown, Root confessed that he was too much engrossed in the law as a game of skill. To another close friend, he declared that his work as Secretary of War under McKinley had brought "a thousand new interests" into his life. And to a former law partner, he exclaimed that his practice seemed to him futile in contrast to the sense of accomplishment that he had from his work in the War Department. Within the frame of a conservative morality his attitude toward the practice of law was frankly manipulative; there were times when he laid down the law to clients, but there is little evidence that he often felt his public policy views as a limitation on his professional services. Yet he represented much of the best that lawmen contributed to society in the United States. He was a leader in the battle to improve standards of legal education and of admission to the bar; he was a blunt critic of the lawyer's tendency toward blindly adhering to the *status quo*, for he appreciated that a living conservatism required readiness not only to accept but to lead in changes that the facts dictated; he was one of the first lawmen to make realistic acceptance of expanded administrative regulation; he put farsighted emphasis on the imperative need for more efficient organization of government business. Despite the distinctive quality of mind which led him to such views, he was also representative of conventional success at the bar in his time. The element of paradox in this went back to his readiness to practice law simply as a technician, leaving to clients the choice of the values which his craftsman's skill should serve.

Lesser men were technicians only. To understand the role of the bar in the United States after 1870, we must emphasize lawyers' preoccupation with the immediacies of the day more than any evil motives or Machiavellian skills. Out of his knowledge of his own generation of the late nineteenth century, Judge Dillon observed somewhat sadly that: "Reform is a plant of slow growth in the sterile gardens of the practicing and practical lawyer." In the first generation after 1790 a Parsons, a Wilson, or a Kent instinctively set discussion of domestic law in a framework provided by jurisprudence and the law of nations. Seventy-five years later it was typical of the times for a leader of the bar — a president of the American Bar Association — to address the bar only on such strictly practical topics as "The Inviolability of Telegrams," "American State Constitutions," and "General Corporation Laws."

How far lawyers had divorced themselves from public leadership, and how far the public had lost confidence in lawyers' leadership, were reflected in Governor Franklin Roosevelt's veto of the first law by which the New York legislature undertook to create a permanent law revision commission. The governor's objection was that the legislature proposed a commission most of whose members would be lawyers:

> The personnel of such a commission in all probability would be interested only in strictly legal and technical phases of judicial administration rather than broad general questions of policy and fundamentals. No substantial benefit could possibly result from such a survey. . . .

> In the study of the broad question of bringing our system of justice to the standards of business efficiency, and to the meeting of modern conditions of life, it is essential to bring to bear the experience of lay as well as technical legal experts.

But even in the commanding figure of a Root, the technician did not alone set the tone of the American bar after the '70s. He shared leadership with the partisan of the now dominant managers of concentrated industrial and financial power. The technician supported the *status quo* with the colorless, implacable force of inertia. The partisan wielded the sword, whether in the hot blood of Guthrie, the complacent arrogance of Choate, or the reasoned ruthlessness of Cravath.

Like the technician, the partisan lawyer showed little evidence that he guided his course by anything save the requirements of his client; prudence for the client might dictate concessions to policies declared in law, but the important fact was that prudence was the test. In 1916 six months of hot blood, cold fury, and calculated pressure swirled about the confirmation of Louis D. Brandeis as an associate justice of the United States Supreme Court. The deepest meaning of that episode was that it brought out the working ideals of the successful bar in the sharply etched lines with which such a crisis may reveal forces generally imperceptible. A banker, testifying before the investigating Senators, told of the answer which Brandeis gave to the request that he represent the interests of a great investment banking group in a proxy fight involving the Illinois Central. Brandeis not only had to be convinced that the proffered retainer was not conceivably inconsistent with his then current public activities devoted to exposing the financial mismanagement of the New Haven. He also required "to be satisfied of the justness of our position." "It was an unusual experience," the witness observed. "I had occasion to retain other lawyers, and no one ever raised that question." Austen Fox, a leader among the lawyers who campaigned against the confirmation, explained his position to Amos Pinchot: "It is true that nothing unethical has been proved against Mr. Brandeis. What has been proved against him is that he does not act according to the canons of the Bar. The trouble with Mr. Brandeis is that he never loses his judicial attitude toward his clients. He always acts the part of a judge toward his clients instead of being his clients' lawyer, which is against the practices of the Bar." This commentary on professional philosophy should be compared with the public letter of contemporary date in which seven former presidents of the American Bar Association recorded their opinion that the nominee lacked the qualities that would fit him for high judicial office.

Partisanship thus summed up professional obligation, in the working philosophy of at least an important part of the modern bar in the United States. The reality of this attitude, and its limitations, even when weighed simply in the scales of the client's interests, were attested by a distinguished practitioner and teacher of law, then president of a great insurance company. From the retrospect of 1935, Thomas I. Parkinson reviewed the practice of law, and put a caution to lawyers:

The lawyer who serves his client without regard to the public welfare, although he succeed in getting the decision in a particular case, in the long run does his client no real service, and, if you want an illustration, let me briefly refer to the extraordinary service which insurance lawyers rendered the insurance business in years gone by, in exaggerating warranties to the point where they were almost one hundred per cent protection against claims, only to develop a public atmosphere resulting in judicial decision and legislation which puts the insurer under his contract in a worse position today than is any other contracting party. That is overservice by the profession.

Undoubtedly there was a tangle of motives behind the partisan spirit of the bar. Critical contemporaries within the profession sometimes felt that lawyers were dominated by excessively prudent regard for getting business. George Templeton Strong was impatient with the slowness of lawyers to take the field against a corrupt local bench in New York City. In December, 1871, he wrote into his journal a tart judgment of the new city bar association:

> Its members are afraid to get up a case against Barnard, Cardozo & Co., though abundant proof of corruption is within their reach. If they should fail, Barnard & Co. would be hostile to them & they would lose clients. The Counsel of the VII *Bishops* had more backbone. I feel inclined to resign from this Bar Association.

Strong's pessimism was not wholly warranted, however; the Association subsequently made charges, and these were sustained after an inquiry by the legislature. Fifty years later the directors of the Cleveland Crime Survey noted that to an increasing extent the abler lawyers disdained court work; hence leaders of the bar had ceased to care much about the quality of the administration of justice, and had become "possessed of a fear of offending judges or prosecutors or political leaders, lest their displeasure have a harmful effect upon the amount of 'business' which flows into their offices. This destroys their willingness or ability to combat aggressively the abuses in courts and public offices." Albert M. Kales, successful and distinguished leader of the Chicago bar, appraised the profession of the early twentieth century in no more flattering terms. He commented on the "notorious" restraining influence of lawyers upon desirable legislative change; this, he felt, came either from inertia or from a reactionary outlook. ". . . nevertheless," he proceeded, "in private one sees the best intelligence, and even excellent reform principles in leading members of the bar. It is the profession of client care-taking that chokes it down. The more important and able the lawyer, the more he is in touch with the most important business interests of the community, and the more clear it is that he cannot propose or advocate any reform of an extensive character which will not be unwelcome to some particular client's interest."

A man might also be content with the simple role of partisan because he was unaware that a changing world called on him to take a larger part. This naïveté was no less real because it might mark a man who was active in large affairs. It was implicit in the moral complacency which could lead Joseph H. Choate to say that the contingent fee was "the chief cause of detraction" from the bar's "absolute independence and disinterestedness as advocates . . ." It was natural in men who handled the same types of business, dealt with the same relatively small circle of law firms, belonged to the same clubs, were part of the same inner circles of bar association activities, or played on the same outer edges of party politics.

Bryce detected this naïveté, or provincialism, in the upper brackets of the bar in the United States. His testimony is the more impressive because his view of this country was colored by contact mainly with the upper strata of its society. He found that in general politics lawyers in the United States were markedly more conservative than the English bar. This he attributed to a "defensive attitude" of the "upper part of the profession" in the United States, reflecting its sensitivity to the pressure of a mass electorate. In contrast, the English legal profession had not felt the stimulus to extreme conservatism that might have come in reaction to sustained popular demand for legal change:

> The defensive attitude which the upper part of the profession is thus led to assume fosters those conservative instincts which a system of case law engenders, and which are further stimulated by the habit of constantly recurring to a fundamental instrument, the Federal Constitution. Thus one finds the same dislike to theory, the same attachment to old forms, the same unwillingness to be committed to any broad principle which distinguished the orthodox type of English lawyers in the first half of last century. Prejudices survive [1893] on the shores of the Mississippi which Bentham assailed when those shores were inhabited only by Indians and beavers; and in Chicago, a place which living men remember as a lonely swamp, special demurrers, replications *de iniuria*, and various elaborate formalities of pleading which were swept away by the English Common Law Procedure Acts of 1850 and 1852, flourish and abound to this day.

What Bryce perceived fitted into a pattern with the basic economic fact of the legal profession in mid-twentieth-century United States — that it got the bulk of its clients and business from about the top 13 per cent of the population, measured by income. Bryce's insight caught one aspect of a point of view to which a leading New York lawyer of the day gave clear expression. With obvious sincerity William D. Guthrie wrote a Chicago colleague (1898) concerning an attack on Illinois's graduated inheritance tax, that: "If graduated taxation is sanctioned, it will lead to the most arbitrary and confiscatory law, and if we could convince the Court of this inevitable tendency of progressive taxation, we should succeed." Subsequently the Supreme Court of the United States decided, 8–1, against Guthrie's position. Despondent over the revealed trend of the times, Guthrie wrote to his colleague Winston, in Chicago:

> The result intensely disappoints me. The opinion is very weak and contains expressions which will do immeasurable injury in the future. I had hoped that the opinion would in any event be reasonably conservative, but such is not the case. I feel with you . . . that the Court has lost some of its courage since the Income Tax decision. The decisions in tax cases since then have been very prejudicial to vested interests. It is impossible to say where the injurious effects of the Trans-Missouri decision will end. That case could have been decided without the socialistic expressions used in the opinion of Mr. Justice Peckham and these Illinois Inheritance Tax Cases could also have been decided without some of the expressions which McKenna has used.

To one of his clients he wrote:

> So far as the question of fee goes, pray do not give it a thought. I would gladly have served for nothing in such a matter for I am deeply interested in these great problems of constitutional law and have for years studied them, fancying that I may some day render a service to the country in helping to keep the courts straight on points so vital to the future of the Union. Personally I am deeply chagrined that I had not sufficient force to lift the Court up to the realization of the danger involved in graduated taxation in a democracy where the majority rules.

From the vantage point of 1950 — in a country newly conscious of how sensitively interrelated were men's interests and institutions — it might appear that for one hundred years past the bar had not fulfilled the constructive role open to it; it might appear that lawyers had been too preoccupied with law as a game, or an instrument for private ends. If an observer were measurably justified in passing this judgment, he was not thereby entitled to any moral complacency. Lawyers had shared the going values and vision of their times. With other people in the United States, they had joined in economic and social growth that was daring and constructive, and also in growth that was ruthless and wasteful. With others they had — after the creative generation that produced the Constitution — been indifferent, hostile, or timid toward adapting their political institutions to the sweep of change. As a group or organized guild, lawyers had stood inert or antagonistic before some imperative needs to reform law and its administration. Nonetheless, individual lawyers were counted among the initiators, architects, and administrators of much of the constructive work in social control after the '70s. Many of the counts that might be leveled against the bar must in justice be directed equally at the society which it reflected. Given the avowed ideals of the legal profession, the most just criticism which could be made against it individually was that it asserted an independence and a leadership in the public interest which in practice it had abdicated during most of the years after 1870.

In 1950 it appeared that if the bar was to be taken out of absorption in sheer technique or partisanship — whether these be regarded as naïve or calculated attitudes — it would be mainly because of the simple pressure of government intervention in the economy. Once public policy, as expressed in government action, was a factor which a prudent man could omit from his private economic calculations or which, with equal prudence, he could treat as if it were wholly consistent with prevailing private ends and values. There had been a day when, if prudence could no longer go quite so far, it permitted or even counseled private purpose to meet in headlong conflict with general values declared in law. By 1950 prudence alone, even without the promptings of any felt sense of professional obligation, required that consideration of public policy, at least of that policy expressed in official action, enter into counsel given to clients. Out of this situation the lawyer might find a new independence in dealing with clients who found themselves perforce reshaping their aims and in a measure accepting their values from the law, whose immediate interpreter was their counsel.

VI. The Executive

CHAPTER FOURTEEN

THE USES OF THE EXECUTIVE

1. THE RANGE OF EXECUTIVE ACTION

a. Who Is "The Executive"?

The common use of words implied much of the history of executive power in the United States. What did people mean, when they talked about "the executive"?

(1) Certainly the executive was the President. In the states the executive was the governor; on this point common usage might be less emphatic, but it was no less sure. Ordinary meaning associated executive power with the idea of a chief executive.

(2) Thanks to Alexander Hamilton people early began to regard the Cabinet and the departments it represented as part of "the executive." In common expression the governor did not have a cabinet; and popular notions were hazy as to just who besides the governor made up the executive branch of state government.

(3) Even in the simple days before 1870 there were many people other than the handful named so far, whose business was to execute the law. Consider only local government: the police, the coroner, the public prosecutor, the town, city, and county clerks, the tax assessors, the village presidents and the city mayors; in a later day, the boards of tax assessment, the police and fire commissioners, the boards of zoning appeals, the boards of health, city managers. If pressed, common usage might concede that these officers wielded executive power. But it was a concession to schoolmaster's logic; everyday meaning did not feel that it jibed with the facts as everyday imagination saw them.

(4) In the twentieth century, common usage haltingly learned the term "administrative." As late as 1950 the word was ordinarily an adjective only; people did not easily refer to "the administrative" as they did to "the executive." They associated this new thing with the executive branch; they did not talk of "administrative" proceedings as a part of legislative or judicial action. To this extent people had given the new phenomenon a location. But they had trouble in identifying what they were talking about. Hence they used "administrative" more readily to describe a quality of action than a distinct institution.

In all these respects, common usage fell short of describing reality, but nonetheless responded to some of its main currents.

(1) Measured by functions performed, the state executive branch as a whole overshadowed the governor, and the federal executive branch was at least of equal weight with the President. Yet the increasing importance of policy leadership steadily pushed the chief executive into higher responsibility and command.

(2) The Cabinet rarely had the coherence that the name implied, and the department heads' common responsibility to advise the President produced little co-ordination of policy among the departments. On the other hand, common usage was wholly correct in the distinction it drew between the national and the state governments. If there was a minimum of co-ordination of executive policy in the national government, there was almost no centralized executive program in the states.

(3) People were ordinarily engrossed in the drama of Presidents and Cabinet members. But the law made itself felt in everyday living mainly through policemen, clerks, inspectors, and licensing officers. However, the common attitude pointed to two important realities. We so diffused the responsibility for executing the law that it was not easy to think of all law-enforcing officers as agents of a common task. And we allowed this to happen because usually we were not much interested in law enforcement.

(4) There is a temptation to talk about the growth of the administrative process as a separate development. In such great agencies as the Interstate Commerce Commission or the state industrial commissions, "the administrative" tended to become a distinct branch of government. Yet this was largely by accident — another reflection of our characteristic diffusion of responsibility and indifference toward implementing policy. A leading characteristic of the administrative process was its merger of legislative (policy-making), executive (policy-applying), and judicial (policy-determining) jobs in one agency. However, this equally marked the work of chief executives and heads of departments. There was much sense in the reluctance of common usage to treat "administrative" as a noun; the reality was much more that certain qualities or techniques of operation came to mark all major executive action. Separate discussion of "executive" and "administrative" agencies involves so much duplication as to point the moral. They were both aspects of a common task. We shall use the terms "executive" and "administrative" interchangeably to describe officers in the executive branch subordinate to the chief executive.

Previous chapters sketched the structure of legal institutions before discussing the jobs they did. It makes better sense to reverse this order when we talk about the executive. What executive power came to mean in our law was determined mainly by what it did. Much of the story has already been told; executive action so pervaded our law that we could not talk about the bar, or courts, or legislatures, without taking account of what executive officers were doing.

We know less about the history of executive functions than we do about the functions of any other legal agencies. This does not merely reflect a gap in scholarship. It traces back to our general indifference to the problems of implementing legal policy.

This attitude is a puzzle — perhaps a puzzle more properly for the historian of ideas than of law. We were proud of our Yankee handyman's tradition, preoccupied with technical skill, intent on getting results in factory and market. We diverted ourselves with gadgets and not with musing. Yet we were relatively uninterested in problems of making law work. Probably, again, the explanation is that we were too busy about our economic chances.

Whatever the explanation, the results were clear, and the same in one field after another. We had a limited stock of energy for public affairs. Too often we spent it all in the declaration of policy and had none left over to see policy through to effective operation.

This relative indifference toward the execution of law spelled a lesson of peculiar force for the historian of law in the United States: He could never safely treat the declared policy of law as sufficient evidence of what the law meant in the life of the community.

Clever men knew the popular lack of interest in the enforcement of legal policy. They used it. And this reinforced the need to look beyond declared policy, for full understanding. The full story generally lay also in the weary detail of legislative appropriations hearings, and in the scattering, and usually unsatisfactory statistics of public prosecutors' offices. It was concealed behind the deceptively precise geometry of office organization charts. It was implied, for the knowing reader, in the dry detail of court decrees in equity.

In such material was the last and often the most telling chapter of a story which began with the proud generalities of a statute or judicial decision. Too often we found this chapter hard reading, and closed the book. Out of the realism of a working reformer, Louis D. Brandeis cautioned: ". . . do not pin too much faith in legislation. Remedial institutions are apt to fall under the control of the enemy and to become instruments of oppression."

b. Formal and Functional Definitions
of Executive Power

History furnished no well-defined boundaries for executive power in the United States. This was in contrast to the positions of legislative and judicial authority. There were early years in which the functions of legislatures and courts were not yet sharply defined. But their shape was never as flexibly responsive to pressure as was that of the executive.

Early state legislatures sometimes behaved like executives, because of the detailed scrutiny they gave to the carrying out of policy. They acted like courts, when they passed special acts to allow new trials, to grant divorces, or to extend other individualized relief to particular persons. These proved to be passing matters — results of the practices and the self-confidence of revolutionary years when popular assemblies led the movement for independence.

The early years gave the courts opportunities to claim direct participation with the legislature and the executive in policy making. But the Supreme Court of the United States rebuffed President Washington's request that it advise him in matters affecting foreign policy; and it rejected the effort of Congress to make the judges administrators of veterans' pensions under the supervision of Congress and the Secretary of War. The Federal Convention drew a line between the courts and avowed lawmaking, when it rejected the idea that the Supreme Court review legislation in course of enactment. New York tried such an experiment, but the device failed to make for itself an integral place in the state government; the experiment did not survive the democratic upsurge of the early nineteenth century.

As we shall see, the primary role that fell to executive officers was to co-ordinate ends and means, to give the minimum continuity required to translate general policy into everyday action. This task inherently resisted precise definition.

The difficulty of defining executive power had still deeper roots. The colonists learned to see the executive as a symbol of objectionable policies imposed on them by a remote superior. In contrast the popular assemblies championed the home viewpoint. Independence grew out of reaction against policies that bore Parliament's imprint but were moved by a small group clustered about the Crown. Agencies close to the Crown — the Privy Council, the Board of Trade — issued orders which put these objectionable policies into action. And despite the Revolution of 1688, the royal power was cloaked in vaguely defined and therefore much feared "prerogative" powers.

It was not strange that the first state constitution makers did not want a strong executive, or that they put most positive power in the legislature. In all the first states but two (Massachusetts and New York), the legislature appointed the governor. It appointed many other executive officers, or provided an executive council of its own appointment to share in executive tasks. Only Massachusetts and South Carolina subjected the legislature to executive veto. These early state constitutions said little of the governor's authority to set up or supervise administrative machinery. Given the temper of the times, this silence obviously implied no intention that the governor enjoy the historic prerogatives of the Crown or the newly emerging authority of a parliamentary executive.

Several of the new state constitutions emphatically announced the doctrine of the separation of powers, mainly, it would seem, as a bulwark against extension of executive authority. Out of abundance of caution, the Maryland and Virginia constitutions expressly denied that the executive as such had any inherent authority, whether by historic inheritance or by the logic of its position. Executive power must trace its title to clear constitutional or statutory grant — a proposition which took on added emphasis in the twentieth century with the rise of new statute-made administrative bodies.

The Virginia Constitution of 1776 declared that:

> The legislative, executive, and judiciary department, shall be separate and distinct, so that neither exercise the powers properly belonging to the other: nor shall any person exercise the powers of more than one of them, at the same time . . .

Not content with this, it went on to specify that the governor "shall not, under any pretence, exercise any power or prerogative by virtue of any law, statute or custom of England."

Later state constitutions moved toward the federal model of a stronger executive. They gave the chief executive independent status through popular election. They allowed him a longer term of office. They equipped him with the veto.

Such measures gave strong men a greater chance to wield influence as governors. But they still had to reckon with a popular tradition that distrusted executive power. And state constitutions still left the executive authority divided between a governor and independently elected heads of departments. It was not surprising that the governor emerged as a policy leader only after the turn of the century.

The growth of federal executive power was in marked contrast. By 1787 early uncritical reliance on the legislature had worn off, at least among those concerned to protect order, property, and enterprise. Shays's Rebellion underlined the need of a strong executive to oppose violent resistance to authority. Stay laws emphasized that legislators were apt to prefer the pleas of distressed debtors to the claims of their creditors.

The prevailing view in the Federal Convention was bent on creating a strong executive, just as it was on providing independent judges. *The Federalist* papers bear witness to the new temper. For example, consider the matter of judicial tenure. The first state constitutions guaranteed the judges tenure during good behavior. Plainly they did so in reaction against remembered royal control of the bench. The Federal Constitution likewise guaranteed the tenure of judges during good behavior. But the explanation was different: *The Federalist* explained that tenure must be secure against the danger that the legislative branch would try to dominate the courts.

In 1787 many people feared an attempt to set up a monarchy. Hence the framers could not make fully clear the position they had in mind for the President. But they gave him potential power far surpassing that of any state governor: a four-year term without declared limit on his re-election, selection independent of Congress, no co-ordinate executive officers, the veto power, broad powers of appointment. They made little enumeration of the President's positive authority. Instead they "vested" him with "the executive power," and charged him to "take care that the laws be faithfully executed."

This constitutional background invited men of will, courage, and program to build a Presidential tradition. That was the history of the office, its growth thrown into sharp relief now by charges of usurpation of power, now by bold claims of a national stewardship. The latter proved the more successful of the contending attitudes. This was because it had the more solid grounding in fact; the President was the one national officer who was in effect elected by the people as a whole, and so was relatively insulated from particular pressures. In the judgment of Edward S. Corwin, of the thirty-one men who were President up to 1940, about one in three contributed to develop the powers of the office. What Presidential practice established remained fixed.

2. THE EXECUTION OF THE LAWS

To administer law or any other of their affairs, men have to do three things: (1) They must learn the facts of their social situation sufficiently to reason about cause and effect. (2) They must decide what end results they want to bring about, and in what order of priority.

(3) They must decide what procedures they will use to achieve their ends, and then put their procedures to work and check them against the desired results. The operation of each of our major legal institutions responded in varying measure to these elementary problems. We shall use them as the framework for analysis of executive functions. We shall consider them in reverse of their logical order, since this reverse emphasis marked the way in which executive power grew.

a. Regulation and Service

Whatever the expansion of executive responsibilities, the characteristic and the most engrossing executive job was always to see that legislative and judge-made policy was carried out. This was true both in the states and in the national government, though in the latter participation in policy making competed for executive attention much earlier than in the states.

Executing the laws involved in part regulating people's affairs, and in part offering people services. The relations between these aspects of the job changed greatly over the years and so affected the nature of executive functions as to call for some analysis.

When we say that the law regulates, we mean that it commands people to make or refrain from certain choices of conduct. When we say that the law renders services, we mean that legal agencies make benefits available to all or certain groups of the people, either automatically or on the initiative of those benefited, but in any case without legal compulsion on anyone to take what is offered.

No absolute line separated government regulation and service. Traffic regulation was a necessary incident to the effective rendering of highway service. Cities furnished many services designed in part to reduce the burden of police; parks, recreation programs, health and sanitation work tempered environments favorable to breeding young criminals.

Although regulation and service could not be separated, laymen and lawmen alike were inclined to identify law with regulation alone. Legal history was commonly treated as if it were subject to the same restrictive definition. This behavior stood in odd contrast to the fact that at all times the people of the United States demanded relatively large services from government. This was so in early years when a restlessly ambitious people wanted cheap or free land and better communications. It was so later on, when an urban people felt their individual helplessness in the grip of impersonal economic currents and sought security from government.

Most of the federal government's executive budget always went to support services to the people. Most federal government employees always worked in service activities. Particularly was this true if one counted the armed forces as service agencies; without them, it was still true, though the contrast between service and regulatory budgets was then less dramatic. Military items were never so prominent in state or local government programs. Hence state budgets probably always showed a relatively greater allocation of men and money to regulation than was true in the federal budget. This was especially so in the states during the peacetime years of the nineteenth century; only after 1910 did states embark on major service programs in health and sanitation, highways, education, and conservation.

Data are lacking to support more specific statements about the relation between regulation and service activities in the nineteenth century. Galloway and Kilpatrick point out that between 1913 and 1941 expanded public services on all levels of government, far more than price or population changes, accounted for the growth in public expenditure.

The national, state, and local governments increased their expenditures for services 121 per cent from 1913 to 1932. This increase accounted for $3.9 billion out of a total rise of $12.8 billion in government costs. Between 1932 and 1941 these governments increased their service expenditures 58 per cent, accounting for $8.7 billion out of a total cost increase of $13.8 billion.

The scale of these figures overshadowed the relatively modest amounts spent for police, inspection, and other regulatory agencies. Total government expenditures in the United States (in 1941 dollars) stood at $4.9 billion in 1913, $14.3 billion in 1932, and $23.1 billion in 1941. Expenditure for police protection (in 1941 dollars) went from $158 million in 1913, to $396 million in 1932, to $411 million in 1941. Municipal police expansion accounted for most of this in the years 1913–1932; during the 1932–1941 span, growth in state and federal police was a more important factor. Expenditures for inspection and regulation (in 1941 dollars) mounted from $57 million in 1913, to $102 million in 1932, to $120 million in 1941. These totals covered a wide range of activity, from local building inspection to state liquor regulation to the work of the federal Securities and Exchange Commission.

Viewing the situation as of 1943 an expert observer crisply summarized the relative position that regulation held in contemporary government budgets. From his summary Professor George A. Graham drew a measure of the motives of those who would cut regulatory budgets in the name of economy:

The effect as well as the purpose of reduced appropriations is to withdraw authority, for regulation is the least expensive function of government. It costs the taxpayer little in comparison with the service, guardianship, or protective activities of government. . . . Normally an almost unbelievably small per cent of public employees do work that is primarily regulatory. In peacetime the personnel in regulatory activities was not 5 per cent of the total in the federal service. In all governments — national, state, and local — regulation probably employed less than 1 per cent of the men and women who were public servants. Hence, when regulatory enterprises are starved by meager appropriations, the motive is usually hostility, not economy. The execution is penal, not managerial. It should be so understood.

Both regulatory and service activities involved overhead cost, for the maintaining of the basic agencies of government. This overhead was a minor part of government expense, especially when compared with the budgets for services. In 1941 the general overhead cost of the federal government was about 3 per cent of its expenditures, that of the states about 5 per cent of their expenditures, that of local governments about 9 per cent. This included the costs of legislatures, courts, general executive and administrative agencies, and all staff offices (such as finance and personnel offices), serving more than one department.

b. Trends in Regulation

(1) Executive Adjudication

From 1790 on, both in the national and state governments, executive officers took over an increasing amount of work which might have been done by judges. The trend was a steady one, though after 1887 the great growth of administrative agencies gave it heightened emphasis.

During most of the nineteenth century the staple instrument of regulation was the criminal law, administered by public prosecutor, judge, and jury. In our system judges and petit jurors were not authorized or equipped to take the initiative in law enforcement. Hence the public prosecutor was marked for a leading role. A great deal of regulation was accomplished wholly within the walls of his office. What he thought it best to do settled many more matters than ever came before judge or jury. In effect he decided cases when he decided that a complaint should or should not be further investigated, when he determined to prosecute or not to prosecute, to drop proceedings once begun or to accept pleas of guilty to the charged offense or a lesser crime.

The reach of the prosecutor's function was the more significant after 1870 when we made increasing use of penal sanctions to enforce policies of social and economic regulation. The same development added to the importance of the police. The rise of great cities produced pressures for professionalizing police organization and techniques. The police assumed more and more discretion in disposing of the bulk of day-to-day collisions between the individual and the law. The traffic violations bureau provided a marked example.

Administrative agencies finally disposed of vast numbers of issues under law. In this they went through the same steps that were traditionally associated with judicial business. They weighed evidence, interpreted statutes or regulations, and formally or informally decided the application of the law to the facts found. In at least 90 per cent of the matters disposed of by administrative action there was no contest. This did not alter the fact that executive rather than judicial officers made final decisions on the legal position of private individuals and the government on a grand scale.

In 1939 the United States Treasury received 7,600,000 tax returns regarding incomes, estates, and gifts. Treasury officers made hundreds of thousands of adjustments of these returns. The judicial process touched only a minor percentage of the whole; 4854 appeals were filed in the Board of Tax Appeals, and 900 appeals went to court. In the year ended October 31, 1939 the Interstate Commerce Commission's Bureau of Motor Carriers (Section of Complaints) held formal hearings in 5212 cases; between the enactment of the Motor Carrier Act in 1935 and October 31, 1939, the Commission received 98,734 applications for the issue of certificates of convenience and necessity to permit motor carrier operations. During the fiscal year ended June 30, 1939, the National Labor Relations Board held hearings in 1048 cases, and formally decided 893 cases; 2942 cases were settled before formal action was begun, and 127 cases were settled after formal action was begun but before decision; 5534 cases (including cases settled) were dismissed, withdrawn, or otherwise closed before formal action.

These were the more obvious examples of administrative adjudication. Not so obvious, but nonetheless adjudications, were the hundreds of thousands of final decisions made by federal officers in a typical year like 1939, in the course of applying regulatory laws to particular situations. Federally licensed inspectors tested and graded farm products. The Civil Aeronautics Administrator issued airman certificates to persons found qualified to operate civil aircraft. Officers of the Bureau of Marine Inspection and Navigation determined whether vessels should be certified to be seaworthy. The Post Office decided applications for second-class mailing privileges.

Administrative adjudications ran into high totals. In 1939 the Interstate Commerce Commission made more than 110,000 inspections, to certify railroad locomotives as fit for the road. In one year, the Federal Alcohol Administration passed on more than 93,000 applications for approval or exemption of labels. In quantitative comparison the total annual business of the federal courts was small. In the fiscal year ended June 30, 1939, omitting bankruptcy matters, all federal courts determined a total of 73,448 civil and criminal cases.

Administrative adjudication showed comparable growth in the states. In 1938 a report by the New York State Public Service Commission showed that the Commission annually issued about 2500 orders, held about 900 hearings, and made tens of thousands of inspections. The administration of workmen's compensation provided the most uniformly impressive totals of administrative decisions of a type traditionally made in court proceedings. This kind of business reached stability by the late 1920's. By that time, in a typical year administrators were disposing of about 56,000 claims in Illinois, about 41,000 in Massachusetts, about 85,000 in Pennsylvania, about 21,000 in Wisconsin. A trifling percentage of these administrative decisions were reviewed in court. In a typical year of the late 1920's review was sought in Illinois circuit courts in 237 (about four tenths of 1 per cent), of the 57,535 compensable accident cases reported; the Illinois supreme court granted further review in only 23 cases. In the same year, in Massachusetts review was sought in 183 out of 40,274 cases.

The expansion of administrative adjudication reflected different pressures, according to the field of regulation involved. Sometimes the tendency was to import more of a judicial atmosphere into executive action; sometimes it was to import more of executive vigor into judging.

There were areas in which the extension of administrative adjudication meant the extension of the "rule of law." Administrative rules and decisions sometimes spelled out principles, precedents, and procedures where earlier there had been only a broad and ill-defined executive discretion. This was true of taxation. A less obvious example was the matter of public contracts. Under statutory delegation, executive officers began to erect standards to which contracts with the government must conform. For example, the Public Contracts Division of the United States Department of Labor developed a body of doctrine regarding wages on public contract jobs.

There were other areas in which the legislature committed the application of policy to specialized administrative bodies in order to obtain the full thrust of executive power. In giving an administrative agency one field of policy on which to concentrate, the legislature hoped that the agency would be more alert and sympathetic to the values declared in the governing statutes. Plainly, also, the legislators hoped that these administrators would be vigorous in adjudication as well as in police and prosecution. This was the thinking behind the creation of many state public utility commissions, and the background of the Federal Trade Commission, the Securities and Exchange Commission, the National Labor Relations Board. In their origins such agencies were not designed to be aloof, dispassionate judges, but judges who would be aggressive exponents of legislative policy.

(2) Extension of the Prosecutor's Role

More important than the expansion of adjudication by executive officers were developments that scarcely fitted any of the stereotypes of government action. One of these was the provision of administrative machinery to press claims which an older day left to the initiative of private suitors in court. This development bore some analogy to the familiar prosecutor's role but went far beyond it.

The regulation of life insurance provided one example. In some states the insurance commissioner in effect did the job of an attorney for small policyholders in their disputes with insurers. On their behalf the commissioner would take up questions of alleged overcharge of premiums, failure to credit dividends, reinstatement of lapsed policies, or determination of rights of beneficiaries. Some disputes might still go to court, but ordinarily the commissioner negotiated a settlement that ended the matter.

Another example concerned the collection of wage claims. By 1936 in about one third of the states employees could invoke the help of a labor commissioner to collect money owing them for their labor. Sometimes this assistance was made available by statute, sometimes simply by administrative practice. The labor commissioner would help the claimant frame his demand, would negotiate on his behalf with the recalcitrant employer, and in the last resort would bring civil or criminal action for the failure to pay.

Analogous to such administrative assistance in the pressing of claims was the provision of a public defender in criminal cases. By the 1930's a score of large cities had set up such an office.

In some fields administrators did not limit themselves to doing lawyers' work for people who brought in their troubles. Administrators sometimes took the initiative in originating and pursuing claims on behalf of persons protected by statutory policy. The better state workmen's compensation commissions were outstanding for such activity. They kept their own check on the occurrence of industrial accidents. Where a compensable injury appeared to be involved, they saw that proper claims were filed. Through their own investigators, their own medical and safety experts, their own lawyers and their trial examiners, they took the initiative in exploring the facts and issues in claims. Given such administrative activity, the average claimant need not drain his resources to retain counsel; the commission was his counsel. This, it must be said again, was the situation under the best administrative practice. Where the administrative staff was inadequate, where politics ruled administration, where trial examiners fell into unjudicial relationships to insurance counsel who regularly rode circuit with them, there was real danger that the compensation system substituted only the appearance of help for the zealous attention the claimant could expect from his own lawyer.

Small loans regulation offered another example of administrative initiative. Statutes against usury were old on the books. They gave the oppressed debtor the dubious benefits of a defense, if he were stouthearted enough to force the creditor to sue; and they gave him a complaint which he might try to interest a harassed district attorney in prosecuting. By the 1930's about one half of the states had required that loan companies be licensed, and had created administrative authority (usually in the state banking department) to license them, and to discipline them by suspension or revocation of license. Here was a flexible, summary, and drastic remedy, in the hands of officers specialized in its use, and active to detect the need for it.

Federal administrative agencies were also busy with the representation of individual claimants under the laws. The Interstate Commerce Commission annually adjusted thousands of shippers' claims for reparation against allegedly unlawful charges by carriers. Department of Agriculture inspectors acted for both buyers and sellers in determining thousands of questions of the grade of grains sold, or the quality and condition of perishable foodstuffs delivered to market. The Department of Agriculture decided on behalf of farm-produce sellers a small but not insignificant number of reparations proceedings under the Packers and Stockyards Act; and it held reparations and disciplinary proceedings affecting middlemen's licenses under the Perishable Agricultural Commodities Act.

(3) Extension of the Policeman's Role

By the 1930's the supervisory activity of the executive had grown to a point where — at least in the field of economic regulation — it overshadowed both the adjudicative and prosecuting aspects of law enforcement.

Of course, there was a good deal of the policeman, just as there was of the judge, in the conduct of either the old-style prosecutor's office or the new-style administrative agency. In the close-knit life of twentieth-century cities, the prosecutor's decisions as to what he would investigate and what he would prosecute had regulatory impact much beyond the immediate matters at issue. Moreover, his conduct helped to set the tone of police activity. The mere possession of licensing power, so characteristic of the expanded administrative process, greatly extended the executive's ability to police whole areas of conduct. We noted an aspect of this in the fields of insurance and small loans, where the administrators' reserved licensing powers enabled them to influence the plane of dealing between the regulated companies and their customers. An especially clear-cut example was provided by the regulation of the issue of corporate securities. New stocks or bonds would appeal only to buyers confident of the stability and good faith of the issuing companies. It did not take much to upset this prerequisite of a successful flotation. The mere announcement that the Securities and Exchange Commission had begun proceedings to question a proposed issue would probably suffice. Thus the SEC had a powerful police instrument merely in its power to begin proceedings. Because it had the power, it generally did not need to use it; would-be issuers had great inducement to comply with the administrators' informal suggestions that they confer and endeavor to eliminate potential objections to a proposed filing.

Inspection was a procedure by which the executive enormously extended its range of supervision. In the late nineteenth century inspection preceded licensing as the means of an expanded administrative control of business. Inspection was particularly relied on in industrial safety and health and sanitation legislation. In the twentieth century the legislature learned to strengthen, as it extended, this technique of enforcement. Statutes provided stiffer penalties for failure to comply with inspectors' recommendations, and often made the penalties cumulative. The legislature learned also to support inspection by requiring the regulated business to keep records. In the 1930's federal regulation brought record keeping to a new peak as a method of police, particularly in connection with social security and fair labor standards legislation. In the states and in the nation alike, inspection and record keeping were mainstays of the effort to regulate public utility rates and services. Attention turned particularly to record keeping when the 1930's brought the policy of requiring utilities to keep adequate historical data on the cost of new equipment, the expense of which would be an element in the rate base.

Inspection and record keeping represented the detailed use of fact finding as a technique of law enforcement. In the twentieth century the legislature sometimes empowered the executive to undertake more broad-scale investigation. In part this was to help in formulating general policy. In part, through the discipline of publicity, it was to help police the conduct of government and of industry. New York state led in arming its governor with power to conduct broad fact-finding investigations through "commissioners" specially named to inquire into matters of public concern. Congress employed the Federal Trade Commission to investigate various aspects of business and the concentration of economic power.

Fact finding and publicity were closely linked as sanctions. The legislature was not imaginative in exploring the possible uses of publicity as a means of law enforcement. However, it made some beginnings. Public utilities were required to declare their rates and other terms of service, to abide by announced schedules, and from time to time to issue statements of financial condition. In the 1940's the law was learning how to use open fact-finding procedures to cool the temper of labor disputes and to mobilize public opinion to influence a settlement.

In turn, publicity was related to regulation by education. Conservation authorities did not discharge their game wardens, but they increased emphasis on programs and procedures to enlist the co-operation of sportsmen, guides, and resort owners. Not only in conservation, but also in public health and sanitation, administrators put more and more effort into preventive regulation, spreading information, and educating people to want things and to follow habits that were consistent with public welfare.

Regulation which enlisted the co-operation of the regulated persons presented the most novel problems in areas dominated by organized interests. The twentieth century saw a rising group consciousness among men engaged in a common livelihood. Occupational groups began to formulate professional standards. They sought to use the law for their own purposes, while the law undertook to use them as agents of public policy. Statutes required that those who practiced certain callings must meet professional standards, and the laws designated authorities to enforce standards. Often the statute provided that the administering authority should be named by or in co-operation with the representatives of the regulated occupation. For example, legislation sometimes authorized the state medical society to nominate men for appointment, or even itself to appoint men to the state board of medical examiners. In 1933 the National Industry Recovery Act provided a most dubious experiment in wholesale delegation of self-police to organized business groups. The amended Securities and Exchange Act made a more lasting, and more limited, delegation of police power to a business association. It authorized the creation of a National Association of Securities Dealers, and empowered this private group to do the primary policing of private dealings in corporate securities.

It was efficient to implement legal policy by enlisting the co-operation of the regulated. To delegate the enforcement of policy directly to the regulated interests raised more serious questions, involving not only the efficiency of the program but also public confidence in its integrity. The indications were that this would be one of the great testing grounds of government in the second half of the twentieth century.

(4) The Regulator as Partner of the Regulated

An accounting of the methods the executive used to extend or alter its traditional jobs of police, prosecution, and decision made it clear that a new kind of regulation had emerged, although it was hard to find an adequate shorthand description for this new role of government. Ernest Griffith suggested that the legislative, adjudicative, and administrative activities of the twentieth-century executive added up to a process best called "adjustment." That seemed about as satisfactory a summary as could be had.

In a widening range of regulation, especially affecting the economy, the executive now intervened before rather than after private decisions had been made in matters of public interest. This was contrary to the emphasis of most nineteenth-century legal regulation, which usually acted after the event. As a policeman, the nineteenth-century executive investigated, and brought to book one who had already broken the law. As prosecutor, he assembled evidence, and presented a case against the lawbreaker; or, acting in effect as judge in the matter, he decided to proceed no further, or to accept some tendered reparation on behalf of the public interest. This was a pattern for implementing legal policy which was sanctioned by long practice, and not ill-suited to simple regulation in a simple economy.

The contrast between the nineteenth- and the twentieth-century emphasis in executive action was symbolized in the distinction between a penalty and a license. Licensing or enabling legislation provided the main foundation for the new executive pattern. The statute might require a formal license as prerequisite to lawful pursuit of certain activity — as did an increasing number of laws that controlled admission to various callings and the terms on which they should be practiced. Or the statute might exact the practical equivalent of a formal license — as did the laws that required public utilities, as a condition of operation, to submit their schedules of rates and services and abide by the approved and published terms. From the issue of general licenses or orders, government moved into the issue of orders more closely tailored to a given situation. By 1950, in many fields, executive regulation had made the administrator substantially a partner in formulating and executing business policy.

c. Trends in Service

The development of government services had a simpler history than the growth of regulation. There were two main threads in the story: (1) By undertaking to sell services for a fee, instead of supporting them from general taxes, government undoubtedly extended its service functions faster and more widely than would otherwise have been financially or politically feasible. (2) By delegating the performance of public services to private enterprisers, subject to regulation, government kept the door open to extension of its service functions; as it extended its regulations, government made its administrators to an increasing extent partners in the policy of the regulated enterprises.

Precedents for the government's sale of services went back to 1790, and indeed in some cases much further back. Precedents in early federal practice were the postal service, the patent system, and the General Land Office. In the states inspection fees were the outstanding early precedent: The seller of grain or the maker of nails paid an inspection fee to obtain an official certification of grade or quality that would make his goods more salable in a distant market. In both federal and state governments court fees were an old example of government service rendered for a price.

During the nineteenth century, government made little expansion of its services-for-a-fee. However, from 1790 well into the 1870's state legislatures readily delegated to private enterprisers the authority to render public services for charges which the law usually set or purported to regulate. The commonest examples concerned communications facilities (involving turnpike, plank-road, and canal companies), or the provision of water power (by gristmills and sawmills). Somewhat analogous were the laws that chartered private schools, academies, and colleges, to satisfy the public interest in education; these statutes did not usually control the fees charged.

After 1870 a countertrend set in. The states began to provide canals, roads, and schools out of general tax revenues. About the same time the neighborhood gristmill or sawmill lost its economic importance. Offsetting these developments, the railroads grew to dominate transportation. After their peak of empire came the rise of the electric power industry. In these new fields, government again left the provision of critical public services to private enterprisers, subject to regulation. Whatever the shortcomings of this regulation, it far exceeded the nominal controls imposed by the law of the middle nineteenth century. Now there were specialized administrative agencies to represent the public interest, and from the control of rates and services their regulations extended to supervision of the capital expansion and financial practices of the regulated industries.

The federal government led the way into broader administrative supervision over delegated public service functions. In 1887 it set up the Interstate Commerce Commission to deal with transportation. In 1920, in recognition of the public importance of electric power production, it created the Federal Power Commission; and in 1935 it empowered the Securities and Exchange Commission to reorganize the structure of the power industry, under the Public Utility Holding Company Act.

Thus, through the back door of regulation, twentieth-century government moved toward the direct rendering of services for fees. Several states decided that the way to control the liquor traffic was to make it a monopoly of state-owned, state-operated dispensaries. Under state authorization, there was a considerable extension of municipal ownership of public utilities. Both the states and the federal government became large-scale publishers and sellers of books, pamphlets, and periodicals containing information of public interest. The federal government went into the business of operating the Panama Canal. The depression of the 1930's led both the federal and the state governments into new business ventures. Particularly through the Reconstruction Finance Corporation, the federal government became a large-scale lender to banks and industry. Government entered the vast business of supplying new kinds of social security insurance, and the federal government undertook, for a premium, to insure bank deposits and farmers' crops.

The law began to recognize that consumers should have defined rights to obtain public services, and regular procedures by which to enforce their rights — and this whether the services were paid for by general taxes or by the fees of those who used them. The purpose of public utility regulation through administrative agencies was to give the consumer more effective rights to reasonable and equal access to delegated public services. Government began to subject its own service agencies to controls in the interest of the consumer. During the nineteenth century the individual usually had only ill-defined rights to the benefits of public facilities; his remedy for abuse of executive discretion was ordinarily an expensive and cumbersome lawsuit. By mid-twentieth century, statutes or regulations typically defined the persons entitled to public services, the services to which they were entitled, and the procedures by application, submission of evidence, or hearing, on the basis of which a claim to services would be decided. Ninety per cent of executive action was taken without formal hearing or contest. However, though formality was at a minimum here, the great volume of executive business more and more proceeded against a background of defined principle and procedure.

With the expansion of public services, many matters that once concerned mainly the internal housekeeping of government became important in fixing the rights of great numbers of private persons. Government made contracts with more and more people; it was of broad concern that statutes, regulations, and administrative practice began to develop specialized standards for the making, interpreting, and adjusting of these contract relations. Contracts were only one aspect of a general picture. Whenever lines of authority were defined inside a public agency, whenever it specialized its internal division of labor, such measures directly affected the ability of private persons to make effective claim upon public facilities. Public administration was no longer just government housekeeping; it determined how far the "rule of law" extended into areas once governed by almost undefined, unlimited executive discretion.

3. Making Policy

a. Prerogative Powers of the Executive

Our history emphatically denied any intention to endow our executive with powers inherited from the traditional prerogatives of the Crown. This was as true regarding the executive's role in making policy as it was of his authority to carry out policy. In the Federal Convention James Wilson led the successful drive to create a strong executive. It was also Wilson who forthrightly declared that "he did not consider the prerogatives of the British monarch as a proper guide in defining the Executive powers. Some of these prerogatives were of a Legislative nature."

However, Presidential practice and the sanction of the Supreme Court combined to create in the federal executive an area of what amounted to prerogative power — power inherent in the constitution of the executive. The Court found formal warrant for this primarily in Article II of the Federal Constitution, which vested the President with "the executive power."

Most of this homemade prerogative concerned the execution rather than the making of the laws. But important parts of it involved the authority to make broad policy, or, in effect, to legislate. Congress and the Court conceded this authority to the executive because the concession met the working needs of government.

Apart from foreign affairs, in which the Constitution expressly contemplated that the President should exercise great discretion, the greatest development of Presidential prerogative occurred under the head of the powers of the commander in chief of the armed forces. Lincoln boldly seized on these powers to command national policy in the face of domestic rebellion, raising an army, spending unappropriated funds, and pledging the national credit. Only in 1866, after the war was over, did the Supreme Court put any check on this martial prerogative. In *Ex parte Milligan* a majority of the Justices held that the commander in chief's authority did not permit the creation of military tribunals to try civilians outside the immediate theater of military operations, in places where the civil courts were open.

In practice the commander in chief developed scarcely less sweeping authority to use federal troops in situations far short of war or rebellion. The Federal Constitution contemplated that the states would be primarily responsible for keeping the domestic peace. Out of the fresh memory of Shays's Rebellion, Article IV, Section 4 provided only a residual responsibility in "the United States," to protect each state "on Application of the Legislature, or of the Executive (when the Legislature cannot be convened) against domestic Violence."

In 1849, in *Luther* v. *Borden*, Mr. Chief Justice Taney said for the Court that "It rested with Congress . . . to determine upon the means proper to be adopted to fulfill this guarantee." Congress early delegated this authority to the President, under the conditions outlined by Article IV, Section 4. In the railroad strikes of 1887 President Hayes, and in the Pullman strike of 1894 President Cleveland used federal troops in the states with a freedom that implied some authority outside that delegated under Article IV. There were other major labor disputes — for example, the anthracite strike of 1902 — in which the President used his influence to promote a settlement without using the troops. In all these cases the interests and issues at stake were so immense as to make it clear that in intervening, the President did something more than simply execute the laws or protect government property. His intervention implied an authority and a duty to act as trustee of the general interest. In 1894, in the *Debs* case which grew out of President Cleveland's intervention in the Pullman strike, the Supreme Court sanctioned this theory of Presidential prerogative:

The entire strength of the nation may be used to enforce in any part of the land the full and free exercise of all national powers and the security of all rights intrusted by the Constitution to its care. The strong arm of the national government may be put forth to brush away all obstructions to the freedom of inter-state commerce or the transportation of the mails. If the emergency arises, the army of the nation, and all its militia, are at the service of the nation, to compel obedience to its laws.

There were other precedents of Presidential action which made a bridge from power as commander in chief to power as chief executive. One of these was the Presidential practice of creating or enlarging reservations of public lands. Theodore Roosevelt made particularly bold assertion of this right when he withdrew from private entry great tracts whose preservation he deemed essential to a proper conservation policy.

Two doctrines developed by the Supreme Court contributed to executive prerogative. First, beginning in 1840 with *Decatur* v. *Paulding*, the Court developed a rather vaguely defined policy against the issue of mandamus to command an executive officer to perform an official act where he must exercise judgment on a point open to reasonable doubt or use of discretion. Second, the Court advised deference to the administrative construction of a statute. In the interpretation of a statute, said the Justices, great weight should be given to a uniform, long-continued construction of the act, reflected in its actual application by officers charged with its execution. In theory the judges deferred to the administrative construction because it was some evidence of the probable intention of the legislature. In practice the doctrine often amounted to a judicial license to the executive to shape the content of policy, so long as the legislature did not protest.

Nineteenth-century court decisions conceded to state governors a considerable discretion in declaring and enforcing martial law. This bore some analogy to the President's prerogative as commander in chief, but the governor's practical field of operation was much more limited. State courts, like the federal judiciary, contributed to executive prerogative by fencing in the use of mandamus and according weight to the administrative interpretation of legislation.

Judges sometimes spoke as if such inherent executive powers as there were resided only in the chief executive. In the absence of express constitutional provisions, so ran the theory, all other executive officers must be able to trace an asserted authority to a grant by the legislature. This doctrine extended the grounds on which courts might invalidate executive action; they might find it to lack, or exceed, any constitutional basis; they might find it to lack, or exceed, any statutory basis. But by mid-twentieth century the judicial doctrines which limited interference with executive discretion and commanded deference to executive interpretations of the statutes had worked to create something like an area

of prerogative power in administrators subordinate to the chief executive. In the states twentieth-century legislation delegated to administrative agencies rule-making powers which were often so broadly framed
as to give the administrators within their domain a greater freedom of
action than that enjoyed by the governor. In the federal government
emphasis was more equal. Congress delegated at least as much discretionary power to the President as it did to independent administrative
agencies.

b. Promoting Legislation

The separation of powers held an important place among American
ideas on law. Sometimes, as in the Massachusetts constitution of 1780,
it was affirmed with doctrinaire rigidity. But when it came to setting
up government structure, and making government work, the dogma
yielded to more practical intuitions.

The separation of powers presented no insuperable barriers to a
considerable participation of the executive branch in the work of the
legislature. The Federal Constitution and the typical state constitution
declared it the duty of the chief executive to recommend to the legislature measures for the public welfare. Written amid extreme distrust
of executive power, the first state constitutions usually gave the governor no veto. But the Federal Constitution took care to arm the President
with this power. After the pendulum had swung in the states toward
restraint of the legislature, from the early nineteenth century on the
state constitutions gave the veto to the governor.

Constitutional provisions could create only the potentiality of power.
What built up the executive's role in legislation was the skill and determination with which particular men wielded executive power, and the
use made of the experience and precedent which their successors inherited.

(1) The President

Able and self-confident, Alexander Hamilton set the federal precedent for executive leadership in legislation, when as Secretary of the
Treasury in Washington's first administration he pushed through a
broad fiscal program. As President, Jefferson chose to work through
a tight-knit corps of lieutenants in the Congress. The form was different, but the result was more executive leadership of the legislative program. Jackson also had his lieutenants in Congress. But it was not in his
temper to limit himself to generalship behind scenes; through executive
messages he made the Presidency a platform from which he commanded the attention of the country. The President also had at his

disposal much patronage, mainly through his power of appointment to federal offices. Jefferson used this power, and Jackson wielded it like a broadax, to induce Congress to follow Presidential leadership. Both men linked the use of patronage to the development of the national political party, and made good in action the President's title to leadership of the administration party. Subsequently Polk demonstrated what an effective combination of powers the President had, in his resources as chief executive and party leader.

Lincoln vastly increased the power of the Presidency, but by bold assertion of executive prerogative rather than by legislative leadership. The Congress of the Civil War years was not easily led. During the generation after the war, Congress was in the saddle, and nonetheless so because its direction was uninspired. None of the stodgy men who preceded Theodore Roosevelt added much to executive leadership. Cleveland vetoed more bills than anyone before him, but he used the veto only as a negative instrument, and mainly for the limited purpose of curbing pension abuses. In any case, the party situation in Congress denied him the chance for successful leadership.

Characteristically, Theodore Roosevelt used all the inventions of his predecessors. He asserted party leadership, through his own lieutenants in Congress and by exploiting his opportunities for firsthand relations with influential Senators and Representatives. He put the veto to positive use, treating it as a counter in bargaining over the content of pending legislation. He caused desired legislation to be prepared in detail in executive departments. He made full use of patronage. Well-timed messages dramatized problems, prepared the ground for future planting, fixed on Congress the responsibility for action. To these familiar techniques he added his own contribution — the most complete and adroit use theretofore of the publicity commanded by the President. In this he had the help, which most of his predecessors lacked, of opportunities offered by the growth of cheap, mass-circulation newspapers.

Woodrow Wilson took office with the advantages of a Congress firmly controlled by his party, and a Congressional majority unused to power and eager for patronage long denied. Carefully Wilson focused on one major measure at a time. In pressing each item of his legislative program he practiced his philosophy of the President as prime minister, and dramatized the role by delivering in person his messages to Congress. War interrupted the development of his peacetime leadership. It was characteristic of his idea of the Presidency that, unlike Lincoln, he rested his wartime command largely on broad delegations of power which he requested from Congress.

For a decade after Wilson, Congress, and especially the Senate, took the initiative. Then the depression of the 1930's plunged the country into a period of self-doubt it had known only twice before. In this troubled atmosphere of his first administration, Franklin Roosevelt made the Presidency a more open and decisive force in legislation. More clearly than ever before, major measures were stamped as "administration bills." Helped at the start by the environment of crisis, the President fully exploited previous techniques of leadership. To these he added an unprecedented development of the claim of the President to be the national spokesman.

Theodore Roosevelt claimed for the President the status of "a steward of the people bound actively and affirmatively to do all he could for the people . . ." Wilson implemented the theory by direct appeal to the country, speaking to it as representative of its united interests, over the heads of Congress. Now through masterly use of the press conference and the intimacy of radio, Franklin Roosevelt asserted a greater command of policy and program than had any President in peacetime. However, when war came, the second Roosevelt, like Wilson, based his wartime authority largely on sweeping delegations of power which he asked and received from Congress.

(2) The Governor

The executive in the states was much slower to assert leadership in legislative programs. In part this was a natural consequence of the weak constitutional position of the state executive branch. In part it reflected the fact that during most of the nineteenth century state government was relatively simple; most regulation and services were in the hands of local officials.

Public opinion counted for more than constitutional forms in determining the time when the state executive began to shape policy. The Civil War emergency produced strong war governors in some Northern states. But this was an abnormal situation. It was not until the last quarter of the nineteenth century that the stage was set for a lasting trend toward a stronger executive, and it was after 1900 that the governor definitely shouldered responsibility for a legislative program. People wanted more effective regulation of public utilities. They wanted government to protect consumers against fraud, imposition, and dangers to health and safety. They wanted curbs put upon concentrated economic power. Along with these demands went a tardy but unmistakable reversal of that de-professionalization of government that had been the boast and legacy of the Jackson era. People interested in extension of state regulation or services began to demand that state government be reorganized, its personnel improved, and its lines of authority defined, so that responsibility might be fixed. These demands necessarily implied a stronger executive.

The mid-nineteenth-century trend to grant the governor the veto was prophetic of a new attitude. In the 1880's and 1890's a few strong-willed governors claimed legislative leadership, essentially on the stewardship theory which Theodore Roosevelt later applied to the Presidency. In New York there were Tilden, Cleveland, and Roosevelt himself. Wisconsin provided another example, in Robert M. LaFollette. The solid development of the governor's leadership awaited the early-twentieth-century examples of Charles Evans Hughes in New York and Woodrow Wilson in New Jersey. Both men sought to achieve more efficient administrative organization in the states, particularly through more centralization of responsibility. In their substantive programs, both called for more effective control of the financial and service policies of great corporations. In the interest of their administrative and their substantive programs, both appealed to the people over the heads of boss-ridden legislatures.

The governor rose in legislative influence partly because of improvement of his own position, and partly because of the contrasting weakness of the legislature.

The appeal which a few strong men made to public opinion helped to produce structural changes which strengthened the chief executive's capacity to direct general policy. The outstanding changes related to control of state finance. Creation of the executive budget helped the governor to enforce some co-ordination of policy among diverse agencies of the state. More and more states bulwarked the executive budget by granting the governor authority to veto separate items in appropriation bills; armed with the item veto the chief executive could better protect his program against the distortions wrought by particular interests which got the ear of the legislature.

The governor had the greater opportunity to assert policy leadership because from 1850 on the typical legislature functioned in a negative fashion. Except for a few years of agrarian revolt, late-nineteenth-century legislatures were dominated by bosses who in turn were obedient to the railroads or other major economic interests in their states. Once these interests had consolidated their position with the help of public subsidies and grants of privilege, their strategy was to keep things as they were.

Its own organization handicapped the state legislature in bidding for policy leadership. This was so even into mid-twentieth century. The legislature met at rather widely spaced intervals. Most of its members served only one or two terms. The legislature worked through an unco-ordinated committee system, and it had no central planning agency of its own. Usually the legislature did not even have its own staff to help investigate facts and draft bills.

The legislature itself could have remedied most of these handicaps. But remedy did not serve the interests of its old-style masters. Their veto on reform was reinforced by the characteristic indifference of public opinion toward the arrangement of government institutions. So far as the legislative branch began to improve its capacity to take a positive role in policy making, the credit was due chiefly to reform governors. They played a considerable role in the most tangible effort that was made up to 1950 to reinvigorate the legislature. This was the creation of legislative councils to undertake the long-range investigating and planning which were the conditions of effective policy making.

(3) Departments and Commissions

Both in the federal government and in the states executive departments or administrative agencies originated a substantial amount of legislation. Where new policy of the first rank was involved, the proposals were almost always advanced with the advice and consent of the chief executive; especially in the federal government, therefore, one could count such high-level policy leadership by departments or administrative agencies as part of the role of the President. However, departments and administrative agencies also pressed on Congress and state legislatures many measures which in no substantial sense were part of a program initiated or urged by the chief executive. Officers experienced in the working of laws committed to their charge naturally sponsored additions or corrections which their experience taught them were desirable in the interests of the statutory program. Administrators and legislative committees formed partnerships that shaped a great volume of such supplementary legislation; the legislature and the chief executive entered the picture only to ratify, or occasionally to veto, the work of their agents. Court opinions sometimes recognized these facts as affording solid basis for the doctrine that judges should defer to the administrative interpretation of statutes; often the administrators had written the statutes.

Administrative initiation of second-rank legislation was important in the twentieth century. We have no studies to tell us what role subordinate executive officers played in nineteenth-century legislation. In view of the tardy development of the governor's legislative leadership, it seems likely that in the states such officials had more freedom to press their ideas on the legislature than had their counterparts in the national government. When the governor began to assert leadership in the first half of the twentieth century, he met one practical obstacle which showed that subordinate executive officers had been wielding legislative influence during much of the nineteenth century. In most states the governor confronted departments and independent administrative agencies that already had well-established relations and traditions of cooperation with the important committees of the legislature.

(4) The Weight of Executive Influence

The drama of bold initiative and high conflict surrounded executive leadership in legislative policy. The drama made it hard to weigh realistically the relative influence of the chief executive and the legislature.

Professor Lawrence Chamberlain looked carefully at the history of about 90 major federal statutes of the years 1890–1940 in an effort to reach an objective appraisal of Presidential leadership. He picked laws that dealt with the critical areas of agriculture, banking and currency, business, government credit, immigration, labor, national defense, natural resources, railroads, and tariff.

Chamberlain credited 19, or about 20 per cent, of the 90 laws to the preponderant influence of the President. He found that Congressional influence preponderated in the enactment of 35 of the statutes, or about 40 per cent of the total. He classed 29 statutes, or about 30 per cent, as the product of joint Presidential and Congressional influence. He found that slightly less than 10 per cent (7 acts) resulted mainly from the work of outside pressure groups; 4 of these statutes were tariff acts.

Of course these categories of influence were only approximations. Still, the count showed that in the national government legislation was a joint process, even in years which had seen Presidential power at its peak. Moreover, the bulk of these laws had roots deep in the legislative process; this was so even of many whose final passage was attributed largely to the President's influence. Of the 90 laws, Chamberlain traced 77 to bills that were originally introduced without administration sponsorship and were the subject of hearings and deliberation in legislative committees for periods ranging from a few months to several years before they were finally passed. Of 19 laws for whose final passage the President might be given primary credit, Congress initiated 12, and held extensive hearings on them. Of 29 laws which could be classed as joint products of Congress and the President, 26 had origins in bills introduced without administration support and were considered extensively in committee before Presidential influence came into play.

By mid-twentieth century the executive had risen far in influence on legislation. But the chief executive still could scarcely claim the status of prime minister in the programming and enactment of policy.

c. Delegated Legislation

After 1870 administrators had most influence on policy through the issue of rules or regulations under authority delegated by the legislature. Through such delegated legislation the executive branch as a whole probably had more effect on the everyday lives of people than through all its influence upon the legislature.

(1) Federal Doctrine

Constitutional theory first denied that there could be any lawful "delegation" of legislative power: The legislature could authorize the executive to find facts, on the existence of which the exercise of a statutory power depended; but the courts insisted that it was the exclusive right and duty of the legislature to decide what should be the law. As late as 1892, in *Field* v. *Clark* the Supreme Court repeated this rigid doctrine, though with incongruity typical in this area the Court there held that Congress could give the President discretion to remove from the free list certain products of a country whose own tariff the President found to be "reciprocally unequal and unreasonable."

In 1928, in *Hampton* v. *United States* Mr. Chief Justice Taft cast the principle into new form. There the Court sustained the Flexible Tariff Act of 1922, which authorized the President to adjust tariff rates up to 50 per cent where he found that existing rates did not "equalize . . . differences in costs of production in the United States and the principal competing countries . . ." The Chief Justice tried to minimize the extent of discretion that this grant conferred. But he did not try to rationalize what Congress had done as merely a delegation to the President of a power to find "facts." Rather, he declared that "If Congress shall lay down by legislative act an intelligible principle to which the person or body authorized to fix such rates is directed to conform, such legislative action is not a forbidden delegation of legislative power." Five years later the new judicial frankness had progressed to the point at which Mr. Justice Cardozo, speaking for the Court, could refer to the 1922 statute as "in substance a delegation, though a permissible one, of the legislative power."

Through the years when the Court insisted that legislative power could not be "delegated," it upheld all acts of Congress that were challenged before it on the ground of unlawful delegation. However, in two cases in 1935 the Court held that provisions of the National Industrial Recovery Act were an invalid abdication of legislative responsibility.

The government lost these cases in an atmosphere so unfavorable to it as to cast doubt on the strength of the precedents so established. Congress passed the National Industrial Recovery Act in days of mingled despair, fear, and hope in a new administration. Concerned above all to save the country from economic disaster, Congress granted the President powers of wartime breadth to campaign against depression. The two lawsuits reached the Supreme Court after the country had recovered nerve. By then small businessmen and liberals alike were severely critical of the act, which they felt worked mainly to promote monopoly. A majority of the Justices were emotionally as well as intellectually opposed to the administration's broad intervention in the economy. On top of these factors, one of the lawsuits provided an object lesson in the dangers of loose administrative procedure. At the last minute the Government discovered, and conceded in one of the cases, that the regulation under which the defendant was being prosecuted had by inadvertence been amended out of existence before the charged violations occurred. Against this background the NIRA cases did not prophesy a fundamental change in the Court's general treatment of delegation. On the whole record, the doctrine limiting delegation of legislative power stood more as an admonition of principle than as a substantial curb on Congressional practice.

(2) Federal Practice

In its practical effect, constitutional doctrine reflected the realities of government as it was conducted from 1790 on. From the days of the first Congress there were examples of statutory delegation of rule-making powers to the executive. The subjects involved ranged from control of trading with the Indians to the collection of internal revenue, the appraisal of imported goods for tariff purposes, the taking of fire precautions on passenger and freight vessels, and the prevention of diseases imported from foreign places.

After 1870 government intervened more and more in economic affairs. As it did so, more and more rule-making power was delegated to the executive. This went on regardless of which political party was in power. Plainly the growth of delegated legislation responded to deep needs of government. By 1940 all but four or five of forty-nine major federal administrative agencies held authority to make rules to regulate matters under their jurisdiction; all of them held power to fix procedural rules to govern their disposition of business.

These rule-making powers grew to include areas of life that deeply concerned great numbers of people. Congress authorized the Federal Reserve System to regulate margin requirements in securities transactions, reserve requirements for banks, and maximum rates of interest on bank deposits. The Fair Labor Standards Act permitted the administrator of the Wage and Hour Division of the Department of Labor — on recommendations of industry committees — to fix wages varying from the statutory minima, and to define the range of certain statutory exemptions. Under the Food, Drug, and Cosmetics Act, Congress empowered the Federal Security administrator to set standards of identity, quality, and fill of container for many products, and to fix label and content requirements for various classes of goods. Statutes authorized the Secretary of Agriculture to set standards of quality and condition for certain agricultural commodities when these were sold under stated conditions in interstate or foreign commerce.

A realistic catalog of administrative legislation could not be limited to regulations made under express grant of rule-making power. Executive officers necessarily interpreted the laws in order to apply them. The peculiar facts of the particular case often so hedged in their interpretations as to give the interpretations more the character of judicial decisions than general regulations. This was especially true of Treasury rulings under the tax laws. However, executive officers did issue many general interpretive regulations under the statutes they enforced. In theory interpretive regulations lacked the statutory force of rules issued under an express delegation of rule-making power: A court could substitute its own interpretation of the statute for that made by the executive. But a court could not set aside a regulation made under express delegation of rule-making power unless the court found that the regulation clearly exceeded the delegated authority. However, the courts developed the doctrine that great weight should be accorded the administrative construction of a statute. Under this approach, interpretive regulations often had as much lawmaking force as if they had been made under an express delegation of rule-making power.

(3) State Doctrine and Practice

In the states, after 1900, administrative legislation grew on a scale proportionate to its growth in the federal government. State legislators and administrators were partners in the progressive building of policies that concerned industrial safety, compensation for industrial accidents, the rates and services of public utilities, the issue of securities, and the conservation of natural resources. The relatively weak position of the governor allowed independent administrative agencies to play a larger role in policy making in some states than such agencies did in the federal government.

Though state and federal practice were parallel, constitutional doctrine had a somewhat different history in the state courts from that which it followed in the Supreme Court of the United States. Well into the 1930's some state courts still denied that there could be any lawful "delegation" of legislative power. Other state courts — for example, the Wisconsin court, in a much cited opinion by Mr. Chief Justice Rosenberry in 1928 — went beyond the Supreme Court of the United States in frank recognition of the realities of delegated legislation.

The conservatism of state court doctrine reflected a stiffer application of constitutional limits on delegation. It was not until 1935 that the Supreme Court of the United States upset an act of Congress on this ground. From 1850 on, state Reports were sprinkled with decisions which held state laws unconstitutional because they made unlawful delegations. The tone of opinions and the kinds of cases that provoked the opinions suggested that the judges often thus rationalized their distaste for the substantive policy of the disputed statute. This seemed particularly likely where the legislation regulated economic affairs.

On the whole the state courts tempered their strict doctrine with common sense in application. For example, they uniformly upheld administrative regulation of public utility rates. Sometimes the decisions which upset legislation made more sense than the opinions that went with them. If the judges looked skeptically on broad delegations of the power to license the practice of callings, perhaps they knew that licensing could serve to restrain competition as well as to protect public interest. If they showed distrust of broad delegations to make building codes, or fire regulations, or to set zones for business and residential property, perhaps they took heed of the dubious level of local government administration in such matters. There was little evidence that the state courts had more than delayed the extension of delegated legislation into any areas where the public interest required it.

(4) Why Delegated Legislation?

What was behind this vast growth of delegated legislation? The range of human affairs involved made it unlikely that any one explanation would suffice. Observers emphasized various causes: the need for speed and flexibility in some fields of regulation; the need of more firsthand knowledge than a legislature could provide in areas of tangled, detailed, shifting problems; the value of the continuity, and tested expertness which experienced administrators could bring to the shaping of a policy in evolution; the release of the legislature from encumbering detail, to the consideration of general policy. One could match each of these explanations with examples — but how evaluate their relative force?

Sometimes legislators delegated rule-making power simply because they did not know what else to do, or because opposing forces were in such balance as to preclude putting into a statute anything except the most general declaration of principle. In this aspect delegated legislation was simply a more open form of a practice that the legislature had often followed with the help of the courts. When legislators entrusted the enforcement of any broadly phrased statute to private or public lawsuits, this amounted to a delegation of rule-making power to the judges who would be called on to "interpret" the legislation. So accepted was this partnership of legislature and court that when objection was raised that the vague terms of the Sherman Act called on the judges to legislate, and hence violated the separation of powers, Mr. Chief Justice White summarily dismissed the argument: it was "clearly unsound." He declared that the argument "in substance denies the existence of essential legislative authority and challenges the right of the judiciary to perform duties which that department of the government has exerted from the beginning." This reply — either very naïve or very sophisticated — skirted the fact that stood out in the legislative history of the act: namely, that Congress had passed the statute feeling it must do something, but unable to agree on anything tangible to do.

Much delegated legislation did what the more realistic judicial doctrine declared it to do; it specified rules within the framework of standards defined by the legislature. But even the remodeled judicial doctrine did not realistically describe all that was done by delegated legislation. Under many important statutes the administrators made first-rank policy as well as filling in the details under statutory standards. This was true of railroad regulation under the Interstate Commerce Act and the rules and orders of the Interstate Commerce Commission. It was true of the patterns of regulation spelled out by statute and administrative orders under the Public Utilities Holding Company Act, or under some aspects of the Fair Labor Standards Act.

"Delegation" once implied that a job within a fixed frame of policy had been turned over more or less finally to the administrators. However, as delegated legislation grew in importance, administrators and legislators more and more joined in a continuing process of policy making, by experiment and out of experience. The law that resulted was less and less the product of a definitive act of legislation. What happened oftener fitted this pattern: (1) The legislature entered a new field, with a broad declaration of standards and a delegation of rule-making power to an administrative agency. (2) Administrative legislation began to put content into the broad outlines of the basic statute. (3) In subsequent acts the legislature might refine, approve, or rebuke the administrative policy making. (4) More often, legislative committees heard administrators on their requests for appropriations or new authority, aired complaints about the operation of the law, sought explanations of things done or undone, and in such diverse ways contributed to shape evolving policy. (5) All of this activity following upon the original legislative decision to embark on a new course of policy making was given practical focus in the day-to-day work of administration — in fact finding, rule making, inspecting, form checking, negotiating, conciliating, arguing, warning, prosecuting, interpreting, deciding.

The policy-making partnership of legislator and administrator was largely an unplanned and wasteful accommodation to our failure to provide institutions properly organized and staffed to deal with twentieth-century issues. On the other hand, in some measure the partnership was inevitable. It responded to issues that were too new and too complicated for men to grasp and resolve at first impact in a completed program. Often the partnership was the only way by which law could begin to take hold of a problem while government waited on the growth of the understanding and public consent required for a sound and democratic choice of policy. The approach was not new in our law. As working partners, judges and lawyers, and judges and legislators had built many a principle of common law and court-glossed legislation.

As of mid-twentieth century it appeared that both in the federal government and in the states delegated legislation and the policy-making partnership of legislator and administrator would grow further in importance. Ernst Freund — sympathetic with the growth of the administrative process, but also distrustful of the delegation of broad policy decisions — predicted in 1928 that legislatures would take back the leadership of policy as they gained experience in new fields of regulation. Twenty years' subsequent experience did not support his prediction. However, this did not mean that the legislature had grown weaker in that time. Rather, its partnership with the administrators had strengthened its capacity to deal with contemporary issues. Promise lay not in turning back from, but in more fully exploiting this development. The legislature needed to provide itself with central policy direction, to strengthen its committees, and to provide itself with permanent staff to strengthen its hand in investigation and bill drafting. Thus it might equip itself to make full use of the contributions of the executive. In the Legislative Reorganization Act of 1946 Congress made tardy and modest recognition of this need.

4. FINDING FACTS

Institutions do not grow by the logic of a plan. Government should have set up fact-finding processes before it undertook to make and execute policy. In practice, it took fact finding for granted and treated it as a necessary nuisance, a menial and secondary job. We noted the haphazard growth of the legislature's investigating function. Fact-finding was similarly neglected in the growth of the executive branch.

The courts first gave fact finding an attention that measured up to its importance and difficulty. The common law of procedure and evidence long represented the most deliberate acknowledgment that the law had fact-finding responsibilities. The common law dealt with fact finding in two aspects which marked all later developments. In part the common law provided for authenticating and weighing evidence when it was before the trier of fact. Equally important was its provision of devices which, by allocating the burden of proof or the burden of producing evidence, prodded interested parties into fact-finding activity.

As fact finders courts were inherently hampered by the limiting tradition of their office. It was not the proper work of judges to initiate broad solutions of public problems. The courts inherited no staff which they could use for independent fact finding. They had no independent funds with which to finance inquiries.

Judges claimed inherent power to make rules of court to govern the procedure under which facts should be elicited in trials. But procedural reform encountered deep professional inertia, which was not seriously disturbed even by the challenge of the Field Code in mid-nineteenth century. The courts did not put the rule-making power to significant reform use until after 1910.

At best, court-developed rules of procedure and evidence were of narrow conception. They were almost exclusively designed to bring out facts in order to apply principles or rules of law to particular cases. They developed in a time of relatively simple litigation, when the critical facts of a lawsuit had to do with things that a witness could see, hear, taste, or smell. It was within this framework that the courts built the general rule against admission of hearsay testimony: In general the court would hear only those who were able to bear direct witness to the matter of which they testified.

The conventional rules of evidence might do, when the question was only to decide whether the facts of the parties' conduct fitted within a settled rule of law. But courts were called on, also, to decide whether they should extend a precedent or a principle, or even whether they should make a new rule. Like any policy maker, they needed to know the pertinent facts of the community life into which their policy must fit; for this job, the simple determination of what the particular parties before the court had done or had not done was not enough.

Confronted by the need to find facts preparatory to making law, the courts showed little boldness or imagination. They were all too ready to take judicial notice of matters of community life which were subjects of reasonable debate. But they devised no flexible escapes from the hearsay rule, to facilitate courtroom presentation of evidence on economic or social trends. They were slow to adapt to broader use the common law's familiar techniques for prodding the parties into fact-finding activity. Courts said that a "presumption of constitutionality" protected a statute. But judges put the "presumption" to little practical use to compel counsel to bring into court evidence which would inform the judges of the social context of the legislation. Courts invoked canons of statutory construction to rationalize prejudices of policy, or to conceal the fact that they lacked the imagination or energy to grasp the history of the legislation. On the whole they failed to see that they could use rules of construction as devices to allocate the burden of persuasion or the burden of producing evidence of the legislative history.

Presidents and governors made little use of their position to develop the fact-finding function. What they did do was mainly a by-product of improvements in administrative organization. The exception was President Herbert Hoover, who made broad use of executive authority to set up commissions of inquiry to deal with various public issues. It measured the immaturity of the fact-finding function in our law that many responsible people saw no purpose in these efforts, and criticized and ridiculed Hoover's readiness to commission inquiries.

After 1870 the executive departments and the administrative agencies in the federal government and in the states became the main sources of persistent investigation into the operations of the society. They took this role largely because of their routine accumulation of data in the course of applying the laws; in particular, this development accompanied the wider resort to inspection and licensing as techniques for implementing policy. However, they occasionally sponsored investigations outside the run of the job, and the legislature began to delegate general investigations to executive or administrative agencies.

Most departmental and administrative fact finding bore direct relation only to policy of the second rank; investigations pertaining to major policy were generally by legislative committees. However, if the legislature thus overshadowed the executive, the executive branch as a whole far outstripped the courts in the development of fact-finding procedures. The professionalization of the police, the expanded requirements of record keeping, the use of inspections and licenses, and the fact-finding initiative taken by administrative officers added up to tremendous resources for the gathering of information on the life of the community. But little planning had gone into the effective use of these resources, and in consequence there was a good deal of lost energy.

In England during the nineteenth century the Royal Commissions offered impressive examples of what co-operative investigations might achieve. But, the legislature and the executive in the United States had little experience of collaboration in fact finding. Our indifference to the English example measured our failure to grasp the significance of the fact-finding job in modern government. In 1898 Congress created an Industrial Commission, composed of five members from each house of Congress and nine persons named by the President from civil life. The Commission's procedure was careful, objective, exhaustive; but, largely for lack of any relation to a central policy-programing agency, its findings and recommendations led to little result. In 1938, on recommendation of the President, Congress created a Temporary National Economic Committee, with members drawn from Congress and important departments and administrative agencies, to investigate the concentration of economic power. For lack of an agreed coherent philosophy the TNEC did a mediocre job. However, like the Industrial Commission, in its structure it offered a promising precedent. The policy-making partnership of legislator and administrator suggested that working relationships existed on the basis of which these precedents might be extended.

CHAPTER FIFTEEN

THE STRUCTURE OF THE EXECUTIVE BRANCH: THE CHIEF EXECUTIVE

These essays deal with the lawmaking functions of legal agencies. They do not presume to give a history of government housekeeping. Hence we shall only discuss those aspects of executive structure most closely related to the tasks of making and applying law.

Federal and state constitution makers committed the chief executive power to one man. How firm was the commitment was emphasized by the short history of the alternatives. The Federal Convention gave short consideration to the suggestion of a several-member top executive. New York's "Council of Revision" to oversee legislation was unable to make a lasting place for itself and disappeared after a generation.

The Presidency went through the years substantially without change in formal structure. This was not so of the governorship. The early state constitutions left the governor in so extremely weak a position that some formal changes were inevitable if the office was to amount to anything. We have noted the main items of change as these bore on the governor's legislative leadership and his power to superintend the executive branch. He was made a popularly elected officer; he was granted first the general, and later the item veto; he was authorized to direct administrative reorganizations; he was given control of the preparation of the budget.

But it was constitutional and political practice, rather than formal amendment, that altered the structure of the President's power. Popular attitudes and the rise of national political parties made him in substance an officer elected by direct popular vote, even if the machinery of the Electoral College made a popular majority no guaranty of election.

Practice affected the tenure of the President. In 1868 the Radical Republicans failed by one vote to convict the impeached President Johnson. Their failure probably established for the Presidency a precedent like that set for the Supreme Court in 1805 when the Jeffersonians failed to convict the impeached Justice Samuel Chase. A high officer might not properly be removed under impeachment based merely on political disagreement, however fundamental.

Eligibility for re-election bore on the President's tenure. By mid-nineteenth century the accepted idea was that no one should be President for more than two terms — at least, not for more than two successive terms. The idea was vaguely defined and was not put to the test until 1876. Then it apparently contributed to bar a third term for Grant. Theodore Roosevelt's 1912 candidacy, and the calculated ambiguity of Coolidge's choice not to run in 1928 shook the certainty of the tradition. The re-election of Franklin Roosevelt for third and fourth terms established that the tradition no longer did more than raise a presumption against extended tenure. The presumption could be rebutted by the people's judgment that a sufficient emergency existed to warrant the continuance of a trusted President.

Earlier we discussed the homemade prerogative of the chief executive as a part of his power to shape general policy. Here we must note a development of the prerogative that affected the chief executive's functions with respect to the execution of the laws.

Early constitutional policy left the governor without firm control of the heads of departments or subordinate officers. It required new constitutional and statutory provisions to authorize the governor to coordinate and discipline executive officials. In contrast the Federal Constitution sweepingly vested in the President "the executive power." Hence the later history of the President's authority to discipline his subordinates was written in the practice of the executive and legislative branches and in the decisions of the Supreme Court.

The First Congress began the practice of leaving to the President the discretion to remove executive officers whose term was not set by statute. The President held this power by custom even with reference to officials whose appointment required the consent of the Senate. However, Congress sometimes did set a term of office, occasionally adding the stipulation that the officer might be removed only with the advice and consent of the Senate.

Congress provided in this last fashion for the tenure of first-, second-, and third-class postmasters. In the face of this provision, the postmaster general, by direction of the President, removed a first-class postmaster. In 1926, in *Myers* v. *United States* the Supreme Court held that the removal was valid, and that the statutory limitation on the President's removal power was unconstitutional as in breach of the separation of powers.

The *Myers* case involved an inferior officer, charged only with routine administration. The issue might have been taken to have narrow significance. Mr. Chief Justice Taft, speaking for the Court, did not choose to treat it so. Undoubtedly moved by his experience as President, the Chief Justice spoke far beyond the requirements of the case. He announced that under Article II of the Constitution the President could remove any "executive officers of the United States appointed by him," and that Congress could in no way limit this removal power.

In 1935 the Court repudiated the broad dicta of the *Myers* opinion. The formula announced nine years before encroached on Congress's right to set the framework of policy. In *Humphrey's Executor v. United States* the Court held that the President could not remove a member of the Federal Trade Commission within the commissioner's statutory term of office and for reasons not within those enumerated by statute as cause for removal. The Court's explanation was that:

> The Federal Trade Commission is an administrative body created by Congress to carry into effect legislative policies embodied in the statute in accordance with the legislative standard therein prescribed, and to perform other specified duties as a legislative or as a judicial aid. Such a body cannot in any proper sense be characterized as an arm or an eye of the executive. Its duties are performed without executive leave and, in the contemplation of the statute, must be free from executive control.

The Court thus used the result of the case to explain the result. If the history of executive functions were the test, no sharp line could be drawn between the jobs done by a body like the Federal Trade Commission and those done by the head of a Cabinet-rank department. What the Court actually did was to acknowledge that legislative practice had effectively redefined an area of executive prerogative. Congress could guaranty a limited tenure for new kinds of officers to whom it chose to delegate policy-making powers.

Relations between the chief executive and department and agency heads developed almost wholly outside of constitutional forms. The advisory role of the President's Cabinet was a growth of practice. The Cabinet's role varied sharply with the temper of the President; the Cabinet, or some members of it, exercised more power alongside an average President than under a strong one. In the states the existence beside the governor of independently elected high officers like an attorney general or a secretary of state meant that the governor had little basis on which to build a "cabinet."

Both in the federal government and in the states the twentieth century saw an expansion of government regulation and services that outstripped the growth of established departments. The heads of new agencies became important policy makers though they did not belong to the traditional Cabinet circle. Armed with broad delegations of power from the legislature, accustomed to direct relations on their own account with influential legislative committees, the independent commissions posed new problems for any chief executive who strove to centralize programming and administrative control in his office.

Up to mid-twentieth century neither President nor governor possessed a personal staff adequate to the functions of the chief executive. It took the spur of new demands on government in the depression of the 1930's to produce any substantial growth of an executive secretariat. Over the years Presidents and governors made makeshift arrangements to provide themselves with the minimum assistance they needed; they had their "kitchen cabinets," confidential assistants who had means of support outside government, or for whom the chief executive found sinecure jobs in the departments.

Not until after the 1937 report of the President's Committee on Administrative Management was the President provided with a recognized secretariat. Broad policy planning was done *ad hoc*. The federal government first created a National Planning Board merely as an adjunct to the depression-born Public Works Administration; when a vast social security program was to be planned, the President improvised a special Cabinet committee with its own director and staff, to do the job. The National Planning Board was replaced by a National Resources Committee of Cabinet status. This Committee soon fell before political hostility, but it pointed a possible direction. In 1946 Congress created a permanent Council of Economic Advisers to the President, charged to provide a continuing survey of the economy in aid of policy planning. Characteristically, the Council was not the product of any general consideration of government organization. It emerged as a specific political compromise, to resolve a contest over the extent and nature of the federal government's responsibility for full employment. However, like the short-lived National Resources Committee, the Council of Economic Advisers prophesied mounting concern for the improvement of our central policy planning.

In most states even less was done than in the federal government to bring programming to a focus. The weak constitutional inheritance of the governor, and the persistent distrust of "big city" planning ideas in legislatures dominated by the small towns and the country, made progress slow. There were occasional examples of advances that might be made; conspicuous was the leadership record of Governor Alfred E. Smith, in New York. But in mid-twentieth century it seemed that, largely under the stimulation of federal programs and federal money, the great cities and some rural counties might outstrip the states in their contribution to long-range planning of public policy.

CHAPTER SIXTEEN

THE STRUCTURE OF THE EXECUTIVE BRANCH: THE ADMINISTRATIVE PROCESS

1. Definition

Next in importance to developments that affected the status of the chief executive was the rise of the administrative process. We noted earlier that it was impossible to define the administrative process in terms of functions that were sharply distinct from those performed by traditional executive offices. It was easier to mark certain features of structure which, in combination, identified the emphases in organization and technique which characterized "administrative" agencies.

(1) An administrative agency specialized in matters that centered on one area of policy or an area of closely clustered policies. It might deal with one field in most of its aspects, as the Interstate Commerce Commission regulated transportation. It might deal with one aspect of a wide range of fields, as the National Labor Relations Board dealt with union organization and collective bargaining, and the Federal Trade Commission with unfair methods of competition. (2) An administrative agency had a large measure of legal and practical autonomy in handling its assigned problems. (3) An administrative agency held a complete, or almost complete, array of the kinds of authority useful for regulation or service — including legislative power (the power to make rules), executive power (the power to investigate, negotiate, prosecute, and settle), and judicial power (the power to determine the particular application of law).

The administrative process was important in the federal government from the beginning. In fact, compared with the restricted scope of federal activity before 1870, administrative power bulked about as large as it did later when the federal government vastly expanded its regulation of the economy and its provision of services. Between 1790 and 1870 Congress created administrative authority to deal with some aspects of almost all areas of federal action — the revenue, veterans' pensions, patents, public lands, ship inspection, currency, internal improvements, postal privileges.

On first inspection it appeared that the administrative process took hold more slowly in the states. Before 1870 the only important administrative authority set up in the states was for the inspection of goods and the licensing of occupations. But up to this time the states left to local government the administration of most affairs that touched people's everyday lives. When the states assumed increasing regulatory and service responsibilities after 1870, they began to set up administrative machinery to handle the new responsibilities.

In the 1870's states learned a lesson when they failed to achieve effective railroad regulation through statutory rate making and through lawsuits. About 1900 the Progressives won back ground lost by their agrarian predecessors. The Progressives embodied their victories in variously labeled Railroad Commissions, Public Service Commissions, Industrial Commissions, and Corporation Commissions. As early as 1916 Elihu Root pointed out that these bodies had become an "inevitable" part of our government structure:

We are entering upon the creation of a body of administrative law quite different in its machinery, its remedies, and its necessary safeguards from the old methods of regulation by specific statutes enforced by the courts. As any community passes from simple to complex conditions the only way in which government can deal with the increased burdens thrown upon it is by the delegation of power to be exercised in detail by subordinate agents, subject to the control of general directions prescribed by superior authority. The necessities of our situation have already led to an extensive employment of that method. The Interstate Commerce Commission, the state public service commissions, the Federal Trade Commission, the powers of the Federal Reserve Board, the health departments of the states, and many other supervisory offices and agencies are familiar illustrations. Before these agencies the old doctrine prohibiting the delegation of legislative power has virtually retired from the field and given up the fight. There can be no withdrawal from these experiments. We shall go on; we shall expand them, whether we approve theoretically or not, because such agencies furnish protection to rights and obstacles to wrongdoing which under our new social and industrial conditions cannot be practically accomplished by the old and simple procedure of legislatures and courts as in the last generation.

As Root pointed out, the extent of power vested in these agencies posed new problems in devising safeguards for the rights of the persons affected. This did not alter the fact that the new agencies had won a firm place among our institutions. Their growth was so closely correlated with the growth of government responsibilities as to evidence a response to deep necessities of effective legal action.

The response was more instinctive than planned. Congress debated very little over the structure of the independent commissions it set up. The Civil Aeronautics Act of 1938 was "unique in that most of the major controversies arose on matters of administrative organization." State legislators paid no more attention to problems of administrative structure. The Wisconsin legislature provided a rare example to the contrary: In 1909–1911 it authorized a joint interim committee which held extensive hearings and gave detailed consideration to the organization of an Industrial Commission.

We waited until almost the middle of the twentieth century to make the first adequate official studies of the administrative process. In 1941 an Attorney General's Committee on Administrative Procedure, led by Dean Acheson, made the first comprehensive report on administrative procedures of the federal government. The first notable state study was that reported in 1942 in New York state, by Robert M. Benjamin, as commissioner appointed by Governor Herbert H. Lehman to investigate administrative adjudication.

Studies of federal and state administrative agencies revealed meaningless diversity in details of organization, powers, and procedures. This needless diversity reflected the lack of plan in administrative developments. It made generalization hazardous, and underlined the need for more specific studies. But neither caution nor study was much in evidence in the debates that swirled about the administrative process as it passed through its greatest generation of growth in the years after 1910.

2. SPECIALIZATION

No aspect of structure more sharply distinguished administrative agencies than their specialized areas of action. In contrast, legislators, Presidents, governors, judges must deal with any questions of public policy that could be stated in terms of their procedures. By inheritance this was not only their right but also their duty.

Different reasons led to the creation of specialized agencies. In some fields there was a high premium on expertness. The expertness might derive from professional knowledge, or it might derive from the administrative job itself through the administrator's opportunity for concentrated, continuous experience in one area. Need for the expert explained such specialization as that of the Bureau of Animal Industry or the Bureau of Entomology and Plant Quarantine in the United States Department of Agriculture; it was in large measure the explanation for the Immigration and Naturalization Service of the Department of Justice, or the Office of the Chief of Engineers in the War Department;

it was behind the specialization of boards of health, departments of agriculture, and banking commissions in the states.

Partisans of the administrative process were apt to overwork the explanation in terms of expertness. Much administrative work required specialized attention less because of its technical difficulty than because of its sheer bulk. The government's vast insurance business was an example: the Veterans' Administration, the United States Employees' Compensation Commission, the Railroad Retirement Board, and the Social Security Board. Another example was the enforcement of standards in public contracts, as in the work of the Division of Public Contracts in the United States Department of Labor.

The need for the expert and the need for specialized handling of vast detail were woven together in the creation of some of the most important administrative agencies. This was true of state public utility commissions, of the Interstate Commerce Commission, the Bureau of Marine Inspection and Navigation, the Patent Office, the Federal Communications Commission, the Federal Power Commission. It was true, also, in the administration of tax laws, workmen's compensation, and conservation policy. This combination of factors was implied in the "single generalization" which Louis L. Jaffe suggested could encompass the grounds of all delegated legislative power:

> Power should be delegated where there is agreement that a task must be performed and it cannot be effectively performed by the legislature without the assistance of a delegate or without an expenditure of time so great as to lead to the neglect of equally important business.

However, there were other reasons for administrative specialization. One related to policy planning. In the scanty legislative debates on administrative organization there stood out the persistent hope that administrative agencies might help the legislature construct long-range programs in their special areas of public interest.

Another reason touched the most controversial motive behind the resort to specialized enforcement of policy: the hope that from concentration of responsibility and energy, from the shaping of a single-purpose agency in the same heat in which was forged the policy of its governing statute, would come partisan zeal in implementing the statutory policy. This hope marked the creation of the early public utility commissions in the state; it was part of the history of the Interstate Commerce Commission, the Federal Trade Commission, the Securities and Exchange Commission, the National Labor Relations Board.

In this thinking there was a measure of naïveté that carried the promise of disillusionment. An agency which specialized in the regulation of one industry, and through the sweep of its regulation entered into the industry's management decisions, was apt to learn a partner's rather than a prosecutor's attitude toward the industry's problems. An agency which specialized in problems that cut across many industries was not likely to run this course. But its more abstract specialization might lead it to fall prisoner to its own origins and precedents, robbed of imagination and initiative. Specialization did not guarantee long-lived vigor.

3. INDEPENDENCE

a. Administrators and the Constitution

In rare cases state constitution makers made an administrative body independent even of the legislature, when they established the administrative agency by constitutional fiat. Some state constitutions thus created commissions to regulate public utilities. The men who did this feared that they would lose power in the future, and that a legislature newly dominated by "the interests" would abolish or emasculate an agency which had only statutory authority.

In practice this constitutionally given independence was likely to prove an illusion. Once the constitution makers went home, it was the courts that said what the constitution meant. The agency's constitutional charter might only make the administrators dependent on the word of judges rather than of legislators.

Experience indicated that administrative agencies, as such, had no special need of constitutional protection. In the absence of constitutional barriers, legislatures sometimes abolished offices. This might happen when changes in substantive policy made the offices no longer necessary. It happened in course of administrative reorganizations. Illegitimately, legislatures sometimes abolished an office as it existed under one title only to set it up again under a new name, to put jobs at the disposal of the dominant party. None of this had anything to do with the administrative process as such. No important administrative agency seems ever to have been destroyed because of objections to its distinctive characteristics as an administrative agency.

b. Administrators and the Legislature

Since the structure of administrative agencies was usually fixed by statute, it was the legislature in both the federal and state governments that ordinarily exercised basic control over administration. This was true at least until the 1920's. Then it began to be common for the chief executive to take the lead in administrative reorganization, under delegation from the legislature.

Once it was established, a major administrative agency enjoyed a large margin of freedom from legislative control. Top administrators were usually in office for more years than the average legislator. Legislators' and administrators' years of service overlapped, so that the legislature never confronted a wholly new array of administrators with whom it might make a fresh beginning. Administrative staffs gained experience and expertness in their fields which the average legislator could not match. Legislative committees generally lacked the knowledge, the time, or the staff to exercise any broad or thorough scrutiny of administrative activity. In fields like taxation administrators dealt with problems inherently so complicated as to guaranty the administrators practical freedom from any detailed legislative oversight.

In an unplanned way the appropriations committees grew to exercise the legislature's most regular and detailed check on administration. The recurring hearings on the budget gave committeemen a strategic opportunity to question the administrators. Questions were often sharp and pointed, if haphazard and ill-balanced. So far as it went, this kind of legislative scrutiny made sense. It left general policy to the legislative committees assigned to deal with the major fields of public interest; on questions of general policy, these committees could ask the advice of informed administrators. On the other hand, the appropriations committees — concerned with concrete details of the budget — were logical agents to inquire into specific items of executive action.

Because it controlled the purse, the legislature inevitably had the residual power to question how policy was carried out. However, it was poorly suited to regular surveillance of the details of execution. As Robert Luce pointed out, legislators were not chosen for administrative capacity or experience. The range of problems that pressed on their attention did not give them time for details. They had ties to local constituencies and to party, and they must constantly be alert to the political battle; local, partisan, and personal aims were likely to impair their capacity to exercise objective supervision of an often intricate, technical pattern of administration. The most constructive development in the relation of legislator and administrator was the tendency toward the policy-making partnership that was effected through the interplay of statute, legislative committee, and administrative rule or order.

c. Administrators and the Chief Executive

In no respect was the twentieth century administrative agency more strikingly independent than in its relations to the chief executive. The chief executive appointed top administrators, but usually subject to the advice and consent of one of the chambers of the legislature. The statutes usually fixed the term of important administrators, and set it at a number of years greater than a single executive term of office. The laws often further hedged in the chief executive's choice by requiring that several-member commissions be bipartisan. In practice — and in law so far as *Humphrey's Executor* v. *United States* made it so — the chief executive could remove top administrators only for specified cause amounting to malfeasance. Legislation generally left to agency heads the definition of the number and description of subordinate jobs in their offices. Civil service rules further withdrew control of agency personnel from the chief executive. The responsibilities which statutes assigned to the agencies substantially dictated the size and relative emphasis of agency budgets. And the accretion of precedent in the operation of a major agency tended to give independent weight to the agency's own estimate of its budget needs.

Agencies more or less independent of the chief executive grew to be a considerable part of the whole machinery of government. In 1941 the Attorney General's Committee on Administrative Procedure appraised the fifty-one major federal administrative agencies whose rule making and decisions affected private rights. The Committee classified twenty-two of these agencies as "outside the regular executive departments" and twenty-nine as within them.

After 1920, first in the federal government and later in the states the chief executive asserted a little more control of administrative policies and operating standards. The executive budget was the most effective instrument of this control. This required prior clearance by the chief executive for all requests for funds made to the legislature. During the administration of Franklin Roosevelt the Budget Bureau set up a Division of Legislative Reference whose function was to scrutinize legislative proposals made by departments and agencies to insure their consistency with the President's program. Committees of Congress on their own motion began to refuse to consider proposals that the Budget Bureau had not cleared. These tardily developed clearance procedures emphasized that full co-ordination of executive policy waited upon the provision of adequate staff facilities for the chief executive.

d. Administrators and the Courts

Lawyers, students, and publicists tended to give a disproportionate share of attention to the relations between administrative agencies and the courts. This was especially so in the generation of controversy that began about 1910 when the economy first felt the full new sweep of administrative regulation. For years after courses in "administrative law" first appeared in law school catalogs, they dealt almost exclusively with judicial review of administrative action. To case-trained lawyers judicial review had the attraction of a familiar landmark in new territory. To the pamphleteer it had the attraction of permitting him to import classic political concepts and bywords into novel controversies.

Of course, judicial review had deep roots in our legal tradition. The common law said that any private individual could hold liable in tort an official who abused public power to his damage. It had its classic, if narrowly circumscribed, writs by which to check on official arrogance — quo warranto, mandamus, certiorari. To the common law inheritance the United States added its peculiar stress on rights under written constitutions, declared and enforced by judges.

Actually, however, administrators disposed of the vast bulk of matters before them without contest. Of the minor percentage of contested matters, only a few went on to court review. Moreover, at most the courts did only the negative job of curbing abuse of power. They had neither the authority nor the equipment to superintend in any positive way the effectiveness with which the administrator did his work.

After 1850, in the first reaction against the pinch of expanded regulation, the courts used their reviewing power so broadly as to invade the proper sphere of the executive. The 1890's marked the high point of this judicial overreaching. Thereafter federal and state courts alike, of their own invention, imposed on themselves doctrines to restrain the substitution of judicial for executive discretion. That the courts were impelled to do this was perhaps the best evidence of how far the administrative process responded to urgent needs of modern government. Legislatures began to be more explicit in delegating freedom of choice to the executive, and in defining limits of judicial review. However, this legislation was guided by little formulated principle, and was usually vague enough to leave ample room for judicial invention.

Thus it was primarily judge-made law that fixed the basic doctrines affecting judicial review of administrative action. Three rules particularly concerned review of administrative adjudication. Only a person with defined legal standing, a clear-cut interest in law and in fact in the matter contested, might attack administrative action. Courts generally refused to review preliminary or procedural orders of administrators. Aside from a vague category of "jurisdictional" or "constitutional" facts, courts limited their review to deciding whether the administrators had substantial record evidence to support what they decided.

Where administrative legislation was drawn in question, the courts grew even more reluctant to disturb what the administrators had done.

Judges enforced certain requirements of notice and hearing in connection with administrative adjudication. But if an administrative order
or rule affected so broad a range of persons as to make it more analogous to a statute than to a decision, the courts would not require that
the affected persons have notice and opportunity to be heard before the
order or rule took effect. The judges said, further, that a presumption of
constitutionality like that which surrounded a statute also protected administrative legislation. If the challenge was not that the regulation was
unconstitutional, but rather that it exceeded the power the legislature
meant to delegate, still the courts usually gave the regulation the benefit
of a presumption that it fell within the delegated authority.

The irony of politics dictated that just when administrative-judicial
relations were achieving a workable pattern, demand should arise
that legislatures enact codes of procedure for administrators, and that
these codes should redefine the scope of judicial review. This pressure
came out of the tensions that attended expansion of the government's
role in the depression of the 1930's. The debaters talked of procedural
reform. However, they lined up pretty much according to how they
felt about the substantive merits of the policies that were being enforced by the agencies whose procedure was particularly in question.

The leading contest centered on federal legislation. Seven years of
mounting controversy culminated in December, 1940, when President Roosevelt vetoed the Walter–Logan Bill. As a countermove, and
to relieve the pressure to do something, the President appointed the
Attorney General's Committee on Administrative Procedure. In 1941
a majority of that Committee recommended against any sweeping legislation. The war then shelved the matter. Renewed attention to the issue
finally brought the federal Administrative Procedure Act of 1946. In
the meantime North Dakota (1941) and Ohio and Wisconsin (1943)
enacted administrative procedure codes of varying scope.

So far as judicial review was concerned, different people read the
new laws to forecast quite different results. Some saw in the statutes
mere declarations of previous judicial doctrine. Others saw an expansion of the scope of judicial review, particularly over the fact-finding
aspect of administrative adjudication. How far the courts would take
the legislation as warrant for opening a new chapter in their relations to
the administrators remained to be seen.

4. Merger of Functions

The federal Administrative Procedure Act of 1946 dealt more with
the internal structure and procedures of agencies than it did with judi-

cial review of their actions. The fact was prophetic. The administrative process had apparently grown beyond the stages in which men were content to discuss it in terms of separation-of-powers doctrine and the scope of judicial review. At last they were prepared to give their attention to administrative organization itself and not just to its relations to other institutions of government. This development brought under examination what we noted as the third characteristic of administrative structure — the merger of legislative, executive, and judicial functions.

Attention to administrative structure was tardy and was at first moved more by desire to find political ammunition than to find facts. It was not surprising that there was little objective evidence accumulated by which to weigh even elementary problems. Nor was it surprising that emphasis was misplaced in defining the significant issues.

The choice between the single-member and the several-member agency was an example of an elementary problem on which evidence was lacking. In the early twentieth century the several-member commission became the model for the rapidly expanding administrative process. The precedent was set partly by the Interstate Commerce Commission, as the first great new federal agency; it was set partly by the successful Wisconsin Industrial Commission of 1911. Later opinion varied regarding the merits of the several-member commission. The consensus favored it for administrative legislation, but criticized it from an executive standpoint, as liable to internal division, inertia, and delay.

Wisconsin demonstrated experiments in administrative organization. Despite the early favorable precedent, it did not adhere rigidly to the several-member commission. By 1940 Wisconsin was employing (1) a single commissioner for insurance regulation, (2) a part-time commission with a part-time administrative officer, for its Athletic Commission and its Aeronautics Commission, (3) a part-time commission with a full-time director for its Conservation Commission, its Board of Health, and its Department of Agriculture and Markets, (4) a full-time commission, with no separate administrative officer, for its Banking Commission, its Grain and Warehouse Commission, and its Labor Relations Board, and (5) a full-time commission with full-time executive officers for its Public Service Commission and its Industrial Commission.

In 1937 the President's Committee on Administrative Management recommended that all administrative functions except those of judicial type be assigned to the departments; the independent regulatory commissions would keep only the business of administrative adjudication. The recommendation was evidence that the question of the constitution of top administrative authority had become entangled with the thorny question of the separation of powers within agencies. The provision of separate executive officers in some Wisconsin agencies reflected the same mingling of problems, without the dogmatic sort of solution suggested by the President's Committee.

Demands for sharp separation of functions within agencies provided the outstanding example of misplaced emphasis in discussion of administrative structure. The demands usually boiled down, in particular, to insistence that agencies should not be both "prosecutor" and "judge." Critics sought moral weight for their plea by invoking the maxim that no man should be judge in his own case. Out of such thinking came the concrete suggestion that a staff wholly distinct from those who heard and decided questions of the application of law should do the inspecting and investigating, the bringing of charges, and the preparation and presentation of cases.

The suggestion had at least the merit of stirring the first real consideration of the policies involved in the specialization and merger of functions which marked the administrative process. We noted earlier that varying reasons were behind administrative specialization: the need for the expert, the need for undivided attention to great volumes of detail, the hope of better policy planning or more aggressive execution. Some or all of these factors were typically mingled in the creation of a given agency. The same factors put a premium on a type of organization that would be sensitive to the interrelations of the various aspects of the problems with which the agency dealt. To fulfill its special functions, the administrative agency must keep in view: (1) the general policy of the governing statutes, (2) what that policy meant in terms of individual application, (3) how the disposition of individual cases shaped the evolution of the general policy, (4) the problems posed both for general policy and detailed application, by the recalcitrance of some of the regulated persons. Administrative organization must then be capable of flexible and speedy adaptation of any one aspect of its business to the bearing of that part on the whole policy with which the agency was charged.

These requirements spelled a merger of legislative, executive, and judicial authority. They spelled this particularly for an agency like the Interstate Commerce Commission that had broad regulatory and service responsibilities regarding a particular industry. The decisions of such an agency inevitably became a significant part of the management of the industry regulated or served. This meant that flexibility, speed, and coherence in the various phases of the agency's operations were important to the life of the regulated business. Most pressure for the grant of broad discretion to administrators came not from the administrators but from the regulated businessmen, who feared to become caught in rigid regulation. Senator Robert Taft pointed to this fact in the debate on federal administrative procedure legislation.

Merger of powers was scarcely less needed by an agency like the Federal Trade Commission, whose concern was with particular aspects of a great range of business. The legislature might not always grant rule-making power to such agencies, but the administrators nonetheless made general policy, by accumulation of precedents. Policy making required of them, as it did of the one-industry agency, that they have the means to work the various phases of their job into a more or less consistent pattern.

The demand for a rigid separation of administrators' executive and legislative jobs from their adjudicative jobs was heedless of the requirements for effective functioning. The demanded separation promised to make an agency more prosecutor-minded than policy-minded, and to hinder the pooling of experience and expertness within the organization. Thus it threatened effective handling of the bulk of administrative business — the informal disposition of a great volume of matters without contest. Moreover, much administrative business was inherently not capable of disposition by proceedings patterned on a judicial hearing. This was not the way to negotiate settlement or adjustment of a disputed point; it was not the way quickly and informally to correct defective license applications; it was not the way to get speedy, simply determined reparation for public utility overcharges; it was not the way to conduct inspections of goods or tests of the fitness of men or equipment.

The demand for a formal separation of administrative jobs ignored trends in practice which worked to the same ends, but in a fashion moulded and tested by experience. In natural response to a great volume of business, the larger administrative agencies developed a considerable division of labor within their organizations. The men who heard and decided contested matters were generally not in fact the same men who made inspections or investigations, who filed charges, or prepared cases for argument. Of course, in smaller agencies, typically in many state administrative offices, the volume of business did not warrant elaborate division of labor.

Administrative procedure likewise tended toward regular forms. The Attorney General's Committee and New York's Commissioner Benjamin both found that in practice, in contested matters, administrators developed procedures and followed many principles of proof that were in substance analogous to those used in court. Indeed, some observers thought that the agencies tended to follow courtroom examples too closely, at the expense of the speed and ready use of expert knowledge which were supposed to be strengths of administrative procedure. For example, administrators were criticized because they did not make enough use of written evidence, or enough resort to official notice — the administrative counterpart of judicial notice — in the proof of matters peculiarly within their field of experience or expertness.

How unreal was much of the argument for separation of the jobs of "prosecutor" and "judge" within administrative agencies was attested by a fact as familiar in the routine of a local prosecutor's office as in the operation of a major agency. The overwhelming bulk of questions that arose in the application of any law were inevitably disposed of by executive discretion. This was true whatever might be the formal divisions of functions for disposing of contested matters. Someone had to take the responsibility of deciding in countless instances whether to investigate or not to investigate, to file charges or to drop the matter, to withdraw or dismiss charges or to let them go to hearing, to negotiate an adjustment or to fight for the letter of the law. Such decisions were necessary incidents of carrying out legal policy. They made up most of the work of any administrative agency. In them there could be no division between executive and adjudicative functions.

5. JUDICIAL ANALOGIES

Demands that some administrators put on the judge's robe contrasted ironically with tendencies in the courts toward administrative organization and procedure.

The working partnership between public prosecutor and trial judge was a fact that experienced lawyers took for granted in many a court. It was the judiciary's oldest, continuing analogy to the administrative merger of functions. The reality of the partnership was reflected in the early-nineteenth-century insistence on the autonomy of the jury; the jury was the accused's reliance against an otherwise solid front of officialdom.

The pressures that produced the growth of the administrative process also affected the operation of the courts. The first impact was on policy making. The nineteenth-century judges had learned confidence in policy making out of the experience of building common law on the grand scale. When change speeded up in the 1870's, it was natural that the courts first ventured into closer participation in executive responsibility by assuming more burdens of general policy. Sometimes claiming authority by statute, sometimes building from common law, they made ill-advised efforts to engage in administrative regulation. Through the clumsy forms of lawsuits courts tried to regulate rates and services of public utilities. In actions to abate nuisances they did some limited and ex post facto land-use planning. On occasion they used mandamus to supervise collection of local taxes to pay arrears of interest on public bonds. They gave ready ear to taxpayers' suits to prevent alleged waste of public funds. They lent the prestige of the bench to the conduct of railroads by insiders who operated in the name of a receiver in equity. They were not reluctant to substitute their own weighing of evidence or policy for the judgment of administrators whose action was challenged by suit.

The courts did not have the investigative machinery, the time or specialized knowledge, the philosophy or the range of sanctions, to compete long with the executive in policy making. Their policy-making activity declined after 1900 as the legislature created new administrative agencies and added new duties and powers to older executive offices. The courts acknowledged the new order; they deferred to the administrative construction of statutes, and they developed a body of self-denying ordinances to limit their review of administrative action.

Independence was a character which the courts inherited from their own particular history, with no borrowing from the rise of the administrative process. Specialization of function was a different matter. Through most of the nineteenth century, courts in the United States either held general jurisdiction, or at least jurisdiction over a considerable variety of matters. But the federal government developed its Court of Claims, its Court of Customs and Patent Appeals, its Tax Court, and its short-lived Commerce Court. The twentieth century produced state courts specially set up to handle small claims, domestic relations, traffic offenses, juvenile delinquents, and female offenders. Did these specialized courts represent any common principle, borrowed perhaps from administrative analogies?

Behind the creation of specialized state courts were considerations like those which produced much specialization of administrative agencies. These new state courts were set up to achieve a more positive attitude in action toward given social problems. They expressed the view that justice was something to be created and not merely administered. They represented a demand for speeding up justice, and making it less costly in areas where a great volume of detailed business touched the lives of great numbers of people. Some of these courts responded to an insistent need for specialized professional competence, substituting expert handling for rule of thumb. In these various aspects — at least in their origins and the hopes of their sponsors — these new courts were agents of a positive program; and in that respect they belonged to the current of the administrative process. With the exception of the Commerce Court, the special federal courts were not created out of a similar desire to give positive drive to given policies. Their origins lay usually in the intricacy or the mass of business in given fields, or in a combination of these factors.

Congress designed the Court of Claims to relieve the general courts of business which clogged their dockets not because of its peculiar technicality (most of the work involved familiar contract principles and situations), but because of its volume and time-taking demands. Technical detail in the subject matter was a good deal of the reason for a special customs court. However, it was also important that the revenue flow smoothly, and that executive and judicial action be nicely coordinated for the efficient application of tariff policy; these elements contributed to the customs court some flavor of a body intended to give positive support to a program. The Tax Court (once known as the Board of Tax Appeals), presented a somewhat different emphasis. Congress clearly intended that the Tax Court should do its work with judicial detachment; the detail and technical nicety of the business, rather than any desire to provide an aggressive exponent of policy, were the main reasons for specialization in tax matters.

Federal statutes also provided that special three-judge district courts should be convened to hear challenges to the constitutionality of state or federal legislation or administrative regulation. As part of the price control system set up in World War II, Congress provided an Emergency Court of Price Appeals. These special ad hoc courts were in recognition of the gravity of the issues at stake and the public interest in their prompt disposition. In the matter of price control there was also the imperative need for uniform treatment of a national price policy.

Neither in the federal government nor in the states did any specialized court exist for any length of time to promote policy in a field where a major administrative agency worked for the same purpose. The short life of the Commerce Court contrasted with the durability of the Interstate Commerce Commission. It was notable that no central administrative body existed in the fields occupied by the specialized state courts. Apparently there was no new principle of specialization at work in the development of the judiciary as such. The shape of legal institutions was slowly responding to the demands of the problems they handled.

Not only in the immediate work of judges, but also in their dependence on new kinds of auxiliary officers, judicial developments raised questions of the force of administrative example. Tardily, and in limited measure, the courts began to use administrative assistance to check how effectively legal policy was executed in certain fields.

There were precedents to support the judges' use of what amounted to administrative assistants. The Chancellor had long referred issues in equity to masters, to explore complicated facts, and to consider what the equities required. In the common law action of account the English courts were accustomed to order references in long and tangled accounting issues. Oddly, courts in the United States did not freely borrow these English precedents. Only the federal courts readily applied these techniques without the aid of statutes; with few exceptions, state courts used only such reference proceedings as specific legislation clearly provided. The legislature was much freer than the courts in invention of reference procedures. It provided these particularly where it put on the courts duties of an administrative kind — notably in a wide range of eminent domain proceedings. Probably the distrust of executive power that marked the early nineteenth century made the legislature the more ready to put administrative-type proceedings in the courts.

Both legislatures and courts were slower to experiment with new machinery for disposition of criminal as compared to civil matters. There was little attention to the fixing of sentence, after the accused had been convicted. The trial judge determined sentence almost entirely at his discretion, according to his own philosophy, within such meager framework as the statutes might set. Once sentence was passed, the court's concern ended. This was the typical situation during most of the nineteenth century. From small beginnings at the end of the century there gradually developed a considerable administrative apparatus that affected the fixing and executing of sentence. In form the judge supervised, or was merely advised by, the administrative officers. In operation the administrators began to overshadow the court. They did so to an extent which suggested that sentence might finally become an entirely separate administrative function, in the hands of special investigators, psychiatrists, probation and parole officers, and vocational and personal affairs advisers, responsible to some central board. Trends in juvenile court administration pointed this way.

We need only recall here the earlier references to administrative assistance which legislatures began to attach to some of the specialized state courts. Some domestic relations courts had the help of staff social workers and doctors, as well as providing special clerks to check compliance with decrees involving the payment of money. The clerk of the small claims court helped suitors prepare cases, and sometimes staff was provided to administer a financial settlement over a period of time between debtor and creditors. In line with such developments, legal aid organizations tended to integrate their work with that of other social agencies that dealt with problems of the poor.

In some areas of twentieth-century economic regulation, Congress sought to bring special administrative competence to the help of the courts. Thus it provided that the federal courts might ask the help of the Federal Trade Commission in preparing antitrust decrees. That this procedure was almost never used did not disprove its inherent usefulness; the Commission failed to develop strength, and during most of the years under the Sherman Act neither the Department of Justice nor the courts showed energy or imagination in using the full range of means to implement the antitrust laws. More significant was Congress's requirement that the courts refer financial reorganization plans of distressed railroads or other corporations to the consideration of the Interstate Commerce Commission, or the Securities and Exchange Commission, respectively. The judge could refuse to follow the administrators' advice, but Congress required that he have that advice before he took final action.

As a matter of judicial practice, courts began to recognize that they should sometimes hear an administrative agency on a matter that came to court in the first instance simply as a controversy between private parties. Where the private suit involved laws with whose execution the administrator was charged, he might ask to be heard as a friend of the court, or even as an intervening party; thus he would have a voice in a matter contributing to shape the interpretation of the policy with which he was concerned. On its own initiative, a court occasionally asked administrators to participate in a private suit where public policy was in issue. These various instances followed no plan and had limited effect. Even so, they were one more way in which judicial administration drew closer to executive practice.

We have noted that the executive, like the legislature, was slow to improve its fact-finding facilities. It is not surprising that in this respect there was the least sign that executive example had constructive influence on the courts. Improved fact-finding facilities marked the new specialized courts in the states. But at best these improvements were limited to particular fields, and reflected no co-ordinated plan. Moreover, they related only to the more effective application of law in particular cases; they did not touch fact finding in the making of general policy. The pressure of a society in rapid transition promised to increase government's responsibility to find the facts beneath the swirl of change. There was little indication that the courts would contribute much to this fact-finding function, and much in the record to suggest that their limitations in this respect would contribute to their steady loss of ground to other policy makers.

VII. Conclusion: Prospectus for Legal History

CHAPTER SEVENTEEN

"... TO ... PROMOTE THE GENERAL WELFARE ..."

According to Anglo-American legal tradition, law existed to order social relations, to protect the individual on the one hand, and the community on the other. This was the ideal function of legal agencies, to which other tasks that we have discussed were subsidiary.

Jurisprudence sometimes oversimplified and distorted issues by posing the central problem in our law as simply the reconciliation of the claims of individuals and of the whole. Calhoun, our only first-rank political thinker of mid-nineteenth century, saw more clearly the main challenge to the legal order in this country. He pointed out that:

> ... nothing is more difficult than to equalize the action of the government, in reference to the various and diversified interests of the community; and nothing more easy than to pervert its powers into instruments to aggrandize and enrich one or more interests by oppressing and impoverishing the others; and this too, under the operation of laws, couched in general terms — and which, on their face, appear fair and equal.

This was a problem in all communities, but especially in such a country as ours:

> ... the more extensive and populous the country, the more diversified the condition and pursuits of its population, and the richer, more luxurious, and dissimilar the people, the more difficult is it to equalize the action of the government, — and the more easy for one portion of the community to pervert its powers to oppress and plunder the other.

Law dealt with the individual and the community. It dealt also with groups or blocs, brought together by some close, sharply felt interest, more powerful than individuals, less representative than the community. Group interest was the most dynamic force that played on our law — and this was natural in an association-minded society, preoccupied with opportunities for the diverse growth of ambitions in an extensive, richly varied land.

How hold together such a community? There was danger that the different interests would form ranks for a spurious expression of majority policy — spurious, because it would not speak for the general interest but merely for a working alliance of special interests. Calhoun warned that:

> . . . a struggle will take place between the various interests to obtain a majority, in order to control the government. If no one interest be strong enough, of itself, to obtain it, a combination will be formed between those whose interests are most alike; — each conceding something to the others, until a sufficient number is obtained to make a majority.

He saw only one way to offset the threat of special interests to usurp the title to speak for the community. The central job of law was to bring power into balance sufficiently so that particular blocs could not run roughshod over other interests in society. The only way in which special interest could be curbed, Calhoun was sure, was:

> by taking the sense of each interest or portion of the community, which may be unequally and injuriously affected by the action of the government, separately, through its own majority, or in some other way by which its voice may be fairly expressed; and to require the consent of each interest, either to put or to keep the government in action. This, too, can be accomplished only in one way, — and that is, by such an organism of the government, — and, if necessary for the purpose, of the community also, — as will, by dividing and distributing the powers of government, give to each division or interest, through its appropriate organ, either a concurrent voice in making and executing the laws, or a veto on their execution.

Of course Calhoun's analysis and prescription were colored by an advocate's bias for his cause. His particular solution — a dual executive — spelled such stalemate as could not be indefinitely endured on major issues of policy. Nonetheless, the immediate occasion aside, his analysis prophesied major legal problems dating from 1870 to the present.

Two characteristics of our social life increasingly threatened the individual's right to his full development, and the community's need for solidarity: (1) a diminished political sensitivity, and (2) a growing impersonality in people's dealings with one another. Both worked to give undisciplined freedom to particular interests at the expense of the individual and community life.

At one time or another law in the United States dealt with tensions that traced to differences in religion, race, color, and social class. But no factors bore so powerfully upon the legal order, or so much shaped its problems, as the main currents in the growth of the economy. The '70s saw us turn decisively from a subsistence to a market economy. For the future most people were to depend for a critical part of the needs of life upon what they could buy. To buy they must have money, and to have money they must sell something: goods, cleverness, skill, or labor. Earning a living became a newly distinct, critically important phase of life. The hours spent at one's livelihood were more and more divorced from all the other aspects of living — spent in a different place, among different people, in different pursuits from those that centered about home, church, school, neighborhood. This way of life made men above all else conscious of their interests as producers rather than as consumers. In terms of means-in-relation-to-ends, this made sense: Life depended on production. But in terms of ends-as-superior-to-means, it was a dangerous way of life.

As a function sharply separated from the aspects of life which alone could give it meaning, production — the getting of income and of power that income symbolized — could easily become an end in itself. Separated from close attention to the purposes of consumption, production easily became wasteful of natural resources as well as of human resources. Moreover, production in a market economy was an emphasis which divided men; the aim was to win as big a share of the consumer's dollar as one could, as against not only other sellers in the same industry, but also as against other industries, and also to do whatever was necessary to protect and strengthen the particular bastion from which one sallied forth into the market. In contrast, consumption basically related to things that men had in common, the common need for which tended to bind them together: food, shelter, clothing, recreation.

The richness and rawness of the continent combined to make a second impact on our social life. We found no established western-type society already settled here, on which we could build by slow accretion. The whole job must be done from a standing start, and the size of it was such as naturally to preoccupy men with the economy above all other aspects of the society they were forming. When one added to this the unexampled riches, not only natural resources but also potential markets, it was perhaps inevitable that men's plans and their values, their conscious purposes and their deep-felt emotions should center on economic affairs. "Getting ahead" meant just one thing in this society. As this dominant temper governed, men made political issues and political participation more and more a game. They might argue their politics vehemently, but in the argument they were apt to find merely recreation or a vent for emotion.

As Lincoln Steffens reported of the early-twentieth-century United States, people were content to be righteously indignant about the political boss, and to leave him generally to his business, and to seek his favors when that seemed advantageous. Nothing more clearly demonstrated how far public issues had been pushed off to the borders of men's interests than the mediocrity of our national politics in the generation after the Civil War, in a time when an urban-industrial-financial revolution was remaking the community.

The dominant temper governed not only general political attitudes, but also affected the quality of leadership. Tocqueville detected the beginnings of this condition as early as the 1830's: "In democracies nothing is greater or more brilliant than commerce; it attracts the attention of the public and fills the imagination of the multitude; all energetic passions are directed towards it." The economy not only drained off the best part of the energy of the people; it also drained off the best part of our talent for leadership.

While economic trends worked to diminish general interest in public affairs and the amount of ability that went into them, other developments tended to thin down people's sense of community with one another. We became an urban people. Not only did an increasing percentage of the population live in urban areas (a majority after 1920), but also city-bred standards more and more dominated our values and behavior. Urban living was relatively impersonal, even in the smaller towns and cities, compared to the ready sociability and association-forming habit which so struck Tocqueville in 1831. The neighborhood lost its tight-knit character, and became a place from which one went forth for work and play. There was a lessened sense of loyalty or proprietorship toward one's town or city; local government took on the aspect of just one more shop or industry from which one bought services.

The logic of improved bulk transport, mass production industry, and cheap mass media of communication created national or at least sectional markets for goods and services once handled only on a local basis. The automobile enormously extended the easy range of movement, and by a twist of the dial the radio carried people far outside their home areas. Large-scale business and mobile people spelled problems that pressed urgently, but reached beyond the capacity of government close to home. These developments weakened the sense of belonging to a particular state. People had to shift a good deal of their loyalty, interest, and proprietorship to sections or to the nation. But these were more remote and abstract entities, harder to feel as a source of binding ties.

These two trends made an unfortunately consistent pattern. The most aggressively cohesive forces and attitudes tended to grow out of the inherently divisive interests in production. To keep producer-minded interests in their subordinate place, as means to better living, called for a strong and alert sense of the general welfare — called, in a broad definition of the term, for a consumer-minded people. But at the time that producer-mindedness was on the rise, the sense of common interest was becoming dulled or attenuated.

By 1950 it was apparent that these currents had moved far enough to call into question the capacity of our main legal institutions to mediate. Calhoun had urged the need of a "concurrent majority" — a required agreement of each affected interest in the community — to curb potential abuse of power by the numerical majority. The rise of great organized pressure groups, given thrust and continuity by their own bureaucracies, created something like a concurrent majority, though in a way quite different from that which Calhoun envisaged. Organized spokesmen for industry, commerce, labor, and agriculture wielded a practical veto on measures adverse to their separate concerns, or at least had enough force to modify pending public measures closer to their liking. They used their veto frankly and bluntly in their own interests, and not as trustees for a broader public. In positive action they displayed precisely the danger that Calhoun foresaw, the formation of majorities which expressed not an agreement upon the general interest, but merely a sum of temporary alliances of special interests. The forces in the society which drove in directions away from the central core of common concerns seemed steadily to gain strength relative to the forces that drove toward the center. As blocs pushed their particular programs in legislative chambers, they made a picture of a society which seemed less like a structure of interlocking, mutually supporting parts, than like billiard balls on a table, knocking against each other and rolling apart from the impact, to hit and rebound from others.

The businesslike ordering of any human affairs requires that men: (1) learn the facts of their situation, (2) decide what is best to do, and (3) attend to the details of carrying out their resolution. Insofar as the law was used to help order social relations, all major legal agencies did a share of these things: found facts, made policy, and saw to its execution. In our legal order, as we have noted, these institutions were supposed to operate with substantial neutrality toward special interests, so that law might protect the individual's right to a full life and the community solidarity essential to the individual's well-being. How did the institutions of our law perform their work in the face of the divisive and centrifugal forces that played on them?

Fact finding was peculiarly the province of the expert. To a degree, the required expertness of the job would protect it from intrusion; and, left to his work, the expert could do a good deal to lay open the bases on which policy should be made and the conditions of carrying it out. We have noted that government was the greatest agency for the accumulation of facts about the way in which the society worked. But we noted also that most of this accumulation was routine, unplanned, and dealt with matters of secondary importance. That this was so undoubtedly traced to some of the matters we have discussed. Preoccupied with the economy as a field for private adventure, we were uninterested in the creation of efficient public institutions. Allowing free play to special interests upon our government, we allowed most of our official fact gathering to develop not as part of a co-ordinated scheme to discover what it was in the public interest that we should know, but rather as a patchwork of separate activities responding to the immediate interests of particular groups — facts for business, for agriculture, for labor, because these organized interests demanded services from government for their own ends. Only the tendency of a bureaucracy to develop its own pride in the job saved these specialized fact-finding agencies from becoming mere apologists for the interests which demanded them. For major investigations, we relied on occasional legislative inquiries; and the lack of plan, staff, or traditions of fair and orderly procedure cut seriously into the value of these.

As between policy making and policy execution, experience taught that there was the less danger of corruption of the second process. This might seem at odds with notorious fact: Favor and bribery were most commonly uncovered in connection with law enforcement. But legal history offered a good deal of reason for optimism that there were manageable ways to keep these dangers within bounds. Thus, we learned that some problems were simply the result of imposing unnecessary strain on public machinery. In the mid-nineteenth century the state legislature in effect did an executive job, in the dispensing of special corporate charters, according to no defined pattern of law. The result was corruption which ruined legislative prestige for three generations. But the enactment of general incorporation laws, and the delegation of the issue of charters to executive officers under defined standards, removed this source of strain, and contributed to the rehabilitation of the state legislative branch. We learned, not only in the conduct of the routine police work of the law, but also in the operation of modern administrative machinery, that if we provided adequate security in the job, coupled it with insistence on qualified personnel, and delegated real responsibility, we could trust to the growth of professional spirit to go a long way toward safeguarding the integrity of regulation. Moreover, it was in this area, where the regulated person challenged not the basic validity of the regulation, but rather alleged discrimination in applying it, that our institution of judicial review showed to best advantage.

The breakdown of the sense of community, and the growing divisive influence of blocs or special-interest groups fell with most dangerous force upon the making of general policy. Main currents in the history of all the principal agencies of lawmaking showed this in one fashion or another. The late-nineteenth-century courts yielded uncritically to a producer-minded philosophy, and abused their judicial veto by substituting their own judgments of policy for those of the legislature, in the name of due process of law. The bar fell so far into the governing temper of the time as to be content with the role either of technician or partisan, and forfeited much of its public standing as spokesman of the general interest.

Most critically affected was the legislature; and as the currents of our growth brought the federal government into greater prominence, developments in Congress caused most concern. By law and tradition our legislators were tied most closely to the localities which elected them. There they were most vulnerable to aggressive minorities, which followed voting records and were ready to take the field against a representative who displeased them. Moreover, out of the locality the legislator was apt to draw his own firmest convictions of public welfare, and to identify public interest with home interest. Often out of warm conviction, the legislator was himself a more efficient lobbyist for the prominent concerns of his district than was any unofficial pressure group. Our preoccupation with private business, our prime concern with our interests as producers and with the spokesmen for those interests, our thinned-down sense of community with our fellows in an urban society — these were at least among the factors which made us deprecate "politics" (as if a representative government could work otherwise than through political means), praise action as "nonpolitical," and condemn it for party motives. It was little wonder that, from mid-nineteenth century on, our parties were unable to assert discipline over their members on behalf of general programs. In a clash between party loyalty and interest-group loyalty, more and more often the presumption favored substantial victories for the latter.

Only the executive branch seemed to react with positive force against the divisive forces at work. And, significantly, this was most true of the chief executive. However honest their detailed execution of the laws, when general policy was in the making, the departments and the independent commissions were apt to behave as representatives of the particular interest in the community which most ardently supported their appropriations and with which their own existence was most intimately tied. But the President and the governor had some realistic claim to be responsible to a constituency no narrower than the nation or the state. And the rising prestige of the chief executive in the first half of the twentieth century was strong evidence that great numbers of people felt this distinctive quality of independence and representation of the general interest.

This then was the challenge that faced law in mid-twentieth century, as mediator in the general interest. To trace the manner in which legal institutions had dealt with the resulting tensions in one field of public policy after another was the central theme for legal history in the United States. To that theme this volume forms an introduction.

ACKNOWLEDGMENTS

Grateful acknowledgment is made to the following persons, groups, and firms for their permission to quote from the works noted:

The American Academy of Political and Social Science, for permission to quote from Walter, "Reapportionment and Urban Representation," 195 Annals of The American Academy of Political Science 1 (1938).

The American Bar Association, for permission to quote from Rogers, *American Bar Leaders* (Chicago, 1932); from *Special Committee on the Economic Condition of the Bar: The Economics of the Legal Profession* (Chicago, 1938); and from Swaine, "Impact of Big Business on the Profession: An Answer to Critics of the Modern Bar," 35 American Bar Association Journal 89 (1949).

Banks-Baldwin Law Publishing Co., Cleveland, Ohio, for permission to quote from Dos Passos, *The American Lawyer* (New York, 1907).

Callaghan & Company, Chicago, Illinois, for permission to quote from Jameson, *A Treatise on Constitutional Conventions* (4th ed., 1887).

The Cleveland Foundation, for permission to quote from Pound and Frankfurter, eds., *Criminal Justice in Cleveland* (Cleveland, 1922).

The Columbia Law Review, Columbia University, for permission to quote from Jaffe, "Essay on Delegation of Legislative Power," 47 Columbia Law Review 359 (1947).

The Cornell Law Quarterly, Cornell Law School, for permission to quote from Wickser, "Bar Associations," 15 Cornell Law Quarterly 390 (1930), and from Sutherland, "A New Society and An Old Calling," 23 Cornell Law Quarterly 545 (1938).

Dodd, Mead & Company, Inc., New York City, for permission to quote from Philip C. Jessup, *Elihu Root* (New York. Copyright 1938 by Dodd, Mead & Co., Inc.).

Dr. Claude M. Fuess, for permission to quote from his *Daniel Webster* (Boston, 1930).

Harper & Brothers, New York City, for permission to quote from Auerbach, *The Bar of Other Days* (New York, 1940).

The Harvard Law Review, Cambridge, Massachusetts, for permission to quote from Holmes, "The Path of the Law," 10 Harvard Law Review 457 (1897); Holmes, "Law in Science and Science in Law," 12 Harvard Law Review 443 (1899); Stone, "The Public Influence of the Bar," 48 Harvard Law Review 1 (1934); and Parker, "The Integration of the Federal Judiciary," 56 Harvard Law Review 563 (1943).

Harvard University Press, Cambridge, Massachusetts, for permission to quote from Root, *Addresses on Government and Citizenship* (Bacon and Scott, eds., Cambridge, 1916).

Houghton Mifflin Company, Boston, for permission to quote from Haynes, *The Senate of the United States* (Boston, 1938), and from Woldman, *Lawyer Lincoln* (Boston, 1936).

The Illinois Law Review, Northwestern University School of Law, for permission to quote from Kales, "A Comparative Study of the English and the Cook County Judicial Establishments," 4 Illinois Law Review 303 (1909); Neitzert, "The Judges of the Nisi Prius Courts of Illinois," 30 Illinois Law Review 469 (1935); and Horack, in symposium, "Admission to the Bar: Many Are Chosen," 33 Illinois Law Review 891 (1939).

The Johns Hopkins Press, Baltimore, for permission to quote from Marshall and Marquard, *Unlocking the Treasuries of the Trial Courts* (Baltimore, 1933).

Alfred A. Knopf, Inc., New York City, for permission to quote from Tocqueville, *Democracy in America* (Bradley ed., New York, 1945).

J. B. Lippincott Company, Philadelphia, for permission to quote from *Memoirs of John Quincy Adams* (C. F. Adams ed., Philadelphia, 1874), and from Pepper, *Philadelphia Lawyer* (Philadelphia, 1944).

Little, Brown & Company, Boston, for permission to quote from Dillon, *Laws and Jurisprudence of England and America* (Boston, 1895); Holmes, *Speeches* (Boston, 1918); Holmes, *The Common Law* (Boston, 1881); Pound, *Appellate Procedure in Civil Cases* (Boston, 1941); and Williston, *Life and Law* (Boston, 1941).

Professor Karl Llewellyn, for permission to quote from *The Bramble Bush* (New York, 1930).

The Macmillan Company, for permission to quote from "Legal Profession," by A. A. Berle, Jr., in 9 *Encyclopedia of the Social Sciences* (Copyright 1933 by The Macmillan Company, New York); and from Bryce, *The American Commonwealth* (New ed., 1913. Copyright 1913 by The Macmillan Company, New York).

Professor Reginald C. McGrane, for permission to quote from his edition of the *Biddle Correspondence* (Boston, 1919).

The Oxford University Press, Inc., New York City, for permission to quote from Cushman, *The Independent Regulatory Commissions* (New York, 1941).

Pomona College, Claremont, California, for permission to quote from Swisher, *Motivation and Political Technique in the California Constitutional Convention 1878–1879* (Claremont, 1930).

Charles Scribner's Sons, New York City, for permission to quote from Martin, *Life of Joseph Hodges Choate* (New York, 1920), and from Theodore Roosevelt, *Autobiography* (New York, 1913).

Mr. Reginald Heber Smith, for permission to quote from his *Legal Service Offices for Persons of Moderate Means* (Boston, 1946).

Mr. Robert T. Swaine, for permission to quote from his *The Cravath Firm* (New York, 1946, 1948).

Messrs. William Howard Taft, 2nd, and Walbridge S. Taft, for permission to quote from Taft, *A Century and a Half at the New York Bar* (New York, 1938), and from the *Diary* of Mr. George Templeton Strong.

The University of Chicago Press, for permission to quote from Martin, *The Role of the Bar in Electing the Bench in Chicago* (Chicago, 1936).

The University of Pennsylvania Press, for permission to quote from Winkelman, *John G. Johnson* (Philadelphia, 1942).

The Viking Press, Inc., New York City, for permission to quote from Alpheus Mason, *Brandeis: A Free Man's Life* (New York, 1946).

Mr. Charles Warren, for permission to quote from his *History of the Harvard Law School* (New York, 1908).

The West Publishing Company, St. Paul, for permission to quote from Wickser, "Bar Examinations," 7 American Law School Review 7 (1930); Garrison, "Results of the Wisconsin Bar Survey," 8 *Id.* 116 (1931); and Parkinson, "Are the Law Schools Adequately Training for the Public Service?" 8 *Id.* 291 (1935).

John Wiley & Sons, Inc., New York City, for permission to quote from *Regulatory Administration* (G. A. Graham & H. Reining, Jr., eds. Published by John Wiley & Sons, Inc., 1943).

The John C. Winston Company, Philadelphia, for permission to quote from *Great American Lawyers* (Lewis ed., 8 vols., Philadelphia, 1907).

The Yale University Press, New Haven, for permission to quote from Farrand, *The Records of the Federal Convention of 1787* (New Haven, 1937).

BIBLIOGRAPHICAL NOTES

I: Introduction

CHAPTER ONE

SECTION 1. Data on early law curricula will be found in the essay on James Gould, by Baldwin, in Lewis, ed., *Great American Lawyers* (8 vols., Philadelphia, 1907), Vol. 2, pp. 455, 469–471; Warren, *History of the Harvard Law School* (3 vols., New York, 1908), Vol. 1, pp. 436–437, n. 1; Vol. 2, *id.*, at p. 365.

SECTION 2. *The Thomas Jefferson*, 10 Wheaton 428 (1825); *The Genesee Chief*, 12 Howard 443 (1851).

II: The Legislature

CHAPTER TWO

SECTION 1. See Luce, *Legislative Problems* (Boston, 1935); Chamberlain, *Legislative Processes* (New York, 1936); Landis, "Constitutional Limitations on the Congressional Power of Investigation," 40 Harvard Law Review 153 (1926); Potts, "Power of Legislative Bodies to Punish for Contempt," 74 University of Pennsylvania Law Review 691, 780 (1926), for the general background of this section.

SECTION 2a. The cases holding acts of Congress unconstitutional up to the 1930's are conveniently collected and summarized in Haines, *The American Doctrine of Judicial Supremacy* (Berkeley, 1932), Appendix I; on the New Deal period, see Volumes 293–298 of the U. S. Reports.

SECTION 2b. A classic discussion of the high point of the judicial veto of state legislation is Pound, "Liberty of Contract," 18 Yale Law Journal 454 (1909).

SECTION 2c. The indirect influence of judicial review upon the approach to the interpretation of statutes is discussed by Pound in "Common Law and Legislation," 21 Harvard Law Review 383 (1908). Jackson's interpretation of his constitutional obligations will be found in the veto message of July 10, 1832 regarding the bill to renew the charter of the Bank of the United States, in Richardson, *Messages and Papers of the Presidents* (10 vols., Washington, 1896), Vol. 2, pp. 576, 582; Taft's position is set forth, in conjunction with the Congressional debate evoked by it, in 49 Congressional Record, Part 5, pp. 4291, 4292, 4441, 4446 (63rd Congress, 1st Session, 1913), while the Supreme Court's subsequent action is in *Clark Distilling Co. v. Western Maryland*

Ry. Co., 242 U. S. 311 (1917); Roosevelt's position, and the debate over it, will be found in 79 Congressional Record, Part 12, pp. 13449 ff (74th Congress, 1st Session, 1935).

SECTION 2d. On the evolution of the investigatory power, see Landis, "Constitutional Limitations on the Congressional Power of Investigation," 40 Harvard Law Review 153 (1926); and Potts, "Power of Legislative Bodies to Punish for Contempt," 74 University of Pennsylvania Law Review 691, 780 (1926). *Kilbourn* v. *Thompson* will be found in 103 U. S. 168 (1880), and *McGrain* v. *Daugherty* in 273 U. S. 135 (1927).

SECTION 3a. On the changed status of the legislature in public opinion, see, for example, Luce, *Legislative Procedure* (Boston, 1922), and Luce, *Legislative Assemblies* (Boston, 1924).

SECTION 3c. Walter's findings on the prevalence of unequal apportionment appear in his "Reapportionment and Urban Representation," 195 Annals of the American Academy of Political and Social Science 11, 12, 13 (1938); see also his "Reapportionment of State Legislative Districts," 37 Illinois Law Review 20 (1942).

SECTION 3d. For the position of Kent and Spencer in the New York Constitutional Convention of 1821, see O'Rourke and Campbell, *Constitution-Making in a Democracy* (Baltimore, 1943), pp. 50–53; cf. Colvin, *The Bicameral Principle in the New York Legislature* (New York, 1913), p. 48. Walter's summary of the inequality of representation in the two chambers is contained in "Reapportionment and Urban Representation," 195 Annals of the American Academy of Political Science 11, 19 (1938).

CHAPTER THREE

SECTION 1. On the comparative ages of Congressmen and constituents, see Galloway, *Congress at the Crossroads* (New York, 1946), pp. 28–29. The Illinois record of experience of legislators is set forth in Hyneman and Morgan, "Cumulative Voting in Illinois," 32 Illinois Law Review 12, 27 (1937); Deming's data is most conveniently available in Luce, *Legislative Assemblies* (Boston, 1924), p. 356, and Luce's data on the later situation in Massachusetts and in the Congress will be found at pp. 364–365 of that volume. Hyneman's data on legislative turnover is given in his "Tenure and Turnover of Legislative Personnel," 195 Annals of the American Academy of Political Science 21, 25–27 (1938). The Kentucky example of the influence of turnover is in Stewart, "Introduction and Passage of Bills by the 1932 House of Representatives of Kentucky," 22 Kentucky Law Journal 285 (1934).

SECTION 2d. Data on committee business in Pennsylvania and New York will be found, respectively, in Winslow, *State Legislative Committees* (Baltimore, 1931), Ch. 2, and Zeller, *Pressure Politics in New York* (New York, 1937), p. 277. Cf. McCown, *The Congressional Con-*

ference Committee (New York, 1927), and Burdette, "Conference Committees in the Nebraska Legislature," 30 American Political Science Review 1114 (1936).

SECTION 2f. Chamberlain's comment on the time spent by Congressmen in the departments will be found in his *Legislative Processes* (New York, 1936), p. 46; see *id.*, Ch. 4 in general.

SECTION 3b. See, in general review of legislative contributions to the body of the law, Farnam, *Chapters in the History of Social Legislation in the United States to 1860* (Day, ed., Washington, 1938); Frankfurter, *The Public and Its Government* (New Haven, 1930); Pound, *The Formative Era of American Law* (Boston, 1938); and Stimson, *Popular Law-Making* (New York, 1911). The decision in *The Cargo of the Brig Aurora, Burnside, Claimant* v. *U. S.* will be found in 7 Cranch 382 (1813); that in *Wayman* v. *Southard,* in 10 Wheaton 1 (1825); that in *Panama Refining Co.* v. *Ryan* in 293 U. S. 388 (1935); that in *Schechter Poultry Corp.* v. *U. S.* in 295 U. S. 495 (1935).

SECTION 3c. For *Ex parte McCardle,* see 7 Wallace 506 (1869).

SECTION 3e. Data on the comparative number of legislative investigations of executive departments is given in Galloway, "The Investigative Function of Congress," 21 American Political Science Review 47, 48 (1927).

III: The Courts

CHAPTER FIVE

The "classic" analysis by Pound was the speech entitled, "Causes of Popular Dissatisfaction with the Administration of Justice," Reports of American Bar Association, Vol. 29, Pt. I, p. 395 (1906).

SECTION 1. The background of judicial reform for the Chicago area is traced in Lepawsky, *The Judicial System of Metropolitan Chicago* (Chicago, 1932), especially pp. 94–98.

SECTION 2. *Wayman* v. *Southard* will be found in 10 Wheaton 1 (1825).

SECTION 3. On the comparative numbers of English and American judges, see Lepawsky, *The Judicial System of Metropolitan Chicago* (Chicago, 1932), pp. 107–108, and Wickersham, "The Courts and the Dispatch of Judicial Business" in *Law: A Century of Progress, 1835–1935* (3 vols., New York, 1937), Vol. 1, pp. 274, 278. For the growth and cost of the Ohio court system, see Reticker, *Expenditures of Public Money for the Administration of Justice in Ohio* (Baltimore, 1933), pp. 4–5, 37–38.

SECTION 6. The verdict on the appellate system of the United States as the least efficient in the world is put in Sunderland, "The Proper Function of an Appellate Court," 5 Indiana Law Journal 483, 504 (1930). Pound's opinion on the reasons for our adoption of the writ of error will be found in his *Appellate Procedure in Civil Cases* (Boston, 1941), pp. 59, 66; his comments on "record worship" at pp. 35–36.

CHAPTER SIX

The standard monograph on the history of the federal judiciary is Frankfurter and Landis, *The Business of the Supreme Court* (New York, 1927); all references or citations not here specifically noted may be readily traced in that volume, which forms the central basis for this chapter. The Court fight of 1937 has not yet received adequate analysis; a helpful bibliographical comment will be found in Morison and Commager, *The Growth of the American Republic* (2 vols., 3d ed., New York, 1942), Vol. 2, pp. 727–728.

SECTION 3. The quoted praise for the Administrative Office Act is that of Circuit Judge John J. Parker, in his "The Integration of the Federal Judiciary," 56 Harvard Law Review 563, 564 (1943).

CHAPTER SEVEN

The basic structural facts on selection and tenure are assembled for ready use in Haynes, *The Selection and Tenure of Judges* (Baltimore, 1944); the major incidents concerning tenure may be located through Carpenter, *Judicial Tenure in the United States* (New Haven, 1918), though the discussion therein is disappointing.

SECTION 2. For Story's intervention on behalf of constitutional protection for judicial salaries in the Massachusetts convention of 1820, see Story, *Life and Letters of Joseph Story* (2 vols., Boston, 1851), Vol. 1, p. 388. The income tax case is *Evans* v. *Gore*, 253 U. S. 245 (1920), substantially repudiated by *O'Malley* v. *Woodrough*, 307 U. S. 277 (1939).

SECTION 3. On the Commerce Court battle, see Frankfurter and Landis, *The Business of the Supreme Court* (New York, 1927), pp. 153–174.

SECTION 4. On the Court bill of 1937, see note to Chapter Six; the forecast by Bryce will be found in *The American Commonwealth* (2 vols., new ed., New York, 1913), Vol. 1, p. 276; the admonition by Mr. Justice Stone is contained in his dissenting opinion in *United States* v. *Butler*, 297 U. S. 1, at p. 78 (1936).

SECTION 5. For President Taft's summary of the appointing power, see Haynes, *The Senate of the United States* (2 vols., Boston, 1938), Vol. 2, p. 722; the New Jersey incident is noted in McCormick, "Judicial Selection — Current Plans and Trends," 30 Illinois Law Review 446, 454 (1935). Martin, *The Role of the Bar in Electing the Bench in Chicago* (Chicago, 1936), is a rare example of well-directed inquiry into the functioning of the judicial system, and the source of data herein cited on bar association activity in judicial elections; with implications much broader than its title implies, the book should be examined for its general relevance to an estimation of the modern, metropolitan bench; the observation on qualifications for judicial office will be found at p. 317. The other monograph on the Chicago judiciary mentioned in the text is the valuable book by Lepawsky, *The Judicial System of Metropolitan Chicago* (Chicago, 1932). On the *de facto* system of appointment in Minnesota, see Anderson, "Reorganizing Minnesota's Judiciary," 27 Minnesota Law Review 383, 391, 396 (1943). McCormick, "Judicial Selection — Current Plans and Trends," 30 Illinois Law Review 446, 462 (1935), discusses the Kales proposal for a combined system of appointment and election.

SECTION 6. John Quincy Adams' account of Giles' remarks on the scope of impeachment will be found in his Diary, entry of December 21, 1804, *Memoirs of John Quincy Adams* (6 vols., C. F. Adams, ed., Philadelphia, 1874), Vol. 1, p. 322.

SECTION 7. The adoption of the judiciary article of the Minnesota constitution is described by Schochet, "Minnesota's First State Supreme Court (1858–1865)," 11 Minnesota Law Review 93, 96 (1927). Holmes, *The Common Law* (Boston, 1881), p. 106, contains the judgment on Shaw. On the Cleveland judges, see Smith and Ehrmann, "The Criminal Courts," in Pound and Frankfurter, eds., *Criminal Justice in Cleveland* (Cleveland, 1922), Part 3, Ch. 4, p. 260; cf. Lepawsky, *The Judicial System of Metropolitan Chicago* (Chicago, 1932), pp. 131–133; Bettman, "Criminal Justice Surveys Analysis," in *National Commission on Law Observance and Enforcement: Report on Prosecution*, No. 4, April 22, 1931 (Washington, 1931), pp. 119 ff. On patronage in receiverships in Chicago, see Martin, *The Role of the Bar in Electing the Bench in Chicago* (Chicago, 1936), pp. 289–293. The re-election of Judge Cole in Wisconsin is discussed in Winslow, *The Story of a Great Court* (Chicago, 1912), Ch. 14. For political objections to confirmation of nominees to the Supreme Court of the United States, see Frank, "The Appointment of Supreme Court Justices," 1941 Wisconsin Law Review 172, 343, 461. Neitzert's survey of Illinois trial judges is stated in his "The Judges of the Nisi Prius Courts of Illinois," 30 Illinois Law Review 469 (1935); the Vernier and Selig study is the "The Reversal of Criminal Cases in the Supreme Court of California," 20 Journal of the American Institute of Criminal Law and Criminology 60 (1929). The key constitutional decisions cited in the text are *Powell v. Pennsylvania*, 127 U. S. 678 (1888); *Lochner v. New York*, 198 U. S. 45 (1905); *Adkins v. Children's Hospital of the District of Columbia*, 261 U. S. 525 (1923); *Home Building & Loan Association v. Blaisdell*, 290 U. S. 398 (1934); *Nebbia v. New York*, 291 U. S. 502 (1934); *Ritchie v. People*, 155 Illinois 98, 40 N. E. 454 (1895); *People v. Williams*, 189 New York 131, 81 N. E. 778 (1907).

CHAPTER EIGHT

SECTION 1. The office of the justice of the peace has attracted more recent functional research than any other level of the judiciary. Particularly helpful in this account have been Douglass, *The Justice of the Peace Courts of Hamilton County, Ohio* (Baltimore, 1932); Sunderland, "A Study of Justices of the Peace and Other Minor Courts," Part II, *Fifteenth Annual Report of the Judicial Council of Michigan* (Lansing, 1945); Warren, *Traffic Courts* (Boston, 1942); and Allen, "Administration of Minor Justice in Selected Illinois Counties," 31 Illinois Law Review 1047 (1937).

SECTION 2. On urban developments, the discussion rests chiefly on Willoughby, *Principles of Judicial Administration* (Washington, 1929) for background; Lou, *Juvenile Courts in the United States* (Chapel Hill, 1927); Cooper and Dawson, "The Office of the Friend of the Court in Wayne County, Michigan," Appendix to *Fifth Annual Report of the Judicial Council of Michigan* (Ann Arbor, 1935), pp. 53 ff; Lapp, Cooper, and Dawson, "The Administration of Family Law in Michigan," Appendix to *Seventh Annual Report of the Judicial Council of Michigan* (Chicago, 1937), pp. 57 ff; Smith, *Justice and the Poor* (3rd ed., New York, 1924); Schramm, *Piedpoudre Courts* (Pittsburgh, 1928); "Symposium on the Poor Debtor," 42 Yale Law Journal 473 ff (1933); "Small Claims Courts (Legislation)," 34 Columbia Law Review 932 (1934).

SECTION 3. The quotation from Smith and Bradway, *Growth of Legal-Aid Work in the United States*, will be found at p. 141 of Department of Labor, Bureau of Labor Statistics Bulletin No. 607 (Washington, 1936), and the other cited data on case load and staff at pp. 121 and 145.

SECTIONS 8 & 9. Material on the handling of small claims will be found in the foregoing references. Material on traffic courts is from the admirable study by Warren, *Traffic Courts* (Boston, 1942), which thus far stands as the uniquely complete and functional study of a phase of judicial administration. See also Douglass, *The Justice of the Peace Courts of Hamilton County, Ohio* (Baltimore, 1932), Ch. 8, and the same author's *The Mayors' Courts of Hamilton County, Ohio* (Baltimore, 1933); Blackburn, *The Administration of Criminal Justice in Franklin County, Ohio* (Baltimore, 1935).

CHAPTER NINE

SECTION 1. Marshall's comment is from Marshall and Marquard, *Unlocking the Treasuries of the Trial Courts* (Baltimore, 1933), pp. 1–2. The New Haven County study is Clark and Shulman, *A Study of Law*

Administration in Connecticut (New Haven, 1937); case mortality data will be found at pp. 22–32; jury data at pp. 28–29, and 63–79; appellate data at pp. 43–49.

SECTION 2. A convenient summary of the surveys of criminal justice in the great cities and in some of the states after 1920 will be found in Bettman, "Criminal Justice Surveys Analysis," in *National Commission on Law Observance and Enforcement, Report on Prosecution,* No. 4, April 22, 1931 (Washington, 1931). The figure for jury trials in felony cases in Chicago in 1926, and other data on the prosecutor's role may be found in Moley, *Our Criminal Courts* (New York, 1930), pp. xi, 35 ff, 113 ff. On jury waiver in felony cases, see Grant, "Felony Trials Without a Jury," 25 American Political Science Review 980 (1931); the Supreme Court decision was *Patton* v. *United States,* 281 U. S. 276 (1930), with which compare *Adams* v. *United States ex rel. McCann,* 317 U. S. 269 (1942).

SECTION 3. Results of various surveys on recent trends in litigation are brought together in Garrison, "The Problem of Overcrowding," 16 Tennessee Law Review 658, 666–668 (1941). The federal court study is American Law Institute, *A Study of the Business of the Federal Courts* (2 Parts, Philadelphia, 1934); general civil caseload figures will be found in Pt. 2, *id.,* Ch. 3; figures on the criminal docket, Pt. 1, *id.,* Ch. 4; on criminal and civil appeals, respectively, Pt. 1, *id.,* Ch. 15, and Pt. 2, *id.,* Ch. 11. The data on the recent origin of offenses charged in Chicago in 1912 is from Pound, *Criminal Justice in America* (New York, 1930), p. 23; on California offenses, from Vernier and Selig, "The Reversal of Criminal Cases in the Supreme Court of California," 20 Journal of the American Institute of Criminal Law and Criminology 60, 62–63 (1929).

SECTION 4. The estimate of the relative volume of reported and unreported cases is from Jaffin, "Prologue to Nomostatistics," 35 Columbia Law Review 1, 7 (1935). The proportion of recent criminal appeals in California is shown in Beattie, "Report on California Criminal Appeals 1929–1935," Appendix to *Sixth Report of the Judicial Council of California* (1934–1936), Part II (Sacramento, 1937), pp. 91, 98–99.

SECTION 6. Washington's letter to the Justices is discussed in Warren, *The Supreme Court in United States History* (3 vols., Boston, 1922), Vol. 1, pp. 108 ff; *Hayburn's Case* is reported in 2 Dallas 409 (1792). The statement of the Kansas court is quoted from *State* v. *Mohler,* 98 Kansas 465, 471, 158 Pac. 408, 410 (1916).

SECTION 7. Langdell's statement will be found in Warren, *History of the Harvard Law School* (3 vols., New York, 1908), Vol. 2, p. 374.

SECTION 8. The Supreme Court's late caution in the use of legislative history is to be seen in *United States* v. *Trans-Missouri Freight Association,* 166 U. S. 290, 318 (1897), with which compare, for example, *Wright* v. *Vinton Branch of the Mountain Trust Bank,* 300 U. S. 440

(1937). "The sovereign prerogative of choice" is of course from Holmes, "Law in Science and Science in Law," 12 Harvard Law Review 443, 461 (1899).

SECTION 9. *Swift* v. *Tyson* is reported in 16 Peters 1 (1842), *Erie Railroad Co.* v. *Tompkins* in 304 U. S. 64 (1938). The percentages of diversity jurisdiction cases involving corporate litigants are summarized in Clark, "Diversity of Citizenship Jurisdiction of the Federal Courts," 19 American Bar Association Journal 499, 503 (1933). Holmes drew his distinction between the two realms of judicial review in "Law and the Court," in *Speeches* (Boston, 1918), p. 102. The Supreme Court decisions under the commerce clause are collected in Gavit, *The Commerce Clause of the United States Constitution* (Bloomington, 1932), Appendices A–E.

IV: The Constitution Makers

CHAPTER TEN

SECTION 1. Despite its doctrinaire and formal character, Jameson, *A Treatise on Constitutional Conventions* (4th ed., Chicago, 1887) is indispensable for summation of data on the calling and conduct of the bulk of state conventions. Dodd, *The Revision and Amendment of State Constitutions* (Baltimore, 1910), and Dodd, *State Government* (2d ed., New York, 1928) are the standard modern discussions. None of the general treatises is satisfactory regarding the social functions of the formal constitution-making processes. The best light here is cast by monographs on particular conventions, of which the best are clearly O'Rourke and Campbell, *Constitution-Making in a Democracy* (Baltimore, 1943) concerning the New York convention of 1938, and Swisher, *Motivation and Political Technique in the California Constitutional Convention, 1878–79* (Claremont, 1930). On the Federal Convention of 1787, the basic works are Farrand, ed., *Records of the Federal Convention of 1787* (4 vols., New Haven, 1937), and Farrand, *The Framing of the Constitution of the United States* (New Haven, 1913), together with Beard, *An Economic Interpretation of the Constitution of the United States* (New York, 1913 and 1935). *Luther* v. *Borden* is reported in 7 Howard 1 (1849); the 1912 decision fulfilling the implications of the earlier decision is *Pacific States Telephone & Telegraph Co.* v. *Oregon*, 223 U. S. 118.

SECTION 2a. On the Rhode Island Supreme Court's reversal regarding the power of the legislature to call a constitutional convention, see Bromage, *State Government and Administration in the United States* (New York, 1936), p. 84.

SECTION 2b. Concerning the failure to submit the Virginia constitution of 1902, see McDanel, *The Virginia Constitutional Convention of 1901–02* (Baltimore, 1928), pp. 118 and 141.

Section 2c. Jameson, *A Treatise on Constitutional Conventions* (4th ed., Chicago, 1887), p. 2, expresses the quoted fear of the "menace" of the power inherent in constitutional conventions. Holmes is quoted from his speech, "Law and the Court," in *Speeches* (Boston, 1918), p. 102.

Section 3. The 1895–1908 figures on legislatively proposed constitutional amendments are from Dealey, *Growth of American State Constitutions* (Boston, 1915), p. 90; the later figures are from Dodd, *State Government* (2d ed., New York, 1928), p. 107. On the use of the initiative, see Crouch, "The Constitutional Initiative in Operation," 33 American Political Science Review 634 (1939).

CHAPTER ELEVEN

Section 1a. The legislature's control of the calling of conventions is discussed in O'Rourke and Campbell, *Constitution-Making in a Democracy* (Baltimore, 1943), p. 59; and, regarding Pennsylvania, in Tanger and Alderfer, *Pennsylvania Government* (rev. ed., Harrisburg, 1939), pp. 71 and 73. Data on the minorities which typically decide upon constitutional change will be found in Kettleborough, *Constitution Making in Indiana* (Indianapolis, 1916), p. 71; McDanel, *The Virginia Constitutional Convention of 1901–02* (Baltimore, 1928), p. 142; Combs and Cole, *Tennessee, A Political Study* (Knoxville, 1940), pp. 38, 40 and 44; McKay, *Seven Decades of the Texas Constitution of 1876* (n. p., 1942), p. 189; Sheldon, "The Nebraska Constitutional Convention, 1919–1920," 15 American Political Science Review 391, 397 (1921); Loeb, "The Missouri Constitutional Convention: A Note," 18 American Political Science Review 320 (1924). On the degree of popular understanding of the issues on submission of constitutional change, cf. Swisher, *Motivation and Political Technique in the California Constitutional Convention, 1878–79* (Claremont, 1930), p. 109; Sutherland, "Lawmaking by Popular Vote," 24 Cornell Law Quarterly 1, 11 (1938) [New York, 1938]; and Crouch, "The Constitutional Initiative in Operation," 33 American Political Science Review 634, 635–637 (1939). The difficulties of getting out the vote to call a convention under strict requirements are noted in Swisher's *Motivation and Political Technique*, referred to above, at pp. 17 and 18, and in Anderson and Lobb, *A History of the Constitution of Minnesota* (Minneapolis, 1921), pp. 148 and 149. On the incalculability and momentum of conventions, see Swisher's work, at p. 18; Bridgman, *The Massachusetts Constitutional Convention of 1917* (Boston, 1923), p. 4; Caldwell, *Studies in the Constitutional History of Tennessee* (2d ed., Cincinnati, 1907), pp. 312, 325–328 [Tennessee, 1870]; McDanel, *The Virginia Constitutional Convention of 1901–02* (Baltimore, 1928), pp. 9, 10, 141; Sheldon, "The Nebraska Constitutional Convention, 1919–20," 15 American Political Science Review

391, 392 (1921); Tanger and Alderfer, *Pennsylvania Government* (rev. ed., Harrisburg, 1939), pp. 71, 73.

SECTION 1b. Any of the foregoing references may be consulted for examples of the partisan and interest pressures behind the calling and conduct of conventions. The incident related by George Wharton Pepper will be found in his *Philadelphia Lawyer* (Philadelphia, 1944), at p. 132.

SECTION 2a. On the lack of original creation in the shaping of government structure in the state constitutions, see Erdman, *The New Jersey Constitution of 1776* (Princeton, 1929), p. 43; Caldwell, *Studies in the Constitutional History of Tennessee* (2d ed., Cincinnati, 1907), p. 133; Evans, *A Study in the State Government of Louisiana* (Baton Rouge, 1931), p. 25; Dorr, ed., *The Michigan Constitutional Conventions of 1835-36* (Ann Arbor, 1940), pp. 27 and 28; Verlie, ed., *Illinois Constitutions* (Springfield, 1919), p. xxi; Sheldon, "The Nebraska Constitutional Convention, 1919-1920," 15 American Political Science Review 391 (1921); Goodwin, *The Establishment of State Government in California* (1846-1850) (New York, 1914), p. 242. On Rhode Island's rotten boroughs, see Chafee, *The Constitutional Convention That Never Met: First Part* (Providence, 1938), p. 5. Swisher is quoted from page 93 of his monograph, *Motivation and Political Technique in the California Constitutional Convention, 1878-79* (Claremont, 1930). On the Iowa provisions regarding the selection of judges, see Shambaugh, *The Constitutions of Iowa* (rev. ed., Iowa City, 1934), pp. 138, 140.

SECTION 2b. The "conspiracy theory" of the 14th Amendment is discussed in Boudin, "Truth and Fiction About the Fourteenth Amendment," 16 New York University Law Quarterly Review 19 (1938); Graham, "The 'Conspiracy Theory' of the Fourteenth Amendment," 47 Yale Law Journal 371 (1938), 48 *id.*, 171 (1938); Book Review, 52 Harvard Law Review 851 (1939). *Field* v. *Clark* is reported in 143 U. S. 649 (1892). The litigious aftermath of the tax provisions written by the California convention of 1878-1879 is discussed in Swisher, *Motivation and Political Technique in the California Constitutional Convention, 1878-79* (Claremont, 1930), pp. 78, 84.

SECTION 3a. On suffrage questions, see Selsam, *The Pennsylvania Constitution of 1776* (Philadelphia, 1936), pp. 18-39; Dorr, ed., *The Michigan Constitutional Conventions of 1835-36* (Ann Arbor, 1940), p. 30 [Michigan, 1837]; Kettleborough, *Constitution Making in Indiana* (Indianapolis, 1916), pp. 92-95, 103, 171-172; Swisher, *Motivation and Political Technique in the California Constitutional Convention, 1878-79* (Claremont, 1930), p. 92. Examples of apportionment contests will be found in Morison, *A History of the Constitution of Massachusetts* (Boston, 1917), pp. 40-44; Cary, *The Connecticut Constitution* (New Haven, 1900), pp. 5-14; Chafee, *The Constitutional Convention That Never Met: Second Part* (Providence, 1939), p. 5

[Rhode Island]; Elson, "Constitutional Revision and Reorganization of the General Assembly," 33 Illinois Law Review 15, 19 (Illinois, 1938); Selsam, *The Pennsylvania Constitution of 1776* (Philadelphia, 1936), pp. 18–30; Pate, *State Government in Virginia* (Richmond, 1932), p. 42; McDanel, *The Virginia Constitutional Convention of 1901–02* (Baltimore, 1928), p. 3; Green, *Constitutional Development in the South Atlantic States, 1776–1860* (Chapel Hill, 1930), pp. 152, 164; Hunt, *The Genesis of California's First Constitution* (Baltimore, 1895), p. 50.

SECTION 3b. There is no one reference to be cited for the history of specific policy enactments in the state constitutions, but the various types can be readily documented from such a sampling of studies as those referred to in previous connections.

SECTION 4. The desire for a more permanent enactment of policy, as an expression of distrust of future action by the ordinary agencies of government may be seen in incidents discussed by Swisher, *Motivation and Political Technique in the California Constitutional Convention, 1878–79* (Claremont, 1930), p. 65; O'Rourke and Campbell, *Constitution-Making in a Democracy* (Baltimore, 1943), p. 46 [New York]; McDanel, *The Virginia Constitutional Convention of 1901–02* (Baltimore, 1928), pp. 74, 75, 88. Examples of breaking log-jams may be seen in Bridgman, *The Massachusetts Constitutional Convention of 1917* (Boston, 1923), p. 31; in the McDanel book, at p. 64 [Virginia]; and in Swisher's work at pp. 66–69. *Chisholm* v. *Georgia* is reported in 2 Dallas 419 (1793); *Pollock* v. *Farmers' Loan & Trust Co.*, in 157 U. S. 429 (1895).

V: The Bar

CHAPTER TWELVE

SECTION 1. The liberality of Indiana toward admission to the bar will be found stated in Art. 7, Sect. 21 of its Constitution as it stood prior to 1933. Tocqueville's comment is in *Democracy in America* (2 vols., Bradley ed., New York, 1945), Vol. 1, p. 278; cf. Bryce, *The American Commonwealth* (2 vols., rev. ed., New York, 1913), Vol. 2, pp. 306–307, 672–674; Berle, "Modern Legal Profession," in the *Encyclopedia of the Social Sciences* (12 vols., New York, 1933), Vol. 9, p. 340.

SECTION 2. On the bar's relation to income groups in the 20th century United States, see, in "Report of the Cincinnati Conference on Law and Lawyers in the Modern World," 15 University of Cincinnati Law Review 123 (1941), Garrison on lawyers' incomes, at pp. 166–168, and Harris on untapped business, at pp. 176–180. On the bar and standard American prejudices, see Gregory, "Charles O'Conor," in *Great American Lawyers* (8 vols., Lewis ed., Philadelphia, 1907), Vol. 5, pp. 83, 86; Shea, "Overcrowded? — The Price of Certain Remedies," 39 Columbia Law Review 191 (1939); Rogers, *American Bar Leaders*

(Chicago, 1932), p. 124; *In the Matter of the Motion to Admit Miss Lavinia Goodell*, 39 Wisconsin 232 (1875), and *Application of Miss Goodell*, 48 Wisconsin 693 (1879).

SECTION 3. Statistics on the Litchfield School will be found in Fisher, *Litchfield Law School, 1774–1833: Biographical Catalogue of Students* (New Haven, 1946); information on curriculum in Baldwin, "James Gould," in *Great American Lawyers* (8 vols., Lewis ed., Philadelphia, 1907), Vol. 2, pp. 455, 471, 486. On early instruction at the Harvard Law School, see Curtis, ed., *A Memoir of Benjamin Robbins Curtis* (2 vols., Boston, 1879), Vol. 1, pp. 42, 56; Barrows, *William M. Evarts* (Chapel Hill, 1941), p. 15; Martin, *Life of Joseph Hodges Choate* (2 vols., New York, 1920), Vol. 1, p. 80; on Pomeroy at New York University Law School, see Jessup, *Elihu Root* (2 vols., New York, 1938), Vol. 1, p. 61; on Eliot and Langdell, and Langdell's quoted philosophy of legal education, see Warren, *History of the Harvard Law School* (3 vols., New York, 1908), Vol. 2, pp. 360–361, 374; Ames' comment on the nationwide adoption of the case method is in his essay, "Christopher C. Langdell," in *Great American Lawyers* (8 vols., Lewis ed., Philadelphia, 1907), Vol. 8, pp. 465, 484. Parsons' reading assignment to John Quincy Adams will be found in Warren, *History of the American Bar* (Boston, 1911), at p. 181. Data on law school entrance requirements will be found in Reed, *Training for the Public Profession of the Law* (Carnegie Foundation for the Advancement of Teaching, Bulletin No. 15, New York, 1921), p. 319; Brown, *Lawyers and the Promotion of Justice* (New York, 1938), pp. 45, 51, 79. The New York clerkship figures are from Wickser, "Law Schools, Bar Examiners, and Bar Associations — Co-operation Versus Insulation," 7 American Law School Review 725, 729 (1933). The pessimistic verdict on variations in school standards was by Dean H. Claude Horack of Duke University Law School, in the symposium, "Admission to the Bar: Many Are Chosen," 33 Illinois Law Review 891, 896 (1939). Comparative data on law and medical schools, and data on the number of "approved" law schools are given in Brown, *Lawyers and the Promotion of Justice* (New York, 1938), at pp. 31–33, 39, 48. The New York bar examination data, 1922–1931, are from Wickser's article, at p. 729.

SECTION 4. On the spread of the professional idea, within and without the law, see Reed, "The Opportunities of a Board of Bar Examiners," 7 American Law School Review 591, 593 (1932). For data on the evolution of bar admissions standards, see Reed, *Training for the Public Profession of the Law* (Carnegie Foundation for the Advancement of Teaching, Bulletin No. 15, New York, 1921), pp. 40, 72–73, and Ch. 8. Comparative data for 1800 and 1931 on the training of lawyers in this country will be found in Rogers, "The Epic of the American Lawyer," 24 Reports of the State Bar Association of Wisconsin 77, 84 (1934); and the comment on the "tiny stream" of trained men is from the same article. The story of Chase's examination for the bar is quoted in Wambaugh, "Salmon Portland Chase," in *Great American Lawyers* (8 vols., Lewis ed., Philadelphia, 1907), Vol. 5, pp. 329, 344; that of the examination conducted by Lincoln, in Woldman, *Lawyer Lincoln* (Boston, 1936), pp. 153–154. The verdict on bar examinations as an "informal equalizer of law school standards" is that of Wickser, "Bar Examinations," 7 American Law School Review 7, 16 (1930); and general data on percentages of men passing the bar examinations is found in the same article, at p. 725. On "character" examinations, see Brown, *Lawyers and the Promotion of Justice* (New York, 1938), p. 125.

SECTION 5. For basic data regarding bar organization, see Brown, *Lawyers and Promotion of Justice* (New York, 1938), pp. 127–153, and Reed, *Training for the Public Profession of the Law* (Carnegie Foundation for the Advancement of Teaching, Bulletin No. 15, New York, 1921), pp. 204–228. Stone's comment on the autonomy of the bar is contained in "The Public Influence of the Bar," 48 Harvard Law Review 1, 4–5 (1934). On the "politics" of the internal organization of the American Bar Association, see Rogers, *American Bar Leaders* (Chicago, 1932), pp. vii, 123, 197, 211. The description of a typical American Bar Association annual meeting is that of Wickser, "Bar Associations," 15 Cornell Law Quarterly 390, 416 (1930). Information on the movement for the integrated bar will be found in Harley, "Bar Integration Is a National Movement," 22 Journal of American Judicature Society 211 (1939).

CHAPTER THIRTEEN

SECTION 1a. One work stands pre-eminent for its rich sources on the flow of business through a great, busy law office of the 19th and 20th centuries. This is Swaine, *The Cravath Firm* (3 vols., New York, 1946–48). For the Vermont title difficulties, see Chipman, *The Life of Honorable Nathaniel Chipman* (Boston, 1846), pp. 62–70; on the Kentucky land snarl, see Wolf, "Thomas Alexander Marshall," in *Great American Lawyers* (8 vols., Lewis ed., Philadelphia, 1907), Vol. 4, pp. 301, 313, the other references to lawyers' land business are Walters, *Alexander James Dallas* (Philadelphia, 1943), pp. 161–164; Meade, *Judah P. Benjamin* (New York, 1943), pp. 64, 65, 126; Brigance, *Jeremiah Sullivan Black* (Philadelphia, 1934), pp. 131–142, 226; Flower, *Life of Matthew Hale Carpenter* (3d ed., Madison, 1884), pp. 88–91; Hall, "Seargent Smith Prentiss," in *Great American Lawyers*, Vol. 5, pp. 375, 386–388; Platt, "Matthew P. Deady," in *Great American Lawyers*, Vol. 7, pp. 357, 377, 379; Swaine, *The Cravath Firm*, Vol. 1, pp. 47–50, 70–73. On specialized business types of practice, the references in the text include Fuess, *Daniel Webster* (2 vols., Boston, 1930), Vol. 1, p. 86; Binney, *The Life of Horace Binney* (Philadelphia, 1903), p. 60; Wolf, "Thomas Alexander Marshall," in *Great American Lawyers*, Vol. 4, p. 320; Cowen, "Morrison Remick Waite," in *Great American*

Lawyers, Vol. 7, pp. 89, 94; Barrows, *William M. Evarts* (Chapel Hill, 1941), p. 31; Wambaugh on "Chase" in *Great American Lawyers*, Vol. 5, p. 348. On the "railroad lawyer," see Rogers, *American Bar Leaders* (Chicago, 1932), pp. v, 105, 108, 128–130, 137, 146, 148, 163, 242; Swaine, *The Cravath Firm*, Vol. 1, pp. 15, 16, 140, 212, 248; *Davis, Polk, Wardwell, Gardiner & Reed: Some of the Antecedents* (New York, 1935), p. 20. Regarding Southmayd, see Barrows, *William M. Evarts* (Chapel Hill, 1941), p. 427; on Harding and Wetmore, see Walker, "George Harding," in *Great American Lawyers*, Vol. 8, pp. 45, 60, 67, and Rogers, *American Bar Leaders*, at pp. 110 ff. On lobbying, see Walters, *Alexander James Dallas*, p. 160; Binney, *The Life of Horace Binney*, p. 64; Swaine, *The Cravath Firm*, Vol. 1, pp. 197–199, 245, 654, 757–764; the comment on Guthrie's statement for the Pinkertons is that of Swaine, and will be found in Vol. 1, at p. 483. Data regarding the Illinois law firms is contained in Stephens, "The 'Experienced Lawyer Service' in Illinois," 20 American Bar Association Journal 716 (1934). On government lawyers, see Pfiffner, "The Role of the Lawyer in Public Administration," 20 Southern California Law Review 37, 45 (1946), and *Final Report of the Attorney General's Committee on Administrative Procedure* (Washington, 1941), Chs. 1, 3 and 4.

SECTION 1b. The list of early 19th century leaders of the bar is Pound's, in "The Legal Profession in America," 19 Notre Dame Lawyer 334, 343 (1944); the characterization of Broadhead is from Rogers, *American Bar Leaders* (Chicago, 1932), p. 2. Choate's comments on the rarity of business experience at the mid-19th century bar are in Martin, *Life of Joseph Hodges Choate* (2 vols., New York, 1920), Vol. 1, pp. 86, 87, 115; on the importance of the "office" member of a firm, see Taft, *A Century and A Half at the New York Bar* (New York, 1938), pp. 3, 166, 168, 176; on the rendering of "Opinions," see Curtis, ed., *A Memoir of Benjamin Robbins Curtis* (2 vols., Boston, 1879), Vol. 1, pp. 265–267; Barrows, *William M. Evarts* (Chapel Hill, 1941), p. 47. The characterizations of Cravath will be found in Swaine, *The Cravath Firm* (3 vols., New York, 1946–48), Vol. 1, pp. 573–575.

SECTION 2a. On the size of firms, see Martin, *Life of Joseph Hodges Choate* (2 vols., New York, 1920), Vol. 1, p. 112; Auerbach, *The Bar of Other Days* (New York, 1940), p. 7; Taft, *A Century and A Half at the New York Bar* (New York, 1938), p. 176, n. 6; Swaine, *The Cravath Firm*, Vol. 1, p. 3; Swaine, "Impact of Big Business on the Profession: An Answer to Critics of the Modern Bar," 35 American Bar Association Journal 89, 92 (1949); on a large office's overhead, see Cohen, *The Law: Business or Profession?* (rev. ed., New York, 1924), p. 212; data on partnerships in the 20th century are in *The Economics of the Legal Profession* (American Bar Association Special Committee on the Economic Condition of the Bar, Chicago, 1938), pp. 48–51. The 1947 data on law office organization are reported in Weinfeld, "Incomes of

Lawyers, 1929–1948," in U. S. Dept. of Commerce, Survey of Current Business: August, 1949, p. 21.

SECTION 2c. The American Bar Association committee's comment on specialization will be found in *The Economics of the Legal Profession* (Chicago, 1938) at p. 31, while the Illinois experience is noted by Fisher in "Report of the Cincinnati Conference on Law and Lawyers in the Modern World," 15 University of Cincinnati Law Review 123, 161 (1941). Bryce's comparison of the relative position of the individual lawyer under the English and American systems of bar organization will be found in *The American Commonwealth* (2 vols., rev. ed., New York, 1913), Vol. 2, pp. 668, 673, 677–678.

SECTION 2d. On lawyers' incomes, see Baldwin, "James Gould," in *Great American Lawyers* (8 vols., Lewis ed., Philadelphia, 1907), Vol. 2, p. 458; Walters, *Alexander James Dallas* (Philadelphia, 1943), p. 160; Howe, "Francois Xavier Martin," in *Great American Lawyers*, Vol. 2, pp. 411, 418; Meade, *Judah P. Benjamin* (New York, 1943), p. 91; Jessup, *Elihu Root* (2 vols., New York, 1938), Vol. 1, p. 71; Swaine, *The Cravath Firm* (3 vols., New York, 1946–48), Vol. 1, p. 268; Barrows, *William M. Evarts* (Chapel Hill, 1941), p. 49; Curtis, ed., *A Memoir of Benjamin Robbins Curtis* (2 vols., Boston, 1879), Vol. 1, p. 268; Winkelman, *John G. Johnson* (Philadelphia, 1942), p. 112; Williston, *Life and Law* (Boston, 1941), p. 107; Bryce, *The American Commonwealth* (2 vols., rev. ed., New York, 1913), Vol. 2, p. 674; Garrison, "The Problem of Overcrowding," 16 Tennessee Law Review 658, 660 (1941). The 1949 findings on lawyers' incomes and related factors are reported in Weinfeld, "Income of Lawyers, 1929–1948," in U. S. Dept. of Commerce, Survey of Current Business: August, 1949, p. 18; the data on the relation between size of income and practice involving individuals or business firms is from *id.*, Table 4, p. 20.

SECTION 2e. On competition from within the bar, see Brown, *Lawyers and the Promotion of Justice* (New York, 1938), p. 164; Baldwin, "James Gould," in *Great American Lawyers* (8 vols., Lewis ed., Philadelphia, 1907), Vol. 2, pp. 455, 458; Taft, *A Century and A Half at the New York Bar* (New York, 1938), p. 64; Garrison, "The Problem of Overcrowding," 16 Tennessee Law Review 658, 659 (1941); *The Economics of the Legal Profession* (American Bar Association Special Committee on the Economic Condition of the Bar, Chicago, 1938), pp. 61–70; Smith, "The Overcrowding of the Bar and What Can Be Done About It," 7 American Law School Review 565, 567 (1932); Wickser, "Law Schools, Bar Examiners, and Bar Associations — Cooperation Versus Insulation," 7 American Law School Review 725, 729, 733–734 (1933). The New Haven study of untapped business is summarized in Clark and Corstvet, "The Lawyer and the Public: An Association of American Law Schools Survey," 47 Yale Law Journal 1272 (1938), and in the American Bar Association Special Committee report on *The Economics of the Legal Profession* at pp. 71 ff; lawyers' business in relation to average American family expenditures, and the results of the Columbus, Ohio, study are set out by Harris, "Report of the Cincinnati Conference on Law and Lawyers in the Modern World," 15 University of Cincinnati Law Review 123, 179, 180 (1941); the Philadelphia experiment is described in Abrahams, "The Neighborhood Law Office Experiment," 9 University of Chicago Law Review 406 (1942); the Chicago referral office experience is noted by Smith, *Legal Service Offices for Persons of Moderate Means* (Boston, 1946), p. 29, the New York legal aid experience in referrals is likewise noted in that work at p. 21, and the figures on Army legal assistance cases are also given, at p. 51; the quoted judgment on unsatisfied need for legal services is Smith's and will be found at p. 15. A six-city study of middle-class and working-class family needs for legal service is reported in Koos, *The Family and the Law* (mimeograph, Boston, 1948).

SECTION 2f. Data on "law-list" business are from Otterbourg, "Collection Agency Activities: The Problem from the Standpoint of the Bar," 5 Law and Contemporary Problems 35, 39 (1938); for data from the New Haven and Columbus studies, see citations above; the quoted summary of the Wisconsin findings is from Garrison, "Results of the Wisconsin Bar Survey," 8 American Law School Review 116, 122 (1935). Data on the growth of bar association sponsored lawyer reference plans will be found in Porter, *Lawyer Reference Plans* (Boston, 1949), Ch. III.

SECTION 2g. Kales' appraisal of the comparative efficiency of the English barrister and the American lawyer is stated in his "A Comparative Study of the English and the Cook County Judicial Establishments," 4 Illinois Law Review 303, 312–315 (1909); Bryce's opinion is put in *The American Commonwealth* (2 vols., rev. ed., New York, 1913), Vol. 2, pp. 673–677. On the recency of the Bar's active concern with "unauthorized practice," see Sanders, "The 'Unauthorized Practice of Law' Controversy," 5 Law and Contemporary Problems 1, 2 (1938), and Otterbourg, "Collection Agency Activities: The Problem from the Standpoint of the Bar," 5 Law and Contemporary Problems 35 (1938). On official action by the organized bar in recognition of experiments in reorganization of the economics of the profession, see Smith, *Legal Service Offices for Persons of Moderate Means* (Boston, 1946), pp. 11, 22–25. Stone's concern for the tardy response of the bar to the problem is stated in "The Public Influence of the Bar," 48 Harvard Law Review 1, 8 (1934), and his comments on the moral issues not met by the bar, and on the superficiality of the canons of ethics appear at pp. 8–10; Sutherland's criticism will be found in his "A New Society and an Old Calling," 23 Cornell Law Quarterly 545, 551, 552 (1938).

SECTION 3a. On Johnson and the equipment trust certificate, see Winkelman, *John G. Johnson* (Philadelphia, 1942), p. 238; on Stetson and corporate reorganization, see *Davis, Polk, Wardwell, Gardiner & Reed: Some of the Antecedents* (New York, 1935), p. 20; on Brandeis and *Muller v. Oregon*, see Mason, *Brandeis* (New York, 1946), pp. 248 ff. The difficulties of re-creating the life of a busy law office are noted by Taft, *A Century and A Half at the New York Bar* (New York, 1938), pp. vii–ix.

SECTION 3b. Holmes' distinction of himself from God cannot be traced to a document; the story so fits the character of speaker and situation that it demands acceptance for its validity in spirit if not in letter. Llewellyn's description of the growth of the trust receipt device is from *The Bramble Bush* (New York, 1930), pp. 152–153.

SECTION 3c. Brandeis' memorandum on the practice of law is quoted in Mason, *Brandeis* (New York, 1946), p. 69; Holmes' prophecy of the importance of facts in lawyers' work is contained in "The Path of the Law," 10 Harvard Law Review 457, 469 (1897); for Binney's lament on time given to fact-handling, see Binney, *The Life of Horace Binney* (Philadelphia, 1903), p. 71; on the "constitutional lawyers," see Rogers, *American Bar Leaders* (Chicago, 1932), p. 2; on Lincoln, see Woldman, *Lawyer Lincoln* (Boston, 1936), pp. 78, 92–93. Holmes' remarks on the desirable complexity of civilization will be found in his "Speech at a Dinner Given to Chief Justice Holmes by the Bar Association of Boston on March 7, 1900," *Speeches* (Boston, 1918), pp. 82, 85–86. The analogy of modern law to the under-the-street network of pipes is that of Sutherland, in "A New Society and an Old Calling," 23 Cornell Law Quarterly 545, 548 (1938).

SECTION 3d. Dos Passos' observation on the rise of the business lawyer is in his *The American Lawyer* (New York, 1907), p. 22. On personal business ventures of lawyers from the early 19th century, see *e.g.*, Klingelsmith, "James Wilson," in *Great American Lawyers* (8 vols., Lewis ed., Philadelphia, 1907), Vol. 1, pp. 151, 219; Swaine, *The Cravath Firm* (3 vols., New York, 1946–48), Vol. 1, pp. 43–44, 70–73, 82. Seward's letter on "The Ice Pitcher Case" is quoted in the same work at p. 302; Guthrie's activities are noted there at pp. 370–371, 465–468, 485, 546, 591, 627–629, 632–633, 645; the characterization of stockyard company "intrigues" is Swaine's, and appears at p. 655. For Brandeis' business policy-making, see Mason, *Brandeis* (New York, 1946), pp. 108–117, Chs. 9–11, *passim*, and pp. 70–71, 89–90. Root's comments on litigation and checking clients are given in Jessup, *Elihu Root* (2 vols., New York, 1938), Vol. 1, pp. 132–133. The characterization of Johnson is by Winkelman, *John G. Johnson* (Philadelphia, 1942), p. 75. Guthrie's complaint of his client's intervention in a pending case is noted in Swaine, *The Cravath Firm*, Vol. 1, p. 542. The statement of Vanderbilt, and that variously attributed to Morgan, Ryan, and Whitney, are given in Jessup's *Elihu Root*, Vol. 1, pp. 66, 185. The description of the lawyer who "brought things to pass" is contained in Williston, *Life and Law* (Boston, 1941), p. 108. On Lowry and Edison, see Auerbach, *The*

Bar of Other Days (New York, 1940), p. 68; on Davies in the Elevated cases the same work at p. 115; on the Express Company battles, see Swaine, *The Cravath Firm*, Vol. 1, pp. 327–337; Cravath's letter on the Western Pacific financing negotiations is given in the same volume at p. 721. The tabulation of cases in the Supreme Court of the United States involving more than two parties is contained in *Committee on Legal Education of the Harvard Law School: Preliminary Statement* (Cambridge, 1947), p. 13. On Dallas' political cases, see Walters, *Alexander James Dallas* (Philadelphia, 1943), pp. 77–93; on Black in the Milligan case, Brigance *Jeremiah Sullivan Black* (Philadelphia, 1934), p. 254; for *Brown* v. *Maryland*, see 12 Wheaton 419 (1827); on Johnson's suits, Winkelman, *John G. Johnson*, pp. 150–154; on early corporate control litigation, see Brigance, *Jeremiah Sullivan Black*, pp. 223–225, Barrows, *William M. Evarts* (Chapel Hill, 1941), p. 192, and Mason, *Brandeis* p. 153. Guthrie's comments on control of the Chicago gas litigation will be found in Swaine, *The Cravath Firm*, Vol. 1, p. 748; his activities in the Income Tax Case are set forth in the same volume at pp. 520, 521; *Pollock* v. *Farmers' Loan & Trust Co.* is reported in 157 U. S. 429 (1895).

SECTION 3e. Data on lawyers in public office are summarized by Rogers, "The Epic of the American Lawyer," 24 Reports of the State Bar Association of Wisconsin 77, 82–83 (1934); the characterization of Hagerman is by Rogers, in his *American Bar Leaders* (Chicago, 1932), p. 128; information on federal executive officials is given in MacMahon and Millett, *Federal Administrators* (New York, 1939), pp. 293, 459–462; on professional men as business executives, see Taussig and Joslyn, *American Business Leaders* (New York, 1932), p. 88. On Field and the codification battle, see Rogers, *American Bar Leaders*, p. 53; on Butler, the same at p. 40; and on Storey, the same at p. 88; and in addition Mason, *Brandeis* (New York, 1946), pp. 477, 480, 484, 489. On the "transformation from a profession to a business," see Dos Passos, *The American Lawyer*, p. 25; Wilson, "The Lawyer and the Community," 35 Reports of the American Bar Association 419, 422, 425, 436 (1910); Cohen, *The Law: Business or Profession?* (rev. ed., New York, 1924) p. 31; Rogers, *American Bar Leaders*, p. 128; Berle, "Modern Legal Profession," in *Encyclopedia of the Social Sciences*, Vol. 9, p. 344; Stone, "The Public Influence of the Bar," 48 Harvard Law Review 1, 3 (1934); Swaine's appraisal of the new demands upon the bar's capacity as mediator is stated in his "Impact of Big Business on the Profession: An Answer to Critics of the Modern Bar," 35 American Bar Association Journal 89, 171 (1949).

SECTION 3g. The Brandeis letter to Bruere is quoted in Mason, *Brandeis* (New York, 1946), p. 585. Data on the positions taken by the American Bar Association in public affairs issues will be found in Rutherford, *The Influence of the American Bar Association on Public Opinion and Legislation* (Philadelphia, 1937), and in McCown and Brooks,

"The American Bar Association and Social Issues, 1896–1925, 1925–1937," 5 Duke Bar Association Journal 75 (1937). For the debate on Pound's paper before the 1906 meeting of the Association, see *Report of the 29th Annual Meeting, American Bar Association,* 35 Reports of American Bar Association, Part 1, p. 65 (1906).

SECTION 3h. The quoted appraisals of Webster are in Fuess, *Daniel Webster* (2 vols., Boston, 1930), Vol. 1, pp. 176, 278; the letter to Biddle is that of December 21, 1833, *Biddle Correspondence* (McGrane ed., Boston, 1919), p. 218. On George W. Strong, see Taft, *A Century and A Half at the New York Bar* (New York, 1938), Ch. 3; on William H. Seward, Swaine, *The Cravath Firm,* Vol. 1, Part 3; on Davis and Lincoln, Beveridge, *Abraham Lincoln* (2 vols., Boston, 1928), Vol. 1, pp. 513–514; on Miller, Fairman, *Justice Samuel F. Miller* (Cambridge, 1935); on George Grover Wright, Rogers, *American Bar Leaders* (Chicago, 1932), p. 46; on Black and the railroads, Brigance, *Jeremiah Sullivan Black* (Philadelphia, 1934), pp. 266, 286; on Hagerman, Farrar, and Gregory, respectively, Rogers, *American Bar Leaders,* pp. 130, 163, 167–168. The quoted appraisal of Johnson is from Pepper, *Philadelphia Lawyer* (Philadelphia, 1944), p. 59. Root's quoted opinion on economic reforms is given in Jessup, *Elihu Root* (2 vols., New York, 1938), Vol. 1, p. 206, and his comment on the stimulation of public office in the same volume at p. 218. The biographies by Winkelman of Johnson and by Jessup of Root are essential studies for appraisal of the modern American bar. Dillon's remark is quoted in a suggestive context in Hamlin's essay on the law reform work of John Appleton, in *Great American Lawyers* (8 vols., Lewis ed., Philadelphia, 1907), Vol. 5, pp. 41, 48; the original source is Dillon, *Laws and Jurisprudence of England and America* (Boston, 1895), p. 340; the addresses cited as typical of the narrow practicality of the time are those of Henry Hitchcock, as to whom see Rogers, *American Bar Leaders,* p. 59; Governor Roosevelt's veto will be found in *Public Papers of Governor Roosevelt, 1929* (Albany, 1929), p. 210; cf. Cheatham, "What the Law Schools Can Do to Raise the Standards of the Legal Profession," 7 American Law School Review 716, 717 (1933). On the ideas and values of the opposition to the Brandeis appointment, see Mason, *Brandeis* (New York, 1946), pp. 478, 489, 506. Parkinson's comment on the partisan lawyer are in his "Are the Law Schools Adequately Training for the Public Service?", 8 American Law School Review 291, 294 (1935); George Templeton Strong's comment is in Taft, *A Century and A Half at the New York Bar* (New York, 1938), p. 148; the Cleveland study comment is in Pound and Frankfurter, eds., *Criminal Justice in Cleveland* (Cleveland, 1922), pp. 219–220; Kales' views are stated in his "A Comparative Study of the English and the Cook County Judicial Establishments," 4 Illinois Law Review 303, 319–320 (1909). For Choate on the contingent fee, see Cohen, *The Law: Business or Profession?* (rev. ed., New York, 1924), p. 206. The appraisal of the conservatism of the American bar is in Bryce, *The*

American Commonwealth (2 vols., rev. ed., New York, 1913), Vol. 2, p. 672; Guthrie's letters on the trend in tax cases are quoted in Swaine, *The Cravath Firm*, Vol. 1, pp. 651, 652, 653.

VI: The Executive

CHAPTER FOURTEEN

SECTION 1a. The quotation is from an informal talk given by Brandeis to a small group interested in social reform, February 25, 1922, set out in Mason, *Brandeis* (New York, 1946), p. 585.

SECTION 1b. For the reference to the Maryland and Virginia constitutional provisions denying executive prerogative, see Corwin, *The President* (New York, 1940), p. 5, and Thorpe, ed., *American Charters, Constitutions, etc.* (7 vols., Washington, 1909), Vol. 7, p. 3816. Corwin's judgment on the number of Presidents contributing to develop the powers of the office will be found in *The President* at p. 29.

SECTION 2a. Data regarding increase in the service functions of government will be found in Galloway and Kilpatrick, "Government Expenditures," in Dewhurst and Associates, *America's Needs and Resources* (New York, 1947), pp. 471–472 (and Table 157, p. 472), 483, 484 (and Table 154, pp. 568–569). Graham's comment on the relation between regulatory and service expenditures will be found in his essay on "Regulatory Administration," in Graham and Reining, eds., *Regulatory Administration* (New York, 1943), p. 10.

SECTION 2b. Data on the volume of business handled by federal administrative agencies will be found in *Final Report of the Attorney General's Committee on Administrative Procedure* (Washington, 1941), pp. 35–39, 314–326; the 1938 report of the New York State Public Service Commission is commented on in Graham and Reining, eds., *Regulatory Administration* (New York, 1943), p. 137; data on disposition of workmen's compensation claims will be found in Dodd, *Administration of Workmen's Compensation* (New York, 1936), pp. 117, 387. The "adjustment" function in modern government is sketched in Griffith, *The Impasse of Democracy* (New York, 1939), pp. 106, 109, 110.

SECTION 3a. James Wilson's denial that the Presidency inherited any of the Crown prerogative was called to my attention by Corwin, *The President* (New York, 1940), p. 319, n.36; see Farrand, *The Records of the Federal Convention of 1787* (4 vols., New Haven, 1937), Vol. 1, p. 65. For *Ex parte Milligan* see 4 Wallace 2 (1866); *Luther* v. *Borden* is reported in 7 Howard 1 (1849); *In re Debs* is reported in 158 U. S. 564 (1895); *Decatur* v. *Paulding*, in 14 Peters 497 (1840).

SECTION 3b. The study of Presidential leadership in major legislation, 1890–1940, is that of Chamberlain, *The President, Congress and Legislation* (New York, 1946), especially Chs. I and XII.

SECTION 3C. As to the evolution of Supreme Court theory concerning delegation of powers, see *Field* v. *Clark*, 143 U. S. 649 (1892); *Hampton & Co.* v. *United States*, 276 U. S. 394, 409 (1928); *Norwegian Nitrogen Products Co.* v. *United States*, 288 U. S. 294, 305 (1933); the National Industrial Recovery Act cases are, of course, *Panama Refining Co.* v. *Ryan*, 293 U. S. 388 (1934), and *Schechter Poultry Corp.* v. *United States*, 295 U. S. 495 (1935). Mr. Chief Justice White's approval of the delegation of power to the courts under the Sherman Act will be found in *Standard Oil Co.* v. *United States*, 221 U. S. 1, 69 (1911). The opinion of Rosenberry, C. J., on delegation of powers is that in *State ex rel. Wisconsin Inspection Bureau* v. *Whitman*, 196 Wis. 472, 220 N. W. 929 (1928). Freund's prediction of a trend toward legislative recapture of areas of discretion committed to the administrative arm may be found in his *Administrative Powers over Persons and Property* (Chicago, 1928), p. 70.

CHAPTER FIFTEEN

On the President's removal power, see *Myers* v. *United States*, 272 U. S. 52 (1926), and *Humphrey's Executor* v. *United States*, 295 U. S. 602 (1935).

CHAPTER SIXTEEN

SECTION 1. Elihu Root's comments on the permanency of the new administrative process will be found in the address, "Public Service by the Bar," in his *Addresses on Citizenship and Government* (New York, 1916), pp. 534–535. The characterization of the "unique" history of the Civil Aeronautics Act of 1938 is that given in Cushman, *The Independent Regulatory Commissions* (New York, 1941), p. 403. The cited official studies of administrative law in action are *Final Report of the Attorney General's Committee on Administrative Procedure* (Washington, 1941), and *Administrative Adjudication in the State of New York* (Albany, 1942), by Robert M. Benjamin, as Commissioner under Section 8 of the Executive Law.

SECTION 2. Jaffe's "single generalization" is put in his "Essay on Delegation of Legislative Power," 47 Columbia Law Review 359, 361 (1947).

SECTION 3b. Luce's unfavorable appraisal of the legislature as a continuing check upon executive or administrative action is stated in his review of Willoughby's treatise on "Legislative Organization," 29 American Political Science Review 294 (1935).

SECTION 4. Senator Taft's observation on the pressure exerted by the regulated persons for the grant of discretion to administrators is pointed out by Frank, in *If Men Were Angels* (New York, 1942), pp. 148–149.

VII: Conclusion: Prospectus for Legal History

CHAPTER SEVENTEEN

The quotations from Calhoun will be found in his "Disquisition on Government," *Works of John C. Calhoun* (4 vols., New York, 1863), Vol. 1, pp. 15, 16, 25. Tocqueville's estimate of the pre-eminence of commerce in our society is in *Democracy in America* (2 vols., Bradley ed., New York, 1945), Vol. 2, p. 155.

Index

INDEX

New York State Public Service Commission, 389
New York University Law School, 261
Neutrality, 181
Nevada, 210
Nicholas, George, 257
Nolle prosequi, 174, 175
Nonsupport proceedings, 149, 156, 158, 179; *see also* DOMESTIC RELATIONS
Norris, George W., 18, 53, 56
North Carolina, 92, 109, 224, 239
North Dakota, 71, 427
Northern Securities case, 368
Northwest Territory, 95, 101, 148
Notary public, 320, 321
Notice and hearing, 36, 77, 427
Noyes, William Curtis, 303
Nuisance, 150, 432
Nullification, 116
Nye, Bill, 39

O'CONOR, CHARLES, 255
Official notice, 431
Ohio, 92, 94, 112, 122, 137, 151, 152, 224, 227, 228, 259, 277, 281, 427
Oil, 7, 307, 406–407
Oklahoma, 8, 214
Old age insurance, 10
"Old court" battle in Kentucky, 125, 140
Old World contributions to United States law, 3; *see also* ENGLISH HERITAGE IN UNITED STATES LAW
Oleomargarine, 349
"Opinions" by lawyers, 181, 303, 309, 343
Order, need for with increasing settlement, 3
Oregon, 214, 219
Original jurisdiction, 75; *see also* JURISDICTION OF FEDERAL COURTS; JURISDICTION OF STATE COURTS
O'Rourke, Vernon A., 221
Orphans Court, Pennsylvania, 151
Oxford University, 257

PACKERS AND STOCKYARDS ACT, 391
Packing courts: *see* COURTS, FEDERAL, packing of Supreme Court; JUDGES, packing of courts
Panama Canal, 396
Panama Refining Co. v. *Ryan*, 73, 406–407
Parking offenses, 168

Parkinson, Thomas I., 371–372
Parks, 385
Parole, 179, 434
Parsons, Theophilus, 253, 261, 266, 267, 370
Parties, political, 7, 38, 42, 45, 47, 55, 56, 59, 61, 67, 68, 69, 76, 77, 81, 89, 129, 132, 133, 135, 138, 142, 150, 208, 209, 212, 214, 215, 216, 218, 219, 220, 221, 225, 231, 236, 237–239, 266, 299, 320, 349, 353, 354, 369, 372, 401, 407, 415, 424, 440, 442, 445; *see also* PARTICULAR PARTIES BY NAME
Parties to lawsuits, 349
Partition, 300
Partnership, 5, 259, 306
Passivity of law, in United States growth, 4
Patent Office, 80, 422
Patents, 3, 4, 5, 72, 80, 298, 311, 343, 395, 419, 422
Paterson, William, 18
Patronage, 401
Paupers' suits, 151
Peckham, Rufus Wheeler, 374
Penal statutes, strict construction of, 186
Penalties, compared with licenses, 394
Pennsylvania, 38, 53, 60, 88, 92, 95, 115, 137, 151, 159, 180, 202, 204, 205, 207, 211, 216, 220, 230, 235, 239, 253, 287, 299, 349, 367, 389
Pensions, 180, 320, 401, 419, 422
People v. *Williams*, 146
Pepper, George Wharton, 220, 254, 368
Perishable Agricultural Commodities Act, 391
Permanent Court of International Justice, 364
Personnel experts, 341
Peters, Richard, 180
Petit jury: *see* JURY, PETIT
Pettigru, James Louis, 302
Pharmacy, 277
Philadelphia, 96, 161, 254, 287, 299, 311, 318, 319, 326, 345, 368
Philippine Islands, 120
Physical setting of law in the United States, 6–9
Pickering, John, 135
Pinchot, Amos, 371
Pinkerton agency, 300
Pinkney, William, 302
Pittsburgh, 96
Plank roads, 395